The Essential Guide to
Dreamweaver CS3
with CSS, Ajax, and PHP

David Powers

friendsof

DESIGNER TO DESIGNER™

an Apress® company

The Essential Guide to Dreamweaver CS3 with CSS, Ajax, and PHP

Credits

Lead Editor
Chris Mills

Technical Reviewer
Tom Muck

Editorial Board
Steve Anglin, Ewan Buckingham, Gary Cornell, Jonathan Gennick, Jason Gilmore, Jonathan Hassell, Chris Mills, Matthew Moodie, Jeffrey Pepper, Ben Renow-Clarke, Dominic Shakeshaft, Matt Wade, Tom Welsh

Project Manager
Tracy Brown Collins

Copy Edit Manager
Nicole Flores

Copy Editor
Heather Lang

Assistant Production Director
Kari Brooks-Copony

Production Editor
Kelly Winquist

Compositor
Dina Quan

Artist
April Milne

Proofreader
April Eddy

Indexer
Julie Grady

Interior and Cover Designer
Kurt Krames

Manufacturing Director
Tom Debolski

In memory of my sister, Nimbia
November 21, 1941–April 24, 2007

CONTENTS AT A GLANCE

CONTENTS

Chapter 3: Getting the Work Environment Ready 67

Chapter 8: Sprucing Up Content with Spry Widgets **209**

Chapter 9: Building Online Forms and Validating Input **247**

Chapter 19: Using Spry to Display XML 653

Chapter 20: Getting the Best of Both Worlds with PHP and Spry 693

FOREWORD

The Macromedia community was unique. There was a synergy among developers, designers, marketers, and the Macromedia product teams that kept the product line alive and growing year after year. I say "was," because Macromedia is now part of Adobe. Since Adobe acquired Macromedia, the community has gotten larger. Adobe did not previously have a reputation for fostering a community spirit, however, even though the Adobe umbrella is now over the entire former-Macromedia product line, the community has flourished and become even more pervasive. Adobe now feels more like Macromedia than even Macromedia did, because Adobe has somehow taken the best of Macromedia and made it even better.

With that acquisition, we have one of the largest software rollouts ever—the CS3 release, which combined all of Macromedia's biggest product lines with Adobe's biggest product lines into one massive release. If it were a normal product release cycle, that would be big news by itself, but with all the major enhancements in most of the products in the line, it's even bigger. Dreamweaver CS3 contains some great new features, most of which are covered extensively in this book, including the Spry tools, page layouts, and CSS tools. Dreamweaver CS3 (or Dreamweaver 9, if you're counting) is the first Adobe version of Dreamweaver, but aside from the Adobe name and the Photoshop integration, it is instantly recognizable as the same great program.

One of the things that make the community great is the involvement of the company (Macromedia, now Adobe) with the designer/developer community. Adobe actively seeks feedback on products and welcomes give and take; it doesn't just pay lip service to the concept of a developers' community. The feedback forms on the website go directly to the product team, and product engineers contact customers directly. This kind of involvement brought PHP into Dreamweaver in the first place, and this kind of involvement keeps Dreamweaver at the top of the heap of all the web development tools available.

To give an example of the Adobe community involvement, Adobe sent a team of representatives to meet with everyone at the recent TODCon convention, which typically attracts a small, closely knit group of Dreamweaver designers and developers. They didn't just send a couple of marketing people or low-level operatives; they flew in over a dozen of the cream of the crop, including product managers, development team managers, quality assurance managers, and others from locations in San Jose, San Diego, Romania, and Germany. On the first day of the conference, Dreamweaver product manager Kenneth Berger introduced the team, which looked like a wall of Adobe at the front of the room, and led a session about what is right and wrong with Dreamweaver, and the attendees of the conference got to give their input as to what Dreamweaver is doing well and what could be improved. There was plenty of praise along with plenty of venting that the product team will use directly. That wasn't the end of it though. The team was in attendance for the bulk of the conference, walking around with notebooks, getting valuable feedback that will help shape the next version of the product. This is the kind of personal contact that keeps the community and the product thriving.

Couple the company involvement with the extensibility of Dreamweaver, which keeps the development community buzzing with creativity by extending the program to do things that it won't do out of the box, and you have a program that gets exponentially better with each release. I say the same thing every time a new version of Dreamweaver comes out: I could never go back to the previous version. I feel the same way about the latest CS3 release.

I've never met David Powers, but know him well through the Adobe Dreamweaver community. He is a fellow Adobe Community Expert who freely shares his knowledge of the product in Adobe support forums, among other places. I know David by reputation as one of the most thorough yet easy-to-read authors on the scene today and as one of the most passionate and vocal Dreamweaver experts in the world. Among the scores of Dreamweaver books, David's are the books that I personally recommend to people as the best. This book is no exception. Having written a few books in the past myself, I know it's no easy task. As the technical reviewer of this book, it was frequently a challenge for me to find things to say about it—David leaves no stone unturned in his quest to provide the best instructional material on the shelves today. That is exactly what you are holding in your hands right now.

Tom Muck
June 2007

ABOUT THE AUTHOR

 **David Powers** is an Adobe Community Expert for Dreamweaver and author of a series of highly successful books on PHP, including *PHP Solutions: Dynamic Web Design Made Easy* (friends of ED, ISBN-13: 978-1-59059-731-6) and *Foundation PHP for Dreamweaver 8* (friends of ED, ISBN-13: 978-1-59059-569-5). As a professional writer, he has been involved in electronic media for more than 30 years, first with BBC radio and television and more recently with the Internet. His clear writing style is valued not only in the English-speaking world; several of his books have been translated into Spanish and Polish.

What started as a mild interest in computing was transformed almost overnight into a passion, when David was posted to Japan in 1987 as BBC correspondent in Tokyo. With no corporate IT department just down the hallway, he was forced to learn how to fix everything himself. When not tinkering with the innards of his computer, he was reporting for BBC TV and radio on the rise and collapse of the Japanese bubble economy. Since leaving the BBC to work independently, he has built up an online bilingual database of economic and political analysis for Japanese clients of an international consultancy.

When not pounding the keyboard writing books or dreaming of new ways of using PHP and other programming languages, David enjoys nothing better than visiting his favorite sushi restaurant. He has also translated several plays from Japanese.

ABOUT THE TECHNICAL REVIEWER

Tom Muck is the coauthor of nine Macromedia-related books. Tom also writes extensions for Dreamweaver, available at his site www.tom-muck.com. Tom is also the lead PHP and ColdFusion programmer for Cartweaver, the online shopping cart software package, and a founding member of Community MX, who has written close to 100 articles on PHP, ColdFusion, SQL, and related topics.

Tom is an extensibility expert focused on the integration of Adobe/Macromedia products with ColdFusion, ASP, PHP, and other languages, applications, and technologies. Tom was recognized for this expertise in 2000 when he received Macromedia's Best UltraDev Extension Award. He has also written numerous articles for magazines, journals, and websites and speaks at conferences on this and related subjects.

ACKNOWLEDGMENTS

For an author, writing a book means long, lonely hours at the keyboard, but the volume you're holding in your hands—or reading onscreen if you've got the electronic version—is very much a collaborative effort. The idea of writing an expanded book on the dynamic features of Dreamweaver came from my editor, Chris Mills, who was gracious enough not to complain each time I changed my mind about the final shape of the book. My thanks go to him and all the production staff at Apress/friends of ED for keeping this mammoth project on target.

I'm also indebted to the development team at Adobe, who gave me a sneak preview of their plans for Dreamweaver CS3 very early in the development process and helped me understand how many of the new features work. At times, I'm sure they were exasperated by my persistent questions and the occasionally hectoring tone of my suggestions for improvements, but they never let it show.

A particular thank you goes to my technical reviewer, Tom Muck. I'm deeply honored that such a respected expert on Dreamweaver agreed to undertake this role. Tom's in-depth knowledge of Dreamweaver, PHP, and SQL saved me from some embarrassing mistakes (any that remain are my responsibility entirely). He also provided helpful advice when he thought my explanations were too oblique.

My biggest thanks of all go to you, the reader. Without you, none of this would be worthwhile. If you enjoy this book or find it useful, tell all your friends and get them to buy a copy. Don't lend it to them. You might never get it back!

INTRODUCTION

The Essential Guide to Dreamweaver CS3 with CSS, Ajax, and PHP . . . Wow, the title's almost as long as the book! And what's that "essential" doing in there? "Essential" suggests that it's a book you can't do without. So, who's it for and why should you be reading it?

Dreamweaver isn't a difficult program to use, but it's difficult to use *well*. It's packed with features, and more have been added with each new version. The user interface has barely changed in the last few versions, so it's easy to overlook some great productivity boosters if you don't know where to find them. I have been using Dreamweaver on a daily basis for about seven years, pushing it to the limit and finding out its good points—and its bad ones, too.

So, the idea of this book is to help you get the best out of Dreamweaver CS3, with particular emphasis on building dynamic web pages using the improved CSS management features, Spry—the Adobe implementation of Ajax—and the PHP server behaviors. But how can you get the best out of this book?

Who this book is for

If you're at home with the basics of (X)HTML and CSS, then this book is for you. If you have never built a website before and don't know the difference between an <a> tag and your Aunt Jemima, you'll probably find this book a bit of a struggle. You don't need to know every tag and attribute by heart, but I frequently dive into Code view and expect you to roll up your sleeves and get to grips with the code. It's not coding for coding's sake; the idea is to adapt the code generated by Dreamweaver to create websites that really work. I explain everything as I go along and steer clear of impenetrable jargon. As for CSS, you don't need to be a candidate for inclusion in the CSS Zen Garden (www.csszengarden.com), but you should understand the basic principles behind creating a style sheet.

What about Ajax and PHP? I don't assume any prior knowledge in these fields. Ajax comes in many different guises; the flavor used in this book is Spry, the Adobe Ajax framework (code library) that is integrated into Dreamweaver CS3. Although you do some hand-coding with Spry, most features are accessed through intuitive dialog boxes.

Dreamweaver also takes care of a lot of the PHP coding, but it can't do everything, so I show you how to customize the code it generates. Chapter 10 serves as a crash course in PHP, and Chapter 11 puts that knowledge to immediate use by showing you how to send an email from an online form—one of the things that Dreamweaver doesn't automate. This book doesn't attempt to teach you how to become a PHP programmer, but by the time you reach the final chapter, you should have sufficient confidence to look a script in the eye without flinching.

Do I need Dreamweaver CS3?

Most definitely, yes. Although the PHP features in Dreamweaver CS3 are identical to Dreamweaver 8.0.2, you'll miss out on roughly half the book, because the chapters devoted to CSS and Spry are based on CS3. In a pinch, you could download the free version of Spry from http://labs.adobe.com/technologies/spry/ and hand-code everything in an earlier version of Dreamweaver, but the focus in this book is on using the CS3 interface for Spry. If you want to use PHP in an earlier version, I suggest you read my *Foundation PHP for Dreamweaver 8* (friends of ED, ISBN-13: 978-1-59059-569-5) instead.

How does this book differ from my previous ones?

I hate it when I buy a book written by an author whom I've enjoyed before and find myself reading familiar page after familiar page. This book is intended to replace *Foundation PHP for Dreamweaver 8*, so a lot of material is inherited from that book. There's also some overlap with *PHP Solutions: Dynamic Web Design Made Easy* (friends of ED, ISBN-13: 978-1-59059-731-6), but I estimate that at least 60 percent of the material was written exclusively for this book. Every chapter has been completely revised and rewritten, and the chapters on CSS and Spry are brand new.

Even where I have recycled material from the two previous books, I have revised and (I hope) improved the scripts. For example, the mail processing script has increased protection against email header injection attacks, and I have adapted it so that it can be reused more easily with different online forms. The script also inserts the form content into a database after sending the email.

I have added a section on using Dreamweaver templates in a PHP site. There's a new chapter on building search queries, and the chapter on multiple database tables tells you how to use foreign key constraints if your MySQL server supports InnoDB. The final chapter shows you how to generate XML on the fly from a database and enhance a PHP site by integrating some features of Spry data management.

How this book is organized

My previous books have taken a linear approach, but I have structured this one to make it easier for you to dip in and out, using the Table of Contents and Index to find subjects that interest you and going straight to them. So, if you want to learn how to create tabbed panels with Spry, you can go directly to Chapter 8. Although the example pages use a design that was created in an earlier chapter, you don't need to have worked through the other chapter first. Nevertheless, there is a progressive logic to the order of the chapters.

Chapters 1 and 2 serve as an overview of the whole book, explaining what's new and what has changed in Dreamweaver CS3. Chapter 2 also explains in detail how to use Spry effects. They are simple to apply and don't require knowledge of CSS or PHP. If you're new to Dreamweaver, these chapters help you find your way around essential aspects of the Dreamweaver interface.

Chapters 3 and 4 show you how to set up your work environment for PHP and Dreamweaver. If you already have a local testing environment for PHP, you can skip most of the material in these chapters. However, I urge you to follow the instructions at the end of Chapter 3 to check your PHP configuration. The section in Chapter 4 about defining your testing server in Dreamweaver is also essential reading. These two subjects are the most frequent causes of problems. A few minutes checking that you have set up everything correctly will save a lot of heartache later.

Chapters 5 and 6 cover in depth how Dreamweaver handles CSS. If you're relatively new to CSS, Chapter 5 shows you how *not* to use Dreamweaver to create style rules. For more advanced readers, it provides a useful overview of the various CSS management tools, including the ability to reorder the cascade and move rules to different style sheets without ever leaving Design view. Chapter 6 uses one of the 32 built-in CSS layouts to create an elegant site, and in the process, unravels the mysteries of the CSS Styles panel.

Chapters 7 and 8 return to Spry, exploring the Spry Menu Bar and the tabbed panels, accordion, and collapsible panel user interface widgets. Because these widgets make extensive use of CSS, you'll find these chapters easier to follow if you're up to speed on the previous two chapters. Of course, if you're already a CSS whiz kid, jump right in.

Chapter 9 sees the start of practical PHP coverage, showing you how to construct an online form. The second half of the chapter completes the roundup of Spry widgets, showing you how to use Spry to check user input before a form is submitted. This is client-side validation like you've never seen before. If you want to concentrate on PHP, you can skip the second half of the chapter and come back to it later.

As noted earlier, Chapter 10 is a crash course in PHP. I have put everything together in a single chapter so that it serves as a useful quick reference later. If you're new to PHP, just skim the first paragraph or so of each section to get a feel for the language and come back to it later to check on specific points.

Chapters 11 and 12 give you hands-on practice with PHP, building the script to process the form created in Chapter 9. Newcomers to PHP should take these chapters slowly. Although you don't need to become a top-level programmer to use PHP in Dreamweaver, an understanding of the fundamentals is vital unless you're happy being limited to very basic dynamic pages. If you're in a hurry, you can use the finished mail-processing script from Chapter 12. It should work with most online forms, but you won't be able to customize it to your own needs if you don't understand how it works. Chapter 12 also looks at using Dreamweaver templates in a PHP site.

Chapter 13 gets you ready to bring out Dreamweaver's big guns by guiding you through the installation of the MySQL database and a graphic interface called phpMyAdmin. This chapter also covers database backup and transferring a database to another server.

Chapters 14 through 17 show you how to build database-driven web pages using PHP, MySQL, and Dreamweaver's PHP server behaviors. You'll also learn the basics of SQL (Structured Query Language), the language used to communicate with all major relational databases. To get the most out of this section, you need to have a good understanding of the material in the first half of Chapter 9. You'll learn how to create your own content management system, password protect sensitive parts of your site, and build search forms.

The final three chapters (18–20) introduce you to working with XML (Extensible Markup Language), the platform-neutral way of presenting information in a structured manner. XML is often used for news feeds, so Chapter 18 sets the ball rolling by showing you how to use Dreamweaver's XSL Transformation server behavior to draw news items from a remote site and incorporate them in a web page.

Chapter 19 explains how to generate a Spry data set from XML and use it to create an online photo gallery. The attraction of Spry is that it provides a seamless user experience by refreshing only those parts of a page that change, without reloading the whole page. The disadvantage is that, like most Ajax solutions, the underlying code leaves no content for search engines to index, or for the browser to display if JavaScript is disabled. So, Chapter 20 shows how to get the best of both worlds by creating the basic functionality with PHP and enhancing it with Spry. The final chapter also shows you how to generate your own XML documents from content stored in your database.

What this book isn't

I like to credit my readers with intelligence, so this book isn't "Dreamweaver CS3 for the Clueless" or "Dreamweaver CS3 for Complete Beginners." You don't need to be an expert, but you do need to have an inquiring mind. It doesn't teach the basics of web design, nor does it attempt to list every single feature in Dreamweaver CS3. There are plenty of other books to fill that gap. However, by working through this book, you'll gain an in-depth knowledge of the most important features of Dreamweaver.

A high proportion of the book is devoted to hands-on exercises. The purpose is to demonstrate a particular technique or feature of Dreamweaver in a meaningful way. Rather than racing through the steps to finish them as quickly as possible, read the explanations. If you understand why you're doing something, you're far more likely to remember it and be able to adapt it to your own needs.

Windows- and Mac-friendly

Everything in this book has been tested on Windows XP SP2, Windows Vista, and Mac OS X 10.4—the minimum required versions for Dreamweaver CS3. The overwhelming majority of screenshots were taken on Windows Vista, but I have included separate screenshots from Windows XP and Mac OS X where appropriate.

Chapters 3 and 13 have separate sections for Windows and Mac to guide you through the setup of PHP and MySQL, so Mac users aren't left trying to adapt instructions written for a completely different operating system.

Keyboard shortcuts are given in the order Windows/Mac, and I point out when a particular shortcut is exclusive to Windows (some Dreamweaver shortcuts conflict with Exposé and Spotlight in the Mac version). The only place where I haven't given the Mac equivalent is with regard to right-clicking. Since the advent of Mighty Mouse, right-clicking is now native to the Mac, but if you're an old-fashioned kind of guy or gal and still use a one-button mouse, Ctrl-click whenever I tell you to right-click (I'm sure you knew that anyway).

Some Mac keyboard shortcuts use the Option (Opt) key. If you're new to a Mac and can't find an Opt key on your keyboard, in some countries it's labeled Alt. The Command (Cmd) key has an apple and/or a cloverleaf symbol.

A note about versions used

Computer software is constantly evolving, and—much though I would like it to do so—it doesn't stand still simply because I have written a 700-odd page book. A book represents a snapshot in time, and time never stands still.

Everything related to Dreamweaver in this book is based on build 3481 of Dreamweaver CS3. This is the version that was released in April 2007. The build number is displayed on the splash screen when you launch Dreamweaver. You can also check the build number by going to Help ➤ About Dreamweaver (Dreamweaver ➤ About Dreamweaver on a Mac) and clicking the credits screen. This build of Dreamweaver shipped with Spry version 1.4. About one month later, Adobe released Spry version 1.5; and Spry 1.6 was released in October 2007.

You can download a Dreamweaver extension from http://labs.adobe.com/technologies/spry/ to update Spry. The extension makes it easy to install the most recent version of the Spry library files and code hints. However, it does not add any new features to Dreamweaver CS3, nor does it affect any of the instructions in this book.

Check my website at http://foundationphp.com/egdwcs3/updates.php for any updates concerning PHP, MySQL, and phpMyAdmin. The instructions in this book are based on the following versions:

- PHP 5.2.1
- MySQL 5.0.37
- phpMyAdmin 2.10.1

Using the download files

All the necessary files for in this book can be downloaded from www.friendsofed.com/downloads.html. The files are arranged in five top-level folders, as follows:

- examples: This contains the .html and .php files for all the examples and exercises, arranged by chapter. Use the File Compare feature in Dreamweaver (see Chapter 2) to check your own code against these files. Some exercises provide partially completed files for you to work with. Where indicated, copy the necessary files from this folder to the workfiles folder so you always have a backup if things go wrong.
- images: This contains all the images used in the exercises and online gallery.
- SpryAssets: This contains the finished versions of Spry-related style sheets. With one exception, it does *not* contain the external JavaScript files needed to display Spry effects, widgets, or data sets. Dreamweaver should copy the JavaScript files and unedited style sheets to this folder automatically when you do the exercises as described in this book.
- tools: This contains a Dreamweaver extension that loads a suite of useful PHP code fragments into the Snippets panel, as well as a saved query for the Find and Replace panel, and SQL files to load data for the exercises into your database.
- workfiles: This is an empty folder, where you should build the pages used in the exercises.

Copy these folders to the top level of the site that you create for working with this book (see Chapter 4).

Support for this book

Every effort has been made to ensure accuracy, but mistakes do slip through. If you find what you think is an error—and it's not listed on the book's corrections page at www.friendsofed.com—please submit an error report to www.friendsofed.com/errataSubmission.html. When ED has finished with the thumbscrews and got me to admit I'm wrong, we'll post the details for everyone's benefit on the friends of ED site. I also plan to post details on my own website at http://foundationphp.com/egdwcs3/updates.php of changes to Dreamweaver or other software that affect instructions in the book.

I want you to get the best out of this book and will try to help you if you run into difficulty. Before calling for assistance, though, start with a little self-help. Throughout the book, I have added "Troubleshooting" sections based heavily on frequently asked questions, together with my own experience of things that are likely to go wrong. Make use of the File Compare feature in Dreamweaver to check your code against the download files. If you're using a software firewall, try turning it off temporarily to see whether the problem goes away.

If none of these approaches solves your problem, scan the chapter subheadings in the Table of Contents, and try looking up a few related expressions in the Index. Also try a quick search on the Internet: Google and the other large search engines are your friends. My apologies if all this sounds obvious, but an amazing number of people spend more time waiting for an answer in an online forum than it would take to go through these simple steps.

If you're still stuck, visit www.friendsofed.com/forums/. Use the following guidelines to help others help you:

- Always check the book's updates and corrections pages. The answer may already be there.
- Search the forum to see if your question has already been answered.
- Give your message a meaningful subject line. It's likely to get a swifter response and may help others with a similar problem.
- Say which book you're using, and give a page reference to the point that's giving you difficulty.
- Give precise details of the problem. "It doesn't work" gives no clue as to the cause. "When I do so and so, x happens" is a lot more informative.
- If you get an error message, say what it contains.
- Be brief and to the point. Don't ask half a dozen questions at once.
- It's often helpful to know your operating system, and if it's a question about PHP, which version of PHP and which web server you're using.
- Don't post the same question simultaneously in several different forums. If you find the answer elsewhere, have the courtesy to close the forum thread and post a link to the answer.

The help I give in the friends of ED and Adobe forums is not limited to problems arising from my books, but please be realistic in your expectations when asking for help in a free online forum. Although the Internet never sleeps, the volunteers who answer questions certainly do. They're also busy people, who might not always be available. Don't post hundreds of lines of code and expect someone else to scour it for mistakes. And if you do get the help that you need, keep the community spirit alive by answering questions that you know the answer to.

Layout conventions

To keep this book as clear and easy to follow as possible, the following text conventions are used throughout.

Important words or concepts are normally highlighted on the first appearance in **bold type**.

Code is presented in `fixed-width` font.

New or changed code is normally presented in **`bold fixed-width font`**.

Pseudo-code and variable input are written in *`italic fixed-width font`*.

Menu commands are written in the form Menu ➤ Submenu ➤ Submenu.

Where I want to draw your attention to something, I've highlighted it like this:

> *Ahem, don't say I didn't warn you.*

Sometimes code won't fit on a single line in a book. Where this happens, I use an arrow like this: ➥.

```
This is a very, very long section of code that should be written all ➥
on the same line without a break.
```

1 DREAMWEAVER CS3—YOUR CREATIVE PARTNER

After 8, comes . . . not 9, but CS3. In the confusing world of marketing, Dreamweaver versions have gone from straightforward numbers to a couple of meaningless letters (MX), to MX 2004 (which didn't reflect the year of release accurately), and back to numbers again. So why CS3? And does it make any sense?

In one respect, the change symbolizes the fact that Dreamweaver is under new ownership. Macromedia, the company that turned Dreamweaver, Flash, and Fireworks into must-have tools for web developers, was acquired by Adobe at the end of 2005. And Dreamweaver (together with former Macromedia stable mates Fireworks and Flash) is now part of Creative Suite, Adobe's family of web and print design tools that includes Photoshop, Illustrator, and InDesign. Creative Suite is now in its third iteration; hence CS3. Although each program has a long history, the idea of Creative Suite is to promote greater integration to make it easier to switch to the best tool for a particular job, such as Photoshop for photo manipulation and retouching, and import the results into another program. And that's what's happened to Dreamweaver: although it's available as a stand-alone program, it's now closely integrated with its new Adobe brothers and sisters as part of Adobe Web Suite CS3 and Design Suite CS3.

Even the stand-alone version of Dreamweaver CS3 comes bundled with three other programs:

- **Extension Manager CS3**: An updated version of the program that lets you install third-party add-ons to extend the functionality of Dreamweaver, Flash, and Fireworks.
- **Adobe Bridge CS3**: As the name suggests, this is intended to facilitate communication between the various parts of Creative Suite, but it also works with the stand-alone version of Dreamweaver. At one level, it's like a super-charged version of Windows Explorer or Finder on the Mac, but it shines in the handling of visual assets. It allows you to see inside a wide variety of formats, making it easy to find an image by what it looks like.
- **Adobe Device Central CS3**: This is a brand new program that allows you to visualize what your websites will look like in a wide range of mobile devices, not only from the layout point of view but also simulating mobile backlight and sunlight reflections.

The integration goes further through the ability to copy and paste directly from a Photoshop PSD file into Dreamweaver. When you do so, Dreamweaver optimizes the file for the Web. So, yes, the "CS3" does make sense. It's not just change for the sake of change.

Once installed, Extension Manager, Bridge, and Device Central are separate programs and can be launched independently, but you have no choice whether to install them. The installer simply lists them as "Shared Components." As a result, this version of Dreamweaver occupies roughly four times more disk space than previous versions. Personally, I like Bridge and think that Device Central is likely to become increasingly useful as mobile Web access grows in popularity. Others may disagree.

If you're a long-term Dreamweaver user, though, the program that you know and love hasn't changed beyond recognition. As Figures 1-4 and 1-5 show, the workspace layout is identical to Dreamweaver 8. The development team moved with Dreamweaver to Adobe, and the improvements to the program are a logical progression. Adobe accompanied its decision to include Dreamweaver in Creative Suite 3 with the bold step of dropping its own web design program, GoLive. Although GoLive has been updated, it's not in any of the CS3 packages. What's more, Adobe has created an online tutorial to help GoLive users migrate to Dreamweaver (www.adobe.com/go/learn_dw_golive). This sends a clear message that Adobe now regards Dreamweaver as its prime tool for developing standards-compliant websites.

In this chapter, we'll take a look at the most important features and changes in Dreamweaver CS3, with particular emphasis on cascading style sheets (CSS) and creating standards-compliant Extensible HyperText Markup Language (XHTML), both of which are essential for building any modern website. Then, in the following chapter, we'll take a look at the tools Dreamweaver offers for building dynamic websites: Spry—Adobe's implementation of Asynchronous JavaScript + XML (Ajax)—and PHP.

What this chapter covers

- Finding out what's new in Dreamweaver CS3
- Exploring and organizing the Dreamweaver workspace
- Using Bridge to manage visual assets
- Taking a first look at Dreamweaver's support for cascading style sheets
- Getting the best out of Code view

Getting your bearings in Dreamweaver

As the title of this book says, this is an *essential* guide to Dreamweaver CS3. So I don't intend to bore you to death with descriptions of every menu and submenu. However, all readers may not be familiar with Dreamweaver, so I'll start with a few signposts to guide you around the Dreamweaver interface and help set basic program preferences. Most of this will be familiar to experienced users of Dreamweaver, but there are some important changes. To identify these changes, look for the New and Changed graphics in the margin.

Starting up

When you launch Dreamweaver CS3, the first thing you see after the program has finished loading is the welcome screen shown in Figure 1-1. The three columns in the top section provide quick access to a recently opened document (this list is empty the first time you launch Dreamweaver), create a new document or Dreamweaver site (site definition is covered in Chapter 4), or select from a predefined layout. The Dreamweaver Exchange option at the foot of the right column takes you directly to the Adobe Dreamweaver Exchange (www.adobe.com/cfusion/exchange/index.cfm?view=sn120), where you can obtain extensions to add extra functionality to Dreamweaver (many are free; others are sold on a commercial basis). The bottom section of the welcome screen takes you to various parts of the Adobe website and displays what Adobe considers useful information, for example, available updates to the program.

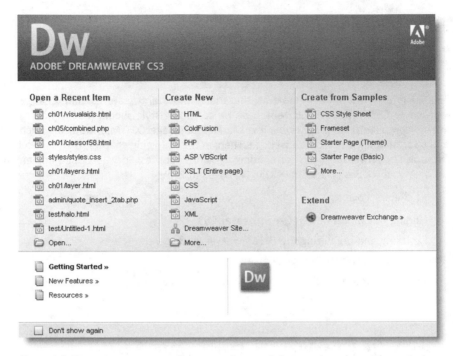

Figure 1-1. The welcome screen offers access to recent documents and a quick way to create new ones.

The Dreamweaver welcome screen reappears whenever you close all documents in the workspace and connects to Adobe to see if there are any new announcements. In previous versions, leaving the welcome screen enabled was a resource hog, so many developers chose the Don't show again option at the bottom left. This means what it says: once you select it, the welcome screen disappears forever. If you want it back, go to Edit ➤ Preferences (Dreamweaver ➤ Preferences on a Mac), choose the General category, and select Show welcome screen.

Although the welcome screen no longer appears to be a resource hog, you may prefer to switch it off because you get a much better range of options from the New Document dialog box. You can also configure Dreamweaver to reopen on startup any documents that are still open when you close the program. Just select Reopen documents on startup in the General category of the Preferences panel.

Changed

Creating a new document

To create a new document, select File ➤ New or press Ctrl+N/Cmd+N. This opens the New Document dialog box, which has been considerably revamped, as shown in Figure 1-2.

The biggest change is that, in addition to a completely blank page, you can now select one of 32 CSS layouts. There are also options to change the page's document type definition (DTD)—by default, Dreamweaver CS3 uses XHTML 1.0 Transitional—and to attach an external style sheet to the page at the time of creation. We'll look at the CSS layouts and style sheet options in Chapters 5 and 6.

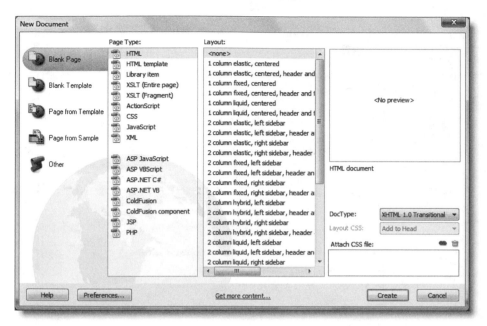

Figure 1-2. The New Document dialog box offers a massive range of options and preset layouts.

By selecting the appropriate option from the menu on the left side of the New Document dialog box, you can also create new templates from scratch or a page from an existing template (templates are covered in Chapter 12). The Page from Sample option offers a wide range of preset layouts, but I don't recommend using them, as many of them use old-style presentational elements and deprecated attributes. The final option, labeled Other, contains a variety of pages for programming languages such as ActionScript, C#, and VBScript, none of which are used in this book.

Setting new document preferences

Click the Preferences button at the bottom left of the New Document dialog box. Alternatively, choose Preferences from the Edit menu (Dreamweaver menu on a Mac), and select the New Document category. Either presents you with the New Document Preferences dialog box shown in Figure 1-3.

The dialog box lets you set the following global preferences:

- Default document lets you choose the type of document that will be created when you use the keyboard shortcut for a new document (Ctrl+N/Cmd+N). For this to work, you must deselect the option at the bottom labeled Show New Document dialog box on Control+N/Cmd+N. Otherwise, the dialog box shown in Figure 1-2 will appear.

- Default extension affects only (X)HTML files. Change the value only if you want to use .htm to maintain unity with the naming convention of older sites.

- Default Document Type (DTD) sets the default DOCTYPE declaration for all new web pages. You cannot set one value for, say, .html and another for .php pages.

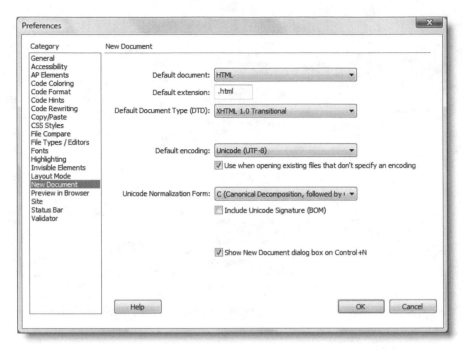

Figure 1-3. The New Document category of the Preferences panel

- Default encoding lets you choose the character set to be used in all web pages. The Dreamweaver CS3 default is Unicode (UTF-8). (In the Mac version, this is listed as Unicode 4.0 UTF-8.) This is different from previous versions. The checkbox below this option tells Dreamweaver to use the same character set to display existing pages that don't specify a particular encoding. It doesn't insert any extra coding in such pages.

- Unicode Normalization Form is required only when using UTF-8 for encoding. It should normally be set to C (Canonical Decomposition, followed by Canonical Composition), and the Include Unicode Signature (BOM) checkbox should be deselected. If you use any other encoding, set Unicode Normalization Form to None.

Changed

Choosing the default document type Many people misunderstand the purpose of the DTD (the DOCTYPE declaration before the opening <html> tag). It simply tells the browser how you have coded your page and is intended to speed up the correct rendering of your design. It's not a badge of honor or magic spell that somehow renders your web pages future-proof. The default setting in Dreamweaver CS3 is XHTML 1.0 Transitional, and this is the appropriate choice for most people when creating a new web page *as long as you understand the stricter rules imposed by XHTML.*

> Visit www.w3.org/TR/xhtml1/#diffs *to learn about the differences between HTML and XHTML. Also read the frequently asked questions at* www.w3.org/MarkUp/2004/xhtml-faq.

The full range of options is as follows:

- **None:** Don't use—all pages should have a DOCTYPE declaration.

- **HTML 4.01 Transitional:** Choose this if you don't want to use XHTML.

- **HTML 4.01 Strict:** This excludes deprecated elements (those destined for eventual elimination)—use this only if you have a good knowledge of HTML and have made a conscious decision not to use XHTML.

- **XHTML 1.0 Transitional:** This offers the same flexibility as HTML 4.01 Transitional by permitting the use of deprecated elements but applies the stricter rules of XML.

- **XHTML 1.0 Strict:** This excludes all deprecated elements—use this only if you are competent with XHTML.

- **XHTML 1.1:** Don't use—this DTD should not be used on pages delivered using the text/html MIME type, the current standard for web servers.

- **XHTML Mobile 1.0:** This is a subset of XHTML Basic for mobile devices—you can find the full specification at www.openmobilealliance.org/tech/affiliates/wap/wap-277-xhtmlmp-20011029-a.pdf.

If you choose an HTML document type, Dreamweaver automatically creates code according to the HTML specification. Similarly, if you choose XHTML, your code automatically follows the stricter rules, using lowercase for tag names and event handlers and inserting a closing slash in empty tags such as <img>. You need to be careful when copying and pasting code from other sources. If you're not sure about the quality of the code, run Commands ➤ Clean Up XHTML, which should correct most, if not all, problems.

If you select a Strict DTD, it's important to realize that Dreamweaver does *not* prevent you from using deprecated elements or attributes. Dreamweaver expects you to understand the difference yourself.

Choosing the default encoding The decision to switch the default encoding in Dreamweaver CS3 to Unicode (UTF-8) makes a lot of sense. Unicode supports nearly every known writing system, so—as long as you have the right fonts on your computer—you can combine Spanish, Russian, Chinese, and English all on the same web page. All modern browsers support UTF-8, so there is no reason you shouldn't use it. But—and it's a big but—this book concentrates heavily on using PHP and the MySQL database. Versions of MySQL prior to the 4.1 series do not support UTF-8. If your hosting company uses MySQL 3.23 or 4.0, you might need to change the default encoding for your web pages. See "Understanding collation" in Chapter 14.

Exploring the workspace

Figure 1-4 shows the default Windows workspace with a web page under construction and all the main areas labeled. The main part of the workspace is occupied by the Document window, which includes everything from the Document toolbar to the Tag selector.

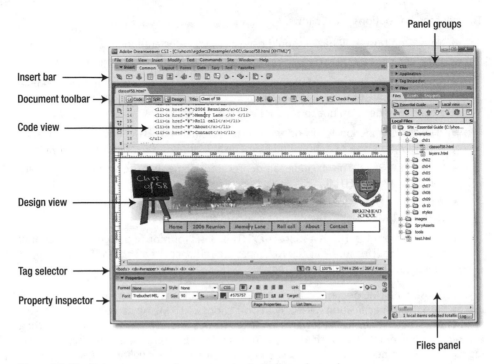

Figure 1-4. The Dreamweaver workspace remains basically unchanged.

As you can see from Figure 1-5, the Mac workspace is virtually the same. In harmony with other Mac programs, the Close, Minimize, and Zoom buttons are at the top left of the Document window. The Document window's tabbed interface is displayed only when more than one document is open. If you want the Mac version to display tabs all the time, open Preferences from the Dreamweaver menu, select the General category, and check the option labeled Always show tabs. Alternatively, if you don't want the tabbed interface, de-select the Open documents in tabs option.

Two other points to note about the Mac workspace: you can close a tab by clicking the ✕ in a circle to the left of the file name; and the Property inspector overlaps the Files panel on a 1024✕768 resolution monitor (the minimum display required for Dreamweaver CS3). As a result, on a small monitor the Property inspector flops in front of or behind the Files panel, depending on whether it has focus. This results in some icons being hidden, but you can bring them back into view by clicking in any blank space in the Property inspector. Alternatively, resize the Files panel to make room.

The main menus run across the top just below the title bar. The menus provide access to all features, but I prefer to work directly in the workspace with Dreamweaver's visual tools, each of which I'll describe briefly.

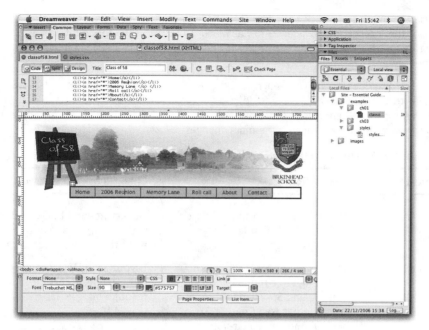

Figure 1-5. Apart from a few minor differences, the Mac workspace is identical to Windows.

Insert bar

The Insert bar is really a collection of toolbars used to perform the most frequently used operations in building web pages. It's organized as a tabbed interface. Figure 1-6 shows the Common tab. When you first launch Dreamweaver, there are six other tabs (or categories). Additional, context-sensitive tabs are displayed only when the features can be used in a particular page, such as when using PHP or the XSL Transformation server behavior. The tabs organize program features in logical groups, so some commonly used features, such as tables and <div> tags, are duplicated on more than one tab to save time switching back and forth.

Figure 1-6. The Common tab of the Insert bar houses some of the most frequently used operations.

If space is at a premium, you can save a few pixels of vertical space by switching to the menu style shown in Figure 1-7. Click the name at the left end to reveal a menu of available categories. However, it takes two clicks to change categories, so you'll probably find the tabbed interface more convenient. Alternatively, you can put frequently used items in the Favorites category as described shortly.

Figure 1-7. The Insert bar has an alternative menu style that saves a little space.

To use the menu style, click the panel Options menu button (shown alongside) at the top right of the Insert bar, and select Show as Menu. To restore the tabbed interface, click the category name at the left end of the Insert bar, and select Show as Tabs from the bottom of the menu.

Table 1-1 describes briefly what each category contains. Although the Insert bar will look familiar to users of previous versions of Dreamweaver, it has been revamped with many new items and the removal of some old ones. For the benefit of readers upgrading from Dreamweaver 8, I have indicated the main changes.

Table 1-1. The main features of Insert bar tabs (categories)

Tab/category	Description	Changes from Dreamweaver 8
Common	Inserts the most commonly used objects, such as tables, images, and `<div>` tags.	Now contains all tags related with `<head>` and `<script>` from the old HTML category.
Layout	Offers various tools for layout, including table modification, frames, and Spry widgets, such as menu bar (see Chapter 7), and tabbed and collapsible panels (see Chapter 8).	Layout Mode was removed but remains accessible through View ➤ Table Mode ➤ Layout Mode.
Forms	Creates forms and inserts all form elements, including Spry validation widgets (forms and Spry validation are covered in Chapter 9).	No change, apart from the addition of Spry validation widgets.
Data	Offers access to most dynamic features, including Spry data sets (see Chapter 19) and PHP server behaviors (see Chapter 14 onward). Also imports data from comma-separated value (CSV) files into a static web page.	Previously the Application category. Import Tabular Data (for CSV files) has been relocated here from the Layout category. Addition of Spry data features.
Spry	All Spry features gathered in a single category.	New.
Text	Provides an alternative to the Property inspector for common formatting options. Also, home to definition list and HTML entities.	Font Tag Editor was removed.
Favorites	Left blank for you to customize.	For backward compatibility, gives access to the HTML and Flash elements categories, which have been removed from the main Insert bar.

Selecting options from the Insert bar To see what each button is for, hold your mouse pointer over it, and a tooltip appears. Some buttons have a little down arrow alongside them to the right. The first time you click one of these buttons, Dreamweaver displays a menu showing all options, as shown in the screenshot alongside. Dreamweaver remembers your selection and always displays the most recently used option. If you want to use the same option again, click the button itself. To select a different option, click the arrow to the right to reveal the menu again.

Customizing the Favorites category If switching among categories becomes too time-consuming, you can populate the Favorites category with your most frequently used items. Select the Favorites tab, right-click, and select Customize Favorites from the context menu. The drop-down menu at the top left of the Customize Favorite Objects dialog box (shown in Figure 1-8) lets you choose either from a master list or from individual categories. In the left panel, select one item at a time, and click the button with the double chevron to add it to the Favorite objects panel on the right. To remove an item, select it in the right panel, and click the trash can button at the top right. The up and down arrows can be used to change the position of the selected item, and the Add separator button inserts a separator after the current item.

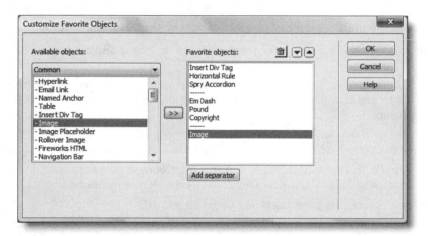

Figure 1-8. You can customize the Favorites category of the Insert bar for quick access to frequently used options.

The Customize Favorite Objects dialog box gives access to all Insert bar categories, including context-sensitive ones, such as PHP, as well as to items that have been removed since Dreamweaver 8.

To copy your Favorites to a different computer, follow the instructions at the end of the next section.

Document window

By default, Dreamweaver displays each web page in a tabbed interface. Tabs are created left to right in the same order as the pages are opened, but you can drag and drop them into any order. You can also tidy up the workspace by right-clicking any tab to reveal a context menu that, among other things, lets you close the individual tab, close all tabs, or close them all except the current one.

Document toolbar Running across the top of the Document window is the Document toolbar, shown in Figure 1-9. The three buttons on the left are the most important, as they let you switch quickly between Code view, Design view, and a combination of both called Split view, as shown in Figures 1-4 and 1-5. The Live Data view button is displayed only in dynamic pages, such as a PHP page. It processes server-side code to show you a good approximation of what the page will look like when parsed by a web server. Before you can use Live Data view, you need to define a testing server as described in Chapter 4.

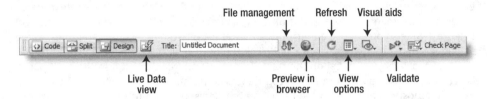

Figure 1-9. The Document toolbar mainly controls how your main work environment looks.

The following list briefly describes the other options on the Document toolbar:

- Title: This is where you enter the document title that is displayed in the browser title bar.

- File management: This offers a quick way of uploading and downloading the current file to and from your remote server. Setting the connection details is covered in Chapter 4.

- Preview in browser: This displays the current page in a browser or Device Central (see "Checking what your page will look like in other media" later in this chapter).

- Refresh: This refreshes Design view. It's used only when you're working in the underlying code in Split view. Otherwise, Design view refreshes automatically.

- View options: This turns rulers and guides on and off.

- Visual aids: This controls the CSS visual aids described in "Using visual aids to understand your CSS structure" later in this chapter.

- Validate: This option checks your document, selected files, or the entire site against World Wide Web Consortium (W3C) standards. Dreamweaver's validator misses some errors, particularly when checking pages against a Strict Document Type Definition (DTD). Double-check against the official W3C Markup Validation Service at http://validator.w3.org.

- Check page: This runs checks for browser compatibility (see "Checking for browser bugs" later in the chapter) and accessibility.

Code view This is where you work directly with all the XHTML, PHP, and other code that controls your web page. Even if you rarely touch the code yourself, it's important to understand what's happening in Code view. PHP code inserted in the wrong place will bring your page down like a house of cards.

Design view This renders your page as it should look in a standards-compliant browser. The CSS rendering in Dreamweaver CS3 is generally very accurate, but don't fall into the trap of regarding Dreamweaver as a WYSIWYG (what you see is what you get) web page builder. It's an excellent visual design tool, but you need a solid understanding of XHTML and CSS to use it to its best advantage.

Tag selector The status bar at the bottom of the Document window displays a hierarchical view of the document indicating where the insertion point is at any given moment. As Figure 1-10 shows, clicking one of the tags in the Tag selector highlights the element in both Design view and Code view. This is extremely useful for editing an element or applying a dynamic behavior to it. Right-clicking a tag in the Tag selector brings up a context menu with a useful selection of editing options, including the ability to add an ID or a class to the element. The Tag selector fulfils a similar role to the GoLive Markup Tree bar.

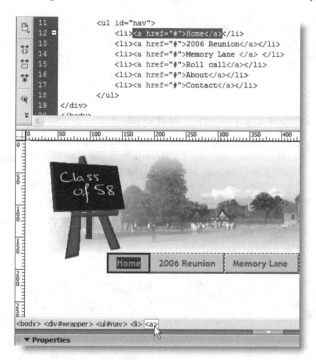

Figure 1-10. Clicking a tag in the Tag selector highlights the element in Design view, as well as the underlying code.

Property inspector This context-sensitive panel gives direct access to all the main attributes of the currently selected element. It's equivalent to the Inspector palette in GoLive.

Panel groups The panel groups, which are displayed by default on the right of the screen, give you access to more detailed or specialized features. Clicking a panel group's title bar toggles it open and closed. The most important one is the Files panel, which not only displays the file hierarchy of your site but also ensures that all internal links are updated and controls uploading and downloading to and from your remote server.

Organizing your workspace

The Windows version of Dreamweaver CS3 comes with three workspace layouts: Designer, Coder, and Dual Screen. Designer is the default layout shown in Figure 1-4. Coder puts the panel groups on the left of the screen with the Property inspector collapsed. Dual Screen detaches the panel groups and Property inspector and opens a separate Code Inspector, ready for you to arrange as you like. The Mac version has two preset options: the Default layout shown in Figure 1-5 and the Dual Screen option.

To select a layout, go to Window ➤ Workspace Layout, and choose the layout you want to use.

Rearranging panels

The preset layouts are just a start. You can undock any panel group by hovering your mouse pointer over the left side of a panel's title bar until it turns into a four-headed arrow, as shown alongside (or a hand on the Mac version). Hold down your mouse button, and drag the panel to wherever you want.

Saving and sharing customized workspace layouts

In addition to undocking panel groups, you can reorganize the panels into different groups to suit your own preferences or to reflect different priorities for various projects. To move a panel, open its parent panel group, and select the panel you want to move. Then right-click the icon on the right of the panel group's title bar to display the Options menu, as shown in the following screenshot. You can choose to move the panel to an existing group or to create a new panel group. The menu also offers other options, including renaming the panel group. (The same options are available from a much larger menu if you use your main mouse button.)

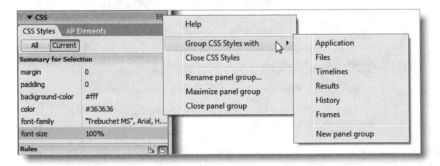

Once everything is the way you want it, save the new layout by choosing Window ➤ Workspace Layout ➤ Save Current. The name of your customized workspace appears at the top of the Workspace Layout submenu. There is no limit to the number of preset layouts that you can create, and you can switch freely between layouts without restarting the program. To rename or remove customized layouts, use the Manage option at the bottom of the Workspace Layout submenu.

You can transfer customized layouts to another computer by copying the XML files that store the details. In Windows XP, the files are in `C:\Documents and Settings\<username>\Application Data\Adobe\Dreamweaver 9\Configuration\Workspace`, where `<username>` is the Windows account to which you are currently logged in. In Vista, they're in `C:\Users\<username>\AppData\Roaming\Adobe\Dreamweaver 9\Configuration\Workspace`. If you can't see the `Application Data` or `AppData` folder, see the next section, "Accessing hidden files and folders in Windows."

On a Mac, they are in `Macintosh HD:Users:<username>:Library:Application Support:Adobe:Dreamweaver 9:Configuration:Workspace`.

The files have the same name that you used to save the layout. Simply copy them to the other computer, and restart Dreamweaver. Since they're XML, you can share them among Windows and Mac users.

Accessing hidden files and folders in Windows

Most Dreamweaver configuration files are hidden by default in Windows XP and Vista. To edit or copy them, you need to enable the option to view hidden files and folders. Once you turn on this option, hidden folders are displayed as dimmed icons to remind you to treat them with care.

In Windows XP, go to Start ➤ My Computer ➤ Tools ➤ Folder Options ➤ View. In Advanced settings, **select** Show hidden files and folders. In Vista, go to Start ➤ Computer ➤ Organize ➤ Folder and Search Options ➤ View. In Advanced settings, **select** Show hidden files and folders.

Displaying optional toolbars

Bizarre though it may seem, the Standard toolbar (see following screenshot) is not displayed by default. To display it, go to View ➤ Toolbars, and select Standard. Alternatively, right-click any toolbar, and select Standard from the context menu.

Dreamweaver automatically locates the Standard toolbar—which contains common file functions such as New Document, Open, Save, Print, Cut, Copy, and Paste—immediately below the Document toolbar. This isn't really very helpful, because it means the toolbar disappears as soon as all documents are closed.

However, on Windows you can move the Standard toolbar by positioning your mouse pointer over the double row of dots at the left edge, holding down the main mouse button, and dragging and dropping the toolbar to a new location. If you have a wide monitor, you can place it alongside the Insert bar. Alternatively, dock it directly underneath the Insert bar. It then remains available at all times.

On a Mac, there appears to be no way of undocking the Standard toolbar from the Document toolbar.

Temporarily hiding all panels

When you want to clear the onscreen clutter to see your design in all its glory, just press F4, and all the panels disappear, leaving the Document window on its own. In Windows, the Document window expands to fill the entire workspace. On a Mac, panels disappear, but the Document window doesn't change size. Press F4 again: the panels return, and on Windows, the Document window shrinks back to fit inside the workspace.

Organizing visual assets with Bridge

New

If you have used Adobe Creative Suite 2, you'll already be familiar with Bridge, although it has undergone a considerable transformation in CS3. It's a powerful file organizer with features designed to appeal to photographers and designers, and it now comes bundled with Dreamweaver CS3. To do Bridge justice would require several chapters, so I'll concentrate on the main points that apply to Dreamweaver.

You can launch Bridge CS3 either from the Start menu in Windows and Applications in Mac OS X or from inside Dreamweaver or any other CS3 program. To launch Bridge from inside Dreamweaver, go to File ➤ Browse in Bridge, or click the Browse in Bridge button on the Standard toolbar (shown alongside).

Bridge is a large program, so it doesn't appear instantly. The advantage of launching Bridge from inside Dreamweaver is that it automatically displays the root folder of the current site in the Content tab. Figure 1-11 shows the default layout of Bridge after navigating to a site's main images folder.

Figure 1-11. Bridge CS3 makes it easy to view and organize a website's visual assets.

The Content tab in the center displays the contents of the selected folder. At first glance, it may not look very different from Windows Explorer or Mac Finder, but the first thing you'll notice is that if you have Flash movies (SWF files) or video (FLV), Fireworks PNG files, Photoshop PSD files, or Adobe Illustrator AI files, you can see a thumbnail of the contents, rather than an icon. You can also play Flash video and see the contents of most PDF files. You can even flip through the pages of a PDF in the Preview panel at the top right.

Two features that will appeal to digital photographers are the abilities to use Bridge to import photos directly from your camera (File ➤ Get Photos from Camera) and to preview photos stored in Camera Raw, the generic name given to the native format of most middle-range and professional-level digital cameras.

Controlling thumbnails

The thumbnails in the Content tab are scalable. Just drag the pointer at the right end of the Bridge status bar to make them bigger or smaller. If the thumbnails look blurred, switch the default to High Quality Thumbnails by opening the Preferences panel (Edit ➤ Preferences or Bridge ➤ Preferences on a Mac) and selecting the Thumbnails category. The Thumbnails category in Preferences also lets you choose other information to be displayed under the thumbnail in addition to the file name.

Once a thumbnail has been generated, Bridge caches it in a central folder to speed up the program's performance. By default, the cache is created in your own user folders, but you can change the location through the Advanced category of Preferences. It's a good idea to purge the cache from time to time to avoid clogging up your hard disk with thumbnails of files no longer in use. You can clear the entire cache by clicking the Purge Cache button in the Advanced category of Preferences. To clear the cached thumbnails for a single folder, go to Tools ➤ Cache, and select Purge Cache for Folder "*foldername*".

As well as the default view shown in Figure 1-11, there are two other layouts: Filmstrip Focus and Metadata Focus (which displays metadata alongside the thumbnail). You can quickly switch between views by clicking one of the numbers at the bottom right of the Bridge status bar.

If you want to display your images in their full glory, Bridge can create a full-screen slideshow (View ➤ Slideshow or Slideshow Options). Press Esc to exit the slideshow.

Adding metadata

To get the most out of Bridge's powerful search capabilities, you need to input information about your images, such as keywords, designer/photographer, ranking (you can give images star ratings), and so on. You fill in these details in the Metadata and Keywords tabs at the bottom right of the default view.

Renaming files

One of the most useful features of Bridge is its ability to rename large numbers of files. Let's say you have just received a batch of photos from a client and they have meaningless names such as DSC_0417.jpg. You can rename them all in seconds by selecting them in

Bridge and going to Tools ➤ Batch Rename. The options allow you to build up complex yet meaningful names. You can rename the existing files in the same folder or make renamed copies in a different folder.

Although you can use the batch rename feature to change the file name extension of all files in a website from .html to .php, the integration with Dreamweaver is not smart enough to update all internal links inside the files. This would be a useful addition to a future version.

Dragging and dropping files

You can drag and drop any file directly from Bridge into Dreamweaver or another CS3 program. If you drag an image into Dreamweaver, it's inserted into the page wherever you drop it, automatically creating the necessary XHTML. If you drag an image into Fireworks, it's immediately ready for editing.

Creating standards-compliant web pages

No sooner was Dreamweaver 8 out of the door than a team of Dreamweaver engineers were recruited for a secret mission known as Project Hoover, a reference to the well-known brand of vacuum cleaners. The team's task has been to sweep up relics of the past, removing obsolete tags and markup from the code that Dreamweaver creates when laying out a web page. Web standardistas will be quick to point out that the job isn't complete, but the team has trodden a delicate path between striving for full standards compliance and maintaining backward compatibility with existing sites. I understand that the team members haven't packed away their coveralls; they plan to keep on vacuuming as they work on the next release. They're not ready to flip the Hoover off switch just yet.

Enhanced CSS support

In spite of some failings, particularly in regard to ensuring full compliance with a Strict DTD—which is still left up to the user—I think it's fair to say that Dreamweaver CS3 is the most standards-compliant version of the program yet. It comes with an impressive array of standard layouts, styled with fully-commented CSS. The handling of CSS style rules and the visual rendering of pages in Design view are much improved. Dreamweaver CS3 is browser-neutral: unlike the previous version, it doesn't attempt to emulate Internet Explorer 6. Instead, it attempts to render styles according to the CSS 2.1 recommendation laid down by W3C—and mostly succeeds.

As part of Project Hoover, Dreamweaver dropped proprietary terminology in favor of more descriptive terms.

Layers are dead . . . Welcome, AP elements

One important change for existing Dreamweaver users and those migrating from GoLive is that layers are dead. Since a layer is really a <div> that has been absolutely positioned with CSS, Dreamweaver CS3 now calls them AP elements. While this may seem a cosmetic change, the idea is to clarify how they fit into a web page. What's more, any tag can be used to create an AP element, not just a <div>.

> *For backward compatibility, "layers" still live on in the name of the JavaScript function associated with one of the Dreamweaver behaviors. Although the* Show/Hide Layers *behavior has been renamed* Show/Hide Elements*, the function is still called* MM_showHideLayers. *However, the behavior now handles any element that has an ID. Behaviors are covered in the next chapter.*

Figure 1-12 shows how Dreamweaver CS3 renders the following code (it's in examples/ch01/classof58.html in the download files):

```
<div id="wrapper">
  <img id="header" src="images/header.jpg" alt="Class of 58" ➥
width="720" height="175" />
  <ul id="nav">
    <li><a href="#">Home</a></li>
    <li><a href="#">2006 Reunion</a></li>
    <li><a href="#">Memory Lane </a> </li>
    <li><a href="#">Roll call</a></li>
    <li><a href="#"</a></li>
    <li><a href="#">Contact</a></li>
  </ul>
</div>
```

The wrapper <div> is relatively positioned to center the whole page in the browser and contains two absolutely positioned elements: an image with the ID header and an unordered list with the ID nav. As you can see, the AP Elements panel on the right of the figure lists both absolutely positioned elements but not the relatively positioned one. In previous versions of Dreamweaver, the Layers panel ignored absolutely positioned elements unless they used a <div> tag.

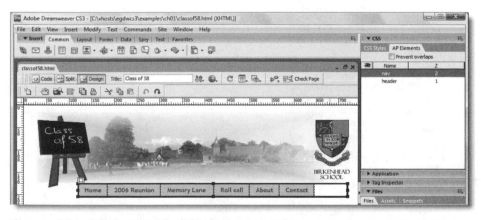

Figure 1-12. Dreamweaver CS3 lists all absolutely positioned elements in the new AP Elements panel.

This new arrangement gives you much greater flexibility and control over your CSS. There's no longer any need to litter your code with unnecessary <div> tags, and the AP Elements panel provides an instant snapshot of the absolutely positioned elements on your page. You can drag and drop elements within the panel to change their z-index property, and the eye icon on the left of the panel changes the visibility property. AP elements nested inside another AP element are indented, and if you realize that the nesting is causing an element to be displayed in the wrong place, you can separate them by dragging the nested element to the left of the panel. Changes made in the AP Elements panel automatically update the element's style rules, even if they are in a separate style sheet.

> *The style rules for* classof58.html *are in* classof58.css *in the* styles *folder. This example has been deliberately designed to demonstrate a new feature of Dreamweaver CS3. I don't necessarily recommend the use of AP elements to achieve this particular layout.*

Seeing the impact of CSS changes in real time

Grouped together with the AP Elements panel is the CSS Styles panel, which lets you inspect and edit style rules without leaving Design view. As a result, you can see immediately how your changes affect the layout of the page and tweak them until you get the desired result. Like many features in Dreamweaver, the CSS Styles panel is context sensitive. Figure 1-13 shows the styles for the nav unordered list in classof58.html. The properties for the #nav ID selector are shown in the lower section of the panel, while the upper sections show all the rules that affect the element currently selected in Design view. This helps you understand how the rules are cascaded down to a particular element, making it easier to troubleshoot styles that don't work the way you expect. Chapters 5 and 6 show you how to make effective use of the CSS Styles panel.

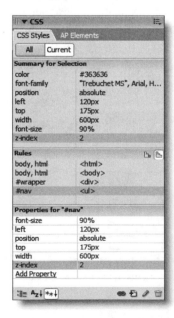

Figure 1-13.
The CSS Styles panel shows which styles in the cascade affect the selected element.

New

Improved style sheet management

A major innovation in Dreamweaver CS3 is the ability to drag and drop selectors in the CSS Styles panel to reorder style blocks in your style sheet. You can also move styles out of the <head> of a document into a new or an existing style sheet with just a couple of mouse clicks. The target style sheet doesn't even need to exist or to be open; everything happens automatically.

If you have old-style layers with inline styles, you can clean up your pages easily by using the Convert Inline CSS to Rule feature to move the rules into the <head> of the document or an external style sheet. It doesn't matter whether you're in Code view or Design view; as long as your cursor is anywhere inside a layer, just right-click and select CSS Styles ➤ Convert Inline CSS to Rule from the context menu. Dreamweaver presents you with the dialog box shown in Figure 1-14.

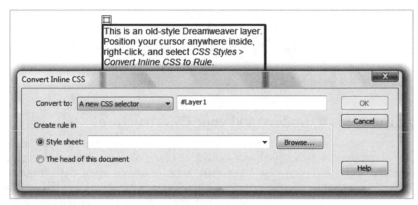

Figure 1-14. As long as your cursor is inside a layer, Dreamweaver can move the inline styles to an external style sheet or the head of the document.

Dreamweaver automatically chooses the ID as the name of the selector for the new rule. Although you can change the name in the dialog box, this affects only the new style rule. It doesn't change the ID of the <div>. You can convert only one layer at a time, but it's a much quicker and more accurate way of tidying up legacy pages than attempting to cut and paste everything manually. The Convert to drop-down menu at the top left of the Convert Inline CSS dialog box has two other options: to create a class based on the inline styles or to apply the styles to all <div> elements. They are there for completeness and should be used rarely, if ever. You can test this feature using layers.html in examples/ch01.

Another small improvement to CSS management in Dreamweaver CS3 is the option to clean up the formatting of style rules by selecting Apply Source Formatting from the Commands menu. The available formatting options are shown in Figure 1-15. They're very basic in comparison with a dedicated CSS editor like TopStyle Pro but are nevertheless a welcome addition. To access the CSS Source Format Options dialog box, go to Preferences on the Edit menu (Dreamweaver menu on a Mac), select the Code Format category, and click the Advanced Formatting CSS button.

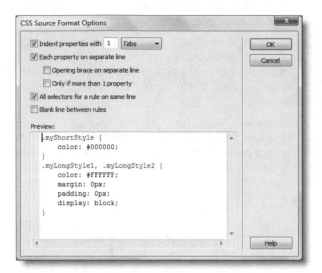

Figure 1-15. You can tell Dreamweaver CS3 how you prefer style sheets to be laid out.

Using visual aids to understand your CSS structure

Dreamweaver's visual aids are a powerful feature that helps you visualize the underlying structure of your page by highlighting individual block elements and their associated padding and margins in Design view. Most visual aids are turned on by default but remain in the background until you select a particular block element, such as a <div> or <table>. Figure 1-16 shows one of the preset layouts with the container <div> selected in the Tag selector (the file is also in examples/ch01/visualaids.html).

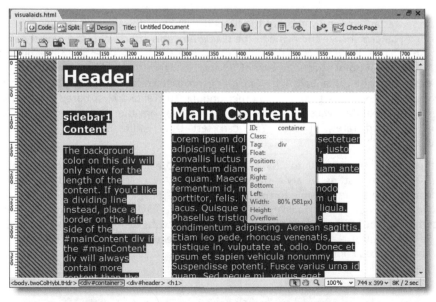

Figure 1-16. Dreamweaver lets you see the underlying structure of your page with powerful visual aids.

When you hover your mouse pointer over different sections of the page, Dreamweaver displays a box containing information about the currently applied style rules. As you can see in Figure 1-16, the width of the container <div> is declared as 80%. The 581px displayed in parentheses is the calculated width that would be displayed in a browser opened to the same size as the current Document window (the size—744×399—is displayed at the right end of the status bar). The selected element has a solid border, and child <div> elements are indicated by a dotted border. Padding and margins are indicated by cross-hatching.

Most of the time, you will find these visual aids a help rather than a hindrance, but if you want to turn them off, open the Visual Aids menu on the Document toolbar (see Figure 1-9 and the screenshot alongside). A check mark alongside an option indicates that it's active. Clicking an option toggles it on and off. The same options are also available from the Visual Aids submenu of the View menu. A quick way to toggle all currently selected visual aids on and off is to use the keyboard shortcut Ctrl+Shift+I/Shift+Cmd+I.

The CSS Layout Backgrounds option is turned off by default. It identifies all box elements on a page by highlighting each one in a different color. It's useful for analyzing a page that you might have inherited from another developer but should normally be disabled. If your page suddenly looks like a five-year-old child's coloring book, make sure CSS Layout Backgrounds hasn't been turned on by mistake.

Checking for browser bugs

Another invaluable aid in CSS troubleshooting is the Check Browser Compatibility feature. This offers much more detailed support than the Check Browser Support option in Dreamweaver 8, which it replaces. Figure 1-17 shows the results of running Check Browser Compatibility on classof58.html.

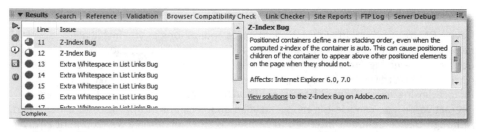

Figure 1-17. Dreamweaver CS3 identifies potential CSS bugs in your pages and links to an online knowledge base.

As you can see, Dreamweaver lists two potential bugs together with the line on which the affected elements are located in the XHTML code. The field on the right of the Results panel gives a brief description of the CSS bug, and at the bottom of the panel, there's a link to an online resource called CSS Advisor, where you can find further information. The site is moderated by Adobe to ensure that the information comes from reliable sources. Clicking the bottom icon in the left margin of the Results panel launches your default browser and presents you with the full report as a single page.

New

Checking what your page will look like on other media

Adobe Device Central CS3 is a major addition to Dreamweaver. In addition to launching a variety of browsers from within Dreamweaver to preview your website, you can now see how it will look in a mobile phone. Figure 1-18 shows classof58.html in a generic device, but you can choose skins from all the main mobile phone manufacturers, and more will be made available on a regular basis as a free upgrade service.

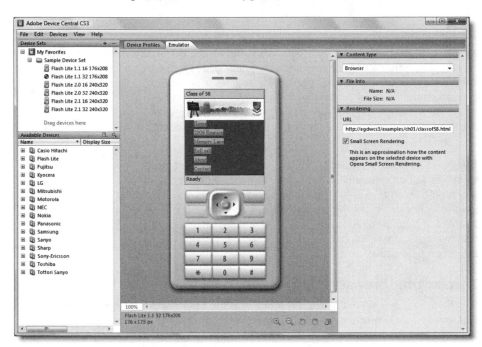

Figure 1-18. Device Central lets you see what your site will look like in a wide range of mobile devices.

Device Central works both with static web pages and, as long as you install a PHP development environment as described in Chapter 4, dynamic PHP pages, too. You access Device Central by selecting File ➤ Preview in Browser ➤ Device Central. The keyboard shortcut (Ctrl+Alt+F12/Ctrl+Opt+F12) is easy to remember because it's so similar to the shortcut for previewing in your default browser (F12/Opt+F12). The display in Device Central is interactive, so you can use the mobile keypad and click links to navigate to other pages. Although Device Central is intended to be used as an emulator in a development environment, you can also view live pages on the Internet. Just type the website address into the URL field in the right panel and press Enter/Return.

Using the Style Rendering toolbar Many people think of style sheets in terms of "one size fits all"—in other words, they create one set of style rules and hope that the site will look just as good in every medium. However, you can specify different style sheets for a variety of media, those with the best support being for ordinary browsers (screen), print, and handheld devices. One of Dreamweaver 8's best-kept secrets—because it wasn't enabled by default—was the Style Rendering toolbar (see Figure 1-19). You still have to enable it yourself in Dreamweaver CS3, but it's well worth doing so if you work with multiple style sheets.

The Style Rendering toolbar lets you see the effect of each media style sheet in Design view. It also allows you to disable CSS entirely, so that you can see the logical flow of your web page in the same way that it would be presented to a visually disabled person using a screen reader.

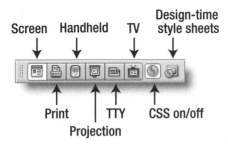

Figure 1-19.
The Style Rendering toolbar lets you see the effect of different style sheets without leaving Design view.

A new addition to the Style Rendering toolbar in Dreamweaver CS3 is the Design Time Style Sheets icon. This gives direct access to the Design Time Style Sheets dialog box, which lets you control which style sheets are applied or hidden while working in Design view. The advantage of this is that it allows you to view two or more style sheets in combination, whereas the Style Rendering toolbar selects only one at a time. Design Time Style Sheets are covered in Chapter 12.

To enable the Style Rendering toolbar, go to View ➤ Toolbars, and select Style Rendering. Dreamweaver parks the toolbar at the top of the Document window, but in Windows, you can detach it and move it to a new location by dragging the double row of dots to the left of the Screen icon.

If you prefer working with menus, you can access the Style Rendering submenu from the View menu. To access Design Time Style Sheets, use Text ➤ CSS Styles ➤ Design-time.

Understanding Dreamweaver's approach to layout

Although many people treat Dreamweaver as a WYSIWYG tool, you'll get the best out of the program if you have a good understanding of the principles of XHTML and CSS, and use Design view to keep track of how your structure is likely to be rendered in standards-compliant browsers. However, Dreamweaver does have some legacy features that are designed to assist with purely visual layout. Most of them are best avoided, but it's useful to know they exist and the problems they can cause.

Drawing absolutely positioned elements

The Draw AP Div button (see alongside) in the Layout tab of the Insert bar lets you "draw" an absolutely positioned <div> in Design view. It's simple to use. The cursor turns to a crosshair pointer. Position the intersection of the crosshair wherever you want to locate a corner of the <div>, hold down the main mouse button, and drag in any direction. When the <div> is how you want it, release the mouse button.

If you need to make any adjustments, click the box-shaped handle at the top left of the <div>. When the cursor turns into a four-headed arrow as shown in the following screenshot (on a Mac, it turns into a hand), hold down the main mouse button to drag and drop the <div> into a new position. You can visually change the dimensions of the <div> by using any of the resize handles at the corners and the center of each side.

This is a very convenient way of creating an absolutely positioned <div>. Dreamweaver automatically assigns the ID apDiv1 to the first one on a page and numbers any subsequent ones sequentially. The style rules for each <div> created this way are automatically inserted into a style block in the <head> of the document. You can also insert an absolutely positioned <div> by choosing Insert ➤ Layout Objects ➤ AP Div, and move and visually resize it the same way.

The problem with creating an absolutely positioned <div> by either of these methods is that you need to keep an eye on what is happening to your underlying code. It doesn't matter where your cursor is when you use the Draw AP Div button on the Insert bar. Dreamweaver always inserts the first new <div> immediately after the opening <body> tag, and any subsequent ones are also inserted ahead of your static (non-absolutely positioned) content. However, if you use the Insert menu to insert an absolutely positioned <div>, the code is inserted wherever your cursor happens to be at the time. Everything may look fine in Design view, but the underlying code can descend into chaos if you're not careful.

Layout Mode goes into exile

Changed

A change that will shock some visual designers is the removal of Layout Mode from the Layout category of the Insert bar. The concept behind Layout Mode was well intentioned: it attempts to treat web page layout like desktop publishing. After drawing a layout table as the page framework, you draw individual layout cells to hold your content, while Dreamweaver looks after building the underlying structure.

Unfortunately, the Web is a fluid medium totally unlike print, and the way Layout Mode achieves a rigid framework is by creating a rat's nest of code glued together by invisible spacer images. The result *can* look very satisfying. The problems arise when you decide to reposition anything or add extra content. The code begins to tie itself in impossible knots, and pleas for help in online forums invariably bring forth hoots of derision followed by the only practical advice: start again, preferably avoiding Layout Mode.

I don't propose to say anything more about Layout Mode other than to advise you to stay well clear. Layout Mode can still be accessed by selecting View ➤ Table Mode ➤ Layout Mode (Alt+F6/Opt+F6), but the complex code that it creates will have you tearing your hair out if you attempt to combine it with dynamic technologies, such as Spry and PHP. You should also avoid all other options on the Table Mode submenu.

Getting the best out of Code view

Many web designers are terrified of working with the code that lies under Dreamweaver's Design view. There's nothing to be worried about. Most of the time you can remain in Design view and leave Dreamweaver to create efficient, standards-compliant code on your behalf. But when you start mixing Spry or PHP dynamic elements with your web pages, you need to understand what is going on in Code view. That doesn't mean you need to learn every single tag and attribute, but you do need to know when something is in the wrong place and where to locate your cursor for Dreamweaver to insert dynamic code. Code view has a number of features to make your life easier.

Using the Coding toolbar

The Coding toolbar is displayed by default on the left side of Code view. It's also available in the Code Inspector (F10/Opt+F10), which allows you to view the underlying code of a page in a separate window. The Coding toolbar can't be undocked, but you can hide it in Code view by deselecting it from the View ➤ Toolbars menu (or from the context menu of any toolbar). In the Code Inspector, it's controlled independently by the View Options menu at the top of the inspector.

Figure 1-20 shows what each button is for, and the same information is displayed as a tooltip whenever you hover your mouse pointer over one of them. A really cool aspect of the Coding toolbar is what happens when there's not enough room to display all the buttons. A double chevron appears after the last button that can fit into the available space. If you click it, the rest of the toolbar sits neatly at the bottom of Code view.

Open documents

Collapse full tag
Collapse selection
Expand all

Select parent tag
Balance braces

Line numbers
Highlight invalid code

Apply comment tags
Remove comment tags
Wrap tag
Recent snippets
Move or convert CSS

Indent code
Outdent code
Format source code

Figure 1-20. The Coding toolbar

Let's take a quick look at what each button does:

- **Open documents**: This displays a list of currently open documents together with the full pathname of each file. This is very useful if you have several pages open, all with the same name (such as index.php from different folders or sites). Click the name of a file, and it comes to the front—no more guessing whether you have the correct file open.

- **Collapse full tag**: This selects the code block in which your cursor is currently located and collapses everything inside including the opening and closing tags. Unfortunately, it works only with XHTML tags; it cannot be used to select a PHP code block. To collapse everything *outside* a full tag, hold down the Alt/Opt key while clicking the Collapse Full Tag button. This is useful for isolating a block of code and hiding the rest of the page.

- **Collapse selection**: This collapses the currently selected code. To collapse all code *outside* the selection, hold down Alt/Opt while clicking the Collapse Selection button.

- **Expand All**: Click this to expand all collapsed sections.

- **Select parent tag**: This selects the parent tag of the current selection or wherever the insertion point is currently located. For example, if your cursor is inside a paragraph, it selects the entire paragraph and the enclosing <p> tags. Clicking again moves up the document hierarchy, always selecting the parent element of the current selection.

- **Balance braces**: This selects all code between matching curly braces, brackets, or parentheses. *This button will help maintain your sanity when working with PHP code.*

- **Line numbers**: This toggles on and off the display of line numbers in Code view.

- **Highlight invalid code**: Dreamweaver highlights incorrectly nested tags in yellow. This can be distracting in Code view, particularly when working with PHP, where conditional structures might result in code that Dreamweaver incorrectly interprets as invalid. This button toggles the yellow highlighting on and off in Code view. The default is off.

- **Apply comment tags**: This lets you apply different types of comment tags to the current line or selection. PHP comments are covered in Chapter 10.

- **Remove comment tags**: This removes comment tags from the current line or selection.

- **Wrap tag**: This provides a quick way to wrap the current selection in an XHTML tag. Dreamweaver lets you select any tag, even if it's inappropriate in the current context. This is based on the principle that, if you're working in Code view, you should know what you're doing. When mixed with PHP conditional logic, apparently invalid code is often perfectly OK, so Dreamweaver makes no attempt to intervene.

- **Recent snippets**: This displays a list of the most recently used items from the Snippets panel, providing quick access to frequently used code snippets.

- **Move or convert CSS**: This provides a quick way to move style rules, as described in "Improved style sheet management" earlier in the chapter.

- **Indent code**: This moves the opening tag of the current selection to the right. If nothing is selected, Dreamweaver automatically selects the parent tag and moves it.

- **Outdent code**: This moves the opening tag to the left.
- **Format source code**: This reveals a menu that lets you apply default formatting to the entire page or the current selection. It also provides quick access to the Code Format category of the Preferences panel and to the Tag Library Editor. The Tag Library Editor gives you control over how every single XHTML tag is formatted in your underlying code. It's mainly of interest to advanced users, but the interface is intuitive and easy to use.

In addition to using the Coding toolbar to collapse sections of code, you can use the keyboard shortcuts in Table 1-2. When you collapse a section of code, it affects only what you see in Code view; the contents remain fully expanded in Design view. Dreamweaver remembers which sections of code are collapsed when a page is saved, so the same layout is visible in Code view the next time you open a document.

Table 1-2. Keyboard shortcuts for collapsing code

Action	Windows shortcut	Mac shortcut
Collapse full tag	Ctrl+Shift+J	Shift+Cmd+J
Collapse outside tag	Ctrl+Alt+J	Opt+Cmd+J
Collapse selection	Ctri+Shift+C	Shift+Cmd+C
Collapse outside selection	Ctrl+Alt+C	Opt+Cmd+C
Expand all	Ctrl+Alt+E	Opt+Cmd+E

To inspect a collapsed section, highlight it and use the plus button in the left margin (it's a triangle in the Mac version) to expand it, or hover your mouse pointer over it and view the content as a tooltip.

To select sections of code in Code view, use the Select Parent Tag or Balance Braces buttons. Alternatively, use your mouse or keyboard in the same way as with any text editor. Double-clicking selects the current word. Triple-clicking selects the parent tag. The GoLive selection shortcuts *do not work* in Dreamweaver.

Setting Code view options

Code view has a number of options that you can set by accessing View ➤ Code View Options or from the View options menu on the Document toolbar (see Figure 1-9 and the screenshot alongside). You toggle the options on and off by clicking them. A check mark alongside an option indicates that it's active.

Controlling word wrapping in Code view The way Dreamweaver wraps text in Code view confuses many people. There are two options: soft and hard wrapping. Soft wrapping is *on* by default and works like a word processor. When code would normally extend beyond the right edge of Code view, Dreamweaver automatically wraps it to the next line. If you resize the Code view window, the code reorganizes itself to fit the viewport. No new line characters are inserted into the code until you press Enter/Return. If you prefer your code to be in a single line and don't mind scrolling horizontally, deselect Word Wrap.

Hard wrapping is *off* by default. When turned on, it automatically inserts a new line character a preset distance from the left margin. Although this makes code look tidy, it causes serious problems with JavaScript and is *not* recommended. It's controlled by the Automatic wrapping option in the Code Format category of the Preferences panel (Edit ➤ Preferences or Dreamweaver ➤ Preferences). If you have turned this option on, I strongly recommend that you turn it off and rely on soft wrapping instead.

Displaying line numbers Dreamweaver displays line numbers in the left margin of Code view. They are generated automatically and don't become part of your code. The line numbers are particularly useful for locating problems with PHP code. You can also toggle them on and off from the Coding toolbar.

Displaying hidden characters This option reveals characters that aren't normally visible in your code. It should normally be turned off but can be useful for debugging problems caused by unwanted new line characters in PHP or JavaScript.

Highlighting invalid code This menu option does the same as the button on the Coding toolbar described in the preceding section.

Syntax coloring Dreamweaver highlights XHTML, PHP, and other code in preset colors according to the role it fulfils, making it easy to identify key sections of code quickly. Forgetting to close a pair of quotes results in the subsequent code being displayed in the wrong color, alerting you to the mistake. In normal circumstances, this option should always be on. You can adjust the colors to your liking by going to Edit ➤ Preferences (Dreamweaver ➤ Preferences on a Mac) and selecting Code Coloring. Choose the appropriate Document type, and click Edit Coloring Scheme.

Automatically indenting code With the Auto Indent option selected, Dreamweaver automatically indents your code according to the settings in the Code Format category of the Preferences panel and the Tag Library Editor, as described in the preceding section.

Using code hints and auto completion

By default, Dreamweaver displays context-sensitive code hints in Code view. For example, if you type an opening angle bracket after the <body> tag of an XHTML page, a context menu pops up displaying all valid XHTML tags, as shown in the screenshot alongside. You can either scroll down to find the tag you want and double-click to insert it or continue typing. As soon as you type di, the context menu highlights <>div. Press Enter/Return, and Dreamweaver completes the tag name.

When you press the spacebar, another context menu springs up, this time showing you all the valid attributes for the tag. Again, scroll down to select the one you want or continue typing. If you type i and press Enter/Return, Dreamweaver enters id="", as shown alongside, and positions

the insertion point between the quotes ready for you to insert the ID value. Even better, if your page already has a style sheet attached to it, Dreamweaver populates a list of defined IDs. Use your keyboard arrow keys and Enter/Return to insert your choice. Alternatively, select it with your mouse pointer and double-click.

These context menus continue to appear until you type the closing angle bracket of the tag. If you lose the context menu, just press Ctrl+Space anywhere between the opening and closing brackets of a tag.

> *The keyboard shortcut for code hints on the Mac version is the same as Windows (Ctrl+Space) to avoid a conflict with Spotlight, which uses Cmd+Space.*

Automatic completion of closing tags Dreamweaver is smart enough to keep track of which tags are open. As soon as you type </ in Code view, it automatically inserts the correct closing tag. For example, let's say you have the following code in a page:

```
<p>This text is <strong>bold and <em>italicized
```

If you type </ three times, Dreamweaver automatically completes the open tags in the correct order like this:

```
<p>This text is <strong>bold and <em>italicized</em></strong></p>
```

Fine-tuning code hints Most people find code hints invaluable, but if they annoy you or get in your way, you can delay their appearance by up to five seconds or turn them off altogether. However, Dreamweaver is much more responsive if you leave the delay at its default setting of zero. To change the default settings, go to Edit ➤ Preferences (Dreamweaver ➤ Preferences on a Mac), and select the Code Hints category. The Menus option lets you turn off code hints for individual categories. For example, you may decide that you want code hints only for XHTML tags and CSS properties. All categories are enabled by default.

For compatibility with Dreamweaver MX 2004, you can get Dreamweaver to insert the matching closing tag as soon as you type the closing angle bracket of an opening tag. So, if you enter <p>, Dreamweaver inserts </p> and places the insertion point between the opening and closing tags. This setting can be useful when working with PHP because Dreamweaver sometimes gets confused as to which tag should be completed if dynamic code lies in between. You can also tell Dreamweaver never to complete tags.

Dynamic too . . .

So far, I've covered the basic things you need to know about Dreamweaver in order to start building static web pages using XHTML and CSS, but Dreamweaver is capable of much more. A major new feature in Dreamweaver CS3 is the integration of the Spry Ajax framework. Dreamweaver also has support for creating dynamic websites using server-side technology. The one I have chosen to concentrate on in this book is PHP in combination with the MySQL database, both widely available and highly popular open source technologies. The next chapter explains how they fit into the bigger picture of web development and how Dreamweaver makes them easy to use.

2 BUILDING DYNAMIC SITES WITH AJAX AND PHP

Foundation ActionScri
Powers, and Eric Doleck

<u>Buy new</u>: $~~$44.99~~ **$29.6**

Get it by **Monday, Mar. 5,**

★★★★★

PHP Solutions: Dynam
(**Paperback** - Nov 20,

<u>Buy new</u>: $~~$34.99~~ **$23.0**

Get it by **Monday, Mar. 5,**

★★★★★

 To get this behavior to work properly,
of the content tag you want to slide. (I
an <image> tag that is wrapped with a
<div> tag. The container tag must hav

Please select a container tag as your ta
behavior, wrap your target element wi
tag a unique ID, and reapply the behav
behavior, select the new div tag as you

The action will not be added to your d

In the last chapter, I discussed many of the new and improved features in Dreamweaver CS3, but the one with the real "wow factor" is Spry, Adobe's implementation of Ajax. Although Ajax started out as an acronym for Asynchronous JavaScript + XML, it's taken on a broader meaning. In simple terms, it's a combination of existing technologies that allow you to change the content of a web page without the need to reload it in a browser, and rival implementations have mushroomed at a breathtaking pace. Ajax is not without problems, particularly with regard to accessibility and search engine optimization, so in this chapter, I'll explain what Ajax is, what its pluses and minuses are, and how Dreamweaver has implemented the Adobe version called Spry. I'll also be discussing PHP, the most popular server-side language, which—among other things—activates online forms to send email, communicate with a database, and make websites searchable.

What this chapter covers

- Exploring different ways of adding dynamic features to a website
- Understanding the strengths and weaknesses of Ajax and PHP
- Using Dreamweaver's built-in JavaScript behaviors
- Applying Spry effects to different page elements
- Wrapping a selection in a <div>
- Removing a tag cleanly without losing its contents
- Taking a look at Dreamweaver server behaviors
- Comparing files with a third-party utility

Understanding how dynamic pages work

Back in the early 1990s, web pages consisted of nothing but text. Things didn't stand still for long, and it soon became possible to add images and scrolling text. But even if some things moved around the page in an irritating way, everything on the Web was **static** in the sense that the content was fixed at the time the page was created. Genuinely dynamic features began to be added around 1995 with the help of two distinct types of technology: client-side and server-side. The primary distinction between the two is concerned not with *how* dynamic features are generated but with *where*.

At its most basic level, the Internet involves a simple request and response between the user's computer (the **client**) and the remote website (the **server**), as illustrated in Figure 2-1. Client-side technology works entirely on the client computer. When used in conjunction with a website, server-side technology dynamically generates content on the server and usually sends the result to the client. (Server-side technology encompasses a much broader range, but I'm concerned here with the way it integrates with the Web.)

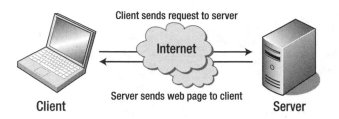

Figure 2-1. The basic relationship on the Internet is between client and server.

Making pages dynamic with client-side technology

In December 1995, Netscape incorporated into its browser the ability to handle JavaScript. Microsoft followed shortly afterward, and before long, web pages were using features such as image rollovers, pop-up windows, and interactive forms for calculations. These types of dynamic features rely on a script being downloaded from the server at the same time as the web page. The script runs exclusively on the client computer without any further contact with the server, hence the name **client-side** technology.

Unfortunately, Netscape and Microsoft implemented incompatible versions of the Document Object Model (DOM), which—among other things—allows a browser to interact with a web page. This forced developers to write convoluted scripts to get dynamic effects to work consistently in all browsers. Programs like Dreamweaver came to the rescue with cross-browser JavaScript behaviors, but they're limited to simple dynamic effects. JavaScript looked as though it would never fulfill its original promise.

> *Despite the similarity of names, JavaScript is totally unrelated to Java. It was originally going to be called LiveScript, but the name was changed at the last moment in an apparent attempt to cash in on the popularity of Java. The decision has caused confusion ever since.*

JavaScript isn't the only client-side technology. In Flash, the animation and interactive code are embedded into a SWF file and downloaded to the client. However, Flash also has the ability to communicate with the server, something that was rarely done with JavaScript until the technique was popularized by Ajax.

Increasing user interactivity with server-side technology

With a static web page, everything is fixed at the time of design. All text, links, images, and client-side scripts are hard-coded into the underlying markup. Dynamic web pages built with a **server-side** language like PHP work in a very different way. Instead of all content being embedded in the underlying code, much of it is automatically generated by the server-side language or drawn from a database. Figure 2-2 illustrates this extra stage in the process.

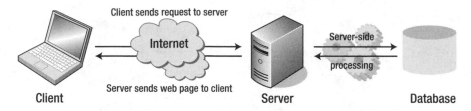

Figure 2-2. Server-side technology involves processing on the server before the web page is sent back to the client.

Generating content dynamically on the server makes it possible to offer the user a much richer variety of content. Perhaps the best known example is www.amazon.com. Even though the Amazon catalog contains many thousands of items, you can search its website for your favorite author (well, mine anyway), and seconds later it presents you with something like Figure 2-3.

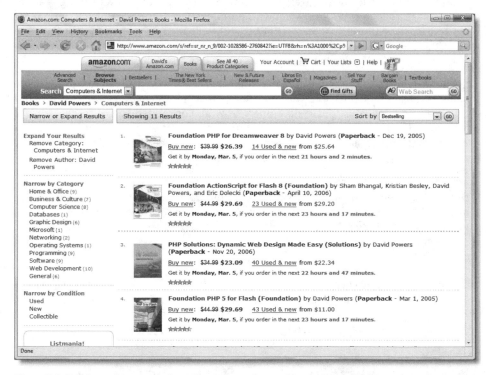

Figure 2-3. Database-driven websites tailor information to the user's requirements through server-side techology.

Amazon and international news providers, such as the BBC (www.bbc.com/news) or CNN (www.cnn.com), constantly update their pages in response to sales figures or breaking news stories. It would be impossible for them to create and store a separate web page for every item. Instead, most of the content is stored in a database, and the web server extracts the relevant information. Although this involves extra processing, it's normally very quick, and the whole sequence appears seamless to the user.

Dreamweaver CS3 supports the following server-side technologies:

- **Active Server Pages (ASP):** Now often referred to as Classic ASP, this is a Microsoft technology that's no longer under development. Although still in widespread use, its limited future makes it a poor choice for anyone starting to develop dynamic websites.

- **ASP.NET:** This is Microsoft's replacement for ASP. Although Dreamweaver CS3 supports ASP.NET with C# and Visual Basic (VB), it doesn't support ASP.NET 2.0.

- **ColdFusion**: This is Adobe's own server-side technology. It's powerful and easy to learn, but not as widely available as most other server-side solutions.

- **JavaServer Pages (JSP)**: This has a steep learning curve, and tends to be used mainly by large organizations.

- **PHP**: PHP is powerful, very widely used, easy to learn—and the choice for this book.

Why choose PHP?

Arguments of an almost religious nature often break out when discussing which server-side technology is the best. All the languages supported by Dreamweaver are fine, but it's a good idea to pick one and get to know it well. Once you have become proficient at one server-side language, you'll find the transition to another a lot easier, because they share many elements in common.

So, why choose PHP in preference to the others? PHP is the Web's most widely available server-side language. Although it fell back from a peak of more than 22 million domains in mid-2005 (www.php.net/usage.php), it remains the most popular module on Apache, the software that runs 60 percent of web servers in the world today (http://news. netcraft.com/archives/web_server_survey.html). Dreamweaver supports PHP in conjunction with MySQL, the most popular open source database (www.mysql.com). Apache, PHP, and MySQL run on just about every operating system, including Windows, Mac OS X, and Linux. This flexibility is one of the great advantages of developing with PHP/MySQL. Let's quickly look at the others:

- **Cost**: They're free. Don't be fooled into thinking this means they're just for hobbyists. MySQL is used by many leading organizations, including NASA, the U.S. Census Bureau, Yahoo!, and the New York Stock Exchange.

- **Open source**: Apache, PHP, and MySQL all benefit from a rapid upgrade policy based on need rather than commercial pressures. If a bug or security risk is identified, the input of many volunteers helps the core development teams solve problems rapidly.

- **Cross-platform capability**: You can develop on your personal computer and deploy the same code on the production server, even if it's running on a different operating system. While the goal is 100 percent cross-platform compatibility, some hosts run PHP on Windows servers in CGI mode, which lacks some features. I point out such differences whenever they affect the code in this book and offer alternative solutions.

One thing missing from that list is "ease of learning." That's not because they're difficult—far from it. All are relatively easy to pick up, but they do require a bit of effort on your part. If you have experience with other programming languages, your progress is likely to be much faster than if you are a complete beginner. This book is designed to ease your progress, whatever your level of expertise.

> *Although Apache is the recommended web server for PHP, you can also use Microsoft IIS on some Windows systems. Instructions for setting up both are in Chapter 3.*

Taking dynamic functionality a stage further with Ajax

Ajax is a fusion of client-side and server-side technology that has been made possible thanks, in part, to the end of the browser wars, and to the efforts of developers of extensive code libraries that make remaining differences invisible to the user. You can read the original article that launched the term Ajax at www.adaptivepath.com/publications/essays/archives/000385.php.

The client-side and server-side technologies that I have described so far are **synchronous**. All interaction between client and server happens at the same time. The client sends a request and the server responds; that's the end of the communication. Ajax, on the other hand, is capable of **asynchronous** communication with the server. It can send requests to the server in the background, and when it receives the response, just the affected part of the page is redrawn, usually providing a much more seamless user experience. Ajax frequently employs sophisticated effects, such as color transitions, glides, and fades.

This type of functionality requires complex scripting, so most developers rely on a JavaScript **framework** or **code library**—a collection of tried and tested code. Spry is one such framework, first released by Adobe in mid-2006. Anyone can download it from http://labs.adobe.com/technologies/spry, but the free version requires everything to be coded by hand. Dreamweaver CS3 automates the entire process, putting Ajax features at your fingertips without the need to touch a line of code. However, before rushing to use Spry on every web page, you need to be aware of the limitations of Ajax, some of them serious.

Understanding the limitations of Ajax

All mainstream modern browsers as far back as Internet Explorer 5.0 (Windows only), Mozilla/Firefox 1.0, Netscape 7, Safari 1.2, and Opera 7.6 support the level of DOM manipulation required by Ajax but with one important condition: *JavaScript must be enabled*. This may not seem to be a major obstacle, but published statistics seem to indicate that the proportion of people browsing with JavaScript disabled has consistently remained in the region of 10 percent for several years (www.w3schools.com/browsers/browsers_stats.asp). Many developers dispute these figures, contending that the figures are almost certainly distorted by search engine spiders, which don't use JavaScript.

Hopefully, the last point rang alarm bells in your head. Since search engine spiders don't use JavaScript, they can't index any content or links on your site that rely on Ajax—or, indeed, any other client-side script. You should implement Ajax with care and ensure that your site remains navigable and meaningful even with JavaScript turned off. Fortunately, many aspects of Spry do leave your content accessible, but Spry data sets are more of a problem, as I'll demonstrate later in the chapter.

See http://en.wikipedia.org/wiki/Ajax_%28programming%29#Pros_and_cons for a good summary of the pros and cons of Ajax.

Other considerations you should take into account when deciding whether to use Spry are as follows:

- The Spry code libraries are much bigger than the scripts used by Dreamweaver behaviors. The code that controls a Spry data set runs to nearly 6,000 lines, adding approximately 160KB to the size of your page download. Adding a Spry effect, such as fading an image, increases the download by more than 60KB. The libraries remain in the browser's memory, so you don't need to worry about this being added to every page, but you should consider carefully whether a single effect is worth the extra burden or at least consider avoiding heavy use of Spry on the site's opening page.

- Changes made to the content of a page by Spry cannot be bookmarked, nor do they become part of the browser's history, so the back button may not work as expected.

- With server-side technology, all processing is done on the server, so you can be sure that your intended content is delivered to everyone. If you can achieve the same results with server-side code, you should consider using it instead of Spry.

Use Spry to enhance your website and not just because Ajax sounds cool. Ajax *is* cool. What's *not* cool is making your website less user friendly because you don't know how to use the right tools for the job.

Dynamic terminology 101

Dreamweaver greatly speeds up the development of dynamic pages by generating most of the code for you, but you'll find life a lot simpler if you have at least a basic understanding of what's happening in Code view, as it makes troubleshooting much easier. Also if you rely on Dreamweaver to do everything for you with PHP, you'll be restricted to very basic features.

This section explains some basic concepts. There's a more detailed explanation of PHP in Chapter 10.

Variable A variable acts as a placeholder for an unknown or changeable value, which may come from user input, a database, the result of a calculation, and so on. Although this sounds abstract, we use variables all the time in everyday life. My name is David, and my editor's name is Chris. In this case, "name" plays the same role as a variable—the word "name" always remains the same, but the *value assigned* to it can change.

Function Functions can be regarded as the verbs of programming languages; they do things. Many functions are built into the language, but you can also build your own functions by combining a series of commands. In both JavaScript and PHP, function names are always followed by a pair of parentheses. Often, the parentheses contain variables, known as **parameters** or **arguments**. Passing a variable as an argument tells the function to do something with it, such as perform a calculation or format text.

Event handler JavaScript is triggered by **events**, such as when the page has finished loading or the user clicks a link. You tell the browser to run a function by assigning it (plus any arguments, if necessary) to an event handler such as onclick, onmouseover, or onmouseout. To give a trivial example, the following code pops up an annoying message when the link is clicked:

```
<a href="#" onclick="alert('You clicked!')">Click me quick</a>
```

String This is the name that programming languages give to text. A string is always enclosed in quotes.

Number Normally, numbers should not be enclosed in quotes. When they are, both JavaScript and PHP treat them as strings, sometimes with surprising results.

Array An array is a variable that can hold multiple values, rather like a shopping list.

Object An object is like a super variable, which can have variables (called **properties**) and functions (called **methods**) of its own. New instances of an object are created using a constructor function, which looks and works very much like any other function.

Changed

Using Dreamweaver behaviors and Spry effects

Behaviors are ready-made JavaScript functions that you can add to your web pages. Most behaviors in Dreamweaver CS3 are showing signs of advanced age and should be pensioned off, but have been retained for backward compatibility. However, the Spry team has contributed seven new behaviors—called Spry effects—breathing new life into the Behaviors panel.

Third-party developers are also an important source of up-to-date client-side (and server-side) functionality through Dreamweaver extensions. To install a Dreamweaver extension, double-click the MXP file you get from the developer, and follow the instructions onscreen. You can also install and manage extensions with the Extension Manager (Help ➤ Manage Extensions). The following is a short—and by no means exhaustive—list of some of the most respected third-party developers (some extensions are free; others are sold on a commercial basis):

- Community MX (http://communitymx.com/)
- DMXzone (http://dmxzone.com/)
- Kaosweaver (http://kaosweaver.com/)
- Project Seven (www.projectseven.com)
- Tom Muck (http://tom-muck.com/)

You can visit their sites to see what they have to offer, but first let's take a look at how you use behaviors by using some of the built-in ones.

Accessing the Behaviors panel

Although the coding methods behind the Spry effects are very different from all the other built-in behaviors (they're based on Ajax), they are applied in exactly the same way as any other behavior. So let's use one of the new Spry effects to see how to work with behaviors.

2

Shortly before Dreamweaver CS3 began shipping, Adobe decided to make a fundamental change in the main code library for Spry effects, using JavaScript objects instead of functions. This will make it easier to combine effects. However, the new code library (Spry 1.5) was not completed in time, and Dreamweaver CS3 shipped with version 1.4. To ensure that effects applied through the Dreamweaver Behaviors *panel continue to work when Spry 1.5 becomes available (expected in mid-2007), Dreamweaver uses wrapper functions to create the JavaScript objects. This means you can apply Spry effects without worrying about the changes.*

Spry is still evolving. To keep up with developments, visit http://blogs.adobe.com/ spryteam/. *Adobe says updates to Spry will be incorporated into Dreamweaver, although at the time of this writing no decision had been made whether this would be through the automatic updater or the release of extensions. Check my website at* http://foundationphp.com/egdwcs3/updates.php *for details of changes that affect the instructions in this book.*

If you open effects_start.html in examples/ch02 in the default Dreamweaver workspace, it should look like Figure 2-4. The page contains an <h1> heading, a series of dummy links in an unordered list, a paragraph containing a photo of the Golden Pavilion in Kyoto, and a paragraph of dummy text.

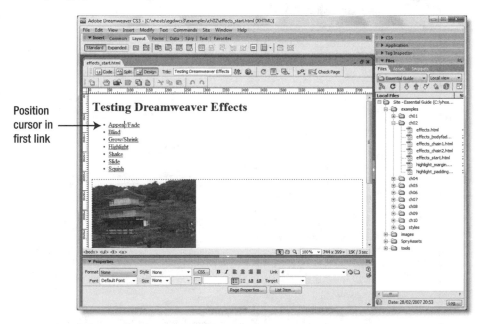

Figure 2-4. The test page for Spry-based effects

Because behaviors need to be triggered by an event, you need to select the tag you want to use as the trigger. I'm going to use the Appear/Fade link in effects_start.html, so I've placed the cursor inside that link, as shown in Figure 2-4. You apply behaviors through the

Behaviors panel, which is inside the Tag Inspector panel group (it's the third from the top on the right side of Figure 2-4).

Press Shift+F4 to open the Behaviors panel. Alternatively, click the title bar of the Tag Inspector panel group to open it, and select the Behaviors tab. Note how the text in the panel group title bar changes to reflect the name of the parent tag of the cursor's current location, as shown in Figure 2-5. If a whole tag is selected, the Tag Inspector indicates the currently selected tag, rather than its parent.

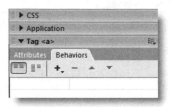

Figure 2-5.
The Tag Inspector title bar changes to indicate the current tag.

Click the plus (+) button at the top of the Behaviors panel to reveal the menu. As Figure 2-6 shows, some items are grayed out. Only those behaviors that can be applied to the current tag are accessible.

Figure 2-6.
Behaviors that cannot be applied to the current tag are grayed out.

The ~Deprecated category at the bottom of the menu includes the notorious Dreamweaver pop-up menus, which produce the most complex, search-engine-unfriendly code imaginable. If you have never used Dreamweaver pop-up menus before, don't even think about it. They have been replaced by the standards-compliant Spry Menu Bar, which is much lighter and produces fully accessible links (see Chapter 7). Use behaviors in the ~Deprecated category only to maintain code on existing sites.

Applying a Dreamweaver behavior

This exercise assumes that you have downloaded the accompanying files for this book from www.friendsofed.com/download.html?isbn=1590598598 and stored them in a Dreamweaver site.

> *If you're new to Dreamweaver, site definition is covered in detail in Chapter 4. At this stage, you need to define only the* Local Info *and* Spry *categories in the* Site Definition *dialog box.*

1. Open effects_start.html in examples/ch02. Select File ➤ Save As, and save it as effects.html. You'll need the same start file as the basis for later exercises.

2. Click inside the first item in the unordered list: Appear/Fade. It's not necessary to select the whole link; it's sufficient for your cursor to be inside the <a> tags. It's also unimportant whether you're in Design view or Code view; either will do.

3. If the Behaviors panel is not already open, press Shift+F4 or open it through the Tag Inspector panel group.

4. Click the plus (+) button in the Behaviors panel, move down to Effects, and select Appear/Fade from the submenu. As Figure 2-7 shows, the submenu may appear on the left, even though the arrow points to the right. Submenus appear on either side of the main menu depending on available screen space.

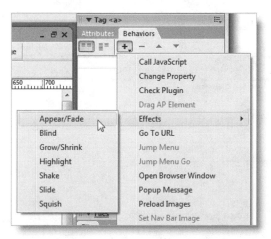

Figure 2-7. Apply behaviors by clicking the plus (+) button in the Behaviors panel and selecting them from the menu.

In Spry 1.5, Appear/Fade *and* Grow/Shrink *will be renamed* Fade *and* Grow *respectively. It's not known whether the Dreamweaver interface will be updated to reflect this change.*

5. This opens the following dialog box:

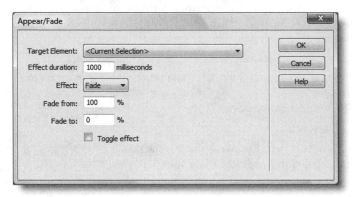

Each behavior has its own dedicated dialog box, where you set the available options. For the time being, just put a check mark in the Toggle effect **checkbox,** and click OK.

6. Save effects.html. The Spry-based effects require an external file called SpryEffects.js, which contains the Spry effects library. The first time that you apply a Spry effect in a site, Dreamweaver presents you with the following dialog box:

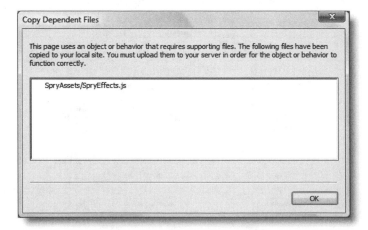

Click OK. Dreamweaver saves SpryEffects.js to the folder you designated for all Spry scripts in the site definition (see "Setting up for Spry" in Chapter 4).

> *Although Spry effects use an external code library, most other Dreamweaver behaviors embed the JavaScript in the document* <head>. *If you want to move the code for other behaviors to an external file, you need to do it manually.*

7. Press F12/Opt+F12 to preview the page in a browser. When the page loads, click the Appear/Fade link. The link should gradually fade and disappear. Click the space where the link should be, and it should fade back into view. Impressive, but hardly useful—it would be much better if the image faded instead.

Behaviors frequently need a way of identifying the target element. This is done by adding an id attribute to the target element's tag. Unfortunately, this is one area where Dreamweaver is inconsistent and can be confusing for the newcomer. So, before showing you how to amend an existing behavior, a little diversion into the mysteries of setting id attributes is necessary.

Giving elements a unique identity

An id attribute is like an ID in real life: to provide a positive method of identification, an id attribute must be unique in the same way as a Social Security number. Once you have assigned an id, you must not reuse it within the same page. You *can* reuse it elsewhere in the same site, but only once in each page.

Many web designers blithely ignore this rule, because CSS usually works perfectly well even if the same id is used several times on a page. Moreover, in spite of its commitment to generating standards-compliant code, Dreamweaver won't actually stop you from reusing an ID. Behaviors, Spry, and any JavaScript that relies on manipulating the DOM are different: they need to identify the target element accurately. Even if duplicate use of an id attribute works in one browser, you cannot guarantee it will work in others.

> *When building PHP pages later in the book, you need to remain alert to the problems caused by duplicate IDs. If you put an ID in a loop (Dreamweaver calls it a repeat region), you end up with multiple instances of the same ID and—most likely—JavaScript that no longer works.*

The reason for Dreamweaver's inconsistent approach lies in the fact that the id attribute has acquired significance only in recent years through widespread use in JavaScript and CSS. The most logical place to assign the id attribute is the Property inspector, but it's already crammed so full of other attributes, there's not always room to fit a text field for it. However, when there *is* room, Dreamweaver consistently places the id field at the top left of the Property inspector. You can assign an id through the Property inspector for <img>, <div>, <table>, <form>, and most <input> elements (see Chapter 9 for details about how Dreamweaver treats name and id attributes in forms).

Assigning an id attribute through the Property inspector

The following instructions show you how to assign an id attribute to the image in effects.html from the previous exercise.

1. Select the image of the Golden Pavilion by clicking it in Design view. The Property inspector should look like Figure 2-8. As the figure shows, the field where you set the id attribute is not labeled.

Set id attribute here →

Figure 2-8. The field for an element's id attribute is not always labeled in the Property inspector.

2. Type pavilion into the field indicated, and press Tab or Enter/Return. The <img> tag in the Tag selector changes to <img#pavilion> to show that the id attribute of the selected image has now been set.

Using the Quick Tag Editor to set an id attribute

If you can't find the field to enter an id in the Property inspector, the simplest way is to use the Quick Tag Editor (this works for all tags). Let's use the page's <h1> element to see how it's done.

1. Continue working with effects.html from the preceding exercise, and position your cursor anywhere inside the <h1> heading that reads Testing Dreamweaver Effects.

2. Right-click the <h1> tag in the Tag selector to open the context menu as shown in the following image:

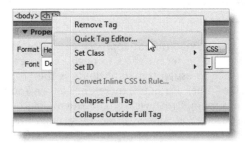

3. Contrary to what you might expect, do *not* select Set ID (I'll explain what it does shortly). Click Quick Tag Editor. This opens the <h1> tag in a small Edit tag window, with the cursor immediately to the left of the closing angle bracket, as shown here:

4. Press the spacebar, and Dreamweaver opens a code hint menu with all valid attributes for the tag. As soon as you type i, the menu selects id. Press Enter/Return, and Dreamweaver automatically completes the attribute followed by an equal sign and a pair of quotes, with the cursor between the quotes ready for you to type the attribute's value: pageTitle.

5. Press Enter/Return to close the Edit tag window. The id attribute is now set.

6. Select <h1#pageTitle> in the Tag selector, right-click to access the context menu, and select Set ID. As the following screenshot shows, only two options are shown: None and the current id value, which has a check mark alongside it but is grayed out.

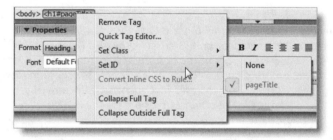

Why is this? After all, you have set three id attributes: pavilion, container, and pageTitle. It's because Set ID (and Set Class on the same context menu) are part of Dreamweaver's CSS features. The submenu is intended to work only with ID (or class) selectors that have already been defined in your style rules. We'll take an in-depth look at CSS management in Dreamweaver in Chapter 5.

Removing an id attribute

As you have probably guessed from the preceding exercise, the way to remove an id from an element is to right-click the element's tag in the Tag selector, and select Set ID ➤ None.

Editing behavior and effect settings

Now that you know how to set the id attribute for individual elements, let's apply the Appear/Fade effect to a specific element.

Amending an existing behavior

This exercise continues working with effects.html and the Spry Appear/Fade effect, but the same technique applies to editing any Dreamweaver behavior after it has been applied to a web page.

1. Position your cursor inside the Appear/Fade link in effects.html, and open the Behaviors panel (Shift+F4) if it's not already open. The panel lists all behaviors applied to the current tag. At the moment there's only one, as shown here:

2. The left side of the panel shows the JavaScript event that triggers the behavior. Click the name of the event (onClick) or just to the right of it to reveal a drop-down menu of available events. Select onMouseOver, as shown in the following screenshot:

The drop-down menu displays only those events that can be applied to the current tag. If the event you're looking for isn't listed, click the plus (+) button in the Behaviors *panel, and select* Show Events For *at the bottom of the menu (see Figure 2-6). Make sure there's a check mark alongside* HTML 4.01. *If there's a check mark against any other setting, select* HTML 4.01 *to reset it. Otherwise, click anywhere outside the menu to leave it unchanged. The other settings are for the benefit of developers who need to work with obsolete browsers.*

The drop-down menu spells the event names in camel case (mixed lowercase and uppercase) for ease of reading. If you have selected an XHTML Document Type Definition (DTD) for your page, Dreamweaver automatically uses the correct lowercase version in the underlying code.

When you select an image, the drop-down menu contains a duplicate set of events preceded by <A>, for example, <A> onClick. This option inserts the event handler in a pair of <a> tags wrapped around the image. This is necessary for some older browsers that don't recognize event handlers attached directly to an image.

3. Save `events.html`, and press F12/Opt+F12 to view the page in a browser again. Move your mouse pointer over the Appear/Fade link. It should gradually fade. Move the mouse away and back again, and the link should fade back into view. Again, not the most useful of effects, but it demonstrates how to change the trigger event.

4. Return to Dreamweaver, and change the event back to onClick.

5. Now let's take a look at editing the other settings for a behavior. Reopen the behavior's dialog box by using any of the following methods:

  ▪ Double-click the name of the behavior in the right side of the Behaviors panel.

  ▪ Highlight the behavior in the Behaviors panel list, and press Enter/Return.

  ▪ Right-click the behavior in the Behaviors panel list, and select Edit Behavior from the context menu, as shown in the following screenshot.

  ▪ Highlight the behavior in the Behaviors panel list, and click the panel group Options menu icon (see following screenshot) with the main mouse button. Select Edit Behavior.

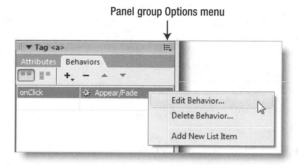

The context menu and the panel group Options *menu both have an option labeled* Add New List Item, *which serves no practical purpose. This is an "undocumented feature" of Dreamweaver—in other words, a bug. Just ignore it.*

6. With the behavior's dialog box open, you can apply any changes you want to the settings. For the purposes of this exercise, activate the Target Element drop-down menu, and select img "pavilion" as shown in the following screenshot.

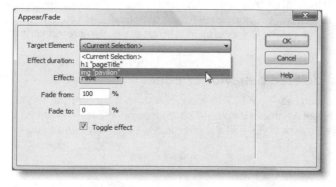

Click OK to save the change and close the behavior dialog box.

7. Save `effects.html`, and test it in a browser again. This time, when you click the Appear/Fade link, the image of the Golden Pavilion in Kyoto should fade to nothing. Click the link again, and it should fade back into view. Notice that the paragraph of text below the image remains in its original position throughout.

Dreamweaver automatically detects which elements a behavior can affect. If the dialog box doesn't list the element you want, it usually indicates that you have forgotten to give it an ID or that you have applied the behavior to an inappropriate element in the first place. Each behavior has different options. To find out how a behavior works, click the Help button in the behavior's dialog box. This launches the Adobe Help Viewer, and opens the relevant page in Dreamweaver Help.

Removing behaviors and effects cleanly

A common question in online forums is "Why does my browser report errors on the page?" Almost invariably the answer is that a behavior has been removed, but the event handler that triggers it has been left behind. Another cause is the removal of a page element, such as an image or a `<div>`, that a behavior is attempting to find. If you treat Dreamweaver purely as a WYSIWYG tool, you're likely to end up with similar problems. If you remove an element that either triggers a behavior or is the target of one, you must first remove the behavior in the correct manner.

Removing a behavior involves three simple steps, as follows:

1. Select the page element that the behavior is applied to.

2. Select the behavior in the Behaviors panel.

3. Click the minus (–) button as shown in the following screenshot:

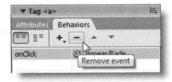

Instead of clicking the minus button, you can right-click and select Delete Behavior. You can even just press Delete (but make sure the behavior is selected in the Behaviors panel first).

Everything is removed cleanly, preventing errors from popping up later in your page. However, `SpryEffects.js` is *not* deleted from the SpryAssets folder, in case it's needed by other pages. The link to the external JavaScript file is also preserved if it's required by other effects in the page.

Restoring a deleted behavior or effect

If you delete a behavior by mistake, you can restore it by pressing Ctrl+Z/Cmd+Z or by selecting Edit ➤ Undo Remove Behavior (Edit ➤ Undo on a Mac). This always undoes the last action, so it won't work if you edit the page in any other way before you use it.

To undo several steps, use the History *panel. The* History *panel is not displayed by default but is automatically added to the bottom of the panel groups the first time you open it (*Window ➤ History*). The keyboard shortcut (Shift+F10) is available on Windows only. To learn more about the* History *panel, open* Help *(F1), and select* History Panel *from the* Index.

Another useful way of retracing your steps is the Revert *command on the* File *menu. This undoes all changes in a document and restores it to the last saved state.*

2

Exploring Spry effects

New

Let's take a quick look at each of the Spry effects. Use `effects.html` from the previous section to experiment or just inspect the finished code and effects in `examples/ch02/ effects_done.html`.

Table 2-1 summarizes what each Spry effect does and which target elements it can be used with. Appear/Fade and Highlight can be used with almost any tag, but the others are more restricted. The complete list of supported target elements is reproduced mainly for reference. Most effects can be applied only to a block element, such as a heading, paragraph, or <div>. Appear/Fade, Highlight, and Shake can be applied directly to an <img> tag. If in doubt, wrap the target element in a <div>, and assign it an ID.

Table 2-1. Spry effects and supported target elements

Effect	Action	Supported targets	Not supported
Appear/Fade	Fades an element in or out	Most tags	`applet`, `body`, `iframe`, `object`, `tbody`, `th`, `tr`
Blind	Reveals or conceals an element, like pulling a window blind up or down	`address`, `applet`, `center`, `dir`, `dd`, `div`, `dl`, `dt`, `form`, `h1–6`, `li`, `menu`, `p`, `pre`, `ol`, `ul`	Any other tag
Grow/Shrink	Grows or shrinks an element to either the center or top left	`address`, `applet`, `center`, `dd`, `dir`, `div`, `dl`, `dt`, `form`, `img`, `menu`, `p`, `pre`, `ol`, `ul`	Any other tag
Highlight	Applies a color transition to the element's background	Most tags	`applet`, `body`, `frame`, `frameset`, `noframes`

Continued

Table 2-1. Spry effects and supported target elements *(continued)*

Effect	Action	Supported targets	Not supported
Shake	Shakes an element horizontally for half a second	address, applet, blockquote, dd, dir, div, dl, dt, fieldset, form, h1–6, hr, iframe, img, li, menu, object, p, pre, ol, table, ul	Any other tag
Slide	Slides an element up or down to conceal or reveal it	blockquote, center, dd, div, form, img	Any other tag
Squish	Collapses or expands an element to or from its upper left corner	address, applet, center, dd, dir, div, dl, dt, form, img, menu, p, pre, ol, ul	All other tags

All Spry effects are accessed by selecting the trigger element, clicking the plus button in the Behaviors panel, and then selecting the effect from the Effects submenu.

The dialog box for each effect is very similar, and the options are very intuitive, so there's no need to go through each effect in detail. Here are the common settings:

- Target Element: Dreamweaver automatically identifies every element on the page that the effect can be applied to. Select the element from the drop-down list. Unless the effect is being applied to the trigger element, the target must have an ID. In the case of the Shake and Squish effects, this is the only setting.

- Effect duration: This is the length of the effect, measured in milliseconds. The default setting is 1000—in other words, one second.

- Effect: The available options depend on the effect but normally specify the direction in which the target element will move.

- Toggle effect: Selecting this option reverses the effect the next time the event is triggered.

The best way to learn how to use Spry effects is to experiment with them. However, the hints in the following sections should help you.

Appear/Fade

This effect can be applied to just about any element on a page, and it affects everything inside the target element. As you saw earlier in the chapter, making an element fade to nothing does not alter the layout of the page. An empty space remains where the element originally was.

The <body> tag cannot be used as the target element of this effect. To get the whole page to fade in after it finishes loading, wrap the entire contents of the page in a <div>. Use the <body> tag as the trigger, set the <div> as the target element, and set the event to onLoad. You can see this in effects_bodyfade.html in examples/ch02. A <div> called wrapper has been selected as the target element, the effect duration set to 3000 (3 seconds), and the effect set to Appear.

Blind

This is very similar to Slide, except that Blind acts like a mask scrolling up or down in front of the target element, whereas Slide moves the whole target element. Blind up results in the target element disappearing from the bottom; with Blind down, the target element is normally hidden, and the mask moves down to reveal it. Content below the target element moves up and down in time with the effect.

Images need to be wrapped in a block element such as a paragraph or <div> to use Blind.

Grow/Shrink

This effect works with a wide range of block elements and images, but it can have unexpected results (see Figure 2-9), so you need to test your pages and CSS carefully when using it.

There are two options for the direction of movement: to and from the center of the target element (see Figures 2-9A and 2-9B), or to and from its top-left corner (see Figures 2-9C and 2-9D). Grow/Shrink can be applied directly to an image or its containing element. Each screenshot shows what happens when the target element is shrunk to 25 percent of its original size but in a variety of circumstances. (You can test the results in shrinkA.html, shrinkB.html, shrinkC.html, and shrinkD.html in examples/ch02.)

- Figure 2-9A shows what happens when the image itself is selected as the target element and shrunk to its center. Any content below the target element moves up, but the image moves down, resulting in an overlap. The same happens if the effect is applied to a surrounding element with the same width and height as the image.

- Figure 2-9B shows what happens if the effect is applied to a surrounding block element with no fixed width or height and is shrunk to its center: the parent element and its contents shrink together but move to the center of the page.

- Figure 2-9C shows what happens if the effect is set to move to the top left and is applied to the surrounding <div>, regardless of whether the <div> has fixed dimensions. The same happens if the image is selected as the target but *only* if the surrounding <div> has no height.

- Figure 2-9D shows the gap created by applying the effect directly to the image and shrinking it to its top-left corner when the surrounding <div> has a fixed height. The text remains in its original position, much further down the page.

A Image shrunk to center

B Container with no set width shrunk to center

C Image or container shrunk to top left

D Image shrunk to top left, container has height

Figure 2-9. The Grow/Shrink Spry effect can produce unexpected changes to your layout (see text for details).

Test your layout carefully if you use this effect.

Highlight

Highlight changes the background color of the target element. As the following screenshot shows, the Highlight dialog box has three color settings: Start Color, End Color, and Color After Effect. You can set these either by typing the hexadecimal color value in the text field (preceded by #) or by clicking the color picker to the left of the text field.

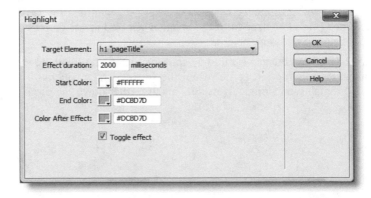

The meanings of Start Color and End Color are what you would expect. Effect duration sets the time taken (in milliseconds) to transition from one color to the other—2000 (or 2 seconds) seems to be the optimal choice—and the transition follows a visually pleasing curve. Color After Effect is the color to which the background is set after the transition, and it cuts in immediately. You need to choose this color carefully. I find it's best to set this value either to the same as Start Color or End Color. Otherwise, the transition appears unnaturally abrupt.

When Highlight is applied directly to an image, there must be padding around the image for the background color to be visible. Adding only margins to the image has no effect, because background color does not affect the margin of an element. See highlight_padding.html and highlight_margin.html in examples/ch02.

Shake

This is my least favorite effect. It has only one option: the target element, which it shakes horizontally for half a second. It might be appropriate in advanced Ajax contexts to indicate that an element has been updated asynchronously, but it would be more useful if you could set the speed and duration of the movement. The danger is that it will become the modern equivalent of the <blink> tag—mercilessly abused because it looks "cool." Use with care. Depending on your layout, this effect sometimes spawns a horizontal scrollbar in the browser.

Slide

Slide is similar to Blind, but rather than a mask moving over the target element, the element itself moves. As Table 2-1 shows, this effect can be applied to only a small range of block elements or images. You need to wrap a <div> around the element you want to apply the effect to and select the wrapper <div> as the target element. If you don't do this, you get the following warning:

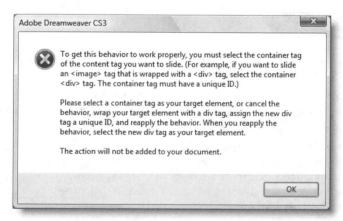

I'll show you how to create a wrapper <div> after briefly describing the final effect.

Squish

This collapses the target element from the bottom-right corner toward the top left until it disappears completely and is very easy to apply. The Squish dialog box has only one setting: the target element. Any content below the target element moves up to fill the gap. If you select the Toggle effect option, the target element reappears and expands back to its original size, moving down any content below it.

Creating a wrapper <div> for the Slide effect

The Slide effect is unusual in that you cannot apply it directly to the element you want to slide in and out of view. Instead, the target element must be a <div> wrapped around it. Although that's straightforward, what makes matters slightly complicated is that the Slide effect is very picky about the elements it accepts immediately inside the wrapper. The child element of the wrapper <div> *must* be one of the following: <blockquote>, the deprecated <center> element, <dd>, <form>, <img>, or another <div>.

The image of the Golden Pavilion in effects.html is wrapped in a paragraph. Even though this is a block element, it's not in the list accepted by Slide. This leaves you with two options, namely:

- Wrap the paragraph in two <div> tags, and use the outer one as the target element.
- Replace the paragraph with a <div>. The immediate child element then becomes an <img> tag, allowing you to use the <div> as the target element.

Since the second option requires less code, let's use that approach. It also gives me the opportunity to show you two important techniques: how to wrap a selection in a <div> and how to remove a tag without losing its contents.

Applying the Slide effect

This exercise uses effects.html from the previous exercises. Alternatively, use effects_start.html in examples/ch02. The final code is in effects_done.html.

1. Begin by selecting the image in Design view. You can then see the <p> tag immediately to the left of <img#pavilion> in the Tag selector. Click the <p> tag to select both the image and its enclosing paragraph.

2. Click the Insert Div Tag button in the Common tab of the Insert bar, as shown in the screenshot shown alongside (it's also available in the Layout tab, or you can use the menu option Insert ➤ Layout Objects ➤ Div Tag).

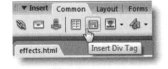

3. Because you have selected part of the layout, the Insert Div Tag dialog box automatically selects Wrap around selection as the value for the Insert drop-down menu (we'll examine the other options in later chapters). Type container in the ID field, as shown in the following screenshot, and click OK.

4. If you switch to Code view, you'll see that Dreamweaver has wrapped the paragraph and image in a new container `<div>`, as shown in the following screenshot (the line numbers may be different in your version, depending on whether you have applied any other effects to the page):

```
28  <div id="container">
29      <p><img src="../../images/kinkakuji.jpg" alt="Golden Pavilion in Kyoto" name="pavilion"
    width="270" height="346" id="pavilion" /></p>
30  </div>
```

If you try to apply the Slide effect to the container `<div>` at this stage, you'll get the lengthy warning message shown in the preceding section. You need to get rid of the `<p>` tags surrounding the image. It's easy enough to do it manually in Code view, but I want to show you another, cleaner way to remove a tag without losing its contents.

5. Repeat step 1 to select the `<p>` tag in the Tag selector again, right-click, and select Remove Tag from the context menu, as shown here.

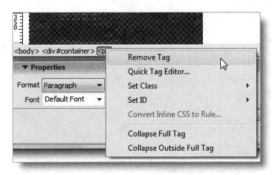

The paragraph disappears, but the image remains intact. It's now the direct child of the container `<div>`, so you can apply the Slide effect to its parent element.

6. Place your cursor inside the Slide link; click the plus button in the Behaviors panel; and select Effects ➤ Slide from the menu. Set the options in the Slide dialog box as shown in the following screenshot, and click OK.

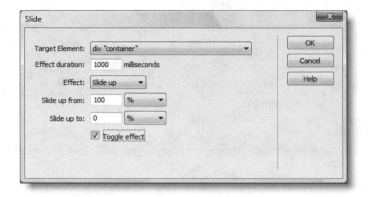

7. Save `effects.html`, and press F12/Opt+F12 to test the page in a browser. Slide away!

Applying multiple events to a trigger element

You're not limited to applying a single event to the trigger element for a behavior or Spry effect. For example, in `events_done.html`, I have applied the onmouseover and onmouseout events to the image. The first event applies the Highlight effect to the pageTitle `<h1>` tag, giving it a blue background when you mouse over the image. The second event applies the same effect but turns the background back to white. To apply multiple events to the same trigger, just apply the behavior or effect again, and select a different event from the drop-down menu in the Behaviors panel, as shown in Figure 2-10.

Figure 2-10.
You can apply more than one behavior or effect to the same tag by choosing a different event handler.

If you choose different event handlers, the order that behaviors or effects are listed doesn't matter. However, you may need to change the order when you use the same event handler for more than one behavior. This sometimes happens when adding several behaviors to the <body> tag to be executed when the page first loads. You do this by selecting an event in the Behaviors panel and moving it up or down the list with the up and down arrows at the top of the panel.

There's a lot more to Spry than these six effects. In Chapters 7 and 8, we'll come back to explore the Spry user interface widgets: the Spry Menu Bar, accordion, tabbed panels, and collapsible panels. The widgets make it easy to display a lot of information on your pages in a compact space. And in Chapter 9, we'll put Spry to work validating user input in an online form.

Handling dynamic data with Spry and PHP

Working with dynamic data drawn from an XML file or a database is the subject of the second half of this book. Treat this section as just a taster of things to come.

Comparing how Spry and PHP handle data sets

In one respect, Spry data sets are the crowning glory of the Spry framework. They enable you to draw information stored in XML files to generate photo galleries, product catalogs, news feeds, and so on with just a few clicks inside Dreamweaver. The screenshot on the left of Figure 2-11 shows a photo gallery Adobe created to demonstrate what Spry is capable of doing (http://labs.adobe.com/technologies/spry/demos/gallery/index.html).

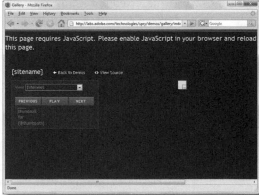

Figure 2-11. This Spry gallery uses just a few lines of code to draw the photo details from an XML file, but fails completely if JavaScript is not supported.

It's a stunning display of what Spry can do. However, you get a very different result if you visit the site with JavaScript disabled, as you can see in the screenshot on the right.

Even if you choose not to serve the tiny minority of users who disable JavaScript in their browsers, you cannot afford to ignore the fact that the information in the screenshot on the right of Figure 2-11 is just about all that a search engine would see when visiting a page created with a Spry data set. This may not be very important for a photo gallery, but it would be a disaster if your main page or a product catalog depended on this technology.

The Web Content Accessibility Guidelines (WCAG) are another important consideration. Checkpoint 6.3 of WCAG 1.0 says: "Ensure that pages are usable when scripts, applets, or other programmatic objects are turned off or not supported. If this is not possible, provide equivalent information on an alternative accessible page" (www.w3.org/TR/WCAG10/#gl-new-technologies). This is classified as Priority 1—in other words, a checkpoint that a web developer *must* satisfy.

Adobe is aware of this, and Spry is not alone in suffering from accessibility problems. It's a subject of intense debate regarding Ajax. Using Spry to manipulate data sets may be appropriate in a closed environment, such as an intranet, where you know that JavaScript is enabled and search engines are not a consideration. However, manipulating data sets with server-side technology avoids all the problems inherent in Ajax, because the server generates all the necessary XHTML to display your website's content. Everyone receives a complete page, regardless of whether JavaScript is enabled, making your site accessible.

In the second half of this book, I'll show you how to use both Spry and PHP to work with data sets, enabling you to make your own informed choice as to which technology suits the job in hand.

Building PHP sites with Dreamweaver

PHP code is very different from standard XHTML markup. It consists of a series of instructions that tell the PHP engine what to output to the browser. Most of the time, you'll use it in combination with XHTML, but sometimes you use it on its own, such as to send an email. Dreamweaver speeds up working with PHP by automatically generating the code for a wide range of common tasks, such as connecting to a MySQL database, inserting, updating, and deleting records, user authentication, and building navigation systems to page through a long set of database results.

Once you have defined a PHP site in Dreamweaver (see Chapter 4), the starting point of working with most server behaviors is creating a **MySQL connection** (covered in Chapter 14). This tells Dreamweaver (and your web pages) where to find MySQL, the correct username and password, and the name of the database that you want to use. Once you have connected to a database, you can insert, update, and delete records (see Chapters 14 and 15). Dreamweaver gives you the choice of automating the whole process with a wizard that builds the necessary online forms and associated PHP code. Alternatively, you can design your own forms and get Dreamweaver to generate the PHP needed to activate them.

Once you have entered some records in your database, you can get Dreamweaver to create a **recordset**, which queries the database and stores the results ready for display in your web page (see Chapter 14). The following server behaviors and data objects simplify that process:

- **Repeat Region:** When displaying a list of database records, you just create a single row, and the Repeat Region server behavior loops through all the results and creates the code automatically. You can choose whether to display all results or limit the page to just a specific number (see Chapter 14).

- **Show Region:** Sometimes, your recordset may not contain any relevant results. The Show Region server behavior creates the "smart" code that decides whether to display certain parts of the page when that happens (see Chapter 17).

- **Recordset Paging:** This automates the construction of a navigation system that lets users move backward and forward through a long set of database results by spreading them over several pages (see Chapter 16).

- **Display Record Count:** This is normally used in conjunction with Recordset Paging to display information such as Showing items 21 to 30 of 48 (see Chapter 17).

- **Dynamic Form Elements:** Dreamweaver makes it easy to populate online forms with the results of a database query, automatically setting drop-down menus, radio buttons, and checkboxes to the correct value. This is particularly useful for updating database records.

- **User Authentication:** The User Authentication suite of server behaviors makes light work of password-protecting sections of your site, such as a members-only area or the administrative back-end of a database. It also lets you set different access levels for groups of users (see Chapter 15).

- **XSL Transformation:** This uses Extensible Stylesheet Language Transformations (XSLT) to display XML data in a web page. It differs from Spry in that the output doesn't rely on JavaScript being enabled in the browser. Although the code created by Dreamweaver is compatible with both PHP 4 and PHP 5, you will need PHP 5 to make full use of this feature, as XSLT support is not enabled by default in PHP 4 (see Chapter 18).

No computer program, however sophisticated, can completely automate everything for you. So, before diving into working with server behaviors, I'll show you how to process and email the input from an online form in Chapter 11. As well as showing you how to implement one of the most useful features of PHP, this will arm you with the basic knowledge necessary to dive into the code generated by Dreamweaver and adapt it to your own requirements.

Comparing different versions of files

Working with dynamic code is not particularly difficult once you have learned the basic principles, but spotting mistakes can be a major headache. A missing comma, quote, or curly brace can bring your page crashing down. When you run into a problem in this book, the first thing you should do is compare your code with the download files. But the prospect of checking hundreds of lines of code is enough to make grown men cry—unless, of course, they already know the secret of file comparison utilities.

Dreamweaver CS3 lets you specify a third-party application, which can be used to compare two local files, two remote files, or the local and remote versions of a file—all from within the Dreamweaver interface. Take a few minutes to set up File Compare. It will save you hours of agony.

Setting up the File Compare feature

If you already have a file comparison utility installed on your computer, all that's necessary is to register the program inside the Dreamweaver Preferences panel. If you don't yet have one, here are some suggestions:

- **Windows**
  - **WinMerge:** A good utility, free from http://winmerge.sourceforge.net/.
  - **Beyond Compare:** An excellent tool from www.scootersoftware.com. It's moderately priced, but you can try it free for 30 days.
- **Mac OS X**
  - **TextWrangler:** Not just a file comparison utility, it's an excellent script editor, and it's free from www.barebones.com.
  - **BBEdit:** BBEdit (also from www.barebones.com) is expensive if you only need it for file comparison but is widely recognized as the Rolls Royce of Mac script editors.

Once you have installed a file comparison utility, open Edit ➤ Preferences (Dreamweaver ➤ Preferences on a Mac), and select File Compare. Click the Browse button, and navigate to the executable file for the program. Windows users should have little difficulty recognizing the correct file to select; it will normally be in a subfolder of Program Files.

On a Mac, the location is somewhere you may never even have known existed:

- **TextWrangler:** Macintosh HD:usr:bin:twdiff
- **BBEdit:** Macintosh HD:usr:bin:bbdiff (this is the BBEdit file comparison utility—make sure you choose bbdiff and not bbedit, which is listed just below it)

Even though the usr:bin directory is normally hidden on a Mac, the Dreamweaver Select External Editor dialog box will display it by default. All you need to do is select the correct file name and click Open. If you can't find twdiff or bbdiff, open Preferences from the TextWrangler or BBEdit menu, select Tools, and click the Install Command Line Tools button.

Using File Compare

File Compare allows you to compare the contents of two files. Individual utilities offer different features, but the way you launch them from Dreamweaver is the same for all of them. Figure 2-12 shows how Beyond Compare handles two versions of a file that's nearly 600 lines long.

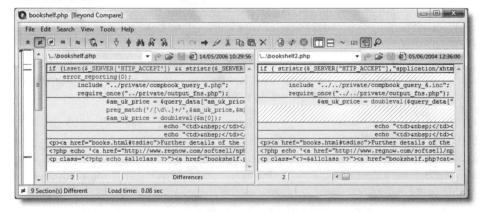

Figure 2-12. Using the Dreamweaver File Compare feature with a third-party utility like Beyond Compare makes light work of identifying differences between two files.

You can hide all matching lines and concentrate solely on the differences, which are highlighted in a way that's easy to comprehend. No more searching in vain for a missing comma or closing quote. You don't even have to do any typing to resolve the differences between files. All file comparison programs allow you to synchronize the content of two files, line by line, section by section, or in their entirety.

Comparing two local files in the same site

To compare two files in the same site, highlight both in the Files panel, right-click, and select Compare Local Files. This can be useful if you operate a simple form of version control, such as saving each version of a file with an incremental number. By comparing the two, you can see any differences, and use the comparison utility's merge function to update one file from another.

Comparing two local files in different sites

Although Dreamweaver allows you to open files in the workspace from as many sites as you want, the Files panel can display only one site at a time. However, as long as both files are on the same disk in your local file system, you can still compare them without leaving Dreamweaver.

Open the drop-down menu at the top of the Files panel, as shown in the screenshot alongside, and select the disk on your local file system where both files are located. You can then select files from different sites. In fact, you can select files that aren't even in Dreamweaver sites. Once both target files have been selected, right-click and select Compare Local Files.

Comparing local and remote files

If you select just one file in the Files panel and right-click, the context menu will display either Compare with Remote or Compare with Local, depending on the location of the selected file. If the file you want to compare is already open in the Document window, it's even faster to right-click the document tab and select Compare with Remote (or Compare with Testing, if you don't have a remote server defined).

For this type of comparison, Dreamweaver will only select a file of the same name and in the same location on the other computer. So you can compare the local or remote equivalent of myfile.php in myfolder in the same Dreamweaver site but not myotherfile.php or the same file in a different folder or different site. The reason for this restriction is that Dreamweaver uses the details in the Remote Info section of your site definition to locate the remote file (Dreamweaver site definition is covered in Chapter 4).

Beyond Compare produces a false negative when comparing the remote and local versions of a file. This is easily remedied by opening the main Beyond Compare window, and selecting Tools ➤ Options ➤ Startup. Set Show dialog with quick comparison results to Rules-based quick compare.

You cannot use the merge or copy feature of your file comparison program to make changes to a remote file, because Dreamweaver works with a temporary copy of the remote file rather than the original. Local files can be changed, because you always work with the original.

On Windows, you can merge local and remote versions of a file by launching Beyond Compare outside Dreamweaver. Select New *from the Beyond Compare* Session *menu, and choose* Synchronize with FTP site.

Failure of BBEdit to display results If BBEdit isn't running, Dreamweaver launches it and displays a blank page when both pages are identical. If BBEdit is already running, nothing happens at all—the focus doesn't even switch to the file comparison program. This is BBEdit's way of saying there is nothing to compare.

TextWrangler keeps focus on first use You may see the Dreamweaver icon bouncing furiously in the Dock while a blank TextWrangler page hogs the screen. This happens *only* if both files are identical *and* TextWrangler wasn't running when you compared them. Switch back to Dreamweaver, and you should see a Dreamweaver alert box reporting No differences found between these files.

Meet Mark of the Web

There's an item at the bottom of the Commands menu that may have you scratching your head: Insert Mark of the Web. Click it, and it inserts the following code immediately after the DOCTYPE declaration:

```
<!-- saved from url=(0014)about:internet -->
```

This cryptic piece of code prevents Internet Explorer on the latest versions of Windows from popping up that annoying message that blocks JavaScript and other active content from running when you preview a web page locally—simple, effective, and useful. You can find out more at the following site: http://msdn.microsoft.com/library/default. asp?url=/workshop/author/dhtml/overview/motw.asp.

Once Mark of the Web has been inserted into a page, the menu option changes to Remove Mark of the Web. Although it won't do any harm if you leave it in, it doesn't look very professional, so use this command to remove Mark of the Web after local testing and before uploading the page to a live server.

Even though this is a Windows issue, Commands ➤ Insert Mark of the Web is also on the Mac version of Dreamweaver. After all, Mac developers still need to test their pages on what's currently still the world's most popular browser.

The next step

Now that you have a good idea of the features Dreamweaver CS3 provides for dynamic website development, it's time to get your computer ready to work with PHP. Although it's not absolutely essential to install PHP and a web server on your local computer, it speeds up the development process considerably. The next chapter describes in detail how to do this, both for Windows and Mac OS X. The setup process is not difficult, but it's important to get it right. Follow the steps carefully, and you should be up and running in no time at all. If you already have a fully operational PHP setup on your computer, you can skip to Chapter 4 to see how to define a PHP site in Dreamweaver.

2

3 GETTING THE WORK ENVIRONMENT READY

Although Dreamweaver lets you use a remote server—such as a hosting company—to test PHP pages, it's usually more efficient to set up a testing environment on your local computer. All the necessary software can be downloaded free of charge from the Internet, and it's not difficult to set up. Don't worry about the length of this chapter. It contains separate instructions for Windows and Mac OS X, and the Windows section covers both XP and Vista, as well as Apache and IIS. There are also troubleshooting hints in the unfortunate event that anything goes wrong.

Read only the sections relevant to your setup. However, do read them carefully and check the book's companion website at http://foundationphp.com/egdwcs3/updates.php for any updates. Setting up your development environment correctly is essential to working with dynamic websites in Dreamweaver.

If you already have a functional web server configured to run PHP, there is probably no need to reinstall, but you should take a look at the section titled "Checking your PHP configuration" toward the end of the chapter and make sure that your setup meets the minimum requirements.

What this chapter covers

- Deciding whether to build a local testing server
- Installing the Apache web server and PHP on Windows
- Configuring PHP to work with Apache or IIS on Windows
- Setting up Apache and PHP on Mac OS X
- Learning to read the PHP configuration page

Deciding where to test your pages

Building PHP pages involves a lot of testing—much more than you might normally do with a static website. It's not only a question of what your pages look like; you also have to check that the dynamic code is working as expected. Dreamweaver doesn't mind where your testing server is, as long as it knows where to find it, there's an available connection, and, of course, the server is capable of handling PHP pages. This means that you can test on your local machine, another computer on a local network, or a remote host.

These are the advantages of creating a local test environment:

- **Safety:** If an error in your code causes the server to slow down or even crash, the only person affected is you. Keep your mistakes to yourself; don't inflict them on others.
- **Speed:** There's no waiting. Even with a broadband connection, the response is usually slower from a remote server.
- **Convenience:** You can continue work even if there is a disruption to your Internet service.
- **Knowledge:** By setting up your own testing environment, you get a better understanding of how a web server and PHP work.

There are also disadvantages to creating a local test environment:

- **Setup time:** Each piece of software requires a multimegabyte download, which then has to be set up and configured.

- **Complexity:** Some people find configuring the software daunting. This chapter is designed to eliminate any such fears.

Wherever you decide to test your PHP pages, you also need to confirm that your remote server supports PHP, so that you're ready to deploy your handiwork once it's ready.

Checking that your remote server supports PHP

In Dreamweaver, select File ➤ New ➤ Blank Page. Choose PHP as the Page Type and <none> as the Layout. Switch to Code view, delete all existing code, and replace it with the following:

```php
<?php phpinfo(); ?>
```

Save the file as test.php, upload it to your website, and view it in a browser. If you see a page similar to Figure 3-1, you're in business. If all you see is the raw code, you need to move to a server that supports PHP. If you see a blank screen or an error message, try using the version of test.php in examples/ch03.

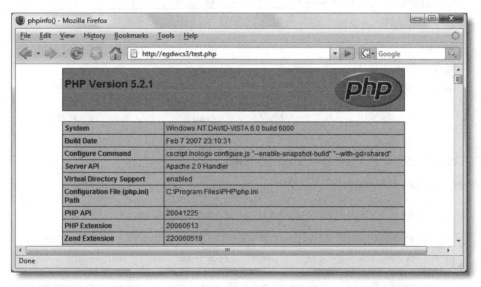

Figure 3-1. The phpinfo() command confirms that PHP is enabled and provides a wealth of information about supported features.

The screenshot in Figure 3-1 was taken in a local testing environment on a Windows computer, so the Configure Command section may look very different on a remote Linux server. This is perfectly normal. As the name suggests, phpinfo() provides information about the PHP setup on your server, so the contents of the resulting page differ from machine to machine.

Check that the version number at the top left of the screen is a minimum of 4.3.1. This is the absolute minimum supported by Dreamweaver. Important security fixes were made to PHP in February 2007, so you should ideally be using PHP 5.2.1 or higher. If your hosting company still uses PHP 4, the same security fixes were added to PHP 4.4.5. All the code generated by Dreamweaver CS3 is backward compatible with PHP 4.3.1 and MySQL 3.23.31, so PHP 5 isn't essential. However, PHP 5 has been a stable release since July 2004, and the features required by the XSL Transformation server behavior in Chapter 18 are not enabled by default in PHP 4. So, if your hosting company hasn't upgraded yet, pressure it to do so.

For security reasons, it's a good idea to delete test.php from your remote server after checking the details, or to store it in a password-protected folder. Don't delete it from your local computer, as you'll need it to check your testing environment.

> If you don't want to create a local testing environment, skip ahead to "Checking your PHP configuration" later in the chapter to make sure that your remote server has the necessary features.

Creating a local testing server

To create a local test environment, you need three things:

- PHP
- A web server—Apache or IIS
- MySQL

This chapter deals with the first two. MySQL is covered in Chapter 13.

Choosing which versions to install

There are two schools of thought about the software versions you should use for local testing. Some say that you should match the setup on your remote server. Others, myself included, believe it's better to install the latest versions available for the following reasons:

- **It's easier:** You don't need to scramble around in archives to find older versions.
- **It's forward compatible:** Using the most recent versions on your testing computer gives you confidence that your code will still work when your remote server is upgraded. You can also experiment with new features and put pressure on your host to upgrade.

Of course, using the latest versions for your testing environment isn't without danger: you might fall into the trap of using features that aren't supported on your remote server. Nevertheless, I believe that the advantages of testing for forward compatibility outweigh this danger. To give a couple of examples, changes in PHP 5 and MySQL 5 affect the way that data is handled from forms and how database tables are joined. Code written in the old style breaks in newer versions, but the newer style is backward compatible with the minimum versions required by Dreamweaver CS3.

> All code in this book that requires a higher version than PHP 4.3.1 or MySQL 3.23.31 is clearly marked as such.

Choosing individual installation or an all-in-one package

Setting up a local PHP testing environment has undeservedly gained a reputation for being fiendishly complicated, particularly on Windows. Installation is quite simple, but it does need to be done correctly. It's no different from a battery: it works when you put it in the right way; put it in the other way around, it doesn't. The problem is that, once you install PHP the wrong way, it can be difficult to put right. It's not as simple as turning around a battery; you may have made changes to your computer's configuration that need to be reversed before everything works.

As a result, many people prefer to use an all-in-one package that automates the installation of Apache, PHP, MySQL, and the phpMyAdmin interface to MySQL. However, the PHP website at www.php.net/manual/en/install.windows.php carries the following warning:

Warning

There are several all-in-one installers over the Internet, but none of those are endorsed by PHP.net, as we believe that the manual installation is the best choice to have your system secure and optimised.

Although this warning applies mainly to live Internet servers, rather than a local testing environment, I still prefer to install each program separately, as I feel it gives you more control. What's more, installation on Windows has been streamlined with the release of a new Windows installer for PHP in November 2006. Mac OS X comes with the Apache web server preinstalled, and Mac packages are available for both PHP and MySQL. If you follow the instructions in this chapter, you should be up and running in next to no time.

If you decide against individual installation, an all-in-one package that has a very good reputation for Windows is XAMPP (www.apachefriends.org/en). MAMP (www.mamp.info/en/index.php) has a similar reputation for Mac OS X. If you would like to use either of these packages, follow the instructions on the relevant website. If you run into difficulties, seek help in the XAMPP or MAMP support forum.

There are separate instructions for Windows and Mac OS X. Mac users should skip ahead to the section titled "Setting up on Mac OS X."

Setting up on Windows

The minimum requirement for Dreamweaver CS3 is Windows XP with Service Pack 2 or higher. It also runs on Windows Vista Home Premium, Business, Enterprise, and Ultimate. Vista Home Basic and Vista Starter are *not* supported. Although Dreamweaver may run on 64-bit systems, support is not guaranteed. These instructions assume that you are running one of the supported versions of Windows.

> *Make sure you're logged into Windows as an Administrator before starting.*

Getting Windows to display file name extensions

By default, Windows hides the three- or four-letter file name extension, such as .doc or .html, so all you see in dialog boxes and Explorer is thisfile, instead of thisfile.doc or thisfile.html. The ability to see these file name extensions is essential for working with PHP.

To change the default setting, you need to open the Folder Options dialog box. In Windows XP, go to Start ➤ My Computer ➤ Tools ➤ Folder Options. In Vista, go to Start ➤ Computer ➤ Organize ➤ Folder and Search Options.

Select the View tab, and uncheck the box marked Hide extensions for known file types, as shown in Figure 3-2. Click OK. (The Folder Options dialog box looks slightly different in Windows XP, but this option and the View tab are common to both XP and Vista.)

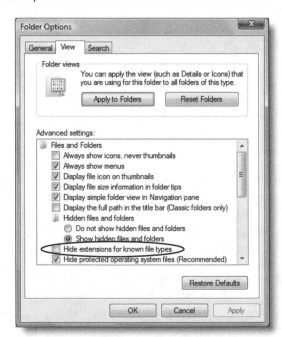

Figure 3-2. Setting Windows so that it automatically displays the extension on all file names

I recommend you leave your computer permanently at this setting, as it is more secure—you can tell if a virus writer has attached an EXE or SCR executable file to an innocent-looking document.

Choosing the right web server

Before installing PHP, you need to have a web server running on your computer. There are no two ways about it: *Apache is the web server of choice for PHP*. If you don't have a web server installed on your computer, install Apache. It's simple and reliable.

However, a lot of developers want to work with ASP or ASP.NET, which requires IIS. The good news is that you can install PHP on top of IIS. The bad news is that IIS doesn't support all features of PHP. So, if your remote server runs on Apache, you may want to consider the possibility of running Apache and IIS in parallel. If you want to run both web servers in parallel, you must make sure that they don't both try to use the same port on your computer (see "Checking that port 80 is free").

Downloading the software

Windows installer packages are available for both Apache and PHP from the following locations:

- **Apache**: Go to `http://httpd.apache.org/download.cgi`. Scroll down to the section for Apache 2.2.x, and select the file marked Win32 Binary (MSI Installer). The x in the number represents the most recent version of the 2.2 series. If a later series is available, please check `http://foundationphp.com/egdwcs3/updates.php` to see whether it's compatible with the current version of PHP.

- **PHP**: Go to `www.php.net/downloads.php`, and select the PHP 5.x.x Installer from the Windows Binaries section, where x.x represents the latest version.

  Do *not* use a Windows PHP installer earlier than version 5.2.0. Older versions run PHP in a very restricted way and are totally unsuitable for use with this book. If, for any reason, you need to use an older version of PHP, follow the instructions for installing the ZIP package by visiting `http://foundationphp.com/egdwcs3/`.

Basic installation is the same on Windows XP and Vista, but the security system and software compatibility issues in Windows Vista involve a few extra steps. If you're running XP, skip ahead to "Before you begin."

Preparing for installation on Windows Vista

Whenever you attempt to install software or change protected files, User Account Control (UAC) asks you to confirm that you want to go ahead. UAC is designed to help prevent unauthorized changes to your computer, but an unfortunate side effect is that some programs not yet optimized for Vista are installed in a nonstandard location. At the time of this writing, this applies to Apache and PHP. To get around this, you need to turn off UAC temporarily while installing and configuring Apache and PHP. I also suggest you do the same for MySQL, so you might want to install it at the same time (MySQL installation instructions are in Chapter 13).

Once installation is complete, you can turn UAC back on, and your testing environment should run smoothly. Some people find UAC so intrusive that they turn it off permanently. It's not a good idea, as it exposes you to viruses or malware making changes to your system without your knowledge.

Turning off User Account Control temporarily on Vista

Turning off UAC exposes your computer to greater risk, so I suggest that you download the software first and then disconnect from the Internet.

1. Log into Vista as an Administrator. Close any programs that are running.

2. Go to Start ➤ Control Panel, and select Classic View. Double-click the User Accounts icon shown alongside.

3. In the screen that opens, click Turn User Account Control on or off at the bottom of the menu titled Make changes to your user account. Click Continue when prompted.

4. Deselect the Use User Account Control (UAC) checkbox, and click OK.

5. Vista prompts you to restart your computer for the changes to take effect. Click Restart Now. If you click Restart Later, you need to reboot your computer before proceeding with the installation of Apache and PHP.

Once you have finished installation and configuration, turn UAC back on by repeating steps 1–5, but put a check mark in the Use User Account Control (UAC) checkbox in step 4.

Before you begin . . .

For the vast majority of people, installation goes without a hitch. Things normally go wrong when a conflict arises with existing programs or if you have previously installed PHP on your computer. Until mid-2004, the recommended way to install PHP involved copying files to your Windows system folders. If you have an old installation like this, you need to remove a file called php.ini from the C:\WINDOWS folder and all files beginning php_ from C:\WINDOWS\system32. Also remove the main PHP folder.

If you installed PHP using the instructions in my previous books—*Foundation PHP 5 for Flash*, *Blog Design Solutions*, *Foundation PHP for Dreamweaver 8*, or *PHP Solutions*—there is no need to reinstall. If you want to upgrade, I suggest you follow the same installation method as recommended in those books. It's still perfectly valid. However, if you do want to remove such an installation, follow these steps:

1. Delete the PHP folder and all its contents.

2. Uninstall Apache using Control Panel ➤ Add or Remove Programs.

3. Delete C:\Program Files\Apache Group\Apache, C:\Program Files\Apache Group\ Apache2, or C:\Program Files\Apache Software Foundation\Apache2.2, depending on the version you installed. (Adjust the path if you installed Apache on a different drive.)

   If you followed my instructions, all your web pages will be outside the Apache folder, but if you left the Apache DocumentRoot at its default setting, move your pages to a safe location before deleting the folder.

4. Remove the PHP folder from the Windows path, and delete the PHPRC setting from the computer's system variables. You do this by double-clicking System in the Windows Control Panel. Select the Advanced tab, and click Environment Variables at the bottom of the panel. In the System variables pane at the bottom of the dialog box that opens, select Path, and click Edit. Remove the pathname of your PHP folder (C:\php5 or C:\php), and click OK. Then select PHPRC, and click Delete. Click OK to save the changes.

5. Use the Windows Search feature to find all instances of php.ini and remove them.

Checking that port 80 is free

By default, web servers listen for requests on port 80. It's important to make sure that nothing else is using port 80. The most common culprit is Skype. Check its configuration. If it is running on port 80, select a different port number to free up 80 for the web server.

If IIS is installed, it will already be using port 80. Although the Apache installation setup has an option to select port 8080, I recommend stopping IIS temporarily and installing Apache on port 80 instead. This installs Apache as a Windows service, making it easier to control. After you have installed Apache, you can switch either Apache or IIS to port 8080 and run them in parallel. Alternatively, you can switch both to manual startup and run only one of them at any given time.

To prevent conflicts during installation, open the Windows Services panel (Start ➤ Control Panel ➤ Administrative Tools ➤ Services) to stop IIS and switch it to manual operation.

Inside the Services panel, highlight IIS Admin in Windows XP, or World Wide Web Publishing Service in Vista, right-click, and select Properties. Click the Stop button to stop the web server, and when it has stopped, select Manual from the Startup type drop-down menu, as shown in Figure 3-3.

Figure 3-3.
If you want to install Apache in parallel with IIS, temporarily disable IIS by stopping the service and setting Startup type to Manual.

Before restarting IIS, you must *either close down Apache or switch one of them to port 8080 (instructions are given later in the chapter). You can then reset* Startup type *to* Automatic *in* IIS Admin *(Windows XP) or* World Wide Web Publishing Service *(Vista).*

Installing Apache on Windows

The Apache web server is installed like any ordinary Windows program. There's just one dialog box for you to fill in. The rest of the process is fully automated. The following instructions show you how to install Apache as a Windows service, which starts automatically whenever you switch on your computer. You can change this later to a manual startup, but installing it initially as a Windows service also installs the Apache Service Monitor, a useful utility that lets you control Apache from the Windows taskbar.

1. Close all open programs, and temporarily disable virus-scanning software. Double-click the Apache installer package icon. On Vista, you will see a warning that the publisher could not be verified. You can ignore this if you downloaded Apache from the Apache site or an official mirror site. Click Run.

2. Click Next to start the installation wizard. The first thing to appear is the Apache License agreement. Select the Accept terms radio button, and click Next.

3. The following dialog box contains information about Apache. Click Next to continue.

4. The Server Information dialog box, as shown in Figure 3-4, follows. This is where you enter the default settings for your web server. In the Network Domain and Server Name fields, enter localhost, and in the last field, enter an email address. The localhost address tells Apache you will be using it on your own computer. The email address does not need to be a genuine one. It has no bearing on the way the program runs.

   Select the option labeled for All Users, on Port 80, as a Service, and click Next.

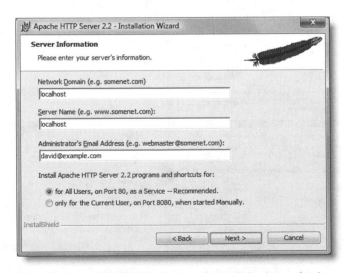

Figure 3-4. Selecting port 80 in the installation dialog box makes it easier to control Apache, but you need to resolve any conflicts.

5. In the next dialog box, select the option for a Typical setup, and click Next to continue.

6. You are given an opportunity to change where Apache will be installed. The default location, C:\Program Files\Apache Software Foundation, is fine. Click Next. Finally, click Install to finish the Apache installation.

7. The process is quite quick, but don't be alarmed if you see a Command Prompt window open and close several times while the program is being installed. This is perfectly normal. If a software firewall, such as Norton Internet Security or ZoneAlarm, displays any warnings, you must select the option to allow connections to Apache.

   On Vista, you will see the Error alert shown alongside. It's nothing to worry about, just click OK, and follow the instructions in "Running the Apache Monitor on Vista."

8. If Windows attempts to block Apache, choose the Unblock option.

9. After the installation has finished, open a browser, and type http://localhost/ into the address bar. If all has gone well, you should see the test page shown in Figure3-5.

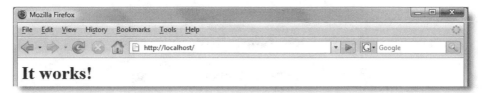

Figure 3-5. A simple, reassuring message that Apache 2.2 is running

Troubleshooting If you get an error message, it probably means that the Apache server is not running. Start up the server as described in the next section, and try again. Other causes of failure include the following:

- A software firewall is blocking Apache. Launch your firewall management panel, and allow communication to and from Apache.

- Another program is using port 80. Download a free utility called Fport from www. foundstone.com/index.htm?subnav=resources/navigation.htm&subcontent=/ resources/proddesc/fport.htm. Save fport.exe to the top level of your C drive, open a Windows Command Prompt, and type the following commands, each followed by Enter:

```
cd C:\
fport
```

   This displays a list of ports being used by various programs. Identify which program is using port 80. If possible, change the other program's configuration to move it to a different port. If you can't move the other program, reconfigure Apache to use port 8080, as described in "Changing the default Apache port" later in the chapter.

Running the Apache Monitor on Vista

This section applies to Windows Vista only. If you are running Windows XP, skip to the next section.

At the time of this writing, the Apache Monitor hasn't been optimized for running on Vista, so you need to run it in compatibility mode. The following instructions show you how:

1. Go to Start ➤ All Programs. You need to locate the Apache Monitor. It may be listed separately as Apache HTTP Server Monitor, or you might find it listed as Monitor Apache Servers inside Apache HTTP Server 2.2.x ➤ Control Apache Server.

2. Right-click Apache HTTP Server Monitor (Monitor Apache Servers), and select Properties.

3. Select the Compatibility tab, and check the option to run the program in compatibility mode for Windows XP (Service Pack 2), as shown in the following screenshot:

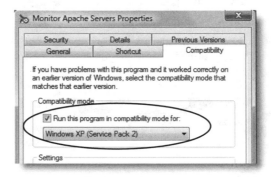

4. Click OK and restart your computer.

5. When you log back into Vista, the task tray should display a message saying that it has blocked some startup programs. Click the message, and select Run blocked program ➤ Apache HTTP Server Monitor, as shown here.

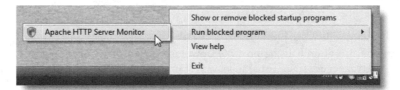

Vista should register it as a permitted program. If you see the Error alert shown in step 7 of "Installing Apache on Windows," check that compatibility mode hasn't been deselected by accident. After resetting compatibility mode, you should be able to start the Apache Monitor by selecting it from Start ➤ All Programs.

Starting and stopping Apache on Windows

Apache 2.2 places a tiny icon like a red feather with a white circle in the tray at the right end of the Windows taskbar. This is the Apache Monitor, which shows you at a glance whether Apache is running. If it's running, there is a green, right-facing arrow in the white circle.
When Apache has stopped, the arrow turns to a red dot (see the screenshots immediately above). Click the icon once with the *left* mouse button to reveal a context menu to start, stop, and restart Apache.

Changing startup preferences or disabling Apache

3

If you stop developing PHP sites for a while or decide you want to experiment with IIS, you can switch Apache to manual operation or disable it like this:

1. Open the Windows Services panel by right-clicking the Apache Service Monitor icon, and selecting Open Services from the context menu.

2. Highlight Apache2.2 in the Services panel, right-click, and select Properties.

3. From the Startup type drop-down menu, select Automatic, Manual, or Disabled, as shown in Figure 3-6. If you want to start or stop Apache at the same time, click the appropriate Service status button before clicking OK.

Figure 3-6. If you decide you don't need Apache for a while, you can switch off automatic startup.

Installing PHP on Windows

Now that you have a web server running, you can install PHP. These instructions work with Apache on Windows XP and Vista and with IIS on Windows XP.

> In my testing, the PHP 5.2.1 installer failed with IIS7 on Vista. I expect a future version will rectify the problem. Check my website at http://foundationphp.com/egdwcs3/updates.php for the current situation. The site gives details of a workaround I used to get PHP working successfully on IIS7.

1. Make sure all programs are closed, and double-click the php-5.x.x-win32-installer.msi icon to launch the installation wizard. Click Next to start the installation.

2. Accept the PHP License Agreement, and click the Next button.

3. The next dialog box allows you to choose where PHP should be installed. The default is C:\Program Files\PHP\. Accept the default or specify another location, and click Next.

4. You now get the chance to select the web server that you want to use in conjunction with PHP. As you can see from the next screenshot, there's a wide selection.

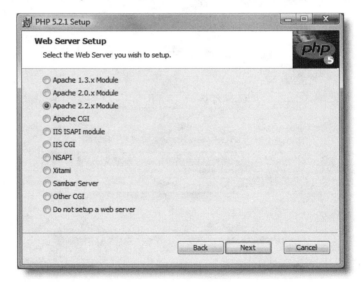

- If you plan to use Apache with PHP, select Apache 2.2.x Module.
- Although there are two options for IIS, only IIS CGI is supported at the moment. (Check http://foundationphp.com/egdwcs3/updates.php for the current situation.)

Make your selection, and click Next.

5. If you chose IIS in the preceding step, skip to step 6.

If you chose Apache, specify the location of the Apache configuration file by browsing to C:\Program Files\Apache Software Foundation\Apache2.2\conf\ (adjust the path if you installed Apache in a different location). Click OK, and then click Next.

6. The next dialog box lets you select which PHP extensions will be enabled. PHP offers a huge range of noncore extensions, so it's best to choose only those that you know you'll need. Click inside the dialog box to expand the Extensions tree menu. You need to enable the following extensions:

- **GD2:** This enables PHP's image manipulation functions.
- **Multi-Byte String:** This allows you to handle Unicode (UTF-8) and is needed for communication with MySQL.
- **MySQL:** This allows you to interact with the MySQL database.
- **MySQLi:** This offers enhanced MySQL features.
- **XSL:** This is required for the Dreamweaver XSL Transformation server behavior.

To enable an extension, click the down arrow next to the extension name, and select Will be installed on local hard drive, as shown in the following screenshot. The red X is replaced by a hard drive icon, indicating that the extension will be enabled.

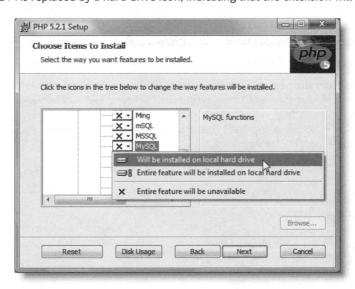

Click Next when you have made your choices.

7. The wizard is now ready to install PHP. If you selected Apache, it asks whether you want it to configure Apache. (On Vista, this alert may be hidden behind the main dialog box; select it from the Windows task bar when it flashes.) Click Yes.

After the installation, you should see two alert boxes telling you that the Apache configuration and mime.types files were successfully updated. Click OK and then click Finish to close the wizard.

If you selected IIS, there are no further dialog boxes. Just click Finish when the installation is complete. If you selected IIS on Vista and see the following warning, click OK and visit http://foundationphp.com/egdwcs3/updates.php for details of a workaround.

Keep the .msi file after you have finished, as you will need it again if you want to add new features to PHP. The installer copies only those files needed for the features you selected.

Testing your PHP installation (Windows XP and Vista)

Before you can test your PHP installation, you must reboot your computer.

Use test.php from the beginning of the chapter or from examples/ch03 in the download files to make sure that the installation succeeded. Because PHP is a server-side language, you need to locate all files within what's known as the **server root** or the server's **document root**. This is simply a top-level folder where Apache or IIS automatically looks for files. The default location for Apache 2.2 is

    C:\Program Files\Apache Software Foundation\Apache2.2\htdocs

For IIS, it's

    C:\Inetpub\wwwroot

Copy test.php to the appropriate folder for your web server, launch a browser, and type the following URL in the browser address bar:

    http://localhost/test.php

If everything went well, you should see the page of PHP configuration data shown in Figure 3-1 at the beginning of the chapter. Congratulations, you're nearly finished. Unless you need to run Apache on a different port from the default 80, or you want to run Apache and IIS in parallel, skip ahead to the section "Checking your PHP configuration."

Troubleshooting Unfortunately, sometimes things go wrong. If you fail to see the PHP configuration page, the first thing to check is that your web server is running. Copy an ordinary .html web page to the server root, and view it by typing http://localhost/ followed by the file name in the browser address bar. If it displays correctly, the problem is with the PHP installation. If it doesn't display, the problem is with your web server.

■ If you are using IIS, uninstall PHP through the Windows Control Panel like any other Windows program, and remove C:\Program Files\PHP, if it isn't removed automatically. Check IIS and make sure it is working properly before reinstalling PHP.

■ If you are using Apache, open the main Apache configuration file (C:\Program Files\ Apache Software Foundation\Apache2.2\conf\httpd.conf) in Notepad, and scroll down to the bottom of the file. You should see a section that starts with #BEGIN PHP INSTALLER EDITS, as shown in Figure 3-7.

```
httpd.conf - Notepad

File  Edit  Format  View  Help

SSLRandomSeed startup builtin
SSLRandomSeed connect builtin
</IfModule>


#BEGIN PHP INSTALLER EDITS - REMOVE ONLY ON UNINSTALL
PHPIniDir "C:\\Program Files\\PHP\\"
LoadModule php5_module "C:\\Program Files\\PHP\\php5apache2_2.dll"
#END PHP INSTALLER EDITS - REMOVE ONLY ON UNINSTALL
```

Figure 3-7. The Windows PHP installer places all edits in one convenient block at the end of the Apache configuration file.

If your file doesn't look like that, replace the PHP installer edits with the code shown in Figure 3-7.

Apache is case sensitive; the commands in the second and third lines must contain the correct combination of uppercase and lowercase letters. The pathnames must be in quotes, and there should be no spaces in PHPIniDir and LoadModule.

Also open C:\Program Files\Apache Software Foundation\Apache2.2\conf\ mime.types in Notepad. The PHP installer should have added the following two lines at the bottom:

```
application/x-httpd-php          php
application/x-httpd-php-source   phps
```

If they're missing, add them on separate lines as shown here. After making any changes to httpd.conf and mime.types, save both files, and restart Apache.

If PHP still fails in Apache, remove the four lines of code from httpd.conf and the two lines from mime.types. Uninstall PHP through the Windows Control Panel like any Windows program, delete the C:\Program Files\PHP folder if it's still there, and restart Apache. Make sure Apache is running properly before attempting to reinstall.

Changing the default Apache port

By default, web servers like Apache and IIS listen for requests on port 80, but they cannot share the same port. So, if you plan to run Apache and IIS in parallel, you must switch one of them to listen on a different port. Equally, if another program is already using port 80 and cannot be moved, you need to switch your web server to a different port. This is how you change the default setting for Apache.

1. Open C:\Program Files\Apache Software Foundation\Apache2.2\conf\httpd. conf in Notepad, and locate the line indicated by the arrow in the following screenshot:

```
49  # Change this to Listen on specific IP addresses as shown below to
50  # prevent Apache from glomming onto all bound IP addresses (0.0.0.0)
51  #
52  #Listen 12.34.56.78:80
▶ 53  Listen 80
54
```

2. Change it to this:

   Listen 8080

3. Save httpd.conf, and restart Apache. After making this change, you should always use http://localhost:8080/ in place of http://localhost/.

Changing the default IIS port

The following instructions show you how to change the default port for IIS. The setup is slightly different for Windows XP and Vista. Use the appropriate set of instructions.

Changing the IIS port on Windows XP

1. Open the Internet Information Services panel (Start ➤ Control Panel ➤ Administrative Tools ➤ Internet Information Services), expand the tree menu on the left to highlight Default Web Site, and click the Stop Item icon, as shown here:

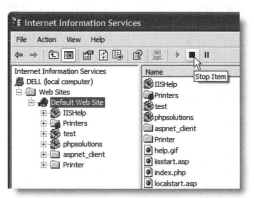

2. Right-click Default Web Site, and choose Properties from the context menu.

3. Select the Web Site tab, and change TCP Port to 8080, as shown in the next screenshot.

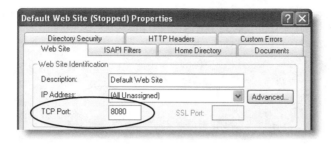

4. Click OK to save the change, and restart IIS by clicking the Start Item icon (the right-facing arrow immediately to the left of the Stop Item icon).

Changing the IIS port on Vista

1. Open the Internet Information Services (IIS) Manager by going to Start ➤ Control Panel ➤ Administrative Tools ➤ Internet Information Services(IIS) Manager (see Figure 3-8). Expand the tree menu on the left to highlight Default Web Site.

Figure 3-8. The Internet Information Services (IIS) Manager in Vista

2. In the Actions panel on the right, click Stop under Manage Web Site. Then click Bindings under Edit Site. This opens the Web Site Bindings dialog box.

3. Select the existing entry in the Web Site Bindings dialog box, and click Edit. In the Edit Web Site Binding dialog box, change the value of Port to 8080, as shown in the next screenshot, and click OK.

4. Confirm that Port displays 8080 in the Web Site Bindings dialog box, and click Close.

5. Restart IIS by clicking Start under Manage Web Site in the Actions panel.

> *After making this change, you should always use* http://localhost:8080/ *in place of* http://localhost/. *If you switched IIS to manual startup before installing Apache, you can now reinstate automatic startup, as long as Apache and IIS are listening on different ports. Reopen the dialog box shown in Figure 3-3, and reset* Startup type *to* Automatic.

Setting up on Mac OS X

The good news about Mac OS X is that Apache and PHP are already installed. The not quite so good news is that the preinstalled version of PHP is very restricted and not suitable for working with this book. Fortunately, an excellent Mac PKG file is available for free download, and it will provide you with a full-featured, up-to-date version of PHP 5.

> *These instructions have been tested on Mac OS X 10.4 (Tiger), the minimum requirement for Dreamweaver CS3. They do* not *cover Mac OS X Server.*

Starting and stopping Apache on Mac OS X

Make sure you are logged into Mac OS X with Administrative privileges.

1. Open System Preferences, and click Sharing in Internet & Network.

2. In the dialog box that opens, click the lock in the bottom left corner, if necessary, to allow you to make changes, and enter your password when prompted. Highlight Personal Web Sharing on the Services tab, as shown in Figure 3-9, and then click the Start button on the right. A message will appear informing you that personal web sharing is starting up. Once it's running, the label on the button changes to Stop. Use this button to stop and restart Apache whenever you install a new version of PHP or make any changes to the configuration files. Click the lock again, if you want to prevent accidental changes.

Figure 3-9. The Apache web server on a Mac is switched on and off in the Sharing section of System Preferences.

3. Open your favorite browser, and type http://localhost/ into the address bar. You should see a page like the one shown in Figure 3-10, confirming that Apache is running.

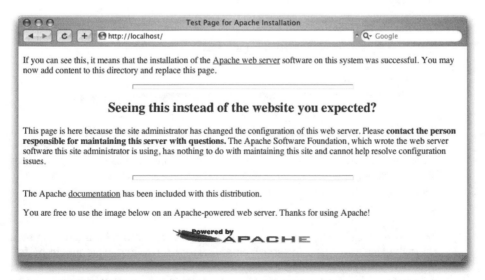

Figure 3-10. Confirmation that Apache is running successfully on Mac OS X

Upgrading PHP on Mac OS X

The engine underlying Mac OS X is Unix, a very stable multitasking operating system that's been around for more than 30 years. While that's a good thing, it means that installing PHP the traditional way involves compiling it from source code. Without a solid understanding of Unix, this can turn into a nightmare if anything unexpected happens.

Thankfully, it's a route you don't have to take. A software engineer named Marc Liyanage is highly respected in the Mac PHP community for the packages he creates for all major upgrades of PHP. Marc's packages are not only easy to install, he takes the trouble to configure them to support a wide range of extra features. The only drawback is that they involve a large download (nearly 50MB). Even if you have a slow Internet connection, the large download is worth it. You get a full-featured version of PHP that works straight "out of the box." If you run into problems, there's a searchable support forum on Marc's website, where answers tend to be fast and accurate. It should be your first port of call in case of installation problems.

> *PHP relies heavily on the availability of external code libraries. It is essential that you have installed all the latest Apple system software updates before proceeding. Marc Liyanage has a policy of supporting only the most recent version of Mac OS X. At the time of this writing, his package is a Universal Binary (suitable for both PowerPC and Mac Intel processors) that works on Mac OS X 10.4, the minimum required for Dreamweaver CS3.*

1. There are different packages for Apache 1.3 and Apache 2. The default installation in Mac OS X at the time of this writing is Apache 1.3, but it's important to check whether it's the same in your case. In Finder, open the Utilities folder within the Applications folder, and launch Terminal.

2. A window like the one shown here will open:

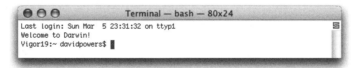

It doesn't look very impressive, but if you've ever worked on a Windows or DOS computer, it should be as familiar as the Command Prompt, and it performs the same function. All instructions to the computer are inserted as written commands at the **shell prompt**. This is the final line in the preceding screenshot, and it looks something like this:

```
Vigor19:~ davidpowers$
```

The first part (before the colon) is the name of your Macintosh hard disk. The tilde (~) is the Unix shorthand for your home directory (or folder). This should be followed by your username and a dollar sign. As you navigate around the hard disk, your location is indicated in place of ~. All commands in Terminal are followed by Return.

3. To find out which version of Apache is running on your Mac, type the following command:

```
httpd -v
```

After pressing Return, you should see something like this:

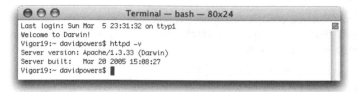

This tells you the version of Apache and when it was built. Check the first two numbers of the version—in this case, 1.3—to ensure that you download the correct PHP package.

4. Go to www.entropy.ch/software/macosx/php/, scroll about halfway down the page to the section labeled PHP 5 for Mac OS X, PPC and Intel, and select the link for the same version of Apache as you have on your computer. Read any installation instructions on the site, as they'll contain the most up-to-date information about special requirements or restrictions.

5. The Universal Binary is in a compressed file called entropy-php-5.x.x-x.tar.gz, where x represents the version number. Double-click the compressed file's icon. This extracts two icons to your Desktop: entropy-php-5.x.x-x.tar and entropy-php.mpkg. Double-click entropy-php.mpkg, and follow the instructions onscreen.

6. Copy the test.php from the beginning of the chapter or the download files to Macintosh HD:Library:WebServer:Documents. Launch a browser, and type http://localhost/test.php in the address bar. You should see a screen similar to Figure 3-11 confirming that PHP has been installed successfully. If it fails to appear, stop Apache, and restart it as described in the preceding section.

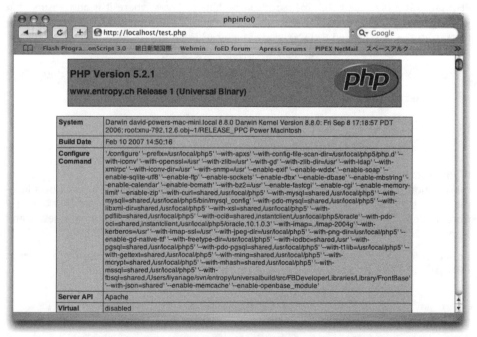

Figure 3-11. Confirmation that a full-featured version of PHP has been installed on Mac OS X

Checking your PHP configuration

Whichever method you used to install PHP, you need to make sure not only that it's running but also that it's configured correctly for working with Dreamweaver CS3. This involves the following two steps:

1. Checking the output of `phpinfo()`

2. Making any necessary changes to the PHP configuration file, `php.ini`

Understanding the output of phpinfo()

The screen full of information produced by `phpinfo()`, as shown in Figures 3-1 and 3-11, may appear overwhelming at first sight, but it's a very user-friendly way of checking the features available in your PHP setup. Everything is grouped together logically and usually in alphabetical order. The top section contains mainly technical details. Windows users will notice that the section labeled Configure Command is far shorter than that shown in Figure 3-11 for Mac OS X or on a remote Linux server. This simply reflects the different way Windows handles PHP extensions. Most of the important information is further down the page.

The first item you should check is right at the top. It's the PHP version number. It must be a minimum of 4.3.1, and preferably 5.2.1 or higher. If it's below the minimum, you have no option but to reinstall PHP.

Checking the location of php.ini

Although `phpinfo()` displays the details of your configuration, what actually controls your PHP setup is a file called `php.ini`, so it's important to know where it is and ensure that your operating system is reading the correct file. This information is displayed in the sixth item from the top, labeled Configuration File (php.ini) Path. In PHP 5.2.3 or later, check the seventh item, labeled Loaded Configuration File.

If you accepted the default installation location on Windows, it should display this:

```
C:\Program Files\PHP\php.ini
```

On Mac OS X, you should see this:

```
/usr/local/php5/lib/php.ini
```

If you installed XAMPP or MAMP, or chose a different installation location on Windows, make a note of where `php.ini` is located, as you will need to make a few minor adjustments to it shortly. If `php.ini` is where you expect it to be, skip ahead to "Checking PHP Core settings." If `php.ini` is in an unexpected location, or if the pathname doesn't end with `php.ini`, read on.

Both problems arise almost exclusively with Windows, and are usually caused by a previous installation of PHP (or all-in-one package) that hasn't been completely removed.

If php.ini is in the wrong place Until mid-2004, the recommended location for php.ini was in the main Windows folder. If you still have a copy of php.ini in C:\WINDOWS or in some other, unexpected location, remove it, and restart Apache or IIS. Reload test.php in your browser, and check whether it now shows the correct location or if you now have the next problem.

If the pathname doesn't end with php.ini This means that the operating system isn't reading the configuration file. This results in PHP applying a restricted set of default values, which are unsuitable for working with Dreamweaver CS3 or MySQL. *You must fix this before attempting to go any further.*

On Mac OS X, this normally occurs only if you have enabled the preinstalled version of PHP. The problem should disappear if you install the PHP Mac package as described earlier in the chapter.

On Windows, it usually means there is a problem with the Windows path, which tells the operating system where to find programs. Open a Windows Command Prompt (Start ➤ Accessories ➤ Command Prompt), type path, and press Enter. You should see a list of folder names separated by semicolons.

Inspect the list of folders to see if it includes the location of a previous PHP installation, such as C:\php5. If it does, you need to edit the path to remove the old location and add the new one, if necessary.

To edit the Windows path in Windows XP, double-click System in the Windows Control Panel. Select the Advanced tab, and click Environment Variables. In the System variables pane at the bottom of the dialog box that opens, select Path, and click Edit. Make any edits, and click OK to save them.

To edit the Windows path in Vista, double-click System in the Windows Control Panel in Classic View. Then click Change settings under Computer name, domain, and workgroup settings. In the System Properties panel, select the Advanced tab, and click Environment Variables. In the System variables pane at the bottom of the dialog box that opens, select Path, and click Edit. Make any edits, and click OK to save them.

> *Be careful when editing the Windows path. If you make a mistake, it could prevent other programs from functioning correctly. Each entry must be separated by a semicolon.*

After editing the path, you need to restart your computer. If you have entered the correct path to the PHP folder, and the folder contains php.ini, the correct pathname should be displayed by test.php.

If you still don't see the correct path, copy php.ini from the PHP folder to C:\WINDOWS, and restart your computer. This is a last resort but should always work.

Checking PHP Core settings

With test.php still displayed in your browser, scroll down to the section labeled PHP Core, as shown in Figure 3-12. This section tells you the value of each basic configuration setting on your server. It contains details of more than 80 configuration directives, most of which you need never worry about. However, you need to check the following three, indicated by arrows in Figure 3-12:

- **display_errors**: This needs to be On.
- **error_reporting**: For PHP 5.2.0 and higher, this should be 6143. For earlier versions of PHP, it should be at least 2047.
- **log_errors**: This needs to be Off.

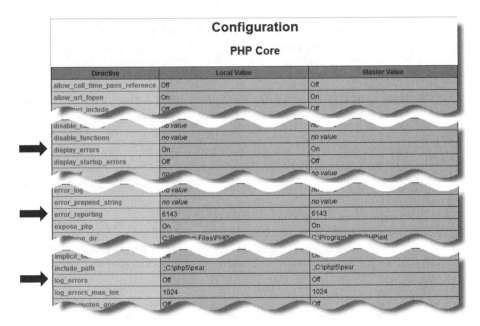

Figure 3-12. The PHP Core section shows all the basic PHP settings on your server.

If you used the PHP Windows installer or the Mac package created by Marc Liyanage, you need to change display_errors and log_errors. If you used an all-in-one package, you may need to change all three. Instructions are given in "Editing php.ini" later in the chapter.

Although you don't need to worry about the PHP Core directives now, Table 3-1 describes the most important ones. Refer to this table if you get unexpected results when deploying PHP pages on your remote server. Hosting companies frequently restrict what you're allowed to do by altering the default configuration.

Table 3-1. The main PHP Core directives

Directive	Default value	Remarks
allow_url_fopen	On	This allows your scripts to read files, such as news feeds, on other sites. Prior to PHP 5.2.0, it also allowed you to include the contents of remote files directly within scripts. This is potentially dangerous, so many hosting companies turn this setting off.
allow_url_include	Off	This was introduced in PHP 5.2.0 to overcome the security problem with allow_url_fopen (see preceding entry). It's hoped that hosting companies will turn allow_url_fopen back on once they upgrade to PHP 5.2.0 or higher.
display_errors	Off	This setting should be on when developing but off on a live production server, as error messages can provide useful information to malicious users. However, many hosting companies turn this setting on to prevent filling up their error logs. Always test scripts thoroughly to eliminate errors before deployment on a live server.
error_reporting	6143	This is the equivalent of E_ALL in php.ini. It displays all error messages, except E_STRICT, a category mainly of interest to advanced users. Prior to PHP 5.2.0, E_ALL is displayed as 2047.
file_uploads	On	This allows you to upload files to the remote server, a subject not covered in this book. For a detailed explanation of PHP file uploads, see my book *PHP Solutions: Dynamic Web Design Made Easy* (friends of ED, ISBN-13: 978-1-59059-731-6).
log_errors	On	This setting should normally be the opposite of display_errors, so that errors are either displayed onscreen or written to a log file, but not both. For a local development environment, display_errors should be on, and log_errors should be off, to prevent filling up your hard disk with unnecessary files.
magic_quotes_gpc	Off	When turned on, this setting automatically inserts backslashes in front of single and double quotes in data submitted from a form. Code generated by Dreamweaver CS3 automatically detects whether this setting is on and handles the data appropriately. This subject is discussed in Chapter 11.

Continued

Table 3-1. The main PHP Core directives *(continued)*

Directive	Default value	Remarks
max_execution_time	30	The maximum time, in seconds, that a script will attempt to run. If your scripts take longer than 30 seconds, it's normally a sign there's something wrong with them.
open_basedir		For security reasons, some hosting companies restrict files that can be opened by PHP to a specific directory (folder) and its subfolders. If a value is displayed here, your scripts will not have access to files in other folders.
post_max_size	8M	The maximum size of data sent using the post method, including upload files. K indicates kilobytes; M indicates megabytes. If no suffix is given, the size is measured in bytes.
register_globals	Off	The default setting has been off since 2002, but some hosting companies switch it back on because many poorly written scripts break without it. Do not be tempted to change this setting, as scripts that rely on register_globals are extremely insecure. Moreover, register_globals will be permanently disabled in PHP 6, so you need to future-proof your scripts.
safe_mode	Off	As a security measure, some hosting companies enable safe mode, which disables many PHP features. For details, see www.php.net/manual/en/features.safe-mode.php.
short_open_tag	Off	Some scripts use <? instead of <?php, and <?= instead of <?php echo. This causes confusion with XML, so the shorter form is now discouraged. Dreamweaver CS3 and this book always use the longer, recommended form.
upload_max_filesize	2M	This is the maximum size of an individual upload file.
upload_tmp_dir		This is where upload files are stored temporarily until moved to their final location. See my book, *PHP Solutions*, for more details.

Checking installed extensions

The rest of the configuration page shows you which PHP extensions are enabled. They're listed alphabetically and provide considerable information about the features installed on your server. Figure 3-13 shows part of the details listed for a server that supports the original MySQL extension and MySQL Improved (mysqli). Although Dreamweaver CS3 doesn't offer support for MySQL Improved, if you install PHP 5 as recommended here, you need to make sure that test.php lists both mysql and mysqli, as shown in Figure 3-13. The value of Client API Version determines the maximum version of MySQL you will be able to install in Chapter 13. It should be at least 5.0.x. PHP 4 does not support mysqli, and the Client API Version will be lower, restricting you to running an older version of MySQL.

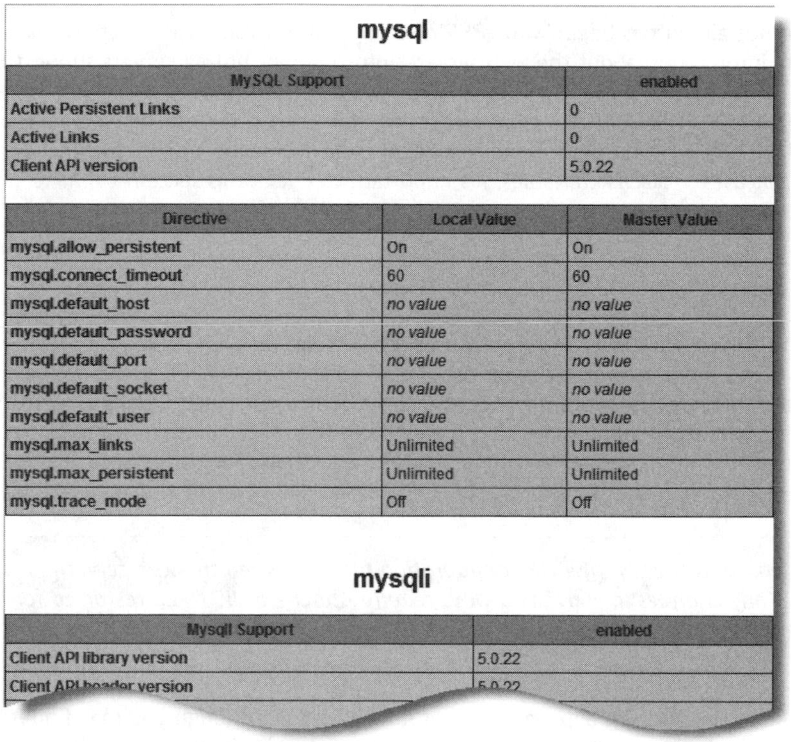

mysql

MySQL Support	enabled
Active Persistent Links	0
Active Links	0
Client API version	5.0.22

Directive	Local Value	Master Value
mysql.allow_persistent	On	On
mysql.connect_timeout	60	60
mysql.default_host	*no value*	*no value*
mysql.default_password	*no value*	*no value*
mysql.default_port	*no value*	*no value*
mysql.default_socket	*no value*	*no value*
mysql.default_user	*no value*	*no value*
mysql.max_links	Unlimited	Unlimited
mysql.max_persistent	Unlimited	Unlimited
mysql.trace_mode	Off	Off

mysqli

Mysqli Support	enabled
Client API library version	5.0.22
Client API header version	5.0.22

Figure 3-13. It's important to check that you have correctly installed support for the MySQL database in PHP.

Scroll down the rest of test.php, and check that the following extensions are also enabled:

- gd
- mbstring
- pcre
- session
- xsl

> *If any of these entries are missing, fix your installation before attempting to go any further. On a Mac, this means a complete reinstallation, because PHP extensions must be compiled into the program at the time of installation. Windows users should refer to "Enabling PHP extensions in Windows" later in the chapter, as the method depends on how you originally installed PHP.*

Checking supported $_SERVER variables

The final section output by phpinfo() is titled PHP Variables. You don't need to worry about this section when first working with PHP, but it comes in very handy later.

Most, if not all, entries begin with _SERVER. These are preset PHP variables that contain valuable information about the web server. Unfortunately, not all servers support the full range. For example, a Windows server running in CGI mode does not normally support $_SERVER['DOCUMENT_ROOT'], which contains the pathname of the server root, and $_SERVER['SCRIPT_FILENAME'], which contains the file name of the current script. If a PHP script uses $_SERVER variables, it's important to check this section to make sure that your remote server supports the particular variables you need.

Editing php.ini

The configuration file, php.ini, controls all the settings on your server. Although you can edit php.ini in your own testing environment, you normally have no control over most settings on a remote server, unless it's your own dedicated server. Editing php.ini is easy, because it's a text file, albeit a very long one (more than 1,200 lines). Most lines begin with a semicolon, which indicates a comment. Directives that your computer reads when the web server starts up are always on separate lines that don't begin with a semicolon.

> *Your computer reads the PHP configuration file only when the web server first starts up, so any changes to php.ini always require Apache or IIS to be restarted for them to take effect.*

Windows users can open php.ini and edit it in Notepad, although you may find it helpful to use a script editor—such as TextPad (www.textpad.com) or EditPlus (www.editplus.com)—that displays line numbers. Things are slightly more complicated on Mac OS X.

Accessing php.ini on Mac OS X

On a Mac, php.ini is a hidden file, so it's best to use a script editor capable of handling hidden files, such as BBEdit (www.barebones.com). If you don't have a suitable editor, I suggest that you download TextWrangler (also from www.barebones.com), a free, cut-down version of BBEdit that's ideal for editing php.ini.

1. Open BBEdit or TextWrangler. To make it easier to identify the correct place in the files you edit, choose Preferences from the BBEdit or TextWrangler menu, and select Text Status Display. Make sure the Show Line Numbers checkbox is selected. Close the Preferences panel.

2. From the File menu, choose Open Hidden, and navigate to Macintosh HD:usr: local:php5:lib:php.ini. Because php.ini is a protected file, you need to select All Files from the Enable drop-down menu at the top of the Open dialog box, as shown in the following screenshot. Click Open.

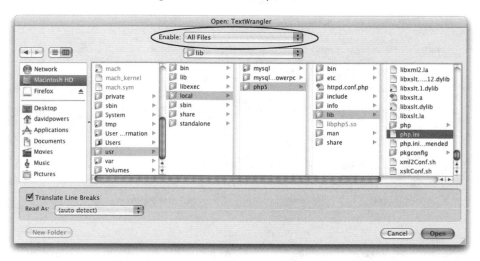

3. At the top left of the toolbar, a pencil with a line through it indicates that php.ini is a read-only file. To edit it, click the pencil icon. You will see the following prompt:

4. Click Yes. You can then edit php.ini normally.

5. When you save the file, you will be prompted for your Mac administrator password. This is because the file belongs to your computer's super administrator known as "root."

Configuring PHP to display errors

If phpinfo() shows that display_errors is turned off in your local testing environment, you need to make a couple of simple text edits to php.ini. Locate the section in php.ini shown in the following screenshot, and edit the directives shown on lines 349, 356, and 366 so they are the same as in the image.

```
345  ;error_reporting = E_COMPILE_ERROR|E_RECOVERABLE_ERROR|E_ERROR|E_CORE_ERROR
346  ;
347  ;    - Show all errors, except coding standards warnings
348  ;
349  error_reporting  =  E_ALL
350
351  ; Print out errors (as a part of the output).  For production web sites,
352  ; you're strongly encouraged to turn this feature off, and use error logging
353  ; instead (see below).  Keeping display_errors enabled on a production web site
354  ; may reveal security information to end users, such as file paths on your Web
355  ; server, your database schema or other information.
356  display_errors = On
357
358  ; Even when display_errors is on, errors that occur during PHP's startup
359  ; sequence are not displayed.  It's strongly recommended to keep
360  ; display_startup_errors off, except for when debugging.
361  display_startup_errors = Off
362
363  ; Log errors into a log file (server-specific log, stderr, or error_log (below))
364  ; As stated above, you're strongly advised to use error logging in place of
365  ; error displaying on production web sites.
366  log_errors = Off
367
```

The line numbers should be taken only as a guide to identifying the correct section of php.ini. They may be different in your version of PHP.

Enabling PHP extensions on Windows

PHP offers a large number of extensions to its core functionality. Many extensions are built into the Windows version of PHP. Others rely on dynamic link libraries (.dll files). If the extension you want to use isn't listed when you run phpinfo(), you need to enable it. How you do so depends on how you installed PHP.

If you used the Windows installer for PHP 5.2.0 or higher The changes need to be made by running the installer again.

1. To launch the installer, go to Start ➤ Control Panel.

2. In Windows XP, double-click Add or Remove Programs, and select PHP. Click the Change button, and follow the instructions onscreen.

   In Vista, select Programs and Features in Classic View. Highlight PHP, click Change at the top of the panel, and follow the instructions onscreen.

3. Select any new extensions in the same way as when you originally installed PHP.

The .msi file that you used to install PHP must still be available. If it's no longer in the original location, Windows prompts you to browse for it. If the file is missing, the update procedure will terminate without making any changes.

If you have previous experience of PHP, it's important to realize that you cannot simply uncomment the appropriate extension in php.ini, because the Windows installer needs to install the corresponding .dll file(s) as well. Unlike the ZIP version of PHP, the extension folder contains only those .dll files actually required.

If you installed PHP any other way You should be able to enable extensions by uncommenting the appropriate directive in php.ini. Open php.ini, and remove the semicolon from the beginning of the line that lists the appropriate .dll file in the section labeled Windows Extensions (around line 625). See www.php.net/manual/en/install.windows.extensions.php for details of extensions that are dependent on others.

Enabling file uploads and sessions (Windows installer)

The Windows installer designates two folders in your user area as the values for upload_tmp_dir and session.save_path. However, file uploads and sessions won't work unless you create the folders yourself. (Sessions are covered in Chapter 15.)

In Windows XP, go to C:\Documents and Settings\<username>\Local Settings\Temp. In Vista, go to C:\Users\<username>\AppData\Local\Temp.

Create a new folder called php, and inside that folder, create two subfolders called upload and session.

Alternatively, edit php.ini to set the values of upload_tmp_dir and session.save_path to point to folders of your choosing. If the folder pathname includes any spaces, enclose the entire pathname in quotes. Make sure you edit the correct versions of these directives in php.ini. You can identify them because they don't have a semicolon at the beginning of the line.

Overriding settings on your remote server

Although I said earlier that you normally have no control over settings on your remote server unless it's your own dedicated server, it is possible to override some of them. This is not something that you need to worry about at this stage, but this information may be useful later.

Suppressing error messages

If your remote server has display_errors turned on, you can suppress all error messages by adding the following line of code to the top of your pages:

```php
<?php error_reporting(0); ?>
```

Overriding default settings with ini_set()

Some PHP directives can also be overridden by using a function called ini_set() in your scripts (if you're new to PHP, functions and other basic structures are covered in Chapter 10). There's a full list of php.ini directives at www.php.net/manual/en/ini.php. Those marked PHP_INI_ALL can be used with ini_set(). The function takes two arguments: the directive and the new value, both in quotes. So this is how you increase the maximum time a script is allowed to run from the default 30 to 45 seconds:

```php
ini_set('max_execution_time', '45');
```

Using .htaccess to change default settings

If your remote server runs on Apache *and* the server is configured to allow you to change settings, you can override many more by creating .htaccess files. Unlike ini_set(), which must be included in every script, this has the advantage that the new settings are applied automatically to all files in the affected directory (folder). Directives marked PHP_INI_ALL or PHP_INI_PERDIR in the list at www.php.net/manual/en/ini.php can be overridden in this way. For directives that have an on/off value, use php_flag followed by the directive name and the new value. To turn off magic quotes, use the following command in an .htaccess file:

```
php_flag magic_quotes_gpc off
```

Directives that have a value other than on/off use a different command: php_value followed by the directive and the new value. So, changing max_execution_time to 45 seconds through .htaccess would look like this:

```
php_value max_execution_time 45
```

For more details, see www.php.net/manual/en/configuration.changes.php.

Summary

By now, you should have a testing environment compatible with Dreamweaver CS3. At the risk of sounding repetitive, you must check that display_errors is turned on and that phpinfo() lists mysql among the enabled extensions. Nobody likes seeing error messages, but they're indispensable when developing with PHP. Also, many people are confused by the fact that, although support for MySQL is automatically built into PHP 4, you need to enable it explicitly in PHP 5.

Before you can build web pages with PHP, you need to define your server root and tell Dreamweaver where to find your local files, testing server, and remote server. That's the subject of the next chapter.

If you're using Windows Vista, you may want to install MySQL (see Chapter 13) at this stage. You should also read the section in the next chapter about creating virtual hosts. Once you have finished configuring your testing environment, you should turn User Account Control back on.

4 SETTING UP A PHP SITE

If you're a regular Dreamweaver user, I don't need to tell you the importance of site definition; it's how Dreamweaver organizes your web files and makes sure that links point to the right place. If you're in a hurry, and working with static web files, Dreamweaver will let you create a quick page without saving it within a defined site. That won't work with PHP pages. Dreamweaver uses the site definition to determine which tools to make available to you. Unless you choose the correct server model, all the PHP server behaviors will be inaccessible, and you won't be able to test your files.

This is because web pages that use a server-side language like PHP need to be processed—**parsed**, to use the correct technical expression—by the PHP engine on the web server before they can be sent to the browser. As a result, the web server has to know not only where to find your PHP pages, but also the correct URL to send them to after they have been processed. Defining a PHP site in Dreamweaver is simple, but a lot of people seem to get it wrong. This chapter guides you through the various options for storing PHP pages, and then shows you how to define your site correctly in Dreamweaver CS3.

What this chapter covers

- Choosing the best location for your files
- Understanding the difference between document- and root-relative links
- Moving the Apache server root on Windows
- Creating virtual hosts on Windows and Mac OS X
- Registering virtual directories on IIS
- Setting up Dreamweaver to communicate with your remote server
- Defining the PHP testing server in Dreamweaver
- Testing your site definition
- Backing up your Dreamweaver site definitions

Deciding where to locate your sites

There are two ways you can organize web files—in a centralized location known as the **server root**, or in separate locations using **virtual hosts** or virtual directories. Both have merits, and your choice is likely to be dictated by your work habits. Another consideration is the type of links in your pages.

Understanding document- and root-relative links

When you insert a link or an image in a web page the <a> or <img> tag needs to point to the correct resource. Let's say you have a simple website structure like that shown in Figure 4-1.

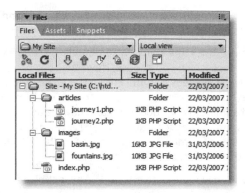

Figure 4-1.
A simple website structure displayed in the Dreamweaver Files panel

Document-relative links

The most common way to indicate the path to a resource on the same site is with links that are relative to the document. For example, if index.php, contains a link to journey1.php, the code looks like this:

```
<a href="articles/journey1.php">Read more</a>
```

And a link back to index.php inside journey1.php looks like this:

```
<a href="../index.php">Back to main page</a>
```

Similarly, if index.php contains the image called fountains.jpg, the <img> tag looks like this (I have omitted all attributes other than src, because that's the only one we're interested in at the moment):

```
<img src="images/fountains.jpg" . . . />
```

A reference to the same image in journey1.php, however, looks like this:

```
<img src="../images/fountains.jpg" . . . />
```

The ../ before index.php and the images folder name tells the web server that it needs to look one level higher in the website hierarchy to find the correct folder. If you change the structure of the website using the Files panel, Dreamweaver automatically updates all links, adding or removing the requisite number of ../ to ensure that everything works as intended.

Root-relative links

An alternative way of indicating the path to a resource on the same site is to make the links relative to the site root, rather than the document. With root-relative links, the two links look like this:

```
<a href="/articles/journey1.php>Read more</a>
<a href="/index.php">Back to main page</a>
```

The <img> tag in *both* index.php and journey1.php looks like this:

```
<img src="/images/fountains.jpg" . . . />
```

105

The difference is that the pathname always begins with a leading forward slash, which indicates the top level of the site—in other words, the site root.

Why does this matter? After all, both achieve the same thing. When building static sites with .html pages, it doesn't make any difference which you choose. However, root-relative links can be extremely useful with PHP. The advantage is that the link to the image is identical in index.php and journey1.php, even though the pages are at different levels of the site hierarchy. This means that you can put some of your code, such as a navigation menu, in an external file and the links will always work. As you'll see in Chapter 12, the menu can be included in multiple pages using a simple PHP command, and changes to the external file are automatically propagated to all of them—a great time saver.

Because root-relative links are so useful, you may think that they're the best choice for a PHP site. Unfortunately, life is not quite so simple. Although *root*-relative links are essential inside external files, PHP expects the include command to use a *document*-relative link. Moreover, Dreamweaver uses code that fails on IIS if you select root-relative links as the default for your site. I'll show you how to get around these problems at the appropriate points later in the book.

First, let's look at the alternative ways of organizing your files.

Keeping everything together in the server root

The **server root** is a directory or folder where the web server expects to find all public files. The simplest way of organizing a test environment is to create a subfolder for each site inside the server root. You can then test the site in a browser by adding the subfolder's name after http://localhost/. So, a site in a subfolder called egdwcs3 is accessed by the address http://localhost/egdwcs3/.

Putting everything in the server root has the advantage that the web server automatically recognizes any new subfolders inside the server root, eliminating the need for any further setup.

There are, however, two significant disadvantages:

- All files need to be in the same parent folder, so if your web files are in different parts of your system, you need to move them before working with PHP.
- Because each site is in a subfolder of the server root, you cannot test pages locally if they use root-relative links.

One way round this is to create your site in the server root, but this restricts you to only one site. A better solution—although only if you're using Apache as your local testing server—is to use virtual hosts.

Working with virtual hosts

Without getting into technical details, the web server treats a site in a virtual host as though it's in a dedicated server root of its own, even though everything is outside the main server root. You can emulate this setup on your development computer so that instead of http://localhost/egdwcs3/, the address becomes simply http://egdwcs3/. This has two main advantages:

- It doesn't matter whether your web files are scattered in different parts of your system—as long as each individual site is inside a single parent folder.

- Because a virtual host is treated as a dedicated server root, there is no problem with testing links relative to the site root.

There are no prizes for spotting that the advantages of virtual hosts overcome the disadvantages of keeping everything in the server root. So why don't I just tell you to create virtual hosts? Three reasons:

- Virtual hosts are slightly more complicated to set up. Each new one needs to be added to the web server's main configuration.

- To support virtual hosts with IIS, you must be running a server version of Windows. The version of IIS that runs on Windows XP or Vista supports only virtual *directories*, which are not the same as virtual hosts.

- Even if you never put anything in the server root, you still need one.

Don't worry if you're not sure which to choose. Using the server root is simpler, faster, and adequate for most local development.

Finding the server root

On Windows, Apache 2.2 creates the server root at the following location:

> C:\Program Files\Apache Software Foundation\Apache2.2\htdocs

I don't think it's a good idea to store your web files in among all your program files, so I suggest that you move the Apache server root on Windows to a different location, as described in the next section.

The IIS server root is located at

> C:\Inetpub\wwwroot

On Mac OS X, you have two choices of server root. The main one is located at

> Macintosh HD:Library:WebServer:Documents

Every user account on a Mac also has its own dedicated server root at

> Macintosh HD:Users:*username*:Sites

Any site within this folder can be viewed in a browser using the address http://localhost/~*username*/ followed by the name of the site's subfolder, where *username* is the name of your home folder. The address for the main server root is simply http://localhost/, so it is probably the most convenient to use unless you share the computer with others and want to keep things separate.

Moving the Apache server root on Windows

To avoid clogging up C:\Program Files with unrelated files, it's a good idea to move the Apache server root on Windows. All it involves is creating a new folder and a couple of simple edits to the main Apache configuration file, httpd.conf. I normally create a folder called htdocs at the top level of my C drive, but if you have another hard disk, it's a good idea to use a drive other than C, as—among other things—it makes it easier to recover your files in case of a hard drive failure. The name of the folder is unimportant. I use htdocs because that's the traditional name for an Apache server root.

After you have created the new folder, open C:\Program Files\Apache Software Foundation\Apache2.2\conf\httpd.conf in Notepad or a text editor and locate the following section:

```
144 #
145 # DocumentRoot: The directory out of which you will serve your
146 # documents. By default, all requests are taken from this directory, but
147 # symbolic links and aliases may be used to point to other locations.
148 #
149 DocumentRoot "C:/Program Files/Apache Software Foundation/Apache2.2/htdocs"
150
```

Change the pathname shown on line 149 of the preceding screenshot to the same as your new folder (use the line numbers simply as a guide. They are not part of the file and may be different in a later version of Apache). In my case, I change it to this:

DocumentRoot **"C:/htdocs"**

Scroll down about 30 lines until you find this section:

```
174 #
175 # This should be changed to whatever you set DocumentRoot to.
176 #
177 <Directory "C:/Program Files/Apache Software Foundation/Apache2.2/htdocs">
```

The instruction shown on line 175 is pretty straightforward: change the pathname to match the previous change. In my case, I end up with this:

<Directory **"C:/htdocs"**>

> Make sure that you use forward slashes in the pathname, instead of using the Windows convention of backward slashes.

That's all you need to do. While you have httpd.conf open, though, it's a good idea to add a default PHP page to your Apache configuration.

Setting a default file for Apache on Windows

With httpd.conf still open, scroll down to the following section:

```
208 # DirectoryIndex: sets the file that Apache will serve if a directory
209 # is requested.
210 #
211 <IfModule dir_module>
212     DirectoryIndex index.html
213 </IfModule>
```

This setting tells web servers what to display by default if a URL doesn't end with a file name but contains only a folder name or the domain name (for instance, www.friendsofed.com). Apache will choose the first available page from a space-separated list. Add a space followed by index.php at the end of the command shown on line 212 of the preceding screenshot like this:

```
DirectoryIndex index.html index.php
```

If you want to create one or more virtual hosts, leave httpd.conf open, and skip to "Creating virtual hosts on Apache." Otherwise, save httpd.conf, and restart Apache for the changes to take effect.

Adding a default PHP file to IIS

Since you'll be working with PHP, it's useful to add index.php to the list of default documents that IIS serves up whenever you enter a URL in the browser address bar that doesn't include a file name (such as www.friendsofed.com). The following instructions explain how to do it.

1. Open the Internet Information Services panel (Start ➤ Control Panel ➤ Administrative Tools ➤ Internet Information Services), and expand the tree menu in the left pane. Select Default Web Site.

2. In Windows XP, right-click, and choose Properties from the context menu. Then select the Documents tab of the Default Web Site Properties dialog box, and click Add. In the dialog box that opens, type index.php in the Default Document Name field, and click OK. Use the up and down arrows to move index.php to the position you want in the list, as shown in the following screenshot. If there are any default documents listed that you never intend to use, highlight them, and click Remove. Make sure that Enable Default Document is checked, and click OK.

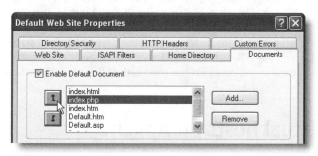

In Windows Vista, double-click Default Document in the IIS section of Default Web Site Home, as shown in the following screenshot:

Add index.php to the comma-separated list in the File name(s) field. Remove any document types that you have no intention of using, and click Apply in the Actions panel at the top right of the Internet Information Services (IIS) Manager.

3. Before your changes can take effect, you need to restart the web server. In Windows XP, with Default Web Server still highlighted in the Internet Information Services panel, click the Stop Item button (a black square) in the toolbar. After the web server stops, click the Start Item button (a right-facing arrow). In Windows Vista, return to the Default Web Site Home screen, and click Restart under Manage Web Site in the Actions panel (at the top right of the preceding screenshot).

Creating virtual hosts on Apache

This section is entirely optional. If you don't want to set up virtual hosts, skip ahead to the section "Defining a PHP site in Dreamweaver." You can come back and set up virtual hosts at any time.

Apache allows you to create as many virtual hosts as you want. It's a two-stage process. First, you tell the operating system the names of the virtual hosts, and then you tell Apache where the files will be located. There are separate instructions for Windows and Mac OS X.

Registering virtual hosts on Windows

Although you can locate your virtual hosts anywhere on your hard drive system, it's a good idea to keep them in a single top-level folder, as this makes it easier to set the correct permissions in Apache. The following instructions assume that all your virtual hosts are kept in a folder called C:\vhosts and show you how to create a virtual host called egdwcs3 within that folder.

1. Create a folder called C:\vhosts and a subfolder inside it called egdwcs3.

2. Open C:\WINDOWS\system32\drivers\etc\hosts in Notepad or a script editor. It's normally a very short file. Look for the following line at the bottom:

   127.0.0.1   localhost

   127.0.0.1 is the IP address that every computer uses to refer to itself.

> *In Vista, you need to open Notepad using the* Run as administrator *option. Otherwise, you won't be able to save the file. From the Windows* Start *menu, right-click* Notepad *(it's in the* Accessories *folder), and select* Run as administrator *from the context menu. Click* Continue *when prompted. In Notepad, choose* File ➤ Open, *and set the drop-down menu alongside* File name *to* All Files (*.*). *Navigate to the* hosts *file and click* Open.

3. On a separate line, enter 127.0.0.1, followed by some space and the name of the virtual host. For instance, to set up a virtual host for this book, enter the following:

   127.0.0.1   egdwcs3

4. If you want to register any further virtual hosts, add each one on a separate line, and point to the same IP address. Save the hosts file, and close it.

The remaining steps involve editing two Apache configuration files. On Windows XP, you don't need to take any special steps. Just edit them in Notepad or a text editor.

If you are using Vista and User Access Control (UAC) is still turned off from the previous chapter, you can edit these files in the normal way. If you want to add additional virtual hosts after turning UAC back on, run Notepad as administrator as described in step 2.

5. Open C:\Program Files\Apache Software Foundation\Apache2.2\conf\httpd.conf in a text editor, scroll down to the Supplemental configuration section at the end, and locate the following section:

```
462  # Virtual hosts
463  #Include conf/extra/httpd-vhosts.conf
```

6. Apache uses the hash or pound sign (#) to indicate comments in its configuration files. Uncomment the command shown on line 463 in the preceding screenshot by removing the #, like this:

   Include conf/extra/httpd-vhosts.conf

   This tells Apache to include the virtual host configuration file, which you must now edit. Save httpd.conf, and close it.

111

7. Open C:\Program Files\Apache Software Foundation\Apache2.2\conf\extra\ httpd-vhosts.conf in Notepad or a text editor. The main part of the file looks like this:

```
13  # You may use the command line option '-S' to verify your virtual host
14  # configuration.
15
16  #
17  # Use name-based virtual hosting.
18  #
19  NameVirtualHost *:80
20
21  #
22  # VirtualHost example:
23  # Almost any Apache directive may go into a VirtualHost container.
24  # The first VirtualHost section is used for all requests that do not
25  # match a ServerName or ServerAlias in any <VirtualHost> block.
26  #
27  <VirtualHost *:80>
28      ServerAdmin webmaster@dummy-host.home
29      DocumentRoot /www/docs/dummy-host.home
30      ServerName dummy-host.home
31      ServerAlias www.dummy-host.home
32      ErrorLog logs/dummy-host.home-error_log
33      CustomLog logs/dummy-host.home-access_log common
34  </VirtualHost>
35
36  <VirtualHost *:80>
37      ServerAdmin webmaster@dummy-host2.home
38      DocumentRoot /www/docs/dummy-host2.home
39      ServerName dummy-host2.home
40      ErrorLog logs/dummy-host2.home-error_log
41      CustomLog logs/dummy-host2.home-access_log common
42  </VirtualHost>
```

8. Position your cursor in the blank space shown on line 15 in the preceding screenshot, and insert the following four lines of code:

```
<Directory C:/vhosts>
  Order Deny,Allow
  Allow from all
</Directory>
```

This sets the correct permissions for the folder that contains the sites you want to treat as virtual hosts. If you chose a location other than C:\vhosts as the top-level folder, replace the pathname in the first line. Remember to use forward slashes in place of backward slashes. Also surround the pathname in quotes if it contains any spaces.

9. Lines 27–42 in the preceding screenshot are examples of virtual host definitions. They show all the commands that can be used, but only DocumentRoot and ServerName are required. When you enable virtual hosting, Apache disables the main server root, so the first definition needs to reproduce the original server root. You then add each new virtual host within a pair of <VirtualHost> tags, using the location of the site's web files as the value for DocumentRoot and the name of the virtual host for ServerName. If the path contains any spaces, enclose the whole path in quotes. If your server root is located, like mine, at C:\htdocs, and you are adding egdwcs3 as a virtual host in C:\vhosts, change the code shown on lines 27–42 so they look like this:

```
<VirtualHost *:80>
  DocumentRoot c:/htdocs
  ServerName localhost
</VirtualHost>
```

```
<VirtualHost *:80>
  DocumentRoot c:/vhosts/egdwcs3
  ServerName egdwcs3
</VirtualHost>
```

10. Save httpd-vhosts.conf, and restart Apache. All sites in the server root will continue to be accessible through http://localhost/sitename/. Anything in a virtual host will be accessible through a direct address, such as http://egdwcs3/.

Registering virtual hosts on Mac OS X

This is a two-stage process. First, you register the names of any new hosts in NetInfo Manager, and then you add the details of where to find them to the Apache configuration file.

1. Create a new folder on your hard disk to house your virtual hosts. I created a folder called vhosts in my home folder.

2. Open NetInfo Manager, which is in the Utilities subfolder of Applications.

3. Click the lock at the bottom left of the dialog box that opens, and enter your administrator's password when prompted.

4. Select machines, then localhost, and click the Duplicate icon. When prompted, confirm that you want to make a copy.

5. Highlight the copy, and double-click the name in the lower pane, as shown in the following screenshot.

6. Change localhost copy to whatever you want to call the virtual host. For example, to create a virtual host for this book, enter egdwcs3.

7. Click any of the other entries in the left column of the top pane. The operating system will ask you twice if you really want to make the changes. You do. This registers the name of the virtual host with your computer. The next stage is to tell Apache where to find the web files.

8. Repeat steps 4–7 for any other virtual hosts you want to create. When you have finished, click the lock icon in the bottom-left corner of the NetInfo Manager, and close it.

9. Open BBEdit or TextWrangler, and select File ➤ Open Hidden. In the Open dialog box, select All Files from the Enable drop-down menu, and open Macintosh HD:etc:httpd:httpd.conf.

10. Scroll almost to the bottom of httpd.conf, and locate the following section:

```
1073  #
1074  # Use name-based virtual hosting.
1075  #
1076  #NameVirtualHost *:80
1077
1078  #
1079  # VirtualHost example:
1080  # Almost any Apache directive may go into a VirtualHost container.
1081  # The first VirtualHost section is used for requests without a known
1082  # server name.
1083  #
1084  #<VirtualHost *:80>
1085  #     ServerAdmin webmaster@dummy-host.example.com
1086  #     DocumentRoot /www/docs/dummy-host.example.com
1087  #     ServerName dummy-host.example.com
1088  #     ErrorLog logs/dummy-host.example.com-error_log
1089  #     CustomLog logs/dummy-host.example.com-access_log common
1090  #</VirtualHost>
```

11. Click the pencil icon at the top left of the editor window, and confirm that you want to unlock the document, entering your administrator password when prompted. Uncomment the command shown on line 1076 in the screenshot by removing the hash sign (#). This enables virtual hosting but disables the main server root, so the first virtual host needs to reproduce the Mac's server root. The example (on lines 1084–90) is there to show you how to define a virtual host. The only required commands are DocumentRoot and ServerName. After uncommenting the NameVirtualHost command, your first definition should look like this:

NameVirtualHost *:80

```
<VirtualHost *:80>
  DocumentRoot /Library/WebServer/Documents
  ServerName localhost
</VirtualHost>
```

12. Add any further definitions for virtual hosts. To create one for this book, I used this:

```
<VirtualHost *:80>
  DocumentRoot /Users/davidpowers/vhosts/egdwcs3
  ServerName egdwcs3
</VirtualHost>
```

13. Save `httpd.conf`, and restart Apache. All sites in Macintosh `HD:Library:WebServer:Documents` can still be accessed using `http://localhost/` and those in your Sites folder using `http://localhost/~username/sitename/`, but named virtual hosts can be accessed directly, such as `http://egdwcs3/`. Of course, a site must exist in the location you defined before you can actually use a virtual host.

Registering virtual directories on IIS

The version of IIS that runs in Windows workstations (the vast majority of personal computers) does not support virtual hosts. Instead, it allows you to set up virtual directories. However, `localhost` always remains the basic address of the web server, so you cannot use root-relative links with virtual directories. The main advantage of using virtual directories is that they avoid the need to locate all web files in the default IIS server root at `C:\Inetput\wwwroot`. This means you can leave your sites wherever they are on your hard disk but still get IIS to parse your PHP scripts when viewed through a browser. A virtual directory can be anywhere, but don't use spaces or special characters in the virtual directory name. Also, putting virtual directories on your desktop is likely to lead to permission problems.

To set up a virtual directory in IIS, open the Internet Information Services **panel** (Start ➤ Control Panel ➤ Administrative Tools ➤ Internet Information Services), **highlight** Default Web Server, **right-click, and select** New ➤ Virtual Directory **(XP) or** Add Virtual Directory **(Vista). On XP, a wizard will appear and walk you through the process.** In Vista, type the name of the virtual directory in the Alias field, and click the button alongside the Physical path field to browse to the folder where the files are kept. If you create a virtual directory called egdwcs3, the URL becomes `http://localhost/egdwcs3/`.

Defining a PHP site in Dreamweaver

Site definition is fundamental to working successfully with Dreamweaver. It allows you to create an exact copy of your website on your development computer, update existing files and create new ones locally, test them, and then upload them to the remote server on the Internet. For the benefit of Dreamweaver newcomers, I will go through the whole process step by step. Old hands should take particular notice of the sections titled "Defining the testing server" and "Setting up for Spry."

By this stage, you should have decided where you are going to store your local files. The setup process is basically the same whether you test your PHP files locally or on your remote server.

Opening the Site Definition dialog box

There are several ways to open the Site Definition dialog box. If the Dreamweaver Welcome screen is open, you can choose Dreamweaver Site from the bottom of the Create New column. It's probably more convenient, though, to choose New Site from the Site menu, because the menu is always available, even if you have web pages open in the Document window. Another convenient way is to select Manage Sites from the bottom of the site list at the top left of the Files panel.

Dreamweaver has been designed with both beginners and more advanced users in mind, so you may see either the basic dialog box shown on the left of Figure 4-2 or the advanced one on the right.

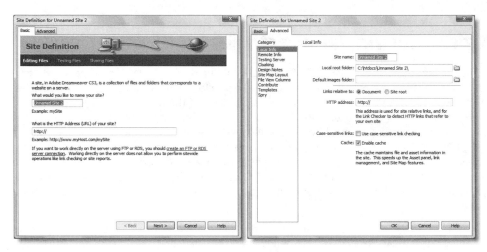

Figure 4-2. The Site Definition dialog box has two interfaces: Basic (left) and Advanced (right).

If you see the screen on the left of Figure 4-2, click the Advanced tab at the top left (it's in the center of the Mac version). Dreamweaver is good at remembering your previous choices, so, if you use the Site menu to open the Site Definition dialog box, it will automatically display the advanced version after the first time. Opening it from the Dreamweaver Welcome screen always displays the basic version.

If you select Site ➤ Manage Sites by mistake, you will be presented with the dialog box shown in Figure 4-3. This presents you with a list of sites that you have already defined in Dreamweaver. The buttons on the right let you perform a variety of management functions that are described in "Managing Dreamweaver sites" later in the chapter. To create a new site, click the New button at the top right, and select Site from the mini menu that appears.

Figure 4-3.
The Manage Sites dialog box lets you create a new site or edit an existing one.

Telling Dreamweaver where to find local files

The first stage of site definition involves defining the basic details of the site. Open the Site Definition dialog box, and make sure the Advanced tab is selected. If necessary, select Local Info from the Category column on the left. You should see the same screen as shown on the right of Figure 4-2.

Let's take a look at what each option means, with particular reference to defining a PHP site for use with this book. If you plan to use a virtual host in your local development environment, I assume that you have set up a virtual host called egdwcs3 in C:\vhosts\egdwcs3 on Windows or in a folder called vhosts inside your home folder on a Mac.

Site name This identifies the site within Dreamweaver. The name appears in the dropdown menu at the top of the Files panel (Figure 4-1) and in the Manage Sites dialog box (Figure 4-3), so it needs to be reasonably short. It's used only within Dreamweaver, so spaces are OK. I used Essential Guide.

Local root folder This is the top-level folder of the site. Everything should be stored in this folder in exactly the same hierarchy as you want to appear on the live website. When testing a PHP site locally, this folder should either be inside your server root, a virtual host, or a virtual directory (IIS only). Click the folder icon to the right of the Local root folder field and navigate to the appropriate location on your hard disk. If the folder doesn't exist, navigate to your server root or virtual host's top-level folder, and click Create New Folder in the Choose local root folder dialog box. Depending on your setup, your local root folder for this book should be one of the following:

- **Server root on Windows**: C:\htdocs\egdwcs3\
- **Virtual host on Windows**: C:\vhosts\egdwcs3\
- **Main server root on Mac OS X**: Macintosh HD:Library:WebServer:Documents:egdwcs3:
- **Server root inside your home folder on Mac OS X**: Macintosh HD:Users:*username*:Sites:egdwcs3:
- **Virtual host on Mac OS X**: Macintosh HD:Users:*username*:vhosts:egdwcs3:

If you plan to use a remote server or an IIS virtual directory to test your files, the local root folder can be anywhere on your local computer.

> With large sites, it's sometimes convenient to create a site definition in Dreamweaver for just part of the site. If the local root folder is already in another defined site, Dreamweaver warns you that some functions, such as site synchronization, won't work. However, it won't prevent you from creating the subsite.

Default images folder This field is optional but is very useful if you plan to use images that are on other parts of your file system or even in other Dreamweaver sites. Whenever you insert an image in a web page, Dreamweaver automatically copies it to this folder and creates the correct link in the <img> tag's src attribute. To set this option, click the folder icon to the right of the Default images folder field, navigate to the local root folder that you selected for the previous option, and select the images folder. If the folder doesn't exist, click the Create New Folder button to create it.

Links relative to This option lets you select the default style of links used in the site (see "Understanding document- and root-relative links" earlier in the chapter). Unless your testing server and remote server both run on Apache, I strongly advise you to accept the default Document. When you select root-relative links as the site default, Dreamweaver attempts to connect to your database using code that works only on Apache. Although you can amend the code manually, it's easier to use document-relative links throughout the site, and switch to root-relative ones only when necessary.

> *If in doubt, select* Document. *You can always change this option later or override the site default for individual links. If you change the site default later, it affects only links created afterward. Dreamweaver gives you the freedom to mix different types of links in the same site and will not override existing code. The implications of this choice with relation to PHP includes and connection to MySQL are discussed in Chapters 12 and 14, respectively.*

HTTP address This field should contain the URL of the final site on the Internet. If you are using the site only for local testing, you can leave this field empty. If you have selected root-relative links, Dreamweaver will display the following warning:

You can safely ignore this warning for local testing, and click OK. However, it is important to get the URL correct for remote testing or a site that you plan to deploy on the Internet.

Case-sensitive links I recommend that you select this option since the vast majority of PHP websites are hosted on Linux servers, which treat products.php and Products.php as completely different file names. Even if your remote server runs on Windows, selecting this option maintains internal integrity of your file structure.

Cache As the Site Definition dialog box explains, this speeds up various aspects of site management in Dreamweaver. Very large sites (with several hundred pages) tend to slow down dramatically if the site cache is enabled. However, with a PHP site, you should draw content from a database into a dynamically generated page, rather than create a new page every time. I suggest that you leave this option selected, and disable it only if you run into performance problems.

After you have completed the Local Info category, select Remote Info from the Category list on the left of the Site Definition dialog box.

Telling Dreamweaver how to access your remote server

When you first open the Remote Info category, you're presented with a single drop-down menu labeled Access. It has six options, as shown in the following screenshot (the final option—Microsoft Visual SourceSafe—is not available in the Mac version).

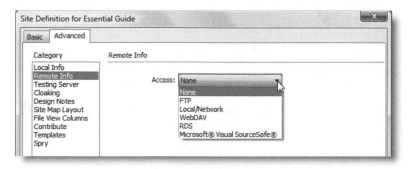

First, let's take a look at the Access options:

- **None:** Choose this if you don't plan to deploy the site on the Internet, or if you don't want to set up your remote server immediately. If you choose this option, you can skip ahead to the "Defining the testing server" section.

- **FTP:** This is the most common choice. It sets up Dreamweaver's built-in FTP (File Transfer Protocol) program to communicate with your remote server.

- **Local/Network:** This allows you to deploy your live website to another folder on your local computer or network. This is normally done only by organizations that run their own live web servers.

- **WebDAV:** This uses the WebDAV (Web-based Distributed Authoring and Versioning) protocol to communicate with the remote server. It requires a remote server that supports the WebDAV protocol.

- **RDS:** This uses Remote Development Services, which is supported only by ColdFusion servers. You cannot use it with a PHP site.

- **Microsoft Visual SourceSafe:** This requires access to a Microsoft Visual SourceSafe database and is not appropriate for the Dreamweaver PHP MySQL server model.

Since FTP is the most common method of connecting to a remote server, that's the only one I'll describe. Click the Help button at the bottom of the Remote Info category of the Site Definition dialog box for detailed descriptions of the options for the other methods.

When you select the FTP option from the Access drop-down menu, the Remote Info category of the Site Definition dialog box presents you with the options shown in Figure 4-4. Most of them are very straightforward, but I'll describe each one briefly.

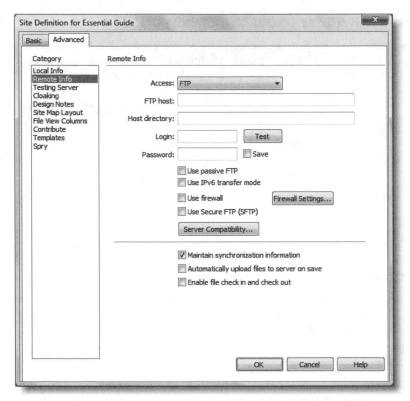

Figure 4-4. The FTP options for the Remote Info category of the Site Definition dialog box

FTP host Enter your remote server's FTP address in this field. You should normally get this from your hosting company. It usually takes either of the following forms: `ftp.example.com` or `www.example.com`.

Host directory This is the pathname of the top level of your website. The important thing to realize is that the directory (folder) that you enter in this field should contain only those files that will be accessible to the public through your site's URL. Often it will be named `htdocs`, `public_html`, or `www`. If in doubt, ask your hosting company or server administrator.

Login This is the username given to you by your hosting company or server administrator.

Password Enter your remote server password in this field. Dreamweaver displays your password as a series of dots. It also automatically saves your password, so deselect the Save checkbox if you want to be prompted for the password each time you connect to the remote server. Click the Test button to make sure that Dreamweaver can connect successfully.

If the test fails, make sure Caps Lock isn't turned on, as passwords are normally case sensitive. Other reasons for failure include being behind a firewall, so check the remaining options before trying again.

Use passive FTP Try this option if a software firewall prevents you from connecting to the remote server. For more details, see `www.adobe.com/go/15220`.

Use IPv6 transfer mode This option is designed to prepare Dreamweaver for the future. Select this option only if you have been told that your remote FTP server uses Internet Protocol version 6 (IPv6).

Use firewall Select this option if you are behind a firewall. Then click the Firewall Settings button to open the Site Preferences dialog box. Enter the firewall host and firewall port (if it's different from 21) in the appropriate fields, and click OK to return to the Site Definition dialog box.

Use Secure FTP (SFTP) Select this option if your remote server supports Secure FTP, which gives you a more secure connection but is not supported by all servers. Selecting this option automatically disables these other options: Use passive FTP, Use IPv6 transfer mode, Use firewall, Firewall Settings, and Server Compatibility.

Server Compatibility Click this button if you are still having problems connecting through FTP. The two options in the dialog box that opens are self-explanatory.

Maintain synchronization information This is selected by default and enables you to synchronize your remote and local files through the Files panel.

Automatically upload files to server on save This is self-explanatory. I don't recommend its use, because you should always test files locally before uploading them to your remote server. Otherwise, all your mistakes will go public. It overwrites your original files, so you can no longer use them as backup.

Enable file check in and check out Select this option only if you are working in a team and want to use Dreamweaver's Check In/Check Out system. For more information, launch Dreamweaver Help (F1) and select Check In/Check Out from the Index, or go to www.adobe.com/go/15447. *All* team members must have this option enabled for it to work. Failure to do so results in chaos.

After you have completed the Remote Info category, select Testing Server from the Category list on the left of the Site Definition dialog box.

Defining the testing server

This is probably the most important dialog box when building dynamic sites in Dreamweaver. It's quite easy to fill in, but if you get the details wrong, Dreamweaver cannot communicate with any of your databases. When you first open the Testing Server category, it looks similar to the Remote Info category in its initial state, but with two drop-down menus instead of one, as shown in the following screenshot.

Activate the Server model drop-down menu, and select PHP MySQL. What you choose for Access depends on whether you want to test your PHP pages locally or by using your remote server. The options are different, so I'll cover them separately—first, local testing.

Selecting options for local testing

The Access drop-down menu determines how you communicate with the testing server. If you have a local test environment on your computer or another computer on a LAN, choose Local/Network. This reveals two options that Dreamweaver attempts to fill in automatically. Figure 4-5 shows what happened when I had defined the local root folder in the Local Info category as a virtual host on Windows.

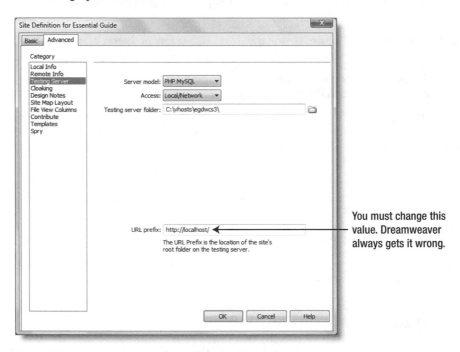

Figure 4-5. Dreamweaver attempts to fill in the Testing Server details automatically.

Dreamweaver usually gets the value for Testing server folder correct but invariably gets URL prefix wrong. Getting both right is crucial, so let's take a look at what they represent.

Testing server folder This should normally be the same folder that you selected as the Local root folder in the Local Info category. The only exception is if you want to use a testing server elsewhere on your local network. In this case, click the folder icon to the right of the field to browse to the correct location.

URL prefix This needs to reflect the structure that you have chosen for your testing environment. If your testing server folder is in the server root or a virtual directory, it will be http://localhost/*sitename*/. If you are using a virtual host, it will simply be http://*sitename*/. If the testing server is on another computer on a local network, substitute localhost with the correct IP address.

It's critical that URL prefix is set correctly, as it controls all dynamic aspects of Dreamweaver. Because so many people seem to get this wrong, here are the values for Testing server folder and URL prefix for the various scenarios described earlier:

- If the site is in a subfolder of the server root of the same machine on Windows:
  - **Testing server folder**: C:\htdocs\egdwcs3\
  - **URL prefix**: http://localhost/egdwcs3/
- If the site is in a virtual host called egdwcs3 on Windows:
  - **Testing server folder**: C:\vhosts\egdwcs3\
  - **URL prefix**: http://egdwcs3/
- If the site is in a subfolder of the main server root of the same machine on a Mac:
  - **Testing server folder**: Macintosh HD:Library:WebServer:Documents:egdwcs3:
  - **URL prefix**: http://localhost/egdwcs3/
- If the site is in a subfolder of your Sites folder of the same machine on a Mac:
  - **Testing server folder**: Macintosh HD:Users:*username*:Sites:egdwcs3:
  - **URL prefix**: http://localhost/~*username*/egdwcs3/
- If the site is in a virtual host called egdwcs3 on a Mac:
  - **Testing server folder**: Macintosh HD:Users:*username*:vhosts:egdwcs3:
  - **URL prefix**: http://egdwcs3/
- If the site is in an IIS virtual directory:
  - **Testing server folder**: Can be anywhere
  - **URL prefix**: http://localhost/egdwcs3/

In simple terms, Testing server folder and URL prefix must both point to the site's root folder. Testing server folder is the physical address, while URL prefix is the address you enter in a browser.

Selecting options for remote testing

The Access drop-down menu in the Testing Server category offers fewer options than the Remote Info category, because RDS and Microsoft SourceSafe are not appropriate for working with the Dreamweaver PHP MySQL server model. If you decide you want to use a remote server to test your files, the most common choice is FTP. Dreamweaver is intelligent enough to copy across the main details from the Remote Info category and presents you with the dialog box shown in Figure 4-6. Although most details should be correct, the URL prefix is almost certain to need editing.

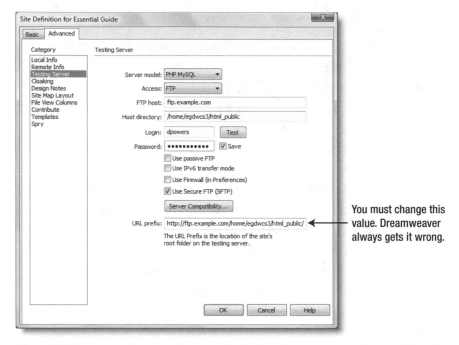

Figure 4-6. When you select a remote server for testing, Dreamweaver copies details from the Remote Info category, but you normally need to change at least the URL prefix.

As you can see from Figure 4-6, Dreamweaver combines the values in the FTP host and Home directory fields. This produces the following value for URL prefix:

        http://ftp.example.com/home/egdwcs3/html_public/

It's vital that the URL prefix and Host directory fields point to the same place. However, this does *not* mean that the values should be the same. The distinction is explained in the following sections.

Host directory This is the pathname that the FTP program uses for the top level of your site.

URL prefix This is the address that anyone surfing the Internet uses to reach the top level of your site. In other words, it's normally http:// followed by the domain name and a trailing slash.

So, if /home/egdwcs3/html_public/index.php is your home page, and users access it by typing http://www.example.com/index.php in their browser address bar, the correct value for URL prefix should look like this:

        http://www.example.com/

One thing to note about Figure 4-6 is that, even though the Use Secure FTP (SFTP) checkbox is selected, the three checkboxes above and the Server Compatibility button are not grayed out as in the Remote Info category. This is a known bug in Dreamweaver CS3. Make sure you don't accidentally select them if you're using SFTP. The settings should be the same as in the Remote Info category.

Points to watch when using a remote server for testing Dreamweaver tries to make everything seamless, regardless of whether you use a local or a remote web server for testing. However, there are several important differences that you should be aware of with a remote testing server.

- Some software firewalls prevent FTP access when running Dreamweaver as a standard user on Windows Vista. You may need to log in as administrator or turn off UAC to use your remote server for testing.

- You miss the main benefit of Live Data view, which allows you to view dynamic output inside the Dreamweaver Document window without the need to load your page into a browser. This is because Dreamweaver still needs to transfer the script across the Internet to your remote server, rather than just handle it locally.

- Live Data view uses temporary files that are removed automatically when you switch to another site in Dreamweaver or close the program. If you test a file that's in a new folder, Dreamweaver creates a folder with the same name on the remote server but not the file itself.

- When you preview a page in a browser, it may not display correctly if the browser can't find dependent files, such as images and style sheets (see "Setting options for Preview in Browser" later in this chapter).

- If you're on dial-up and have chosen to use your remote server for testing, be aware that Dreamweaver automatically connects to the Internet every time you use Live Data view, and it doesn't automatically disconnect when you toggle Live Data view off. Unless you are careful, you could end up with very large communications charges.

Setting up other site options

There are seven more categories in the Site Definition dialog box. Most of the time, you should leave them at their default values. To find out what each one is for, select it in the Category list on the left, and click the Help button at the bottom of the dialog box to launch context-sensitive help. Perhaps the most useful category is Cloaking, which lets you specify folders of file types that you don't want to be uploaded to your remote server. Since a large part of this book deals with Spry, which is new to Dreamweaver CS3, the Spry category needs a brief description.

Setting up for Spry

Adobe's Ajax framework, Spry, relies on code libraries that need to be uploaded to your remote server. By default, Dreamweaver inserts these files in a folder called SpryAssets at the top level of your site root. For most people, this is ideal. However, if you want to locate the code libraries elsewhere, you need to specify the folder name in the Spry category of the Site Definition dialog box. This is so that Dreamweaver can update or remove the files when you make changes to elements that use Spry.

As you can see from Figure 4-7, there's just one field in the Spry category. If you want to use a different folder, click the folder icon to the right of the field labeled Spry assets folder, and navigate to the new location or create a new folder within your site root.

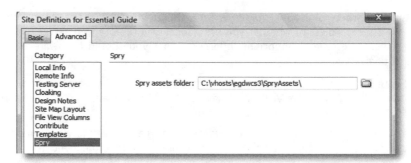

Figure 4-7. Change the setting for the Spry assets folder if you don't want to use the default location.

Saving the site definition

After entering all the necessary details, click OK at the foot of the Site Definition dialog box. This returns you to the Manage Sites dialog box (see Figure 4-3). Click Done at the bottom left (it's on the right in the Mac version, as shown in Figure 4-10). Dreamweaver creates the site cache (unless you deselected that option in Local Info) and opens the site in the Files panel ready for you to start work. If there were any files in the root folder, they will be listed as a tree menu in the Files panel.

> *If you didn't enter a value for* HTTP address *in the* Local Info *category, you might see a warning that the URL prefix for the testing server doesn't match the URL prefix for the site's HTTP address. You can safely ignore this by clicking* OK.

You can change your site definition at any time by reopening the Manage Sites dialog box (see "Managing Dreamweaver sites" later in this chapter).

Testing your PHP site

If you have followed the instructions carefully, you should now have a PHP site within Dreamweaver that will give you access to all the PHP server behaviors and other PHP features. Before moving on, it's wise to do a quick test to make sure everything's working as expected.

There are two ways of testing dynamic code: using Live Data view, which displays the dynamic output inside the Dreamweaver Document window, and by previewing the page in a browser. These instructions cover both methods.

1. In Dreamweaver, select File ➤ New, and in the New Document dialog box (see Figure 1-2 in Chapter 1), select Blank Page from the options on the left side. In the Page Type column, choose PHP (it's the final item). For Layout, choose <none> (at the top of the column), and then click Create.

2. Save the page as datetest.php in the Essential Guide site you have just created.

3. Open Split view, and type the following code between the <body> tags:

```
<?php
echo date('l, F jS, Y');
?>
```

Sure, it looks pretty cryptic, but I have never understood why so many books and tutorials feel obliged to start by showing you how to display "Hello, world" or "Hi, Mom!" onscreen. I want to show you the real power of PHP by demonstrating something really useful. Make sure you copy the code exactly (the first character after the opening quote is a lowercase "L"), or use datetest.php in examples/ch04.

The first thing you should notice is that Dreamweaver displays the opening and closing PHP tags in a bold red font, while echo and date are pale blue. This is Dreamweaver Syntax Coloring at work. If this doesn't happen, check that your file name ends with .php. Also select View ➤ Code View Options, and make sure that there's a check mark next to Syntax Coloring. If there isn't, click Syntax Coloring to toggle the setting on.

4. Click inside Design view, and a gold shield labeled PHP should appear, as shown in the next screenshot. This marks the location of your PHP script.

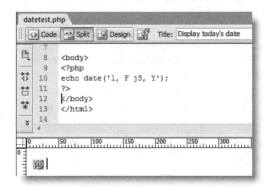

5. Click the Live Data button, as shown in Figure 4-8 (if you're a keyboard shortcut fetishist, press Ctrl+Shift+R/Shift+Cmd+R). As long as your web server is running, you should see today's date displayed in Design view. It will be highlighted in a different color (the default is pale yellow) to indicate that it's dynamically generated output. You'll learn about the first part of the script—echo—in Chapter 10; it's one of the most basic commands that displays PHP output onscreen. The rather cryptic aspects of the rest of the script will be covered in Chapter 17 when we delve into the mysteries of working with dates in PHP.

As soon as you click the Live Data button again (or use the keyboard shortcut), the date will disappear and be replaced by the PHP gold shield.

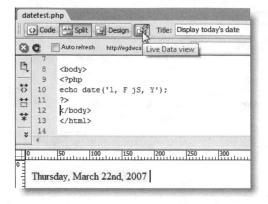

Figure 4-8.
If Live Data view displays the current date, you're ready to start working with PHP in Dreamweaver.

6. Now press F12 (Opt+F12 on a Mac). Depending on your settings in Preferences, you may see the following alert (see "Setting options for Preview in Browser" below).

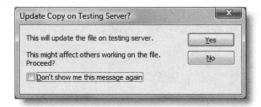

This warns you that Dreamweaver is about to overwrite the file on your testing server. Since it's only a test file, click Yes. You will then probably see this dialog box:

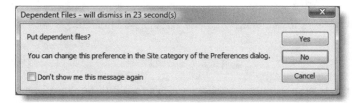

Click No. The significance of these two alerts is explained in "Setting options for Preview in Browser" shortly.

Your default browser should launch and display datetest.php. The result will be similar to that shown in Figure 4-8, except that the output won't be highlighted in a different color. More importantly, if you view the page's source code in the browser, you'll see only XHTML. PHP is a server-side language: *only the output of the PHP code is sent to the browser; the code itself remains on the server.*

Troubleshooting

This is the part of the chapter that I hope nobody ever needs to read. As I said earlier, PHP site definition in Dreamweaver is not difficult, but a lot of people do seem to get it wrong. Troubleshooting is basically a process of elimination: find out what is working, and it frequently helps identify where the problem lies. If you're banging your head on the keyboard at this point, try the following suggestions:

- The first thing to check is whether your web server is running. Try an ordinary .html page first. If it doesn't display, Apache or IIS needs to be restarted.

- Then check that PHP is properly configured. Use test.php as described in the previous chapter. If the page of PHP configuration information doesn't display, go back to Chapter 3, and fix your PHP setup.

- If the web server and PHP are OK, do you get any error messages? If you got a blank screen, check your PHP configuration as described in the previous chapter, and make sure that display_errors is turned on.

- If an error message says something like Parse error or Fatal error, the mistake is in the PHP code. Use the version of datetest.php from the download files instead.

- If you get an error message about the URL prefix not mapping correctly, the problem lies in the details you entered in the Testing Server category of the site definition.

- If the web server and PHP are OK, but you see nothing in Live Data view, check that a software firewall, such as Norton Internet Security or ZoneAlarm, isn't blocking communication between Dreamweaver and the web server.

Setting options for Preview in Browser

Pressing F12/Opt+F12 or using the menu option File ➤ Preview in Browser automatically launches your default browser and displays the page currently open in the Document window. Dreamweaver normally detects your default browser the first time that you use this option, but you can also designate other browsers by opening Preferences from the Edit menu (Dreamweaver menu in a Mac) and selecting the Preview in Browser category (see Figure 4-9). If Dreamweaver has detected other browsers on your system, they are listed in the Browsers field. You can designate one of them as your secondary browser, which can be launched using Ctrl+F12/Cmd+F12 as a shortcut.

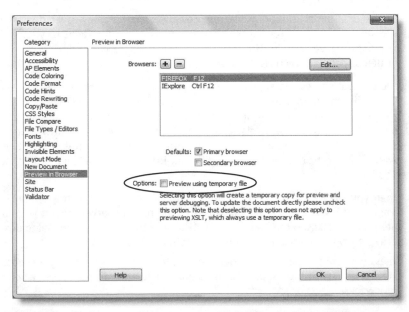

Figure 4-9. When previewing pages, Dreamweaver gives you the option to use a temporary file.

Add other browsers by clicking the plus (+) button. Type the browser's name in the Name field, click the Browse button to locate its executable file, and then click OK to register it. The Edit button lets you change the details of the selected browser. Click the minus (–) button to remove the selected browser from the list. Although default keyboard shortcuts exist for only two browsers, you can launch the current page in one of the other browsers by using File ➤ Preview in Browser or clicking the Preview/Debug in browser icon on the Document toolbar, as shown in the following screenshot.

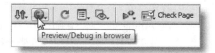

The most important setting is the checkbox highlighted in Figure 4-9. It determines whether Dreamweaver creates a temporary file for the preview. This often causes confusion among PHP beginners, because if they make a mistake in their code, they might see an error message like this:

The file TMP2erxjfculq.php isn't some mysterious, hidden aspect of the PHP engine, but a random file name created by Dreamweaver for previewing the page. It's automatically deleted as soon as you preview another file or close Dreamweaver.

The advantage of using a temporary file for preview is that Dreamweaver doesn't overwrite the existing file on your testing server. You can also see the effects of your changes without needing to save the file. However, you cannot test server behaviors that insert, update, or delete database records this way.

If you leave this option deselected, you must always save your file before using Preview in Browser. You will also see the alerts shown in step 6 of "Testing your PHP site." If you have set up a local testing environment and use your local root folder as the testing server folder, you can safely ignore these alerts and check the option not to show them again. Your local files and testing ones are actually the same files, so you're not overwriting anything. However, if your testing server is in a different location, such as on a remote server, you need to be aware of the following consequences:

- When you preview a file in a browser, if you haven't selected the option to use temporary files, Dreamweaver uploads it to the remote server even if you haven't entered any details in the Remote Info category of the Site Definition dialog box. This permanently overwrites the existing file on the remote server.

- Unless you use temporary files, dependent files, such as images, style sheets, and external JavaScript files, must also be uploaded to the remote server when using Preview in Browser.

Managing Dreamweaver sites

To change any settings in your site definition, select Manage Sites from the Site menu to open the Manage Sites dialog box (Figures 4-3 and 4-10 show the Windows and Mac versions, respectively). Select the name of the site that you want to change, and click Edit. This reopens the Site Definition dialog box ready for you to update the settings. If you're feeling really impatient, though, the quickest way of opening the Site Definition dialog box is to double-click the site's name in the drop-down menu at the top left of the Files panel.

Figure 4-10.
The position of the Help and Done buttons is reversed in the Mac version.

The other buttons on the right side of the Manage Sites dialog box are fairly self-explanatory. However, the following is a quick guide to each one:

- New: This offers two options: Site and FTP & RDS Server. The first opens the Site Definition dialog box. The second option is rarely used, but lets you create a direct FTP connection to a remote site (RDS is for ColdFusion only). You might want to use this to upload a single file without defining a local site in Dreamweaver.

- Duplicate: This creates an exact copy of the site definition for whichever site is highlighted in the left panel. You might find this useful if a new site shares common settings with an existing one. It's important to understand that creating a new site definition doesn't make a mirror version of the common files and folders. Editing or deleting a shared file in one site affects both sites, as there is only one set of files.

- Remove: This removes only the site definition from Dreamweaver. The actual files and folders remain untouched.

- Export: This exports your site definition as an XML file (Dreamweaver gives it an .ste file name extension). You can export multiple site definitions by using Shift-click or Ctrl/Cmd-click to select several sites in the left panel.

Dw
Changed

If any of the site definitions contain login details for a remote server, Dreamweaver presents you with the following dialog box:

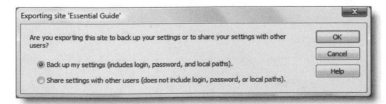

This dialog box is shown only for the first site that contains login details, and the export option you choose applies to all sites being exported at the same time. Dreamweaver then asks you where to save the file. Just browse to the folder where you want to store the .ste files and accept the default value for File name. Definitions for all selected sites are exported in a single operation.

- Import: This imports site definitions from .ste files. If the .ste files are in the same folder, you can import multiple sites simultaneously. If a site of the same name already exists, Dreamweaver creates a duplicate site definition with a number after the name, rather than overwriting the existing definition.

It's a good idea to back up your site definitions from time to time, just like any other valuable data. The vastly improved Export and Import options in this version of Dreamweaver make it a lot easier.

Now let's get on with it . . .

The last two chapters have been full of some pretty heavy but essential stuff. Getting your work environment set up doesn't offer the same excitement as developing websites, but if you have ever repainted your house, you'll know the value of preparation. Skimp on the preparation, and the paint starts peeling off in next to no time. If everything is set up properly now, you're less likely to find yourself coming suddenly unstuck later in this book.

Keeping in mind the importance of laying a solid foundation, I don't plan to start working with PHP until Chapter 9. Dynamic websites that use Ajax and server-side languages like PHP demand a much more disciplined approach to web standards than static websites built solely with HTML. So the next two chapters provide your essential guide to creating standards-compliant websites using cascading style sheets (CSS).

5 ADDING A TOUCH OF STYLE

Judging by the runaway success of books such as *CSS Mastery* by Andy Budd with Simon Collison, and Cameron Moll (friends of ED, ISBN-13: 978-1-59059-614-2), web designers have finally got the message that Cascading Style Sheets (CSS) are *the* way to design a website. Getting the message is the easy part, but many designers rapidly find their initial enthusiasm takes a severe dent when they run into the reality of creating a CSS-driven site. Creating a style rule is simple enough, and most CSS properties have intuitive names. The difficulty lies in the infinite number of ways in which style rules can be combined. And *that's* what makes it so powerful and worthwhile. You need only visit the CSS Zen Garden at www.csszengarden.com to see why—the underlying XHTML of every page is identical; what makes each one so different is the CSS.

Whether you're capable of designing a masterpiece worthy of the CSS Zen Garden or just a beginner, the improved handling of CSS in Dreamweaver CS3 should make your life easier by showing you the impact of your style rules without needing to load the page in a browser every few minutes. Another welcome new feature is the addition of 32 ready-made CSS layouts that you can use as the basis for designing your own pages. In the next chapter, I'll take one of these basic layouts and show you how to transform it into a good-looking, standards-compliant page, but before you can do that, you need to understand the nuts and bolts of how Dreamweaver handles CSS. So that's what this chapter is all about. In particular, it examines the CSS Styles panel—an extremely powerful tool that takes a little getting used to, but once you know how it works, it speeds up the design process immensely.

What this chapter covers

- Understanding the limitations of styles created by the Property inspector
- Creating basic style rules for a page
- Using the CSS Styles panel in All mode
- Exporting style rules from the <head> of a document
- Using drag and drop to move style rules
- Setting Dreamweaver preferences for CSS

To start off, though, I want to show you how *not* to use Dreamweaver to create style rules.

Avoiding bad habits

A well established program like Dreamweaver needs to add new features but risks the wrath of existing users if old features are taken away or the program is changed radically. In the bad old days, when everybody used <font> tags and other presentational markup, the Property inspector was where all the action was. It remains one of the most important tools in Dreamweaver, but its handling of text is a compromise between the old and the new—a brave compromise but one that doesn't really work.

For the past couple of versions of Dreamweaver, the Property inspector has generated CSS instead of <font> tags. But don't be fooled into using it to build your style rules. Instead of littering your pages with <font> tags, it litters them with meaningless classes that make sites a nightmare to maintain.

Stay away from the Property inspector for fonts

Let's say that you have an <h1> heading that you want displayed in 24-pixel Verdana. Select the text of the heading in Design view or the <h1> tag in the Tag selector, set Font in the Property inspector to Verdana, Arial, Helvetica, sans-serif, and choose

24 pixels as Size. As the screenshot alongside shows, Dreamweaver automatically generates a style name and displays it in the Style field.

The style is applied to the heading as a class like this:

```
<h1 class="style1">How not to use CSS</h1>
```

The following class definition is placed in a <style> block and embedded in the <head> of the document:

```
.style1 {
  font-family: Verdana, Arial, Helvetica, sans-serif;
  font-size: 24px;
}
```

As far as it goes, it's not bad. The class definition is perfectly valid, and you can easily move it to an external style sheet later. The problem is that you don't need a class to style <h1> tags. It's much more efficient to create an h1 selector in your style sheet and apply the style automatically to all <h1> tags. Moreover, when using the Property inspector to format text, you need to select the entire text before you can apply the style. If you accidentally miss part of the heading, Dreamweaver takes your instructions literally and applies the style as a <span> only to the selected characters like this:

How not to use CSS

Figure 5-1 shows a simple page styled using the Property inspector (badCSS.html in examples/ch05). The design isn't particularly inspiring, not because I deliberately wanted to show an example of poor design, but because I didn't want to waste a lot of effort. If you examine the page in Code view, you'll see classes everywhere and four style rules in the <head>.

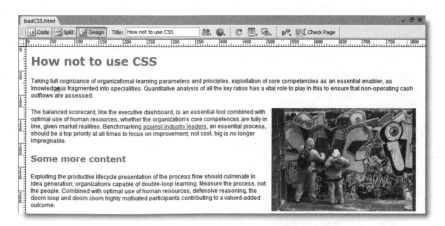

Figure 5-1. The design is basic, but using the Property inspector involved a lot of effort and created bad CSS.

Classes are the first thing most beginners learn about CSS. They draw beginners unwittingly into a love affair—just like George Segal and Glenda Jackson in the movie *A Touch of Class*. In the end, it all becomes too much and ends in failure but is nowhere near as funny as the movie. Classes play only a minor role in well-designed CSS, but Dreamweaver's automatically generated CSS relies on them exclusively. Because it has no way of knowing the purpose of the styles it's creating, it gives them only generic names: style1, style2, etc. With just three or four, you might be able to remember what each one is for, but how on earth are you going to remember what style32 is for?

The Property inspector is great for a lot of things. It's the quickest way to apply XHTML format tags, such as <h1>, <h2>, <p>, <strong>, <em>, and <blockquote>. And as you'll see in the rest of the book, it's where you set the values of many XHTML attributes. But the Property inspector falls down when it comes to styles. The CSS it creates is both crude and inefficient. *Don't use it.*

Creating simple CSS for beginners

If you're new to CSS, Dreamweaver offers a simple dialog-based interface to create basic styles that are automatically applied to the entire page without the need for meaningless classes. It's not capable of anything sophisticated, but provides a gentle starting point. If you're already up to speed with CSS, I suggest that you skip forward to the next section, "Introducing the CSS Styles panel."

> *Although this section shows you how to get started on the right footing with CSS in Dreamweaver, it's not intended to teach you CSS. For that, you need a book like* Beginning CSS Web Development: From Novice to Professional *by Simon Collison (Apress, ISBN-13: 978-1-59059-689-0). Also, any book by Eric Meyer will give you a solid grounding in CSS.*

Using Page Properties to create basic style rules

This exercise shows you how to create a basic set of style rules for a page. I've removed all style markup from badCSS.html (see Figure 5-1) and saved it as betterCSS_start.html. Copy the file from examples/ch05 to workfiles/ch05, and save it as betterCSS.html.

1. Open betterCSS.html in the Document window, and click the Page Properties button in the Property inspector as shown in the following screenshot. If you can't see the button, click the expander triangle at the bottom right of the Property inspector.

If the Property inspector is closed, use Window ➤ Properties or Ctrl+F3/Cmd+F3 to open it. Alternatively, select Modify ➤ Page Properties (Ctrl+J/Cmd+J).

2. This opens the Appearance category of the Page Properties dialog box, as shown in Figure 5-2. This is a multiple category dialog box that sets a wide range of options.

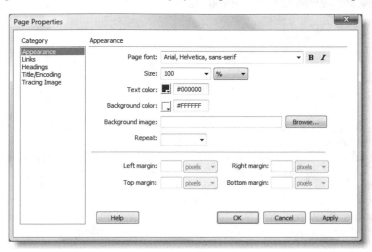

Figure 5-2. The Page Properties dialog box offers a simple way of setting basic style rules for a page.

It's a good idea to set a default font for the page, which you can override in special cases, such as headings or pull quotes. Setting the font size to 100 percent uses the browser's default for all text elements, which you can again override later. You should also always set default colors for the text and page background. Use the settings shown in Figure 5-2, and then select the Links category from the column on the left.

3. The Links category lets you set the font and colors for hyperlinks. The color options are the equivalent of the following CSS pseudo-classes:

- Link color: a:link
- Visited links: a:visited
- Rollover links: a:hover
- Active links: a:active

The Underline style option lets you choose whether your links are always underlined, never underlined, show an underline on hover, or hide the underline on hover. If you decide not to underline links, it's a good idea to choose a distinctive color and select the Bold icon alongside Link font. Use the settings shown in the following screenshot, and select the Headings category from the column on the left:

4. The Headings category lets you choose a different font for headings (the same choice applies to all six levels). You can also set the size and color separately for each level. Using percentage sizes gives visitors more freedom to adjust your page to their visual needs and preferences, so is better from the accessibility point of view, but you can use pixels if you prefer. I used the following settings:

5. When you have finished, click OK to close the Page Properties dialog box. Your styles are immediately applied to the page in Design view. What's more, they're automatic. Position your cursor anywhere inside the first paragraph, and select Heading 2 from the Format menu in the Property inspector; the paragraph is transformed into a large, brown Verdana. Select Paragraph again from the Format menu, and it switches back to normal black Arial. This is because the Format menu changes the surrounding tags from <p> to <h2> and back again. Everything is controlled by CSS type selectors that Dreamweaver has embedded into the <head> of the page (type selectors change the default style of HTML tags).

6. Select some text in one of the paragraphs, and type # in the Link field of the Property inspector to create a dummy link. The text is automatically styled as a link. If you have been used to the old-school way of selecting everything and applying colors and fonts, this should be an exciting revelation that convinces you of the power of CSS.

7. Save betterCSS.html. You'll improve it later in the chapter.

Unfortunately, the Page Properties dialog box creates only the most basic rules. To change the size of the paragraph font and wrap the text around the image, you need to create a couple of style rules yourself. For that, you need the CSS Styles panel.

Introducing the CSS Styles panel

To get the most out of the CSS Styles panel, you need a solid understanding of CSS. Although that statement is likely to provoke sighs of despair—or even anger—from readers expecting Dreamweaver to do everything for them, it's true of any tool or piece of software. The greater your understanding of the tools you're working with, the easier the job becomes. Also, with a little persistence, using the CSS Styles panel should help beginners improve their skills, because it shows you exactly which rules affect a particular part of the page. And even if the theory behind CSS taxes your brain, the almost perfect rendition in Design view shows you how your page will look 99 percent of the time.

Opening the CSS Styles panel

To open the CSS Styles panel, click the title bar of the CSS panel group (in the default workspace layout, it's at the top right of the screen), and select the CSS Styles tab. Alternatively, select Window ➤ CSS Styles. On Windows, there's also the keyboard shortcut Shift+F11. Mac keyboard shortcut enthusiasts are out of luck, because the same combination runs Exposé in slow motion on OS X.

The CSS Styles panel is so useful you can also open it by clicking the CSS button in the center of the Property inspector whenever your cursor is in a position to enter text. If you have a <div> selected, the button is labeled Edit CSS.

Viewing All and Current modes

The CSS Styles panel has two modes, All and Current, which are toggled by clicking the button at the top of the panel. Figure 5-3 shows both modes with an explanation of the icons at the bottom of the panel and in the middle pane of Current mode. Current mode (on the right of Figure 5-3) is more powerful, but it's also more complex, so beginners should try to get used to working in All mode first.

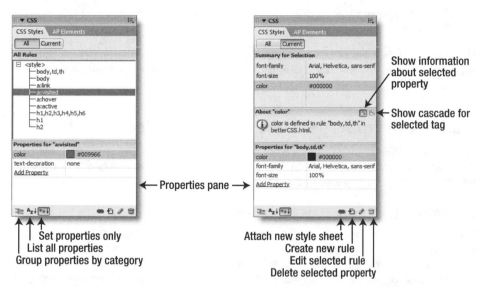

Figure 5-3. The CSS Styles panel crams a lot of tools and information into a small space.

A good way of regarding All mode is as a window into all CSS rules available to the page, regardless of whether they are embedded in the <head> of the document or in multiple external style sheets. The top pane (labeled All Rules) displays the hierarchy of style rules as a tree menu. If the rules are embedded in the <head> of the document, the root of the tree (at the top) is displayed as a <style> tag, as in Figure 5-3. If they're in an external style sheet, the file name appears at the root. The tree menus are collapsible to make it easier to work when multiple style sheets are attached to the page. The only style rules that you cannot inspect or edit in All mode are inline styles, although you can see them in Current mode.

The Properties pane at the bottom of the CSS Styles panel is common to both modes. It displays details of the currently selected style rule and lets you edit or delete properties and add new ones.

> *Don't confuse the* Properties *pane of the* CSS Styles *panel with the Property inspector, which is normally docked at the bottom of the Document window. If you're not familiar with Dreamweaver, the names are easy to mix up, because the title bar of the Property inspector says "Properties." When working with CSS, any reference to the* Properties *pane means the pane at the bottom of the* CSS Styles *panel as shown in Figure 5-3.*

Use All mode when you need to do any of the following:

- View the overall structure of the styles attached to a page
- Change the order of rules
- Inspect or edit the contents of a style rule identified by its selector
- Add a new style rule (you can do this in both modes)
- Attach a style sheet to the current page (this is one of several places you can do this)

I'll describe the features of Current mode in the next chapter. For the moment, let's take a look at the seven icons at the bottom of the CSS Styles panel, as they apply to both modes.

Exploring the Properties pane of the CSS Styles panel

The default setting of the Properties pane is to display only those CSS properties that have been set in a particular style rule, as shown in Figure 5-3. However, the two leftmost icons let you display properties grouped by category or alphabetically.

Displaying CSS properties by category

If you select the leftmost icon (see alongside) at the bottom of the CSS Styles panel, the Properties pane lists all available CSS properties grouped together in easily identifiable categories, as shown in Figure 5-4. Click the plus (+) and minus (–) symbols (triangles in the Mac version) to expand or close each category, and click in the right column alongside the property name to edit it. If a fixed range of options is available, a drop-down menu appears. Similarly, a folder icon or color picker appears if the property requires a pathname or color. To remove a property, highlight it and click the trash can icon at the far right. Unlike the default display, the property remains listed, but the value is deleted. If you're new to CSS and find it difficult to remember the names of the various properties, I recommend that you use this display until you gain sufficient confidence to use the less cluttered default view.

Figure 5-4.
Displaying all available CSS properties organized
by category makes life easier for beginners.

Displaying CSS properties alphabetically

 Clicking the middle icon (shown alongside) at the bottom left of the CSS Styles panel lists virtually all available CSS properties in alphabetical order, as shown in Figure 5-5. Properties that have already been set move to the top of the list, but to set a new one, you need to scroll down to find it, making this view the least user-friendly.

This alphabetical list omits a small number of poorly supported CSS properties, such as counter-increment and counter-reset, but as you can see from Figure 5-5, nonstandard properties beginning with -moz are also listed. These are supported mainly by Firefox and Mozilla, but are expected to become part of CSS 3. Dreamweaver also lists some Microsoft-only properties, such as layout-grid, and properties that were dropped from the CSS 2.1 specification, such as font-stretch. This wide choice is useful if you are a CSS expert, but could lead you astray if you're a novice. Use the alphabetical display with care.

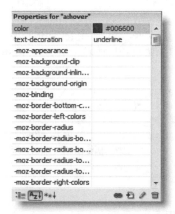

Figure 5-5.
You can also display all available CSS
properties in alphabetical order.

Displaying only CSS properties that have been set

 To restore the Properties pane to its default display of only those properties that have been set (see Figure 5-3), click the third icon from the left at the bottom of the CSS Styles panel (shown alongside).

143

Attaching a new style sheet

The chain icon at the bottom right of the CSS Styles panel opens the Attach External Style Sheet dialog box (see Figure 5-6). This lets you attach the file using either <link> or @import and set the media type.

The File/URL field lists recently used style sheets as a drop-down menu. Click the Browse button to navigate to a new style sheet. Select a media type from the drop-down menu in the Media field or enter a comma-separated list of valid types (all, aural, braille, hand-held, print, projection, screen, tty, tv). Choose screen for visual browsers, or all to apply your styles to all types of media. If you leave the Media field empty, browsers apply your styles to all media.

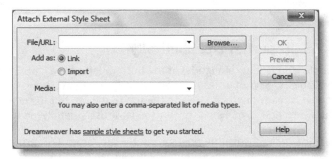

Figure 5-6. You can attach an external style sheet using <link> or @import.

If you choose a media type other than screen or all, use the Style Rendering toolbar, which was described in "Checking what your page will look like on other media" in Chapter 1, to see the effect of your styles in Design view.

If you type the file name of a nonexistent style sheet in the File/URL field, Dreamweaver displays a warning, and asks if you want to create the link/import statement anyway. If you click Yes, you can create the necessary style sheet afterward, and it becomes immediately available inside your page.

> There are several other ways of attaching external style sheets. As you'll see in the next chapter, you can attach style sheets in the New Document dialog box when first creating a page. There is also an option to attach a new style sheet at the bottom of the Style drop-down menu in the main Property inspector and in the New CSS Style dialog box (see Figure 5-7).

Adding, editing, and deleting style rules

The final three icons at the bottom right of the CSS Styles panel let you add new rules, edit existing rules, and delete existing rules and properties. Most editing and deletion is done directly in the CSS Styles panel, and I'll show you how to do that in the next chapter, but the creation of new rules involves the use of two dialog boxes. Let's take a look at how you define a new style rule.

Creating new style rules

Creating a style rule involves two steps: first define the selector, and then add property/value pairs to the style block. The selector determines which parts of the page the rule applies to.

The main types of CSS selectors are as follows:

- **Type**: A type selector uses the name of the HTML tag that you want to style. For instance, using h1 as the selector for a style rule applies the rule to all <h1> tags. Dreamweaver calls this a **Tag selector**.

- **Class**: A class can be applied to many different elements in a page. The selector name always begins with a period, for example, .warning.

- **ID**: An ID selector applies the rule to an element identified by its id attribute. If the element, such as a list, has child elements, the rule also applies to the children. The name of an ID selector always begins with the hash or pound sign, for example, #mainContent.

- **Pseudo-classes and pseudo-elements**: These selectors style elements according to their positions or roles in a document, such as a link when the mouse passes over it or the first line of a paragraph. They consist of a type selector followed by a colon and the name of the pseudo-class or pseudo-element, for example, a:hover or p:first-line.

- **Descendant**: A descendant selector combines two or more of the previous types to target elements more precisely. For instance, you may want to apply a different style to links inside a <div> with the id attribute footer. Descendant selectors are separated by a space between the individual parts of the selector, like this: #footer a.

- **Group**: When you want to apply the same set of rules to several selectors, you can group them together as a comma-separated list, for example, h1,h2,h3,h4,h5,h6.

Dreamweaver refers to anything that isn't a Class or Tag (Type) selector as an **Advanced selector**.

Defining a selector

 To create a new style rule, click the New CSS Rule icon (shown alongside) or right-click inside the CSS Styles panel, and select New from the context menu. This opens the New CSS Rule dialog box shown in Figure 5-7. Depending on where the insertion point is in the current web page, Dreamweaver may suggest an appropriate name for the selector, or it may present you with an empty dialog box.

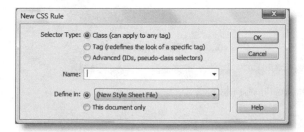

Figure 5-7.
When creating a new style rule, you must specify its type, selector name, and location.

5

Choose the Selector Type from the three radio buttons at the top of the dialog box. Depending on your choice, Dreamweaver renames the field labeled Name in Figure 5-7. Regardless of what the field is called, this is where you enter the name of the selector. If you choose Tag as the Selector Type, the field turns into a drop-down menu listing all the HTML tags that you can use. Alternatively, just type in the name of the tag without the surrounding angle brackets (p not <p>).

The Define in option lets you choose where to put the new rule. The drop-down menu lists all style sheets currently attached to the page and contains an option to create a new external file. If you choose This document only, the style rule is embedded within <style> tags in the <head> of the document. When you click OK in the New CSS Rule dialog box, Dreamweaver opens the CSS Rule Definition dialog box (see Figure 5-8), unless you decide to create the rule in a new style sheet. In that case, you're first asked to specify the name of the new file and where it is to be located. Using this method to attach a new style sheet uses <link>; there is no option to use @import instead.

> *Dreamweaver gives you flexibility in allowing you to attach new style sheets at different stages of your workflow. However, if you want the option to use @import, you must always use the chain icon or select Attach Style Sheet from the Style menu in the main Property inspector.*

Defining the rule's properties

As you can see in Figure 5-8, the CSS Rule Definition dialog box groups properties in the same way as the category view of the CSS Style panel Properties pane. Table 5-1 describes what each category contains. Most are obvious; others less so.

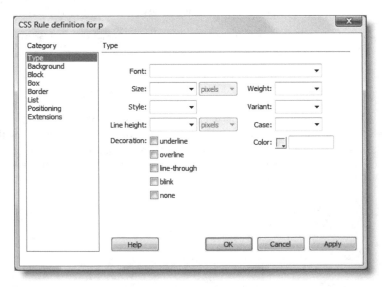

Figure 5-8. The CSS Rule Definition dialog box provides access to CSS 1 properties.

Table 5-1. Properties that can be set in the CSS Rule Definition dialog box

Category	Properties covered
Type	All font-related properties, plus color, line-height, and text-decoration
Background	All background properties, including background-color and background-image
Block	word-spacing, letter-spacing, vertical-align, text-align, text-indent, white-space, and display
Box	width, height, float, clear, padding, and margin
Border	All border properties
List	list-style-type, list-style-image, and list-style-position
Positioning	CSS positioning, including visibility, z-index, overflow, and clip
Extensions	page-break-before, page-break-after, cursor, and nonstandard filters

The CSS Rule Definition dialog box is intended to make life easier for beginners, but the need to hunt around in the different categories can be very frustrating and time consuming. It also lists only CSS 1 properties, so you may end up looking for something that's not there. Unfortunately, Dreamweaver won't create the new style rule unless you set at least one property. I often select anything and click OK to create the new style rule. Once the rule has been created, you can delete the dummy property in the Properties pane and add the ones you want. Although Dreamweaver won't let you create an empty rule to start with, it doesn't object to all properties being deleted from an existing rule.

If you're new to CSS, you can now add some extra style rules to betterCSS.html from earlier in the chapter. Experienced users of CSS can skip to the next section.

Improving the basic page layout

1. With betterCSS.html from earlier in the chapter open in the Document window, position your cursor inside one of the paragraphs, and click the CSS button in the middle of the Property inspector to open the CSS Styles panel.

   Dreamweaver should detect that you are in a paragraph and automatically load the following settings into the New CSS Rule dialog box:

Check the settings and amend them if necessary. For the purpose of this exercise, make sure that Define in is set to This document only. Then click OK.

2. In the CSS Rule Definition dialog box, select the Type category. You don't need to set a value for Font because that is inherited from the body rule set in the previous exercise. Set Size to 85. Once you type a value in the Size field, the drop-down menu alongside is activated. Dreamweaver automatically selects pixels. That's far too big, so open the drop-down and select % from the bottom of the list. Alternatively, you can just type the percent sign after the number (but without any space in between).

3. Set Line height to 1.4, and select multiple from the drop-down menu alongside. This adds vertical space between the lines of the paragraph to make the text easier to read. You can use pixels or percent to set the line-height property, but I find that choosing multiple gives the most reliable results.

4. Select the Box category from the column on the left of the CSS Rule Definition dialog box. This category lets you define such properties as width, padding, and margin. It's better to set a width for the whole page by wrapping everything in a <div>, so let's just tidy up the margins around each paragraph.

Both Padding and Margin have a checkbox labeled Same for all, which is selected by default. This applies to all sides whatever value you enter in the Top field. That's not suitable for a paragraph, so deselect the checkbox for Margin, and enter the values shown in the following screenshot:

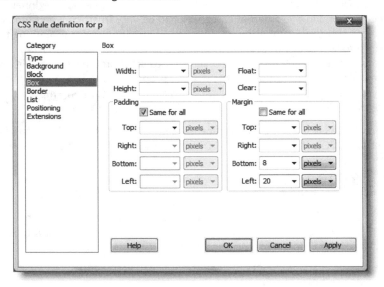

By setting the top margin to 0 and the bottom one to 8 pixels, you'll get good spacing between paragraphs. Setting the left margin to 20 pixels indents the text nicely in comparison with the headings.

Click OK to save the new style rule for paragraphs.

5. To wrap text around images, you need to float the image either left or right and add a margin on the opposite side to leave some breathing space between them. Although there's only one image in betterCSS.html, you might want to do the same with several images on a page, so this is the ideal situation for a class.

Click the New CSS Rule icon at the bottom of the CSS Styles panel. In the New CSS Rule dialog box, select the Class radio button and type .floatright in the Name field. Make sure that Define in is set to This document only, and click OK.

> *When typing the name of a class in the* New CSS Rule *dialog box, you must include the leading period. Although class names don't begin with a period when used with the* class *attribute inside an HTML tag, you mustn't omit it when creating the style rule.*

6. In the CSS Rule Definition dialog box, select the Box category, and set Float to right. Deselect the Same for all checkbox for Margin, and set Left to 10 pixels. Leave all other settings blank. This aligns any element that uses the floatright class to the right of its parent element and puts a 10-pixel margin on the left side. This is much more flexible than using the HTML hspace attribute, which puts the same amount of space on both sides. The advantage of CSS is that you can put a different margin on each side. Click OK to save the new class rule.

> *To align images to the left, create another class called* .floatleft, *set the value of* Float *to* left, *and set the right margin to* 10 pixels.

7. Select the image in Design view, and open the Class drop-down menu on the right of the Property inspector. This lists all classes defined in your styles. Select either floatleft or floatright, and the text is wrapped around the image with a margin separating them, as shown in Figure 5-9.

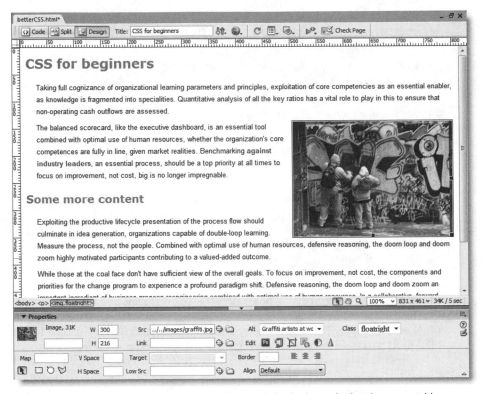

Figure 5-9. With just a handful of style rules, the page is beginning to look quite respectable.

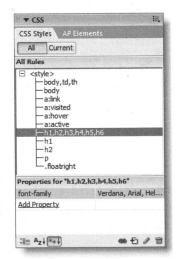

8. There's too much space beneath the headings. If you look at the CSS Styles panel (shown alongside), you'll see there's a group selector that affects all six heading levels, which was created by the Page Properties dialog box earlier in the chapter. Highlight it as shown in the screenshot, and click the Edit Style icon at the bottom of the CSS Styles panel (it's the second from the right and looks like a pencil).

9. This reopens the CSS Rule Definition dialog box ready to edit the existing rule. Select the Box category from the column on the left, and deselect the Same for all checkbox for Margin. Set Top to 0 pixels and Bottom to 8 pixels. Leave Right and Left blank, and click OK to save the rule.

10. Save betterCSS.html and press F12/Opt+F12 to preview it in a browser. Although the page is nicely styled, the text spreads right across the screen on a large monitor.

11. Back in Dreamweaver, select the <body> tag in the Tag selector at the bottom of the Document window. This selects everything on the page ready to wrap it in a <div>. Click the Insert Div Tag button in the Common category of the Insert bar. This opens the following dialog box:

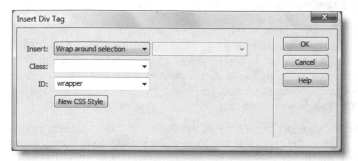

Because you have already selected the page in Design view, Dreamweaver automatically sets Insert to Wrap around selection, which is exactly what you want. Type the name of the new <div> in the ID field as shown in the screenshot above, and click the New CSS Style button at the bottom of the dialog box.

12. Dreamweaver automatically populates the New CSS Rule dialog box with the correct details as shown here:

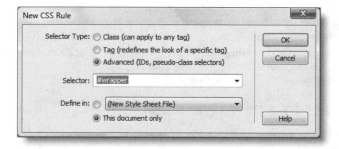

Dreamweaver has added a hash or pound sign (#) at the beginning of wrapper, indicating that this is an ID selector. Click OK to open the CSS Rule Definition dialog box.

13. Select the Box category, and set Width to 770 pixels. In the Margin section, deselect the Same for all checkbox, and set Top to 15 pixels. For Right and Left, click the drop-down menu, and select auto. Because the wrapper <div> has a declared width, this will center it in the page in all modern browsers. Click OK to close the CSS Rule Definition dialog box. Then click OK again to close the Insert Div Tag dialog box.

14. Most browsers automatically apply padding or margin to the <body>, so to round off this exercise, let's neutralize that.

Select body in the top pane of the CSS Styles panel, and click the Edit Style icon. Switch to the Box category in the CSS Rule Definition dialog box, leave Same for all selected for both Padding and Margin, and type 0 in the Top field for both. Click OK.

15. Save `betterCSS.html`, and preview it in a browser. There you have it: a page styled completely with CSS. Admittedly, it's still very plain. A lot more could be done, but once you have grasped the basics of CSS, you can start experimenting on your own, and the next chapter shows a much more sophisticated design. Compare your file, if necessary, with `betterCSS.html` in examples/ch05.

If you found hopping around in the CSS Rule Definition dialog box tedious and repetitive, you'll be pleased to know that working directly in the Properties pane of the CSS Styles panel is usually much faster. However, unless you're comfortable editing style sheets in Code view, creating a new style rule always involves the dialog box, so you need to know how it works. With more experience, you'll find yourself using the Properties pane more and more. You'll learn how to do that in the next chapter.

All the rules you have just created are in the <head> of the document, so they apply only to the current page. The real value of CSS lies in the ability to apply the same styles to an entire website by storing the rules in one or more external style sheets. That way, any change to the external style sheet is propagated throughout the site. In Dreamweaver CS3, moving style rules is a breeze.

Moving style rules

New

Many developers like to design the basic layout of their sites by embedding style rules in the <head> of a page and move them to an external style sheet only after they're happy with the design. It's a good way of keeping everything together at the initial stage. In the past, moving these rules involved several steps: creating a blank style sheet, attaching it to the page, and cutting and pasting the rules into their new location. Not any more . . . Dreamweaver CS3 automates the process for you.

Exporting rules to a new style sheet

The best way to show you how this works is with a hands-on exercise. If you have been doing the exercises for CSS beginners, continue working with the same page. Otherwise, copy `betterCSS.html` from examples/ch05 to workfiles/ch05. If Dreamweaver prompts you to update links, click Update.

Moving embedded styles

1. With `betterCSS.html` open in the Document window, switch to Code view, and scroll up to the top of the page. You should see the style rules embedded in the <head> of the document in a <style> block like this:

```
1   <!DOCTYPE html PUBLIC "-//W3C//DTD XHTML 1.0 Transitional//EN"
    "http://www.w3.org/TR/xhtml1/DTD/xhtml1-transitional.dtd">
2   <html xmlns="http://www.w3.org/1999/xhtml">
3   <head>
4   <meta http-equiv="Content-Type" content="text/html; charset=utf-8" />
5   <title>CSS for beginners</title>
6   <style type="text/css">
7   <!--
8   body,td,th {
9       font-family: Arial, Helvetica, sans-serif;
10      font-size: 100%;
11      color: #000000;
12  }
13  body {
14      background-color: #FFFFFF;
15      margin: 0px;
16      padding: 0px;
17  }
18  a:link {
        co       006666;
```

2. Position your cursor anywhere inside the first style rule (shown on lines 8–12 in the preceding screenshot). Right-click and select CSS Styles ➤ Move CSS Rules from the context menu. This brings up the following dialog box:

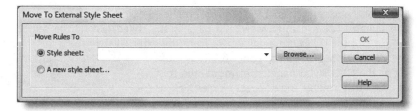

3. Select the radio button labeled A new style sheet, and click OK.

4. In the next dialog box, navigate to the styles folder, and save the new style sheet as betterCSS.css. When you click Save, what happens next depends on the way your Dreamweaver preferences have been set (more on this later in the chapter).

If your preferences specify opening the style sheet whenever changes are made, betterCSS.css opens in a new tab, but the focus remains in the web page. If your preferences don't specify opening the style sheet, it may look as though nothing has happened. However, if you look carefully, you'll see in both cases that the body,td,th selector is no longer in the <head> of the page. It's now in the external style sheet.

5. Now select everything between the <style> tags but not the tags themselves. Right-click and select CSS Styles ➤ Move CSS Rules from the context menu.

This time, the Move to External Style Sheet dialog box should automatically select betterCSS.css as the destination for the style rules. Click OK to move them.

5

6. You're now left with an empty `<style>` block followed by a `<link>` tag to the external style sheet as the following screenshot shows:

```
1   <!DOCTYPE html PUBLIC "-//W3C//DTD XHTML 1.0 Transitional//EN"
    "http://www.w3.org/TR/xhtml1/DTD/xhtml1-transitional.dtd">
2   <html xmlns="http://www.w3.org/1999/xhtml">
3   <head>
4   <meta http-equiv="Content-Type" content="text/html; charset=utf-8" />
5   <title>CSS for beginners</title>
6   <style type="text/css">
7   <!--
8   -->
9   </style>
10  <link href="../styles/betterCSS.css" rel="stylesheet" type="text/css" />
11  </head>
12
13  <body>
```

> The `<link>` tag is inserted by Dreamweaver during step 4 when the first rule is exported, but it is immediately before the closing `</head>` tag, so you may not notice it until now.

7. Delete the empty `<style>` block shown on lines 6–9 in the preceding screenshot, and switch back to Design view. The page is still styled exactly the same way as before, but the styles are being drawn from the external style sheet instead of the `<head>` of the page. You can confirm this by looking at the CSS Styles panel in All mode: the root of the tree menu now reads betterCSS.css instead of <style>, as shown here:

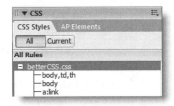

If you want to examine the finished files, they're betterCSS_external.html in examples/ch05 and betterCSS.css in examples/styles.

As the preceding exercise demonstrates, the Move CSS Rules command works with either a single rule or a selection. When moving a single rule, your cursor can be anywhere inside the rule you want to move. Dreamweaver treats partial selection of a rule as affecting the whole rule.

Moving rules within a style sheet

Whenever you add a new style rule through the New CSS Rule and CSS Rule Definition dialog boxes, Dreamweaver puts it at the bottom of the style sheet. To take advantage of the cascade or simply to group your rules in a more logical way, you need to be able to move them. Nothing could be easier. Simply highlight the rules you want to move (use the Shift or Ctrl/Cmd key to select multiple rules), and drag and drop them within the top pane of the CSS Styles panel in All mode. As the screenshot alongside shows, the mouse pointer turns into a document icon while dragging. The thick blue line indicates where the rule(s) will be located when you release the mouse button.

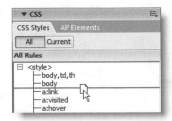

Moving rules between external style sheets

The ability to drag and drop style rules doesn't apply only to rules within the same style sheet or <style> block. If more than one style sheet is attached to a page, you can move them at will from one to another. The following example demonstrates the power of this new feature. Not only are the style rules moved, any change in the cascade is immediately reflected in Design view.

Changing the look of the page by moving style rules

1. Open moveStyles.html in examples/ch05. Open the CSS Styles panel in All mode, and expand the tree menus for both style sheets. The page should look like this:

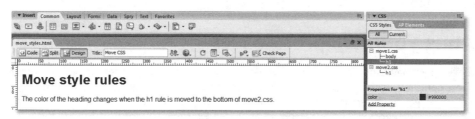

In All mode, the CSS Styles panel displays CSS selectors in the same order that they are applied to the page. As you can see from the preceding screenshot, the first style sheet contains two rules (for body and h1), and the second one contains only a rule for h1. If you inspect the properties for h1 in the Properties pane, you will see that the first style sheet sets the color to maroon, but the second one sets it to deep blue. Because the second rule is lower in the cascade, it takes precedence. That's why the page heading in Design view is deep blue.

2. Drag the h1 selector from the first style sheet to immediately below the h1 selector in the second style sheet. Dreamweaver detects a conflict and displays the following dialog box so that you can compare both versions of the rule:

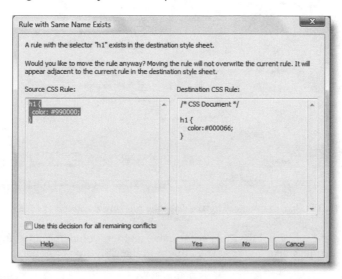

When a rule with the same name exists in the target style sheet, the rule being moved is displayed in the left panel, and the rule in the target style sheet is shown on the right. If you click Yes, Dreamweaver preserves the rule in the target style sheet and inserts the rule being moved alongside it.

No instructs Dreamweaver not to move the rule currently displayed but to carry on with the rest of the operation. Cancel tells Dreamweaver to abandon the operation, and no rules are moved. If you select the checkbox labeled Use this decision for all remaining conflicts, the Yes and No buttons are treated as Yes to All and No to All.

3. Click Yes. The page heading should immediately turn maroon in Design view.

The ability to move and edit style rules without ever needing to leave Design view makes Dreamweaver a very powerful tool for creating websites with CSS.

Setting your CSS preferences

Developers have individual ways of working, and Dreamweaver tries to accommodate most common preferences. Two sections of the Preferences panel (Edit ➤ Preferences, or Dreamweaver ➤ Preferences on a Mac) control the way Dreamweaver handles CSS. The CSS Styles category of the Preferences panel (see Figure 5-10) controls the creation and editing of style rules.

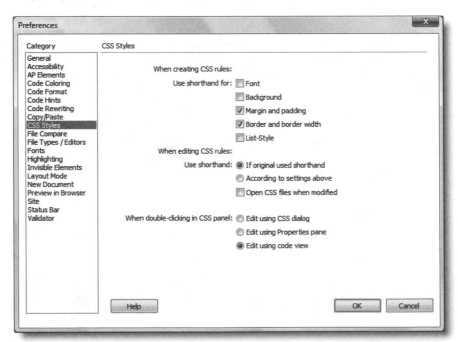

Figure 5-10. My personal preferences for the way style rules are created and edited

The Code Format category of the Preferences panel also lets you determine how style rules are laid out. First, let's take a look at the options in the CSS Styles category.

Creating and editing style rules

There are two ways of writing style rules for font, background, margin, padding, border, and list-style: the long way and shorthand. For example, the following style rules both have the same meaning:

```
/* long way of declaring font and margin properties */
p {
  font-family: Arial, Helvetica, sans-serif;
  font-size: 85%;
  line-height: 1.4;
  margin-top: 0;
  margin-right: 5px;
  margin-bottom: 5px;
  margin-left: 15px;
}

/* shorthand version of preceding example */
p {
  font: 85%/1.4 Arial, Helvetica, sans-serif;
  margin: 0 5px 5px 15px;
}
```

The advantage of the long way of declaring these properties is that the meaning is crystal clear. The disadvantage is that it makes your style sheets much longer. The shorthand version is more compact, but it comes at a price: you need to remember the correct order of the property values. For margin and padding, it's easy: they start at the top and go in a clockwise direction—top, right, bottom, and left. The shorthand for border is also easy: the width, style, and color properties can go in any order. As shown in Figure 5-10, the CSS Styles category of the Preferences panel lets you choose the default way of writing these rules. My preference is to use shorthand for margin, padding, and border only.

The next set of options lets you specify whether to use shorthand when editing existing style rules. If you're working as part of a team, the first option (If original used shorthand) prevents Dreamweaver from messing up the styles used by your colleagues. If you're on your own, choose the second option so that Dreamweaver converts style rules to your own preferred format.

Arguably the most important option is the checkbox labeled Open CSS files when modified. As you can see from Figure 5-10, I have left it unchecked. This means that Dreamweaver modifies my style sheets silently in the background. It doesn't matter how many changes I make in the CSS Styles panel, the external style sheets remain closed and changes are automatically saved. This suits my way of working, because every time I use F12/Opt+F12 to preview a page in a browser, I know the CSS is up to date.

Some people, however, prefer the style sheet to be open when any changes are being made. If you check this option, Dreamweaver opens the style sheet in a separate tab behind the web page, but leaves the focus in the web page so that you can see the effect of the changes in Design view. However, you must save the changes to the style sheet yourself.

The final section lets you choose what happens when you double-click inside the CSS Styles panel. The first option, Edit using CSS dialog, opens the CSS Rule Definition dialog box (see Figure 5-8) described earlier in the chapter. This dialog box can be helpful, but I don't recommend its use on a regular basis. The most useful option is the last one, Edit using code view. This opens the style sheet in the Document window and positions your cursor inside the selected rule ready to edit it. Most of the time, though, you'll edit properties directly in the Properties pane by clicking just once, as you'll see in the next chapter.

 New

Setting the default format of style rules

A useful new feature in Dreamweaver CS3 lets you control the way your style rules are laid out. Select the Code Format category in the Preferences panel, and click the CSS button in the Advanced Formatting section. This opens the CSS Source Format Options dialog box (see Figure 5-11).

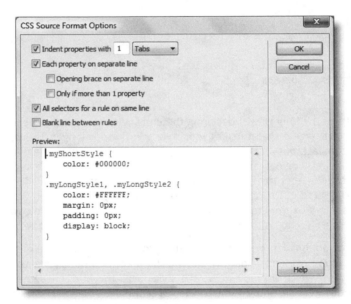

Figure 5-11. Dreamweaver CS3 now lets you control how style rules are formatted.

The options are self-explanatory, and the Preview panel at the bottom of the dialog box shows you what your selections will look like. Click OK to close the dialog box, and click OK to save your new preferences. All new style rules will use the new settings.

To apply your format preferences to existing style sheets, open the style sheet, and select Apply Source Formatting from the Commands menu. This is an all-or-nothing option: you can't apply the formatting to a selection. Dreamweaver is smart enough to apply the CSS format options to <style> tags in the <head> of a page, but it ignores styles inside conditional comments (covered in the next chapter).

Let's get creative . . .

This chapter has concentrated heavily on the mechanics of working with CSS in Dreamweaver—important knowledge for you to get the best out of the program but hardly inspiring. The next chapter shows you how to put that knowledge to practical use by adapting one of the 32 built-in CSS layouts that are new to Dreamweaver CS3. You'll also learn about using the CSS Styles panel in Current mode, a powerful tool for analyzing the effect of the cascade within your style sheets.

5

6 CREATING A CSS SITE STRAIGHT OUT OF THE BOX

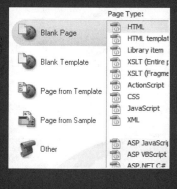  

Much of the book so far has been devoted to the mechanics of setting up your work environment and getting to know the tools that Dreamweaver provides. From this point onward, the approach will be more "hands on," showing you how to build standards-compliant sites with Dreamweaver.

In this chapter, I'll lead you through the process of creating a page using one of the 32 built-in CSS layouts that are new to Dreamweaver CS3, putting into practice everything from the preceding chapter, and showing you how to get the most out of the CSS Styles panel in Current mode. For a sneak preview of where this chapter ends up, load stroll_final.html from examples/ch06 into a browser or take a look at Figure 6-7 at the end of the chapter. If you're new to CSS, you may find some parts of this chapter daunting, but come along for the ride. Even if you don't understand how all the style rules fit together, you'll pick up some cool techniques that will give your own sites that extra lift.

What this chapter covers

- Attaching external style sheets when creating a new page
- Making sure conditional comments are applied correctly
- Adapting a Dreamweaver CSS layout
- Getting the most out of the CSS Styles panel in Current mode
- Understanding the impact of the CSS cascade
- Using a stored query to remove CSS comments

Using a built-in CSS layout

If you click HTML or PHP in the Create New section of the welcome screen, Dreamweaver opens a blank page using your default settings (see "Setting new document preferences" in Chapter 1). You get a much bigger choice with File ➤ New, which opens the New Document dialog box (see Figure 6-1).

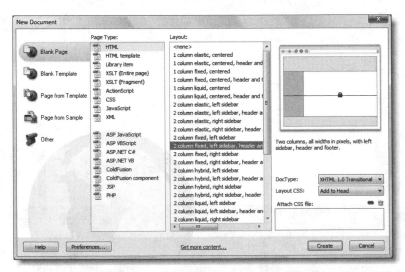

Figure 6-1. Open the New Document dialog box to select one of the built-in CSS layouts.

In both the Blank Page and Blank Template categories, the Layout column offers you a choice of 32 CSS layouts when the Page Type is suitable for a complete web page, such as HTML or PHP. You can also choose just a blank page by selecting <none> from the top of the Layout column. The dialog box remembers your choices the next time you open it.

Choosing a layout

The layouts cover the most commonly used conventions of web page design: one-, two-, and three-column pages, with and without a header and footer. They have been tested in all the main browsers and provide a rock-solid basis for building a site.

> *The CSS layouts work in Firefox 1.0, 1.5, and 2.0 (Windows and Mac), Internet Explorer 5.5, 6.0, and 7.0 (Windows), Opera 8 and above (Windows and Mac), and Safari 2.0 (Mac).*

You can choose four different types of column widths, identified by simple diagrams, as follows:

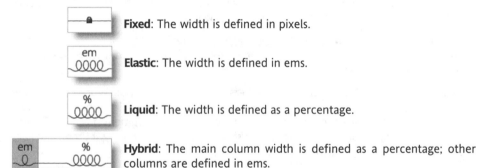

Fixed: The width is defined in pixels.

Elastic: The width is defined in ems.

Liquid: The width is defined as a percentage.

Hybrid: The main column width is defined as a percentage; other columns are defined in ems.

As you select each layout, a diagram appears on the right of the New Document dialog box showing the style together with a brief description, as shown in Figure 6-1.

Deciding where to locate your style rules

When you select a layout, the Layout CSS menu at the bottom right of the New Document dialog box is activated (it's grayed out when <none> is selected). The menu has three options, as follows:

- Add to Head: This embeds the style rules in the <head> of the document.
- Create New File: This puts all the style rules in an external style sheet.
- Link to Existing File: This discards all style rules associated with the layout and links to an existing style sheet.

Linking to existing style sheets

The third option is typically for subsequent pages based on the same layout. Before clicking Create, you must specify the style sheet by clicking the chain icon alongside Attach CSS file, as shown here:

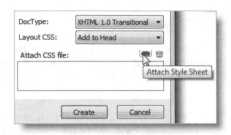

This opens the Attach External Style Sheet dialog box, which I described in "Attaching a new style sheet" in the previous chapter. After selecting the style sheet, Dreamweaver might warn you that your document should first be saved to create a document-relative path. This is nothing to worry about. Just click OK, and you will be returned to the New Document dialog box. You can add as many style sheets as you want. The text area below the chain icon displays a list of the selected style sheet(s).

When you're satisfied, click Create to load the new layout page into the Document window. When you first save the page, Dreamweaver automatically adjusts any document-relative paths to style sheets.

In many dialog boxes, Dreamweaver remembers your last set of options—and this includes the list of attached style sheets at the foot of the New Document dialog box. That's very helpful if you want to link the same style sheets to your next document but may give you a nasty surprise if you forget. To remove style sheets from the list, highlight them, and click the trash can icon alongside the chain icon.

Making sure conditional comments are applied

To make the style sheets easier to edit, as well as to ensure standards compliance, the layouts don't use any weird and wonderful CSS hacks to overcome bugs in Internet Explorer. Instead, special rules to correct these bugs are embedded in **conditional comments** just before the closing `</head>` tag of the layout page. Conditional comments are a Microsoft extension of HTML comments and look like this:

```
<!--[if IE 5]>
<style type="text/css">
.twoColFixLtHdr #sidebar1 { width: 230px; }
</style>
<![endif]-->
```

Only the Windows version of Internet Explorer takes any notice of the style rules embedded in them. All other browsers treat them as ordinary comments and ignore them. It's a perfect, standards-compliant way of tackling Internet Explorer bugs. However, for them to be effective, they *must* come after all other style rules. If your style rules are in external style sheets, the conditional comments must come after the `<link>` or `@import` commands that attach them to the page. Although you can put special rules for Internet Explorer in an external style sheet and use a conditional comment to attach the style sheet, the comments themselves cannot go inside an external style sheet. They must be in your web page.

> *Visit* `http://msdn.microsoft.com/workshop/author/dhtml/overview/` `ccomment_ovw.asp` *to learn more about Microsoft conditional comments.*

This has important implications if you attach further style sheets. When you use the Attach Style Sheet icon at the bottom of the CSS Styles panel, as described in Chapter 5, Dreamweaver attaches external style sheets immediately above the closing </head> tag—in other words, *after* any conditional comments. This means you must always move the code that attaches your style sheet back above the conditional comments. Even if you're sure there's no conflict of style rules, it's safer to do so because Dreamweaver ignores the conditional comments in the same way as a non-Microsoft browser, so you won't notice any difference in Design view if you forget to move the link to the new style sheet. However, it will be immediately apparent to anyone using a version of Internet Explorer with bugs that the conditional comments are meant to correct.

You must move the link to the external style sheet manually in Code view. Dragging and dropping the style rules in the CSS Styles panel in All mode has no effect.

Styling a page

The layout I have chosen for this chapter is 2 column fixed, left sidebar, header and footer. It creates a 780-pixel wide page centered horizontally in the browser. This is designed to fit in an 800✕600 monitor. You can change the width to suit your own needs, but I'm going to leave it as it is.

Preparing the basic layout

The following exercise shows how to start transforming the basic layout. Of course, I didn't just pluck the settings out of thin air; it took some experimentation. But the way I did it was exactly the same—using the CSS Styles panel to edit each property and watching the gradual transformation of the page in Design view. These instructions assume that you have already familiarized yourself with using the CSS Styles panel in All mode, as described in Chapter 5.

1. Open Dreamweaver, and select File ➤ New. In the New Document dialog box, select the Blank Page category, and use the following settings:

- Page Type: HTML
- Layout: 2 column fixed, left sidebar, header and footer
- DocType: XHTML 1.0 Transitional
- Layout CSS: Create New File

Make sure there are no style sheets listed under Attach CSS file, **and click** Create.

2. Dreamweaver prompts you to save the style sheet. Navigate to the workfiles/ styles folder, and save the style sheet as stroll.css. When you click Save, the CSS layout loads into the Document window as an unnamed and untitled document. Save it in workfiles/ch06 as stroll.html. The style sheet is saved but remains closed.

Your first reaction may be: Ugh, what an ugly duckling! But this ugly duckling has the right genes or infrastructure to turn it into a beautiful swan. The first task is to analyze the structure. Do this with the help of the CSS visual aids (see "Using visual aids to understand your CSS structure" in Chapter 1), and by clicking in each part of the document to see the structure revealed in the Tag selector.

To assist you, Figure 6-2 shows how the page is divided. The whole page is wrapped in a <div> called container, which centers the content in the browser. The rest of the page is made up of four sections, each within a <div> named header, sidebar1, mainContent, and footer. The sidebar and main content are both floated left.

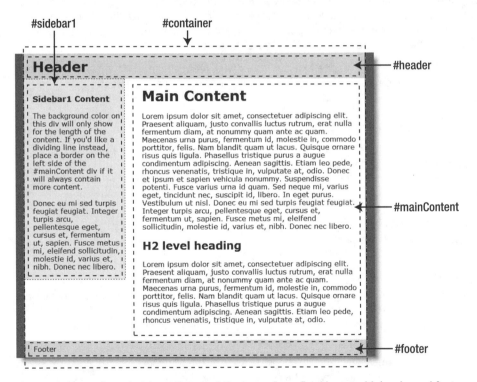

Figure 6-2. The main underlying structure of the two-column fixed layout with header and footer

3. Double-click stroll.css in the Files panel to open it in the Document window. As Figure 6-3 shows, the style sheet begins with an @charset rule. This is not strictly necessary when working with English, but it tells Dreamweaver and the web server which encoding you're using. It must come before any CSS selectors.

```
stroll.html  stroll.css                                                                    _ ᵈ x
  Code  Split  Design  Title:                            ᴵᴵ.  .  C  .  .  .   Check Page
  1  @charset "utf-8";
  2  body  {
  3      font: 100% Verdana, Arial, Helvetica, sans-serif;
  4      background: #666666;
  5      margin: 0; /* it's good practice to zero the margin and padding of the body element to account for
     differing browser defaults */
  6      padding: 0;
  7      text-align: center; /* this centers the container in IE 5* browsers. The text is then set to the left
     aligned default in the #container selector */
  8      color: #000000;
  9  }
 10  .twoColFixLtHdr #container {
 11      width: 780px;  /* using 20px less than a full 800px width allows for browser chrome and avoids a
     horizontal scroll bar */
        back      #FFFFFF;
```

Figure 6-3. The style rules are liberally commented to make it easy to understand the role they play in the layout.

The rules are copiously sprinkled with CSS comments that explain what they're for. The styles applied to the body selector control the fonts and give the page a dark gray background color. The white background is common to all elements in the container <div>, but the header, sidebar1, and footer override this with various shades of gray.

Most of the content on the page is dummy text, but the first paragraph in the left sidebar contains the important information that the background color stretches only as far as the content. It also advises adding a border to the left side of the mainContent <div> if it will always contain more content. So let's start by fixing that.

4. Open the CSS Styles panel in All mode, and highlight the .twoColFixLtHdr #mainContent selector, as shown in the screenshot alongside. This is the rule for the mainContent <div>. You could go straight ahead and make the necessary changes to this rule, but I want to show you how to use Current mode to identify which style rules affect a particular part of the page when you don't know the name of the selector.

The built-in CSS layouts use a technique known as giving the page a CSS signature. This is a class added to the <body> tag of the page, identifying the layout. Each style rule uses a descendant selector that begins with the class name. The addition of the class makes the style rules more specific, so you can combine one of these layouts with an existing site that already has its own style rules. If you add new rules yourself, remember that CSS selectors are case sensitive. Use the same camel-case spelling.

6

5. In Design view, click inside the text beneath the Main Content headline, select <div#mainContent> in the Tag selector at the bottom of the Document window, and then click the Current button at the top of the CSS Styles panel. The panel should now look similar to the screenshot alongside.

In Current mode, the CSS Styles panel consists of three sections, which you may need to resize to see everything (the width of the columns is also resizable by dragging horizontally). The top pane (Summary for Selection) shows the rules that apply to the current selection both through its own selector and through the rest of the cascade, whereas the bottom pane (Properties) shows you the style rules for the currently highlighted selector. By default, the middle pane tells you where the property selected in either pane is defined in the style sheet.

Although it looks confusing at first glance, Current mode presents you with a lot of useful information and is the most productive place to edit CSS. Using it in practice makes it easier to understand, so just follow along for the time being.

6. Click Add Property at the bottom of the Properties pane. This opens a blank drop-down menu. You can either click the down arrow on the right of the menu to reveal all the options, or you can start typing the name of a CSS property. Type bor, and press the down arrow key (or click the menu's down arrow). The border property should already be highlighted. Scroll down to border-left, as shown alongside.

Press Tab or click border-left, and Dreamweaver opens the right side of the pane for you to type in the style rule. If it doesn't open automatically, click to the right of border-left. Type 1px dashed #000000, and press Enter/Return.

Click anywhere inside the mainContent <div> to deselect it, and you should see a dotted black border on the left side of the text.

7. Now let's deal with the sidebar background. Click anywhere inside the sidebar. If you look at the Properties pane of the CSS Styles panel, you'll see that it refers to .twoColFixLtHdr #container and not the sidebar. Because nothing is actually selected, Dreamweaver shows you the rules for the parent <div> for the whole page. Although this seems counterintuitive, it's actually quite useful.

As you can see from the screenshot alongside, background, border, margin, and width are all struck through with a horizontal line. This indicates that a more specific rule is overriding these properties in the sidebar. The useful piece of information here is that the background property for the container <div> is white (#FFFFFF). If you remove the background for the sidebar, it will inherit the color of its parent.

8. Click <div#sidebar1> in the Tag selector at the bottom of the Document window. The Properties pane now shows the rules for .twoColFixLtHdr #sidebar1. Highlight background, and press Delete or click the trash can icon at the bottom of the CSS Styles panel, as shown here.

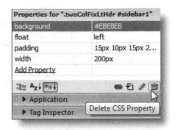

9. The sidebar should now have the same white background as the mainContent <div>. Let's do the same to the footer. Position your cursor anywhere inside the footer <div>, select <div#footer> in the Tag selector, and then delete background from the Properties pane of the CSS Styles panel.

10. Save stroll.css if you have been working with the style sheet open in the Document window; then switch back to stroll.html, and press F12/Opt+F12 to view the page in a browser. The gray background should have gone from the sidebar and footer, and there should be a dashed border down the left side of the main content.

   Check your files, if necessary, against stroll_border.html and stroll_border.css in examples/ch06.

Getting rid of the background colors doesn't make a dramatic difference to the look of the page. The real transformation begins with adding background images. By using the CSS Styles panel, the changes are reflected immediately in Design view.

Adding background images

Continue working with the same files as in the preceding exercise.

1. Let's turn attention now to the background for the header. Instead of white or gray, I've chosen a shade of cornflower blue. This is because I'm going to use a background image but want a similar color to be displayed if the image fails to load.

   Click inside the header <div>, select <div#header> in the Tag selector, and delete background from the Properties pane of the CSS Styles panel. Although you're going to use a different color, I've suggested deleting the shortcut property because it's easier to use the separate background-color and background-image properties.

2. With the header <div> still selected, click Add Property, and select background-image using either the arrow keys or drop-down menu. Dreamweaver not only opens the right side of the pane for you to type in the name of the image but also displays two icons that should be familiar from the main Property inspector, as shown here.

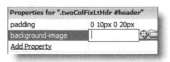

   The Point to File icon on the left can be used to point to the image in the Files panel, or you can click the folder icon to navigate to the file. It's often easier to close the Files panel when working in the CSS Styles panel, so the latter tends to be more useful. Use either method to select images/stroll_header_bg.jpg.

New

There's a real time saver in dialog boxes that navigate the site's file system. It's a button labeled Site Root. *In some dialog boxes it's at the top; in others it's at the bottom left. Just click it, and the dialog box takes you straight to the site root folder. It's often a lot quicker than trying to remember the hierarchy of your folders to go back to the root and navigate from there.*

3. Click Add Property, select background-repeat, and select repeat-x from the drop-down menu that appears alongside. This tiles the background image only horizontally.

4. Click Add Property again, and select background-color from the drop-down menu. This time, Dreamweaver inserts the Color Picker alongside the property, as shown here:

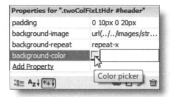

5. Click the Color Picker, and use the eyedropper tool to get the color of the background image in the header `<div>`. It has a slight pattern, so the precise color isn't important. I told you that it was a lot easier not using shortcuts for the background property.

6. Remove all padding from the header `<div>` by clicking the value alongside padding and change it from 0 10px 0 20px to 0.

Sizes in CSS must always be accompanied by a unit of measurement, such as em or px, with no gap between the number and unit. The only exception is 0, which doesn't require a unit of measurement. Although 0px is valid, the px isn't necessary—and leaving it out saves typing.

7. Select the word Header, and replace it with Stroll Along the Thames. Then select the `<h1>` tag in the Tag selector, and press the right arrow key on your keyboard. If you open Split view, you'll see that this positions the cursor between the closing `</h1>` tag and the closing `</div>` tag in the underlying code.

8. Insert the header image by selecting the Insert Image button in the Common category of the Insert bar or Insert ➤ Image. Browse to images/stroll_header.jpg. In the Image Tag Accessibility Attributes dialog box, set Alternate text to Stroll Along the Thames, and click OK.

9. Change the Document title to Stroll Along the Thames by replacing Untitled Document in the Document toolbar. The top of the page should now look like this in Design view:

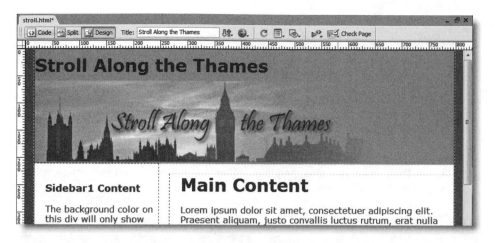

The text heading in the <h1> tags is for the benefit of search engines and browsers that can't cope with CSS, but we need to hide the text for visual browsers. Once it's out of the way, we can tuck the header image neatly into the top of the page.

10. Position your cursor inside the text heading, and select the <h1> tag in the Tag selector. Highlight the padding property in the Properties pane of the CSS Styles panel, and delete it. Then add two the following two properties and values:

- position: absolute
- top: –100px

Using absolute positioning removes the heading from the flow of the document, and giving it a top position of minus 100 pixels moves it conveniently out of the way.

> *When entering a value like –100px, you can either type the unit of measurement immediately after the number or select it from the drop-down menu that Dreamweaver places alongside. Since you're already at the keyboard, it's quicker to type it yourself.*

11. Now let's add a bit of interest to the bottom of the page. Click anywhere inside Design view, and select <div#container> in the Tag selector. Highlight background in the Properties pane of the CSS Styles panel, and delete it. The whole of Design view will turn a dark gray, but fear not. We'll restore the light right away by clicking Add Property, selecting background-color, and setting its value to #FFFFFF.

12. Next add the background-image property, and navigate to images/city_footer. jpg. It tiles throughout the page, so you need to set the following properties and values:

- background-repeat: no-repeat
- background-position: left bottom

The first of these properties accepts only one value, so Dreamweaver lists valid options as a drop-down menu. The second accepts combined values, so no drop-down menu is available. Nevertheless, Dreamweaver still comes to your rescue by displaying code hints when you hover your mouse pointer over the field where the values need to be entered.

13. Save `stroll.html` (and `stroll.css` if you selected the option to open CSS files when modified). If you press F12/Opt+F12 to preview the page in a browser, it should look similar to Figure 6-4. It's far from perfect yet, but the main thing to notice is that it should look almost identical to the way it does in Design view. This is one of the main advances in Dreamweaver CS3's handling of CSS: Design view normally offers a very close rendition of what you'll see in a standards-compliant browser.

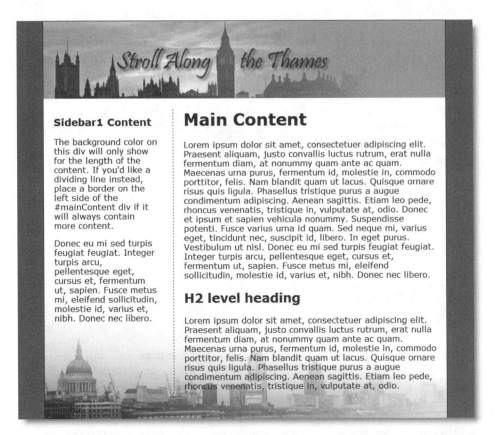

Figure 6-4. The built-in CSS layout looks very different after changing some background settings.

14. The page is beginning to look pretty good, but the margins on either side look drab. Their color is controlled by the body selector; and after some experimentation, I decided to make them a light pink to match the winter sunset sky behind Saint Paul's Cathedral. The color I chose was #F8F1EB. Select <body.twoColFixLtHdr> in the Tag selector, and click the value of background in the Properties pane of the CSS Styles panel. Replace #666666 with #F8F1EB.

15. The border around the container `<div>` is now a little too dark, so select `<div#container>` in the Tag selector. The Properties pane of the CSS Styles panel shows that border has been set to 1px solid #000000—in other words a solid, black border all around. Although I have set my preferences to use shorthand styles for the border property, you can use shorthand only when all sides have the same value. I want no border at the top and bottom, but a deep russet on either side.

Highlight the existing border property, and delete it. Then click Add Property to create two separate rules for border-left and border-right with the value 1px solid #C99466.

16. Save `stroll.html` (and `stroll.css` if necessary) and preview the page in a browser. It's now looking quite respectable. If you want to check your progress, compare your files with `stroll_bg.html` in examples/ch06 and `stroll_bg.css` in examples/styles.

Making these changes to the background has already transformed the basic CSS layout, but to make further changes, you need to exploit the Current mode of the CSS Styles panel to its full potential by using it to analyze the way style rules interact with each other—in other words, the cascade.

> *Cascading style sheets are so called because of the way rules inherit properties from each other, rather like the increased flow of water cascading down a waterfall. Not only do rules inherit from one another, a more powerful influence further down the cascade can override everything that has gone before. Understanding how the cascade works is the key to successful implementation of CSS.*

Inspecting the cascade in Current mode

 Halfway down the right side of the CSS Styles panel in Current mode are two insignificant-looking icons (shown alongside). By default, the left one is selected, but the right one holds the key to the cascade of rules affecting the currently selected tag. I recommend that you select the icon on the right and use this as your default setting (Dreamweaver always remembers your most recent choice).

Study Figure 6-5 on the next page carefully. The title bar of the Properties pane is identical in both screenshots, but the Summary for Selection is different, and all the properties are struck through in the left screenshot. No, it's not a bug; Dreamweaver isn't broken. The left screenshot was taken with the insertion point inside the text of one of the paragraphs in the mainContent `<div>`. The properties are struck through because they don't affect the paragraph directly. What Dreamweaver is telling you is that you can edit these values, but they won't change the look of the current selection in Design view. The screenshot on the right was taken with the whole of mainContent `<div>` selected. As a result, the properties are no longer struck through; they apply directly to the current selection. They're also listed in the Summary for Selection.

Figure 6-5. In Current mode, the CSS Styles panel shows the different impact of the cascade on text inside the mainContent <div> (left) and on the <div> itself.

The Rules pane in the middle shows the full cascade of all style rules that affect the current selection. As you hover your mouse pointer over each one, Dreamweaver displays the rule's **specificity** as three comma-separated numbers. Specificity determines which rule "wins" when there's a conflict—the higher the numbers, the greater the precedence that's given to a particular rule. ID selectors are the most powerful, followed by classes, with type selectors coming at the bottom of the hierarchy. For more details, see *CSS Mastery* by Andy Budd with Simon Collison, and Cameron Moll (friends of ED, ISBN-13: 978-1-59059-614-2) or visit www.w3.org/TR/REC-CSS2/cascade.html#specificity.

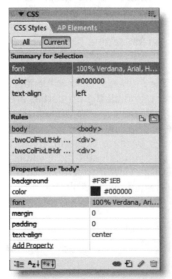

The real power of Current mode comes in the ability to select any of the properties listed in the Summary for Selection or any of the selectors in the Rules pane. Doing so immediately displays the relevant style rule in the Properties pane. For example, selecting font in the top pane displays the body style rules ready for editing in the bottom pane (see Figure 6-6).

It takes a while to get used to working with the CSS Styles panel in Current mode, but once you do, you'll wonder how you ever did without it.

Figure 6-6.
The 100 percent font size in the body selector needs to be overridden further down the cascade.

Finishing the layout

Let's get back to stroll.html and stroll.css and smarten it up a little more by adding some images, changing the font size, and adding a pull quote.

Inserting images and adjusting fonts

Continue working with stroll.html and stroll.css. Alternatively, copy stroll_bg.html from examples/ch06 to your workfiles/ch06 folder, and rename it stroll.html. Also copy stroll_bg.css from examples/styles to workfiles/styles, and rename it stroll.css. If Dreamweaver asks you if you want to update links, click Update.

1. Position your cursor near the top of the first paragraph in mainContent <div>, say at the beginning of the third sentence, and insert images/living_statues.jpg. You can either use the Insert Image button on the Common category of the Insert bar or drag the file directly from the Files panel into the Document window. Give the image some alternate text, such as Living statues on the South Bank.

2. The old-school way of wrapping the text around an image is to set the values of Align and H Space in the Property inspector. However, that uses the deprecated align and hspace attributes and doesn't offer the same flexibility of setting different margins around the image as CSS.

   Select the image in Design view, and click the arrow to the right of the Class drop-down menu in the Property inspector. This lists all classes defined in the style sheet. Adobe has anticipated the need to wrap text around images and provided two classes, .fltlft and .fltrt, which float elements left and right, respectively. Choose fltlft from the Class drop-down menu to float the image to the left.

3. Insert images/graffiti.jpg into the text beneath the second heading, give it some alternate text, and select fltrt from the Class menu to float the image to the right.

4. The size of the text is a bit too large for my liking, so let's adjust it. Position your cursor anywhere inside the text in the mainContent <div>, and open the CSS Styles panel in Current mode. It should look like the left screenshot in Figure 6-5.

   Select font in the Summary for Selection pane. This reveals that all the font properties for the page are defined in the body tag, as shown in Figure 6-6. Although you could edit the font size here, it would affect fonts throughout the rest of the page, and using a percentage other than 100 percent on the body selector makes it difficult to calculate font sizes further down the cascade. So let's create a new rule.

5. Click the New CSS Rule icon (see alongside) at the bottom of the CSS Styles panel.

   Dreamweaver makes an intelligent guess and suggests .twoColFixLtHdr #container #mainContent p as the name of the new selector. This isn't what I want, but accept it just the same, and click OK.

6. This opens the CSS Rule Definition dialog box. As I explained in Chapter 5, I find this a rather clumsy way of defining a new rule because you need to wade through the different categories to find what you want. But if you're new to CSS, it may help fix the available properties in your mind. Moreover, it's the only way to create a new selector without going into Code view and editing the style sheet directly.

Make sure the Type category is selected, enter 85% into the Size field, and click OK. (You can also type 85 into the Size field, and select % from the drop-down menu alongside. Choose whichever method suits you.)

7. The text in the `mainContent` `<div>` is now the right size, but the sidebar is still too big. If you're thinking "new rule" or "class," stop it. Redefining the `<p>` tag is all that's needed. You could have done that in the first case, but I wanted to show you how to change the name of a selector in the CSS Styles panel.

   Switch to All mode, highlight `.twoColFixLtHdr #container #mainContent p`, and gently click the name once. You should now be able to edit the selector name. If you have difficulty, right-click and choose Edit Selector from the context menu. Change the selector to `p` (just the letter on its own). Press Enter/Return. The rule now applies to all paragraphs in the page.

8. The footer text is obscured by the background image, so let's adjust that too. Click anywhere inside the `footer` `<div>`, and switch to Current mode in the CSS Styles panel. The Dreamweaver CSS layout has already defined a selector called `.twoColFixLtHdr #footer p` with values for `margin` and `padding`.

   Click Add Property, and use the following settings:

   - color: #8A5B31

   - text-align: right

   Moving the text across to the right and giving it a dark brown color makes it stand out against the lighter part of the background image. Save `stroll.html` (and `stroll.css` if necessary), but keep them open for the next exercise.

Since it's a page about London, there's just one final touch that I'd like to add: Samuel Johnson's famous assertion that when a man is tired of London, he's tired of life.

Adding a pull quote

In the bad old days, the `<blockquote>` tag was misused by all and sundry to indent text. Well, let's be honest, it still is, but you know better, don't you? You're going to use `<blockquote>` for its real purpose—to highlight a quotation—and then style it with CSS to turn it into a distinctive pull quote.

1. Place your cursor at the end of the first paragraph in the sidebar, and press Enter/Return to create a new paragraph. Type: No, Sir, when a man is tired of London, he is tired of life; for there is in London all that life can afford. Press Enter/Return again, and type the attribution: Samuel Johnson, 1777.

2. Select both paragraphs in Design view, and click the Text Indent button in the Property inspector as shown here:

This wraps the paragraphs in a pair of `<blockquote>` tags.

The names of the Text Indent *button and the one to its left (*Text Outdent*) still reflect the old presentational type of markup that you should avoid in a standards-compliant site. When applied to ordinary text, think of them as "blockquote" and "remove blockquote" buttons. When used inside an ordered or unordered list, they create or remove a nested list.*

3. Click the New CSS Rule icon at the bottom of the CSS Styles panel. In the New CSS Rule dialog box, choose Tag as the Selector Type, select blockquote from the Tag drop-down menu, and click OK.

4. In the CSS Rule Definition dialog box, select the Type category, and set Font to Georgia, Times New Roman, Times, serif and Color to #FFFFFF. Next, select the Background category, and set Background color to #999999. You need to add a few more properties, but it's much easier to do the rest in the CSS Styles panel, because you can see exactly how they affect the look of the pull quote in Design view.

Click OK to save the current rules. The pull quote should now look like the one shown alongside.

> #mainContent div if it will always contain more content.
>
> No, Sir, when a man is tired of London, he is tired of life; for there is in London all that life can afford.
>
> Samuel Johnson, 1777
>
> Donec eu mi sed turpis feugiat feugiat. Integer turpis

5. The default margin around the <blockquote> is too wide, so position your cursor anywhere inside the quote, and select <blockquote> in the Tag selector. With the CSS Styles panel in Current mode, click Add Property to add the following settings:

- margin: 10px
- padding: 0

6. The text in the pull quote, now needs to be pulled in from the edges. Click the New CSS Rule icon, and use the following settings in the New CSS Rule dialog box:

- Selector Type: Advanced (IDs, pseudo-class selectors)
- Selector: blockquote p
- Define in: stroll.css

The descendant selector blockquote p restricts the rule to paragraphs inside a <blockquote>. Click OK, select the Box category in the CSS Rule Definition dialog box, and use the following settings for Padding and Margin:

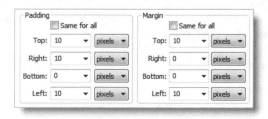

7. When you click OK to save the settings for the blockquote p rule, you'll see that the bottom line is flush with the gray background. Everything comes right in a moment.

   Select <blockquote> in the Tag selector again, and click Add Property in the Properties pane of the CSS Styles panel. Select background-image, and navigate to images/top_quote.gif. The image tiles horrendously, so add two further properties as follows:

   - background-repeat: no-repeat
   - background-position: left top

8. Just a couple more tweaks and you're there. The beginning of the pull quote overlaps the quotation marks of the background image, so click inside the first paragraph of the quote, and add the following property to the blockquote p style rule:

   - text-indent: 20px

9. CSS doesn't let you apply two background images in the same rule (you'll have to wait for CSS 3 to do that), so you need to create a new rule for the quote attribution within the <blockquote>. Position your cursor inside the paragraph that reads Samuel Johnson, 1777, and select the <p> tag in the Tag selector. Right-click and select Quick Tag Editor from the context menu to assign the paragraph an id attribute of quote_attrib (see "Using the Quick Tag Editor to set an id attribute" in Chapter 2).

10. Use the ID selector #quote_attrib to create a new CSS rule (choose Advanced as the Selector Type and #quote_attrib as Selector). In the CSS Rule Definition dialog box, select the Background category, and set Background image to images/btm_quote.gif, Repeat to no-repeat, Horizontal position to right, and Vertical position to bottom.

    Then use either the CSS Rule Definition dialog box or the CSS Styles panel to set the remaining properties:

    - font-size: 70%
    - margin-top: 0
    - padding-bottom: 30px
    - text-align: right
    - text-indent: 0

11. Save stroll.html (and stroll.css if necessary), and press F12/Opt+F12 to preview the page in a browser. It should look similar to Figure 6-7 (I've changed the headings to give the page a more authentic look). The ugly duckling in Figure 6-2 is now an elegant swan. You can compare your files with stroll_final.html and stroll_final.css in examples/ch06.

Figure 6-7. With a little imagination and work, the basic CSS layouts can be transformed into attractive pages.

Removing the CSS comments

The comments in the Dreamweaver CSS layouts are deliberately verbose—they're there to help you understand what each rule is for. Although commenting style sheets is a good idea, you'll probably want to get rid of the Dreamweaver comments once you're familiar with the layouts. It's very easy to do with Edit ➤ Find and Replace and a **regular expression**. Regular expressions describe patterns of text and other characters. They are like wildcard characters but much more powerful. The regular expression (regex) to describe a CSS comment looks like this:

```
/\*.+(?=\*/)\*/
```

Using a stored query in Find and Replace

Because this regex is so useful—and easy to mistype—I have created a stored query to automate the process. The following instructions show you how to remove the CSS comments from a style sheet:

1. Open the style sheet in the Document window. If the styles are embedded in the <head> of the document, switch to Code view.

2. Launch Find and Replace from the Edit menu (or press Ctrl+F/Cmd+F).

3. Click the Load Query icon at the top right of the Find and Replace dialog box (see Figure 6-8).

4. In the Load Query dialog box, browse to the tools folder, select css_comments_remove.dwr, and click Open. This loads the query into the Find and Replace dialog box and sets all the necessary options, as shown in Figure 6-8.

Load Query

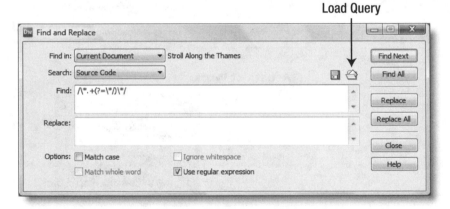

Figure 6-8. Regular expressions make complex find and replace operations possible.

5. To remove all the CSS comments in a single operation, click Replace All. You should be aware that this removes *all* comments, including any CSS hacks that look like comments. If you're in any way uncertain, use the following, more selective approach.

   To remove comments selectively, click Find Next to highlight the first one. Click Replace to remove it or Find Next to move to the next one.

6. Click Close to return to the Document window. After find and replace operations, Dreamweaver always opens the Results panel at the bottom of the workspace. To collapse it, press F7 or right-click the Options menu icon at the top right of the Results panel title bar and select Close Panel Group from the context menu.

Dreamweaver always remembers your last find and replace operation, so these settings will be displayed the next time you open the Find and Replace panel. Delete the regular expression from the Find field, and *deselect* the Use regular expression checkbox (unless you plan to use another regex). This final point is very important. When a find operation fails for no obvious reason, it's usually because you have selected the Use regular expression checkbox by accident.

> *You can save your own queries for reuse in the same way. Just click the* Save Query *icon to the left of the* Load Query *icon, create a suitable folder, and give the query a name.*

How was it for you?

Depending on your knowledge of CSS, this chapter is likely to have been relatively easy or something of a nightmare. If you fall into the latter category, I encourage you to persevere. It can take a long time for CSS to sink in. If you find it difficult to understand how to build your own style sheets, download a page from a site that you admire, complete with images and style sheets. Then use the CSS Styles panel to change or delete individual properties. Watch the effect of each change. Also select different parts of the page to analyze the cascade of styles.

Mastering the CSS Styles panel takes time and patience, but in combination with the greatly improved CSS rendering in Dreamweaver CS3, it will reward you in the end. Remember that Current mode shows the cascade as it affects the current insertion point or selection. Use the Tag selector at the bottom of the Document window to highlight specific elements, and then use the Summary for Selection and Rules panes to drill down to the CSS rules you want to inspect or edit.

You'll get some more practice with the CSS Styles panel in the next chapter when you use Spry widgets to spice up page layout. The widgets come with their own predefined style sheets, so you need to know how to adapt them to blend in with your own design.

6

7 BUILDING SITE NAVIGATION WITH THE SPRY MENU BAR

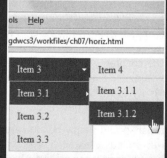

Efficient and attractive navigation is an important element in every website. The Spry menu bar is one of eight Spry widgets new to Dreamweaver CS3 (the others are described in the next two chapters). Its aim is create a flexible menu with flyout submenus that remains accessible even if JavaScript is turned off. In essence, it's an unordered list with optional nested lists for submenus. Styling is done with CSS, and the submenu flyouts are controlled by a combination of CSS and JavaScript. It comes in two versions: horizontal and vertical. Figure 7-1 shows what the horizontal version of the Spry menu bar looks like when integrated into the page built in the last chapter.

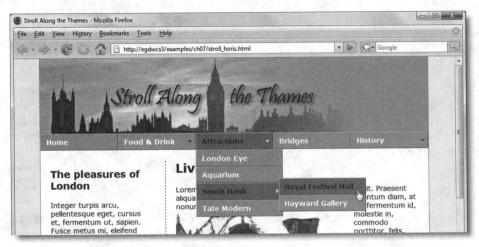

Figure 7-1. The Spry menu bar can be easily integrated into a page by making a few adjustments to the CSS.

Although you can insert a Spry menu bar in seconds, the downside is that styling it requires a good understanding of CSS. Knowing which style rules to change—and which to leave alone—presents more of a challenge. To help you, this chapter

- Describes the structure of the Spry menu bar
- Shows you how to insert and remove a Spry menu bar
- Explains the style rules that control a Spry menu bar
- Shows you how to customize a Spry menu bar

By the end of the chapter, you'll be able to transform the rather bland default design of a menu bar into something much more elegant like the menu in Figure 7-1. Because the Spry menu bar is styled with CSS, this chapter assumes you're familiar with the CSS Styles panel, which was described in detail in Chapter 5.

The Spry menu bar should finally put to rest the horrendous problems caused by the old JavaScript pop-up menus created in Fireworks MX 2004 and earlier. If you don't know about the old menus, ignorance is bliss. All you need to know about them is that they rendered your site totally inaccessible if JavaScript was disabled. Not only that, they prevented search engines from indexing anything beyond the first page. If you're interested in the sad, inside story of how they were developed, see www.losingfight.com/blog/2006/08/11/the-sordid-tale-of-mm_menufw_menujs.

Examining the structure of a Spry menu bar

New

Like all Spry widgets, the Spry menu bar relies on external files to control the way it looks and works, so you must always save your page in a Dreamweaver site (see Chapter 4 for site definition) before attempting to insert a menu bar. If you forget, Dreamweaver tells you to save your page, and opens the Save As dialog box.

The best way to understand how a Spry menu bar works is to launch Dreamweaver and start experimenting. Let's begin with a horizontal menu bar.

Inserting a horizontal menu bar

1. Create a blank HTML page in Dreamweaver by selecting File ➤ New. In the New Document dialog box, select Blank Page, HTML as the Page Type, and <none> for Layout. Make sure that no style sheets are listed under Attach CSS file before clicking Create. Alternatively, just select New ➤ HTML from the welcome screen. Save the file as horiz.html in workfiles/ch07.

2. Select the Spry tab on the Insert bar, and click the Spry Menu Bar button (it's the fourth from the right) as shown in the following screenshot:

3. This opens the Spry Menu Bar dialog box. There are just two options: Horizontal and Vertical. Select Horizontal, and click OK.

4. Dreamweaver inserts a horizontal Spry menu bar at the top of the page, as shown in Figure 7-2. Like all Spry widgets, the menu bar is surrounded in Design view by a turquoise border and a tab at the top-left corner. The tab tells you what type of widget it is, followed by the widget's id attribute. Dreamweaver calls the first menu bar on a page MenuBar1. The next one is MenuBar2, and so on. This means you can have as many menu bars on a page as you want (don't go mad—think of usability).

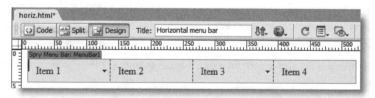

Figure 7-2. The Spry menu bar is given basic styling ready for you to customize.

7

5. Save `horiz.html`. If this is the first time you have inserted a Spry menu bar in the current site, Dreamweaver prompts you to save the dependent files. It locates the files in the Spry assets folder. By default, this is called SpryAssets, but you can specify a different location in your site definition (see "Setting up for Spry" in Chapter 4).

The dependent files are the external JavaScript file, `SpryMenuBar.js`, the external style sheet, `SpryMenuBarHorizontal.css`, and four arrow images that indicate the presence of submenus. Once the files have been copied to the Spry assets folder, they are shared with further instances of the menu bar in the same site.

6. Click OK to save the dependent files, and press F12/Opt+F12 to preview `horiz.html` in a browser. As you can see in Figure 7-3, you already have a fully working menu bar ready for you to customize. You can freely add or remove items and submenus and change the default colors. I'll show you how to do that shortly, but first let's take a look at the vertical menu bar.

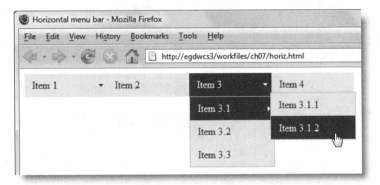

Figure 7-3. The structure and styling of the default menu bar are fully customizable.

Inserting a vertical menu bar

1. Create another blank page, and save it as `vertical.html` in `workfiles/ch07`.

2. Select the Spry Menu Bar button on the Spry tab of the Insert bar. Alternatively, choose Insert ➤ Spry ➤ Spry Menu Bar.

3. Select the Vertical radio button in the Spry Menu Bar dialog box, and click OK.

4. Dreamweaver inserts a vertical menu bar, as shown in the following screenshot:

5. Save vertical.html. This time, Dreamweaver prompts you to save only one dependent file: the style sheet, SpryMenuBarVertical.css. All other dependent files are identical to those used by the horizontal menu bar.

6. Press F12/Opt+F12 to preview the page in a browser. It looks identical to the horizontal menu bar shown in Figure 7-3. The only differences are that the menu items are stacked vertically and the first-level submenus fly out to the right rather than beneath the main menu.

Looking at the XHTML structure

The Spry menu bar is a series of nested unordered lists (<ul>) styled with CSS to look like a series of buttons. The submenu flyouts are controlled by JavaScript. You can see the underlying structure of the menu either by switching to Code view or by toggling the Turn Styles Off/On button in the Property inspector. (If you can't see the button, click the Spry Menu Bar tab at the top left of the menu bar.) Figure 7-4 shows the horizontal menu bar in horiz.html, but the structure is identical in vertical.html. The different look and functionality are controlled entirely by JavaScript and CSS.

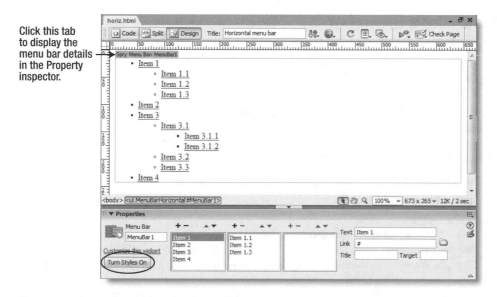

Click this tab to display the menu bar details in the Property inspector.

Figure 7-4. When styles are turned off, you can see the underlying list structure of the menu bar.

If you switch to Code view, you'll see that Dreamweaver has added links to the external JavaScript file and style sheet (see lines 6 and 7 in Figure 7-5, on the next page). To save space, I have used Code collapse (see "Using the Coding toolbar" in Chapter 1) to hide the XHTML code for the nested lists on lines 11–33.

Immediately below the nested lists (on lines 34–38), Dreamweaver has inserted a block of JavaScript. This initializes the widget object. All Spry widgets are JavaScript objects, which need to be initialized when the page first loads. Dreamweaver locates the initialization script just before the closing </body> tag. If a widget stops working, you should always check that you haven't deleted this script by mistake. If you have, you need to go back and reinsert the widget from scratch.

Figure 7-5. Dreamweaver adds three sections of code in addition to the list structure (hidden using Code collapse).

Removing a menu bar

Removing a menu bar is quite simple: click the Spry Menu Bar tab at the top left of the menu (see Figure 7-4), and press Delete. That's it—not only is the XHTML removed but so too are the links to the external JavaScript file and style sheet, as well as the initialization script at the bottom of the page.

Try it now with horiz.html. Switch to Code view, and you'll see just the default code for a blank page. However, if you look in the Files panel, you'll see that the six dependent files in the Spry assets folder have *not* been removed. This ensures that they remain accessible to other pages that may rely on them.

The links to the external JavaScript file and style sheet are not removed if another instance of the same widget exists on the page.

> It's important to remove menu bars and other widgets cleanly by selecting the Spry Menu Bar tab and pressing Delete. Otherwise, the widget initialization script remains in the underlying code and might trigger errors when the page is loaded into a browser.

Editing a menu bar

Since the menu bar is just a series of nested unordered lists, you can turn off the styles, as shown in Figure 7-4, and edit the menu directly in Design view. However, it's much more convenient to do it in the Property inspector. Place your cursor anywhere inside the menu bar, and click the Spry Menu Bar tab at the top left to display the menu bar details in the Property inspector. The following screenshot shows how you might build a menu bar for stroll.html from the previous chapter:

The three columns in the center of the Property inspector show the menu hierarchy, with the top level on the left. When you select an item in this column, the middle one displays the contents of the related submenu. The right column displays the next level down from whatever is selected in the middle one.

To edit a menu item, highlight it, and fill in the fields on the right of the Property inspector as follows:

- Text: This is the label that you want to appear on the menu button.

- Link: This is the page you want to link to. Either type the file name directly into the field or click the folder icon to the right of the field to browse to the target page.

- Title: This adds a `title` attribute to the link. Most browsers display this as a tooltip. It can also improve accessibility for visually impaired people using a screen reader by describing the link's destination more fully.

- Target: This adds a `target` attribute to the link. This should normally be used only with frames. A value of _blank opens the linked page in a new browser window. Although there are sometimes legitimate reasons for wanting to do so, the practice is widely frowned upon, so use with care.

To add an item, click the plus (+) button at the top of the relevant column. To delete an item, select it and click the minus (–) button. You can also change the order of items by highlighting them and using the up and down arrows at the top of each column.

As the preceding screenshot shows, the Property inspector lets you work on two levels of submenus. To create a submenu at a deeper level, insert another nested list either by turning off styles as shown in Figure 7-4 or editing directly in Code view. Two levels of submenus should be sufficient for most purposes. If your menus require more levels, it's probably time to rethink the structure of your site.

After editing a menu bar in an existing page, select one of the items in the left column before moving to another part of the page. If you forget to do this, the submenus remain exposed in Design view, preventing you from working on the underlying part of the page.

If this happens, position your cursor inside any part of the menu bar, and select the Spry Menu Bar tab at the top left. This populates the Property inspector with the menu bar details again. You can then select an item in the left column to hide the submenus.

Maintaining accessibility with the Spry menu bar

The Spry menu bar is much more accessible than the old JavaScript pop-up menus, because the underlying structure and links are written in XHTML, rather than being obscured in JavaScript that search engines can't follow. However, it's important to realize

7

that JavaScript still controls the submenu flyouts. If someone visits your site with JavaScript disabled or an ancient browser that can't understand the Spry code, the only parts of the menu that remain accessible are the top-level items.

This means that you should always link the top-level items to a real page and not just use dummy links to act as triggers for the submenus. So, for instance, if anyone clicks Attractions in the menu shown in Figure 7-1, it should link to an introductory page leading to that section. Unless you do so, some visitors may never be able to get to the pages about London Eye and so on.

Customizing the styles

Although the color scheme of the default style sheets isn't exactly inspiring, the structural layout has been carefully thought out, so you don't need to change many properties to achieve a rapid transformation of the menu bar. Open SpryMenuBarHorizontal.css and SpryMenuBarVertical.css in the Document window. Both are divided into the following sections:

- **Layout information**: This controls the structure, such as font size and menu widths.
- **Design information**: This styles the color scheme and borders.
- **Submenu indication**: The rules in this section control the display of the arrows that indicate the existence of a submenu. Change these only if you need to make adjustments to the submenu arrows.
- **Browser hacks**: These rules deal with bugs in Internet Explorer. You should leave them alone.

The first thing to note is that both style sheets contain almost identical rules, although the names of the CSS selectors reflect the orientation of the menu. The horizontal bar uses the class MenuBarHorizontal, and the vertical one uses MenuBarVertical. There are a few other things to note:

- All the measurements use relative units (ems and percentages).
- The width of the horizontal menu is set to auto, but the vertical menu has a fixed width of 8em.
- The width of the menu items in both versions is fixed at 8em; submenus are 8.2em.

Changing the menu width

The use of ems for the width of the menu and submenu items makes the menu bar very fluid. For a fixed layout, such as that used in stroll.html in the previous chapter, you need to change all instances of 8em and 8.2em in the Layout Information section to a fixed width in pixels.

Changing colors

All colors are defined in the Design Information section of the style sheet. Changing them is simply a matter of substituting the existing hexadecimal numbers for background-color and color in the relevant style rules. The default colors are light gray (#EEE) for the background and dark gray (#333) for the text of menu items in their normal state, and navy blue (#33C) for the background and white (#FFF) for the text of items in a rollover state.

> The Spry menu bar style sheets use hexadecimal shorthand, which uses just three digits instead of six to denote colors. Hexadecimal colors can be shortened when the six-digit version consists of three pairs in which both numbers are the same. So #FFFFFF becomes #FFF and #3333CC becomes #33C, but numbers like #3333C0 cannot be shortened. Using shorthand is a matter of personal preference. It makes no difference to the way the styles are rendered.

The menu bar uses JavaScript to assign a class dynamically to the links when the mouse pointer moves over them. For some reason, Adobe has put the selectors for this dynamic class in a separate style rule, which duplicates the a:hover and a:focus rules like this:

```
ul.MenuBarHorizontal a:hover, ul.MenuBarHorizontal a:focus
{
  background-color: #33C;
  color: #FFF;
}
ul.MenuBarHorizontal a.MenuBarItemHover, ul.MenuBarHorizontal
a.MenuBarItemSubmenuHover, ul.MenuBarHorizontal a.MenuBarSubmenuVisible
{
  background-color: #33C;
  color: #FFF;
}
```

This makes it difficult to edit the rules in the CSS Styles panel. Since both rules contain the same properties and values, it's simpler to combine the selectors like this:

```
ul.MenuBarHorizontal a:hover, ul.MenuBarHorizontal a:focus,
ul.MenuBarHorizontal a.MenuBarItemHover, ul.MenuBarHorizontal
a.MenuBarItemSubmenuHover, ul.MenuBarHorizontal a.MenuBarSubmenuVisible
{
  background-color: #33C;
  color: #FFF;
}
```

Don't forget to add a comma after a:focus in the first line of the selector. Otherwise, it won't work. The rules for the vertical menu bar are identical, except for the class name MenuBarVertical.

Adding borders

By default, a light gray border is added to the outer edge of the submenu containers in both the horizontal and vertical menu bars. In addition, the vertical menu bar has the same border around the entire menu. Change the following rules to alter the menu and submenu borders:

```
ul.MenuBarHorizontal ul
ul.MenuBarVertical
ul.MenuBarVertical ul
```

Individual menu items don't have any borders, so the menu looks seamless. If you want to give your menu a more button-like feel, apply a border to the following rules:

```
ul.MenuBarHorizontal a
ul.MenuBarVertical a
```

The links in the menu bar are styled to display as a block and have no fixed width. Consequently, applying a border to the link style has the advantage of surrounding the individual menu items without affecting either height or width. You'll see how this is done when inserting a menu bar into stroll.html.

Changing the font

The font-size property is set to 100% in two separate rules: ul.MenuBarHorizontal and ul.MenuBarHorizontal li (ul.MenuBarVertical and ul.MenuBarVertical li). Change the wrong one and you get the mysterious shrinking text shown in Figure 7-6.

Figure 7-6. The text gets progressively smaller if you change font-size in the li selector.

The style rules that affect the size of the text in the horizontal menu bar are ul.MenuBarHorizontal and ul.MenuBarHorizontal li. Both of them set font-size to 100%. The shrinking text in Figure 7-6 was caused by changing font-size in ul.MenuBarHorizontal li to 85%.

Although this reduces the text in the main menu items to 85 percent of its original size, the nesting of the submenus results in the first-level submenu being displayed at 85 percent × 85 percent—in other words, 72.25 percent. The second-level submenu is further reduced by another 85 percent—resulting in 61.4 percent.

To prevent this happening, leave the ul.MenuBar Horizontal li selector at 100%, and change only the first one. The following rules produce a consistent text size:

```
ul.MenuBarHorizontal
{
  font-size: 85%;
}
ul.MenuBarHorizontal li
{
  font-size: 100%;
}
```

The rules for the vertical menu bar are identical, except for the class name MenuBarVertical.

If you decide to use pixels instead of percentages, it doesn't matter which rule you change. You should be aware, however, that using pixels for fonts can cause accessibility problems for people with poor eyesight. Many designers mistakenly believe that using pixels for font sizes "locks" their design. It doesn't, because all browsers—apart from Internet Explorer for Windows—permit users to adjust font sizes by default, and Internet Explorer's accessibility features have an option to ignore font sizes. If a change in font size causes your page to fall apart, you need to rethink your design criteria—fast.

Styling a Spry menu bar

If you're completely at home editing style sheets in Code view, the preceding sections tell you all that you need to know about customizing the CSS for a Spry menu bar. The disadvantage of working in Code view is that you can't see how your changes affect the design and fit in with the rest of your page until you save the style sheet and switch back to the web page in Design view. So, I'm going to devote the rest of the chapter to showing you how to customize a Spry menu bar using the CSS Styles panel. Although it involves more steps than editing the style sheet directly in Code view, working through the next few pages should give you a much better understanding of how the CSS Styles panel works.

I'm going to show you how to add a horizontal menu bar to stroll.html, the CSS layout that you styled in the last chapter. You can see the finished menu in Figure 7-1 at the beginning of this chapter.

To wrap or not to wrap, that is the question . . .

Two common diseases are prevalent in the CSS community: "classitis" and "divitis." The first usually afflicts beginners, who style everything with a class, creating a new form of tag soup little better than <font> tags. Then they learn that ID selectors are more powerful, so they start wrapping everything in a <div>, cluttering up the page with lots of meaningless and unnecessary wrapper elements.

I've suffered from both diseases in my time, so my first instinct was to use the horizontal Spry menu bar without a <div>. After all, it's an unordered list, which is a block element, and it has its own ID, so it should be possible to drop one into a page without the need for a wrapper. After much experimentation, though, I discovered that the only reliable way to insert a horizontal menu bar in a fixed-width design like stroll.html is to wrap it in a <div> and give the <div> both a width and a height. The height is needed because all the menu items are floated. Without the fixed size <div>, the design behaves unpredictably in some browsers. Figure 7-8 later in the chapter shows the sort of problem avoided.

Inserting a <div> for the horizontal menu bar

Continue working with your files from the last chapter. Alternatively, copy stroll_horiz_start.html from examples/ch07 to workfiles/ch07 and stroll_horiz_start.css from examples/styles to your styles folder. Rename the files stroll_horiz.html and stroll_horiz.css, and update any links when prompted.

1. With stroll_horiz.html open in the Document window, select the Layout tab of the Insert bar, and click the Insert Div Tag button, as shown here:

> *Frequently used features are duplicated in several places in Dreamweaver. Although the* Insert Div Tag *button is on the* Common *tab of the Insert bar, the reason I'm using the* Layout *tab this time is because it offers access to both* Insert Div Tag *and* Spry Menu Bar *(two buttons further to the right). It's useful to get to know the alternative locations of features you use the most.*

2. The Insert Div Tag dialog box lets you specify where the <div> is to be located. It offers the following options:

   - At the current insertion point
   - Before a specific tag
   - After the start of a tag—in other words, nested inside
   - Before the end of a tag—again, nested inside just before the closing tag
   - After a specific tag
   - Wrapped around the current selection (available only when a section of code is selected in the Document window)

   You need to insert the menu after the header <div>, so select After tag from the Insert drop-down menu. Dreamweaver automatically populates the drop-down menu alongside with all elements that have an ID. Select <div id="header"> as shown here:

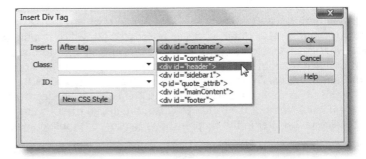

3. Let's call the new `<div>` nav. Type nav in the ID field, and click the New CSS Style button at the bottom of the Insert Div Tag dialog box.

Dw

Changed

4. Dreamweaver CS3 now populates the New CSS Rule dialog box automatically with the correct details, selecting the Advanced radio button, naming the selector #nav, and suggesting defining the rule in the existing style sheet. Click OK to accept.

   If more than one style sheet is attached, you can select another from the drop-down menu. Alternatively, you can create a new style sheet or opt to define the rule in the `<head>` of the page.

5. In the CSS Rule Definition dialog box, select the Box category, and set Width to 780px and Height to 2.2em. Click OK to save the rule. This returns you to the Insert Div Tag dialog box. Click OK again to close it. You should now have a `<div>` with some placeholder text inside it just beneath the header, as shown here:

I calculated the height for the nav `<div>` by adding together the top and bottom padding (0.5em each) for the links in the menu bar. The font-size is set to 100%, which is the same as 1em. The extra .2em was needed to make sure everything fits. By using a fixed pixel width, the menu bar remains snugly inside the container `<div>`, even if the user increases the font size. Equally, using relative units for the height ensures that the nav `<div>` expands vertically to accommodate enlarged text.

> *When using a vertical menu bar, you can simply drop it into a sidebar, which provides the necessary wrapper. Unless the sidebar is particularly wide, there is no need for a separate `<div>` for the menu itself.*

Building the navigation structure

Now that you have created space for it, the next step is to insert the menu bar and create the links.

Inserting and editing the menu bar

1. You need to get rid of the placeholder text for the nav `<div>`. Normally, pressing Delete when the text is highlighted is sufficient. However, it's a good idea to open Split view to make sure that it's only the text between the `<div>` tags that is selected, as shown in the following screenshot:

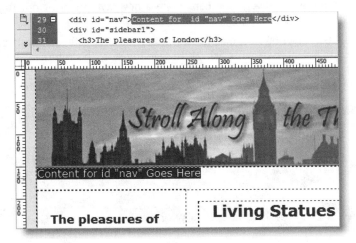

If necessary, go into Code view to adjust the selection and press Delete. Make sure that your cursor is between the empty `<div>` tags.

2. Click the Spry Menu Bar button on the Layout tab of the Insert bar, and insert a horizontal menu bar.

3. Save `stroll_horiz.html`. If you did the other exercises earlier in this chapter, Dreamweaver won't prompt you to save dependent files this time, as they have already been copied to the Spry assets folder. Figures 7-7 and 7-8 show why it was necessary to give a height to the nav `<div>`.

Figure 7-7. With a height, the nav `<div>` maintains the integrity of the page layout.

Giving the nav `<div>` both a width and a height keeps the structure of the page intact (see Figure 7-7). If you give it just a width, the nav `<div>` collapses vertically and the sidebar attempts to move up into the empty space, as shown in Figure 7-8.

Figure 7-8. The nav `<div>` needs a height to prevent the sidebar from attempting to float into any empty space.

4. Select the Spry Menu Bar tab, and edit the menu items as described in "Editing a menu bar" earlier in the chapter. If you want to follow my structure, here it is:

```
Home
Food & Drink
        Restaurants
        Bars
Attractions
        London Eye
        Aquarium
        South Bank
            Royal Festival Hall
            Hayward Gallery
            Tate Modern
Bridges
History
        St Paul's Cathedral
        Tower of London
        Houses of Parliament
```

In a live website, you need to create links to real pages, but for the purposes of the example page, I have left the value of each link as # so the menu bar displays correctly, even though it doesn't link to other pages.

5. Save stroll_horiz.html, and press F12/Opt+F12 to view the page in a browser. If you have used the same menu structure as me, you'll see that a long item, such as Food & Drink, wraps onto a second line. In Internet Explorer, the sidebar still displays in its correct position, but in more standards-compliant browsers, such as Firefox and Opera, the sidebar is pushed across to the right, as shown in Figure 7-9 on the next page.

7

Figure 7-9. Long menu items prevent subsequent floated elements from moving to the left of the viewport.

6. To rectify this, you need to add a clear: left rule to the sidebar's style block. Open the CSS Styles panel in All mode, and expand the stroll_horiz.css tree menu if necessary. Select .twoColFixLtHdr #sidebar1 in the All Rules pane, and click Add property in the Properties pane. Select clear, and then select left as its value. Save the external style sheet, if necessary, and preview the page in a browser again. This time the sidebar should be back in its proper place.

Customizing the design

The final stage is to customize the design features of the menu bar to fit the rest of the page.

Editing the default selectors

1. All style rules exclusive to the menu bar are in SpryMenuBarHorizontal.css in the Spry assets folder. Since this is common to all horizontal menu bars, it's a good idea to give it a different name. Select SpryMenuBarHorizontal.css in the Files panel, and gently click the file name once to open its name for editing (alternatively, press F2 or right-click and select Edit ➤ Rename from the context menu). Change the style sheet's name to SpryMenuBarHorizontal_stroll.css, and press Enter/Return.

   Accept the option to update links when prompted. This updates the link to the external style sheet in both horiz.html and stroll_horiz.html. Since horiz.html was only a test page, it doesn't matter on this occasion, but in a working project, you need to check which links are being updated.

2. Open stroll_horiz.html in Code view. As explained in the last chapter, Dreamweaver adds new style sheets immediately before the closing </head> tag. This puts the styles in SpryMenuBarHorizontal_stroll.css lower in the cascade than the style rules in the conditional comments. Although nothing is likely to clash, it's good practice to cut and paste the link above the conditional comments. Place it immediately after the link to stroll_horiz.css.

3. Double-click SpryMenuBarHorizontal_stroll.css in the Files panel (it should be in the Spry assets folder, the default name is SpryAssets) to open it in Code view, and locate the following section:

```
98   /* Menu items that have mouse over or focus have a blue background and white text */
99   ul.MenuBarHorizontal a:hover, ul.MenuBarHorizontal a:focus
100  {
101      background-color: #33C;
102      color: #FFF;
103  }
104  /* Menu items that are open with submenus are set to MenuBarItemHover with a blue background
     and white text */
105  ul.MenuBarHorizontal a.MenuBarItemHover, ul.MenuBarHorizontal a.MenuBarItemSubmenuHover,
     ul.MenuBarHorizontal a.MenuBarSubmenuVisible
106  {
107      background-color: #33C;
108      color: #FFF;
109  }
```

4. Insert a comma after a:focus at the end of line 99 in the preceding screenshot, and delete lines 100–104 (use the line numbers in the screenshot only as a guide; it's the code that matters). You should end up with this:

```
98   /* Menu items that have mouse over or focus have a blue background and white text */
99   ul.MenuBarHorizontal a:hover, ul.MenuBarHorizontal a:focus,
100  ul.MenuBarHorizontal a.MenuBarItemHover, ul.MenuBarHorizontal a.MenuBarItemSubmenuHover,
     ul.MenuBarHorizontal a.MenuBarSubmenuVisible
101  {
102      background-color: #33C;
103      color: #FFF;
104  }
```

This change makes it possible to edit the rollover colors of the menu bar in the CSS Styles panel, as explained earlier. Save SpryMenuBarHorizontal_stroll.css, and close it. I'll come back to customizing the colors in the next section, but first let's sort out the width of the menu and submenus.

The remaining changes to the styles will be made through the CSS Styles panel. With stroll_horiz.html open in the Document window, click anywhere inside the menu bar, and open the CSS Styles panel in Current mode. Make sure that the Show cascade of rules for selected tag icon is selected, as recommended in "Inspecting the cascade in Current mode" in the last chapter (see Figure 6-5). The menu bar has a lot of style rules, so you may find it best to collapse all other panels and expand the CSS Styles panel so that you can see everything without the need to scroll.

Customizing the menu bar: setting widths

The default width of the menu items is 8em, but this is a fixed width design, so you need to adjust the menu bar to fit. There are five top-level items, and the width of the container <div> is 780 pixels. A quick calculation reveals that dividing 780 by 5 equals 156. So that's the width each item needs to be.

1. The menu bar is a styled unordered list, so the width of each item is controlled by the `<li>` element. With your cursor inside the menu bar, select `<li>` in the Tag selector at the bottom of the Document window. This highlights the current `<li>` element and displays the relevant style rule in the Properties pane of the CSS Styles panel.

   The width property for `ul.MenuBarHorizontal li` is set to 8em. Click inside the value field for width. It should change into two drop-down menus like this:

   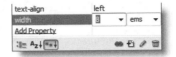

   Type 156px into the left drop-down, and press Enter/Return to save the new value.

   The menu should now fit neatly across the page, as shown in Figure 7-10. Press F4 to hide the panel groups if you can't see the full width of the design. To bring the panel groups back, press F4 again.

Figure 7-10. Giving the `<li>` elements a fixed pixel width matches the width of the container `<div>`.

> *The Property inspector at the bottom of the workspace might still display the width as 8em. This is unimportant, as it's sometimes slow to refresh values changed in an external style sheet. The values that matter are those displayed in the CSS Styles panel. If you toggle F4, the value in the Property inspector will be refreshed.*

2. The width of the submenus is controlled independently. The default is 8.2em, just a little wider than the top-level items. Some of my submenu items are long, so I decided to set the submenu width to 175px. Since the submenus aren't normally displayed in Design view, you need to coax one of them out of hiding to work on the style rules.

The following diagram shows how you do it:

1. Click the tab at the top left of the menu bar to display its details in the Property inspector.

2. Select an item that has a submenu.

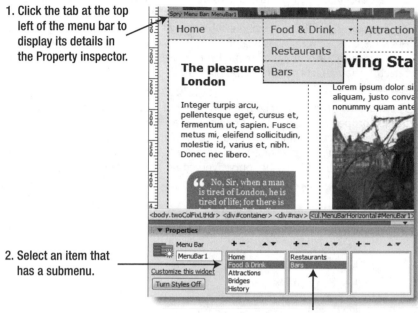

3. Select one of the submenu items.

3. Now position your cursor inside one of the submenu items in Design view. The details of the menu bar will disappear from the Property inspector, but that doesn't matter. Your interest now lies in selecting the submenu <li> element to edit its style rule in the CSS Styles panel. The Tag selector at the bottom of the Document window displays the hierarchy of tags leading to the current selection. As you can see in Figure 7-11, with the cursor inside one of the submenu items, the hierarchy of the menu bar runs like this:

<ul.MenuBarHorizontal#MenuBar1> <li> <ul> <li> <a>

To access the style rule for the submenu, select the second <li> in the Tag selector. This reveals the width property as 8.2em, as shown in Figure 7-11. Change this value to 175px.

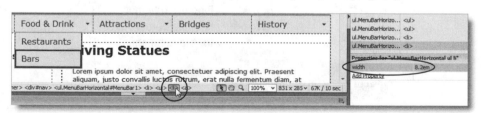

Figure 7-11. Accessing the style rule for submenu items

4. The default menu bar adds a light gray border to the submenus, but I'm going to add a border to each menu item instead, so let's get rid of the default border. Select the <ul> tag immediately to the left of the currently highlighted tag in the Tag selector. This selects the whole submenu. As you can see from Figure 7-12, the Rules pane lists several rules beginning with ul.MenuBarHorizontal. Drag the left column wider to make it easier to find ul.MenuBarHorizontal ul. This is a descendant selector that affects all unordered lists nested inside the menu bar—in other words, all submenus.

There are two rules for `ul.MenuBarHorizontal ul`. The second one contains the border property. Select it, select border in the Properties pane, and press Delete or click the trash can icon at the bottom right of the CSS Styles panel. This leaves an empty style rule, but that doesn't matter. You can leave it in case you want to add different properties later. Of course, you could add a different style border to the submenus here, if you prefer.

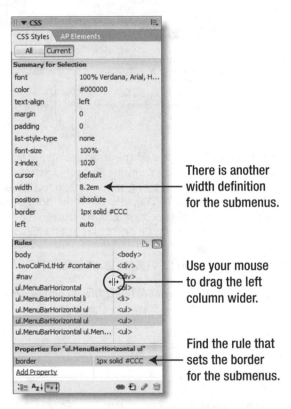

There is another
width definition
for the submenus.

Use your mouse
to drag the left
column wider.

Find the rule that
sets the border
for the submenus.

Figure 7-12. Current mode reveals precisely which rules affect the current selection.

5. Now, this is where a solid understanding of CSS and of how the CSS Styles panel works in Current mode comes in handy. Take a close look at the Summary for Selection pane at the top of the panel. It says the `width` property is `8.2em` (see Figure 7-12). But surely you changed that in step 3! What's going on?

The answer is that the width property for the submenus is set in two places: the rule for nested list items *and* the rule for nested lists. The 8.2em you can see now is the second of these two rules. You need to change it, too.

6. Select the width property highlighted in Figure 7-12. This populates the Properties pane at the bottom of the CSS Styles panel with the rules for the first of the two selectors for ul.MenuBarHorizontal ul, as shown here.

Why are there two selectors for ul.MenuBarHorizontal ul? Cast your mind back to "Customizing the styles" earlier in the chapter. The style sheet for the Spry menu bar is divided into sections. The rule that you edited in step 4 belongs to the Design Information section. This rule belongs to the Layout Information section.

Change the width property to 175px.

Keep stroll_horiz.html open, as I'll show you how to adjust the colors next.

Customizing the menu bar: changing colors and fonts

The main colors of the Spry menu bar are controlled in style rules applied to the links. These instructions assume that you have edited the menu bar style sheet as described in "Editing the default selectors."

1. Position your cursor anywhere inside any menu item that *doesn't* lead to a sub-menu. In stroll_horiz.html, this means Home, Bridges, or any ordinary link in a submenu. The title bar of the Properties pane should read Properties for "ul.MenuBarHorizontal a:hover... This displays the rollover colors for the menu items.

   Change background-color from #33C to #7A85AD (dark mauve) and color from #FFF to #333 (very dark gray). Don't forget the hash or pound sign (#) at the beginning of the number. Because these are rollover colors, you won't see any change in Design view.

2. In the Rules pane, highlight ul.MenuBarHorizontal a immediately above the currently selected rule. This displays the rules that apply to all links in the menu bar. Change background-color from #EEE to #A3AAC6 (a slightly lighter mauve) and color from #333 to #FFF (white). This time the colors are immediately reflected in Design view.

3. To make the links look like buttons, you need to put a border around them. Adding a lighter color for the top and left borders and a darker one for the right and bottom borders creates the effect of a raised button. A neat way of finding the right colors is to create a rectangle in a graphics program like Fireworks, give the rectangle the same color as your buttons, and then apply an inner bevel effect. The following illustration shows how it's done in Fireworks CS3.

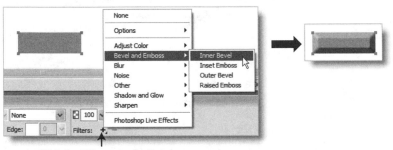

Click the Filters plus button
to apply an inner bevel.

Use an eyedropper tool to find the appropriate colors for the lighter and darker borders, and make a note of the hexadecimal number.

> *In this case, it's probably easier to use the eyedropper tool in your graphics program, but there's a useful trick if you want to copy the color of an object outside Dreamweaver. Adjust the size of the Dreamweaver workspace so that you can see the object, click the Color Picker, and hold down the mouse button. You can then drag the eyedropper outside Dreamweaver. The Color Picker inside Dreamweaver constantly updates to show the color currently being sampled by the eyedropper. Release the mouse button when you find the color that you want.*

4. Now add the border to each side of the links by clicking Add Property and adding the following properties and values:

- border-left: #C4C9DB 1px solid
- border-top: #C4C9DB 1px solid
- border-right: #565968 1px solid
- border-bottom: #565968 1px solid

The values in the CSS Styles panel should now look like this:

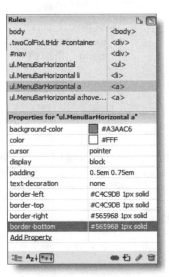

5. There's just one final change: the font would look better if it were bold and slightly smaller. As I explained in "Customizing the styles" earlier in the chapter, the place to change font properties is in the ul.MenuBarHorizontal rule. As you can see from the preceding screenshot, the ul.MenuBarHorizontal selector is listed in the Rules pane. Yet if you select it, the font-size property is struck through. This can be one of the most frustrating aspects of working with the CSS Styles panel in Current mode, but it's also one of its most powerful features.

To understand why font-size is struck through, hover your mouse pointer over the property name. A tooltip should appear, as shown in Figure 7-13, explaining the effect of the CSS cascade.

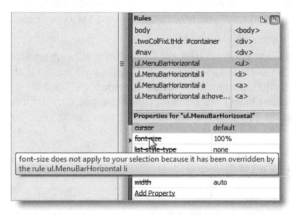

Figure 7-13. The CSS Styles panel in Current mode displays tooltips that explain where a rule is overridden.

Dreamweaver tells you that the property is overridden elsewhere, because Current mode always reflects the cascade as it affects *the current selection in the Document window*. Since your cursor is inside a menu item, the Properties pane doesn't simply show you the ul.MenuBarHorizontal rules; it also explains how they are applied to a menu item. Once you appreciate the subtle ways of how the position of your cursor affects the display in Current mode, your ability to edit complex style rules takes a giant leap forward.

6. As Figure 7-6 showed earlier in the chapter, changing font-size in the wrong rule results in mysteriously shrinking text. So, to make sure you edit the correct rule, click <ul.MenuBarHorizontal#MenuBar1> in the Tag selector at the bottom of the Document window. Change the value of font-size to 90%, click Add Property to add the font-weight property, and set it to bold, as shown here:

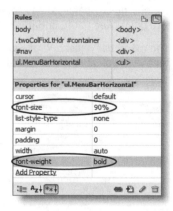

7. Test the page in a browser. If you have been using the settings that I recommended in "Setting your CSS preferences" in Chapter 5, there's no need to save the style sheet unless you had it open in the Document window. Otherwise, save it before viewing the page. You should now have an attractive menu bar as shown in Figure 7-1 at the beginning of this chapter.

You can check your files against stroll_horiz.html in examples/ch07 and SpryMenuBarHorizontal_stroll.css in the SpryAssets folder.

Even if the text size is enlarged, the page structure is preserved, and the dark gray rollover text ensures that spillover text remains reasonably legible. Enlarging the text does disrupt the original design of the page, but certain trade-offs are inevitable in web design. The purpose here has been to show you how to customize a Spry menu bar, rather than seek a definitive answer to accessibility issues.

These instructions have concentrated on customizing a horizontal menu bar, but the process is exactly the same for a vertical one. The main difference is that you don't need to wrap a vertical menu bar in a <div> of its own. However, if you do decide to use a separate <div>, it shouldn't have a fixed height. Otherwise, you may run into display problems if the user enlarges the text in the browser.

A mixed blessing

There's no doubt that the Spry menu bar is much more accessible and search engine-friendly than the old Fireworks pop-up menus. However, I'm sure that many noncoders will find customizing the CSS an uphill struggle. Instead of creating the menu buttons in a graphic environment and letting the software take care of the coding, much more is left up to the designer's individual skill. It's possible that a third-party developer will create an extension to simplify the process of changing the colors in a more intuitive way. Alternatively, it's an enhancement that the Dreamweaver engineers should certainly consider.

In spite of the extra work involved, the Spry menu bar *is* an improvement on the old pop-up menus, which deserve to be consigned to cyber oblivion. Moreover, the CSS skills required to customize a menu bar are essential for building modern standards-compliant sites. In my own experience, CSS is not something you can pick up overnight, but once the various pieces begin to fall together, progress becomes much more rapid. So, if you're struggling, keep at it, and it will all come together in the end.

The menu bar is just one of eight Spry widgets new to Dreamweaver CS3. In the next chapter, we'll look at three more: tabbed panels, the accordion, and collapsible panels.

8 SPRUCING UP CONTENT WITH SPRY WIDGETS

A common dilemma with website design is too little space to display all the content that needs to be on a particular page. Spry widgets to the rescue . . . In common with other Ajax frameworks, Spry makes it easy to build components—such as accordions and tabbed and collapsible panels—that slot into a web page and give it a much more dynamic feel. The Spry Tabbed Panels (see Figure 8-1) and Spry Accordion (see Figure 8-18) are a series of interlinked panels, in which just one panel is open at a time. Spry Collapsible Panels work independently, so they can be opened and closed in any combination.

From the user's point of view, all three are intuitive metaphors that shouldn't need any explanation. Equally important, from the developer's point of view, they are easy to insert and customize. Dreamweaver CS3 does all the Spry coding for you. All you have to do is supply the content and skin the components with CSS. If you struggled with the Spry menu bar in the last chapter, you'll be pleased to know that the style sheets of these Spry widgets are a lot simpler to edit.

What this chapter covers

- Saving space with tabbed panels, accordions, and collapsible panels
- Preserving text formatting with Paste Special
- Selecting harmonious colors
- Styling user interface widgets
- Understanding Spry objects, methods, and properties
- Opening and closing panels from hyperlinks
- Removing widgets cleanly from a page

In this chapter, I'll show you how to insert a set of tabbed panels, an accordion, and a series of collapsible panels in stroll.html, the page that you've been using for the past two chapters (there's a copy in the download files if you haven't built it yourself). I'll also show you how you can change the way the widgets work by making some simple changes to the JavaScript inserted by Dreamweaver.

Features common to all Spry widgets

Several features are common to working with all Spry widgets. If you worked through the last chapter, they should be familiar to you, but it's worth repeating them here:

- Always save your page in a Dreamweaver site before inserting a Spry widget.
- After inserting a widget, save the page to link the external JavaScript file and style sheet, and copy them to the site's Spry assets folder (see "Setting up for Spry" in Chapter 4). All instances of a widget in a site share the same files, so they are copied only when inserting the first instance.
- Dreamweaver attaches the widget's style sheet immediately above the closing </head> tag. If your page has style rules embedded in conditional comments, move the link to the style sheet above the conditional comments.

- Dreamweaver inserts a block of JavaScript at the bottom of the page to initialize the widget when the page loads.

- To see the widget's details in the Property inspector, hover your mouse pointer over the widget in Design view, and click the tab at the top left of the surrounding border.

Although tabbed panels, accordions, and collapsible panels are great space savers, the contents of hidden panels are loaded at the same time as the rest of the page. Don't put lots of heavy graphics in these widgets or overuse them on any individual page. The external JavaScript file and style sheet for each widget add about 20KB to a page but are stored in the browser's cache after loading the first time.

Spry widgets all have methods and properties, which are covered in "Understanding Spry objects" later in this chapter. The method of removing a Spry widget cleanly is covered at the end of the chapter.

Dw Building a tabbed interface

New

Tabbed panels use the common metaphor of tabs at the top of folders in a filing cabinet. Click the tab, and the associated content is displayed in the panel beneath. It's a clean, intuitive way of storing a lot of content in a relatively small space. The example in Figure 8-1 has four tabs, so the total space required to display the information is one-fourth of what it would normally be.

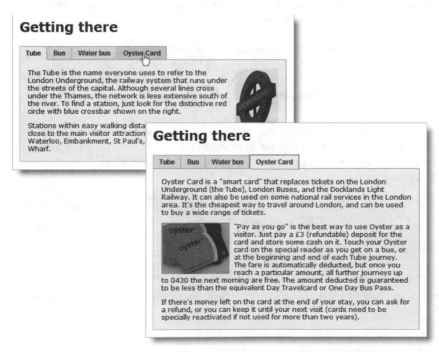

Figure 8-1. Tabbed panels are a familiar website interface that users find easy to use.

The Spry Tabbed Panels widget has two advantages over older methods of creating tabbed panels: it takes only the click of a button to insert, and it degrades gracefully in browsers that have JavaScript turned off or don't understand the document object model recommended by the World Wide Web Consortium (W3C DOM). If a user with an old browser, such as Netscape 4, visits your site, the panels expand to display their contents, as illustrated in Figure 8-2. Although the second and subsequent tabs are no longer directly associated with the panels, everything remains visible. The accordion and collapsible panels expand in a similar way, making all three user interface widgets accessible.

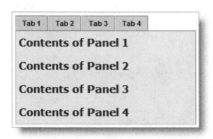

Figure 8-2.
The Spry Tabbed Panels widget expands all panels if the browser cannot interpret the JavaScript.

Let's take a look at the anatomy of a tabbed panels widget.

Examining the structure of the tabbed panels widget

There are three ways to insert a Spry tabbed panels widget: from the Spry tab of the Insert bar (as shown in the following screenshot), from the Layout tab of the Insert bar, or by choosing Insert ➤ Spry ➤ Spry Tabbed Panels.

As soon as you choose one of these methods, Dreamweaver inserts a default two-tab widget (see Figure 8-3) at the current insertion point in the page. Save the page again to copy the dependent files (SpryTabbedPanels.js and SpryTabbedPanels.css) to the site's Spry assets folder.

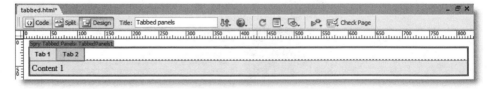

Figure 8-3. The default tabbed panels widget contains two tabs styled with a neutral gray interface.

The underlying XHTML looks like this:

```
<div id="TabbedPanels1" class="TabbedPanels">
  <ul class="TabbedPanelsTabGroup">
    <li class="TabbedPanelsTab" tabindex="0">Tab 1</li>
    <li class="TabbedPanelsTab" tabindex="0">Tab 2</li>
  </ul>
  <div class="TabbedPanelsContentGroup">
    <div class="TabbedPanelsContent">Content 1</div>
    <div class="TabbedPanelsContent">Content 2</div>
  </div>
</div>
```

The whole widget is wrapped in a <div>; the tabs are an unordered list, and the panels are in a nested <div>. Each individual panel is also a <div>, nested one level further down. The only element that has an ID is the overall wrapper <div>. Dreamweaver automatically calls the first tabbed panels widget on a page TabbedPanels1, and numbers subsequent instances TabbedPanels2, and so on. Everything else is controlled by classes. Although each element has a class assigned to it explicitly in the underlying code, other classes are generated dynamically by the external JavaScript file. Table 8-1 explains what each class is for. In common with all user interface widgets, the class names are long, but descriptive.

Table 8-1. The classes used to style the tabbed panels widget

Class	Type	Purpose
TabbedPanels	Explicit	Eliminates margin and padding surrounding the widget and clears any preceding floats. *This class must always have an explicit width.* The default value is 100% to fill all available space.
TabbedPanelsTabGroup	Explicit	Removes margin and padding from the tabs as a group.
TabbedPanelsTab	Explicit	Styles the individual tabs. Uses relative positioning to shift the tabs 1 pixel down and gives the bottom border the same color as the top border of TabbedPanelsContentGroup. This creates the illusion that the tabs are being drawn behind the content panel. Two nonstandard properties (-moz-user-select and -khtml-user-select) are set to none to prevent users from selecting the text in Firefox, Mozilla, and Konqueror.

Continued

8

Table 8-1. The classes used to style the tabbed panels widget *(continued)*

Class	Type	Purpose
TabbedPanelsTabHover	Dynamic	Controls the rollover look of the tabs.
TabbedPanelsTabSelected	Dynamic	Sets the background color and bottom border of the currently selected tab to the same as the TabbedPanelsContentGroup to create the illusion that the tab is part of the panel.
TabbedPanelsContentGroup	Explicit	Ensures that the panels sit beneath the tabs. Sets the background and border colors for the panels.
TabbedPanelsContent	Explicit	Styles the content of an individual panel. By default, only adds 4px padding.
TabbedPanelsContentVisible	Dynamic	Empty style rule that can be used to give a different style to the currently visible panel.

Sharp-eyed readers will have noticed that the <li> tags contain the tabindex attribute, which makes the code invalid according to the W3C specifications. Although Spry generates classes dynamically, Internet Explorer doesn't support setting tabindex through JavaScript, so this was the compromise adopted to make it possible to navigate the panels with the Tab key. If W3C validation is vital to you, remove the tabindex attributes. However, this will make your page less accessible to assistive technology for the disabled and keyboard users. Occasionally bending the rules like this makes sense and has no adverse effect in any browser.

Editing a tabbed panels widget

Unlike the Spry menu bar, there's no option to turn off the styling in Design view. The Property inspector has only three settings for the tabbed panels widget (see Figure 8-4): ID, number and order of panels, and the default panel. The Customize this widget link opens Dreamweaver help at the page listing the style settings.

Figure 8-4. The Property inspector for the tabbed panels widget is very simple.

Use the plus (+) and minus (–) buttons to add or remove panels, and the up and down arrows to reorder them. The name of each panel changes when you edit the tabs in Design view. The Default panel drop-down menu on the right determines which panel is open when the page first loads.

There are two ways to open a tab or panel for editing, as follows:

- Bring up the details of the widget in the Property inspector, and select the panel name in the Panels list.

- Position your mouse pointer over the right side of the tab until an eye symbol appears, as shown in Figure 8-5, and click.

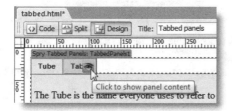

Figure 8-5.
Click the eye symbol at the right side of a tab to reveal its associated panel for editing.

The panel is a <div>, so you can insert anything you like: text, images, etc.

Inserting and editing a tabbed panels widget

Right, roll up your sleeves and insert a tabbed panels widget into stroll.html. To make it easier to dip into individual chapters, the download files use the version of stroll.html from Chapter 6 without the Spry menu bar, as it involves fewer dependent files.

1. Copy stroll.html from examples/ch08 to workfiles/ch08 and stroll_final.css from examples/styles to workfiles/styles. Update links if prompted by Dreamweaver. Save a copy of stroll.html as stroll_tabbed.html.

2. Scroll down to the end of the first block of text in the mainContent <div> (just above the Artists at Work heading). Press Enter/Return to insert a new paragraph. Type Getting There, and convert it to a heading by selecting Heading 2 from the Format drop-down menu on the left of the Property inspector.

3. With your cursor at the end of the new heading, click the Spry Tabbed Panels button on the Spry tab of the Insert bar (or use the Layout tab or Insert menu as described earlier). You should now have a tabbed panels widget in the middle of the page, as shown in Figure 8-6.

As long as your cursor is at the beginning or end of an existing element when you insert a widget, Dreamweaver correctly places the widget outside the existing element. If your cursor is anywhere else, Dreamweaver splits the existing element by creating closing and opening tags and inserting the widget between them.

8

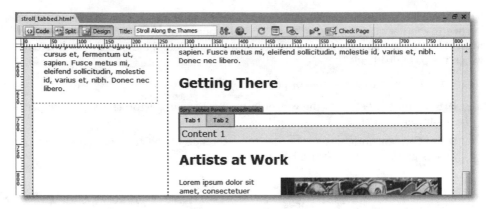

Figure 8-6. By default, the tabbed panels widget fills the available horizontal space.

4. Save `stroll_tabbed.html`, and click OK when prompted to copy the dependent files.

5. Rename `SpryTabbedPanel.css` in the Spry assets folder as `SpryTabbedPanel_stroll.css`, and update the links when prompted. Move the link to `SpryTabbelPanel_stroll.css` above the conditional comments in the <head> of the page. There won't be any conflicts of style rules, but this is a good habit to get into.

6. Place your cursor inside the first tab, delete Tab 1, and type Tube.

7. Open `getting_there.doc` in examples/ch08, and copy the paragraphs labeled Tube to your clipboard. If you can't open a Word document, the text is in `getting_there.txt`, but Dreamweaver won't do the automatic formatting in the next step.

8. Highlight Content 1 in the tabbed panels widget, and press Ctrl+Shift+V/ Shift+Cmd+V or go to Edit ➤ Paste Special. This brings up the dialog box in Figure 8-7.

Figure 8-7. Paste Special preserves a lot of formatting when importing text from word processor documents.

This lets you preserve the original formatting of a word-processed document. It also has an option to remove extra spacing between paragraphs in Microsoft Word. Use the settings shown in Figure 8-7 and click OK. The imported text should replace the placeholder text and be nicely formatted in paragraphs.

If you used the plain text in getting_there.txt, you need to format it manually as paragraphs with the Format drop-down menu in the Property inspector. Dreamweaver places a <br /> tag between the paragraphs, so you need to split them by pressing Enter/Return and then remove the extra line created by the <br /> tag.

9. Position your cursor inside the second tab, and rename it Bus.

10. Open the second panel for editing by selecting it in the Property inspector (click the turquoise tab at the top left of the widget, if necessary) or clicking the eye icon as shown earlier in Figure 8-5. Copy the Bus paragraphs from getting_there.doc, and use Paste Special to replace the placeholder text in the second panel.

11. Click the turquoise Spry Tabbed Panels tab at the top left of the widget to bring up its details in the Property inspector, and click the plus button in the Property inspector to add two more panels. Rename them Water bus and Oyster Card, and repeat steps 7 and 8 to replace the placeholder text with copy from getting_there.doc.

12. With the Oyster Card panel open, insert oystercard.jpg at or near the beginning of the second paragraph. (You can drag and drop it from the Files panel, use the Insert Image button on the Common tab of the Insert bar, or go to Insert ➤ Image.) Enter Oyster Card as the Alternate text when prompted.

13. To make the text wrap around the image, with the image still highlighted, select fltlft from the Class drop-down menu in the Property inspector.

14. Open the first panel (Tube) for editing, and insert underground.jpg at the beginning of the first paragraph. Set Alternate text to Underground station sign and Class to fltrt.

15. Save stroll_tabbed.html, and press F12/Opt+F12 to view the page in a browser. The bottom half of the page should look like Figure 8-8. Click the various tabs to display the other panels. You'll see that the height of the panels expands and contracts depending on the amount of content. All content below the tabbed panels is repositioned according to the height of the selected panel, so you need to be careful when incorporating this widget in a design where the layout needs to be pixel perfect.

Check your code if necessary with stroll_tabbed.html in examples/ch08. The version in the download files contains a link that will be added later, but is otherwise identical.

8

Figure 8-8. Even without customizing the styles, Spry Tabbed Panels look at home in most pages.

The neutral gray styling fits in easily with many designs, so you could leave it as it is. However, I don't imagine that you'll let me get away with that, so let's restyle the panels. The bottom of the panels is too close to the following headline, so that needs fixing, too.

Selecting harmonious colors

A good way to find colors to fit your website is to select a dominant image and use the eyedropper tool of a graphics program, such as Fireworks, to select colors. You can then use a color wheel to generate color schemes. There's a free one online at http://labs.adobe.com/technologies/kuler/.

There's also a useful little tool inside Dreamweaver that I used to find colors for the tabbed panels. I decided to use as base colors the pink (#F8F1EB) from the page background and the russet (#C99466) border down both sides of the container <div>. In a blank page, I entered the base color in the Text Color field of the Property inspector and launched the System Color Picker as described in Figure 8-9. By moving the luminosity slider on the right of the Color panel you can select brighter or darker shades.

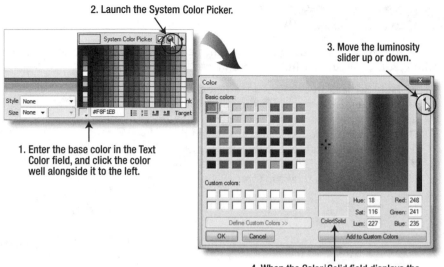

2. Launch the System Color Picker.

3. Move the luminosity slider up or down.

1. Enter the base color in the Text Color field, and click the color well alongside it to the left.

4. When the Color|Solid field displays the desired color, click Add to Custom Colors and then click OK.

Figure 8-9. The Dreamweaver System Color Picker can be useful in picking different shades of a base color.

The Color panel shows color values only in terms of hue, saturation, and luminosity, or red, green, and blue, but as soon as you click OK, you can copy the hexadecimal equivalent from the Text Color field of the Property inspector. Table 8-2 lists the colors that I finally decided on.

Table 8-2. Conversion chart for Dreamweaver defaults and substituted colors

Default color	Replacement	Applies to
Light gray (#EEE)	Light pink (#FAF3ED)	Panel background color and selected tab
Medium gray (#DDD)	Darker pink (#F2E1D2)	Nonselected tabs
Darker gray (#CCC)	Dusky pink (#ECD3BD)	Tabs on rollover
Darker gray (#CCC)	Light brown (#DFBD9F)	Lighter borders
Dark gray (#999)	Russet (#C99466)	Darker borders

To simplify customization of a Spry widget, make a similar chart of the default colors and your chosen replacements. You can then go through the style rules quite quickly to make the substitutions. Dreamweaver uses the same shade of gray for the tabs on rollover and the lighter borders. I wanted a darker border, so you need to take care when replacing #CCC. Otherwise, each color is a straight swap.

Styling a tabbed panels widget

Let's style the tabbed panels using the color scheme outlined in Table 8-2. Continue working with `stroll_tabbed.html` from the previous exercise.

1. As Table 8-1 indicates, several important classes are generated dynamically, so they don't show up in the CSS Styles panel in Current mode. Open the panel in All mode instead, expand the SpryTabbedPanels_stroll.css tree menu, if necessary, and select the first selector (.TabbedPanels), as shown in Figure 8-10.

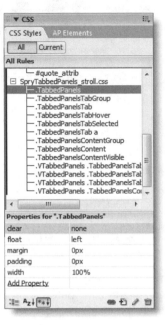

Figure 8-10.
The easiest way to restyle a tabbed panels widget is to go through each selector in turn.

This class controls the horizontal and vertical space around the tabbed panels, as well as their overall width. As Figure 8-8 shows, there's no gap between the bottom of the panel and the following heading. So you need to adjust the margin property. Click the margin value field, and change 0px to 0px 0px 15px 0px. This adds a 15-pixel margin on the bottom but leaves the other sides with a 0-pixel margin.

In Chapter 6, I said that it wasn't necessary to add the unit of measurement after 0. So, why am I being inconsistent and using it here? During testing, I discovered what must qualify as one of the most bizarre bugs ever. Using 0 consistently caused Dreamweaver to crash, and Dreamweaver could not be relaunched until the style sheet was deleted. This bug is triggered by a style sheet being exactly 8,192 bytes or a multiple thereof. It affects only Windows, and only if you make the changes in the CSS Styles panel. Adobe has isolated the problem, and it will be fixed in an updater, so it may have been resolved by the time you read this. However, since 0px is valid, I suggest that you use it here, rather than risk a crash.

If you want to constrain the width of the panels, this is where you should edit the width property. Do *not* delete the width property, as it's required for the widget to display correctly in Internet Explorer.

2. Move to the next selector (.TabbedPanelsTabGroup). It doesn't affect background colors or borders, so move to the next one without making any changes.

3. The third selector (.TabbedPanelsTab) is the most complex. The default settings are shown in the left screenshot of Figure 8-11.

As Table 8-1 shows, this selector sets the styles for the individual tabs. There's a special style for the currently selected tab, so set the background-color property to darker pink (#F2E1D2).

The color of the border-left property is lighter than the other three borders, so use light brown (#DFBD9F), and set the others to russet (#C99466).

The default setting for font uses the shorthand version like this:

`font: bold 0.7em sans-serif`

Since this uses only the generic sans-serif for font-family, it's a good idea to change it, but editing shorthand can be tricky. So delete it, and use Add Property to create separate properties for font-weight, font-size, and font-family.

By the time you have made all the changes, the Properties pane should look like the right screenshot in Figure 8-11.

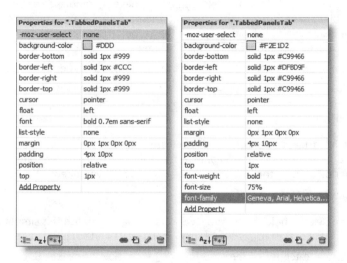

Figure 8-11. The default styles for the tabs (left) and styles after editing (right)

Newly added properties are initially displayed at the bottom of the Properties *pane, but when the pane is refreshed, Dreamweaver shows them in alphabetical order for ease of editing.*

4. Move to the fourth selector (.TabbedPanelsTabHover). This class name is self explanatory. I want the tabs to be dusky pink on rollover, so change background-color to #ECD3BD.

5. The next selector (.TabbedPanelsTabSelected) is the dynamic class that styles the currently selected tab. Both background-color and the color of border-bottom need to be the same as the panel—in other words, light pink (#FAF3ED).

6. The sixth selector (.TabbedPanelsTab a) doesn't actively affect the widget in its default state. If you put a dummy link around the text in a tab, this style rule limits the focus lines around the text, rather than around the entire tab. You can leave it unchanged and move on to the next selector.

7. The seventh selector (.TabbedPanelsContentGroup) is the last one that you need to edit. It controls the background-color property of the panel and the surrounding border. Change the values like this:

Properties for ".TabbedPanelsContentGroup"	
background-color	#FAF3ED
border-bottom	solid 1px #DFBD9F
border-left	solid 1px #DFBD9F
border-right	solid 1px #C99466
border-top	solid 1px #C99466
clear	both
Add Property	

8. Press F12/Opt+F12 to preview stroll_tabbed.html in a browser (save the style sheet if you have been working with it open in the Document window). You now have a nicely styled set of tabbed panels that blend in better with the design.

9. There's one further improvement you could make by reducing the size of the text and adding some horizontal padding to the paragraphs. Position your cursor anywhere inside one of the paragraphs in the tabbed panels widget, and click the New CSS Rule icon (see alongside) at the bottom right of the CSS Styles panel.

The New CSS Rule dialog box suggests this horrendous dependent selector:

```
.twoColFixLtHdr #container #mainContent #TabbedPanels1 ➥
.TabbedPanelsContentGroup .TabbedPanelsContent ➥
TabbedPanelsContentVisible p
```

Apart from the complexity of this selector, TabbedPanelsContentVisible is not preceded by a period, presumably because it's dynamically generated. The lack of the period renders the selector invalid. However, all you need is the following:

```
.TabbedPanelsContent p
```

Edit the Selector field in the New CSS Rule dialog box to use this simplified version; make sure that Define in is set to SpryTabbedPanels_stroll.css, and click OK.

10. In the Type category of the CSS Rule Definition dialog box, set Size to 75%. Then select the Box category, deselect Same for all in the Padding section, set Right and Left to 10 pixels, and click OK.

11. Refresh the page in a browser. The contents of the tabbed panels should now look more compact but with more breathing space on either side. If necessary, compare your style sheet with SpryTabbedPanels_stroll_horiz.css in the SpryAssets folder.

Opening a tabbed panel from a link

As well as opening a panel by clicking its tab, you can open one remotely, as this exercise shows. Continue working with stroll_tabbed.html from the previous exercise.

1. In Design view, select the tab named Bus in the Property inspector, or click its eye icon to reveal the panel content.

2. Select the words Oyster Card in the final sentence, and type javascript:; in the Link field of the Property inspector to create a dummy link.

3. With the words Oyster Card still highlighted, open Split view to reveal the underlying code, and position your cursor just before the closing angle bracket of the `<a>` tag.

4. Press the spacebar. Code hints should pop up. Type onc, and press Enter/Return when onclick is highlighted. The link surrounding Oyster Card should now look like this (with the cursor between the quotes following onclick):

```
<a href="javascript:;" onclick="">Oyster Card</a>
```

5. To call one of the Spry methods (functions) on a widget, type the ID of the widget followed by a period and the name of the method. The ID of this widget is TabbedPanels1. As soon as you type the period after the ID, Dreamweaver pops up code hints for the selected widget, showing the available methods (see Figure 8-12).

```
<a href="javascript:;" onclick="TabbedPanels1.">Oyster Card</a>, which can
                                              ● getContentPanelGroup()
                                              ● getContentPanels()
                                              ● getCurrentTabIndex()
PanelsContent">                               ● getTabGroup()
, Londoners ignored the Thames  as a way of tr ● getTabIndex(element)
k was  a  depressing succession of empty wareh ● getTabbedPanelCount(element)
                                              ● getTabs()
|250    |300    |350    |400    |450    |500  |55● showPanel(elementOrIndex)
```

Figure 8-12. Code hints in Dreamweaver CS3 recognize Spry widgets and display available functions.

Use your mouse or keyboard arrow keys to select showPanel(elementOrIndex) and double-click or press Enter/Return. This inserts showPanel followed by an opening parenthesis. Type 3 followed by a closing parenthesis.

Following JavaScript convention, Spry counts the panels from 0, so 3 represents the fourth panel (Oyster Card). The Oyster Card link code should now look like this:

```
<a href="javascript:;" onclick="TabbedPanels1.showPanel(3)">Oyster ➥
Card</a>
```

6. Save stroll_tabbed.html, and reload it in a browser. Select the Bus tab, and click the Oyster Card link within the displayed panel. The fourth panel should open.

The link to open another panel doesn't need to be inside the widget; it can be anywhere in the page. The use of Spry methods is explained further in "Understanding Spry objects" later in the chapter.

Converting to vertical tabs

If you look at the CSS Styles panel in All mode with stroll_tabbed.html open, you'll see four descendant selectors all beginning with .VTabbedPanels at the bottom of the tree menu for SpryTabbedPanels_stroll.css (see Figure 8-10 earlier). These are a default set

8

of rules that let you change the orientation of a tabbed panels widget. Instead of tabs running across the top, you can have them running down the left side of the panel. Table 8-3 describes the purpose of each selector.

Table 8-3. Style rules for vertical tabs

Selector	Type	Notes
.VTabbedPanels .TabbedPanelsTabGroup	Explicit	Vertical tabs are displayed in a column. This selector sets the background color, border, height, and width of the column. The height (default 20em) needs to be the same as in .VTabbedPanels .TabbedPanelsTabGroup. Don't use a pixel height unless the panels contain elements of fixed dimensions, such as images.
.VTabbedPanels .TabbedPanelsTab	Explicit	Works in combination with .TabbedPanelsTab. Overrides top, left, and right borders, float, and margin. All other rules, such as background color and font, are preserved from the .TabbedPanelsTab class.
.VTabbedPanels .TabbedPanelsTabSelected	Dynamic	Overrides the background and bottom border colors of the selected tab. With horizontal tabs, the bottom border is set to the same color as the panel to create the illusion that the tab is part of the panel, but with vertical tabs, a solid bottom border is needed.
.VTabbedPanels .TabbedPanelsTabGroup	Explicit	Sets the height and width of the panels but inherits the background color and borders from the .TabbedPanelsTabGroup class.

These descendant selectors work in conjunction with the classes listed in Table 8-1. Because basic colors are set in the main classes, this makes it slightly trickier to style vertical tabbed panels if you haven't already styled the default horizontal widget.

Another problem with vertical tabs is the need to set a height, which must be sufficient to accommodate the content of the biggest panel. It should be specified in ems so that the panels can expand if the user increases the size of text in the browser. It is possible to omit the height to create a flexible layout, but the result doesn't look as good, as you'll see shortly.

Switching the orientation of tabbed panels

Let's convert the tabbed panels widget in stroll_tabbed.html to use vertical tabs. Continue working with the same files as in the previous exercise.

1. Click anywhere inside the tabbed panels widget in Design view, and select <div.TabbedPanels#TabbedPanels1> in the Tag selector at the bottom of the Document window. This is the main <div> that wraps around the tabbed panels widget. Right-click and choose Set Class ➤ VTabbedPanels from the context menu, as shown in Figure 8-13.

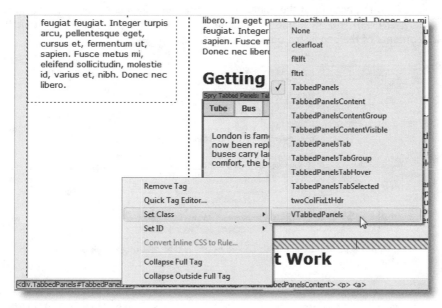

Figure 8-13. The first step in converting to vertical tabs is to change the class of the surrounding <div>.

This changes the class of the <div> from TabbedPanels to VTabbedPanels, and the widget immediately inherits the default rules for vertical tabs. Because the default widths (10em + 30em) are too great, the design falls apart completely in Design view.

2. Adjust the width by highlighting the first vertical tab selector (.VTabbedPanels .TabbedPanelsTabGroup) in the CSS Styles panel. Change the width property from 10em to 20%.

3. Next highlight the final selector (.VTabbedPanels .TabbedPanelsContentGroup), and change the width property from 30em to 78%. The widget springs back into shape. Choosing figures that add up to less than 100 percent avoids rounding errors. To display a web page, the browser needs to convert percentages to whole pixels. If it rounds up, floated content no longer fits and is pushed down the page, breaking your design.

4. The vertical tabs have inherited most of the colors from the original classes, but you still need to make a couple of adjustments. Highlight the first vertical tab selector (.VTabbedPanels .TabbedPanelsTabGroup), and change #EEE to light pink (#FAF3ED). Also change the border colors: #CCC to light brown (#DFBD9F) and #999 to russet (#C99466). This is the same color scheme as in Table 8-2.

5. Change the colors in .VTabbedPanels .TabbedPanelsTabSelected. Change #EEE to light pink (#FAF3ED) and #999 to russet (#C99466).

6. Save stroll_tabbed.html and the style sheet, if necessary, and press F12/Opt+F12 to reload the page in your browser. You'll probably notice two things: the fixed height makes the first panel (Tube) look rather bare, and there's hardly any gap between the bottom of the panel and the following headline. Click the fourth tab (Oyster Card) and, in a standards-compliant browser at least, you'll see that the contents of the panel spill out, as shown in Figure 8-14.

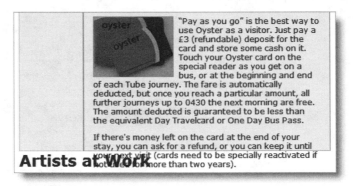

Figure 8-14. The danger with a fixed height is that text might spill out of the panel.

7. Fixing the gap between the tabbed panel widget and the next headline is easy. Add the margin-bottom property to the .VTabbedPanels .TabbedPanelsContentGroup selector, and set its value to 15 pixels.

8. Dealing with the text overspill problem is not so easy. One solution is to change the height property of the .VTabbedPanels .TabbedPanelsTabGroup and .VTabbedPanels .TabbedPanelsContentGroup selectors to 23.5em. The problem with this is that the panels with less content begin to look decidedly empty.

9. The alternative is to remove the height property from both selectors. This causes each panel to expand or contract according to its contents. However, the background color of the column of tabs stretches down only as far as the last tab, as shown in Figure 8-15. You can't give a background color to the surrounding <div>, because both the tabs and panels are floated inside, so the <div> itself has no height.

To revert to horizontal tabs, repeat step 1, changing the class back to TabbedPanels. Compare your style sheet with SpryTabbedPanels_stroll_both.css in the SpryAssets folder, if you need to check your own code. It contains the styles for both horizontal and vertical tabs.

The tabs are no longer in a column the same height as the panels.

The panels expand and collapse to match the height of the content.

Figure 8-15. Removing the height makes the panels flexible but removes the background from the tab column.

Avoiding design problems with tabbed panels

As the previous exercise demonstrates, content overspill creates problems with the panels. You also need to take care with the tabs, because on a horizontal layout, they are floated left. If you make the labels too long, you might end up with the effect shown in Figure 8-16.

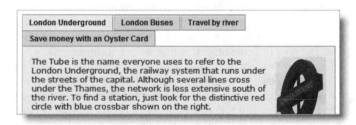

Figure 8-16. Too much content in the tabs breaks the design.

The result can look even more disastrous if you attempt to constrain the width of the tabs by setting a width property in the .TabbedPanelsTab class, as Figure 8-17 shows.

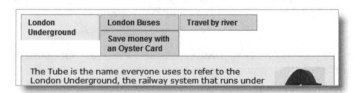

Figure 8-17. Setting a fixed width on the tabs leads to even more unpredictable results.

When using Spry Tabbed Panels, always keep the tab labels short. Don't try to get them to fit exactly across the top of the panels, because some visitors are likely to increase the text size, forcing one or more tabs to drop down in the same way as too much content does in

8

Figure 8-16. In this sense, Spry Tabbed Panels aren't 100 percent bulletproof, but the original short labels (Tube, Bus, Water bus, and Oyster Card) don't cause any problem even when the largest font size is chosen in Internet Explorer. In Firefox, you need to increase the text size four times before the last tab slips down. Somebody who needs to make the text so large is unlikely to be concerned by design aesthetics. Still, if you are worried about overflow, you might consider adding the following properties to the .TabbedPanelsTab class:

```
max-width: /* less than total width divided by number of tabs */
white-space: nowrap;
overflow: hidden;
```

This keeps all the tabs on one line, regardless of how much the text is enlarged. The disadvantage is that the end of the label may be hidden if it's too long. Web pages cannot be controlled as rigidly as print, so you need to take into account the need for flexible design. Alternatively, avoid using design elements such as tabbed panels if you need to maintain pixel-perfect accuracy in your layout.

Understanding Spry objects

To get the most out of Spry Tabbed Panels, Spry Accordion, and Spry Collapsible Panels, you need to dive into Code view from time to time, as you did when creating the link to open the fourth panel. So, let's pause briefly to consider the technology. Spry widgets are **JavaScript objects**. The idea of using objects is that all the complex coding remains locked away in the object definition, so you need concern yourself only with parts exposed through the object's **methods** and **properties**. Methods are functions that can be used to get the object to perform particular actions. For example, "Opening a tabbed panel from a link" used the showPanel() method of a TabbedPanels object to open a panel. Properties define the state of an object, such as whether a panel is open or whether the panels have a fixed height.

> *Of course, the object definitions aren't literally locked away. You can study them by opening the external JavaScript file. However, you should never attempt to edit the JavaScript in the external files unless you really know what you're doing.*

When you insert a Spry widget, Dreamweaver initializes the JavaScript object at the bottom of the page just before the closing </body> tag like this:

```
<script type="text/javascript">
<!--
var TabbedPanels1 = new Spry.Widget.TabbedPanels("TabbedPanels1");
//-->
</script>
</body>
```

The line of JavaScript highlighted in bold uses the new keyword to construct a new TabbedPanels object. The Spry.Widget.TabbedPanels() method is passed just one argument, the ID of the widget's wrapper <div>. The var TabbedPanels1 at the beginning of the line means that the new tabbed panels object is being stored in a JavaScript variable with the same name as the <div>. The ID and the JavaScript variable don't need to be the same, but Dreamweaver adopts this convention to make it easy to use Spry properties and methods.

Dreamweaver normally handles all the coding for you, but if you want to get more adventurous with Spry widgets, you need to know how to pass new properties to the JavaScript object when it's initialized. If you change the value of the Default panel in the Property inspector in stroll_tabbed.html to Water bus, Dreamweaver changes the initialization code like this:

```
var TabbedPanels1 = new Spry.Widget.TabbedPanels("TabbedPanels1", ➥
{defaultTab:2});
```

The second argument enclosed in curly braces lists the name of the property you want to define, followed by a colon and the value you want to give it. If you want to change more than one property, separate each property/value pair with a comma like this:

```
var TabbedPanels1 = new Spry.Widget.TabbedPanels("TabbedPanels1", ➥
{property1:value1, property2:value2, property3:value3});
```

Technically speaking, this type of construction is an **object literal**. In other words, the argument is a JavaScript object in its own right. You can put whitespace around the colons and insert new lines after the commas for ease of reading. Don't worry if the terminology sounds intimidating, you'll see shortly how a little bit of hand coding makes the Spry Accordion more flexible.

8

Dw Using the accordion widget

New

The Spry Accordion is another convenient way of storing a lot of information in a compact space. Figure 8-18 shows the same set of travel information as in the tabbed panels displayed in a Spry Accordion. Instead of a tab, each panel has an individual title bar. When the user clicks the title bar of a closed panel, it glides open and simultaneously closes the panel that was previously open. By default, the panels are a fixed height and automatically display scrollbars if the content is too big. However, it's quite simple to change this so that the panels expand and contract in line with the content.

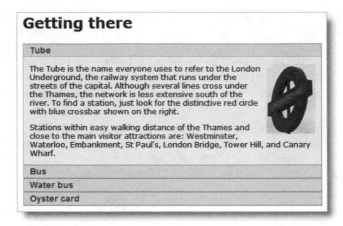

Figure 8-18. The accordion widget displays a series of interlinked panels one at a time.

Examining the structure of an accordion

To insert an accordion widget, click the Spry Accordion button on the Spry tab of the Insert bar, as shown in the following screenshot. Alternatively, use the Layout tab of the Insert bar or the main menu: Insert ➤ Spry ➤ Spry Accordion.

Dreamweaver inserts a default two-panel accordion. The layout in Design view is very similar to the tabbed panels widget, and you access closed panels for editing in exactly the same way, by moving your mouse pointer over the right edge of the title bar and clicking the eye icon, as shown in Figure 8-19.

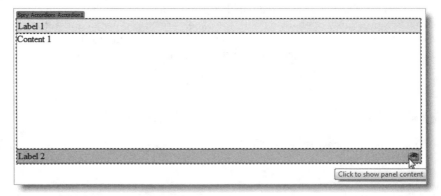

Figure 8-19. The first accordion panel is open for editing; click the eye icon (bottom right) to edit the next one.

The underlying XHTML looks like this:

```
<div id="Accordion1" class="Accordion" tabindex="0">
  <div class="AccordionPanel">
    <div class="AccordionPanelTab">Label 1</div>
    <div class="AccordionPanelContent">Content 1</div>
  </div>
  <div class="AccordionPanel">
    <div class="AccordionPanelTab">Label 2</div>
    <div class="AccordionPanelContent">Content 2</div>
  </div>
</div>
```

It's a simple structure consisting of a wrapper <div>, inside which each panel is a <div> with two more nested inside: one each for the title bar and the content panel. Like the tabbed panels widget, the use of tabindex makes the code technically invalid. Remove it from the opening <div> tag if W3C validation is a requirement, but doing so will disable keyboard navigation of the accordion.

All the styles are controlled by classes and descendant selectors, which are described in Table 8-4. As with Spry Tabbed Panels, some classes are declared explicitly in the XHTML; others are generated dynamically by JavaScript.

Table 8-4. Style rules for the accordion widget

Selector	Type	Notes
.Accordion	Explicit	Sets all borders for the accordion, except for the top border, which is taken from the first title bar. Also sets overflow to hidden to prevent the content of hidden panels from being displayed. Add the background-color property to this rule if you want the panels to be shaded. By default, accordion widgets expand horizontally to fill all available space. Add the width property to this selector to constrain the space it occupies.
.AccordionPanel	Explicit	Eliminates padding and margin for each panel so the accordion displays as a single unit.

Continued

8

Table 8-4. Style rules for the accordion widget *(continued)*

Selector	Type	Notes
`.AccordionPanelTab`	Explicit	Sets the default background color and border of the title bar of each panel. The top border of the first title bar becomes the top border of the whole widget. Change this rule to style the text in the title bar. The nonstandard properties `-moz-user-select` and `-khtml-user-select` prevent users from selecting the title bar label in Mozilla, Firefox, and Konqueror browsers.
`.AccordionPanelContent`	Explicit	Sets the height and overflow properties of the open panel. Change these properties if you want a different or flexible height. Do *not* change or delete the padding property, which is set to 0. Always add padding or margins to elements inside the accordion panel, rather than to the `<div>` itself.
`.AccordionPanelOpen .AccordionPanelTab`	Dynamic	Sets the background color of the title bar for the currently open tab. However, this is overridden by later dynamic rules if the accordion has focus.
`.AccordionPanelTabHover`	Dynamic	Sets the background color of the title bar in rollover state.
`.AccordionPanelOpen .AccordionPanelTabHover`	Dynamic	Sets the background color of the title bar of the currently opened panel when the mouse rolls over the title bar.
`.AccordionFocused .AccordionPanelTab`	Dynamic	Sets the background color of the title bar of all panels when the accordion has focus.
`.AccordionFocused .AccordionPanelOpen .AccordionPanelTab`	Dynamic	Sets the background color of the title bar of the currently open panel when the accordion has focus.

Editing and styling a Spry Accordion

Although the structure of the accordion makes it relatively easy to style, the proliferation of dynamic classes and selectors can be confusing. It's easier to understand how they work through hands-on experimentation. So let's get to work.

Inserting the accordion and adding content

The following exercise is based on stroll.html, which you should have copied to your workfiles/ch08 folder for the Spry Tabbed Panels exercises earlier in the chapter. If you don't have the file, copy stroll.html from examples/ch08 to workfiles/ch08 and stroll_final.css from examples/style to workfiles/style. Update links if prompted by Dreamweaver.

1. Open stroll.html in the Document window, and save it as stroll_accordion. html.

2. Create the new level 2 heading Getting There just above the Artists at Work heading.

3. With your cursor at the end of the new heading, click the Spry Accordion button on the Spry or Layout tab of the Insert bar. The page should look the same as Figure 8-6, except there's an empty accordion widget instead of tabbed panels.

   As Figure 8-20 shows, the Property inspector for a Spry Accordion has very few options (hover your mouse pointer over the accordion in Design view, and click the Spry Accordion tab at the top left, if the Property inspector is showing something else). Dreamweaver automatically assigns Accordion1 as the ID of the first accordion in a page and numbers subsequent instances Accordion2 and so on. The Property inspector displays the ID in the field on the left, where you can change it if you want. The only other options are to add, remove, and reorder panels using the plus, minus, and arrow buttons. Clicking Customize this widget opens Dreamweaver help at the page with details of the style rules that control an accordion.

Figure 8-20. The Property inspector for a Spry Accordion is mainly for changing the number and order of panels.

4. Save stroll_accordion.html, and click OK to copy the dependent files.

5. Rename SpryAccordion.css in the Spry assets folder as SpryAccordion_ stroll.css, and update the links when prompted. Since the web page contains style rules embedded in conditional comments, move the link to SpryAccordion_ stroll.css from just before the closing </head> tag to above the conditional comments.

6. You edit an accordion in the same way as a tabbed panels widget. The only difference is that instead of Tab 1, etc., the accordion uses Label 1, etc. Follow steps 6 through 11 of "Inserting and editing a tabbed panels widget" to populate the accordion with four panels labeled Tube, Bus, Water bus, and Oyster Card.

7. When you paste the text into the third and fourth panels, the end appears to be cut off. This is because the default styles set a height of 200 pixels on the panels and hide the overflow. To display the accordion content for editing when this happens, double-click inside one of the panels that have an overflow (sometimes you need to double-click twice). Alternatively, right-click and select Element View ➤ Full from the context menu. This expands the whole accordion in Design view.

With the accordion fully expanded, insert underground.jpg in the first panel and oystercard.jpg in the fourth panel, and apply the fltrt and fltlft classes to them, respectively (see steps 12–14 of "Inserting and editing a tabbed panels widget").

8. To collapse the accordion after editing, press F5, or right-click and select Element View ➤ Hidden from the context menu.

9. Save stroll_accordion.html, and press F12/Opt+F12 to preview the page in a browser. You should see the accordion in the middle of the page with the first panel open, as shown in Figure 8-21. The addition of the image to the first panel causes it to overflow, so a vertical scrollbar automatically appears inside the panel.

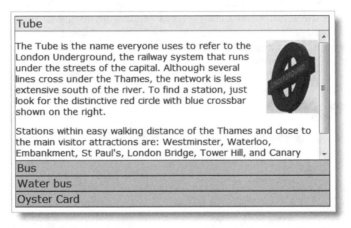

Figure 8-21. The accordion panel automatically displays a scrollbar if the content doesn't fit.

10. Use the Tab key to shift focus to the accordion. As soon as it has focus, the color of the title bars changes from neutral grays to rather ghastly shades of blue. This is the effect of the last two selectors listed in Table 8-4. We'll sort out the colors next, but first press the down arrow on your keyboard. As long as you haven't removed the tabindex, the next panel should glide open, closing the previous one behind it. While the accordion has focus, you can navigate through the panels in sequence with the up and down keyboard arrows. Alternatively, you can click any title bar to open a particular panel. Click anywhere outside the accordion and the colors revert to gray.

Changing the default colors of an accordion

The following instructions show you how to change the colors of stroll_accordion.html from the preceding exercise, but they apply equally to any accordion. Just use your own colors in place of those suggested here. The color scheme I have used is essentially the same as in Table 8-2.

1. Open the CSS Styles panel in All mode, and expand the SpryAccordion_stroll. css tree menu if necessary.

2. Highlight the first selector (.Accordion), and change the color for the border-bottom and border-left properties from gray to #DFBD9F (light brown). Change the color for the border-right property from black to #C99466 (russet).

   Currently, the panels have no background color, so add the background-color property, and set it to #FAF3ED (light pink).

3. The second selector (.AccordionPanel) needs no changes, so move to the third selector (.AccordionPanelTab). As the class name suggests, this styles the tab or title bar of each panel. Change the background-color property from #CCCCCC to #F2E1D2 (darker pink). Also change the gray and black border colors in the same way as in step 2.

   This is also where you can make changes to the text in the title bars. Add the following properties and values:

   - font-family: Geneva, Arial, Helvetica, sans-serif
   - font-size: 90%
   - font-weight: bold
   - color: #555555

   The text could also do with a bit of horizontal space, so change the value of the padding property from 2px to 2px 10px. This gives 2 pixels of padding top and bottom, and 10 pixels on either side.

4. The next color change is to the .AccordionPanelOpen .AccordionPanelTab selector. Change the background-color property to #F2E1D2 (darker pink).

5. The next selector (.AccordionPanelTabHover) controls the rollover state of the title bars, but only when the accordion doesn't have focus. Change the color property to a slightly darker gray (#333333). Also add the background-color property, and set it to #ECD3BD (dusky pink). This keeps the rollover color in harmony with the rest of the accordion when the focus is elsewhere in the page.

6. Give the next selector (.AccordionPanelOpen .AccordionPanelTabHover) the same values as in step 5. This makes the rollover colors the same, regardless of whether the accordion has focus or not.

7. In the final two selectors (.AccordionFocused .AccordionPanelTab and .AccordionFocused .AccordionPanelOpen .AccordionPanelTab), select the background-color property, and delete it. This leaves both style rules empty. Of course, you can apply your own styles to these selectors, but it's not necessary unless you need to make a distinction in the way the title bars look depending on whether the accordion has focus.

8

8. One final change: because you cannot add padding to the AccordionPanelTab class, it's a good idea to create a new rule for .AccordionPanelContent p. By this stage, I expect you should have sufficient experience of creating new style rules, but select Advanced as the Selector Type, and define it in SpryAccordion_stroll. css. Set the following properties and values:

- font-size: 75%

- padding-left: 10 pixels

- padding-right: 10 pixels

This makes the text slightly smaller than in the rest of the page, and gives 10 pixels breathing space on either side of the paragraphs inside the accordion. You can check your code against SpryAccordion_stroll_done.css in the SpryAssets folder.

Using the object initialization to change accordion defaults

As Figure 8-20 showed earlier, the Property inspector for an accordion lets you change only the ID and the number and order of panels. Unlike Spry Tabbed Panels, there's no option to select a panel to be displayed by default when the page first loads. What's more, changing the default behavior of using fixed-height panels isn't just a question of tweaking the style sheet. To make both changes, you need to tweak the object initialization (see "Understanding Spry objects" earlier in the chapter).

Changing the default open panel

The following instructions continue working with stroll_accordion.html, but apply equally to any accordion widget.

1. To change the default open panel, open the page in Code view, and scroll down to the bottom. Locate the following line of code, which initializes the accordion object:

```
var Accordion1 = new Spry.Widget.Accordion("Accordion1");
```

2. Insert your cursor just before the closing parenthesis, and type a comma. Dreamweaver displays the following code hint:

```
83   <script type="text/javascript">
84   <!--                                          Accordion(element, {options})
85   var Accordion1 = new Spry.Widget.Accordion("Accordion1",);
```

This code hint tells you that Spry expects the constructor function to take two arguments: element (the ID of the <div> that houses the accordion) and options. Because options is highlighted in bold, that's what Dreamweaver now expects you to enter. The curly braces remind you that options must be a JavaScript object literal.

3. Type an opening curly brace. This pops up a second code hint, as shown here:

```
83  <script type="text/javascript">
84  <!--
85  var Accordion1 = new Spry.Widget.Accordion("Accordion1",{};
86  //-->
87  </script>
88  </body>
89  </html>
90
```

This shows you some of the available options. Double-click defaultPanel, or use the down arrow key to select it and press Enter/Return. Dreamweaver inserts the defaultPanel property followed by a colon ready for you to insert the value. JavaScript numbers the panels from 0, so to open the third panel, type 2 followed by a closing curly brace. The code should now look like this:

```
var Accordion1 = new Spry.Widget.Accordion("Accordion1", ➥
{defaultPanel:2});
```

4. Save stroll_accordion.html, and reload it in a browser. The third panel (Water bus) should open instead of the first one.

Converting an accordion to flexible height

Using a fixed height for an accordion is very useful when you need to keep different parts of a page in alignment, but the scrollbars tend to look unsightly (only Internet Explorer for Windows supports the nonstandard CSS properties for styling scrollbars).

Converting an accordion to flexible height involves two stages: editing the CSS and adding a new property to the Accordion object when it's initialized.

1. With stroll_accordion.html from the preceding exercise open in the Document window, open the CSS Styles panel in All mode, expand the SpryAccordion_ stroll.css tree menu if necessary, and select .AccordionPanelContent in the All Rules pane. Select height in the Properties pane, and press Delete or click the trash can icon at the bottom right of the panel.

2. Change the value of overflow from auto to hidden. If you leave the overflow property set to auto, some longer panels still spawn a scrollbar. You need to set it to hidden so that only the currently open panel is visible. That takes care of the CSS. Now you need to tell the Accordion object to use flexible height.

3. Switch to Code view in stroll_accordion.html, and scroll right to the bottom of the page and locate the code that initializes the Accordion object (see step 1 in the preceding exercise).

4. If you changed the default open panel in the preceding exercise, amend the constructor function like this (new code is in bold):

```
var Accordion1 = new Spry.Widget.Accordion("Accordion1", ➥
{defaultPanel:2, useFixedPanelHeights:false});
```

8

If you just want to remove the fixed panel heights, amend the code like this:

```
var Accordion1 = new Spry.Widget.Accordion("Accordion1", ➥
{useFixedPanelHeights: false});
```

Make sure you don't omit the comma after "Accordion1".

> The useFixedPanelHeights *property isn't listed in the code hints. This is probably because it was a late addition to the accordion widget properties. I expect it will be added in a later version or through the Adobe Updater.*

5. Save `stroll_accordion.html`, and reload it in your browser. You now have a flexible-height accordion and no ugly scrollbars.

Opening an accordion panel from a link

With Spry Tabbed Panels, it's easy to open a specific panel from a link using the showPanel() method. Spry Accordion works slightly differently. There is an openPanel() method, but it won't accept the index number of the panel on its own. The following exercise shows you how get around this.

Using a link to open the fourth panel

Continue working with `stroll_accordion.html` from the previous exercises.

1. Repeat steps 1–4 of "Opening a tabbed panel from a link" earlier in the chapter to create a dummy link in the second panel and add an onclick attribute to the <a> tag.

2. With your cursor between the quotes of the onclick attribute, type Accordion1 followed by a period. As soon as you type the period, Dreamweaver pops up code hints of the available methods, as shown in the following screenshot.

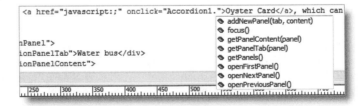

Note that there are three methods that target specific panels: openFirstPanel(), openNextPanel(), and openPreviousPanel(). Although it's not listed, there's also openLastPanel(). Since the details about the Oyster Card are in the last panel, you can use this. Type openLastPanel(). Because these four methods target specific panels, you don't need to add anything between the parentheses.

> *JavaScript is case sensitive. You must use the right combination of uppercase and lowercase.*

3. Save `stroll_accordion.html`, and load the page into a browser. Open the second panel, and click the Oyster Card link to open the last panel.

It works, but what happens if you decide to add another panel to the end of the accordion? You can't use openLastPanel() any more. Nor is openNextPanel() of any use, because you want to open the fourth panel from the second. The answer is to use one of the other methods listed in the code hints: getPanels().

4. Change the value of the onclick attribute like this (new code is in bold):

onclick="**var p=Accordion1.getPanels();** Accordion1.**openPanel(p[3])**"

What this does is create a variable called p that stores a list (an array) of the panels. You can then refer to the fourth panel as p[3] and pass that reference to openPanel(). Remember, JavaScript always starts counting from 0, so the reference needs to be p[3], not p[4], which would indicate the fifth panel if it existed. You can check your code, if necessary, against `stroll_accordion.html` in `examples/ch08`.

It's a little more complicated than opening a specific panel in the tabbed panels widget, but still quite easy. The only thing you need to change in your own code is the number between the square brackets to indicate the panel you want to open.

Using collapsible panels

New

The last of the user interface widgets is the Spry Collapsible Panel. You can use collapsible panels on their own, but when several are used in succession, they look like an accordion. The difference is that each panel is separately controlled, so they can be all open, all closed, or any combination in between.

Examining the structure of a collapsible panel

To insert a collapsible panel, click the Spry Collapsible Panel button in the Spry tab of the Insert bar, as shown in the following screenshot. Alternatively, select the same button in the Layout tab of the Insert bar or use the menu option: Insert ➤ Spry ➤ Spry Collapsible Panel.

This inserts a default collapsible panel (see Figure 8-22) at the current insertion point of the page.

Figure 8-22. A collapsible panel consists of a single tab and content area.

The underlying XHTML is extremely simple: a <div> for the tab, and another for the content, both nested in a wrapper <div> like this:

```
<div id="CollapsiblePanel1" class="CollapsiblePanel">
  <div class="CollapsiblePanelTab" tabindex="0">Tab</div>
  <div class="CollapsiblePanelContent">Content</div>
</div>
```

This simple structure makes for equally simple CSS styling. Table 8-5 lists the default selectors. As with the tabbed panels and accordion widgets, the use of tabindex is technically invalid but is a compromise to make the panels accessible through keyboard navigation.

Table 8-5. Style rules for the collapsible panel widget

Selector	Type	Notes
.CollapsiblePanel	Explicit	This zeros margin and padding on the widget and sets a light-colored border on the left and bottom and a darker-colored on the right and top. By default, collapsible panels expand horizontally to fill the available space, so set a width here if required. Set a background color for the panel here.
.CollapsiblePanelTab	Explicit	This styles the tab. Only the bottom border is set, as the top, left, and right border styles come from the preceding selector. Change this rule to style the text in the title bar. The nonstandard properties -moz-user-select and -khtml-user-select prevent users from selecting the title bar label in Mozilla, Firefox, and Konqueror browsers.
.CollapsiblePanelContent	Explicit	This zeros padding and margins. Do *not* change or delete the padding property. Always add padding or margins to elements inside the panel, rather than to the <div> itself.

Selector	Type	Notes
`.CollapsiblePanelTab a`	Explicit	This doesn't actively affect the widget in its default state. If you put a dummy link around the text in a tab, this style rule limits the focus lines around the text, rather than around the entire tab.
`.CollapsiblePanelOpen` `.CollapsiblePanelTab`	Dynamic	Sets the background color of the tab when the panel is open.
`.CollapsiblePanelTabHover,` `.CollapsiblePanelOpen` `.CollapsiblePanelTabHover`	Dynamic	Sets the background color of the tab in rollover state.
`.CollapsiblePanelFocused` `.CollapsiblePanelTab`	Dynamic	Sets the background color of the tab when the panel has focus.

Editing and styling collapsible panels

When you insert a collapsible panel widget, it's open by default, ready for editing. However, since you can have collapsible panels open and closed in any combination, the options in the Property inspector need a little explanation. As you can see in Figure 8-23, there are two drop-down menus that are set to Open by default. The first one—labeled Display—controls whether the content of the collapsible panel is visible in Design view. The second—labeled Default state—controls whether the panel is open or closed when the web page first loads.

Figure 8-23. Two settings control the state of a collapsible panel—one for Design view, the other for the web page.

The Display setting is purely for your convenience when editing the page in Dreamweaver. If you set Default state to Closed, Dreamweaver sets the contentIsOpen property of the collapsible panel object to false (see "Understanding Spry objects" earlier in the chapter for an explanation of properties).

8

An alternative way to close a collapsible panel in Design view is to click the closed eye icon at the right end of the panel tab as shown here:

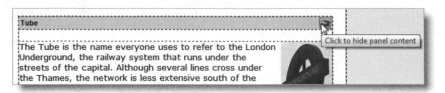

You can also open a collapsible panel in Design view using the open eye icon, which the collapsible panel widget shares in common with tabbed panels and the accordion.

The Enable animation option at the bottom of the Property inspector is checked by default. If you deselect it, the collapsible panel snaps open and closed, rather than gliding.

If you have more than one collapsible panel on a page, Dreamweaver initializes each one independently, so you need to set the options individually for each panel. There is no way of setting global options for all panels on a page.

Customizing the styles of collapsible panels

Since collapsible panels are so similar to the other Spry widgets, I won't give step-by-step instructions for inserting and editing them. For this exercise, copy stroll_collapsible_start.html from examples/ch08, and rename it stroll_collapsible.html in workfiles/ch08. The external JavaScript file, SpryCollapsiblePanel.js, and style sheet, SpryCollapsiblePanel_stroll.css, are already in the SpryAssets folder.

1. With stroll_collapsible.html open in the Document window, open the CSS Styles panel in All mode, and expand the SpryCollapsiblePanel_stroll.css tree menu. Highlight the first selector (.CollapsiblePanel), and change the colors of the borders. The left border uses the lighter color (#DFBD9F), while the right and top borders use the darker color (#C99466).

   Currently, the panels have no background color, so add the background-color property, and set it to #FAF3ED (light pink).

2. Highlight the second selector (.CollapsiblePanelTab). Change the background-color property to light pink (#FAF3ED), and the color of border-bottom to light brown (#DFBD9F).

   The default styles use shorthand for font, which is hard to edit, so delete the font property, and add the following styles:

   - color: #555555
   - font-family: Geneva, Arial, Helvetica, sans-serif
   - font-size: 90%
   - font-weight: bold

3. The next two selectors (.CollapsiblePanelContent and .CollapsiblePanelTab a) require no changes.

4. In the fifth selector (.CollapsiblePanelOpen .CollapsiblePanelTab), change background-color to darker pink (#F2E1D2).

5. Make the same change in the next selector (.CollapsiblePanelTabHover, .CollapsiblePanelOpen .CollapsiblePanelTabHover). Also add the color property, and set it to #333333.

6. In the final selector (.CollapsiblePanelFocused .CollapsiblePanelTab), change background-color to dusky pink (#ECD3BD).

7. One final change: because you cannot add padding to the CollapsiblePanelTab class, it's a good idea to create a new rule for .CollapsiblePanelContent p in the same way as you did for Spry Accordion. Select Advanced as the Selector Type, and define it in SpryCollapsiblePanel_stroll.css. Set these properties and values:

- font-size: 75%

- padding: 5px 10px

- margin: 0

You need to control the space around the paragraphs with padding, rather than margins, to get a similar effect cross-browser.

You can check your code against SpryCollapsiblePanel_stroll_done.css in the SpryAssets folder.

Opening a collapsible panel from a link

Since each panel works independently, opening one from a link is simply a matter of applying the open() method to the JavaScript variable that identifies the target panel. As Figure 8-24 shows, Dreamweaver has initialized four CollapsiblePanel objects at the bottom of stroll_collapsible.html, and the variable that identifies the fourth one is, predictably enough, CollapsiblePanel4.

```
84  var CollapsiblePanel1 = new Spry.Widget.CollapsiblePanel("CollapsiblePanel1");
85  var CollapsiblePanel2 = new Spry.Widget.CollapsiblePanel("CollapsiblePanel2", {contentIsOpen:false});
86  var CollapsiblePanel3 = new Spry.Widget.CollapsiblePanel("CollapsiblePanel3", {contentIsOpen:false});
87  var CollapsiblePanel4 = new Spry.Widget.CollapsiblePanel("CollapsiblePanel4", {contentIsOpen:false});
```

Figure 8-24. Each collapsible panel is initialized independently.

Using the open() method on a collapsible panel

Continue working with stroll_collapsible.html from the previous exercise.

1. Repeat steps 1–4 of "Opening a tabbed panel from a link" earlier in the chapter to create a dummy link in the second panel, and add an onclick attribute to the <a> tag.

2. With your cursor between the quotes of the onclick attribute, type CollapsiblePanel4 followed by a period. As soon as you type the period, Dreamweaver pops up code hints of the available methods, as shown in the following screenshot:

8

```
<a href="javascript:;" onclick="CollapsiblePanel4.">Oyster Card</a>
                                                        close()
                                                        focus()
                                                        getContent()
                                                        getTab()
nel13" class="CollapsiblePanel">                        isOpen()
psiblePanelTab" tabindex="0">Water bus</div>            open()
psiblePanelContent">
```

3. Double-click open() or use the down arrow key to select it, and press Enter/Return. That's it. When clicked in a browser, the Oyster Card link opens the fourth panel.

4. Unlike the accordion, the second panel remains open. If you want to close the second panel at the same time as opening the first, change the onclick attribute like this:

```
onclick="CollapsiblePanel4.open();CollapsiblePanel2.close()"
```

Adding the semicolon after a JavaScript command lets you chain two or more together. You can check your code with stroll_collapsible_done.html in examples/ch08.

Removing a Spry widget

Removing a Spry widget is very easy: just click the turquoise tab at the top left of the widget, and press Delete. Dreamweaver removes the object initialization script from the bottom of the page and, if no other instances of the same widget are on the page, the links to the external JavaScript file and style sheet. However, if you have renamed the style sheet (as in the exercises in this chapter), the link to the style sheet *isn't* removed. Dreamweaver removes only style sheets that retain the default name.

While this sounds simple and convenient, it comes with a big downside: *removing a widget also removes all its contents*. So, think carefully before pressing Delete. Do you need to display the contents in some other format? If so, make sure you have a copy before blasting everything to cyber oblivion.

The alternative is to select each part of the widget individually in the Tag selector at the bottom of the Document window, right-click, and select Set Class ➤ None. If you follow this route, you should also manually remove the object initialization script from the bottom of the page, as well as the links to the JavaScript file and style sheet (assuming they're not required by other widgets).

Yet more widgets . . .

In addition to the user interface widgets, Dreamweaver CS3 has four more, designed to improve user experience when entering information into online forms. This is where real interactivity begins, as online forms are essential for interaction with a database. So, in the next chapter, I'll show you how to build an online form to gather user feedback or place an online order. Then we'll use the Spry validation widgets to check the user information, and finally bring PHP into the mix in Chapter 11 by using it to send the form's contents to your mailbox.

8

9 BUILDING ONLINE FORMS AND VALIDATING INPUT

Online forms are the gateway to the server, and lie at the very heart of working with PHP, the focus of most of the remaining chapters. You use forms for logging into restricted pages, registering new users, placing orders with online stores, entering and updating information in a database, and sending feedback by email. But gateways need protection.

You need to filter out incomplete or wrong information: a form isn't much use if users forget to fill in required fields or enter an impossible phone number. It's also important to make sure that user input doesn't corrupt your database or turn your website into a spam relay. That's what **input validation** is all about—checking that user input is safe and meets your requirements. This is different from validating your XHTML or CSS against W3C standards, and it's much more important because it protects your data.

Validating user input is a theme that will run through much of the rest of this book. In this chapter, we'll look at client-side validation with the assistance of Spry. Then, in Chapter 11, I'll show you how to process the form and validate its content on the server with PHP. Server-side validation is more important, because it's possible for users to evade client-side filters. Even so, client-side validation is useful for catching errors before a form is submitted, improving user experience.

What this chapter covers

- Creating forms to gather user input
- Understanding the difference between GET and POST
- Passing information through a hidden form field
- Making online forms accessible
- Using the Tag Inspector
- Using Spry widgets to validate input
- Displaying and controlling the number of characters in a text area

Building a simple feedback form

All the components for building forms are on the Forms tab of the Insert bar. They're also on the Form submenu of the Insert menu, but for the sake of brevity, I'll refer only to the Insert bar in this chapter.

Most form elements use the `<input>` tag, with their function and look controlled by the type attribute. The exceptions are the multiline text area, which uses the `<textarea>` tag, and drop-down menu and scrollable lists, which use the `<select>` tag. Dreamweaver handles all the coding for you, but you need to dive into Code view frequently when working with forms and PHP, so if your knowledge of the tags and attributes is a bit rusty, brush it up with a good reference book, such as *Web Designer's Reference* by Craig Grannell (friends of ED, ISBN-13: 978-1-59059-430-8).

Choosing the right page type

XHTML contains all the necessary tags to construct a form, but it doesn't provide any means to process the form when submitted. For that, you need a server-side solution, such as PHP. In the past, you may have used FormMail or a similar script to send the contents of a form by email. Such scripts normally reside in a directory called `cgi-bin` and work with `.html` pages. The `action` attribute in the opening `<form>` tag tells the form where to send the contents for processing. It usually looks something like this:

```
<form id="sendcomments" method="post" action="/cgi-bin/formmail.cgi">
```

You can do the same with PHP: build the form in an `.html` page and send the contents to an external PHP script for processing. However, it's far more efficient to put the form in a page with a `.php` file name extension and use the same page to process the form. This makes it a lot easier to redisplay the contents with error messages if any problems are found. So, from now on, we'll start using PHP pages. Before going any further, you should have specified a PHP testing server, as described in Chapter 4.

Creating a PHP page

There are several ways to create a PHP page in Dreamweaver, namely:

- Select Create New ➤ PHP in the Dreamweaver welcome screen.

- Select File ➤ New to open the New Document dialog box, and select Blank Page and PHP as the Page Type. As Figure 9-1 shows, this offers the same choice of CSS layouts as an HTML page. Click Create when you have made your selection.

- Right-click in the Files panel, and select New File. If you have defined a PHP testing server, Dreamweaver creates a default blank page with a `.php` file name extension.

- Change the file name extension of an existing page to `.php` in the Files panel or Save As dialog box.

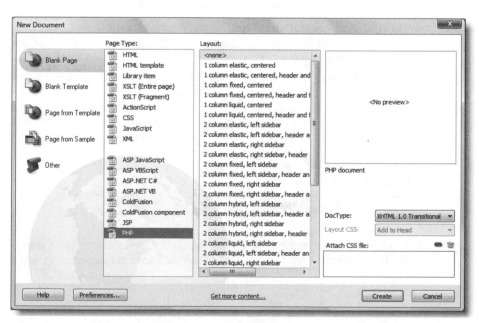

Figure 9-1. You have access to the same wide range of CSS layouts for a PHP page as for an HTML one.

The file name extension is the only difference between a blank PHP page and an HTML one. If you switch to Code view, you'll see the same DOCTYPE declaration and XHTML tags. The .php extension tells the server to send the page to the PHP engine for processing before sending it to the browser.

Mixing .php and .html pages in a site

It's perfectly acceptable to mix .html and .php files in the same site. However, when building a new site, it's a good idea to create all pages with a .php extension, even if they don't contain dynamic code. That way, you can always add dynamic content to a page without needing to redirect visitors from an .html page. If you are converting an old site, you can leave the main home page as a static page, and use it to link to your PHP pages.

A lot of people ask if you can treat .html (or any other file name extension) as PHP. The answer is yes, but it's not recommended, because it places an unnecessary burden on the server and makes the site less portable. Also, reconfiguring Dreamweaver to treat .html files as PHP is messy and inconvenient.

Inserting a form in a page

It's time to get to work and build a feedback form. To concentrate on how the form is validated and processed, let's work in a blank page and keep the styling to a minimum.

Building the basic form

The final code for this page is in feedback.php in examples/ch09.

1. Create a new PHP page as described in the previous section, and save it in workfiles/ch09 as feedback.php. If you use the New Document dialog box, set Layout to <none>, and make sure no style sheets are listed under Attach CSS file.

2. Add a heading, followed by a short paragraph. Make sure that you're in Design view or, if Split view is open, that the focus is in Design view. Inserting a form is completely different when the focus is in Code view, as explained in "Inserting a form in Code view" later. With the insertion point at the end of the paragraph, select the Form button on the Forms tab of the Insert bar. It's the first item, as shown here:

3. This inserts the opening and closing <form> tags in the underlying code. In Design view, the form is surrounded by a red dashed line, as shown in the next screenshot:

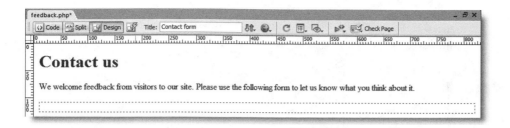

If you try to insert a form element outside the dashed red line, Dreamweaver asks you if you want to insert a form tag. Unless you want to create two separate forms, this is normally an indication that your insertion point is in the wrong place. Although you can have as many forms as you like on a page, each one is treated separately. When a user clicks a form's submit button, only information in the same form is processed; all other forms are ignored.

4. The Property inspector displays the form's settings, as shown here:

Dreamweaver gives forms a generic name followed by a number. This is applied to both the name and id attributes in the underlying code. If you change the name in the Property inspector, Dreamweaver also updates the id attribute.

The Action field is where you enter the path of the script that processes the form. Since this will be a self-processing form, leave the field empty.

The Method menu has three options: Default, GET, and POST. This determines how the form sends data to the processing script. Leave the setting on POST. I'll explain the difference between GET and POST shortly. The confusingly named Default option removes the method attribute from the <form> tag and should not be used.

You can ignore the Target and Enctype options. Target should normally be used only with frames, and Dreamweaver automatically selects the correct value for Enctype if required. The only time it needs a value is for uploading files. Dreamweaver server behaviors don't handle file uploads. See my book *PHP Solutions: Dynamic Web Design Made Easy* (friends of ED, ISBN-13: 978-1-59059-731-6) for details of how to do it by hand-coding.

Inserting a form in Code view

If you insert a form in Code view or in Split view with the focus in Code view, Dreamweaver displays the Tag Editor (see Figure 9-2). This offers the same options as the Property inspector, but you need to fill in all the details yourself. Inserting a form in Design view is much more user friendly.

251

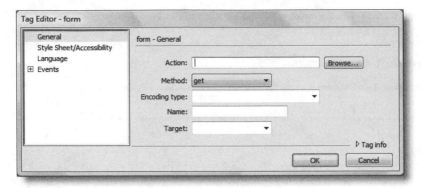

Figure 9-2. The Tag Editor is a less user-friendly way to insert a form.

The Tag Editor selects get as the default value for Method. (GET and POST are case-insensitive in the XHTML method attribute.) If you enter a value in the Name field, Dreamweaver inserts the name attribute, even if you're using a strict DTD, and doesn't assign the same value to the id attribute. To insert an ID, you need to select Style Sheet/Accessibility in the left column, and enter the value manually.

Adding text input elements

Most online forms have fields for users to enter text, either in a single line, such as for a name, password, or telephone number, or a larger area, where the text spreads over many lines. Let's insert a couple of single-line text fields and a text area for comments.

Opinions vary on the best way to lay out a form. A simple way to get everything to line up is to use a table, but this creates problems for adding accessibility features, such as <label> tags. The method that I'm going to use is to put each element in a paragraph and use CSS to tidy up the layout.

Inserting text fields and a text area

Continue working with the form from the preceding exercise.

1. With your insertion point inside the red outline of the form, press Enter/Return. This inserts two empty paragraphs inside the form. Press your up arrow key once to return to the first paragraph, and click the Text Field button in the Insert bar, as shown here:

Changed

2. By default, this launches the Input Tag Accessibility Attributes dialog box (see Figure 9-3), which has been improved since it was first introduced in Dreamweaver 8. You can now enter an ID for the form element, which is also used for its name attribute.

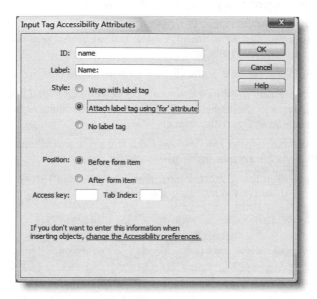

Figure 9-3. Dreamweaver makes it easy to build forms that follow accessibility guidelines.

In the Label field, enter the label that you want to appear next to the form element, including any punctuation, such as a colon, that you want to appear onscreen.

The Style option lets you choose whether to wrap the <label> tag around the form element like this:

```
<label>Name:
<input type="text" name="name" id="name" />
</label>
```

use the for attribute like this:

```
<label for="name">Name:</label>
<input type="text" name="name" id="name" />
```

or have no label at all. This option is sticky, so Dreamweaver remembers whichever you chose the last time.

The Position option, on the other hand, isn't sticky. It automatically chooses the recommended position for a form label. In the case of a text field, this is in front of the item, but with radio buttons and checkboxes, it's after the item. You can, however, override the default choice if you want to.

9

The final two options let you specify an access key and a tab index. Finally, if you don't want to use these accessibility features, there's a link that takes you to the relevant section of Dreamweaver preferences to prevent this dialog box from appearing. However, since accessibility is such an important issue in modern web design, I recommend that you use these attributes as a matter of course.

An important improvement in Dreamweaver CS3 is that the value in the ID field is assigned to both the id and for attributes. You no longer need to dive into Code view to adjust the for attribute.

Use the settings in Figure 9-3, and click OK to insert a text field and label in the form.

3. Move your insertion point into the empty paragraph below and insert another text field. Enter email in the ID field, and Email: in the Label field. Leave the other settings the same as in Figure 9-3, and click OK.

4. Position your cursor after the new text field, and press Enter/Return twice to insert two more blank paragraphs inside the form.

5. Put your cursor in the first blank paragraph, and click the Text Area button on the Insert bar, as shown in the following screenshot:

In the Input Tag Accessibility Attributes dialog box, set ID to comments and Label to Comments:, leave the other settings as before, and click OK.

6. Move into the final blank paragraph, and select Button in the Insert bar as shown:

In the Input Tag Accessibility Attributes dialog box, set ID to send, leave the Label field empty, select No label tag as Style, and click OK. This inserts a submit button.

7. In the Property inspector, change Value from Submit to Send comments. This changes the label on the button (press Enter/Return or move the focus out of the Value field for the change to take effect). Leave Action on the default Submit form. The form should now look like this in Design view:

> *If you select* Reset form *in the Property inspector, this creates a reset button that clears all user input from the form. However, in Chapter 11, you'll learn how to pre-serve user input when a form is submitted with errors. This technique relies on setting the* value *attribute of each form element, which prevents* Reset form *from working after the form has been submitted.*

If you switch to Code view, the underlying XHTML for the form should look like this:

```
<form action="" method="post" name="form1" id="form1">
  <p>
    <label for="name">Name:</label>
    <input type="text" name="name" id="name" />
  </p>
  <p>
    <label for="email">Email:</label>
    <input type="text" name="email" id="email" />
  </p>
  <p>
    <label for="comments">Comments:</label>
    <textarea name="comments" id="comments" cols="45" rows="5"> ➡
</textarea>
  </p>
  <p>
    <input type="submit" name="send" id="send" value="Send comments" />
  </p>
</form>
```

The XHTML 1.0 specification (www.w3.org/TR/xhtml1) lists a number of elements, including <form>, for which the name attribute has been deprecated. If you select a strict document type declaration (DTD), Dreamweaver omits the name attribute from the <form> tag. However, it's important to realize that this applies only to the opening <form> tag and *not* to elements within a form, where name plays a vital role.

> *The* name *attribute not only remains valid for* <input>, <select>, *and* <textarea>; *PHP and other scripting languages cannot process data without it. Although the* id *attribute is optional, you must use the* name *attribute for each element you want to be processed. The* name *attribute should consist only of alphanumeric characters and the underscore and should contain no spaces.*

Setting properties for text input elements

In the preceding exercise, you inserted two text fields and a text area. A text field permits user input only on a single line, whereas a text area allows multiple lines of input. The Property inspector offers almost identical options for both types of text input, and even lets you convert from one to the other. Figure 9-4 shows the Property inspector for the Name text field. Notice that Type is set to Single line. In one respect, this is Dreamweaver trying to be user friendly by adopting descriptive terms, rather than using the official attribute names. Unfortunately, if you're familiar with the correct XHTML terminology, the labels in the Property inspector can be more confusing than enlightening. Single line is the equivalent of type="text" in an <input> tag.

Figure 9-4. The Property inspector for a text field lets you convert it into a text area and vice versa.

The Char width option specifies the width of the input field. For a text field, this is the equivalent of the size attribute, which is measured in characters, so it just takes a number. I normally use CSS to style the width of input fields, so you can leave this blank.

Max chars sets the maximum number of characters that a field accepts. This sets the maxlength attribute of a text field. If left blank, no limit is imposed.

If you change Type to Password, the browser obscures anything typed into the field by displaying a series of stars or bullets. It doesn't encrypt the input but prevents anyone from seeing it in plain text. This is the equivalent of type="password" in an <input> tag.

Init val lets you specify a default value for the field. It sets the value attribute, which is optional and normally left blank.

Figure 9-5 shows the Property inspector for the Comments text area. As you can see, it looks almost identical to Figure 9-4, although Type is set to Multi line and the Wrap option is no longer grayed out. This time, Type has no direct equivalent in the underlying XHTML. Selecting Multi line changes the tag from <input> to <textarea>.

Changed

The other important differences are that Max chars has changed to Num lines and default values have been set for Char width and Num lines. These determine the width and height of the text area by inserting the rows and cols attributes in the opening <textarea> tag. Previous versions of Dreamweaver didn't do this, but both attributes are required for valid XHTML and should be left in, even if you plan to use CSS to set the dimensions of the text area.

Figure 9-5. When you insert a text area, Dreamweaver gives it a default width and height.

All modern browsers automatically wrap user input in a text area, so you should always leave Wrap set to Default. Selecting any other option inserts the invalid wrap attribute that doesn't work in most browsers. Wrap is likely to be removed from the next version of Dreamweaver.

Converting a text field to a text area and vice versa

Although text fields and text areas use completely different tags, Dreamweaver lets you convert from one type to the other by changing the Type option in the Property inspector. If you change Type from Single line to Multi line, the <input> tag is replaced by a pair of <textarea> tags and vice versa. Dreamweaver makes the process seamless by changing or removing attributes. For example, if you convert a text area to a text field, the cols attribute changes to size, and the rows attribute is deleted.

This is convenient if you change your mind about the design of a form, as it saves deleting one type of text input field and restarting from scratch. However, you need to remember to set both Char width and Num lines if converting a single-line field to a text area; Dreamweaver sets the defaults only when inserting a text area from the Insert bar or menu.

The Password option works only with single-line input. It cannot be used with a text area.

Styling the basic feedback form

The form looks a bit unruly, so let's give it some basic styling.

Styling the form

With the exception of a single class, all the style rules use type selectors (see "Creating new style rules" in Chapter 5 for a definition). Rather than using the New CSS Style dialog box to create them, it's quicker and easier to type them directly into a new style sheet in Code view.

1. Create a new style sheet by going to File ➤ New. In the New Document dialog box, select Blank Page and CSS as the Page Type. Insert the following rules, and save the page as contact.css in the workfiles/styles folder. (If you don't want to type everything yourself, there's a copy in the examples/styles folder. The version in the download files contains some extra rules that will be added later.)

```
body {
  background-color:#FFFFFF;
  color:#252525;
  font-family:Arial, Helvetica, sans-serif;
  font-size:100%;
  }
h1 {
  font-family:Verdana, Arial, Helvetica, sans-serif;
  font-size:150%;
  }
p {
  font-size:85%;
  margin:0 0 5px 25px;
  max-width: 650px;
  }
form {
  width:600px;
```

9

```
      margin:15px auto 10px 20px;
      }
label {
   display:block;
   font-weight:bold;
   }
textarea {
   width:400px;
   height:150px;
   }
.textInput {
   width:250px;
   }
```

The style rules are very straightforward, mainly setting fonts and controlling the size and margins of elements. By setting the display property for label to block, each <label> tag is forced onto a line of its own above the element it refers to.

2. Switch to feedback.php in the Document window, click in a blank area of the page, and open the Style drop-down menu in the Property inspector. Select Attach Style Sheet. Browse to contact.css, and attach it to feedback.php. The form should now look a lot neater.

3. Select the Name text field, and set its class to textInput to set its width to 250 pixels. Do the same with the Email text field.

4. Save feedback.php, and press F12/Opt+F12 to preview it in a browser. It should look like Figure 9-6.

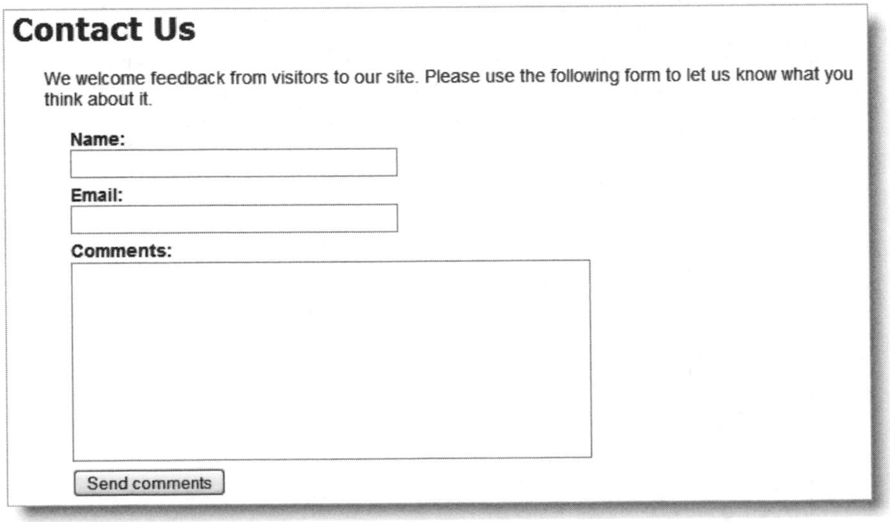

Figure 9-6. The basic feedback form is ready for business.

Understanding the difference between GET and POST

Now that you have a form to work with, this is a good time to see how information is passed from the form and demonstrate the difference between choosing GET and POST as the method attribute. With feedback.php displayed in a browser, type anything into the form, and click the Send comments button. Whatever you typed into the text fields should disappear. It hasn't been processed because there's no script to handle it, but the content of the text fields hasn't entirely disappeared. Click the browser's reload button, and you should see a warning that the data will be resent if you reload the page.

If the action attribute is empty, the default behavior is to submit the data in the form to the same page. As the warning indicates, the data has been passed to the page, but since there's no script to process it, nothing happens. Processing the data is the subject of Chapter 11, but let's take a sneak preview to see the different ways POST and GET submit the data.

Examining the data submitted by a form

In this exercise, you'll add a simple PHP conditional statement to display the data transmitted by the POST method. You'll also see what happens when the form is submitted using the GET method. Use feedback.php from the preceding exercise. If you just want to test the code, use feedback_post.php in examples/ch09.

1. Save a copy of feedback.php as feedback_post.php in workfiles/ch09. Open it in Code view, and scroll to the bottom of the page.

2. Add the following code shown in bold between the closing </form> and </body> tags:

```
</form>
<pre>
<?php if ($_POST) {print_r($_POST);} ?>
</pre>
</body>
```

As soon as you type the underscore after the dollar sign, Dreamweaver pops up a PHP code hint, as shown in the screenshot alongside. Type p (uppercase or lowercase—it doesn't matter), and press Enter/Return. Dreamweaver completes $_POST and automatically places an opening square bracket after it. Delete the square bracket.

$_POST is a PHP superglobal array, which is created automatically. As the name suggests, it contains data sent by the POST method. (The role of superglobal arrays is explained in Chapter 11.)

Don't worry about the meaning of the PHP code. Just accept it for the moment, and concentrate on what it does.

3. Save the page, and load it into a browser. Enter some text in the form, and click Send comments. This time, you should see the value of each field identified by its name attribute displayed at the bottom of the page as in Figure 9-7.

```
Send comments

Array
(
    [name] => David
    [email] => david@example.com
    [comments] => Hi there!
    [send] => Send comments
)
```

Figure 9-7.
The PHP $_POST superglobal array contains the data submitted from the form.

The values gathered by the $_POST array contain not only the information entered into the text fields but also the label of the submit button.

4. Change the value of method in the opening <form> tag from post to get like this:

```
<form action="" method="get" name="form1" id="form1">
```

5. Save the page, and display it again in the browser by clicking inside the address bar and pressing Enter/Return. Don't use the reload button, because you don't want to resend the POST data.

6. Type anything into the form, and click Send comments. This time, nothing will be displayed below the form, but the contents of the form fields will be appended to the URL, as shown in Figure 9-8. Again, each value is identified by its name attribute.

Figure 9-8. Data sent using the GET method is appended to the URL as a series of name/value pairs.

As you have just seen, the GET method sends your data in a very exposed way, making it vulnerable to alteration. Also, some browsers limit the maximum length of a URL, so it can be used only for small amounts of data. The POST method is more secure and can be used for much larger amounts of data. By default, PHP permits up to 8MB of POST data, although hosting companies may set a smaller limit.

Because of these advantages, you should normally use the POST method with forms. The GET method is used mainly in conjunction with database searches and has the advantage that you can bookmark a search result because all the data is in the URL.

> *Although the POST method is more secure than GET, you shouldn't assume that it's 100 percent safe. For secure transmission, you need to use encryption or the Secure Sockets Layer (SSL).*

Passing information through a hidden field

Frequently, you need to pass information to a script without displaying it in the browser. For example, a form used to update a database record needs to pass the record's ID to the update script. You can store the information in what's called a **hidden field**.

Adding a hidden field

Although you don't need a hidden field in this feedback form, let's put one in to see how it works. Hidden fields play an important role in later chapters. Continue working with feedback_post.php from the preceding exercise. The finished code is in feedback_hidden.php.

1. Set the value of method back to post. Do this in Code view or by selecting the form in Design view and setting Method to POST in the Property inspector.

2. A hidden field isn't displayed, so it doesn't matter where you locate it, as long as it's inside the form. However, it's normal practice to put hidden fields at the bottom of a form. Switch back to Design view, and click to the right of the Send comments button.

3. Click the Hidden Field button on the Insert bar, as shown here:

4. Dreamweaver inserts a hidden field icon alongside the Send comments button. Type a name for the hidden field in the left text field in the Property inspector and the value you want it to contain in the Value field, as shown in Figure 9-9.

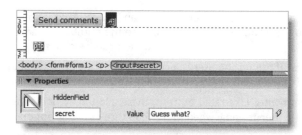

Figure 9-9. Select a hidden field's icon in Design view to edit its name and value in the Property inspector.

Note that the PHP script at the bottom of the page is indicated by a gold PHP icon. If you can't see the hidden field or PHP icons in Design view, select View ➤ Visual Aids ➤ Invisible Elements.

> *The option on the* View *menu controls the display of invisible elements only on the current page. To change the default, open the* Preferences *panel from the* Edit *menu (*Dreamweaver *menu in a Mac), and select the* Invisible Elements *category. Make sure there's a check mark alongside* Hidden form fields *and* Visual Server Markup Tags, *and then click* OK. *The* Visual Aids *submenu is useful for turning off the display of various tools when they get in the way of the design of a page. You can toggle currently selected visual aids on and off with the keyboard shortcut Ctrl+Shift+I/Shift+Cmd+I.*

5. Switch to Code view. You'll see that Dreamweaver has inserted the following code at the end of the form:

```
<input name="secret" type="hidden" id="secret" value="Guess what?" />
```

6. Save feedback_post.php, and press F12/Opt+F12 to load the page in a browser (or use feedback_hidden.php in examples/ch09). The hidden field should be, well . . . hidden. Right-click to view the page's source code. The hidden field and its value are clearly visible. Test the form by entering some text and clicking Send comments. The value of secret should be displayed with the rest of the form input.

Just because a hidden field isn't displayed in a form doesn't mean that it really is hidden. Frequently, the value of a hidden field is set dynamically, and the field is simply a device for passing information from one page to another. Never use a hidden field for information that you genuinely want to keep secret.

Using multiple-choice form elements

Useful though text input is, you have no control over what's entered in the form. People spell things wrong or enter inappropriate answers. There's no point in a customer ordering a yellow T-shirt when the only colors available are white and black. Multiple-choice form elements leave the user in no doubt what the options are, and you get answers in the format you want.

Web forms have four multiple-choice elements, as follows:

- **Radio buttons**: These are often used in an either/or situation, such as male or female and yes or no, but there's no limit to the number of radio buttons that can be used in a group. However, only one option can be chosen.

- **Checkboxes**: These let the user select several options or none at all. They're useful for indicating the user's interests, ordering optional accessories, and so on.

- **Drop-down menus**: Like radio buttons, these allow only one choice, but are more compact and user-friendly when more than three or four options are available.

- **Multiple-choice lists**: Like checkboxes, these permit several options to be chosen, but present them as a scrolling list. Often, the need to scroll back and forth to see all the options makes this the least user-friendly way of presenting a multiple choice.

Let's add them to the basic feedback form to see how they work.

Offering a range of choices with checkboxes

There are two schools of thought about the best way to use checkboxes. One is to give each checkbox a different name; the other is to give the same name to all checkboxes in the same group. My preference is to use the second method, as it makes it easy to identify selected checkboxes as related to each other. Unfortunately, Dreamweaver uses the same values for the id and name attributes of form elements. An ID must always be unique, so you need to adjust the name attribute of each checkbox in Code view after creating the individual checkboxes.

Inserting a group of checkboxes

Laying out a group of checkboxes in an attractive and accessible manner is quite tricky. I have decided to organize five checkboxes in two columns using a floated <div> for each column. Continue working with feedback_post.php from the preceding exercise. Alternatively, copy feedback_multi_start.php from examples/ch09 to workfiles/ch09. The finished code for this exercise is in feedback_checkbox.php.

1. Save the page as feedback_checkbox.php in workfiles/ch09.

2. With the page open in Design view, click immediately to the right of the Comments text area. Press Enter/Return to insert a new paragraph.

3. Each checkbox has its own label, so you need a heading for the checkbox group that uses the same font size and weight as the <label> tags.

   Click the Bold button in the Property inspector (the large B just to the right of the CSS button). Although the tooltip says Bold, this inserts the <strong> tag in accordance with current standards, rather than the presentational <b> tag. Type a heading for the checkbox group. I used What aspects of London most interest you? Click the Bold tag again to move the cursor outside the closing </strong> tag in the underlying code.

4. Checkboxes usually have short labels, so it's often a good idea to display them in columns. You could use a table, but I'm going to use a couple of <div> tags instead. They'll be floated left, so you need to create a style rule for them, but you can do this at the same time as inserting the first <div>. The same rule will be used for both checkboxes and radio buttons, so I've called the class chkRad.

   With your insertion point at the end of the paragraph you entered in step 3, click the Insert Div Tag button on the Common tab of the Insert bar or use Insert ➤ Layout Objects ➤ Div Tag. In the Insert Div Tag dialog box, set Insert to At insertion point, and type chkRad (*without* a leading period) in the Class field.

   If you're using contact.css from the download files, the chkRad class is already defined in the style sheet, so click OK, and skip to step 6.

   If you created your own version of contact.css, click the New CSS Style button in the Insert Div Tag dialog box.

5. The New CSS Style dialog box should select the correct options, as shown here:

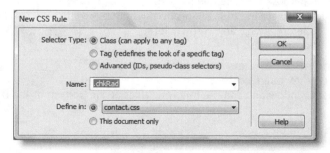

9

There's an inconsistency in the way that Dreamweaver expects you to specify the name of a class. The New CSS Rule *dialog box correctly identifies the class name and automatically adds a period in front of it* only *if you omit the period in the* Insert Div Tag *dialog box. If you use a period in the* Insert Div Tag *dialog box, the* Name *field remains blank when the* New CSS Rule *dialog box opens.*

Click OK to open the CSS Rule Definition dialog box, and select the Box category. Set Float to left. Deselect Same for all under Margin, and set Bottom to 8 pixels and Left to 30 pixels. Click OK twice to close both dialog boxes.

6. You should now have a new `<div>` with some placeholder text in it like this:

Don't worry about the button floating up alongside the `<div>`. We'll fix that soon.

Press Delete to remove the placeholder text, followed by Return/Enter twice to create three empty paragraphs in the `<div>`. Use the up keyboard arrow to move into the first one, and click the Checkbox button on the Forms tab of the Insert bar, as shown here:

7. Use the settings shown alongside in the Input Tag Accessibility Attributes dialog box.

This inserts the label in the recommended position *after* the checkbox.

When you click OK, you'll see that the label is on a new line beneath the checkbox. This is because the style rule for labels in `contact.css` sets the display property to block. Before going any further, let's sort out the style rules.

8. The form needs three new style rules, so it's quicker to open `contact.css` in the Document window and add the following rules at the bottom of the page:

```css
.chkRad label {
  display:inline;
  }
.clearIt {
  clear:both;
```

```
  }
select {
  margin:5px 0 8px 30px;
  }
```

The first rule resets `<label>` elements to display inline when a descendant of the chkRad class. The `.clearIt` selector uses the `clear` property, which prevents other elements from moving up into empty space alongside a floated element. By setting the value of `clear` to both, this works with both left-floated and right-floated elements. The final rule puts a 5px top margin, an 8px bottom margin, and a 30px left margin on `<select>` elements, so that they line up with the chkRad class.

9. Save `contact.css`, and close it. The label should now be alongside the checkbox, but the Send comments button is still causing a problem. Select the button, and right-click the `<p>` tag in the Tag selector at the bottom of the Document window. Select Set Class ➤ clearIt from the context menu, as shown here:

10. With the layout sorted out, you can finish the first checkbox. It needs a value that will be sent to the PHP script if a user selects the checkbox. Click the checkbox in Design view to bring up its details in the Property inspector, and set Checked value to Classical concerts. Leave Initial state at the default Unchecked, as shown here:

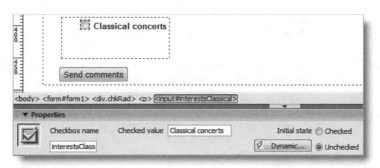

11. Insert two more checkboxes in the second and third paragraphs that you created inside the <div> in step 6. Give them the following settings:

- ID: interestsRock

  Label: Rock/pop events

  Checked value: Rock/pop

- ID: interestsDrama

  Label: Drama

  Checked value: Drama

12. The second column of checkboxes needs to be another <div> immediately after the existing one. Because the existing <div> uses a class, rather than an ID, you need to position your cursor manually at the insertion point. Although you could dive into Code view to do this, it's easy enough in Design view.

Click anywhere inside the <div> that contains the checkboxes, and click <div.chkRad> in the Tag selector at the bottom of the Document window to select the whole <div>, as shown alongside. Press your right keyboard arrow once. The insertion point is now immediately outside the closing </div> tag ready for you to insert the new <div>.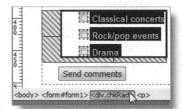

You can now insert a new <div> (Insert ➤ Layout Objects ➤ Div Tag or use the Common tab of the Insert bar). In the Insert Div Tag dialog box, make sure Insert is set to At insertion point, and set Class to chkRad (you can select it from the Class drop-down menu because it was defined in the style sheet earlier).

13. When you click OK, Dreamweaver inserts the <div> with placeholder text alongside the existing checkboxes in the right position for a second column, as shown here:

Press Delete followed by Enter/Return to remove the placeholder text and create two empty paragraphs. Insert two more checkboxes in them, using the following settings:

- ID: interestsWalks

  Label: Guided walks

  Checked value: Guided walks

- ID: interestsArt

  Label: Art

  Checked value: Art

14. Just one more thing: adjust the name attributes of the checkboxes so that PHP knows to treat them as a group. Open Code view. Each checkbox should look like this:

```
<p>
  <input name="interestsClassical" type="checkbox" ➡
id="interestsClassical" value="Classical concerts" />
  <label for="interestsClassical">Classical concerts</label>
</p>
```

Change the name attribute of all five checkboxes like this:

```
<input name="interests[]" type="checkbox" id="interestsClassical" ➡
value="Classical concerts" />
```

The empty square brackets tell PHP to treat this group as an array (or a list of related values). Make sure there is no space between interests and the square brackets.

15. Save the page, and load it into a browser. Select some of the checkboxes, and click the Send comments button. The checked values should appear at the bottom of the page. Try it with no boxes checked. This time, interests isn't listed.

If you think that was rather fiddly, you're right. Building a checkbox group isn't as easy as it might be, since each ID must be unique, but the whole group must share the same name. You can't change the name attributes in the Property inspector, because Dreamweaver automatically links both values together. You'll be relieved to know that other multiple-choice form elements are easier to handle.

Offering a single choice from a drop-down menu

Drop-down menus and multiple-choice lists both use the XHMTL <select> tag, with each individual item in an <option> tag. Apart from two attributes in the opening <select> tag, their underlying structure is identical, so Dreamweaver uses the same tools to insert and configure them. First, let's take a look at a single-choice menu. The following instructions show you how to add one to the feedback form.

9

Inserting and configuring a drop-down menu

Continue working with the form from the preceding exercise or copy feedback_checkbox.php from examples/ch09 to workfiles/ch09. The finished code is in feedback_select.php.

1. Save feedback_checkbox.php as feedback_select.php.

2. To insert the drop-down menu after the checkboxes, insert your cursor anywhere in the second checkbox <div> in Design view, click <div.chkRad> in the Tag selector at the bottom of the Document window, and press your right keyboard arrow once to move the insertion point outside the closing </div> tag.

> *This is the same technique as in step 12 of the preceding section. Selecting an element in the Tag selector and pressing the right arrow key once is a quick and accurate way of moving the insertion point to immediately after the closing tag of an element. If you want to move the insertion point to immediately before the opening tag, press the left arrow key once instead.*

3. Press Enter/Return to insert a paragraph. The cursor will appear not to move because the <div> that contains the checkboxes is floated. So right-click the <p> tag in the Tag selector, and choose Set Class ➤ clearIt from the context menu.

4. The paragraph is now in the right place for you to insert a drop-down menu by clicking the List/Menu button on the Forms tab of the Insert bar, as shown here:

5. Enter the following settings in the Input Tag Accessibility Attributes dialog box:

- ID: visited
- Label: How often have you been to London?
- Style: Attach label tag using 'for' attribute
- Position: Before form item (Dreamweaver selects this automatically)

6. When you click OK, Dreamweaver inserts the label and a blank menu element in Design view. Click the menu element to select it and display its details in the Property inspector, as shown in the following screenshot:

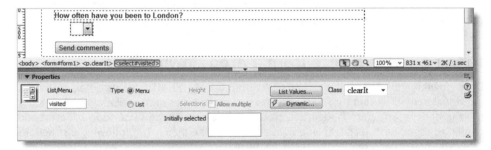

Type is set by default to Menu, which builds a single-choice drop-down menu. The List option creates a scrolling list. You'll see how that works in the next section.

7. To populate the menu, click the List Values button in the Property inspector. This opens the List Values dialog box, as shown in the following screenshot. Item Label is what you want to be shown in the menu, and Value is the data you want to be sent if the item is selected when the form is submitted.

The easiest way to fill in the dialog box is to tab between the fields. Tabbing from the Value field creates the next item. You can also click inside an existing field to edit it. Use the minus (–) button to delete a selected item, and the up and down arrows to reorder the list. Click OK when you are finished.

8. Dreamweaver normally displays the longest label in Design view. To specify the one you want to be displayed when the form first loads, select it in the Initially selected field in the Property inspector. This adds selected="selected" to the <option> tag.

   By default, browsers show the first item in the menu if you don't set the Initially selected field. However, it's often useful to select an item that's lower down the list. For example, you may want to display a list of countries in alphabetical order, but if most of your visitors are from the United States, it's a courtesy to display that by default rather than forcing them to scroll all the way down the list to select it.

9. Save feedback_select.php, and load it in a browser. Select a menu item, and click Send comments. The value should be displayed as visited at the bottom of the page.

   If you did the same as me in step 7 and left the Value field blank for the first item, the contents of Item Label are displayed when you submit the form with the first item selected. This is because Dreamweaver omits the value attribute from the <option> tag. To get around this, always set an explicit value in the List Values dialog box, or go into Code view and add value="" in the code like this:

   ```
   <option value="" selected="selected">-- Select one --</option>
   ```

   I clicked the List Values button in the Property inspector to edit the first item and set the Value field to 0. It doesn't really matter what value you use. The important thing when designing a form is to know what values to expect when the form is submitted.

9

> The value attribute of the <option> tag is optional and needs to be set only if you want the label and the data to be different (www.w3.org/TR/html4/interact/forms. html#edef-OPTION).

Creating a multiple-choice scrollable list

The way you build a multiple-choice list is almost identical to a drop-down menu. It involves only a couple more steps to set the size and multiple attributes in the opening <select> tag. Strictly speaking, the multiple attribute is optional. If it's omitted, the user can select only a single item.

You could convert the menu from the preceding section by changing Type from Menu to List in the Property inspector. However, the way you process data from a multiple-choice list is different, so let's add a separate list to the same form.

Inserting and configuring a scrollable list

Continue working with the form from the preceding exercise, or copy feedback_ select.php from examples/ch09 to workfiles/ch09. The finished code is in feedback_ multiselect.php.

1. Save feedback_select.php as feedback_multiselect.php.

2. In Design view, click immediately to the right of the drop-down menu you inserted in the previous exercise, and press Enter/Return to insert a new paragraph. Because the clearIt class was applied to the preceding paragraph, Dreamweaver applies the same class to the new paragraph. Leaving it does no harm, but you don't really need it either, so reset Style to None in the Property inspector.

3. Click the List/Menu button on the Forms tab of the Insert bar.

4. Enter the following settings in the Input Tag Accessibility Attributes dialog box:

- ID: views
- Label: What image do you have of London?
- Style: Attach label tag using 'for' attribute
- Position: Before form item (Dreamweaver selects this automatically)

5. When you click OK, Dreamweaver inserts a blank drop-down menu into the page in the same way as in step 6 of the preceding exercise. Select the menu element in Design view to display its details in the Property inspector.

Change Type to List. This activates the Height and Selections options. These are more examples of Dreamweaver's attempt at user-friendly names instead of using the XHTML attributes. Height sets the size attribute, which determines the number of items visible in the list; the browser automatically adds a vertical scrollbar. Change the value to 6, and put a check mark in the Selections checkbox to permit multiple choices. This adds multiple="multiple" in the <select> tag. The menu is converted into a tall, narrow rectangle, as shown here:

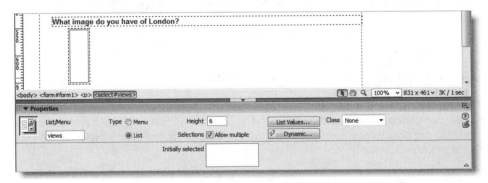

6. Click the List Values button to enter the labels and data values the same as for a drop-down menu. Leave Value blank if you want the data sent by the form to be the same as the label. The following screenshot shows the first five values I used:

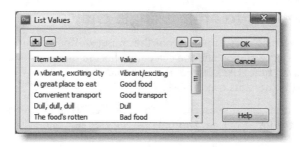

I set the sixth Item Label to A transport nightmare, and its Value to Transport nightmare.

7. Save the page, and load it into a browser. Select several items in the list (holding down the Shift or Ctrl/Cmd key while clicking), and click the Send comments button.

Uh, oh . . . something's wrong. Only the last selected item appears at the bottom of the page. To get all items, you need to use an array in the same way as with the checkbox group by appending a pair of square brackets to the end of the name attribute. Fortunately, this time, there's only one name attribute to change.

The problem with the Property inspector is that it uses the same field for the name and id attributes. If you add the square brackets to views in the Property inspector, it affects both name and id. You could dive into Code view to fix the problem, but let me show you another way—using the Tag Inspector.

8. Make sure the list is selected in Design view, and open the Tag Inspector (F9/Shift+Opt+F9 or Window ➤ Tag Inspector). If the Behaviors panel is displayed, click the Attributes tab to reveal the Attributes panel. This gives you direct access to the attributes of the element currently selected in the Document window. It has two views: listing attributes by category or in alphabetical order.

Expand the General and CSS/Accessibility categories in category view to reveal the name and id attributes. Click inside the name field to add a pair of square brackets after views, as shown in the following screenshot. (Depending on your monitor's resolution, they might appear to merge into an upright rectangle. This doesn't matter.)

9. Press Enter/Return to save the change. Save the page, and test it again in a browser. This time, all selected items from the multiple-choice list should be displayed as an array at the bottom of the page.

10. Click Send comments without selecting anything in the list. This time, views won't be among the items displayed at the bottom of the page. This is the same as with a checkbox group, and it has important implications for how you process the output of a form, as you'll see in Chapter 11.

Using radio buttons to offer a single choice

The term "radio buttons" is borrowed from the preset buttons common on radios: you push a button to select a station and the currently selected one pops out; only one can be selected at any given time. Like a radio, there shouldn't be too many buttons to choose from. Otherwise, the user gets confused.

Although radio buttons limit the user to only one choice, Dreamweaver is more generous. The Forms tab of the Insert bar has two options: Radio Button and Radio Group, as shown here:

Radio Button

Radio Group

The same options exist on the Form submenu of the Insert menu, although they are not adjacent to each other as they are on the Insert bar.

The difference is that Radio Button inserts radio buttons one at a time, while Radio Group inserts them in a single operation. Although doing everything in a single operation sounds better, there's no way of relaunching the Radio Group dialog box to edit the radio buttons or add a new one to the group. Also, I find this method less flexible in the way it lays out radio buttons and attaches the labels. So, I plan to show you how to insert individual radio buttons. Once you know how they work, you should have no difficulty experimenting with the Radio Group option to see if it suits your way of working.

Creating a radio button group with individual buttons

Continue working with the form from the preceding exercise or copy feedback_ multiselect.php from examples/ch09 to workfiles/ch09. The finished code is in feedback_radio.php.

1. Save feedback_multiselect.php as feedback_radio.php.

2. In Design view, click immediately to the right of the scrollable list you inserted in the previous exercise, and press Enter/Return to insert a new paragraph. Like checkboxes, each radio button has its own label, so you need to create a heading to indicate the question being asked. Click the Bold button in the Property inspector and type a question. I used Would you like to receive regular details of events in London?

3. At the end of the line, click the Bold button again to move the insertion point outside the closing </strong> tag. To keep the radio buttons in line with the other form elements, you need to put them in a <div> and apply the chkRad class to it.

    Select Insert Div Tag from the Common tab of the Insert bar, set Insert to At insertion point, and select chkRad from the Class drop-down menu.

4. With the placeholder text in the `<div>` still highlighted, select Paragraph from the Format menu in the Property inspector, and then press Delete to remove the placeholder text. This leaves an empty paragraph to hold the radio buttons.

5. Click Radio Button in the Forms tab of the Insert bar, and enter the following settings in the Input Tag Accessibility Attributes dialog box:

- ID: subscribeYes

- Label: Yes

- Style: Attach label tag using 'for' attribute

- Position: After form item (Dreamweaver selects this automatically)

6. When you click OK, Dreamweaver inserts the radio button and its associated label. Press your right keyboard arrow to move the insertion point to the right of the label, and press the spacebar to insert a space.

7. Repeat step 5, entering subscribeNo in the ID field and No in the Label field.

8. Click OK to insert the second radio button and its label. Select the second radio button element to display its details in the Property inspector, which should look like this:

The field on the left immediately below Radio Button sets the name attribute for the radio button. Change it to subscribe. Unlike other form elements, the name and id attributes of radio buttons aren't automatically linked in the Property inspector because Dreamweaver CS3 is smart enough to know that all buttons in a radio group share the same name, but must have unique IDs.

Dreamweaver automatically enters the same value as the ID in Checked value. While this is OK, you can change the value here without affecting the ID. Just type the letter n in the Checked value field.

Although you can build a form in which no radio button is checked when the page first loads, there isn't a Spry validation widget for radio buttons, so it's a good policy to have a default value. Set Initial state to Checked.

9. Select the Yes radio button, change its name from radio to subscribe, and shorten Checked value to the letter y. Leave Initial state as Unchecked.

10. Save the page, and load it in a browser. Test it to make sure that the value of subscribe is y or n depending on the radio button selected.

9

Organizing form elements in logical groups

An important element in designing a usable form is making sure that everything is laid out logically so that users can see at a glance what sort of information is required. It can also help to divide the form into a number of clearly labeled sections. XHTML provides two tags for this purpose: <fieldset> and <legend>, which most browsers automatically style with a border (see Figure 9-10).

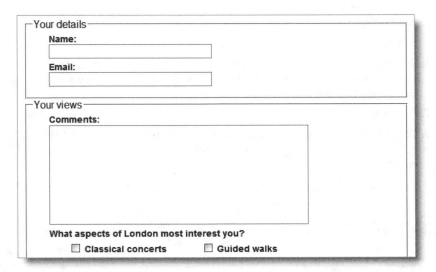

Figure 9-10. Fieldsets give forms a visual and logical structure that help make them more accessible to all users.

Inserting a fieldset

You can add fieldsets to your form before inserting the individual form elements or after you have finished. To insert a fieldset, click the Fieldset button on the Forms tab of the Insert bar, as shown here:

This opens the Fieldset dialog box. It has just one field: Legend, which is the title that you want to give to the group of form elements within the fieldset.

When you click OK, Dreamweaver inserts the following code in your form:

```
<fieldset>
<legend>Your details</legend>
</fieldset>
```

If you create the fieldset before inserting the individual form elements, press your right keyboard arrow after clicking OK in the Fieldset dialog box. This positions the insertion point between the closing </legend> and </fieldset> tags ready for adding the form elements that belong to the fieldset.

To add a fieldset to existing form elements, select the elements that you want to include by dragging your mouse across them in Design view. If you have Split view open, you will see that Dreamweaver doesn't select the opening and closing tags of your selection. However, when you insert the fieldset, it's smart enough to put the <fieldset> and <legend> tags in the correct place. If the fieldset border and legend appear in the wrong place, it probably means that you failed to select the form elements correctly. Press Ctrl+Z/Cmd+Z or Edit ➤ Undo and try again. Alternatively, go into Code view, and make sure that the target form elements are between the closing </legend> and </fieldset> tags.

To see the effect of adding fieldsets to the form you have been using throughout this chapter, and study the code, take a look at feedback_fieldsets.php in examples/ch09. You can alter the look of fieldsets with CSS by adding fieldset and legend type selectors to your style sheet.

Now that you've covered all the main form input and layout elements, let's turn attention to checking user input before submitting the form to the server for processing.

Validating user input before submission

Validation on the client side relies on JavaScript. A visitor simply needs to turn off JavaScript in the browser and press the submit button; all your client-side filters are rendered useless. Consequently, some developers argue that client-side validation is a waste of time. Nevertheless, most visitors to your sites aren't deliberately trying to abuse your forms and are likely to have JavaScript enabled. So, it's generally a good idea to detect errors before a form is submitted. JavaScript validation is conducted locally and is usually instantaneous.

Nevertheless, the fact that client-side validation can be so easily evaded raises the question of how thorough it should be. Since the real checks need to be done on the server, there's a strong argument for keeping client-side checks to the absolute minimum. Dreamweaver CS3 offers both approaches.

Doing minimal checks with the Validate Form behavior

The Validate Form behavior has been part of Dreamweaver for many years. It's quick and easy to apply and performs only the most rudimentary of checks. The following exercise shows you how to use it.

9

Applying the Validate Form behavior

This exercise uses the completed form from the previous exercises. Copy feedback_fieldsets.php from examples/ch09 to workfiles/ch09. If you just want to inspect the code, the finished file is feedback_validate.php in examples/ch09.

1. Save a copy of feedback_fieldsets.php as feedback_validate.php, and open it in the Document window. Switch to Design view, if necessary.

2. Select the form in feedback_validate.php by clicking the red outline or by positioning your cursor anywhere inside the form and clicking <form#form1> in the Tag selector at the bottom of the Document window.

3. Open the Behaviors panel by pressing Shift+F4 or by going to Window ➤ Behaviors. Alternatively, expand the Tag Inspector panel group, and select the Behaviors tab. Click the plus (+) button at the top of the Behaviors panel, and select Validate Form from the menu that appears.

4. This opens the dialog box shown in Figure 9-11.

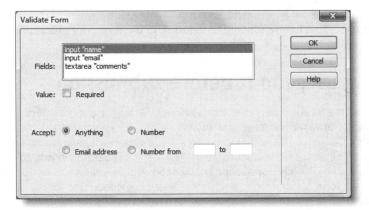

Figure 9-11. The original Dreamweaver Validate Form behavior performs a very limited range of checks.

Dreamweaver automatically detects text fields and text areas in the form and displays their name attributes in the Fields section. But what about the multiple-choice elements? I told you the Validate Form behavior is rudimentary; it works only with text input, and as you'll see shortly, it doesn't check very much.

5. Highlight each field in turn to set its validation requirements. If you want the field to be required, click the Value checkbox to insert a check mark.

The Accept radio buttons let you specify whether to accept anything, an email address, any number, or a number within a specified range.

Make all fields required, and set Accept to Email address for the email field. Set the other fields to accept anything.

6. Click OK to apply the Validate Form behavior. Dreamweaver lists it in the Behaviors panel with the event handler set to onSubmit, as shown in the screenshot alongside.

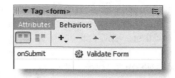

Although the Behaviors panel displays onSubmit in camel case, Dreamweaver inserts the correct lowercase onsubmit attribute in the `<form>` tag if you're using XHTML. If you want to edit the behavior, select the form and double-click its name to reopen the Validate Form dialog box. To remove the behavior, select it in the Behaviors panel, and click the minus (–) button.

7. Save the page, and load it into a browser. Click Send comments without filling in any of the fields. You should see a simple warning like this:

8. As long as JavaScript is enabled, this simple validation prevents the form from being submitted unless all required text input fields have a value. But to see just how crude a test this is, enter a single space in the Name or Comments field, and click Send comments again. When the Validate Form dialog box says Anything, it means just that—entering the single space satisfies its criteria. The email check is equally crude: an @ mark with a space on either side passes validation.

The Validate Form behavior is useful in preventing accidental submission of incomplete text fields. It does nothing about checkboxes, drop-down menus, or lists. This means it can't stop submission of a form without the user checking a box that signifies acceptance of terms and conditions. The sole advantage of this behavior is that's it's ultra-light. The JavaScript code that it inserts into the `<head>` of the page is only a dozen or so lines long, and it adds a mere 1KB to the size of the page.

Using Spry validation widgets for sophisticated checks

The Spry validation widgets, which are new to Dreamweaver CS3, are anything but rudimentary. They're capable of performing a wide range of checks and use a combination of JavaScript and CSS to display customized alerts alongside the affected field. There are four widgets, as follows:

- Spry Validation Text Field widget
- Spry Validation Text Area widget
- Spry Validation Checkbox widget
- Spry Validation Select widget (for single-choice menus and lists)

9

The text field widget is particularly impressive, as it lets you test for a wide range of formats, including numbers, currency, IP addresses, Social Security numbers, and credit card numbers. You can even set up your own custom patterns without the need to master the complex subject of regular expressions. The text area validation widget also provides one of the most frequently requested features—the ability to display how many characters the user has entered or still has left before reaching a predetermined limit. The validation widgets also display warning messages that you can easily edit and style with CSS.

Sure, they're impressive, but before you get carried away, let's take a look at their drawbacks.

Understanding the limitations of Spry validation widgets

Spry validation widgets are certainly powerful, but they greatly increase page size. If you add all four widgets to a form, the external JavaScript files and style sheets weigh in at more than 150KB. The text field widget is responsible for roughly half that amount because of its extensive pattern-matching features. It's overkill for a very basic form, but could be extremely useful in validating user input on a form for a job application or an insurance policy quote.

Dreamweaver CS3 doesn't have Spry validation widgets for radio buttons or multiple-choice <select> elements. A widget for radio buttons has been developed but was too late for inclusion in the program. I expect it will be made available at some stage through an update.

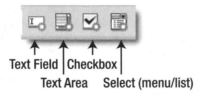

Text Field | Checkbox
Text Area   Select (menu/list)

Figure 9-12. Spry validation widgets have an orange sunburst on the same icons as their related form elements.

Spry validation widgets can also be accessed through the Spry *tab of the Insert bar (confusingly, though, the positions of the* Text Area *and* Select *buttons have been swapped) or the* Spry *submenu of the* Insert *menu.*

If you insert a widget into a blank part of a form, Dreamweaver inserts both the validation code and the form element. Alternatively, you can apply a widget to an existing form element. Whichever approach you use, the method of configuration is exactly the same. In the remaining pages of this chapter, I'm going to show you how to apply validation widgets to an existing form.

I suggest you study carefully the first section of "Validating a text field with Spry," because it contains most of the knowledge you need to work with all validation widgets, particularly with regard to editing and controlling the display of alert messages.

Inserting a Spry validation widget

As with all Spry widgets, the page must have been saved at least once before you can apply a validation widget. Save the page again immediately afterward to attach the external JavaScript code and style sheet and copy them to the Spry assets folder if necessary.

Don't mix the Validate Form behavior with Spry validation widgets. If you apply a validation widget in a form that already triggers JavaScript when submitted, Dreamweaver displays the following warning:

In spite of the warning, Dreamweaver takes the view that a developer with advanced knowledge of JavaScript may have good reasons for combining the widget with other code. So it still goes ahead and inserts the widget. However, if you're not a JavaScript whiz kid, just click OK followed immediately by Ctrl+Z/Cmd+Z or Edit ➤ Undo to remove the widget cleanly. Remove the Validate Form behavior (or other conflicting code), and reapply the validation widget.

Removing a validation widget

Removing a widget immediately after you have applied it is easy. Unfortunately, the standard method of removing a widget (selecting its turquoise tab and pressing Delete) removes the form element with it. The simple way to get around this problem is to select the form element (and label, if necessary) in Design view, and cut it to your clipboard (Ctrl+X/Cmd+X). Then select the turquoise tab to delete the widget. If you see the following warning that the widget has been damaged, you can safely ignore it.

Once you have removed the widget, paste (Ctrl+V/Cmd+V) the form element back into the page.

> *Dreamweaver is context sensitive. If you cut from Design view, always paste back into Design view; the same with Code view. If you don't, Dreamweaver is likely to mess up your page.*

9

Validating a text field with Spry

To validate a text field, either select an existing text field or position your cursor inside a form where you want to insert a new text field, and click the Spry Validation Text Field button on the Insert bar. If you are inserting a new text field, fill in the ID and Label fields in the Input Tag Accessibility Attributes dialog box as described earlier in the chapter.

Figure 9-13 shows what happens when you apply a validation widget to the first text field in the form that you have been working with throughout the chapter. The screenshot was taken with the Document window open in Split view, so you can see the underlying code (the section highlighted on lines 21–23).

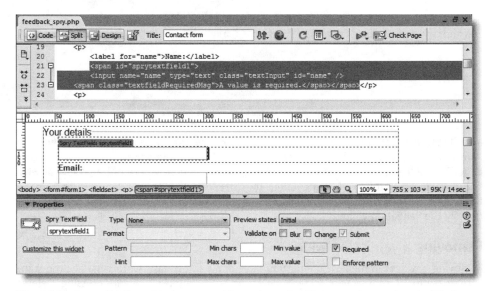

Figure 9-13. Spry validation widgets surround form elements with <span> tags and control their display with JavaScript.

The <input> tag has been surrounded by a <span> tag with the ID set to sprytextfield1. Immediately after the <input> tag is another <span>, which contains the text: A value is required. As you can see in Figure 9-13, that text isn't displayed in Design view. This is because the display of all validation messages in Spry widgets is controlled by JavaScript.

The Preview states drop-down menu on the right of the Property inspector controls the display of these messages in Design view, allowing you to see what they look like, and edit them and their associated style rules. The following exercise shows you how to control the display of validation alerts in a form.

Editing and controlling the display of validation alerts

1. Copy feedback_spry_start.php from examples/ch09, and save it in workfiles/ch09 as feedback_spry.php.

2. Select the Name text input field in Design view, and click the Spry Validation Text Field button in the Insert bar (or use the Insert menu).

3. Make sure there's a check mark in the Required checkbox in the Property inspector (it should be selected by default), and choose Required from the Preview states drop-down menu. The text field should now look like this in Design view:

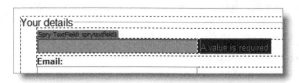

Not only is the text displayed, the background color of the text field has turned an alarming shade of pink.

4. Both the text field and the validation message are highlighted, so click inside the message so you can edit it. Shorten the text to Required.

5. With your cursor still inside the validation message, open the CSS Styles panel in Current mode (the quickest way is to click the CSS button in the center of the Property inspector). As you can see from the following screenshot, the Properties pane shows the styles for the current selection as having a 1-pixel crimson border, crimson text, and the display property set to inline.

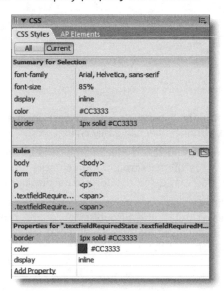

6. Click Add Property, and set font-weight to bold. Design view immediately updates.

7. Select the text field in Design view. You can now change background-color to a less dramatic pink. I chose #FFDFDF.

8. Click the turquoise tab at the top left of the widget. In the Property inspector, change Preview states to Valid. The background color of the text field changes to green.

9. Select the text field to display the style rule for the current selection in the CSS Styles panel, and change background-color to a different shade of green. I chose #E3FBE1.

10. Save the page (and style sheet if necessary), and load feedback_spry.php into a browser. Click inside the Name field. Assuming you're using a modern browser and JavaScript is enabled, the field should turn yellow, indicating that it has focus.

11. Don't enter anything in the field, but move the focus to another field. The Name field reverts to its previous state.

12. Click the Send comments button. The background of the text field turns pink, and the word Required is displayed alongside in bold crimson text. Also note that nothing is displayed below the Send comments button. The file feedback_spry.php contains the PHP script used earlier to display the data submitted by the form, so this is confirmation that the validation widget prevented the form from being submitted.

13. Type your name in the Name field, and move the focus to another field. Although the field turns yellow while you're typing, it turns pink again when the focus moves to another field, and the Required alert isn't cleared, as the following screenshot shows.

This is because the default behavior is to validate form elements only when the form is submitted, although you can easily change that.

14. Click the Send comments button. If your monitor is large enough for you to still see the text field, you'll see the background momentarily turn green indicating that it passed validation. You'll also see the form data displayed at the bottom of the page.

15. Back in Dreamweaver, select the turquoise tab at the top left of the validation widget to display its details in the Property inspector. Directly beneath the Preview states drop-down menu are three checkboxes, as shown here:

Selecting the Blur checkbox runs the validation script when the focus moves to another element on the page. Selecting Change runs the script on every keystroke in the text field. Often, validating on every keystroke is guaranteed to drive users insane, so use with care. The Submit checkbox is automatically selected and grayed out, since there's no point in validation if you don't check the form when it is submitted.

16. Select Validate on Blur, save the page, and repeat steps 10–14 to test it again. This time, the field turns green, and the Required message disappears in step 13.

The styles changed in the preceding exercise affect all text field validation widgets in the same page, and they apply equally to all text field validation alerts. As you'll see shortly, selecting other options in the Property inspector creates a range of different validation alerts.

Although the Preview states menu gives you access to most style rules, two selectors need to be edited either in the CSS Styles panel in All mode or by opening SpryValidationTextField.css in Code view. The first is .textfieldFocusState input, input.textfieldFocusState, which gives the text field a yellow background when it has focus. The default color is #FFFFCC. The other selector is .textfieldFlashText input, input.textfieldFlashText. This applies only when you enable character masking, and it makes the text briefly flash red if an invalid character is inserted.

Now, let's run through the other options for text field validation.

Hint This displays default text that disappears as soon as the text field has focus or anything is entered into it. It's useful for indicating the type of input or format expected. The value is displayed dynamically, so it won't be submitted as part of the form data if the user enters nothing in the field.

Min chars This lets you specify the minimum number of characters required for validation. It adds an alert message in a <span>, and the Preview states menu is updated to include a Min. # of Chars Not Met option. The alert is displayed if the length of user input falls below the number of characters specified in this field. Select this option from the Preview states menu to inspect and edit the alert.

Max chars This works the same way as Min chars, but lets you set a maximum number of characters. The alert is displayed if the length of user input exceeds the number specified in this field.

Type This is where the real power of the text field validation widget lies. It lets you check user input against a wide range of formats, which are summarized in Table 9-1. All options, except None, insert an Invalid format <span> in the underlying code. Use the Preview states menu to display this in Design view for editing and/or styling.

Table 9-1. Formats that the text field validation widget can recognize

Type	Available formats	Notes
None		Use this when no other suitable format is available.
Integer		This validates whole numbers only. Negative numbers are accepted but not decimal fractions or thousands separators. Use Real Number/Scientific Notation for decimals or Currency for whole numbers with thousands separators.
Email address		This performs only a rudimentary check for an email address, making sure that it contains a single @ mark followed by at least one period.

Continued

9

Table 9-1. Formats that the text field validation widget can recognize *(continued)*

Type	Available formats	Notes
Date	mm/dd/yy mm/dd/yyyy dd/mm/yyyy dd/mm/yy yy/mm/dd yyyy/mm/dd mm-dd-yy dd-mm-yy yyyy-mm-dd mm.dd.yyyy dd.mm.yyyy	This checks not only the format but also the validity of the date, rejecting impossible dates, such as September 31. Leap years are recognized, but a bug in version 1.4 of SpryValidationTextField.js incorrectly rejects February 29, 2000.
Time	HH:mm HH:mm:ss hh:mm tt hh:mm:ss tt hh:mm t hh:mm:ss t	HH represents the 24-hour clock, hh the 12-hour clock. Hours before 10 *must* have a leading zero. When using the 12-hour clock, tt stands for AM or PM; t stands for A or P. Lowercase is not accepted.
Credit Card	All Visa MasterCard American Express Discover Diner's Club	Matches known patterns for major credit cards. Numbers must be entered without hyphens or spaces.
Zip Code	US-5 US-9 UK Canada Custom Pattern	This tests only that the right combination of numbers and/or letters is used. It doesn't check whether the code exists or matches other parts of an address. See "Building your own custom pattern" for details of how to use the Custom Pattern format.
Phone Number	US/Canada Custom Pattern	US/Canada must be in the same format as (212) 555-0197. For Custom Pattern, see "Building your own custom pattern."
Social Security Number		This matches only U.S. Social Security numbers.
Currency	1,000,000.00 1.000.000,00	In both formats, the thousands separator is optional, as is the decimal fraction. This makes it possible to validate currencies, such as yen, which aren't normally quoted with a smaller unit.

Type	Available formats	Notes
Real Number/ Scientific Notation		Used for numbers with a decimal fraction, which can optionally be expressed in scientific (exponential) notation, for example, 3.14159, 1.56234E+29, or 1.56234e29. The letter *E* can be uppercase or lowercase, but it must not be preceded by a space.
IP Address	IPv4 only IPv6 only IPv6 and IPv4	Covers all formats of IP address.
URL		This converts the URL to punycode (http://en.wikipedia.org/wiki/ Punycode) before validation, so it should also accept international URLs that contain non-Latin characters.
Custom		This allows you to define your own format as described in "Building your own custom pattern."

Building your own custom pattern

Spry makes it easy to build custom patterns using special pattern characters that act as a mask for the user's input. Spry custom patterns aren't as powerful as regular expressions, but they're a lot easier to use, so it's a reasonable trade-off for most people. Table 9-2 describes the special pattern characters.

Table 9-2. Special characters used for building custom patterns in Spry

Character	Matches	Case sensitivity
0	Any number 0–9	
A	Any letter A–Z	Converted to uppercase
a	Any letter a–z	Converted to lowercase
B	Any letter A–Z	Original case preserved
b	Any letter A–Z	Original case preserved
X	Any alphanumeric character (A–Z and 0–9)	Letters converted to uppercase
x	Any alphanumeric character (A–Z and 0–9)	Letters converted to lowercase

Continued

Table 9-2. Special characters used for building custom patterns in Spry (continued)

Character	Matches	Case sensitivity
Y	Any alphanumeric character (A–Z and 0–9)	Letters preserve original case
y	Any alphanumeric character (A–Z and 0–9)	Letters preserve original case
?	Any character	

Although there are ten special pattern characters, you need concern yourself with only eight of them, because uppercase and lowercase B are identical. So are uppercase and lowercase Y.

Any other character included in a custom pattern is treated as an auto-complete character. For example, let's say you have a stock code that looks like this: BC-901/c. If all stock codes follow the same pattern of two uppercase letters followed by a hyphen, three digits, a forward slash, and a lowercase letter, you could use the following custom pattern:

AA-000/a

Immediately after the first two letters are inserted, Spry automatically inserts the hyphen. Then after the next thee digits, it inserts the forward slash ready for the user to insert the final letter.

If you want to use any of the special characters listed in Table 9-2, you must precede them with a backslash (e.g., \A). To insert a backslash as part of an auto-complete sequence, use a double backslash (\\).

> When using a custom pattern, you must select the Enforce pattern checkbox at the bottom right of the Property inspector (see Figure 9-13 earlier in the chapter).

Validating a text area with Spry

Unlike a text field, the <textarea> tag doesn't have any way to control the acceptable number of characters, so the text area validation widget optionally displays a counter that tells the user how many have been entered or can still be entered. This is important when inserting text in a database, because the text is truncated if the user inputs more than the maximum accepted by the database column. With Spry, this is no longer a problem, as you can block further input once the maximum has been reached.

To validate a text area, either select an existing text area or position your cursor inside a form where you want to insert a new text area, and click the Spry Validation Text Area button on the Insert bar. If you are inserting a new text area, fill in the ID and Label fields in the Input Tag Accessibility Attributes dialog box as described earlier in the chapter. Figure 9-14 shows what happens when you apply a validation widget to the Comments text area in the form that you have been working with throughout the chapter.

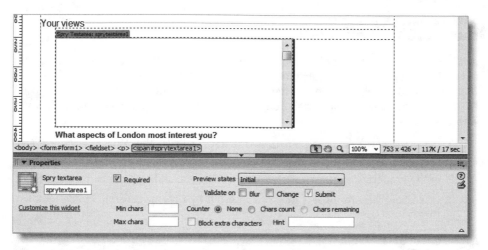

Figure 9-14. The text area validation widget has options to control and monitor the number of characters entered.

The layout of options in the Property inspector is slightly different, but Required, Preview states, Validate on, Min chars, Max chars, and Hint all work exactly the same as for a text field, so I won't explain them again (refer to "Validating a text field with Spry" if you need to refresh your memory).

Let's take a look at the two new options: Counter and Block extra characters.

Counter There are three settings to choose from, as follows:

- None: This is the default. It turns off automatic counting of characters entered.
- Chars count: This displays the total number of characters entered. If you combine this with Validate on Change, it displays a constantly updated total (see Figure 9-15).
- Chars remaining: This is grayed out until you enter a value in Max chars. It uses this value to calculate how many more characters can be accepted. If combined with Validate on Change, it displays a running total of characters left (see Figure 9-15).

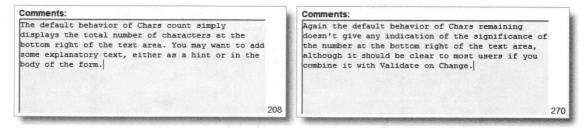

Figure 9-15. The character counter appears at the bottom right of the text area, but gives no indication of its meaning.

Block extra characters This is self-explanatory. It prevents the user from entering more characters than the number specified in Max chars. The checkbox remains grayed out if Max chars is not specified.

Improving the character counter

As Figure 9-15 shows, the Spry character counter simply displays a number at the bottom right of the text area. Although most users will probably guess its meaning, it's user friendlier to add a label to the counter. The following instructions show you how to do this. I have used feedback_spry.php from the previous exercise, but you can use any form with a text area.

1. In Design view, select the Comments text area, and click the Spry Validation Text Area button on the Insert bar.

2. In the Property inspector, select Validate on Change, and set Counter to Chars count.

3. Open Split view to inspect the code inserted by Dreamweaver. It should look like this:

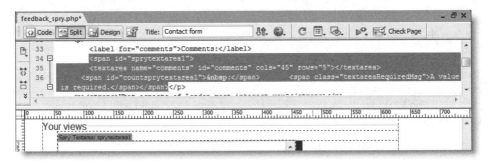

The first <span> shown on line 36 in the preceding screenshot contains a non-breaking space ( ). Spry uses this to display the character count. Because the content of the <span> is generated dynamically, the label needs to go outside.

4. Click inside Code view, position your cursor immediately to the left of the first <span> shown on line 36, and insert the following code shown in bold:

```
<span> Count: </span><span id="countsprytextarea1"> </span>
```

5. Save the page and test it. You should now see a more user-friendly display like this:

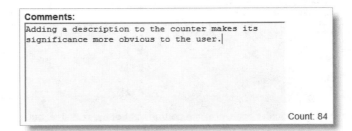

When using the Chars remaining option, change the text inside the new <span> to Remaining:.

> *By default, Dreamweaver puts all alerts in <span> tags and styles them to display inline alongside the form element. This can result in the alert splitting across two lines, which makes the default border look very messy. Either shorten the text or change the style rules so that they blend in with your design. In fact, there is nothing to stop you from moving the alerts to a different position. As long as you keep the classes and IDs assigned by Dreamweaver, you can change the <span> tags to other XHTML elements, as demonstrated in the next exercise.*

Validating a single checkbox with Spry

A common requirement on forms is a checkbox to confirm that the user agrees with certain terms and conditions. Creating this with Dreamweaver couldn't be simpler. If you already have the checkbox in your form, select it, and click the Spry Validate Checkbox button on the Insert bar. Save the page to copy the external JavaScript file and style sheet to your Spry assets folder.

If you don't have a checkbox, position your cursor where you want it to go inside the form, and click the Spry Validate Checkbox button on the Insert bar. Fill in the ID and Label fields in the Input Tag Accessibility Attributes dialog box, and save the page.

That's all there is to it.

Validating a checkbox group with Spry

Validating a checkbox group is easy, but the default use of <span> tags makes it difficult to create a layout that uses valid code and looks halfway decent. However, this is also a good opportunity to show you that you don't need to be constrained by Dreamweaver's way of doing things. The best way to explain is with a practical example based on the form you have been using throughout the chapter.

The form has a group of five checkboxes displayed in two columns, each of which is formed by a <div> floated left. The Dreamweaver documentation tells you to add multiple checkboxes inside the <span> created by the validation widget, but <span> tags cannot contain block-level elements like <div>, <table>, or <p>. So the best way to validate a checkbox group is to apply the widget first to a single checkbox. You can then convert the Dreamweaver code to wrap the entire group in <div> tags.

Adapting a checkbox validation widget

Use feedback_spry.php from the preceding exercise, or copy feedback_spry_start.php from examples/ch09 to workfiles/ch09 and save it as feedback_spry.php.

1. In Design view, select the checkbox labeled Classical concerts, and click the Spry Validation Checkbox button on the Insert bar.

2. In the Property inspector, select the Enforce range (multiple) radio button, and type 2 in the Min # of selections field. Press Enter/Return or Tab to make sure that Dreamweaver updates the validation code.

9

3. Open Split view to inspect the code inserted by Dreamweaver. It should look like this:

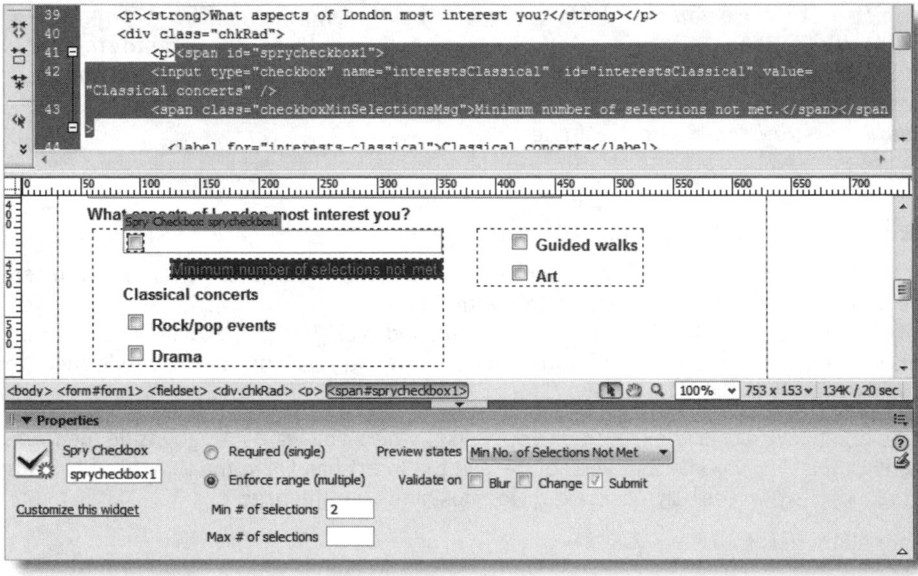

As you can see on line 41 in the preceding screenshot, Dreamweaver creates an opening `<span>` tag with the ID sprycheckbox1 to wrap the checkbox (the closing `</span>` tag is at the end of line 43). Another `<span>` at the beginning of line 43 is assigned the class checkboxMinSelectionsMsg and contains the alert message.

With Preview states set to Min No. of Selections Not Met, you can see that the alert is displayed between the checkbox and its label. It looks a mess, but not for long . . .

4. Switch to Code view, and amend the code as shown in the following screenshot by moving the highlighted sections and deleting the closing `</span>` tag:

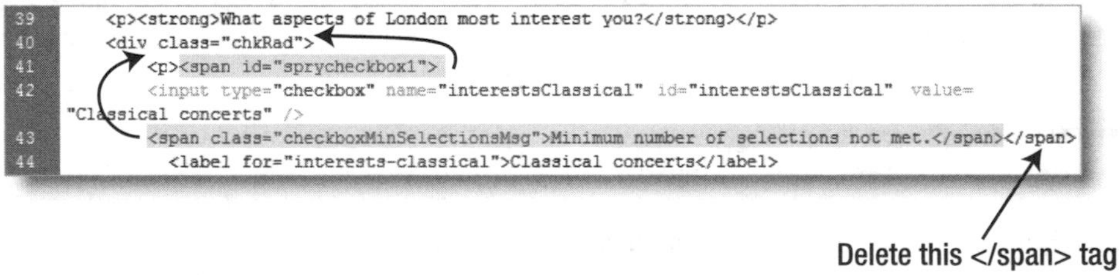

Delete this `</span>` tag

Change the `<span>` tags to `<div>` tags so that it looks like this:

```
<p><strong>What aspects of London most interest you?</strong></p>
  <div id="sprycheckbox1">
    <div class="chkRad">
```

```
<div class="checkboxMinSelectionsMsg">Minimum number of ➡
selections not met.</div>
    <p>
        <input type="checkbox" name="interestsClassical" ➡
id="interestsClassical" value="Classical concerts" />
        <label for="interestsClassical">Classical concerts</label>
```

5. You now need to replace the closing </span> tag that you deleted at the end of line 43. It needs to go right at the end of the checkbox group, and because you're using <div> tags for the validation widget, it needs to be a closing </div> tag.

This is where a good understanding of XHTML and your page structure comes in. Although it's just a case of moving a closing tag, you must get it in the correct position after the closing tag of the second chkRad class <div> (it should now be on line 65). The following code shows the new tag in bold in its surrounding context:

```
        <label for="interestsArt">Art</label>
    </p>
    </div>
</div>
<p class="clearIt">
    <label for="visited">How often have you been to London?</label>
```

6. Switch back to Design view, and click the turquoise tab at the top left of the checkbox validation widget. The checkbox group should now look like this:

You can still display and hide the alert message using the Preview states menu in the Property inspector. The heavy blue outline around the validation widget doesn't enclose the checkboxes because they're floated. If you put the checkbox group in a nonfloated element, such as a table, the outline would enclose the whole group.

7. Select Validate on Change in the Property inspector, save the page, and test it in a browser. Select one checkbox, and the alert message should appear above the checkbox group. Select a second checkbox, and the alert disappears.

You might want to add a 40px left margin to the checkboxMinSelectionMsg class in the CSS Styles panel, and make some other changes to the CSS, but this shows you how you can adapt the basic code created by Dreamweaver. This is something that you will appreciate even more during the second half of this book when working with PHP. Dreamweaver provides a solid basis, but the rest is up to you.

So, what have you done? Just two things, namely:

- Each validation widget is enclosed in an overall <span>. Because <span> tags can only be used for inline elements, you have converted the overall <span> into a <div> and moved the checkbox group inside.

- Each alert message is also contained in a <span>, which is displayed inline wherever it happens to be. By converting the <span> to a <div>, you have turned it into an independent element that can be relocated wherever it best suits your layout.

This exercise just lifts the lid on the possibilities. I'll leave you to experiment with other variations.

Validating a drop-down menu with Spry

Applying a select validation widget is very simple. Highlight the menu object in Design view, and click the Spry Validation Select button in the Insert bar. The following instructions use the same form as throughout the rest of the chapter.

Applying a validation widget to an existing drop-down menu

Use feedback_spry.php from the preceding exercise, or copy feedback_spry_start.php from examples/ch09 to workfiles/ch09 and save it as feedback_spry.php.

1. In Design view, select the existing drop-down menu, and then click the List Values button in the Property inspector. The first item (– Select one –) is an invalid choice, so you need to take a note of its Value (0). Close the List Values dialog box.

2. With the menu still selected, click the Spry Validation Select button in the Insert bar.

3. In the Property inspector, select the Invalid value checkbox, and replace the default -1 with 0 in the field alongside. This is the invalid value you confirmed in step 1. Also select Validate on Change.

4. Save the page, and test it in a browser. An alert message should be displayed if you select nothing or an invalid value.

As with the checkbox group, you can convert <span> tags to <div> tags. Spry isn't concerned with the type of element used, but with the class and id attributes.

Styling the alert messages follows the same principles as for a text field in the various validation widgets. Study the style sheets in the Spry assets folder, or click the Customize this widget link in the Property inspector to display Dreamweaver help, which explains which style rules to change.

Next, let's move to the server side . . .

This has been a long chapter, crammed with detail, but it's an important one. You'll use forms time and again when building dynamic sites, and making sure that user input is in the right format saves endless headaches later on. Spry does a lot to help with validation and is fairly easy to use, but the Dreamweaver interface could still do with some improvement. However, it's important to remember that client-side validation is only half the story.

Because JavaScript can be turned off in the browser, you also need to check user input on the server side with PHP.

Moreover, forms are useless without a script capable of processing the data. The next chapter serves as a crash course in PHP basics for readers new to PHP. Then in Chapter 11, we get down to the nitty-gritty of server-side programming, using PHP to validate user input and then send it to your mail inbox.

9

10 INTRODUCING THE BASICS OF PHP

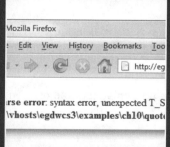

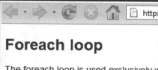

This chapter is a cross between a crash course in PHP and a handy reference. It's aimed at readers who are completely new to PHP or who may have dabbled without really getting to grips with the language. The intention is not to teach you all there is to know but to arm you with sufficient knowledge to dig into Code view to customize Dreamweaver code with confidence. Dreamweaver's automatic code generation does a lot of the hard work for you, but you need to tweak the code to get the best out of it, and when it comes to sending an email from an online form, you have to do everything yourself.

By the end of this chapter, you'll learn about

- Writing and understanding PHP scripts
- Using variables to represent changing values
- Understanding the difference between single and double quotes
- Organizing related information with arrays
- Creating pages that make decisions for themselves
- Using loops and functions for repetitive work

If you're already comfortable with PHP, just glance at the section headings to see what's covered, as you might find it useful to refer to this chapter if you need to refresh your memory about a particular subject. Then move straight to the next chapter and start coding.

If you're new to PHP, don't try to learn everything at one sitting, or your brain is likely to explode from information overload. On the first reading, look at the headings and maybe the first paragraph or two under each one to get a general overview. Also read the section "Understanding PHP error messages."

Introducing the basics of PHP

PHP is a **server-side language**. This means that the web server processes your PHP code and sends only the results—usually as XHTML—to the browser. Because all the action is on the server, you need to tell it that your pages contain PHP code. This involves two simple steps, namely:

- Give every page a PHP file name extension—the default is .php. Do not use anything other than .php unless you are told to specifically by your hosting company.
- Enclose all PHP code within PHP tags.

The opening tag is <?php and the closing tag is ?>. You may come across <? as a short version of the opening tag. However, <? doesn't work on all servers. Stick with <?php, which is guaranteed to work.

Embedding PHP in a web page

When somebody visits your site and requests a PHP page, the server sends it to the PHP engine, which reads the page from top to bottom looking for PHP tags. XHTML passes through untouched, but whenever the PHP engine encounters a <?php tag, it starts processing your code and continues until it reaches the closing ?> tag. If the PHP code produces any output, it's inserted at that point. Then, any remaining XHTML passes through until another <?php tag is encountered.

> You can have as many PHP code blocks as you like on a page, but they cannot be nested inside each other.

PHP doesn't always produce direct output for the browser. It may, for instance, check the contents of form input before sending an email message or inserting information into a database. So some code blocks are placed above or below the main XHTML code. Code that produces direct output, however, always goes where you want the output to be displayed.

A typical PHP page uses some or all of the following elements:

- Variables to act as placeholders for unknown or changing values
- Arrays to hold multiple values
- Conditional statements to make decisions
- Loops to perform repetitive tasks
- Functions to perform preset tasks

Ending commands with a semicolon

PHP is written as a series of commands or statements. Each **statement** normally tells the PHP engine to perform a particular action, and it must always be followed by a semicolon, like this:

```php
<?php
do this;
now do something else;
finally, do that;
?>
```

PHP is not like JavaScript or ActionScript. It won't automatically assume there should be a semicolon at the end of a line if you leave it out. This has a nice side effect: you can spread long statements over several lines and lay out your code for ease of reading. PHP, like XHTML, ignores whitespace in code. Instead, it relies on semicolons to indicate where one command ends and the next one begins.

> To save space, I won't always surround code samples with PHP tags.

10

Using variables to represent changing values

A **variable** is simply a name that you give to something that may change or that you don't know in advance. The *name* that you give to a variable remains constant, but the *value* stored in the variable can be changed at any time.

Although this concept sounds abstract, we use variables all the time in everyday life. When you meet somebody for the first time, one of the first things you ask is, "What's your name?" It doesn't matter whether the person you've just met is Tom, Dick, or Harry, the word "name" remains constant, but the value we store in it varies for different people. Similarly, with your bank account, money goes in and out all of the time (mostly out, it seems), but it doesn't matter whether you're scraping the bottom of the barrel or as rich as Croesus, the amount of money in your account is always referred to as the balance.

Naming variables

You can choose just about anything you like as the name for a variable, as long as you keep the following rules in mind:

- Variables always begin with $ (a dollar sign).
- The first character after the dollar sign cannot be a number.
- No spaces or punctuation are allowed, except for the underscore (_).
- Variable names are case sensitive: $name and $Name are not the same.

A variable's name should give some indication of what it represents: $name, $email, and $totalPrice are good examples. Because you can't use spaces in variable names, it's a good idea to capitalize the first letter of the second or subsequent words when combining them (sometimes called **camel case**). Alternatively, you can use an underscore (e.g., $total_price).

Don't try to save time by using really short variables. Using $n, $e, and $tp instead of descriptive ones makes code harder to understand. More important, it makes errors more difficult to spot.

> *Although you have considerable freedom in the choice of variable names, you can't use* $this, *because it has a special meaning in PHP object-oriented programming. It's also advisable to avoid using any of the keywords listed at* www.php.net/manual/en/reserved.php.

Assigning values to variables

Variables get their values from a variety of sources, including the following:

- User input through online forms
- A database
- An external source, such as a news feed or XML file
- The result of a calculation
- Direct inclusion in the PHP code

Wherever the value comes from, it's always assigned in the same way with an equal sign (=), like this:

```
$variable = value;
```

Because it assigns a value, the equal sign is called the **assignment operator**. Although it's an equal sign, get into the habit of thinking of it as meaning "is set to" rather than "equals." This is because PHP uses two equal signs (==) to mean "equals"—something that catches out a lot of beginners (experienced PHP programmers are not immune to the occasional lapse, either).

Use the following rules when assigning a value to a variable:

- Strings must be enclosed in single or double quotes (the distinction between the different types of quotes is explained later in the chapter).
- Numbers should not be in quotes—enclosing a number in quotes turns it into a string.

You can also use a variable to assign a value to another variable, for example:

```
$name = 'David Powers';
$author = $name;  // both $author and $name are now 'David Powers'
```

If the value of $name changes subsequently, it doesn't affect the value of $author. As this example shows, you don't use quotes around a variable when assigning its value to another. However, as long as you use double quotes, you can embed a variable in a string like this:

```
$blurb = "$author has written several best-selling books on PHP.";
```

The value of $blurb is now "David Powers has written several best-selling books on PHP." There's a more detailed description on the use of variables with double quotes in "Choosing single or double quotation marks" later in the chapter.

Displaying PHP output

The most common ways of displaying dynamic output in the browser are to use echo or print. The differences between the two are so subtle you can regard them as identical. I prefer echo, because it's one fewer letter to type. It's also the style used by Dreamweaver.

Put echo (or print) in front of a variable, number, or string like this to output it to the browser:

```
$name = 'David';
echo $name;     // displays David
echo 5;         // displays 5
echo 'David';   // displays David
```

You may see scripts that use parentheses with echo and print, like this:

```
echo('David');  // displays David
print('David'); // displays David
```

10

The parentheses make no difference. Unless you enjoy typing purely for the sake of it, leave them out.

> *The important thing to remember about* echo *and* print *is that they work only with variables that contain a single value. You cannot use them to display more complex structures that are capable of storing multiple values.*

Commenting scripts for clarity and debugging

Even if you're an expert programmer, code is not always as immediately understandable as something written in your own human language. That's where comments can be a life-saver. You may understand what the code does five minutes after creating it, but when you come back to maintain it in six months' time—or if you have to maintain someone else's code—you'll be grateful for well-commented code.

In PHP, there are three ways to add comments. The first will be familiar to you if you write JavaScript. Anything on a line following a double slash is regarded as a comment and will not be processed.

```
// Display the name
echo $name;
```

You can also use the hash sign (#) in place of the double slash.

```
# Display the name
echo $name;
```

Either type of comment can go to the side of the code, as long as it doesn't go onto the next line.

```
echo $name;    // This is a comment
echo $name;    #  This is another comment
```

The third style allows you to stretch comments over several lines by sandwiching them between /* and */ (just like CSS comments).

```
/* You might want to use this sort of comment to explain
the whole purpose of a script. Alternatively, it's a
convenient way to disable part of a script temporarily.
*/
```

As the previous example explains, comments serve a dual purpose: they not only allow you to sprinkle your scripts with helpful reminders of what each section of code is for; they can also be used to disable a part of a script temporarily. This is extremely useful when you are trying to trace the cause of an error.

Choosing single or double quotation marks

As I mentioned earlier, strings must always be enclosed in single or double quotes. If all you're concerned about is what ends up on the screen, most of the time it doesn't matter which quotes you use, but behind the scenes, PHP uses single and double quotes in very different ways.

- Anything between single quotation marks is treated as plain text.
- Anything between double quotation marks is processed.

Quotation marks need to be in matching pairs. If a string begins with a single quote, PHP looks for the next single quote and regards that as the end of the string. Since an apostrophe uses the same character as a single quote, this presents a problem. A similar problem arises when a string in double quotes contains double quotes. The best way to explain this is with a practical example.

Experimenting with quotes

This simple exercise demonstrates the difference between single and double quotes and what happens when a conflict arises with an apostrophe or double quotes inside a string.

1. Create a new PHP page called quotes.php in workfiles/ch10. If you just want to look at the finished code, use quotes.php in examples/ch10.

2. Switch to Code view, and type the following code between the <body> tags:

```php
<?php
$name = 'David Powers';
echo 'Single quotes: The author is $name<br />';
echo "Double quotes: The author is $name";
?>
```

3. Save the page, and load it into a browser. As you can see from the following screenshot, $name is treated as plain text in the first line, but is processed and replaced with its value in the second line, which uses double quotes.

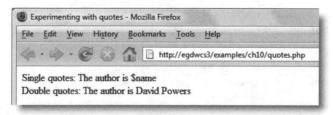

> To display the output on separate lines, you have to include XHTML tags, such as <br />, because echo outputs only the values passed to it—nothing more.

10

4. Change the text slightly in lines 3 and 4 of the code, as follows:

```
echo 'Single quotes: The author's name is $name<br />';
echo "Double quotes: The author's name is $name";
```

As you type, the change in Dreamweaver syntax coloring should alert you to a problem, but save the page nevertheless, and view it in a browser (it's quotes2.php in examples/ch10). You should see something like this:

As far as PHP is concerned, an apostrophe and a single quote are the same thing, and quotes must always be in matching pairs. What's happened is that the apostrophe in author's has been regarded as the closing quote for the first line; what was intended as the closing quote of the first line becomes a second opening quote; and the apostrophe in the second line becomes the second closing quote. All quite different from what was intended—and if you're confused, is it any wonder that PHP is unable to work out what's meant to be going on?

> *The meaning of parse error and other error messages is explained in "Understanding PHP error messages" at the end of the chapter.*

5. To solve the problem, insert a backslash in front of the apostrophe in the first sentence, like this (see quotes3.php in examples/ch10):

```
echo 'Single quotes: The author\'s name is $name<br />';
```

You should now see the syntax coloring revert to normal. If you view the result in a browser, it should display correctly like this:

Using escape sequences in strings

Using a backslash like this is called an **escape sequence**. It tells PHP to treat a character in a special way. Double quotes within a double-quoted string? You guessed it—escape them with a backslash.

```
echo "Swift's \"Gulliver's Travels\""; // displays the double quotes
```

The next line of code achieves exactly the same thing, but by using a different combination of quotes:

```
echo 'Swift\'s "Gulliver\'s Travels"';
```

> *When creating strings, the outside pair of quotes must match—any quotes of the same style inside the string must be escaped with a backslash. However, putting a backslash in front of the opposite style of quote will result in the backslash being displayed. To see the effect, put a backslash in front of the apostrophe in the doubled-quoted string in the previous exercise.*

So what happens when you want to include a literal backslash? You escape it with a backslash (\\).

The backslash (\\) and the single quote (\') are the only escape sequences that work in a single-quoted string. Because double quotes are a signal to PHP to process any variables contained within a string, there are many more escape sequences for double-quoted strings. Most of them are to avoid conflicts with characters that are used with variables, but three of them have special meanings: \n inserts a new line character, \r inserts a carriage return (needed mainly for Windows), and \t inserts a tab. Table 10-1 lists the main escape sequences supported by PHP.

Table 10-1. The main PHP escape sequences

Escape sequence	Character represented in double-quoted string
\"	Double quote
\n	New line
\r	Carriage return
\t	Tab
\\	Backslash
\$	Dollar sign
\{	Opening curly brace
\}	Closing curly brace
\[	Opening square bracket
\]	Closing square bracket

10

> *The escape sequences listed in Table 10-1, with the exception of \\, work only in double-quoted strings. If you use them in a single-quoted string, they are treated as a literal backslash followed by the second character.*

Double quotes are obviously very useful, so why not use them all the time? Many people do, but the official recommendation is to use the quoting method that uses the least processing power—and that's usually single quotes. When PHP sees an opening double quote, it tries to process any variables first. If it finds none, it goes back and treats the string as plain text. On short scripts, such as in this book, the difference in processing time is negligible, but it can make a difference on long, complex scripts.

Joining strings together

PHP has a rather unusual way of joining strings. Although many other computer languages use the plus sign (+), PHP uses a period, dot, or full stop (.) like this:

```
$firstName = 'David';
$lastName = 'Powers';
echo $firstName.$lastName; // displays DavidPowers
```

As the comment in the final line of code indicates, when two strings are joined like this, PHP leaves no gap between them. Don't be fooled into thinking that adding a space after the period will do the trick. It won't. You can put as much space on either side of the period as you like; the result will always be the same, because PHP ignores whitespace in code. You must either include a space in one of the strings or insert the space as a string in its own right, like this:

```
echo $firstName.' '.$lastName; // displays David Powers
```

> *The period—or **concatenation operator**, to give it its correct name—can be difficult to spot among a lot of other code. Make sure the font size in your script editor is large enough to read without straining to see the difference between periods and commas.*

Adding to an existing string

Very often, you need to add more text at the end of an existing string. One way to do it is like this:

```
$author = 'David';
$author = $author.' Powers'; // $author is now 'David Powers'
```

Basically, this concatenates Powers (with a leading space) on the end of $author, and then assigns everything back to the original variable.

Adding something to an existing variable is such a common operation, PHP offers a shorthand way of doing it—with the **combined concatenation operator**. Don't worry about the highfalutin name, it's just a period followed by an equal sign. It works like this:

```
$author = 'David';
$author .= ' Powers'; // $author is now 'David Powers'
```

There should be no space between the period and equal sign. You'll find this shorthand very useful when building the string to form the body of an email message in the next chapter.

> How long can a string be? As far as PHP is concerned, there's no limit. In practice, you are likely to be constrained by other factors, such as server memory; but in theory, you could store the whole of War and Peace in a string variable.

Using quotes efficiently

Award yourself a bonus point if you spotted a better way of adding the space between $firstName and $lastName in the last example. Yes, that's right . . . Use double quotes, like this:

```
echo "$firstName $lastName"; // displays David Powers
```

Choosing the most efficient combination of quotation marks isn't easy when you first start working with PHP, but it can make your code a lot easier to use. Many beginners stick rigidly to double quotes for everything, and end up peppering their scripts with backslashes to escape double quotes in the middle of strings. It not only makes scripts difficult to read, but usually results in PHP errors or broken XHTML.

Special cases: true, false and null

Although text should be enclosed in quotes, three special cases—true, false, and null—should never be enclosed in quotes unless you want to treat them as genuine text (or strings). The first two mean what you would expect; the last one, null, means "nothing" or "no value."

PHP makes decisions on the basis of whether something evaluates to true or false. Putting quotes around false has surprising consequences. The following code:

```
$OK = 'false';
```

does exactly the opposite of what you might expect: it makes $OK true! Why? Because the quotes around false turn it into a string, and PHP treats strings as true. The other thing to note about true, false, and null is that they are *case insensitive*. The following examples are all valid:

```
$OK = TRUE;
$OK = tRuE;
$OK = true;
```

10

Working with numbers

PHP can do a lot with numbers—from simple addition to complex math. Numbers can contain a decimal point or use scientific notation, but they must contain no other punctuation. Never use a comma as a thousands separator. The following examples show the right and wrong ways to assign a large number to a variable:

```
$million = 1000000;     // this is correct
$million = 1,000,000;   // this generates an error
$million = 1e6;         // this is correct
$million = 1e 6;        // this generates an error
```

When using scientific notation, the letter "e" can be uppercase or lowercase and optionally followed by a plus or minus sign. No spaces are permitted.

Performing calculations

The standard arithmetic operators all work the way you would expect, although some of them look slightly different from those you learned at school. For instance, an asterisk (*) is used as the multiplication sign, and a forward slash (/) is used to indicate division.

Table 10-2 shows examples of how the standard arithmetic operators work. To demonstrate their effect, the following variables have been set:

```
$x = 20;
$y = 10;
$z = 3;
```

Table 10-2. Arithmetic operators in PHP

Operation	Operator	Example	Result
Addition	+	$x + $y	30
Subtraction	-	$x - $y	10
Multiplication	*	$x * $y	200
Division	/	$x / $y	2
Modulo division	%	$x % $z	2
Increment (add 1)	++	$x++	21
Decrement (subtract 1)	--	$y--	9

You may not be familiar with the modulo operator. This returns the remainder of a division, as follows:

```
26 % 5    // result is 1
26 % 27   // result is 26
10 % 2    // result is 0
```

A quirk with the modulo operator in PHP is that it converts both numbers to integers before performing the calculation. Consequently, if $z is 4.5 in Table 10-2, it gets rounded up to 5, making the result 0, not 2, as you might expect. (Yes, it was a mistake in my previous books.)

A practical use of the modulo operator is to work out whether a number is odd or even. $number % 2 will always produce 0 or 1.

The increment (++) and decrement (--) operators can come either before or after the variable. When they come before the variable, 1 is added to or subtracted from the value before any further calculation is carried out. When they come after the variable, the main calculation is carried out first, and then 1 is either added or subtracted. Since the dollar sign is an integral part of the variable name, the increment and decrement operators go before the dollar sign when used in front:

```
++$x
--$y
```

You can set your own values for $x, $y, and $z in calculation.php in examples/ch10 to test the arithmetic operators in action. The page also demonstrates the difference between putting the increment and decrement operators before and after the variable.

As noted earlier, numbers should not normally be enclosed in quotes, although PHP will usually convert to its numeric equivalent a string that contains only a number or that begins with a number.

Calculations in PHP follow exactly the same rules as standard arithmetic. Table 10-3 summarizes the precedence of arithmetic operators.

Table 10-3. Precedence of arithmetic operators

Precedence	Group	Operators	Rule
Highest	Parentheses	()	Operations contained within parentheses are evaluated first. If these expressions are nested, the innermost is evaluated foremost.
Next	Multiplication and division	* / %	These operators are evaluated next. If an expression contains two or more operators, they are evaluated from left to right.
Lowest	Addition and subtraction	+ -	These are the final operators to be evaluated in an expression. If an expression contains two or more operators, they are evaluated from left to right.

10

If in doubt, use parentheses all the time to group the parts of a calculation that you want to make sure are performed as a single unit.

Combining calculations and assignment

You will often want to perform a calculation on a variable and assign the result back to the same variable. PHP offers the same convenient shorthand for arithmetic calculations as for strings. Table 10-4 shows the main combined assignment operators and their use.

Table 10-4. Combined arithmetic assignment operators used in PHP

Operator	Example	Equivalent to
+=	$a += $b	$a = $a + $b
-=	$a -= $b	$a = $a - $b
*=	$a *= $b	$a = $a * $b
/=	$a /= $b	$a = $a / $b
%=	$a %= $b	$a = $a % $b

Don't forget that **the plus sign is used in PHP only as an arithmetic operator**.

- **Addition**: Use += as the combined assignment operator
- **Strings**: Use .= as the combined assignment operator

Using arrays to store multiple values

Arrays are an important—and useful—part of PHP. You met one of PHP's built-in arrays, $_POST, in the last chapter, and you'll work with it a lot more through the rest of this book. Arrays are also used extensively with a database, as you fetch the results of a search in a series of arrays.

An array is a special type of variable that stores multiple values rather like a shopping list. Although each item might be different, you can refer to them collectively by a single name. Figure 10-1 demonstrates this concept: the variable $shoppingList refers collectively to all five items—wine, fish, bread, grapes, and cheese.

Individual items—or **array elements**—are identified by means of a number in square brackets immediately following the variable name. PHP assigns the number automatically, but it's important to note that the numbering always begins at 0. So the first item in the array, wine, is referred to as $shoppingList[0], not $shoppingList[1]. And although there are five items, the last one (cheese) is $shoppingList[4]. The number is referred to as the array **key** or **index**, and this type of array is called an **indexed array**.

Figure 10-1. Arrays are variables that store multiple items, just like a shopping list.

Instead of declaring each array element individually, you can declare the variable name once, and assign all the elements by passing them as a comma-separated list to array(), like this:

```
$shoppingList = array('wine', 'fish', 'bread', 'grapes', 'cheese');
```

> *The comma must go outside the quotes, unlike American typographic practice. For ease of reading, I have inserted a space following each comma, but it's not necessary to do so.*

PHP numbers each array element automatically, so this creates the same array as in Figure 10-1. To add a new element to the end of the array, use a pair of empty square brackets like this:

```
$shoppingList[] = 'coffee';
```

PHP uses the next number available, so this becomes $shoppingList[5].

Using names to identify array elements

Numbers are fine, but it's often more convenient to give array elements meaningful names. For instance, an array containing details of this book might look like this:

```
$book['title'] = 'Essential Guide to Dreamweaver CS3';
$book['author'] = 'David Powers';
$book['publisher'] = 'friends of ED';
$book['ISBN13'] = '978-1-59059-859-7';
```

10

This type of array is called an **associative array**. Note that the array key is enclosed in quotes (single or double, it doesn't matter). It mustn't contain any spaces or punctuation, except for the underscore.

The shorthand way of creating an associative array uses the => operator (an equal sign followed by a greater-than sign) to assign a value to each array key. The basic structure looks like this:

```
$arrayName = array('key1' => 'element1', 'key2' => 'element2');
```

So, this is the shorthand way to build the $book array:

```
$book = array('title'     => 'Essential Guide to Dreamweaver CS3',
              'author'    => 'David Powers',
              'publisher' => 'friends of ED',
              'ISBN13'    => '978-1-59059-859-7');
```

It's not essential to align the => operators like this, but it makes code easier to read and maintain.

> *Technically speaking, all arrays in PHP are associative. This means that you can use both numbers and strings as array keys in the same array. Don't do it, though, as it can produce unexpected results. It's safer to treat indexed and associative arrays as different types.*

Inspecting the contents of an array with print_r()

As you saw in the previous chapter, you can inspect the contents of an array using print_r(). This is the code that you inserted at the bottom of feedback.php:

```
<pre>
<?php if ($_POST) {print_r($_POST);} ?>
</pre>
```

It displays the contents of the array like this:

```
Array
(
    [name] => David
    [email] => david@example.com
    [comments] => Hi there!
    [send] => Send comments
)
```

The <pre> tags are simply to make the output more readable. What really matters here is that print_r() displays the contents of an array. As explained earlier, echo and print work only with variables that contain a single value. However, the only real value of print_r() is to inspect the contents of an array for testing purposes. It's no good in a live web page. To display the contents of an array in normal circumstances, you need to use a loop. This gives you access to each array element one at a time. Once you get to an element that contains a single value, you can use echo or print to display its contents. Loops are covered a little later.

Making decisions

Decisions, decisions, decisions . . . Life is full of decisions. So is PHP. They give it the ability to display different output according to circumstances. Decision making in PHP uses **conditional statements**. The most common of these uses if and closely follows the structure of normal language. In real life, you may be faced with the following decision (admittedly not very often if you live in Britain):

```
If the weather's hot, I'll go to the beach.
```

In PHP pseudo-code, the same decision looks like this:

```
if (the weather's hot) {
  I'll go to the beach;
  }
```

The condition being tested goes inside parentheses, and the resulting action goes between curly braces. This is the basic decision-making pattern:

```
if (condition is true) {
  // code to be executed if condition is true
  }
```

> *Confusion alert: I mentioned earlier that statements must always be followed by a semicolon. This applies only to the statements (or commands) inside the curly braces. Although called a conditional statement, this decision-making pattern is one of PHP's control structures, and it shouldn't be followed by a semicolon. Think of the semicolon as a command that means "do it." The curly braces surround the command statements and keep them together as a group.*

10

The code inside the curly braces is executed *only* if the condition is true. If it's false, PHP ignores everything between the braces and moves on to the next section of code. How PHP determines whether a condition is true or false is described in the following section.

Sometimes, the if statement is all you need, but you often want a default action to be invoked. To do this, use else, like this:

```
if (condition is true) {
  // code to be executed if condition is true
  }
else {
  // default code to run if condition is false
  }
```

What if you want more alternatives? One way is to add more `if` statements. PHP will test them, and as long as you finish with `else`, at least one block of code will run. However, it's important to realize that *all* `if` statements will be tested, and the code will be run in every single one where the condition equates to true. If you want only one code block to be executed, use `elseif` like this:

```
if (condition is true) {
  // code to be executed if first condition is true
  }
elseif (second condition is true) {
  // code to be executed if first condition fails
  // but second condition is true
else {
  // default code to run if both conditions are false
  }
```

You can use as many `elseif` clauses in a conditional statement as you like. It's important to note that only the first one that equates to true will be executed; all others will be ignored, even if they're also true. This means you need to build conditional statements in the order of priority that you want them to be evaluated. It's strictly a first-come, first-served hierarchy.

> Although `elseif` *is normally written as one word, you can use* `else if` *as separate words.*

The truth according to PHP

Decision making in PHP conditional statements is based on the mutually exclusive **Boolean values**, true and false (the name comes from a nineteenth century mathematician, George Boole, who devised a system of logical operations that subsequently became the basis of much modern-day computing). If the condition equates to true, the code within the conditional block is executed. If false, it's ignored. Whether a condition is true or false is determined in one of the following ways:

- A variable set explicitly to true or false
- A value PHP interprets implicitly as true or false
- The comparison of two values

Explicit true or false values This is straightforward. If a variable is assigned the value true or false and then used in a conditional statement, the decision is based on that value. As explained earlier, true and false are case insensitive and must *not* be enclosed in quotes.

Implicit true or false values PHP regards the following as false:

- The case-insensitive keywords false and null
- Zero as an integer (0), a floating-point number (0.0), or a string ('0' or "0")
- An empty string (single or double quotes with no space between them)
- An empty array

- An object with no values or functions (PHP 4 only)
- A SimpleXML object created from empty tags

All other values equate to true.

> *This definition explains why "false" (in quotes) is interpreted by PHP as* true. *The value –1 is also treated as* true *in PHP.*

How comparisons equate to true or false is described in the next section.

Using comparisons to make decisions

Conditional statements often depend on the comparison of two values. Is this bigger than that? Are they both the same? If the comparison is true, the conditional statement is executed. If not, it's ignored.

To test for equality, PHP uses two equal signs (==) like this:

```
if ($status == 'administrator') {
  // send to admin page
  }
else {
  // refuse entry to admin area
  }
```

> *Don't use a single equal sign in the first line like this:*
>
> ```
> if ($status = 'administrator') {
> ```
>
> *Doing so will open the admin area of your website to everyone. Why? Because this automatically sets the value of* $status *to administrator; it doesn't compare the two values. To compare values, you must use two equal signs. It's an easy mistake to make, but one with potentially disastrous consequences.*

Size comparisons are performed using the mathematical symbols for less than (<) and greater than (>). Let's say you're checking the size of a file before allowing it to be uploaded to your server. You could set a maximum size of 50KB like this:

```
if ($bytes > 51200) {
  // display error message and abandon upload
  }
else {
  // continue upload
  }
```

Comparison operators These compare two values (known as **operands** because they appear on either side of an operator). If both values pass the test, the result is true (or to use the technical expression, it **returns** true). Otherwise, it returns false. Table 10-5 lists the comparison operators used in PHP.

10

Table 10-5. PHP comparison operators used for decision making

Symbol	Name	Use
==	Equality	Returns true if both operands have the same value; otherwise, returns false.
!=	Inequality	Returns true if both operands have different values; otherwise, returns false.
<>	Inequality	This has the same meaning as !=. It's rarely used in PHP but has been included here for the sake of completeness.
===	Identical	Determines whether both operands are identical. To be considered identical, they must not only have the same value but also be of the same datatype (for example, both floating-point numbers).
!==	Not identical	Determines whether both operands are not identical (according to the same criteria as the previous operator).
>	Greater than	Determines whether the operand on the left is greater in value than the one on the right.
>=	Greater than or equal to	Determines whether the operand on the left is greater in value than or equal to the one on the right.
<	Less than	Determines whether the operand on the left is less in value than the one on the right.
<=	Less than or equal to	Determines whether the operand on the left is less in value than or equal to the one on the right.

Testing more than one condition

Frequently, comparing two values is not enough. PHP allows you to set a series of conditions using **logical operators** to specify whether all, or just some, need to be fulfilled.

All the logical operators in PHP are listed in Table 10-6. **Negation**—testing that the opposite of something is true—is also considered a logical operator, although it applies to individual conditions rather than a series.

Table 10-6. Logical operators used for decision making in PHP

Symbol	Name	Use
&&	Logical AND	Evaluates to true if both operands are true. If the left-hand operand evaluates to false, the right-hand operand is never tested.
and	Logical AND	Exactly the same as &&, but it takes lower precedence.
||	Logical OR	Evaluates to true if either operand is true; otherwise, returns false. If the left-hand operand returns true, the right-hand operand is never tested.
or	Logical OR	Exactly the same as ||, but it takes lower precedence.
xor	Exclusive OR	Evaluates to true if only one of the two operands returns true. If both are true or both are false, it evaluates to false.
!	Negation	Tests whether something is not true.

Technically speaking, there is no limit to the number of conditions that can be tested. Each condition is considered in turn from left to right, and as soon as a defining point is reached, no further testing is carried out. When using && or *and*, every condition must be fulfilled, so testing stops as soon as one turns out to be false. Similarly, when using \|\| or *or*, only one condition needs to be fulfilled, so testing stops as soon as one turns out to be true.

```
$a = 10;
$b = 25;
if ($a > 5 && $b > 20) // returns true
if ($a > 5 || $b > 30) // returns true, $b never tested
```

The implication of this is that when you need all conditions to be met, you should design your tests with the condition most likely to return false as the first to be evaluated. When you need just one condition to be fulfilled, place the one most likely to return true first. If you want a particular set of conditions considered as a group, enclose them in parentheses.

```
if (($a > 5 && $a < 8) || ($b > 20 && $b < 40))
```

Operator precedence is a tricky subject. Stick with && and \|\|, rather than *and* and *or*, and use parentheses to group expressions to which you want to give priority. The xor operator is rarely used.

10

Using the switch statement for decision chains

The switch statement offers an alternative to if . . . else for decision making. The basic structure looks like this:

```
switch(variable being tested) {
  case value1:
    statements to be executed
    break;
  case value2:
    statements to be executed
    break;
  default:
    statements to be executed
}
```

The case keyword indicates possible matching values for the variable passed to switch(). When a match is made, every subsequent line of code is executed until the break keyword is encountered, at which point the switch statement comes to an end.

Dreamweaver uses a switch statement in the GetSQLValueString() function, which it inserts into pages that insert or update records in a database.

The main points to note about switch are as follows:

- The expression following the case keyword must be a number or a string.
- You can't use comparison operators with case. So case > 100: isn't allowed.
- Each block of statements should normally end with break, unless you specifically want to continue executing code within the switch statement.
- You can group several instances of the case keyword together to apply the same block of code to them.
- If no match is made, any statements following the default keyword will be executed. If no default has been set, the switch statement will exit silently and continue with the next block of code.

Using the conditional operator

The **conditional operator** (?:) is a shorthand method of representing a simple conditional statement. The basic syntax looks like this:

```
condition ? value if true : value if false;
```

What this means is that, if the condition to the left of the question mark is true, the value immediately to the right of the question mark is used. However, if the condition evaluates to false, the value to the right of the colon is used instead. Here is an example of it in use:

```
$age = 17;
$fareType = $age > 16 ? 'adult' : 'child';
```

The conditional operator can be quite confusing when you first encounter it, so let's break down this example section by section.

The first line sets the value of $age to 17.

The second line sets the value of $fareType using the conditional operator. The condition is between the equal sign and the question mark—in other words, $age > 16.

If $age is greater than 16, the condition evaluates to true, so $fareType is set to the value between the question mark and the colon—in other words, 'adult'. Otherwise $fareType is set to the value to the right of the colon—or 'child'. You can rewrite the second line using if . . . else like this:

```
if ($age > 16) {
  $fareType = 'adult';
  }
else {
  $fareType = 'child';
  }
```

The if . . . else version is much easier to read, but the conditional operator is more compact, and it's used frequently by Dreamweaver. Most beginners hate this shorthand, but you need to understand how it works if you want to customize Dreamweaver code. Because the conditional operator uses three operands, it's sometimes called the ternary operator.

Using loops for repetitive tasks

Loops are huge time-savers, because they perform the same task over and over again, yet involve very little code. They're frequently used with arrays and database results. You can step through each item one at a time looking for matches or performing a specific task. Loops frequently contain conditional statements, so although they're very simple in structure, they can be used to create code that processes data in often sophisticated ways.

Loops using while and do . . . while

The simplest type of loop is called a while loop. Its basic structure looks like this:

```
while (condition is true) {
  do something
  }
```

The following code displays every number from 1 through 100 in a browser (you can see it in action in while.php in examples/ch10). It begins by setting a variable ($i) to 1, and then using the variable as a counter to control the loop, as well as display the current number onscreen.

```
$i = 1;  // set counter
while ($i <= 100) {
  echo "$i<br />";
  $i++; // increase counter by 1
  }
```

10

A variation of the while loop uses the keyword do and follows this basic pattern:

```
do {
    code to be executed
    } while (condition to be tested);
```

The only difference between a do . . . while loop and a while loop is that the code within the do block is executed at least once, even if the condition is never true. The following code (in dowhile.php in examples/ch10) displays the value of $i once, even though it's greater than the maximum expected.

```
$i = 1000;
do {
   echo "$i<br />";
   $i++; // increase counter by 1
   } while ($i <= 100);
```

Dreamweaver uses a do . . . while loop in its Repeat Region server behavior to loop through the results of a database query (what Dreamweaver calls a recordset) and display them on your page.

The danger with creating while and do . . . while loops yourself is forgetting to set a condition that brings the loop to an end or setting an impossible condition. When this happens, you create an infinite loop that either freezes your computer or causes the browser to crash.

The versatile for loop

The for loop is less prone to generating an infinite loop, because you specify in the first line how you want the loop to work. The for loop uses the following basic pattern:

```
for (initialize counter; test; increase or decrease the counter) {
   code to be executed
   }
```

The three expressions inside the parentheses control the action of the loop (note that they are separated by semicolons, not commas):

- The first expression initializes the counter variable at the start of the loop. You can use any variable you like, but the convention is to use $i. When more than one counter is needed, $j and $k are frequently used.

- The second expression is a test that determines whether the loop should continue to run. This can be a fixed number, a variable, or an expression that calculates a value.

- The third expression shows the method of stepping through the loop. Most of the time, you will want to go through a loop one step at a time, so using the increment (++) or decrement (--) operator is convenient.

The following code does exactly the same as the previous while loop, displaying every number from 1 to 100 (see forloop.php in examples/ch10):

```
for ($i = 1; $i <= 100; $i++) {
    echo "$i<br />";
}
```

There is nothing stopping you from using bigger steps. For instance, replacing $i++ with $i+=10 in this example would display 1, 11, 21, 31, and so on.

Looping through arrays with foreach

The final type of loop in PHP is used exclusively with arrays. It takes two forms, both of which use temporary variables to handle each array element. If you only need to do something with the value of each array element, the foreach loop takes the following form:

```
foreach (array_name as temporary_variable) {
    do something with temporary_variable
}
```

The following example loops through the $shoppingList array and displays the name of each item (see shopping_list.php in examples/ch10):

```
$shoppingList = array('wine', 'fish', 'bread', 'grapes', 'cheese');
foreach ($shoppingList as $item) {
    echo $item.'<br />';
}
```

The preceding example accesses only the value of each array element. An alternative form of the foreach loop gives access to both the key and value of each element. It takes this slightly different form:

```
foreach (array_name as key_variable => value_variable) {
    do something with key_variable and value_variable
}
```

This next example uses the $book array from "Using names to identify array elements" earlier in the chapter and incorporates the key and value of each element into a simple string, as shown in the screenshot (see book.php in examples/ch10):

```
foreach ($book as $key => $value) {
    echo "The value of $key is $value<br />";
}
```

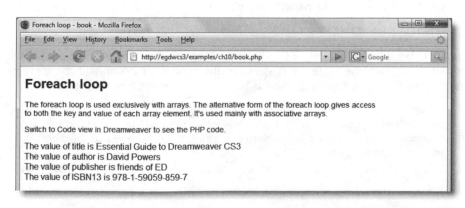

319

> *The* foreach *keyword is one word. Inserting a space between* for *and* each *doesn't work.*

Breaking out of a loop

To bring a loop prematurely to an end when a certain condition is met, insert the break keyword inside a conditional statement. As soon as the script encounters break, it exits the loop.

To skip an iteration of the loop when a certain condition is met, use the continue keyword. Instead of exiting, it returns to the top of the loop and executes the next iteration.

Using functions for preset tasks

Functions do things . . . lots of things, mind-bogglingly so in PHP. The last time I counted, PHP had nearly 3,000 built-in functions, and more have been added since. Don't worry: you'll only ever need to use a handful, but it's reassuring to know that PHP is a full-featured language capable of industrial-strength applications.

The functions you'll be using in this book do really useful things, such as send email, query a database, format dates, and much, much more. You can identify functions in PHP code, because they're always followed by a pair of parentheses. Sometimes the parentheses are empty, as in the case of phpinfo(), which you used in test.php when setting up your testing environment in Chapter 3. Often, though, the parentheses contain variables, numbers, or strings, like this:

```
$thisYear = date('Y');
```

This calculates the current year and stores it in the variable $thisYear. It works by feeding the string 'Y' to the built-in PHP function date(). Placing a value between the parentheses like this is known as **passing an argument** to a function. The function takes the value in the argument and processes it to produce (or **return**) the result. For instance, if you pass the string 'M' as an argument to date() instead of 'Y', it will return the current month as a three-letter abbreviation (e.g., Mar, Apr, May). The date() function is covered in detail in Chapter 17.

Some functions take more than one argument. When this happens, separate the arguments with commas inside the parentheses, like this:

```
$mailSent = mail($to, $subject, $message);
```

It doesn't take a genius to work out that this sends an email to the address stored in the first argument, with the subject line stored in the second argument, and the message stored in the third one. You'll see how this function works in the next chapter.

> *You'll often come across the term "parameter" in place of "argument." There is a technical difference between the two words, but for all practical purposes, they are interchangeable.*

As if the 3,000-odd built-in functions weren't enough, PHP lets you build your own custom functions. Even if you don't relish the idea of creating your own, throughout this book you'll use some that I have made. You use them in exactly the same way.

Understanding PHP error messages

There's one final thing you need to know about before savoring the delights of PHP: error messages. They're an unfortunate fact of life, but it helps a great deal if you understand what they're trying to tell you. The following illustration shows the structure of a typical error message.

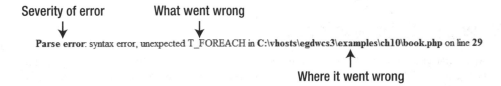

The first thing to realize about PHP error messages is that they report the line where PHP discovered a problem. Most newcomers—quite naturally—assume that's where they've got to look for their mistake. Wrong . . .

What PHP is telling you most of the time is that something unexpected has happened. In other words, the mistake frequently lies *before* that point. The preceding error message means that PHP discovered a foreach command where there shouldn't have been one. (Error messages always prefix PHP elements with T_, which stands for token. Just ignore it.)

Instead of worrying what might be wrong with the foreach command (probably nothing), start working backward, looking for anything that might be missing. Usually, it's a semicolon or closing quote. In this example, the error was caused by omitting the semicolon at the end of line 28 in book.php.

There are four main categories of error, presented here in descending order of importance:

- **Fatal error**: Any XHTML output preceding the error will be displayed, but once the error is encountered—as the name suggests—everything else is killed stone dead. A fatal error is normally caused by referring to a nonexistent file or function.

- **Parse error**: This means there's a mistake in your code, such as mismatched quotes, or a missing semicolon or closing brace. Like a fatal error, it stops the script in its tracks and doesn't even allow any XHTML output to be displayed.

- **Warning**: This alerts you to a serious problem, such as a missing include file. (Include files are covered in Chapter 12.) However, the error is not serious enough to prevent the rest of the script from being executed.

- **Notice**: This advises you about relatively minor issues, such as the use of a nondeclared variable. Although you can turn off the display of notices, you should always try to eliminate the cause, rather than sweep the issue under the carpet. Any error is a threat to your output.

10

Hosting companies have different policies about the level of error checking. If error checking is set to a high level and the display of errors is turned off, any mistakes in your code will result in a blank screen. Even if your hosting company has a more relaxed policy, you still don't want mistakes to be displayed for all to see. Test your code thoroughly, and eliminate all errors before deploying it on a live website.

Another type of error, strict, was introduced in PHP 5.0.0, mainly for the benefit of advanced developers. As of this writing, strict error messages are not displayed by default, but there are plans to change this and introduce a new deprecated category as a prelude to removing outdated parts of the language. If you see a strict or deprecated error message, ignore it at your peril.

Now put it to work . . .

After that crash course, I hope you're feeling not like a crash victim but invigorated and raring to go. Although you have been bombarded with a mass of information, you'll discover that it's easy to make rapid progress with PHP. In the next chapter, you'll use most of the techniques from this chapter to send user input from an online form to your email inbox. To begin with, you'll probably feel that you're copying code without much comprehension, but I'll explain all the important things along the way, and you should soon find things falling into place.

11 USING PHP TO PROCESS A FORM

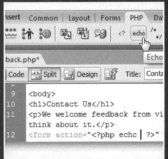

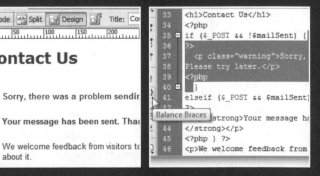

In Chapter 9, I showed you how to build a feedback form and validate the input on the client side with Spry validation widgets. In this chapter, we'll take the process to its next stage by validating the data on the server side with PHP. If the data is OK, we'll send the contents by email and display an acknowledgement message. If there's a problem with any of the data, we'll redisplay it in the form with messages prompting the user to correct any errors or omissions. Figure 11-1 shows the flow of events.

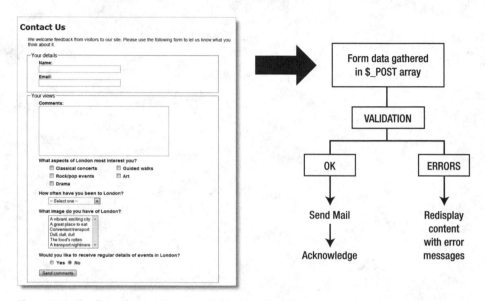

Figure 11-1. The flow of events in processing the feedback form

Sending an email from an online form is just the sort of task that Dreamweaver should automate, but unfortunately it doesn't. Commercial extensions are available to automate the process for you, but not everyone will have—or want to buy—a commercial extension in addition to Dreamweaver CS3, so I think it's important to show you how to hand-code this vital feature. At the same time, it gives you practical experience working with PHP code, which is essential unless you are willing to be limited to very basic tasks. The Dreamweaver server behaviors and data objects that you will use in later chapters take a lot of the hard work out of creating dynamic applications, but like the CSS layout that you used in Chapter 6, they lay a solid foundation for you to build on, rather than do absolutely everything for you.

This chapter shows you how to

- Gather user input and send it by email
- Use PHP conditional logic to check required fields
- Display errors without losing user input
- Filter out suspect material
- Avoid email header injection attacks
- Process multiple-choice form elements

The flow of events shown in Figure 11-1 is controlled by a series of conditional statements (see "Making decisions" in the previous chapter). The PHP script will be in the same page as the form, so the first thing that it needs to know is *if* the form has been submitted. *If* it has, the contents of the $_POST array will be checked. *If* it's OK, the email will be sent and an acknowledgement displayed, *else* a series of error messages will be displayed. In other words, everything is controlled by if . . . else statements.

Activating the form

As you saw in Chapter 9, data entered into the form can be retrieved by using print_r($_POST); to inspect the contents of the $_POST array. This is one of PHP's so-called **superglobal arrays**. They're such an important part of PHP, it's worth pausing for a moment to take a look at what they do.

Getting information from the server with PHP superglobals

Superglobal arrays are built-in associative arrays that are automatically populated with really useful information. They all begin with a dollar sign followed by an underscore. The most important superglobal arrays are as follows:

- **$_POST**: This contains values sent through the post method.
- **$_GET**: This contains values sent through the get method or a URL query string.
- **$_SERVER**: This contains information stored by the web server, such as file name, pathname, hostname, etc.
- **$_SESSION**: This stores information that you want to preserve so that it's available to other pages. Sessions are covered in Chapter 15.
- **$_FILES**: This contains details of file uploads. File uploads are not covered in this book. See www.php.net/manual/en/features.file-upload.php or my book *PHP Solutions: Dynamic Web Design Made Easy* (friends of ED, ISBN-13: 978-1-59059-731-6) for details.

The keys of $_POST and $_GET are automatically derived from the names of form elements. Let's say you have a text input field called address in a form; PHP automatically creates an array element called $_POST['address'] when the form is submitted by the post method or $_GET['address'] if you use the get method. As Figure 11-2 shows, $_POST['address'] contains whatever value a visitor enters in the text field, enabling you to display it onscreen, insert it in a database, send it to your email inbox, or do whatever you want with it.

Figure 11-2. The $_POST array automatically creates variables with the same name and value as each form field.

11

It's important to realize that variables like $_POST['address'] or $_GET['address'] don't exist until the form has been submitted. So, before using $_POST or $_GET variables in a script, you should always test for their existence with isset() or wrap the entire section of script in a conditional statement that checks whether the form has been submitted. You'll see both of these techniques in action in this chapter and the rest of this book.

You may come across old scripts or tutorials that tell you PHP automatically creates variables with the same name as form fields. In this example, it would be $address. This relies on a setting called register_globals being on. The default for register_globals has been off since 2002, but some hosting companies still switch it back on. You should never rely on register_globals, as it leaves your site wide open to malicious attacks. Moreover, register_globals has been removed from PHP 6, so scripts that rely on this setting will break in the future.

Some scripts also recommend the use of $_REQUEST, which is another PHP superglobal. It's much less secure. Always use $_POST for data submitted using the post method and $_GET for the get method or when values are passed through a query string at the end of a URL.

> *Don't forget that PHP is case sensitive. All superglobal array names are written in uppercase. $_Post or $_Get, for example, won't work.*

Dreamweaver code hints make it easy to type the names of superglobals. As soon as you type the underscore after the dollar sign, it displays a list of the array names; and for arrays such as $_SERVER with predefined elements, a second menu with the predefined elements is also displayed, as you'll see when you start scripting the form.

Sending email

To send an email with PHP, you use the mail() function, which takes up to five arguments, all of them strings, as follows:

- The address(es) of the recipient(s)
- The subject line
- The message body
- A list of other email headers
- Additional parameters

The first three arguments are required. Email addresses in the first argument can be in either of the following formats:

```
'user@example.com'
'Some Guy <user2@example.com>'
```

To send to more than one address, use a comma-separated string like this:

```
'user@example.com, another@example.com, Some Guy <user2@example.com>'
```

The second argument is a string containing the subject line. The third argument is the message body, which must be a single string, regardless of how long it is. I'll come back to the final two arguments later.

It's important to understand that mail() isn't an email program. It passes data to the web server's mail transport agent (MTA). PHP's responsibility ends there. It has no way of knowing if the email is delivered to its destination. It doesn't handle attachments or HTML email. Still, it's efficient and easy to use.

These days, most Internet service providers (ISPs) enforce simple mail transfer protocol (SMTP) authentication before accepting email for relay from another machine. However, since mail() communicates directly with the MTA on the same machine, no authentication is required. More important, since mail() doesn't normally need to authenticate itself, it's not capable of doing so when you attempt to use it in your local test environment. What happens is that mail() tries to hand the message to your local MTA. If it finds one, and your ISP accepts the message, you're in luck. More often than not, it can't find one or the ISP rejects the mail without authentication. On Windows, you can edit php.ini (see Chapter 3) and change the SMTP command from localhost to the address of your ISP's outgoing mail server (it's usually something like smtp.example.com). On a Mac, PHP uses the MTA built into OS X, so there is no need to edit php.ini.

> Local testing with mail() *is very much hit and miss. The most reliable approach is to test mail-processing scripts on your remote server. The instructions in this chapter explain which parts of the script can be tested locally.*

Scripting the feedback form

To make things simple, I'm going to break up the PHP script into several sections. To start off, I'll concentrate on the text input fields and sending their content by email. Then I'll move onto validation and the display of error messages before showing you how to handle checkboxes, radio buttons, menus, and multiple-choice lists.

Most readers should be able to send a simple email after the following exercise, but even if you are successful, you should implement the server-side validation described later in the chapter. This is because, without some simple security precautions, you risk turning your online forms into a spam relay. Your hosting company might suspend your site or close down your account altogether. In fact, many hosting companies implement security measures that prevent the first version of the mail script from working. However, you should have a fully working form by the end of this chapter.

This involves a lot of hand-coding—much more than you'll encounter in later chapters. Even if you don't want to do a lot of PHP programming, it's important to get a feel for the flow of a script, as this will help you customize the Dreamweaver code once you start working with a database. The script uses a lot of PHP's built-in functions. I explain the important ones but don't always go into the finer points of how they work. The idea is to give you a working solution, rather than overwhelm you with detail. The finished code for each section is in examples/ch11; and in the next chapter, I'll show you how to put the main part of the script in an external file so that you can reuse it with other forms without the need to hand-code everything from scratch every time.

11

> *This is a long script. Give yourself plenty of time to absorb the details. You can check your progress at each stage with the files in* examples/ch11. *The final code is in* feedback_12.php.

Processing and acknowledging the message

The starting point is in feedback_01.php in examples/ch11. It's the same as feedback_fieldsets.php from Chapter 9 but with the small block of PHP code removed from the bottom of the page. If you want to use your own form, I suggest that you remove any client-side validation from it, as the client-side validation makes it difficult to check whether the more important server-side validation with PHP is working correctly. You can add the client-side validation back at the final stage.

1. Copy feedback_01.php from examples/ch11 to workfiles/ch11, and save it as feedback.php. Also make sure you have a copy of contact.css in your styles folder.

2. Open contact.css, and add the following style rule (it already exists in the version in the examples/styles folder):

```css
.warning {
  font-weight:bold;
  color:#FF0000;
}
```

This adds a class called warning, which displays text in bold red. Close contact.css.

3. Open feedback.php in Split view, click anywhere inside the form, and use the Tag selector to select the entire form. This should bring the opening tag of the form into view in the Code view section of the Document window. Click inside Code view so that your cursor is between the quotes of the action attribute. Although you can set the action for the form through the Property inspector, doing so in Code view greatly reduces the possibility of making a mistake.

4. Select the PHP tab on the Insert bar, and click the Echo button (the menu option is Insert ➤ PHP Objects ➤ Echo). This will insert a pair of PHP tags followed by echo between the quotes of the action attribute, and Dreamweaver positions your cursor in the correct place to start typing, as shown in the following screenshot:

5. To set the `action` attribute of the form to process itself, you need to use a variable from the $_SERVER superglobal array. As noted before, superglobals always begin with $_, so type just that at the current position. Dreamweaver automatically presents you with a pop-up menu containing all the superglobals, as shown here:

You can navigate this pop-up menu in several ways: continue typing "server" in either uppercase or lowercase until SERVER is highlighted or use your mouse or the arrow keys to highlight it. Then double-click or press Enter/Return. Dreamweaver will present you with another pop-up menu. Locate PHP_SELF as shown, and either double-click or press Enter/Return:

6. Although it's not strictly necessary for a single command, get into the habit of ending all statements with a semicolon, and type one after the closing square bracket (]) of the superglobal variable that's just been entered. The code in the opening <form> tag should look like this (new code is highlighted in bold type):

<form action="**<?php echo $_SERVER['PHP_SELF']; ?>**" method="post" ➥ name="form1" id="form1">

The predefined variable $_SERVER['PHP_SELF'] always contains the name of the current page, so using echo between the quotes of the `action` attribute automatically sets it to the current page, making this a self-processing form. As you saw in Chapter 9, leaving out the value of action also results in the form attempting to process itself. So, technically speaking, this isn't 100 percent necessary, but it's common practice in PHP scripts, and it's useful to know what $_SERVER['PHP_SELF'] does.

7. You now need to add the mail-processing script at the top of the page. As you saw in Chapter 9, the $_POST array contains not only the data entered into the form but also the name and value of the submit button. You can use this information to determine whether the submit button has been clicked. From this point onward, it will be easier to work in Code view. Switch to Code view, and insert the following block of PHP code immediately above the DOCTYPE declaration:

11

```php
<?php
if (array_key_exists('send', $_POST)) {
  // mail processing script
  echo 'You clicked the submit button';
  }
?>
<!DOCTYPE html PUBLIC "-//W3C//DTD XHTML 1.0 Transitional//EN" ➥
"http://www.w3.org/TR/xhtml1/DTD/xhtml1-transitional.dtd">
```

This uses the PHP function array_key_exists() to check whether the $_POST array contains a key called send, the name attribute of the form submit button. If you don't want to type out the function name yourself, you can press Ctrl+Space to bring up an alphabetical list of all PHP functions. Type just the first few letters, and then use your arrow keys to select the right one. When you press Tab or Enter/Return, Dreamweaver finishes the rest of the typing and pops up a code hint. Alternatively, just type the function name directly, and the code hint appears as soon as you enter the opening parenthesis after array_key_exists, as shown here:

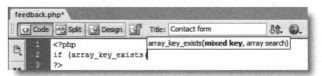

The mixed datatype refers to the fact that array keys can be either numbers or strings. In this case, you are using a string, so enclose send in quotes, and then after a comma, type $_POST. Because it's a superglobal, you are presented with the same pop-up menu as in step 5. If you select POST, Dreamweaver assumes that you want to add the name of an array key and will automatically add an opening square bracket after the T. On this occasion, you want to check the whole $_POST array, not just a single element, so remove the bracket by pressing Backspace. Make sure that you use two closing parentheses—the first belongs to the function array_key_exists(), and the second encloses the condition being tested for by the if statement.

If the send array key exists, the submit button must have been clicked, so any script between the curly braces is executed. Otherwise, it's ignored. Don't worry that echo will display text above the DOCTYPE declaration. It's being used for test purposes only and will be removed eventually.

> Remember, an if statement doesn't always need to be followed by else or elseif. When the condition of a solitary if statement isn't met, PHP simply skips to the next block of code.

8. Save feedback.php, and test it in a browser. It should look no different from before.

9. Click the Send comments button. A message should appear at the top of the page saying "You clicked the submit button."

10. Reload the page without using the browser's Reload button. Click inside the address bar, and press Enter/Return. The message should disappear. This confirms that any code inside the curly braces runs only if the submit button has been clicked.

11. Change the block of code that you entered in step 7 so that it looks like this:

```php
<?php
if (array_key_exists('send', $_POST)) {
  //mail processing script
  $to = 'me@example.com'; // use your own email address
  $subject = 'Feedback from Essential Guide';

  // process the $_POST variables
  $name = $_POST['name'];
  $email = $_POST['email'];
  $comments = $_POST['comments'];

  // build the message
  $message = "Name: $name\n\n";
  $message .= "Email: $email\n\n";
  $message .= "Comments: $comments";

  // limit line length to 70 characters
  $message = wordwrap($message, 70);

  // send it
  $mailSent = mail($to, $subject, $message);
  }
?>
```

The code that does the processing consists of five stages. The first two lines assign your email address to $to and the subject line of the email to $subject.

Next, $_POST['name'], $_POST['email'], and $_POST['comments'] are reassigned to ordinary variables to make them easier to handle.

The shorter variables are then used to build the body of the email message, which must consist of a single string. As you can see, I have used the combined concatenation operator (.=) to build the message and escape sequences to add new line characters between each section (see "Adding to an existing string" and "Using escape sequences in strings" in Chapter 10).

Once the message body is complete, it's passed to the wordwrap() function, which takes two arguments: a string and an integer that sets the maximum length of each line. Although most mail systems will accept longer lines, it's recommended to limit each line to 70 characters.

11

After the message has been built and formatted, the recipient's address, subject line, and body of the message are passed to the mail() function. There is nothing magical about the variable names $to, $subject, and $message. I chose them to describe what each one contains, making much of the script self-commenting.

The mail() function returns a Boolean value (true or false) indicating whether it succeeded. By capturing this value as $mailSent, you can use it to redirect the user to another page or change the contents of the current one.

12. For the time being, let's keep everything in the same page, because the rest of the chapter will add further refinements to the basic script. Scroll down, and insert the following code just after the page's main heading (new code is highlighted in bold):

```
<h1>Contact us</h1>
<?php
if ($_POST && !$mailSent) {
?>
  <p class="warning">Sorry, there was a problem sending your message.
Please try later.</p>
<?php
  }
elseif ($_POST && $mailSent) {
?>
  <p><strong>Your message has been sent. Thank you for your feedback.
</strong></p>
<?php } ?>
<p>We welcome feedback from visitors . . .</p>
```

Many beginners mistakenly think that you need to use echo or print to display XHTML inside a PHP block. However, except for very short pieces of code, it's more efficient to switch back to XHTML, as I've done here. Doing so avoids the need to worry about escaping quotes. Also, Dreamweaver code hints and automatic tag completion speed things up for you. As soon as you type a space after <p in the first paragraph, Dreamweaver pops up a code hint menu like this:

Select class. As soon as you do so, Dreamweaver checks the available classes in the attached style sheet and pops up another code hint menu, as shown in the next screenshot, so you can choose warning.

This makes coding much quicker and more accurate. Dreamweaver's context sensitivity means you get the full range of XHTML code hints only when you're in a section of XHTML code. When you're inside a block of PHP code, you get a list of XHTML tags when you type an opening angle bracket, but there are no attribute hints or auto-completion. So it makes more sense to use PHP for the conditional logic but keep the XHTML separate. The only thing you need to watch carefully is that you balance the opening and closing curly braces correctly. I'll show you how to do that in "Using balance braces" a little later in the chapter.

So what does this code do? It may look odd if you're not used to seeing scripts that mix XHTML with PHP logic, but it can be summarized like this:

```
<h1>Contact us</h1>
<?php
if ($_POST && !$mailSent) {
  // display a failure message
  }
elseif ($_POST && $mailSent) {
  // display an acknowledgment
  }
?>
<p>We welcome feedback from visitors . . .</p>
```

Both parts of the conditional statement check the Boolean values of $_POST and $mailSent. Although the $_POST array is always set, it doesn't contain any values unless the form has been submitted. Since PHP treats an empty array as false (see "The truth according to PHP" in Chapter 10), you can use $_POST on its own to test whether a form has been submitted. So the code in both parts of this conditional statement is ignored when the page first loads.

However, if the form has been submitted, $_POST equates to true, so the next condition is tested. The exclamation mark in front of $mailSent is the negative operator, making it the equivalent of *not* $mailSent. So, if the email hasn't been sent, both parts of the test are true, and the XHTML containing the error message is displayed. However, if $mailSent is true, the XHTML containing the acknowledgment is displayed instead.

11

13. Save `feedback.php`, and switch to Design view. The top of the page should now look like this:

There are three gold shields indicating the presence of PHP code, and both the error and acknowledgement messages are displayed. You need to get used to this sort of thing when designing dynamic pages.

If you don't see the gold shields, refer to "Passing information through a hidden field" in Chapter 9 for details of how to control invisible elements in Design view.

14. To see what the page looks like when the PHP is processed, click the Live Data view button (see alongside) to the right of the Design view button on the Document toolbar.

If you have coded everything correctly, the error message and acknowledgement should disappear. Click the Live Data view button to toggle it off again.

If you got a PHP error message, read "Using balance braces," and then check your code against `feedback_02.php`.

> *The script in step 11 is theoretically all you need to send email from an online form. Don't be tempted to leave it at that. Without the security checks described in the rest of the chapter, you run the risk of turning your website into a spam relay.*

Using Balance Braces

Even if you didn't encounter a problem in the preceding exercise, Balance Braces is a tool that you definitely need to know about. Like quotes, curly braces must always be in matching pairs, but sometimes the opening and closing braces can be dozens, even hundreds, of lines apart. If one of a pair is missing, your script will collapse like a house of cards. Balance Braces matches pairs in a highly visual way, making troubleshooting a breeze.

Let's take a look at the code in step 12 that I suspect will trip many people up. I deliberately removed an opening curly brace at the end of line 41 in the following screenshot. That triggered a parse error, which reported an unexpected closing curly brace on line 45. Now, that could mean either of the following:

- There's a missing opening brace to match the closing one.
- There's an extra closing brace that shouldn't be there.

```
33    <h1>Contact Us</h1>
34    <?php
35 □  if ($_POST && !$mailSent) {
36    ?>
37      <p class="warning">Sorry, there was a problem sending your message.
38    Please try later.</p>
39    <?php
40 □    }
41    elseif ($_POST && $mailSent)
42    ?>
43    strong>Your message has been sent. Thank you for your feedback.
44    </strong></p>
45    <?php } ?>
46    <p>We welcome feedback from visitors to our site. Please use the following
```

The way to resolve the problem is to place your cursor anywhere between a pair of curly braces, and click the Balance Braces button in the Coding toolbar. This highlights the code between the matching braces. I started by placing my cursor on line 37. As you can see, it highlighted all the code between the braces on lines 35 and 40.

Next, I positioned my cursor on line 43. When I clicked the Balance Braces button again, nothing was highlighted, and my computer just beeped. So there was the culprit. All I needed to work out was where the opening brace should go. My first test showed that I had a logical block on lines 35–40, so it was just a process of elimination tracking down the missing brace. If the problem had been an extra curly brace that shouldn't have been there, the code would have been highlighted, giving me a clear indication of where the block ended.

Although it can't tell you whether your code logic is right or where a missing brace should go, you'll find this tool a great timesaver. It works not only with braces, but also with square brackets and parentheses. Just position your cursor inside any curly brace, square bracket, or parenthesis, and click the Balance Braces button to find the other one of the pair. You may need to test several blocks to find the cause of a problem, but it's an excellent way of visualizing code blocks and the branching logic of your scripts.

You can also access Balance Braces through the Edit menu, and if you're a keyboard shortcut fan, the combination is Ctrl+'/Cmd+' (single quote).

Testing the feedback form

Assuming that you now have a page that displays correctly in Live Data view, it's time to test it. As mentioned earlier, testing mail() in a local PHP testing environment is unreliable, so I suggest that you upload feedback.php to a remote server for the next stage of testing. Once you have established that the mail() function is working, you can continue testing locally.

Upload feedback.php and contact.css to your remote server. Enter some text in the Name, Email, and Comments fields. Make sure that your input includes at least an apostrophe or quotation mark, and click Send comments. The form should clear, and you should see a confirmation message, as in Figure 11-3.

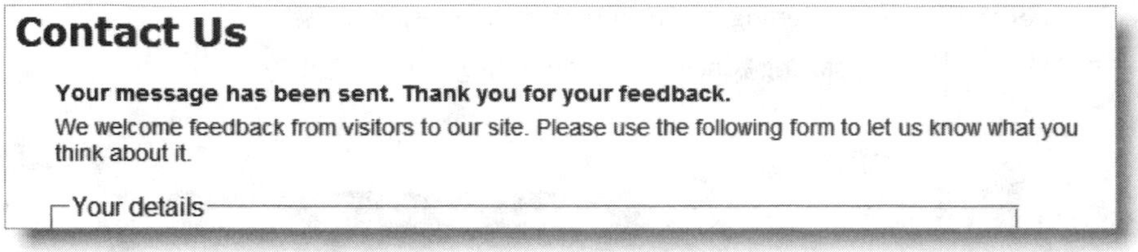

Contact Us

Your message has been sent. Thank you for your feedback.

We welcome feedback from visitors to our site. Please use the following form to let us know what you think about it.

┌─Your details───

Figure 11-3. Confirmation that the mail() function has passed the message to the server's mail transport agent

Shortly afterward, you should receive the message in your inbox. Most of the time, it should work, but there are several things that might go wrong. The next section should help you resolve the problem.

Troubleshooting mail()

If you don't receive anything, the first thing to check is your spam trap, because the email may appear to come from an unknown or a suspicious source. For example, it may appear to come from Apache or a mysterious nobody (the name often used for web servers). Don't worry about the odd name; that will be fixed soon. The main thing is to check that the mail is being sent correctly.

If you see an error message saying that the From header wasn't set or that sendmail_from isn't defined in php.ini, again that's nothing to worry about and will be fixed shortly. Keep building the script as described in each section, and I'll tell you when you can test your page on the remote server again.

Some hosting companies now make it a requirement to use the fifth argument to mail() to ensure that it comes from an entrusted user. If you don't receive mail or see a PHP error message, check your hosting company's instructions and find out the exact format required for the fifth parameter. It normally consists of -f followed (without a space) by your own email address, all enclosed in quotes. You'll see later how to add it to your code. Again, keep building the script as described in each section.

Some mail servers object to new line characters that are not accompanied by carriage returns. If you receive a warning that includes SMTP server response: 451, change the escape sequences in the section that builds the message like this:

```
$message = "Name: $name\r\n\r\n";
$message .= "Email: $email\r\n\r\n";
$message .= "Comments: $comments";
```

Getting rid of unwanted backslashes

Some day back in the mists of time, the PHP development team had the "brilliant" idea of creating a feature known as magic quotes . . . only it wasn't so brilliant after all. When inserting data into a database, it's essential to escape single and double quotes. So the idea of magic quotes was to make life simpler for beginners by doing this automatically for all data passed through the $_POST and $_GET arrays, and cookies. While this seemed like a good idea at the time, it has caused endless problems. To cut a long story short, magic quotes are being officially phased out of PHP (they'll be gone in PHP 6), but they're still enabled on a lot of shared servers. You will know if your server uses them if your test email has backslashes in front of any apostrophes or quotes, as shown in Figure 11-4.

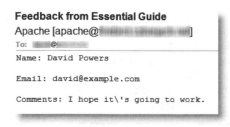

Feedback from Essential Guide
Apache [apache@███████████]
To: ███@███

Name: David Powers

Email: david@example.com

Comments: I hope it\'s going to work.

Figure 11-4. PHP magic quotes insert unwanted backslashes in the email.

Dreamweaver's server behaviors automatically handle magic quotes by stripping the backslashes, if necessary, and preparing data for database input. However, when you're hand-coding like this, you need to deal with the backslashes yourself.

I have created a Dreamweaver snippet, so that you can drop a ready-made script into any page that needs to get rid of unwanted backslashes. It automatically detects whether magic quotes are enabled, so you can use it safely on any server. If magic quotes are on, it removes the backslashes. If magic quotes are off, it leaves your data untouched. It's part of a collection of snippets that I've created for this book and packaged as a Dreamweaver extension so they can be installed in a single operation.

Installing the PHP snippets collection

1. If Dreamweaver is open, you will need to close and restart the program after installing the snippets, so save any files that are open. Access the Extension Manager by choosing Manage Extensions from either the Commands or Help menu.

   If Dreamweaver is closed, launch Adobe Extension Manager CS3 from Start ➤ All Programs (Windows) or Finder ➤ Applications (Mac).

2. Select Dreamweaver CS3 in the drop-down menu on the Extension Manager toolbar, and choose File ➤ Install Extension, or click the Install button. Alternatively, press Ctrl+O/Cmd+O (capital "o," not zero).

3. In the dialog box that opens, navigate to egdwcs3_snippets.mxp in the tools folder of the download files, and click Install.

4. After the extension has been installed, close Dreamweaver if it's open. The snippets will be in the PHP-DWCS3 folder of the Snippets panel when you next open the program.

11

Using the POST stripslashes snippet

1. Open `feedback.php` in Code view. Position your cursor on line 4, just under the `mail processing script` comment, and insert a couple of blank lines.

   Move your cursor onto one of the blank lines, and open the Snippets panel by clicking the Snippets tab in the Files panel group or selecting Window ➤ Snippets. On Windows, you can also use the keyboard shortcut Shift+F9, but this doesn't work on the Mac version.

   Highlight the new POST stripslashes snippet in the PHP-DWCS3 folder, as shown alongside, and double-click it, or click the Insert button at the bottom of the panel.

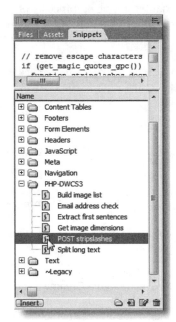

2. This inserts the following block of code into your page:

```php
// remove escape characters from $_POST array
if (get_magic_quotes_gpc()) {
  function stripslashes_deep($value) {
    $value = is_array($value) ? array_map('stripslashes_deep', ➥
$value) : stripslashes($value);
    return $value;
  }
  $_POST = array_map('stripslashes_deep', $_POST);
}
```

   Lying at the heart of this code is the PHP function `stripslashes()`, which removes the escape backslashes from quotes and apostrophes. Normally, you just pass the string that you want to clean up as the argument to `stripslashes()`. Unfortunately, that won't work with an array. This block of code checks whether magic quotes have been turned on; and if they have, it goes through the `$_POST` array and any nested arrays, cleaning up your text for display either in an email or in a web page.

3. Save `feedback.php`, and send another test email that includes apostrophes and quotes in the message. The email that you receive should be nicely cleaned up. This won't work yet if you weren't able to send the first test email.

   If you have any problems, check your page against `feedback_03.php`.

Making sure required fields aren't blank

When required fields are left blank, you don't get the information you need, and the user may never get a reply, particularly if contact details have been omitted. The following instructions make use of arrays and the foreach loop, both of which are described in Chapter 10. So, if you're new to PHP, you might find it useful to refer to the relevant sections in the previous chapter before continuing.

Checking required fields

In this part of the script, you create three arrays to hold details of variables you expect to receive from the form, those that are required, and those that are missing. This not only helps identify any required items that haven't been filled in; it also adds an important security check before passing the user input to a loop that converts the names of $_POST variables to shorter ones that are easier to handle.

1. Start by creating two arrays: one listing the name attribute of each field in the form and the other listing all *required* fields. Also, initialize an empty array to store the names of required fields that have not been completed. For the sake of this demonstration, make the email field optional, so that only the name and comments fields are required. Add the following code just before the section that processes the $_POST variables:

```
$subject = 'Feedback from Essential Guide';

// list expected fields
$expected = array('name', 'email', 'comments');
// set required fields
$required = array('name', 'comments');
// create empty array for any missing fields
$missing = array();

// process the $_POST variables
```

2. At the moment, the $_POST variables are assigned manually to variables that use the same name as the $_POST array key. With three fields, manual assignment is fine, but it becomes a major chore with more fields. Let's kill two birds with one stone by checking required fields and automating the naming of the variables at the same time. Replace the three lines of code beneath the $_POST variables comment as follows:

```
// process the $_POST variables
foreach ($_POST as $key => $value) {
  // assign to temporary variable and strip whitespace if not an array
  $temp = is_array($value) ? $value : trim($value);
  // if empty and required, add to $missing array
  if (empty($temp) && in_array($key, $required)) {
    array_push($missing, $key);
    }
  // otherwise, assign to a variable of the same name as $key
  elseif (in_array($key, $expected)) {
```

11

```
        ${$key} = $temp;
        }
    }
```

```
// build the message
```

If studying PHP code makes your brain hurt, you don't need to worry about how this works. As long as you create the $expected, $required, and $missing arrays in the previous step, you can just copy and paste the code for use in any form.

So what does it do? In simple terms, this foreach loop goes through the $_POST array, strips out any whitespace from user input, and assigns its contents to a variable with the same name (so $_POST['email'] becomes $email, and so on). If a required field is left blank, its name attribute is added to the $missing array.

The code uses several built-in PHP functions, all of which have intuitive names:

- is_array() tests whether a variable is an array.
- trim() trims whitespace from both ends of a string.
- empty() tests whether a variable contains nothing or equates to false.
- in_array() checks whether the first argument is part of the array specified in the second argument.
- array_push() adds a new element to the end of an array.

At this stage, you don't need to understand how each function works, but you can find details in the PHP online documentation at www.php.net/manual/en/index.php. Type the name of the function in the search for field at the top right of the page (see Figure 11-5), and click the right-facing arrow alongside function list. The PHP documentation has many practical examples showing how functions and other features are used.

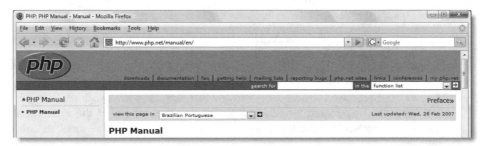

Figure 11-5. Refer often to the excellent PHP online documentation, and your skills will increase rapidly.

Why is the $expected array necessary? It's to prevent an attacker from injecting other variables in the $_POST array in an attempt to overwrite your default values. By processing only those variables that you expect, your form is much more secure. Any spurious values are ignored.

3. You want to build the body of the email message and send it only if all required fields have been filled in. Since $missing starts off as an empty array, nothing is added to it if all required fields are completed, so empty($missing) is true. Wrap the rest of the script in the opening PHP code block like this:

```
// go ahead only if all required fields OK
if (empty($missing)) {

  // build the message
  $message = "Name: $name\n\n";
  $message .= "Email: $email\n\n";
  $message .= "Comments: $comments";

  // limit line length to 70 characters
  $message = wordwrap($message, 70);

  // send it
  $mailSent = mail($to, $subject, $message);
  if ($mailSent) {
    // $missing is no longer needed if the email is sent, so unset it
    unset($missing);
    }
  }
}
```

This ensures that the mail is sent only if nothing has been added to $missing. However, $missing will be used to control the display of error messages in the main body of the page, so you need to get rid of it if the mail is successfully sent. This is done by using unset(), which destroys a variable and any value it contains.

4. Let's turn now to the main body of the page. You need to display a warning if anything is missing. Amend the conditional statement at the top of the page content like this:

```
<h1>Contact us</h1>
<?php
if ($_POST && isset($missing) && !empty($missing)) {
?>
  <p class="warning">Please complete the missing item(s) indicated.</p>
<?php
  }
elseif ($_POST && !$mailSent) {
?>
  <p class="warning">Sorry, there was a problem sending your message.
Please try later.</p>
```

This adds a new condition. The isset() function checks whether a variable exists. If $missing doesn't exist, that means that all required fields were filled in and the email was sent successfully, so the condition fails, and the script moves on to consider the elseif condition. However, if all required fields were filled in, but there was a problem sending the email, $missing still exists, so you need to make sure it's empty. An exclamation mark is the negative operator, so !empty means "not empty."

11

On the other hand, if $missing exists and *isn't* empty, you know that at least one required field was omitted, so the warning message is displayed.

I've placed this new condition first. The $mailSent variable won't even be set if any required fields have been omitted, so you must test for $missing first.

5. To make sure it works so far, save feedback.php, and load it in a browser. You don't need to upload it to your remote server, because you want to test the message about missing items. Don't fill in any fields. Just click Send comments. The top of the page should look like this (check your code against feedback_04.php if necessary):

Contact Us

Please complete the missing item(s) indicated.
We welcome feedback from visitors to our site. Please use the following form to let us know what you think about it.

---

6. To display a suitable message alongside each missing required field, add a PHP code block to display a warning as a <span> inside the <label> tag like this:

```
<label for="name">Name: <?php
if (isset($missing) && in_array('name', $missing)) { ?>
<span class="warning">Please enter your name</span><?php } ?>
</label>
```

Since the $missing array is created only after the form has been submitted, you need to check first with isset() that it exists. If it doesn't exist—such as when the page first loads or if the email has been sent successfully—the <span> is never displayed. If $missing does exist, the second condition checks if the $missing array contains the value name. If it does, the <span> is displayed as shown in Figure 11-6.

7. Insert a similar warning for the comments field like this:

```
<label for="comments">Comments: <?php
if (isset($missing) && in_array('comments', $missing)) { ?>
<span class="warning">Please enter your comments</span><?php } ?>
</label>
```

The PHP code is the same except for the value you are looking for in the $missing array. It's the same as the name attribute for the form element.

8. Save feedback.php, and test the page again locally by entering nothing into any of the fields. The page should look like Figure 11-6. Check your code against feedback_05.php if you encounter any problems.

9. Try one more test. Open Code view, and amend the line that sends the email like this:

```
$mailSent = false; // mail($to, $subject, $message);
```

This temporarily sets the value of $mailSent to false and comments out the code that actually sends the email.

Figure 11-6. The PHP script displays alerts if required information is missing, even when JavaScript is disabled.

10. Reload feedback.php into your browser, and type something in the Name and Comments fields before clicking Send comments. This time you should see the message telling you there was a problem and asking you to try later.

11. Reverse the change you made in step 9 so that the code is ready to send the email.

Preserving user input when a form is incomplete

Imagine you have just spent ten minutes filling in a form. You click the submit button, and back comes the response that a required field is missing. It's infuriating if you have to fill in every field all over again. Since the content of each field is in the $_POST array, it's easy to redisplay it when an error occurs.

When the page first loads or the email is successfully sent, you don't want anything to appear in the input fields. But you do want to redisplay the content if a required field is missing. So that's the key: if the $missing variable exists, you want the content of each field to be redisplayed. You can set default text for a text input field by setting the value attribute of the <input> tag.

At the moment, the <input> tag for name looks like this:

```
<input name="name" type="text" class="textInput" id="name" />
```

To add the value attribute, all you need is a conditional statement that checks whether $missing exists. If it does, you can use echo to display value="" and put the value held in $_POST['name'] between the quotes. It sounds simple enough, but this is one of those situations where getting the right combination of quotes can drive you mad. It's made even worse by the fact that the user input in the text field might also contain quotes. Figure 11-7 shows what happens if you don't give quotes in user input special treatment. The browser finds the first matching quote and throws the rest of the input away.

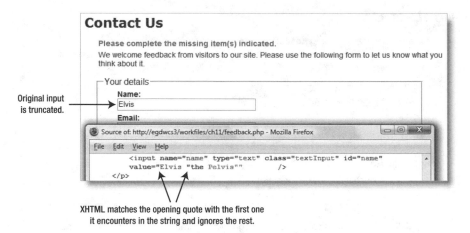

Original input is truncated.

XHTML matches the opening quote with the first one
it encounters in the string and ignores the rest.

Figure 11-7. Quotes within user input need special treatment before form fields can be redisplayed.

You might be thinking that this is a case where magic quotes would be useful. Unfortunately, they won't work either. If you don't use the POST stripslashes snippet, this is what you get instead:

Magic quotes work only with input into a database (and not very well, either, which is why they are being phased out). The browser still sees the first matching quote as the end of the value attribute. The solution is simple: convert the quotes to the HTML entity equivalent ("), and PHP has a function called—appropriately—htmlentities(). Passing the $_POST array element to this function converts all characters (except space and single quote) that have an HTML entity equivalent to that entity. As a result, the content is no longer truncated. What's cool is that the HTML entity " is converted back to double quotes when the form is resubmitted, so there's no need for any further conversion.

Creating sticky form fields

That's the theory—now let's put it into practice.

1. Amend the <input> tag for the Name text field like this:

```
<input name="name" type="text" class="textInput" id="name"
<?php if (isset($missing)) {
  echo 'value="'.htmlentities($_POST['name']).'"';
  } ?>
/>
```

This code is quite short, but the line inside the curly braces contains a tricky combination of quotes and periods. The first thing to realize is that there's only one semicolon—right at the end—so the echo command applies to the whole line. You can break down the rest of the line into three sections, as follows:

- 'value="'.
- htmlentities($_POST['name'])
- .'"'

The first section outputs value=" as text and uses the concatenation operator (a period—see "Joining strings together" in Chapter 10) to join it to the next section, which passes $_POST['name'] to the htmlentities() function. The final section uses the concatenation operator again to join the next string, which consists solely of a double quote. So, if $missing has been set, and $_POST['name'] contains Joe, you'll end up with this inside the <input> tag:

```
<input name="name" type="text" class="textInput" id="name" ➡
value="Joe" />
```

2. Amend the email input field in the same way, using $_POST['email'].

3. The comments text area needs to be handled slightly differently, because <textarea> tags don't have a value attribute. You place the PHP block between the opening and closing tags of the text area like this (new code is shown in bold):

```
<textarea name="comments" id="comments" cols="45" rows="5"><?php
  if (isset($missing)) {
    echo htmlentities($_POST['comments']);
    } ?></textarea>
```

It's important to position the opening and closing PHP tags right up against the <textarea> tags. If you don't, you'll get unwanted whitespace inside the text area.

4. Save feedback.php, and test the page. If the first test message earlier in the chapter was successful, you can upload it to your remote server. If any required fields are omitted, the form displays the original content along with any error messages. However, if the form is correctly filled in, the email is sent, an acknowledgment is displayed, and the input fields are cleared.

If your remote server test didn't succeed earlier in the chapter, just test locally. You'll probably get a PHP error message if all required fields are filled in, but that's nothing to worry about. We're almost at the stage to get your remote server working.

You can check your code with feedback_06.php.

11

By default, htmlentities() *leaves single quotes untouched. Since I chose to wrap the* value *attribute in double quotes, this doesn't matter. To convert a single quote to an HTML entity as well, pass* ENT_QUOTES *(all uppercase) as a second argument to* htmlentities() *like this:* htmlentities($_POST['name'], ENT_QUOTES).

Filtering out potential attacks

A particularly nasty exploit known as email header injection emerged in mid-2005. It seeks to turn online forms into spam relays. A simple way of preventing this is to look for the strings "Content-Type:", "Cc:", and "Bcc:", as these are email headers that the attacker injects into your script in an attempt to trick it into sending HTML email with copies to many people. If you detect any of these strings in user input, it's a pretty safe bet that you're the target of an attack, so you should block the message. An innocent message may also be blocked, but the advantages of stopping an attack outweigh that small risk.

Blocking emails that contain specific phrases

In this section, we'll create a pattern to check for suspect phrases, and pass the form input to a custom-built function that checks for any matches. The function is one of the snippets that you installed earlier in the chapter, so the most complex part of the coding is already done for you. If a match is found, a conditional statement prevents the email from being sent.

1. PHP conditional statements rely on a true/false test to determine whether to execute a section of code. So the way to filter out suspect phrases is to create a Boolean variable that is switched to true as soon as one of those phrases is detected. The detection is done using a search pattern or **regular expression**. Insert the code for both of these just above the section that processes the $_POST variables:

```
// create empty array for any missing fields
$missing = array();

// assume that there is nothing suspect
$suspect = false;
// create a pattern to locate suspect phrases
$pattern = '/Content-Type:|Bcc:|Cc:/i';

// process the $_POST variables
```

The string assigned to $pattern will be used to perform a case-insensitive search for any of the following: "Content-Type:", "Bcc:", or "Cc:". It's written in a format called Perl-compatible regular expression (PCRE). The search pattern is enclosed in a pair of forward slashes, and the i after the final slash makes the pattern case insensitive.

2. You can now use $pattern to filter out any suspect user input from the $_POST array. At the moment, each element of the $_POST array contains only a string. However, multiple-choice form elements, such as checkboxes, return an array of results. So you need to tunnel down any subarrays and check the content of each element separately. In the snippets collection that you installed earlier in the chapter, you'll find a custom-built function to do precisely that.

Insert two blank lines immediately after the $pattern variable from step 1. Then open the Snippets panel, and double-click Suspect pattern filter in the PHP-DWCS3 folder to insert the code shown here in bold:

```
// create a pattern to locate suspect phrases
$pattern = '/Content-Type:|Bcc:|Cc:/i';

// function to check for suspect phrases
function isSuspect($val, $pattern, &$suspect) {
  // if the variable is an array, loop through each element
  // and pass it recursively back to the same function
  if (is_array($val)) {
    foreach ($val as $item) {
      isSuspect($item, $pattern, $suspect);
      }
    }
  else {
    // if one of the suspect phrases is found, set Boolean to true
    if (preg_match($pattern, $val)) {
      $suspect = true;
      }
    }
  }
```

3. I won't go into detail about how this code works. All you need to know is that call-ing the isSuspect() function is very easy. You just pass it three values: the $_POST array, the pattern, and the $suspect Boolean variable. Insert the following code immediately after the code in the previous step:

```
// check the $_POST array and any subarrays for suspect content
isSuspect($_POST, $pattern, $suspect);
```

4. If any suspect phrases are detected, the value of $suspect changes to true, so you need to set $mailSent to false and delete the $missing array to prevent the email from being sent and to display an appropriate message in the form. There's also no point in processing the $_POST array any further. Wrap the code that processes the $_POST variables in the second half of an if . . . else statement like this:

```
if ($suspect) {
  $mailSent = false;
  unset($missing);
  }
else {
  // process the $_POST variables
  foreach ($_POST as $key => $value) {
  // assign to temporary variable and strip whitespace if not an array
    $temp = is_array($value) ? $value : trim($value);
    // if empty and required, add to $missing array
    if (empty($temp) && in_array($key, $required)) {
      array_push($missing, $key);
      }
    // otherwise, assign to a variable of the same name as $key
    elseif (in_array($key, $expected)) {
      ${$key} = $temp;
```

11

```
      }
    }
  }
```

Don't forget the extra curly brace to close the `else` statement.

5. If suspect content is detected, you don't want the code that builds and sends the email to run, so amend the condition in the opening `if` statement like this:

```
// go ahead only if not suspect and all required fields OK
if (!$suspect && empty($missing)) {
  // build the message
```

6. Save `feedback.php`, and check your code against `feedback_07.php`.

Because the `if` statement in step 4 sets `$mailSent` to `false` and unsets `$missing` if it detects any suspect pattern, the code in the main body of the page displays the same message that's displayed if there's a genuine problem with the server. A neutral message reveals nothing that might assist an attacker. It also avoids offending anyone who may have innocently used a suspect phrase.

You can use `isSuspect()` with any array or pattern, but it always requires the following three arguments:

- An array that you want to filter. If the array contains other arrays, the function burrows down until it finds a simple value against which it can match the pattern.

- A regular expression containing the pattern(s) you want to search for. There are two types of regular expression, Perl-compatible (PCRE), and Portable Operating System Interface (POSIX). You must use a PCRE. This function won't work with a POSIX regular expression. A good online source is `http://regexlib.com`.

- A Boolean variable set to `false`. If the pattern is found, the value is switched to `true`.

Safely including the user's address in email headers

Up to now, I've avoided using one of the most useful features of the PHP `mail()` function: the ability to add extra email headers with the optional fourth argument. A popular use of extra headers is to incorporate the user's email address into a Reply-To header, which enables you to reply directly to incoming messages by clicking the Reply button in your email program. It's convenient, but it provides a wide open door for an attacker to supply a spurious set of headers. With the `isSuspect()` function in place, you can block attacks and safely use the fourth argument with the `mail()` function.

The most important header that you should add is From. Email sent by `mail()` is often identified as coming from nobody@servername. Adding the From header not only identifies your mail in a more user-friendly way, but it also solves the problem you might have encountered on the first test of there being no setting for `sendmail_from` in `php.ini`.

You can find a full list of email headers at `www.faqs.org/rfcs/rfc2076`, but some of the most well-known and useful ones enable you to send copies of an email to other addresses (Cc and Bcc) or to change the encoding (often essential for languages other than Western European ones).

Like the body of the email message, headers must be passed to the mail() function as a single string. Each new header, except the final one, must be on a separate line terminated by a carriage return and new line character. This means using the \r and \n escape sequences in double-quoted strings.

Let's say you want to send copies of messages to other departments, plus a copy to another address that you don't want the others to see. This is how you pass those additional email headers to mail():

```
$headers = "From: Essential Guide<feedback@example.com>\r\n";
$headers .= "Cc: sales@example.com, finance@example.com\r\n";
$headers .= 'Bcc: secretplanning@example.com';

$mailSent = mail($to, $subject, $message, $headers);
```

The default encoding for email is iso-8859-1 (English and Western European). If you want to use a different encoding, set the Content-Type header. For Unicode (UTF-8), set it like this:

```
$headers = "Content-Type: text/plain; charset=utf-8\r\n";
```

The web page that the form is embedded in must use the same encoding (usually set in a <meta> tag).

Hard-coded additional headers present no security risk, but anything that comes from user input must be filtered before it's used.

Adding email headers and automating the reply address

This section incorporates the user's email address into a Reply-To header. Although isSuspect() should sanitize user input, it's worth subjecting the email field to a more rigorous check to make sure that it doesn't contain illegal characters or more than one address.

1. At the moment, the $required array doesn't include email, and you may be happy to leave it that way. So, to keep the validation routine flexible, it makes more sense to handle the email address outside the main loop that processes the $_POST array.

   - If email is required but has been left blank, the loop will have already added email to the $missing array, so the message won't get sent anyway.

   - If it's not a required field, you need to check $email only if it contains something. So you need to wrap the validation code in an if statement that uses !empty().

   Insert the code shown in bold after the loop that processes the $_POST array.

   ```
   // otherwise, assign to a variable of the same name as $key
   elseif (in_array($key, $expected)) {
     ${$key} = $temp;
     }
   }
   }
   ```

11

```
// validate the email address
if (!empty($email)) {

}

// go ahead only if not suspect and all required fields OK
if (!$suspect && empty($missing)) {
```

2. Position your cursor on the blank line between the curly braces of the conditional statement you have just inserted. Open the Snippets panel, and double-click Check email PCRE in the PHP-DWCS3 folder. This inserts the following regular expression:

```
$checkEmail = '/^[^@]+@[^\s\r\n\'";,@%]+$/';
```

Designing a regular expression to recognize a valid-looking email address is notoriously difficult. So, instead of striving for perfection, $checkEmail, takes a negative approach by rejecting characters that are illegal in an email address. However, to make sure that the input resembles an email address in some way, it checks for an @ mark surrounded by at least one character on either side.

3. Now add the code shown in bold to check $email against the regular expression:

```
// validate the email address
if (!empty($email)) {
  // regex to ensure no illegal characters in email address
  $checkEmail = '/^[^@]+@[^\s\r\n\'";,@%]+$/';
  // reject the email address if it doesn't match
  if (!preg_match($checkEmail, $email)) {
    $suspect = true;
    $mailSent = false;
    unset($missing);
  }
}
```

The conditional statement uses the preg_match(), which takes two arguments: a PCRE and the string that you want to check. If a match is found, the function returns true. Since it's preceded by the negative operator, the condition is true if the contents of $email *don't* match the PCRE.

If there's no match, $suspect is set to true, $mailSent is set to false, and $missing is unset. This results in the neutral alert saying that the message can't be sent and clears the form. This runs the risk that someone who has accidentally mistyped the email address will be forced to enter everything again. If you don't want that to happen, you can omit unset($missing);. However, the PCRE detects illegal characters that are unlikely to be used by accident, so I have left it in.

> *Many popular PHP scripts use pattern-matching functions that begin with ereg. These work only with POSIX regular expressions. I recommend that you always use the PCRE functions that begin with preg_. Not only is PCRE more efficient, there's a strong likelihood that support for the ereg family of functions will be removed from a future version of PHP.*

4. Now add the additional headers to the email. Place them immediately above the call to the mail() function, and add $headers as the fourth argument like this:

```
// limit line length to 70 characters
$message = wordwrap($message, 70);

// create additional headers
$headers = 'From: Essential Guide<feedback@example.com>';
if (!empty($email)) {
  $headers .= "\r\nReply-To: $email";
  }

// send it
$mailSent = mail($to, $subject, $message, $headers);
```

If you don't want email to be a required field, there's no point in using a nonexistent value in the Reply-To header, so I have wrapped it in a conditional statement. Since you have no way of telling whether the Reply-To header will be created, it makes sense to put the carriage return and new line characters at the beginning of the second header. It doesn't matter whether you put them at the end of one header or the start of the next one, as long as a carriage return and new line separates each header. For instance, if you wanted to add a Cc header, you could do it like this:

```
$headers = "From: Essential Guide<feedback@example.com>\r\n";
$headers .= 'Cc: admin@example.com';
if (!empty($email)) {
  $headers .= "\r\nReply-To: $email";
  }
```

Or like this:

```
$headers = 'From: Essential Guide<feedback@example.com>';
$headers .= "\r\nCc: admin@example.com";
if (!empty($email)) {
  $headers .= "\r\nReply-To: $email";
  }
```

If your hosting company requires you to supply the fifth argument to mail() for security reasons, you should add it after the headers. Normally, it takes the form of -f followed by your email address like this:

```
$mailSent = mail($to,$subject,$message,$headers,'-fdavid@example.com');
```

Use this fifth argument *only* if instructed to do so by your hosting company.

5. Save feedback.php, upload it to your remote server, and test the form. When you receive the email, click the Reply button in your email program, and you should see the address that you entered in the form automatically entered in the recipient's address field. You can check your code against feedback_08.php.

11

> *When building your own forms, don't forget to add the* name *of each text field to the* $expected *array. Also add the* name *of required fields to the* $required *array, and add a suitable alert as described in "Checking required fields."*

Handling multiple-choice form elements

You now have the basic knowledge to process text input from an online form and email it to your inbox. The principle behind handling multiple-choice elements is exactly the same: the name attribute is used as the key in the $_POST array. However, as you saw in Chapter 9, checkboxes and multiple-choice lists don't appear in the $_POST array if nothing has been selected, so they require different treatment.

The following exercises show you how to handle each type of multiple-choice element. If you're feeling punch drunk at this stage, come back later to study how to handle multiple-choice elements when you need to incorporate them into a script of your own.

Getting data from checkboxes

In Chapter 9, I showed you how to create a checkbox group, which stores all checked values in a subarray of the $_POST array. However, the subarray isn't even created if all boxes are left unchecked. So you need to use isset() to check the existence of the subarray before attempting to process it.

1. Add the name of the checkbox group to the $expected array like this:

   ```
   $expected = array('name', 'email', 'comments', 'interests');
   ```

   In the form, interests is followed by square brackets like this:

   ```
   <input type="checkbox" name="interests[]" . . .
   ```

   The square brackets in the form tell the $_POST array to store all checked values in a subarray called $_POST['interests']. However, *don't* add square brackets to interests in the $expected array. Doing so would bury the checked values in a subarray one level deeper than you want. See "Using arrays to store multiple values" in Chapter 10 for a reminder of how arrays are created.

2. If you want the checkboxes to be required, add the name of the checkbox group to the $required array in the same way.

3. Because the checkbox array might never be created, you need to set a default value before attempting to build the body of the email. The following code in bold goes in the section that prepares the message prior to sending it:

   ```
   // go ahead only if not suspect and all required fields OK
   if (!$suspect && empty($missing)) {
     // set default values for variables that might not exist
     $interests = isset($interests) ? $interests : array('None selected');
   ```

This uses the conditional operator (see "Using the conditional operator" in Chapter 10) to check whether $interests has been set. If it has, the existing array of checked values is reassigned to $interests. Otherwise, a single-element array containing the string None selected is created and assigned to $interests. It needs to be an array, even though it contains only one element, because the next step expects an array.

4. To extract the values of the checkbox array, you can use the oddly named implode() function, which joins array elements. It takes two arguments: a string to be used as a separator and the array. So, implode(', ', $interests) joins the elements of $interests as a comma-separated string. Add the following code shown in bold to the script that builds the body of the email:

```
$message .= "Comments: $comments\n\n";
$message .= 'Interests: '.implode(', ', $interests);
```

Note that I added two new line characters at the end of the line that adds the user's comments to the email. On the following line, I put Interests: in single quotes because there are no variables to be processed, and I used the concatenation operator to join the result of implode(', ', $interests) to the end of the email message. You cannot include a function inside a string.

5. The next listing shows the code for the first two checkboxes in the body of the page. The code in bold preserves the user's selections if a required field is missing.

```
<p>
  <input name="interests[]" type="checkbox" id="interests-classical" ➡
value="Classical concerts"
  <?php
  $OK = isset($_POST['interests']) ? true : false;
  if ($OK && isset($missing) && in_array('Classical concerts', ➡
$_POST['interests'])) {
     echo 'checked="checked"';
     } ?>
  />
  <label for="interests-classical">Classical concerts</label>
</p>
<p>
  <input name="interests[]" type="checkbox" id="interests-rock" ➡
value="Rock/pop"
  <?php
  if ($OK && isset($missing) && in_array('Rock/pop', ➡
$_POST['interests'])) {
     echo 'checked="checked"';
     } ?>
  />
  <label for="interests-rock">Rock/pop events</label>
</p>
```

11

The code in the first checkbox contains the following line:

```
$OK = isset($_POST['interests']) ? true : false;
```

This checks whether $_POST['interests'] exists (it won't if the user didn't select any checkboxes). If it does, $OK is set to true.

The PHP code for each checkbox tests three conditions: the value of $OK, whether the $missing variable exists, and whether the value of the checkbox is in the $_POST['interests'] subarray. If all are true, echo inserts checked="checked" into the <input> tag. (If you're using HTML instead of XHTML, use just checked.) Although it looks like a lot of hand-coding, you can copy and paste the code after creating the first one. Just change the first argument of in_array() to the value of the checkbox. The complete code is in feedback_09.php.

If you want to make the checkbox group required, add an alert in the same way as described in "Checking required fields" earlier in the chapter.

Getting data from a drop-down menu

Drop-down menus created with the <select> tag normally allow the user to pick only one option from several. One item is always selected, even if it's only the first one inviting the user to select one of the others. Setting the value of this first <option> to 0 has the advantage that the empty() function, which is used to check required fields, returns true when 0 is passed to it either as a number or string.

1. Add the name of the drop-down menu to the $expected array. Also add it to the $required array if you want a choice to be compulsory.

2. Add the value of the drop-down menu to the email message like this:

```
$message .= 'Interests: '.implode(', ', $interests)."\n\n";
$message .= "Visited: $visited";
```

One option will always be selected, so this doesn't need special treatment. However, change the value of the first <option> tag in the menu to No response if it isn't a required field. Leave it as 0 if you want the user to make a selection.

3. The following code shows the first two items of the drop-down menu in feedback.php. The PHP code highlighted in bold assumes that the menu has been made a required field and resets the selected option if an incomplete form is submitted. When the page first loads, the $_POST array contains no elements, so you can select the first <option> by testing for !$_POST. Once the form is submitted, the $_POST array always contains an element from a drop-down menu, so you don't need to test for it.

```
<label for="visited">How often have you been to London? <?php
if (isset($missing) && in_array('visited', $missing)) { ?>
  <span class="warning">Please select a value</span><?php } ?></label>
  <select name="visited" id="visited">
    <option value="0"
    <?php
    if (!$_POST || $_POST['visited'] == '0') {
```

```
        echo 'selected="selected"';
        } ?>
    >-- Select one --</option>
    <option value="Never"
    <?php
    if (isset($missing) && $_POST['visited'] == 'Never') {
        echo 'selected="selected"';
        } ?>
    >Never been</option>
. . .
</select>
```

When setting the second condition for each <option>, it's vital that you use the same spelling and mixture of uppercase and lowercase as contained in the value attribute. PHP is case sensitive and won't match the two values if there are any differences.

The finished code is in feedback_10.php.

Getting data from a multiple-choice list

Multiple-choice lists are similar to checkboxes: they allow the user to choose zero or more items, so the result is stored in an array. If no items are selected, the $_POST array contains no reference to the list, so you need to take that into consideration both in the form and when processing the message.

1. Add the name of the multiple-choice list to the $expected array. Also add it to the $required array if you want a choice to be compulsory.

2. In the code that processes the message, set a default value for a multiple-choice list in the same way as for an array of checkboxes.

```
$interests = isset($interests) ? $interests : array('None selected');
$views = isset($views) ? $views : array('None selected');
```

3. When building the body of the message, use implode() to create a comma-separated string, and add it to the message like this:

```
$message .= "Visited: $visited\n\n";
$message .= 'Impressions of London: '.implode(', ', $views);
```

4. The following code shows the first two items from the multiple-choice list in feedback.php. The code works in an identical way to the checkboxes, except that you echo 'selected="selected"' instead of 'checked="checked"'. You can reuse $OK here, because its value is reset by the code in the first <option> tag.

```
<select name="views[]" size="6" multiple="multiple" id="views">
    <option value="Vibrant/exciting"
    <?php
    $OK = isset($_POST['views']) ? true : false;
    if ($OK && isset($missing) && in_array('Vibrant/exciting', ➡
$_POST['views'])) {
```

```
    echo 'selected="selected"';
    } ?>
>A vibrant, exciting city</option>
<option value="Good food"
<?php
if ($OK && isset($missing) && in_array('Good food', ➥
$_POST['views'])) {
    echo 'selected="selected"';
    } ?>
>A great place to eat</option>
. . .
</select>
```

The completed code is in feedback_11.php.

If you want to make the multiple-choice list required, add an alert in the same way as described in "Checking required fields" earlier in the chapter.

Getting data from radio button groups

Radio button groups allow you to pick only one value. This makes it easy to retrieve the selected one. All buttons in the same group must share the same name attribute, so the $_POST array contains the value attribute of whichever radio button is selected. However, if you don't set a default button in your form, the radio button group's $_POST array element remains unset.

1. Add the name of the radio button group to the $expected array.

2. If you haven't set a default button and you want a choice to be compulsory, also add it to the $required array. This isn't necessary if a default choice is set in the form.

3. If you haven't set a default button, you need to set a default value before building the body of the email message. You do this in a similar way to a checkbox group or multiple-choice list, but since a radio button group can have only one value, you set the default as a string, not an array, as shown in this example:

   ```
   $radio = isset($radio) ? $radio : 'Not selected';
   ```

4. Add the value of the radio button group to the body of the message like this:

   ```
   $message .= 'Impressions of London: '.implode(', ', $views)."\n\n";
   $message .= "Subscribe: $subscribe";
   ```

5. Assuming a default button has been defined, amend the radio button group like this:

   ```
   <input type="radio" name="subscribe" id="subscribe-yes" value="y"
   <?php
   if (isset($missing) && $_POST['subscribe'] == 'y') {
     echo 'checked="checked"';
   ```

```
    } ?>
  />
  <label for="subscribe-yes">Yes</label>
  <input name="subscribe" type="radio" id="subscribe-no" value="n"
  <?php
  if (!$_POST || isset($missing) && $_POST['subscribe'] == 'n') {
    echo 'checked="checked"';
    } ?>
  />
  <label for="subscribe-no">No</label>
```

The conditional statement for the default radio button begins with !$_POST ||, which means "if the $_POST array is empty or . . ." So, if the form hasn't been submitted, or if the user has selected No and the form is incomplete, this button will be checked.

The completed script is in feedback_12.php.

If no default button has been defined, add the same $OK check as for a checkbox group or multiple-choice list in the first <input> tag, as well as in the conditional statement for each radio button. You need to add a required alert only if no default has been defined in the original form.

Redirecting to another page

Everything has been kept within the same page, even if the message is sent successfully. To redirect the visitor to a different page, change the code at the end of the message-processing section like this:

```
    // send it
    $mailSent = mail($to, $subject, $message, $headers);
    if ($mailSent) {
      // redirect the page with a fully qualified URL
      header('Location: http://www.example.com/thanks.php');
      exit;
      }
    }
  }
```

The HTTP/1.1 protocol stipulates a fully qualified URL for a redirect command, although most browsers will perform the redirect correctly with a relative pathname.

When using the header() function, you must be careful that no output is sent to the browser before PHP attempts to call it. If, when testing your page, you see an error message warning you that headers have already been sent, check there are no characters, including new lines, spaces, or tabs ahead of the opening PHP tag.

11

Time for a breather . . .

If that was your first encounter with PHP, your head will probably be reeling. This has been a tough chapter. In the next chapter, you'll adapt this script so that it can be reused as an external file with most forms. The external file never changes, and the hand-coding is cut down to about a dozen lines. I could, of course, have given you the external file without explanation, but if you don't understand the code, you can't adapt it to your own requirements. Even if you never write an original PHP script of your own, you should know what the code in your page is doing. If you don't, you're storing up trouble for the future.

What makes PHP pages dynamic—and so powerful—is the fact that your code makes decisions, even though you have no way of knowing in advance what is going to be input into the form. The Dreamweaver code that you'll encounter in subsequent chapters tries to anticipate a lot of these unknown factors, but its beauty lies in the fact that it's configurable. If you know how to hand-code, you can get Dreamweaver to do a lot of the hard work for you, and then take it beyond the basics.

However, it's no fun spending all your time churning out code. Life becomes simpler if you can reuse code. So that's what the next chapter is about—saving time with includes and Dreamweaver templates.

12 WORKING WITH PHP INCLUDES AND TEMPLATES

To give a unified look to a website, most pages have common elements, such as a header, navigation menu, and footer. Nobody likes repeating work just for the sake of it, so the ability to build page templates has long been one of Dreamweaver's most popular features. All common features can be defined and locked, but Dreamweaver propagates to all child pages any changes that you make to the master template. The great disadvantage is that every time you make a change all the affected pages must be uploaded again to your remote server. On a large site, this can be a major undertaking.

Wouldn't it be wonderful if you could make changes to just a single page and have them reflected through the site in the same way as CSS? Well, with PHP includes, you can. As the name suggests, the contents of an include file are included and treated as an integral part of the page. They can contain anything that you would normally find in a PHP page: plain text, XHTML, and PHP code. The file name extension doesn't even need to be .php, although for security it's common practice to use it.

Dreamweaver makes working with includes easy thanks to its ability to display the contents of an include in Design view (or Live Data view for dynamic content). Many people find includes so useful that they stop using templates. Nevertheless, templates can be useful, particularly for small sites, so this chapter covers both approaches.

In this chapter, you'll learn how to

- Use PHP includes for common page elements
- Store frequently used code in the Snippets panel
- Apply CSS to page fragments with Design Time Style Sheets
- Export a navigation menu to an external file
- Adapt the mail processing script to work with other forms
- Avoid the "headers already sent" error with includes
- Use Dreamweaver templates in a PHP site

To start with, let's take a quick look at how you create a PHP include.

Including text and code from other files

The ability to include code from other files is a core part of PHP. All that's necessary is to use one of PHP's include commands and tell the server where to find the file.

Introducing the PHP include commands

PHP has four separate commands for creating an include: include(), include_once(), require(), and require_once(). Why so many? And what's the difference?

They all do the same thing, but "require" is used in the sense of "mandatory"; everything comes to a grinding halt if the external file is missing or can't be opened. The "include" pair of commands, on the other hand, soldier bravely on. The purpose of _once is to prevent variables being accidentally overwritten. The PHP engine uses the first instance it encounters and ignores any duplicates. If in doubt about which to use, choose include_once() or require_once(). Using them does no harm and could avoid problems.

Telling PHP where to find the external file

The include commands take a single argument: a string containing the path of the external file. While this sounds simple enough, it confuses many Dreamweaver users. PHP looks for the external file in what's known as the include_path. By default, this always includes the current directory (folder), and PHP expects either a relative or an absolute path. *It won't work with a path relative to the site root.*

If Links relative to is set to Document in the Local Info category of your site definition (see Figure 12-1), Dreamweaver automatically uses the correct path for include files. However, if you have selected Site root as your default style for links, includes won't work unless you override the default setting to change the path to a document-relative one or take alternative measures to set the include_path.

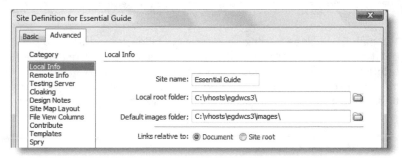

Figure 12-1. Dreamweaver's site definition dialog box lets you specify the default format of internal links.

A practical exercise should clarify the situation.

Including a text file

In this exercise, you'll see what happens if you use the wrong type of path for an include file. You'll also learn how to override the default setting, so that you can use includes successfully even if your site definition specifies using links relative to the site root.

1. Create a new subfolder called includes in your workfiles folder, and copy include.txt from examples/includes to the new folder.

2. Go to File ➤ New. Select Blank Page and PHP as the Page Type. Choose any of the predefined layouts. The one I chose was 2 column fixed, left sidebar. This is only going to be a test page, so you can leave Layout CSS on Add to Head. Click Create and save the file as include_test.php in workfiles/ch12.

3. Position your cursor at the beginning of the first paragraph under the Main Content headline. Press Enter/Return to insert a new paragraph, and then press your up keyboard arrow to move the insertion point into the empty paragraph.

4. Select the PHP tab on the Insert bar, and click the Include button as shown in the following screenshot (alternatively use the menu option Insert ➤ PHP Objects ➤ Include). Dreamweaver opens Split view, inserts a PHP code block complete with an include() command, and positions the insertion point between the parentheses, ready for you to enter the path of the external file.

12

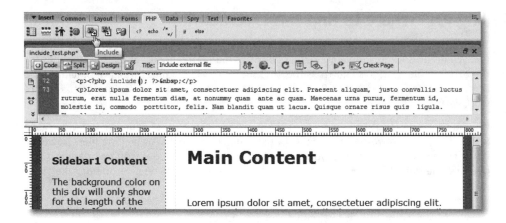

5. The path needs to be a string, so enter a quotation mark (I prefer a single quote, but it doesn't matter, as long as the closing quote matches). Dreamweaver's syntax coloring turns all the subsequent code red, but this reverts to normal once you have finished. Position your mouse pointer over the insertion point, and right-click to bring up a context menu. Select Code Hint Tools ➤ URL Browser, as shown here:

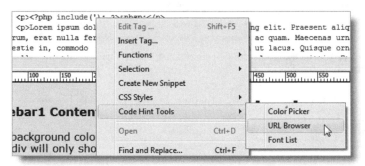

6. This places a tiny Browse icon at the insertion point like this:

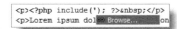

7. Click the Browse icon to open the Select File dialog box. Navigate to the workfiles/includes folder, and select include.txt. Before clicking OK, check the setting of Relative to at the bottom of the dialog box. It displays Document or Site Root, depending on the default in your site definition (see Chapter 4 and Figure 12-1). If necessary, change it to Site Root, as shown here, and click OK:

8. Type a closing quote after the path that has just been entered into the include() command. Syntax coloring turns the rest of the code back to its normal color—a useful reminder of the importance of matching quotes. Move your cursor further along the line to remove the   just before the closing </p> tag.

9. Click inside Design view. The gold PHP shield should disappear and be replaced by the content of the external text file. Magic . . . well, not quite.

10. Save include_test.php, and press F12/Opt+F12 to view it in a browser. You should see something like Figure 12-2.

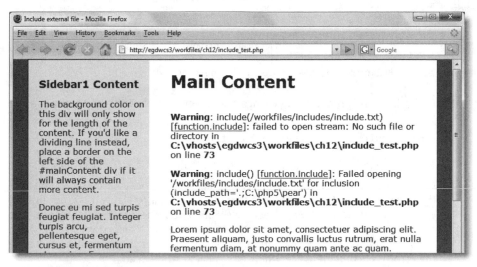

Figure 12-2. If PHP can't find the include file, it displays ugly warning messages.

The first warning says there was no such file or directory, but of course, there is. The second warning gives a cryptic clue as to why PHP can't open the file. The include_path is where PHP looks for include files. The default value on most web servers is . (a period), which is shorthand for the current working directory, and either the main PHP folder or pear (PEAR—the PHP Extension and Application Repository—is a library of extensions to PHP). PHP doesn't understand a leading forward slash as meaning the site root, so it starts from the current folder and ends up in a nonexistent part of the site.

11. Go back to the Dreamweaver Document window, and remove the current path; right-click between the quotes, and use the URL Browser to navigate to include.txt again, but this time make sure that Relative to is set to Document. Save include_test.php, and reload it in a browser. The content of the include file should now be correctly displayed, as shown in Figure 12-3.

12

Figure 12-3. The include file is displayed correctly when a relative path is used.

12. Go back to Dreamweaver, and change the command from include to require like this:

```php
<?php require('../includes/include/txt'); ?>
```

13. Save the page, and load it into a browser. It should look identical to Figure 12-3.

14. Change the path to point to a nonexistent file, such as includ.txt. When you save the page and view it in a browser, it should look similar to Figure 12-2, but instead of the second warning, you should see Fatal error. The other difference is that there's no text after the error message. As explained in "Understanding PHP error messages" in Chapter 10, any output preceding a fatal error is displayed, but once the error is encountered, everything else is killed stone dead.

Using site-root-relative links with includes

As you have just seen, PHP cannot find include files referenced by a site-root-relative link. My recommendation is that, if you have selected links relative to the site root as your default, you simply select Relative to Document in the Select File dialog box (as described in step 10 of the preceding exercise) when creating an include.

Nevertheless, there are a couple of alternatives if you have a pressing reason for wanting to use links relative to the site root. The problem is that they don't work on all servers.

The virtual() function accepts both document-relative and site-root-relative paths and can be used as a direct replacement for include() and require(). It works only when PHP is run as an Apache module.

$_SERVER['DOCUMENT_ROOT'] is a predefined PHP variable that contains the path of the server's root folder, so adding it to the beginning of a site-root-relative link has the effect of turning it into an absolute path. The following works on most servers:

```php
<?php include($_SERVER['DOCUMENT_ROOT'].'/workfiles/includes/ ➡
include/txt'); ?>
```

Unfortunately, `$_SERVER['DOCUMENT_ROOT']` isn't supported by IIS running PHP in CGI mode.

To check whether your server supports either method, run `server_check.php` in examples/ch12. If both are supported, you should see output similar to this.

If neither is supported and you still want to use site-root-relative links, you need to define a **constant** containing the path to the site root. A constant is like a variable, except that once defined in a script, its value cannot be changed. Constants don't begin with a dollar sign, and by convention, they are always in uppercase. You define a constant like this:

```
define('SITE_ROOT', 'C:\inetpub\wwwroot\egdwcs3');
```

You could then use `SITE_ROOT` with a site-root-relative link like this:

```
<?php include(SITE_ROOT.'/workfiles/includes/include/txt'); ?>
```

The disadvantage with this approach is that you need to include the definition of the constant in every page that uses includes.

> *The restriction on site-root-relative links applies only to the include command. Inside include files, all links should be site-root-relative. Document-relative links inside an include file will be broken if the file is included at a different level of the site hierarchy. See "Creating and editing a template-based page" later in the chapter.*

Lightening your workload with includes

So far, you have seen only a fairly trivial use of an include to insert a block of text inside a paragraph. This might be useful in a situation where you want to change the content of part of a page on a frequent basis without going to the bother of building a database-driven content management system. A much more practical use of includes is for content that appears on many pages, for example a navigation menu or footer. Any changes made to the include file are immediately reflected throughout the site.

Choosing the right file name extension for include files

As I explained at the beginning of the chapter, the external file doesn't need to have a `.php` file name extension. Many developers use `.inc` as the default file name extension to make it clear that the file is an include. Although this a common convention, Dreamweaver doesn't automatically recognize an `.inc` file as containing PHP code, so you don't get code hints or syntax coloring. More importantly, browsers don't understand .inc files. So, if anybody accesses an .inc file directly through a browser (as opposed to it being included as part of a PHP page), everything is displayed as plain text.

This is a potential security risk if you put passwords or other sensitive information in external files. One way around this problem is to store include files outside the server root folder. Many hosting companies provide you with a private folder, which cannot be reached by a browser. As long as the PHP script knows where to find the external file *and* has permission to access it, include files can be outside the server root. However, this creates problems for Dreamweaver site management.

A simpler, widely adopted solution is to use .inc.php as the file name extension. Browsers and servers treat only the final .php as the file name extension and automatically pass the file to the PHP engine if requested directly. The .inc is simply a reminder to you as the developer that this is an include file.

As long as you store passwords and other sensitive information as PHP variables within PHP code blocks, and use .php as the final file name extension, your data cannot be seen by anyone accessing the page directly in a browser (of course, it will be revealed if your code uses echo or print to display that information, but I assume that you have the sense not to do that).

Displaying XHTML output

When PHP includes an external file, it automatically treats the contents of the external file as plain text or XHTML. This means that you can cut a section out of an existing page built in XHTML and convert it into an include file. In order to preserve your sanity, it's important to put only complete, logical elements in external files. Putting the opening part of a <div> in one external file and the closing part in another file is a disaster waiting to happen. It becomes impossible to keep track of opening and closing tags, and Dreamweaver is likely to start trying to replace what it regards as missing tags.

Usually, I find the best approach is to build the complete page first, and then convert common elements into include files.

Converting a navigation menu into an include

This exercise shows you how to extract the menu from the "Stroll along the Thames" site in Chapter 7 and convert it into an include file.

1. Copy stroll_horiz.html from examples/ch07 to workfiles/ch12. Also make sure you have the dependent files: styles/stroll_horiz.css, SpryAssets/SpryMenuBar.js, and SpryAssets/SpryMenuBarHorizontal_stroll.css.

2. Save stroll_horiz.html as stroll_horiz.php. You need to change the file name extension so that the PHP engine knows to process it and include the external files you are about to create. Test the page in a browser to make sure that it displays correctly. It should look like Figure 12-4.

Figure 12-4. The menu is the same on every page of the site, so it is a prime candidate for an include file.

3. Create a new PHP file, and save it in the workfiles/includes folder as menu.inc.php. You don't need one of the CSS layouts, as you need a completely blank page. Switch to Code view in menu.inc.php, and delete everything, including the DOCTYPE declaration. There should be nothing left in the page.

4. Switch to stroll_horiz.php in the Document window. Click anywhere inside the navigation menu, and click <div#nav> in the Tag selector to select the entire menu. Switch to Code view, and then cut the menu to your computer clipboard (Ctrl+X/Cmd+X or Edit ➤ Cut).

You must be in Code view when cutting the menu to the clipboard. If you remain in Design view, Dreamweaver cuts all the Spry-related code and pastes it into the include file. You want to move only the XHTML code and the Spry object initialization, but they're in different parts of the page, so it has to be done in two steps. Click No, if Dreamweaver displays the warning shown alongside at any time during the next few steps. Once you move the initialization script, the warning message no longer appears.

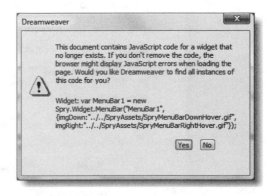

5. Without moving the insertion point, click the Include button on the PHP tab of the Insert bar (or use the menu alternative). This inserts a PHP code block and positions your cursor between the parentheses of an include() command.

6. Type a single quote, right-click, and use Code Hint Tools ➤ URL Browser to navigate to menu.inc.php in the workfiles/includes folder in the same way as in "Including a text file" earlier in the chapter. In the Select File dialog box, make sure that Relative to is set to Document. Click OK, and type a closing quote after the path. Save stroll_horiz.php.

7. Switch to menu.inc.php in the Document window. Make sure you are in Code view, and paste the menu that you cut from stroll_horiz.php. (If you are in Design view, you won't get all the XHTML code. Always cut and paste in the same view in Dreamweaver—Design view to Design view or Code view to Code view.)

8. Go back to stroll_horiz.php, scroll down to the bottom of the page, and cut to your clipboard the section of code highlighted on lines 54–58 in the following screenshot.

```
50    <div id="footer">
51        <p>&copy; Footsore in London </p>
52    <!-- end #footer --></div>
53    <!-- end #container --></div>
54  ⊟ <script type="text/javascript">
55    <!--
56    var MenuBar1 = new Spry.Widget.MenuBar("MenuBar1", {imgDown:"../../SpryAssets/SpryMenuBarDownHover.gif",
      imgRight:"../../SpryAssets/SpryMenuBarRightHover.gif"});
57    //-->
58  ⊟ </script>
59    </body>
60    </html>
```

This is the initialization script for the Spry menu bar. Make sure that you have the opening and closing <script> tags.

9. Paste the Spry object initialization script into menu.inc.php after the closing </div> tag. Save menu.inc.php, and close the file.

10. Switch to Design view in stroll_horiz.php. The menu should be visible as it was before. If you can't see the menu, open Preferences from the Edit menu (Dreamweaver menu on a Mac), select the Invisible Elements category, and make sure there's a check mark in Server-Side includes: Show contents of included file.

11. Hover your mouse pointer over the navigation menu, and click the turquoise Spry Menu Bar tab at the top left corner (see Figure 12-5). The Property inspector recognizes it as a server-side include (SSI) and displays the name of the file, together with an Edit button. Clicking the Edit button opens the include file in the Document window ready for editing.

12. Test stroll_horiz.php in a browser. It should look like Figure 12-4, and the menu should work as before. You can check your code against stroll_horiz_menu.php in examples/ch12 and menu.inc.php in examples/includes.

Figure 12-5. When you select the contents of an include file in Design view, the Property inspector provides a direct link to edit it.

An annoying quirk in the way Dreamweaver handles PHP includes in Design view is that the include command must be in its own PHP code block. If you put any other PHP code in the same block—even a comment—Dreamweaver just displays the gold PHP shield.

Putting the Spry object initialization script at the end of `menu.inc.php` results in it being called earlier than it was in the original page, but it's still in the right order and doesn't result in invalid code. It also prevents the warning in step 4 from being displayed every time that you open the parent page.

An added advantage is that you can edit the Spry menu through the Property inspector in the same way as in Chapter 7. Even though the include file has no direct link to the Spry menu bar external JavaScript file, Dreamweaver automatically finds it because the Spry assets folder is specified in the site definition.

However, what you put in an external file doesn't always have such benign consequences.

Avoiding problems with include files

The server incorporates the content of an include file into the page at the point of the include command. If you pasted all the Spry-related code into `menu.inc.php`, rather than just the constructor, you would end up with the link to the external style sheet within the `<body>` of `stroll_horiz.php`. Although some browsers might render the page correctly, `<style>` blocks are invalid outside the `<head>` of a web page. If it doesn't break now, it probably will sooner or later as browsers get increasingly standards-compliant.

The most common mistake with include files is adding duplicate `<head>` and `<body>` tags. Keep your include files free of extraneous code, and make sure that when everything fits back together that you have a DOCTYPE declaration, a single `<head>` and `<body>`, and that everything is in the right order.

Dreamweaver depends on the DOCTYPE declaration at the top of a page to determine whether to use XHTML rules. Code added to an include will normally use HTML style, so when editing an include, you need to keep a close eye on what is happening in Code view. This is why I recommend extracting code into include files only toward the end of a project or if the external file uses mainly dynamic code.

12

Another common problem is a broken link in an include file. Always use site-root-relative links inside include files. As explained in Chapter 4, site-root-relative links provide a constant reference to a page or an asset, such as an image. If you use document-relative links inside an include file, the relationship—and therefore the link—is broken if the file is included at a different level of the site hierarchy than where it was originally designed.

Applying styles with Design Time Style Sheets

Although Dreamweaver displays the menu normally in `stroll_horiz.php`, it looks completely different in `menu.inc.php`. As Figure 12-6 shows, the menu is completely unstyled; all you can see is the underlying series of nested unordered lists. Design Time Style Sheets let you apply the styles in an external style sheet to a page or code fragment without the need to attach the style sheet directly to the page. As the name suggests, the style sheet is applied only at design time; in other words, in Design view.

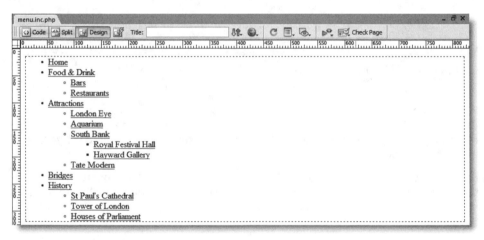

Figure 12-6. The include file is completely unstyled.

To apply Design Time Style Sheets to a page or an include file, select CSS Styles ➤ Design-time from either the Text menu or from the context menu when right-clicking in Design view. This opens the Design Time Style Sheets dialog box, as shown in the following screenshot:

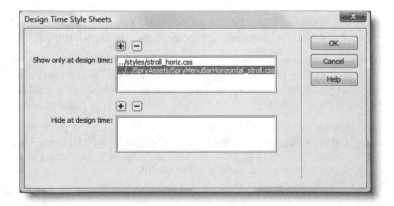

The dialog box has two sections. The first one, Show only at design time, lets you apply a style sheet without attaching it to the file. The second one, Hide at design time, works with style sheets that are attached to a file, letting you hide the effect of selected style sheets while working in Design view. It's particularly useful when working with style sheets for different media, such as print and screen.

Both sections work the same way: add a style sheet to the list by clicking the plus (+) button and navigating to the style sheet in the site file system. The rules of the CSS cascade apply, so add multiple style sheets in the same order as to the original page. To remove a style sheet, highlight it, and click the minus (–) button. Figure 12-7 shows menu.inc.php after applying workfiles/styles/stroll_horiz.css and SpryAssets/SpryMenuBarHorizontal_stroll.css as Design Time Style Sheets. It now looks the same as in the page it was extracted from.

Figure 12-7. After applying Design Time Style Sheets, the include file looks the same as in the original page.

With the Design Time Style Sheets applied, you can manipulate the styles of the include file by changing the class or ID of individual elements. You can also change the style rules in the external style sheets through the CSS Styles panel. But—and it's a rather large one—you should remember that the code fragment that you're working with is no longer in the context of its parent page. As a result, the full effect of the CSS cascade may not be accurately reflected. Also, changes made to the external style sheet may have unexpected consequences on other parts of your design. Although useful, Design Time Style Sheets have their limitations.

Another drawback is that Design Time Style Sheets can be applied to only one page at a time. There is a commercial extension available that lets you apply Design Time Style Sheets to an entire site. See www.communitymx.com/abstract.cfm?cid=61265 for details. Dreamweaver stores details of style sheets applied to a page in this way in a subfolder called _notes. The subfolder is hidden in the Files panel but can be inspected in Windows Explorer or Finder.

Adding dynamic code to an include

The footer of a page frequently contains details that might change, such as company address or telephone number, making it an ideal candidate for an include file.

Automatically updating a copyright notice

The footer in stroll_horiz.php contains only a copyright notice, which normally changes only once a year, but with a little PHP magic, you can get it to update automatically at the stroke of midnight on New Year's Eve every year. Continue working with the files from the previous exercise.

12

1. Create a PHP page, and save it in workfiles/includes as footer.inc.php. Switch to Code view and remove all code, so the file is completely blank. Switch to Design view.

2. Open stroll_horiz.php in Design view, and click anywhere inside the copyright notice at the bottom of the page. Select the entire footer by clicking <div#footer> in the Tag selector, and cut it to your clipboard.

3. Without moving the insertion point, click the Include button on the PHP tab of the Insert bar. Dreamweaver opens Split view with the cursor placed between the parentheses of an include() block. Type a single quote, use the URL Browser as before to insert the path to footer.inc.php, and type a closing quote.

4. Switch to footer.inc.php, and paste the contents of your clipboard into Design view. The footer is unstyled, but if you save footer.inc.php, switch to stroll_horiz.php, and click in Design view, you'll see the footer properly styled as though you had never moved it. Click the copyright notice. The entire text is selected, and the Property inspector displays the path of the include together with an Edit button.

5. Click the Edit button to open footer.inc.php, and switch to Code view. It contains the following XHTML:

```
<div id="footer">
  <p>&copy; Footsore in London</p>
  <!-- end #footer -->
</div>
```

6. A copyright notice should have a year. You could just type it in, but the PHP date() function generates the current year automatically. Add the following code like this:

```
<p>&copy;
<?php
ini_set('date.timezone', 'Europe/London');
echo date('Y');
?>
Footsore in London</p>
```

Chapter 17 explains dates in PHP and MySQL in detail, but let's take a quick look at what's happening here. The core part of the code is this line:

```
echo date('Y');
```

This displays the year using four digits. Make sure you use an uppercase Y. If you use a lowercase y instead, only the final two digits of the year will be displayed.

The reason for the preceding line is because PHP 5.1.0 or higher requires a valid time-zone setting. This should be set in php.ini, but if your hosting company forgets to do this, you may end up with ugly error messages in your page.

What if your hosting company is using an earlier version of PHP? No problem. Earlier versions simply ignore this line.

Setting the time zone like this is not only good insurance against error messages, it also allows you to override the hosting company setting, if your host is in a different time zone from your own. The second argument for ini_set() must be one of the time zones listed at www.php.net/manual/en/timezones.php.

7. Switch to Design view, and click the Live Data view button. You should see the current year displayed alongside the copyright symbol, as shown here.

Click the Live Data view button again to toggle it off.

8. Copyright notices normally cover a range of years, indicating when a site was first launched. To improve the copyright notice, you need to know two things: the start year and the current year. Change the PHP code in the paragraph like this:

```
<p>&copy;
<?php
ini_set('date.timezone', 'Europe/London');
$startYear = 2007;
$thisYear = date('Y');
if ($startYear == $thisYear) {
  echo $startYear;
  }
else {
  echo "{$startYear}-{$thisYear}";
  }
?>
Footsore in London</p>
```

This uses simple conditional logic (if you're new to PHP, see "Using comparisons to make decisions" in Chapter 10, and take particular note of the use of two equal signs in the conditional statement). The static value of $startYear is compared to the dynamically generated value of $thisYear. If both are the same, only the start year is displayed; if they're different, you need to display both with a hyphen between them.

I've used curly braces around the variables in the following line:

```
echo "{$startYear}-{$thisYear}";
```

This is because they're in a double-quoted string that contains no whitespace. The curly braces enable the PHP engine to identify the beginning and end of the variables. Since hyphens aren't permitted in variable names, you could omit the curly braces on this occasion. However, their presence makes the code easier to read.

12

9. Switch back to Design view, and toggle Live Data view on again. Assuming that you used the current year for $startYear, you'll see no difference, so experiment by changing the value of $startYear and alternating between uppercase and lowercase y in the date() function to see the different output, as shown here:

$thisYear = date('Y');   © 2004-2007 Footsore in London

$thisYear = date('y');   © 2004-07 Footsore in London

The values of $startYear, $thisYear, and the name of the copyright owner are the only things you need to change, and you have a fully automated copyright notice. You can check your code against footer.inc.php in examples/includes and stroll_horiz_footer.php in examples/ch12.

Using includes to recycle frequently used PHP code

Up to now, all the examples in this chapter have shown you how to include plain text or XHTML. The last example makes use of PHP code but is specific to one particular site. Includes become really useful when you create PHP code that can be used in any site. A simple example is the POST stripslashes snippet that you used in the last chapter. Instead of putting the code directly inside your script, you could put it in an external file and use include() to incorporate it.

Let's take a look at the code again:

```
// remove escape characters from POST array
if (get_magic_quotes_gpc()) {
  function stripslashes_deep($value) {
    $value = is_array($value) ? array_map('stripslashes_deep', ➥
$value) : stripslashes($value);
    return $value;
    }
  $_POST = array_map('stripslashes_deep', $_POST);
  }
```

It contains nothing but PHP code, and the code itself consists of a conditional statement that removes backslashes from the $_POST array if magic quotes are enabled on the server. To use it successfully as an include, you must do the following two things:

- The code in the external file must be surrounded by PHP tags. Although include() and its related commands are part of PHP, the PHP engine treats everything in an include file as plain text or XHTML until it encounters an opening PHP tag. The opening tag must be matched by a closing one at or before the end of the include file.

- The code must be included at the point in the script where you want to run it. In this respect, it's the same as the text and XHTML includes earlier in the chapter.

PHP can be used in two main ways: as a **procedural** language and as an **object-oriented** one. In a procedural language, everything is usually in the same page and the code is executed from top to bottom. However, to avoid the need to retype frequently used sections of script, you can package them up as custom-built functions. An object-oriented language takes the concept of functions much further, and packages most of the code in libraries called classes.

That's a vast over-simplification, but in both approaches, unless the contents of an external file define functions or classes, the include command must come at the point in the code where you want to run it. The POST stripslashes snippet does include the definition of the stripslashes_deep() function, but it's buried inside a conditional statement. So, the snippet itself is a chunk of procedural code that must be included at the point of the script where it's needed.

However, you can convert the snippet into a new function called nukeMagicQuotes() like this:

```php
<?php
function nukeMagicQuotes() {
  // remove escape characters from POST array
  if (get_magic_quotes_gpc()) {
    function stripslashes_deep($value) {
      $value = is_array($value) ? array_map('stripslashes_deep', ➥
$value): stripslashes($value);
      return $value;
    }
    $_POST = array_map('stripslashes_deep', $_POST);
  }
}
?>
```

If you save this as nukeQuotes.inc.php, you can include the external file at the beginning of your script and run this function at any stage in your script like this (you can see the code in feedback_nuke.php in examples/ch12 and nukeQuotes.inc.php in examples/ includes):

```php
nukeMagicQuotes();
```

The difference of this approach is that the include file initializes the function, but the function doesn't actually run until it's called in the main body of the script. Since this particular piece of code runs only once, there's no immediate advantage of doing it this way. However, let's say that you find a way of improving this script, the changes need to be made only in the external file, saving you the effort of hunting through every page where it might have been used. External files can define more than one function, so you can store frequently used functions together. In this respect, includes are the PHP equivalent of linking external JavaScript files or style sheets.

12

> *When functions or classes are stored in an external file, the include command must come* before *you use the functions or classes in your main script.*

Although building your own function library is an important use of includes, you shouldn't ignore the opportunity to recycle procedural code. The next section shows you how to adapt the mail processing script from the last chapter and make it generic, so that it can handle the output of any feedback form.

Adapting the mail processing script as an include

The mail processing script in the last chapter performs a series of tasks, some of them specific to the feedback form, others more generic in nature.

Analyzing the script

To make the script reusable, you need to identify what's specific, what's generic, and whether any of the specific tasks can be made generic. Once you have identified the nature of each task, you need to concentrate the generic ones into a single unit that can be exported to an external file.

Table 12-1 lists the tasks in the order they are currently performed and identifies their roles. You can study the code in feedback_orig.php in examples/ch12.

Table 12-1. Analysis of the mail processing script

Step	Description	Type
1	Check if form has been submitted	Specific
2	Remove magic quotes	Generic
3	Set to address and subject	Specific
4	List expected and required fields	Specific
5	Initialize missing array	Generic
6	Filter suspect content	Generic
7	Process $_POST variables and check for missing fields	Generic
8	Validate email address	Generic
9	Build the message body	Specific
10	Create additional headers	Specific
11	Send email	Generic

As you can see from Table 12-1, most tasks are generic, but they don't form a single block. However, step 2 can easily be moved after steps 3 and 4. That leaves just steps 9 and 10 that get in the way.

Step 9 builds the body of the message, which would appear to be something that's always specific to each form. Let's take another look at that part of the script:

```
// set default values for variables that might not exist
$interests = isset($interests) ? $interests : array('None selected');
$views = isset($views) ? $views : array('None selected');

// build the message
$message = "Name: $name\n\n";
$message .= "Email: $email\n\n";
$message .= "Comments: $comments\n\n";
$message .= 'Interests: '.implode(', ', $interests)."\n\n";
$message .= "Visited: $visited\n\n";
$message .= 'Impressions of London: '.implode(', ', $views)."\n\n";
$message .= "Subscribe: $subscribe";
```

It doesn't take a genius to work out that the message is built using text labels followed by variables with the same name as the label. Since the variable names come from the name attributes in the form, all you need is a way of displaying the name attributes as well as the values of each input field. That's easily done with PHP. It's also easy to set default values for variables that might not exist.

That leaves just step 10, the creation of additional headers. With the exception of the return email address, it doesn't matter when you specify the additional headers. They simply need to be passed to the mail() function in step 11. So you can move the creation of most headers to the form-specific section at the beginning of the script. Table 12-2 shows the revised order of tasks.

Table 12-2. The revised mail processing script

Step	Description	Type
1	Check if form has been submitted	Specific
2	Set to address and subject	Specific
3	Set form-specific email headers	Specific
4	List expected and required fields	Specific
5	Remove magic quotes	Generic
6	Initialize missing array	Generic
7	Filter suspect content	Generic
8	Process $_POST variables and check for missing fields	Generic
9	Validate email address	Generic
10	Build the message body	Generic
11	Add return email address to headers	Generic
12	Send email	Generic

12

Building the message body with a generic script

Loops and arrays take a lot of the hard work out of PHP scripts, although they can be difficult to understand when you're new to PHP. You may prefer just to use the completed script, but if you're interested in the details, take a look at the following code, and I'll explain how it works:

```php
// initialize the $message variable
$message = '';
// loop through the $expected array
foreach($expected as $item) {
  // assign the value of the current item to $val
  if (isset(${$item})) {
    $val = ${$item};
    }
  // if it has no value, assign 'Not selected'
  else {
    $val = 'Not selected';
    }
  // if an array, expand as comma-separated string
  if (is_array($val)) {
    $val = implode(', ', $val);
    }
  // add label and value to the message body
  $message .= ucfirst($item).": $val\n\n";
  }
```

This replaces the code for step 9 that was listed in the preceding section. It begins by initializing $message as an empty string. Everything else is inside a foreach loop (see "Looping through arrays with foreach" in Chapter 10), which iterates through the $expected array. This array consists of the name attributes of each form field (name, email, etc.).

A foreach loop assigns each element of an array to a temporary variable. In this case, I have used $item. So, the first time the loop runs, $item is name; the next time it's email, and so on. This means that you can use $item as the text label for each form field, but before you can do that, you need to know whether the field contains any value. The code that processes the $_POST variables (step 8 in the revised script) assigns the value of each field to a variable based on its name attribute ($name, $email, etc.). The rather odd-looking ${$item} is what's known as a variable variable (the repetition is deliberate, not a misprint). Since the value of $item is name the first time the loop runs, ${$item} refers to $name. On the next pass through the loop, it refers to $email, and so on.

In effect, what happens is that on the first iteration the following conditional statement

```php
if (isset(${$item})) {
  $val = ${$item};
  }
```

becomes this

```
if (isset($name)) {
  $val = $name;
  }
```

If the variable doesn't exist (which would happen if nothing was selected in a checkbox group), the else clause assigns $val the string Not selected.

So you now have $item, which contains the label for the field, and $val, which contains the field's value.

The next conditional statement uses is_array() to check whether the field value is an array (as in the case of checkboxes or a multiple-choice list). If it is, the values are converted into a comma-separated string by implode().

Finally, the label and field value are added to $message using the combined concatenation operator (.=). The label ($item) is passed to the ucfirst() function, which converts the first character to uppercase. The concatenation operator (.) joins the label to a double-quoted string, which contains a colon followed by the field value ($val) and two new line characters.

This code handles all types and any number of form fields. All it needs is for the name attributes to make suitable labels and to be added to the $expected array.

Converting feedback.php to use the generic script

The following instructions show you how to adapt feedback.php from the previous chapter, so that it can be recycled for use with most forms. If you don't have a copy of the file from the previous chapter, copy feedback_orig.php from examples/ch12 to workfiles/ch12, and save it as feedback.php.

1. Create a new PHP file, and save it as process_mail.inc.php in workfiles/includes. Switch to Code view, and strip out all existing code.
2. Insert the following code:

```
<?php
if (isset($_SERVER['SCRIPT_NAME']) && strpos($_SERVER['SCRIPT_NAME'],➥
'.inc.php')) exit;

?>
```

   This uses the predefined variable $_SERVER['SCRIPT_NAME'] and the strpos() function to check the name of the current script. If it contains .inc.php, that means somebody is trying to access the include file directly through a browser, so the exit command brings the script to a halt. When accessed correctly as an include file, $_SERVER['SCRIPT_NAME'] contains the name of the parent file, so unless you also give that the .inc.php file name extension, the conditional statement returns false and runs the rest of the script as normal.

12

Calling process_mail.inc.php directly shouldn't have any negative effect, but if display_errors is enabled on your server, it generates error messages that might be useful to a malicious attacker. This simple security measure prevents the script running unless it's accessed correctly.

3. Cut the POST stripslashes code from the top of feedback.php, and paste it on the blank line before the closing PHP tag in process_mail.inc.php.

4. Leave $to, $subject, $expected, and $required in feedback.php. Cut the remaining PHP code above the DOCTYPE declaration (DTD), except for the closing curly brace and PHP tag. The following code should be left above the DTD in feedback.php:

```php
<?php
if (array_key_exists('send', $_POST)) {
  //mail processing script
  $to = 'me@example.com'; // use your own email address
  $subject = 'Feedback from Essential Guide';

  // list expected fields
  $expected = array('name', 'email', 'comments', 'interests', ➥
'visited', 'views', 'subscribe');
  // set required fields
  $required = array('name', 'comments', 'visited');
  }
?>
```

5. Paste into process_mail.inc.php just before the closing PHP tag the code you cut from feedback.php.

6. Cut the line that sets the From header, and paste it in feedback.php after the $required array. Replace the code that builds the message with the generic version. The full listing for process_mail.inc.php follows, with the new code highlighted in bold:

```php
<?php
if (isset($_SERVER['SCRIPT_NAME']) && strpos($_SERVER['SCRIPT_NAME'],➥
'.inc.php')) exit;
// remove escape characters from POST array
if (get_magic_quotes_gpc()) {
  function stripslashes_deep($value) {
    $value = is_array($value) ? array_map('stripslashes_deep', ➥
$value) : stripslashes($value);
    return $value;
    }
  $_POST = array_map('stripslashes_deep', $_POST);
  }

// create empty array for any missing fields
$missing = array();
```

```php
// assume that there is nothing suspect
$suspect = false;
// create a pattern to locate suspect phrases
$pattern = '/Content-Type:|Bcc:|Cc:/i';

// function to check for suspect phrases
function isSuspect($val, $pattern, &$suspect) {
  // if the variable is an array, loop through each element
  // and pass it recursively back to the same function
  if (is_array($val)) {
    foreach ($val as $item) {
      isSuspect($item, $pattern, $suspect);
    }
  }
  else {
    // if one of the suspect phrases is found, set Boolean to true
    if (preg_match($pattern, $val)) {
      $suspect = true;
    }
  }
}

// check the $_POST array and any subarrays for suspect content
isSuspect($_POST, $pattern, $suspect);

if ($suspect) {
  $mailSent = false;
  unset($missing);
  }
else {
  // process the $_POST variables
  foreach ($_POST as $key => $value) {
    //assign to temporary variable and strip whitespace if not an array
    $temp = is_array($value) ? $value : trim($value);
    // if empty and required, add to $missing array
    if (empty($temp) && in_array($key, $required)) {
      array_push($missing, $key);
      }
    // otherwise, assign to a variable of the same name as $key
    elseif (in_array($key, $expected)) {
      ${$key} = $temp;
      }
    }
  }

// validate the email address
if (!empty($email)) {
  // regex to identify illegal characters in email address
  $checkEmail = '/^[^@]+@[^\s\r\n\'";,@%]+$/';
```

12

```php
        // reject the email address if it deosn't match
        if (!preg_match($checkEmail, $email)) {
          $suspect = true;
          $mailSent = false;
          unset($missing);
          }
        }

    // go ahead only if not suspsect and all required fields OK
    if (!$suspect && empty($missing)) {
      // initialize the $message variable
      $message = '';
      // loop through the $expected array
      foreach($expected as $item) {
        // assign the value of the current item to $val
        if (isset(${$item})) {
          $val = ${$item};
          }
        // if it has no value, assign 'Not selected'
        else {
          $val = 'Not selected';
          }
        // if an array, expand as comma-separated string
        if (is_array($val)) {
          $val = implode(', ', $val);
          }
        // add label and value to the message body
        $message .= ucfirst($item).": $val\n\n";
        }

      // limit line length to 70 characters
      $message = wordwrap($message, 70);

      // create Reply-To header
      if (!empty($email)) {
        $headers .= "\r\nReply-To: $email";
        }

      // send it
      $mailSent = mail($to, $subject, $message, $headers);
      if ($mailSent) {
        // $missing is no longer needed if the email is sent, so unset it
        unset($missing);
        }
      }
    ?>
```

7. All that remains is to include the mail processing script. Since the form won't work without it, it's a wise precaution to check that the file exists and is readable before attempting to include it. The following is a complete listing of the amended code above the DOCTYPE declaration in feedback.php. The new code, including the $header pasted in the previous step, is highlighted in bold.

```
<?php
if (array_key_exists('send', $_POST)) {
  //mail processing script
  $to = 'me@example.com'; // use your own email address
  $subject = 'Feedback from Essential Guide';

  // list expected fields
  $expected = array('name', 'email', 'comments', 'interests', ➥
'visited', 'views', 'subscribe');
  // set required fields
  $required = array('name', 'comments', 'visited');
  $headers = 'From: Essential Guide<feedback@example.com>';
  $process = '../includes/process_mail.inc.php';
  if (file_exists($process) && is_readable($process)) {
    include($process);
    }
  else {
    $mailSent = false;
    }
  }
?>
```

The path to process_mail.inc.php is stored in $process. This avoids the need to type it out three times. The conditional statement uses two functions with self-explanatory names: file_exists() and is_readable(). If the file is OK, it's included. If not, $mailSent is set to false. This displays the warning that there was a problem sending the message. Because $missing is set inside the processing script, the user's input won't be redisplayed. You could move the initialization of $missing to feedback.php, but if the script can't be accessed, your form is broken anyway.

8. To be super-efficient, send yourself an email alerting you to the problem with the include file by amending the conditional statement like this:

```
if (file_exists($process) && is_readable($process)) {
  include($process);
  }
else {
  $mailSent = false;
  mail($to, 'Server problem', "$process cannot be read", $headers);
  }
```

You can check the final code in feedback_process.php in examples/ch12 and process_mail.inc.php in examples/includes.

12

Because process_mail.inc.php uses generic variables, you can slot this include file into any page that processes a form and sends the results by email. The only proviso is that you must use the same variables as in step 7, namely $to, $subject, $expected, $required, $headers, and $mailSent. You also need to use $missing for the error-checking routine, as described in the previous chapter.

Programming purists would criticize this use of procedural code, arguing that a more robust solution should be built with object-oriented code. An object-oriented solution would probably be better, but it would also be more difficult for a PHP beginner to adapt. The purpose of this exercise has been to demonstrate how even procedural code can be recycled with relatively little effort. It also prepares the ground for customizing the PHP code automatically generated by Dreamweaver. With the exception of the XSL Transformations server behavior (covered in Chapter 18), Dreamweaver uses procedural code.

Avoiding the "headers already sent" error

A problem that you're bound to encounter sooner or later is this mysterious error message:

Warning: Cannot add header information - headers already sent

It happens when you use header() to redirect a page, as described in the previous chapter, or with PHP sessions (covered in Chapter 15). More often than not, the cause of the problem lies in an include file.

Using header() or starting a PHP session must be done before any output is sent to the browser. This includes not only XHTML but also any whitespace. As far as PHP is concerned, *whitespace means any space, tab, carriage return, or new line character*. Why the error message is so mysterious—and causes so much head banging—is because the whitespace is often at the end of an include file. Use the line numbers in Code view, as shown in Figure 12-8, to make sure there are no blank lines at the end of an include file. Also make sure that there is no whitespace after the closing PHP tag on the final line.

Whitespace *inside* the PHP tags is unimportant, but the PHP code must not generate any XHTML output before using header() or starting a session. The same applies to the parent page: there must be no whitespace before the opening PHP tag.

On rare occasions, the error is triggered by an invisible control character at the beginning of the file. Use View ➤ Code View Options ➤ Hidden Characters to check, and delete the character.

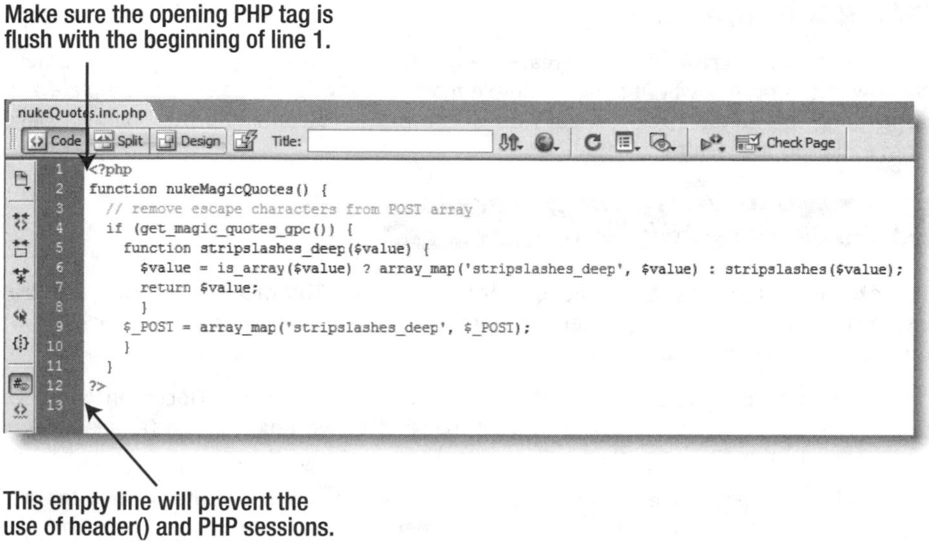

Make sure the opening PHP tag is
flush with the beginning of line 1.

This empty line will prevent the
use of header() and PHP sessions.

Figure 12-8. Eliminate whitespace at the beginning and end of include files to avoid the "headers already sent" error.

Using Dreamweaver templates in a PHP site

Earlier in the chapter, I showed you how to extract two sections from the "Stroll along the Thames" site and turn them into includes. You could go further, and convert the header and fixed parts of the document <head> into includes, so that each page consists of several includes, with just the sidebar and main content forming the actual content of the page. As long as you keep each include as a coherent block, it's relatively easy to manage, and Design view preserves the unified look of the page.

However, it's not an approach that everybody feels comfortable with. That's where Dreamweaver templates can be a useful alternative. A template locks the fixed elements of the design, but lets you designate editable regions for the content that you want to change on each page. Dreamweaver templates allow you to control what can and can't be edited with a great degree of precision, right down to the individual attributes of a tag. If you change anything in a locked region of a master template, Dreamweaver automatically updates all child pages (as long as you accept the option to do so). Although this is convenient, you still need to upload the changed pages manually to the live website.

I don't intend to go into the finer details of working with templates but simply give a broad overview of creating a template, designating editable regions, and creating child pages. I'll also touch on issues that apply specifically to working with PHP in a Dreamweaver template.

12

Creating a template

The easiest way to create a Dreamweaver template is to design a page in the Document window in the normal way. It's then a simple matter of saving the page as a template and designating the editable regions. Let's do that with the "Stroll along the Thames" page from earlier in the chapter.

Converting stroll_horiz_footer.php into a template

This exercise combines the benefits of both approaches. The menu and footer are PHP includes, so can be edited separately, while the rest of the page as a template locks down the main design elements.

1. Open `stroll_horiz_footer.php` from examples/ch12 in the Document window. There is no need to copy or move it, because converting it into a template takes care of that.

2. Choose Make Template from the Common tab of the Insert bar, as shown in the following screenshot. Alternatively, use the menu option File ➤ Save as Template.

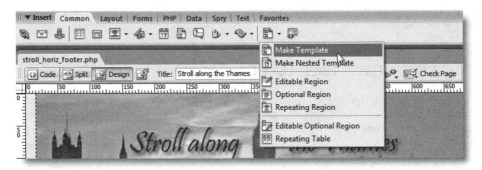

3. This opens the following dialog box:

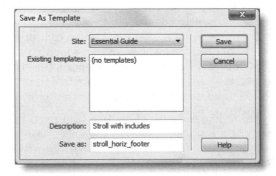

In theory, you can choose to save the template in a different site, but this is likely to cause problems with images, so leave Site unchanged. Existing templates displays a list of templates that you have already defined, if any. Optionally enter a description of the template in the Description field. The Save as field suggests using the current file name. You can change this, if you like, but don't add a file name extension, as Dreamweaver uses a special extension for templates. Click Save.

4. Dreamweaver asks if you want to update links. You must click Yes, or your template will have broken links and cause endless trouble.

5. Although it may appear as though nothing happens, the Dreamweaver title bar changes to display <<Template>> in front of the file name, which now has a .dwt.php extension, as shown here.

Dreamweaver also saves the new template in the Templates folder in the site root. If the folder doesn't exist, Dreamweaver creates it silently.

> *The file with the* .dwt.php *file name extension is now the master template from which you create child pages. Any changes to the design of this page will affect all child pages created from it—as long as you accept the option to update them. You must not move the template from the* Templates *folder. This is perhaps the single most common mistake with templates—moving the master template to another folder will cause you endless grief.* Don't do it.

Adding editable regions to the master template

Everything in a template is locked, except for the <title> tag and an editable region in the <head> of the document. This is needed so that external JavaScript files and style sheets can be added to a child page. It's also where Dreamweaver behaviors insert the JavaScript functions that they require.

> *An important exception to this basic principle is that the area above the DTD and below the closing* </html> *tag is not locked in templates for server-side languages, such as PHP. I'll come back to this issue a little later, as it causes a lot of confusion.*

It goes without saying that you must unlock at least one part of the page for the template to be of any real value. Otherwise, every child page would be identical. Deciding what to lock and unlock depends entirely on the level of control that you want over a page. For instance, you could create separate editable regions for each of the headings on the page.

12

If you select the entire heading, including its surrounding tags, the heading can be replaced by anything: a table, a <div>, an <iframe>, or whatever you like. If you select just the content of an <h2> tag and convert it into an editable region, only the content can be changed in a child page. You can't even change it to an <h1> tag.

Since the remaining chapters of this book are about building dynamic content with PHP, you don't want such rigid control. So you could make everything inside the container <div> one big editable region. However, we'll take a slightly different approach.

Making the sidebar and main content areas editable

This exercise shows you how to create separate editable regions for the sidebar heading and content, as well as for the whole main content area.

1. Open stroll_horiz_footer.dwt.php in the Templates folder if it's not already open.

2. Open Split view. Click immediately to the left of the heading that reads The pleasures of London. Hold down your mouse button and drag to the end of the heading. Alternatively, hold down the Shift key while pressing the keyboard right arrow to select the content of the heading. Make sure you have just the text and not the surrounding <h3> tags, as shown in the following screenshot.

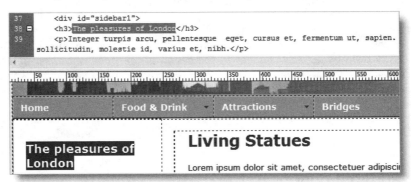

3. There are several ways to make this an editable region. If you're a fan of the Insert bar, click the down arrow next to the Make Template button on the Common tab, and select Editable Region. The Insert bar remembers your last selection, so the Editable Region button remains displayed, ready for the creation of more editable regions.

   Alternatively, right-click and select Templates ➤ New Editable Region from the context menu, or go to Insert ➤ Template Objects ➤ Editable Region.

4. This opens the New Editable Region dialog box. It has just one field for a name for the editable region. It can be anything you like, but each region must have a different name. Enter sidebarHead, and click OK.

5. This wraps the contents of the <h3> tag in two special HTML comment tags, as shown in Figure 12-9. These tell Dreamweaver to treat this as an editable region in child pages. Dreamweaver also displays a turquoise border around the region in Design view, with a tab at the top left indicating the name of the editable region.

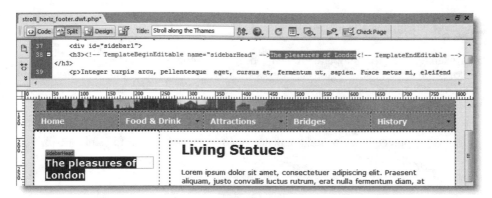

Figure 12-9. Editable regions are easily identified in both Code view and Design view.

Always check the position of the TemplateBeginEditable *and* TemplateEndEditable *comments in Code view, as you can easily move them or any of the surrounding code while still in the template. Checking now saves a lot of frustration later, when you discover that you didn't select the region accurately in Design view, and your child pages don't work the way you expect. These comments are an integral part of the template control mechanism and are propagated to the child pages, where they remain part of the XHTML (see Figure 12-13).*

6. Select the paragraphs and <blockquote> in the sidebar. If you're still in Split view, you'll see that selecting the text in Design view misses the opening tag of the first paragraph and the closing tag of the final one. This doesn't matter. Since more than one paragraph is selected, Dreamweaver is normally clever enough to realize that you want the surrounding tags and includes them when you create the editable region.

7. Use one of the previous methods to make this an editable region named sidebarContent. Switch to Code view to make sure that the opening and closing <p> tags were included. If they weren't, move them inside the template comments.

8. Select all the content in the mainContent <div>, but not the surrounding <div> tags, and create an editable region called mainContent. Check that the template comments are in the right place in Code view, and save stroll_horiz_footer. dwt.php.

9. Dreamweaver should display a warning that sidebarHead is inside a block tag, and that users of the template won't be able to create new blocks in this region. This is because the <h3> tags are outside the sidebarHead editable region, which prevents anything other than a level three heading being created. That's fine. So click OK.

Creating child pages from a template

Now that you have a template, you can build pages based on it. The editable regions can be freely changed, but the other areas remain locked and can be changed only by editing the master template.

12

393

Creating and editing a template-based page

This exercise uses the template from the previous exercise to create a child page and explores the way editable regions are displayed in both Design view and Code view. It also demonstrates the importance of using site-root-relative links in PHP includes,

1. Go to File ➤ New. When the New Document dialog box opens, select Page from Template from the options on the left side. Assuming that you created the template in the preceding exercises, the dialog box should look similar to Figure 12-10.

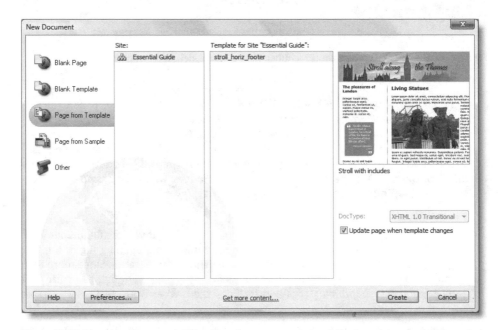

Figure 12-10. The New Document dialog box gives you access to all the templates you have created.

If you have created templates in several sites, select the site and the template that you want to use as the basis for a new page (you can have as many templates as you like in a site, using different designs for pages that serve different functions).

The New Document dialog box shows a preview of the selected template, together with the description you entered when it was first created.

The idea of a template is that all changes to common elements are propagated automatically to child pages when the master template is updated. Unless you want to create a page that doesn't automatically update, make sure that there's a check mark in Update page when template changes, and click Create.

2. A new page is created in the Document window. At first glance, it looks identical to the template, but several features tell you that it's a child page (see Figure 12-11) and that you can make changes only to the editable regions indicated by the turquoise borders and tabs. Whenever your mouse is over a locked part of the page, the pointer turns into a circle with a diagonal bar to warn you that no changes can be made.

Cursor changes shape over locked areas to indicate they cannot be edited

Yellow tab displays name of master template

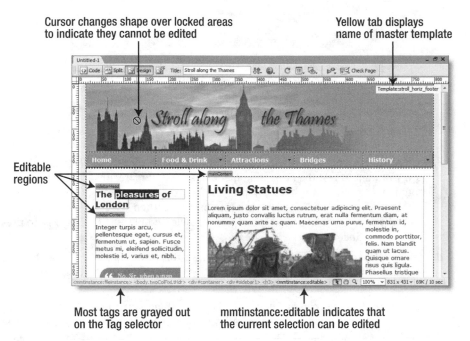

Editable regions

Most tags are grayed out on the Tag selector

mmtinstance:editable indicates that the current selection can be edited

Figure 12-11. The child page is identical to the master template, but locked areas can no longer be edited.

3. Save the page as `stroll_index.php` in `workfiles/ch12`.

4. Repeat step 1 to create another child page from the template. Save it as `stroll_restaurants.php` in a new folder called `workfiles/ch12/food`.

5. Make some changes to `stroll_restaurants.php`. Experiment to see what you can and can't change. For instance, the sidebarHead cannot be changed to a different format, but the <h2> at the top of the mainContent <div> can be changed or deleted altogether. You can also change the Title field in the Document toolbar. Give the pages different titles by adding Home to `stroll_index.php` and Restaurants to `stroll_restaurants.php`. Make sufficient changes to one of the pages so that you can tell them apart, and then save both of them.

6. The navigation menu contains only dummy links at the moment, so open `menu.inc.php` in `workfiles/includes`. Update the link for Home so that it points to `stroll_index.php` and for Restaurants to point to `stroll_restaurants.php`.

Because the navigation menu is shared by files in different levels of the site hierarchy, you must make the links relative to the site root, even if you have set the site default to use links relative to the current document. Use the Browse icon (it looks like a folder) alongside the Link field in the Property inspector to select the target files, and set the Relative to drop-down menu to Site Root as shown in Figure 12-12.

12

Figure 12-12. Links for the navigation menu must be relative to the site root.

7. Save `menu.inc.php`, and switch back to `stroll_index.php` in the Document window. You want to test the navigation menu links, so your Dreamweaver preferences shouldn't use temporary files for preview. (If you're not sure, open Preferences from the Edit menu or Dreamweaver menu on a Mac; then select Preview in Browser, and make sure Preview using temporary file is deselected.) Press F12/Opt+F12 to preview `stroll_index.php` in a browser.

8. Test the Restaurants link. If you have followed the instructions carefully, it *won't* work. Don't worry; I've done something deliberately to demonstrate an important feature of building pages from templates.

9. Open `stroll_index.php` in Code view. The first thing you'll notice is that several parts of code are colored light gray. All the code in gray is locked. Try editing one of these areas. Although Dreamweaver puts the insertion point wherever you click, you cannot type anything. The only exception is between the template comments shown on line 25 of Figure 12-13. This is where you can add extra style sheets or JavaScript. It's also where you should insert any other elements that normally go in the `<head>` of a web page, such as keywords and description `<meta>` tags.

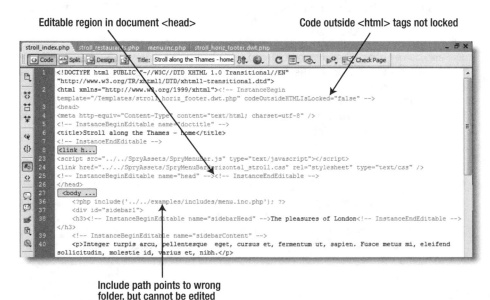

Figure 12-13. Locked areas in a child page cannot be edited (lines 8–22 and 27–35 are hidden using Code collapse).

Another thing to note is the codeOutsideHTMLIsLocked attribute shown on line 2 of Figure 12-13. By default, this is set to false. This is to allow you to apply server behaviors to pages created from a template. When you start working with server behaviors in Chapter 14, you'll see that Dreamweaver puts most of the PHP code outside the <html> tags, so if this were set to true, you wouldn't be able to apply server behaviors to your pages. I'll explain the implications of this shortly.

Finally, look at the include command for menu.inc.php (it's on line 36 in Figure 12-13). It's pointing to the version of the file in examples/includes, but the menu that you edited in step 6 is in workfiles/includes. Because this code is in a locked area, you can't edit it. You need to do that in the master template.

10. Open stroll_horiz_footer.dwt.php in the Templates folder, and click the navigation menu. The Property inspector displays the name of the include file. Click the folder icon to the right of the Filename field, and browse to the workfiles/includes folder. Select menu.inc.php, and make sure that Relative to is set to Document (PHP includes need a relative path).

11. Save stroll_horiz_footer.dwt.php. Dreamweaver will remind you again that sidebarHead is inside a block tag. Just click OK. The next dialog box asks you if you want to update all files based on the template, and lists all of the child pages. The whole point of a template is automatic updating, so click Update.

12. When all the files have been updated, Dreamweaver displays a report like this:

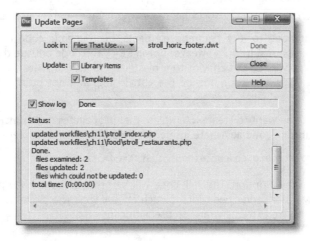

If you don't see the list of updated files at the bottom of the dialog box, select the Show log checkbox. If anything goes wrong, Dreamweaver reports which files it wasn't able to update. As you can see from the preceding screenshot, the update process is almost instantaneous with only a couple of child pages, but the time taken depends on the number of pages and the complexity of the updates. Click Close.

13. Reload stroll_index.php in your browser, and click the Restaurant link. You should be taken to stroll_restaurants.php, and the Home link should take you back to stroll_index.php. You can check your files against the versions in examples/ch12.

12

This is only a trivial example of how a change to the master template is propagated to all child pages, but it should be sufficient to demonstrate how templates control the look and shape of a site. However, the real power of this sample layout lies not so much in the template, but in the use of an include file for the navigation menu. If you were to leave the navigation menu in the main template, you would need to update every single child page each time you edit the menu. With an include, the edits take place in the external file but are immediately available in all pages that include it.

Locking code outside the <html> tags

Often, questions appear in online forums from people puzzled by the fact that the code isn't propagated to child pages when a server behavior is applied to a template. Although coverage of server behaviors begins in Chapter 14, it makes sense to discuss this issue here, while still on the subject of templates.

Dreamweaver uses the space above the DTD and below the closing </html> tag to create the PHP scripts used for server behaviors, such as inserting or updating records in a database. This is the same technique as you used in the last chapter to build the mail processing script. The reason for doing this is quite simple: the PHP engine reads the page from top to bottom and processes the dynamic code in the order that it encounters it. So, if you have a page that displays the results of a database search, it stands to reason that you need to conduct the search before displaying the results as XHTML. Dreamweaver uses the area after the closing </html> tag to clean up any resources used by the script.

Templates are intended to lock common elements, but dynamic code is almost always unique to a page. As a result, Dreamweaver doesn't lock the code outside the <html> tags. So, even if you apply a server behavior to a master template (or write your own custom script above the DTD), the code outside the <html> tags will not be propagated to any child pages.

If, for any reason, you want to create a template that propagates code outside the <html> tags, add the following code anywhere inside the <head> of the master template:

```
<!-- TemplateInfo codeOutsideHTMLIsLocked="true" -->
```

This is an all or nothing option. The PHP code will be propagated to child pages, but you cannot apply any other server behaviors to such child pages. The circumstances in which this option is useful are extremely rare, so use with care—if at all.

Choosing the right tool

The considerably large space I have devoted to PHP includes in this chapter should give you a fair indication of my personal preference for includes. However, some people find the idea of splitting a page into its various component parts a difficult concept to come to terms with. So templates do have an important role to play. They also offer a more secure solution if you work in a team environment. You can generate a child page and hand it to a less experienced developer in the knowledge that only the editable regions can be changed. With includes, nothing is locked. But as a site gets larger, so too do the efficiency savings offered by includes.

13 SETTING UP MYSQL AND PHPMYADMIN

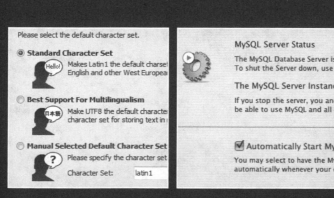

Dynamic websites take on a whole new meaning in combination with a database. Drawing content from a database allows you to present material in ways that would be impractical—if not impossible—with a static website. Examples that spring to mind are online stores, such as Amazon.com; news sites, such as the International Herald Tribune (www.iht.com); and the big search engines, including Google and Yahoo! Database technology allows these websites to present thousands, sometimes millions, of unique pages with remarkably little underlying code. Even if your ambitions are nowhere near as grandiose, a database can increase your website's richness of content with relatively little effort.

Although PHP is capable of interacting with most popular databases (and some less well-known ones, too), Dreamweaver has made the choice for you. All the server behaviors are designed to work with MySQL—a good choice, because it's widely available, free, very fast, and offers an excellent range of features.

In this chapter, you will learn how to

- Install MySQL on Windows and Mac OS X
- Secure access to MySQL
- Set up the phpMyAdmin graphical interface
- Back up and transfer data to another server

Introducing MySQL

If you have ever worked with Microsoft Access, your first encounter with MySQL might come as something of a shock. For one thing, it doesn't have a glossy interface. As Figure 13-1 shows, it looks like a throwback to the old days of DOS before the friendly interfaces of Mac and Windows. Its beauty lies, however, in its simplicity. What's more, most of the time you'll never see MySQL in its raw state like this. You'll either use Dreamweaver or a graphic front end called phpMyAdmin. Best of all, you'll be designing your own personalized interface by creating PHP pages.

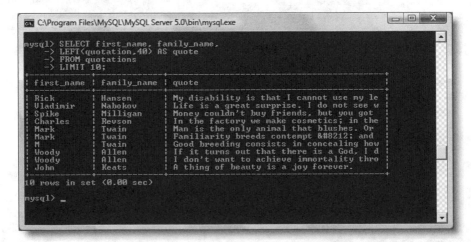

Figure 13-1. The unadorned interface of MySQL as seen in the Windows MySQL Command Line Client

The other thing that comes as a surprise to Access users is that your database is not kept in a single file that you can upload to your remote server. MySQL keeps all databases in a central data folder, and each database table normally consists of three separate files. The way you transfer data from one server to another is by creating a text file that contains all the necessary commands to build the database and its contents—in other words, a backup file. All you need to know now is that there isn't "a database file"—there are lots of them, and normally, you should never handle them directly.

Understanding basic MySQL terminology

If you've not worked with a relational database before, you may find your head spinning with some of the names that crop up throughout the rest of this book. So here's a quick guide:

- **SQL**: Structured Query Language is the international standard behind all major relational databases. It's used to insert and otherwise manipulate data and is based on natural English. For instance, to get the values of first_name and family_name from a database table called members, where username is equal to dpowers, you would use the following command (or SQL query):

```
SELECT first_name, family_name
FROM members
WHERE username = 'dpowers'
```

  As you can see, it's very human readable, unlike many other computer languages. Although SQL is a standard, all of the main databases have added enhancements on top of the basic language. If you have been using Access or Microsoft SQL Server, be prepared for some slight differences in the use of functions. Some people pronounce SQL "sequel," while others say "Ess-queue-ell." Both are right.

- **MySQL**: This refers to the entire database system created by MySQL AB of Sweden. It's always spelled in uppercase, except for the "y," and the official pronunciation is "My-ess-queue-ell." It's not just a single program, but also a client/server system with a number of related programs that perform various administrative tasks. The two main components are mysql and mysqld, with both terms entirely in lowercase.

- mysqld: This is the server (or, to give it its proper technical name, **daemon**) that runs in the background listening for requests made to the database. Once it has been started, you can ignore it.

- mysql: This has three distinct meanings. The first is the client program used to feed requests to the database. mysql is also the name of the main administrative database that controls user accounts, and on Windows, it is the name of the Windows service that starts and stops the database server. Once you start working with MySQL, differentiating between the different meanings of "mysql" is not as confusing as it first seems.

Installing MySQL

So, let's press ahead and install MySQL. There are separate instructions for Windows and Mac OS X. If you plan to use a remote server as your testing server, and already have MySQL and phpMyAdmin set up, you can skip ahead to the next chapter.

You can get MySQL from the downloads page at http://dev.mysql.com/downloads/. Select the Download link for MySQL Community Server, as shown in the following screenshot. This link takes you to the latest stable version of MySQL (currently the 5.0.x series). If, for any reason, you want to install an older version, don't click this link, but scroll down the page to the link to archives of older releases.

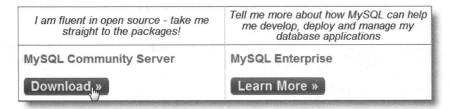

MySQL Enterprise is the commercial version, but the technical features in the Community Server are identical. The main difference is that MySQL Enterprise comes with technical support. With the Community Server, you're on your own, but you have this book to guide you. There is also a large community of MySQL users who are able to offer help online.

The installation instructions for MySQL are different for Windows and Mac OS X, so Mac users should skip ahead to the relevant section of the chapter.

> Because new versions are coming out all the time, I recommend that you check my website at http://foundationphp.com/egdwcs3/updates.php before going ahead. Any major updates to the instructions will be listed there.

Installing MySQL on Windows

MySQL comes in a range of versions, but the one you should choose is **Windows Essentials**. It contains all the important stuff and certainly everything you need for this book. If you have a version older than MySQL 4.1.5 already installed on your computer, you *must* uninstall the old version first.

Deciding whether to enable InnoDB support

MySQL is capable of storing database tables in a variety of formats. Most of the time, you don't need to worry about this. The default MySQL format, MyISAM, is fast and highly reliable. Moreover, if you're on shared hosting, this is frequently your only choice. However, if you have your own dedicated server, you will almost certainly also have the option of InnoDB tables, which offer extra features including foreign key constraints (see Chapter 16 for details). Some hosting companies also offer support for InnoDB, so it's worth checking before installing MySQL on your local computer. The Windows Essentials version of MySQL automatically enables support for InnoDB, but you can save 60MB of disk space if you don't need to use it.

You can either check with your hosting company directly, or you can do a simple test by running a SQL query on your remote server. Most companies provide phpMyAdmin to you to administer your database(s). Launch phpMyAdmin, and click the SQL tab. Delete any existing query in the Run SQL query field, and type the following:

```
SHOW VARIABLES LIKE 'have_inno%'
```

Click Go. If you see a result like the one shown in Figure 13-2, it means InnoDB tables are supported. If your remote server is very old, the Variable_name column may read have_innobase. This is the same as InnoDB.

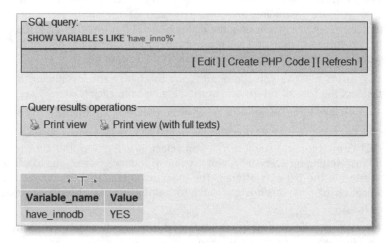

Figure 13-2. Confirmation that the MySQL server supports InnoDB tables

If the Value column says NO, InnoDB is not supported. The instructions in later chapters show you how to emulate foreign key constraints by using PHP conditional logic.

Don't worry if you can't find out whether your remote server supports InnoDB. You can easily add or remove InnoDB from your local setup later.

Installing the Windows Essentials version of MySQL

These instructions are based on the 5.0 series of MySQL, which is installed in C:\Program Files\MySQL\MySQL Server 5.0. *I expect MySQL 5.1 to become the recommended release shortly after publication of this book. On past experience, the default location changes for each series of Windows Essentials, so 5.1 is likely to be installed in* C:\Program Files\MySQL\MySQL Server 5.1, *and Windows treats different series as completely separate programs. If you upgrade from one series to another, any existing databases need to be transferred to the new version as if it were a different server (see the section titled "Backup and data transfer" near the end of this chapter).*

13

1. Go to the MySQL download site, and select the link for MySQL Community Server.

2. In the page that opens, scroll down to find the section marked Windows downloads. Choose Windows Essentials, and click the download link. (You may be invited to Pick a mirror instead. This directs you to a mirror site closer to your location and usually offers a faster download.)

3. Download the MySQL file to your hard disk. It will have a name like `mysql-essential-x.x.x-win32.msi`, where x.x.x represents the version number.

4. Exit all other Windows programs; make sure you are logged in as an administrator (in Windows Vista; turn off User Account Control temporarily—see Chapter 3 for instructions), and double-click the icon of the file you have just downloaded. This is a self-extracting Windows Installer package.

5. Windows Installer will begin the installation process and open a welcome dialog box. If you are upgrading an existing version of the *same series* of Windows Essentials to a more recent one, the dialog box will inform you that it has detected your current installation and will remove it before installing the new one. However, all your databases will remain intact. Click Next to continue.

6. Dialog boxes will give you the opportunity to change the installation destination and select the type of setup. Accept the defaults, and click Next.

7. If you're happy to go ahead with installation, click Install in the next dialog box.

8. Before launching into the actual installation, MySQL invites you to sign up for a free MySQL.com account. I suggest that you select Skip Sign-Up and click Next. After you finish setting up everything, visit www.mysql.com/register.php to see if you're interested in the benefits offered. The main advantage is that you get automatic notification of new versions and links to helpful articles about new features of MySQL.

9. The actual installation now takes place and is normally very quick. When everything's finished, you're presented with a final dialog box.

   ■ If this is a new installation or if you are upgrading from one series to another, click Finish to launch the configuration wizard, which is described in the next section.

   ■ If you are upgrading to a later version of the same series (such as from 5.0.10 to 5.0.37), deselect the checkbox labeled Configure the MySQL Server now before clicking Finish. MySQL should be ready to use but needs to be restarted manually (see "Starting and stopping MySQL manually on Windows" later in the chapter). If you have a software firewall, you might also be prompted to allow connections to and from MySQL. You must permit connections in order to work with the database.

Configuring MySQL Windows Essentials

There are a lot of dialog boxes to go through, although all you usually need to do is accept the default setting. These instructions are based on version 1.0.8 of the Configuration Wizard.

1. The Configuration Wizard opens with a welcome screen. Click Next to proceed.

2. The first dialog box asks whether you want a detailed or standard configuration. Choose the default Detailed Configuration option, and click Next.

3. The three options on the next screen affect the amount of computer resources devoted to MySQL. Accept the default Developer Machine, and click Next. If you choose either of the other options, all other programs will slow down to a crawl.

4. The next dialog box asks you to select from the following three types of database:

   - Multifunctional Database: Allows you to use both InnoDB and MyISAM tables.

   - Transactional Database Only: InnoDB tables only. MyISAM is disabled.

   - Non-Transactional Database Only: MyISAM tables only. InnoDB is disabled.

   Your choice depends on whether your remote server supports InnoDB tables (see "Deciding whether to enable InnoDB support" earlier in the chapter). If it does, choose Multifunctional Database. Otherwise, choose Non-Transactional Database Only. Do *not* choose Transactional Database Only. You should use InnoDB tables only when you need the extra features they provide, so you need support for MyISAM tables as well.

   If you're not sure which to choose, and disk space is not a problem, choose Multifunctional Database. However, you should be aware that this option requires an extra 60MB of disk space to create the InnoDB tablespace.

   > *If you choose* Multifunctional Database, *you need to edit the MySQL configuration file later, as described in "Changing the default table type on Windows Essentials."*

5. What you see next may vary. If you chose Non-Transactional Database Only in the preceding step, you will probably be taken directly to step 6. However, you may see a dialog box inviting you to select a drive for the InnoDB data file. Unless you chose Multifunctional Database, just click Next and move on to step 6.

   If you plan to use InnoDB, you need to tell MySQL where to store the data. The InnoDB engine uses a single **tablespace** that acts as a sort of virtual file system. InnoDB files, once created, cannot be made smaller. The default location for the tablespace is `C:\Program Files\MySQL\MySQL Server 5.0\data`. If you want to locate the tablespace elsewhere, the drop-down menu offers some suggested alternatives. When you have made your choice, click Next.

6. Leave the next dialog box at the default Decision Support (DSS)/OLAP, and click Next.

7. The next dialog box sets the networking options and SQL mode. The important settings are in the top half. Make sure Enable TCP/IP Networking is checked, and leave Port Number on the default setting of 3306. The lower half of the dialog box lets you choose whether to run MySQL in strict mode. In an ideal world, you should accept this default setting, but it may cause problems with some PHP applications written before strict mode was introduced. Deselect the Strict mode checkbox, and click Next.

13

8. MySQL has impressive support for most of the world's languages. The next dialog box invites you to choose a default character set. In spite of what you might think, this has no bearing on the range of languages supported—all are supported by default. The character set mainly determines the order in which data is sorted.

Since Dreamweaver CS3 now uses Unicode (UTF-8) as the default encoding for web pages, choosing the second option, Best Support for Multilingualism, seems the obvious choice. However, support for Unicode was not introduced to MySQL until version 4.1. If your hosting company is still running an earlier version of MySQL, you should stick with the default Standard Character Set. This is also a suitable choice if you work exclusively in English or use a completely different encoding, such as Shift_JIS for Japanese. Click Next after you have made your choice.

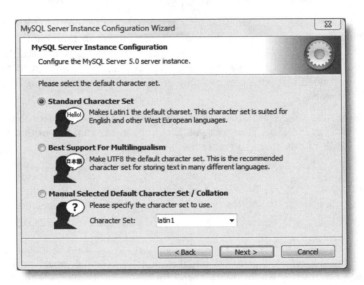

9. The recommended way of running MySQL is as a Windows service. If you accept the defaults as shown in the top half of the next dialog box, MySQL will always start automatically when you boot your computer and run silently in the background. (If MySQL has already been installed as a Windows service, this section will be grayed out.) If for any reason you don't want MySQL to start automatically, uncheck the Launch the MySQL Server automatically option. You can easily change this option later (see the section "Starting and stopping MySQL manually on Windows" later in this chapter).

The lower half of the dialog box gives you the option to include the bin directory in your Windows PATH. This option enables you to interact directly with MySQL and its related utilities at the command line without the need to change directory every time. You won't need to do this very often—if at all—but selecting this option makes life a little more convenient if the occasion ever arises. Click Next.

If you get a warning message that a Windows service with the name MySQL already exists, you will be asked if you want to use this name. You must click No and choose a different name from the drop-down menu in the Service Name *field.*

10. A fresh installation of MySQL has no security settings, so anyone can tamper with your data. MySQL uses the name **root** to signify the main database administrator with unrestricted control over all aspects of the database. Choose a password that you can remember, and enter it in both boxes.

Unless you access your development server from a different computer over a network, leave the Enable root access from remote machines checkbox unchecked.

Do *not* check Create An Anonymous Account. It will make your database insecure.

If you are upgrading an existing version of Windows Essentials and want to keep your current root password, deselect the Modify Security Settings checkbox. If this is a first-time installation, you might not have this checkbox.

Click Next when you have finished.

13

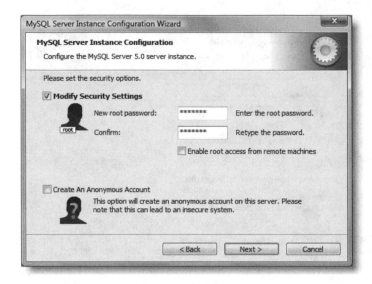

11. At long last, everything is ready. Click Execute. If you have installed a software fire-wall, it will probably warn you that MySQL is trying to connect to a DNS server. You must allow the connection; otherwise, MySQL will never work. If your firewall doesn't list MySQL specifically, make sure that it permits local connections on port 3306, the MySQL default.

12. Assuming that all was okay, you should see a screen confirming that the configura-tion process is complete. MySQL should now be running—even if you selected the option not to start automatically (the option applies only to automatic start on bootup).

13. If you want to change the configuration at a later date—say, to add or remove sup-port for InnoDB—launch the Configuration Wizard from the Windows Start menu by choosing Programs ➤ MySQL ➤ MySQL Server 5.0 ➤ MySQL Server Instance Config Wizard. The dialog box that opens offers the following two options:

- Reconfigure Instance: This takes you through all the dialog boxes again. If you add support for InnoDB, change the default table type, as described in the next section. If you remove support for InnoDB, stop the MySQL server after the wizard has finished, and delete any files with names that begin ibdata and ib_logfile from C:\Program Files\MySQL\MySQL Server 5.0\data. Then restart MySQL.

- Remove Instance: This does not remove MySQL from your system but removes the Windows service that automatically starts MySQL when you boot your com-puter. Unfortunately, it also removes the MySQL configuration file. See "Starting and stopping MySQL manually on Windows" for a less radical solution.

Changing the default table type on Windows Essentials

The instructions in this section are required only if you selected Multifunctional Database in step 4 of "Configuring MySQL Windows Essentials."

The Windows Configuration Wizard sets InnoDB as the default table storage engine for a multifunctional database. This is the opposite of the standard MySQL setup, so it makes sense to switch the default to match the way your remote server works. All it requires is a simple change to the MySQL configuration file: my.ini.

1. Use Windows Explorer to navigate to the folder in which MySQL was installed. The default is C:\Program Files\MySQL\MySQL Server 5.0.

2. Locate the file called my.ini, and double-click it. The file will open in Notepad.

3. Approximately 80 lines from the top, you should find a line that reads as follows:

   default-storage-engine=INNODB

   Change it to the following (the spelling of MyISAM is case insensitive):

   default-storage-engine=**MyISAM**

4. Save the file, and close it. To make the change effective, restart MySQL. MySQL will now create all new tables in the default MyISAM format. To use the InnoDB format for a database or an individual table, you can change the table type in phpMyAdmin, the graphical interface for MySQL that you will install later in the chapter.

Starting and stopping MySQL manually on Windows

Most of the time, MySQL will be configured to start up automatically, and you can forget about it entirely. There are times, however, when you need to know how to start or stop MySQL manually—usually for maintenance or to conserve resources.

1. Select Control Panel from the Windows Start menu. Double-click the Administrative Tools icon, and then double-click the Services icon in the window that opens.

2. In the Services panel, scroll down to find MySQL, and highlight it by clicking once. You can now use the video recorder–type icons at the top of the panel (or right-click to bring up the context menu) to stop or start the server.

3. To change the automatic startup option, highlight MySQL in the Services panel, right-click to reveal a context menu, and choose Properties.

4. In the dialog box that opens, activate the Startup type drop-down menu, and choose Automatic, Manual, or Disabled. Click OK. That's all there is to it.

Using the MySQL monitor on Windows

Although most of your interaction with MySQL will be through phpMyAdmin or your own PHP scripts, it's useful to know how to access MySQL through the MySQL monitor (or the Command Line Client, as it's called in Windows Essentials). It's also a good way to test that your installation went without problems.

To start a session From the Windows Start menu, select Programs ➤ MySQL ➤ MySQL Server 5.0 ➤ MySQL Command Line Client. This will open the Command Line Client, which will ask you for your password. Type the root password that you chose in step 10 of the section "Configuring MySQL Windows Essentials," and press Enter. As long as the server is

13

running—and you typed your password correctly—you will see a welcome message similar to the one shown here (on Windows XP, the title bar says MySQL Command Line Client).

If you get your password wrong, your computer will beep and close the window. If you find this happening repeatedly, even though you're sure you typed in your password correctly, there are two likely explanations. The first is that your Caps Lock key is on—MySQL passwords are case sensitive. The other is that the MySQL server isn't running. Refer to the previous section on how to control MySQL manually before doing too much damage by banging your forehead on the keyboard.

> *Being unable to connect to MySQL because the server isn't running is probably the most common beginner's mistake. The MySQL server runs in the background, waiting for requests. Opening the Command Line Client does not start MySQL; it opens the MySQL monitor, which is a channel for you to send instructions to the server. Equally, closing the Command Line Client does not stop MySQL. The server continues running in the background until the computer is closed down or until you stop it manually.*

Ending your session After you finish working with the MySQL monitor, type exit or quit at the mysql> prompt, followed by Enter. The MySQL Command Line Client window closes automatically.

Setting up MySQL on Mac OS X

MySQL is available as a Mac PKG file, so everything is taken care of for you, apart from some minor configuration.

> *When upgrading an existing installation of MySQL, the Mac installer will not move your data files. You must first create a backup, as described at the end of this chapter, and reload them after upgrading. You must also shut down the MySQL server. If you have never installed MySQL before, you don't need any special preparations; just follow these instructions.*

Downloading and installing MySQL

1. Go to www.mysql.com/downloads, and select the link for MySQL Community Server.

2. Select the Mac OS X (package format) downloads section, and choose the Standard version for your processor and version of OS X—there are separate packages for PowerPC, 64-bit PowerPC, and Intel Macs. The Intel Mac version is labeled x86. As you can see from the screenshot in the next step, the PKG file name includes not only the MySQL version number but also the version of OS X and processor for which it has been compiled (osx10.4-powerpc).

The Mac files are available in two formats. Make sure you don't select a TAR package by mistake. These instructions are for the package format, which uses a Mac installer.

3. Double-click the DMG icon to mount the disk image on your desktop.

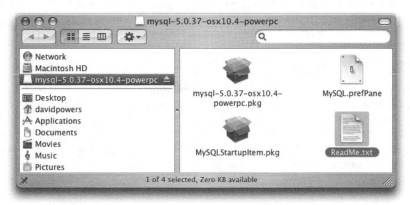

4. Double-click the mysql-standard-x.x.x.pkg icon to start the installation process. The Mac OS X installer opens. Follow the instructions onscreen.

5. Double-click the MySQLStartupItem.pkg icon, and follow the instructions onscreen.

6. Open a Finder window, and drag the MySQL.prefPane icon onto Applications ➤ System Preferences. This installs a MySQL control panel. A dialog box asks whether you want it to be available to yourself or all users. Make your choice, and click Install.

   The MySQL preference pane should open. Click Start MySQL Server, and enter your Mac administrator password when prompted. It may take a few seconds before the preference pane reports that the server is running, as shown here:

13

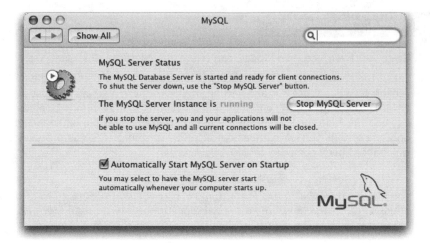

To start or stop the MySQL server in future, open the preference pane by clicking the MySQL icon in the Other section of System Preferences.

Adding MySQL to your PATH

You normally access MySQL through phpMyAdmin (introduced later in this chapter) or your own PHP scripts, but sometimes you need to access it directly in Terminal. To avoid having to type out the full path every time, add it to the PATH in your environmental variables. By default, Terminal uses what is known as the "bash shell." Open Terminal (in Applications ➤ Utilities), and check the title bar. If it says Terminal—bash, as shown in the following screenshot, use the following instructions. In the unlikely event that it says Terminal—tcsh, follow the instructions in the section titled "Amending PATH in the tcsh shell."

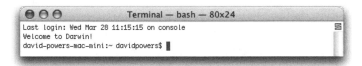

Amending PATH in the bash shell

Use this set of instructions if the Terminal title bar says Terminal—bash:

1. Open BBEdit or TextWrangler.

2. From the File menu, choose Open Hidden, and browse to your home folder. If there is a file called .profile (with a period as the first character), as shown in the screenshot, highlight it, and click Open.

3. The file exists only if you have already made changes to the way Terminal operates. If .profile doesn't exist, click Cancel, and open a blank file.

4. If you have opened an existing version of .profile, add the following code on a separate line at the end. Otherwise, enter it in the blank page.

```
export PATH="$PATH:/usr/local/mysql/bin"
```

5. Select File ➤ Save, and save the file as .profile in your own home folder. The period at the beginning of the file name should provoke the following warning:

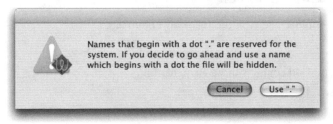

6. Select Use "." and close your text editor.

Amending PATH in the tcsh shell

Use the following, alternative instructions *only* if the title bar says Terminal—tcsh:

1. Open Terminal, and enter the following command at the shell prompt:

```
echo 'setenv PATH /usr/local/mysql/bin:$PATH' >> ~/.tcshrc
```

Make sure you copy everything exactly, including the quotes and spacing as shown.

2. Press Return, and close Terminal. The next time you open Terminal, the MySQL program directory will have been added to your PATH.

Securing MySQL on Mac OS X

Although you have a fully functioning installation of MySQL, by default it has no security. Even if you're the only person working on your computer, you need to set up a similar system of passwords and user accounts as on your hosting company's server. There's one important account that exists by default on all MySQL servers. It's called root, and it is the main database administrator with unlimited powers over database files. When you first install MySQL, access to the root account isn't password protected, so you need to block this security gap. The MySQL root user, by the way, is totally unrelated to the Mac OS X root user, which is disabled by default. Enabling root for MySQL has *no* effect on the OS X root user.

> *If you have just added MySQL to your PATH, you must close and reopen Terminal before embarking on this section. Otherwise, Terminal won't be able to find MySQL.*

Setting the MySQL root password

1. Open Terminal, and type the following command:

```
mysql -u root
```

The command contains three elements:

- `mysql`: The name of the program
- `-u`: Tells the program that you want to log in as a specified user
- `root`: The name of the user

2. You should see a welcome message like this:

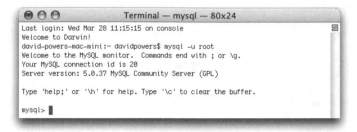

3. The most common problem is getting an error message like this instead:

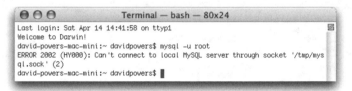

It means that `mysqld`, the MySQL server, is not running. Use the MySQL control panel in System Preferences to start the server.

Another common problem is for Terminal to report command not found. That means you have either mistyped the command or that you haven't added the MySQL program files directory to your PATH, as described in the previous section.

4. Assuming that you have logged in successfully, as described in step 2, type the following command at the mysql> prompt:

```
use mysql
```

This command tells MySQL that you want to use the database called `mysql`, which contains all the details of authorized users and the privileges they have to work on database files. You should see the message Database changed, which means MySQL is ready for you to work on the files controlling administrative privileges.

5. Now enter the command to set a password for the root user. Substitute *myPassword* with the actual password you want to use. Also make sure you use quotes where indicated and finish the command with a semicolon.

```
UPDATE user SET password = PASSWORD('myPassword') WHERE user = 'root';
```

6. Next, remove anonymous access to MySQL:

```
DELETE FROM user WHERE user = '';
```

The quotes before the semicolon are two single quotes with no space in between.

13

7. Tell MySQL to update the privileges table:

```
FLUSH PRIVILEGES;
```

The sequence of commands should produce a series of results like this:

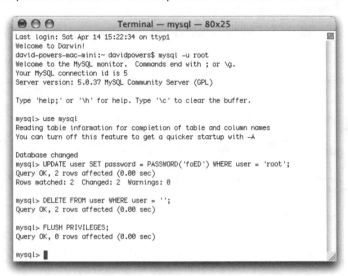

8. To exit the MySQL monitor, type exit, followed by Return. This simply ends your session with the MySQL monitor. *It does not shut down the MySQL server.*

9. Now try to log back in by using the same command as in step 2. MySQL won't let you in. Anonymous access and password-free access have been removed. To get in this time, you need to tell MySQL that you want to use a password:

```
mysql -u root -p
```

10. When you press Return, you will be prompted for your password. Nothing will appear onscreen as you type, but as long as you enter the correct password, MySQL will let you back in. Congratulations, you now have a secure installation of MySQL.

Using the MySQL monitor on Windows and Mac

From this point on, 99.9 percent of everything you do is identical on both Windows and Mac OS X. If you are used to working exclusively with a GUI like Windows or Mac OS, it can be unsettling to work at the command line with MySQL. You won't need to do it very often, if at all. However, it's not difficult, and here are a few pointers to make you feel more at home:

- When you work inside the MySQL monitor, most commands need to end with a semicolon (;). The only exceptions are use *databaseName* and exit. The MySQL monitor is quite happy if you use a semicolon after these two commands, so the simple rule is this: *if in doubt, put a semicolon on the end of each command.*

- If you forget to put a semicolon at the end of a command that needs one, the MySQL monitor will assume that you want to break your command over more than one line, and that you haven't finished typing. It will patiently wait for you to do so, like this:

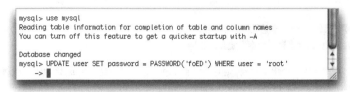

```
mysql> use mysql
Reading table information for completion of table and column names
You can turn off this feature to get a quicker startup with -A

Database changed
mysql> UPDATE user SET password = PASSWORD('foED') WHERE user = 'root'
    -> █
```

This enables you to spread long queries over a number of lines. Not only is this easier to read onscreen, it's also useful if you make an error. The MySQL monitor remembers previous commands line by line, and you can retrieve them by pressing the up and down arrow keys on your keyboard. Once a previous command has been redisplayed, you can use your left and right arrow keys to move along the line and edit it in the normal way. Once you have completed the command, just type a semicolon and press Enter/Return. The MySQL monitor will then process it.

- If you spot a mistake before pressing Enter/Return, use your left and right arrow keys to edit the current line. If the mistake is on a previous line, there is no way to go back. Abandon the command by typing \c. The MySQL monitor will ignore everything you have entered and present you with the mysql> prompt.

Using MySQL with phpMyAdmin

Although you can do everything using MySQL monitor, it's a lot easier to use a graphic interface. There are several to choose from, both commercial and free. Among the free offerings are two from MySQL itself: MySQL Administrator and MySQL Query Browser (www.mysql.com/products/tools). Two other popular graphical front ends for MySQL are the commercial product Navicat (www.navicat.com) and SQLyog (www.webyog.com), which is available in both commercial and free versions.

However, the most popular graphical interface for MySQL is phpMyAdmin (www.phpmyadmin. net). It's a PHP-based administrative system for MySQL that has been around since 1998, and it constantly evolves to keep pace with MySQL developments. It works on Windows, Mac OS X, and Linux and currently supports all versions of MySQL from 3.23.32 to 5.0. What's more, many hosting companies provide it as the standard interface to MySQL.

Because phpMyAdmin has a very intuitive interface, I suggest that you try it first. If you work with databases on a regular basis, you may want to explore the other graphical interfaces later. However, since phpMyAdmin is free, you have nothing to lose—and you may find it does everything you want.

13

Setting up phpMyAdmin on Windows and Mac

These instructions are based on phpMyAdmin 2.10.1. Like a lot of open source applications, phpMyAdmin is constantly evolving. Any changes of a substantial nature will be listed on my website at http://foundationphp.com/egdwcs3/updates.php.

Downloading and installing phpMyAdmin

Since phpMyAdmin is PHP-based, all that's needed to install it is to download the files, unzip them to a website in your local testing environment, and create a simple configuration file.

1. Go to www.phpmyadmin.net, and download the latest stable version. The files can be downloaded in three types of compressed file: BZIP2, GZIP, and ZIP. Choose whichever format you have the decompression software for.

2. Unzip the downloaded file. It will extract the contents to a folder called phpMyAdmin-*x.x.x*, where *x* represents the version number.

3. Highlight the folder icon, and cut it to your clipboard. On Windows, paste it inside the folder designated as your web server root (C:\htdocs, if you followed my example). If you're on a Mac and want phpMyAdmin to be available to all users, put the folder in Macintosh HD:Library:WebServer:Documents rather than in your own Sites folder.

4. Rename the folder you have just moved to this: phpMyAdmin.

5. Like Apache and PHP, phpMyAdmin uses a text file to store all the configuration details. Since version 2.7.0, you no longer edit the phpMyAdmin configuration file but store your personal details in a new file, which should be named config.inc.php. There are two ways of doing this: using a built-in script called setup.php or manually. I prefer the manual method, but instructions for both methods follow.

Configuring phpMyAdmin with setup.php

Use these instructions if you want to use the built-in configuration script.

1. Create a new subfolder called config within the phpMyAdmin folder. Windows users skip to step 3. Mac users continue with step 2.

2. On Mac OS X, use Finder to locate the config folder that you have just created. Ctrl-click and select Get Info. In Ownership & Permissions, expand Details, and click the lock icon so that you can make changes to the settings. Change the setting for Others to Read & Write. Close the config Info panel.

3. Open a browser, and type the following into the address bar:

   http://localhost/phpmyadmin/scripts/setup.php

   If you created the phpMyAdmin folder inside your Sites folder on a Mac, use the following address, substituting *username* with your Mac username:

   http://localhost/~*username*/phpmyadmin/scripts/setup.php

4. You should see the page shown in Figure 13-3.

Figure 13-3. A built-in script automates the configuration of phpMyAdmin.

Ignore any warning about the connection not being secure. This is intended for server administrators installing phpMyAdmin on a live Internet server. If, on the other hand, you see the following warning, it means that you have not set up the config folder correctly and should go back to step 1.

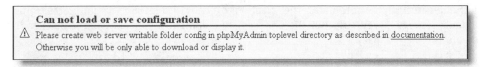

5. Click the Add button in the Servers section. This loads a form with most of the necessary information already filled in. Check the following settings:

- Server hostname: localhost
- Server port: Leave blank unless your web server is running on a nonstandard port, such as 8080
- Server socket: Leave blank
- Connection type: tcp
- PHP extension to use: mysqli

13

6. The default setting for Authentication type is config. If you don't need to password protect access to phpMyAdmin, check that User for config auth is set to root, and enter your MySQL root password in the next field, Password for config auth.

If you want to restrict access to phpMyAdmin by prompting users for a password, change Authentication type to http, and delete root from the User for config auth field.

7. Scroll down to the Actions field, and click Add. As shown here, there are two Add buttons close to each other; click the one circled in the screenshot:

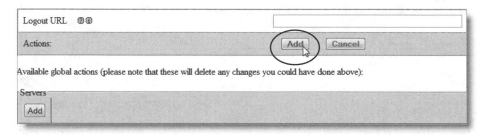

8. The next screen will probably warn you that you didn't set up a phpMyAdmin database, so you won't be able to use all the phpMyAdmin features. This is not important. You can set up one later if you decide to use the advanced features of phpMyAdmin.

9. Scroll down to the Configuration section near the bottom of the page, and click Save.

10. Open the config folder in Explorer or Finder. You should see a new file called config.inc.php. Move it to the main phpMyAdmin folder. The official instructions tell you to delete the config folder, but this isn't necessary in a local testing environment.

Configuring phpMyAdmin manually

Although setup.php automates the creation of config.inc.php, it duplicates some default settings. If you strip out the unnecessary commands, you may find it quicker to create the file manually.

1. If you don't need to password protect access to phpMyAdmin, type the following code into a blank document:

```php
<?php
$i = 1;
$cfg['Servers'][$i]['extension'] = 'mysqli';
$cfg['Servers'][$i]['password']  = 'mysqlRootPassword';
?>
```

Use your own MySQL root password in place of mysqlRootPassword.

If you need password protection for phpMyAdmin, use the following code instead:

```php
<?php
$i = 1;
$cfg['Servers'][$i]['extension'] = 'mysqli';
$cfg['Servers'][$i]['auth_type'] = 'http';
?>
```

2. Save the file as config.inc.php in the main phpMyAdmin folder. Erm . . . that's it.

Launching phpMyAdmin

To use phpMyAdmin, launch a browser, and enter http://localhost/phpMyAdmin/index.php in the address bar (on a Mac, use http://localhost/~username/phpMyAdmin/index.php if you put phpMyAdmin in your Sites folder). If you stored your root password in config.inc.php, phpMyAdmin should load right away, as shown in Figure 13-4. If you chose to password protect phpMyAdmin, enter root as the username and whatever you specified as the MySQL root password when prompted.

If you get a message saying that the server is not responding or that the socket is not correctly configured, make sure that the MySQL server is running.

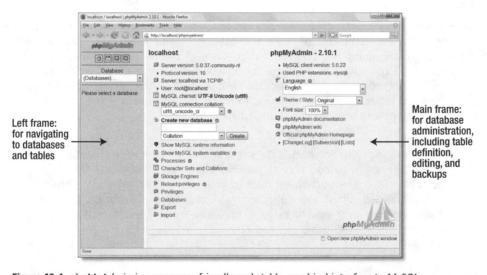

Figure 13-4. phpMyAdmin is a very user-friendly and stable graphical interface to MySQL.

If you're used to glossy software design, your initial impression of phpMyAdmin may not be all that favorable, particularly if you don't have a large monitor. The interface is sorely in need of a facelift, but don't let that fool you; phpMyAdmin is both powerful and easy to use.

Logging out of phpMyAdmin

If you opted to password protect phpMyAdmin, the Log out link is at the bottom left of the front page, just beneath Import (as shown in the screenshot alongside). When you click the link, you are immediately prompted for your username and password. Click Cancel, and you will be presented with a screen informing you that you supplied the wrong username/password—in other words, you have been logged out. Odd, but that's the way it works.

> You cannot log back in to phpMyAdmin from the wrong username/password screen. You must enter the original URL into the browser address bar first.

Backup and data transfer

MySQL doesn't store your database in a single file that you can simply upload to your website. Even if you find the right files (on Windows, they're located in C:\Program Files\ MySQL\MySQL Server 5.0\data), you're likely to damage them unless the MySQL server is turned off. Anyway, most hosting companies won't permit you to upload the raw files, because it would also involve shutting down their server, causing a great deal of inconvenience for everyone.

Nevertheless, moving a database from one server to another is very easy. All it involves is creating a backup **dump** of the data and loading it into the other database with phpMyAdmin. The dump is a text file that contains all the necessary Structured Query Language (SQL) commands to populate an individual table or even an entire database elsewhere. phpMyAdmin can create backups of your entire MySQL server, individual databases, selected tables, or individual tables. To make things simple, the following instructions show you how to back up only a single database.

> If you have just installed MySQL for the first time, bookmark this section for when you need to upload files to your remote server or upgrade MySQL. If you're on a Mac, you must always back up your data before upgrading MySQL. Once the new version has been installed, you can transfer your data to the new server. Windows users need to follow this procedure only when upgrading from one series to another, such as 5.0 to 5.1.

Creating a backup

These instructions show you how to back up an entire database. You can also back up individual tables in the same way by selecting the tables in step 4.

1. Launch phpMyAdmin, and select the database that you want to back up from the drop-down menu in the navigation frame.

2. When the database details have loaded into the main frame, select Export from the tabs along the top of the screen, as shown here.

3. The rather fearsome-looking screen shown in Figure 13-5 opens. In spite of all the options, you need to concern yourself with only a few.

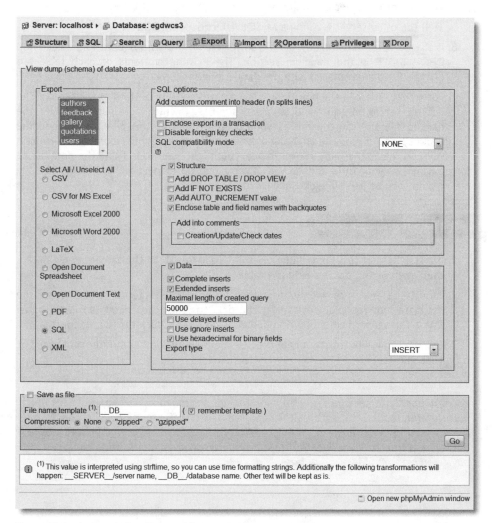

Figure 13-5. phpMyAdmin offers a wide range of choices when exporting data from MySQL.

4. The Export section on the left of the screen lists all the tables in your database. Click Select All, and leave the radio buttons on the default SQL.

5. If the database has *never* been transferred to the other server before, the only option that you need to set on the right side of the screen is the drop-down menu labeled SQL compatibility mode. The setting depends on the version of MySQL on the other server (only the first two numbers, such as 3.23, 4.0, 4.1, or 5.0, are important):

   - If the other server is running the same version of MySQL, choose NONE.
   - If you are transferring between MySQL 4.1 and MySQL 5.0 (in either direction), choose NONE.
   - If the other server is running MySQL 3.23, choose MYSQL323.
   - If the other server is running MySQL 4.0, choose MYSQL40.

6. If the database has *already* been transferred on a previous occasion, select Add DROP TABLE in the Structure section. The existing contents of each table are dropped and are replaced with the data in the backup file.

7. Put a check mark in the box alongside Save as file at the bottom of the screen. The default setting in File name template is __DB__, which automatically gives the backup file the same name as your database. So, in this case, it will become egdwcs3.sql. If you add anything after the final double underscore, phpMyAdmin will add this to the name. For instance, you might want to indicate the date of the backup, so you could add 20070704 for a backup made on July 4, 2007. The file would then be named egdwcs320070704.sql.

Loading data from a backup file

1. If a database of the same name doesn't already exist on the target server, create the database, but don't create any tables.

2. Launch the version of phpMyAdmin that is used by the target server, and select the database that you plan to transfer the data to. Click the Import tab in the main frame (on versions of phpMyAdmin earlier than 2.7.0, click the SQL tab instead).

3. Use the Browse button to locate the SQL file on your local computer, and click Go. That's it!

Because phpMyAdmin uses PHP to upload the file, the maximum size of any backup is normally limited to 2MB, which is the default maximum size for any file upload. If you are transferring a very large database, use the phpMyAdmin export and import tabs to backup and transfer individual tables. Alternatively, contact your hosting company for advice on transferring your database.

Looking ahead . . .

Now that you have MySQL and phpMyAdmin installed, we can finally begin to explore Dreamweaver's server behaviors. In the next chapter, I'll show you how to create a database table in MySQL and insert into it user input from the feedback form in Chapter 9. You'll also learn how to combine it with the mail processing script from Chapters 11 and 12 and how to retrieve and display information stored in a database.

13

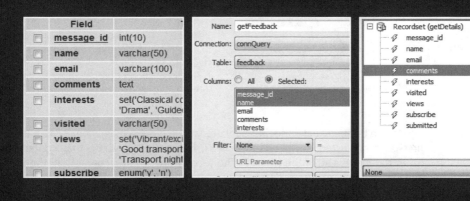

Unlike Access or FileMaker Pro, MySQL doesn't come with predesigned forms. Instead, you build and design everything yourself. While this presents a challenge to the first-time user, MySQL isn't difficult to use, and Dreamweaver takes a lot of the hard work out of integrating MySQL with your website.

Let's say that you decide to start accepting orders for goods and services through your website. As well as getting the orders by email, you need to store that information in a database. Rather than input all the data again manually, it makes much more sense to combine the two operations. So by the end of this chapter, you will be able to input data directly from the feedback form from Chapters 9, 11, and 12, and then send the details to your mail inbox. In the process, you'll learn the basics of database construction, and how to handle different types of data. Specifically, you'll learn how to

- Create MySQL user accounts
- Define a database table
- Create a database connection in Dreamweaver
- Insert form input into a database
- Use a recordset to retrieve data and display database results
- Apply a repeat region to display multiple records
- Merge the mail processing script with database input

Setting up a database in MySQL

If you set up MySQL and phpMyAdmin in a local testing environment, as described in the last chapter, launch phpMyAdmin, and open the Database drop-down menu in the left frame (see Figure 14-1).

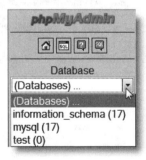

Figure 14-1.
A new installation of MySQL contains three default databases.

MySQL isn't a single database, but a relational database management system (RDBMS). The first database listed, information_schema, is a virtual database that contains details of other databases within the RDBMS. The second one, mysql, contains all the user account and security information and should never be edited directly unless you're really sure what you're doing. The final database, test, contains nothing. The numbers in parentheses indicate how many tables each database contains.

If you're using a remote server, and your hosting company provides phpMyAdmin, the list of databases will be limited to those on your account, or you may be limited to only one database.

Creating a local database for testing

Assuming that you have set up a local testing environment, you need to create a test database to work with the remaining chapters. I'm going to call the database egdwcs3. To make life easier for yourself when it comes to testing pages on the Internet, use the name of a database on your remote server.

Type the name of the database in the field labeled Create new database in the phpMyAdmin welcome screen, and click Create, as shown in Figure 14-2. Leave Collation in its default position. However, if you're working in a language other than English, Swedish, or Finnish, *and* your remote server runs MySQL 4.1 or later, skip ahead to the section "Understanding collation" before going any further.

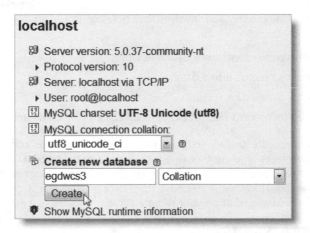

Figure 14-2. To create a new database, just type its name into the phpMyAdmin welcome screen, and click Create.

> *Because phpMyAdmin is a browser-based application, the precise layout of what you see onscreen depends on the size of your monitor and browser viewport.*

The database should be created instantly, and phpMyAdmin will invite you to create a new table. Before doing that, you need to create at least one user account for the database. Leave phpMyAdmin open.

14

Creating user accounts for MySQL

At the moment, your installation of MySQL has only one registered user—the superuser account called "root," which has complete control over everything. A lot of beginners think that once they have set up a password for the root user, they can start building databases. This is a big mistake. The root user should *never* be used for anything other than administration.

MySQL stores all databases in a common directory. So, on shared hosting, your database—with all its precious information—rubs shoulders with everyone else's. Clearly, you need a way to prevent unauthorized people from seeing or altering your data. The answer is to create user accounts that have the fewest number of privileges necessary to perform essential tasks, preferably on a single database.

Granting the necessary user privileges

You normally want visitors to your site to be able to see the information it contains but not to change it. However, as administrator, you need to be able to insert new records, and update or delete existing ones. This involves four types of privileges, all named after the equivalent SQL commands:

- SELECT: Retrieves records from database tables
- INSERT: Inserts records into a database
- UPDATE: Changes existing records
- DELETE: Deletes records but not tables or databases (the command for that is DROP)

In an ideal setup, you create two separate user accounts: one for administrators, who require all four privileges, and another one for visitors, limited to SELECT. If your hosting company lets you set up user accounts with different privileges, I suggest that you create two accounts like this. However, if you have no choice, set up one account and use the same username and password as on your remote server.

Setting up MySQL user accounts

These instructions show you how to set up user accounts in a local testing environment. You can skip this section if you are using your remote server as your testing server.

1. Click the home icon at the top of the left frame in phpMyAdmin to return to the welcome screen, and then click Privileges, as shown in the following screenshot:

1. Click here to return to the welcome screen.

2. Then click the Privileges link in the welcome screen.

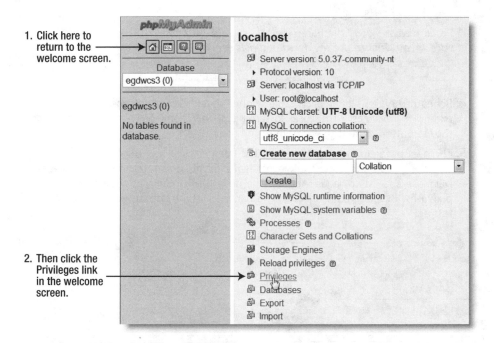

> *The* Privileges *tab at the top of the previous screen displays a list of current user accounts. To create a new user account, you must use the link in the welcome screen.*

2. The User overview screen opens. Click Add a new User halfway down the page.

3. In the page that opens, enter the name of the user account that you want to create in the User name field. Select Local from the Host drop-down menu. This automatically enters localhost in the field alongside. This option restricts the user to connecting to MySQL only from the same computer. Enter a password in the Password field, and confirm it in the Re-type field. The Login Information table should look like this:

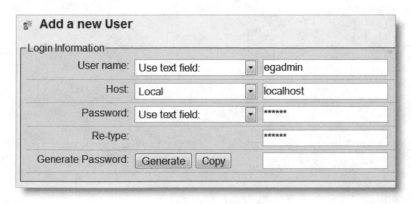

> *Dreamweaver needs these details later to make a connection to the database. If you want to use the download files exactly as they are, use* humpty *as the password for* egadmin.

4. Beneath the Login Information table is one labeled Global privileges. Granting such extensive privileges is insecure, so scroll past the Global privileges table, and click the Go button right at the bottom of the page.

5. The next page confirms that the user has been created and displays many options, beginning with the Global privileges again. Scroll down to the section labeled Database-specific privileges. Activate the drop-down menu, as shown here, to display a list of all databases. Select the name for the database you plan to use for testing.

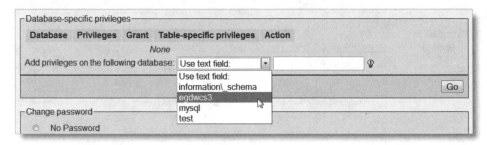

6. The next screen allows you to set the user's privileges for just this database. You want the admin user to have all four privileges listed earlier, so click the checkboxes next to SELECT, INSERT, UPDATE, and DELETE (if you hover your mouse pointer over each option, phpMyAdmin displays a tooltip describing what it's for). After selecting the four privileges, as shown here, click the top Go button.

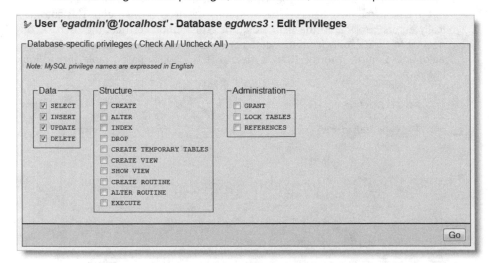

phpMyAdmin frequently offers you a variety of options on the same page, each of which normally has its own Go *button. Always click the one at the foot of or alongside the section that relates to the options you want to set.*

7. phpMyAdmin presents you with the following confirmation that the privileges have been updated for the user account:

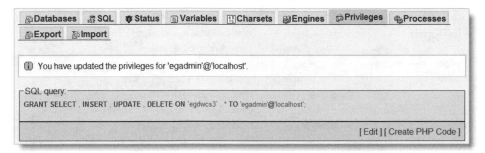

8. The page displays the Database-specific privileges table again, in case you need to change anything. Assuming you got it right, click the Privileges tab at the top right of the page. You should now see the new user listed in the User overview.

If you ever need to make any changes to a user's privileges, click the Edit Privileges icon to the right of the listing, as shown. You can also delete users by selecting the checkbox to the left of the User column, then clicking Go.

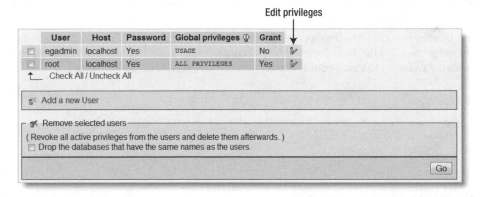

9. If your hosting company permits you to create multiple user accounts, click Add a new User, and repeat steps 3–8 to create a second user account. If you want to use the same username and password as in the download files, call the account eguser, and give it the password dumpty. This user will have restricted privileges, so in step 6, check only the SELECT option.

Now that you have a database and at least one user account, you can build the table to store the feedback information. However, first, you need to understand the principles behind table construction.

14

How a database stores information

All data in MySQL is stored in tables, with information organized into rows and columns very much like a spreadsheet. Figure 14-3 shows a simple database table as seen in phpMyAdmin.

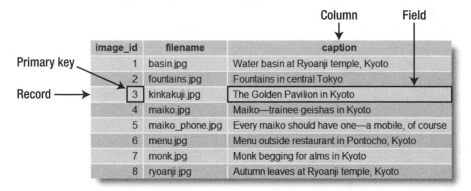

Figure 14-3. Information in a database table is stored in rows and columns, just like in a spreadsheet.

Each **column** has a name (image_id, filename, and caption) indicating what it stores.

The rows aren't labeled, but the first column (image_id) contains a unique identifier known as a **primary key**, which can be used to identify the data associated with a particular row. Each row contains an individual **record** of related data. The significance of primary keys is explained in the next section.

The intersection of a row and a column, where the data is stored, is called a **field**. So, for instance, the caption field for the third record in Figure 14-3 contains the value "The Golden Pavilion in Kyoto" and the primary key for that record is 3.

> *The terms "field" and "column" are often used interchangeably. A field holds one piece of information for a single record, whereas a column contains the same field for all records.*

How primary keys work

Although Figure 14-3 shows image_id as a consecutive sequence from 1 to 8, they're not row numbers. Figure 14-4 shows the same table with the captions sorted in alphabetical order. The field highlighted in Figure 14-3 has moved to the seventh row, but it still has the same image_id and filename.

image_id	filename	caption ▲
8	ryoanji.jpg	Autumn leaves at Ryoanji temple, Kyoto
5	maiko_phone.jpg	Every maiko should have one—a mobile, of course
2	fountains.jpg	Fountains in central Tokyo
4	maiko.jpg	Maiko—trainee geishas in Kyoto
6	menu.jpg	Menu outside restaurant in Pontocho, Kyoto
7	monk.jpg	Monk begging for alms in Kyoto
3	kinkakuji.jpg	The Golden Pavilion in Kyoto
1	basin.jpg	Water basin at Ryoanji temple, Kyoto

Now in the seventh row, but image_id → remains unchanged

Figure 14-4. Even when the table is sorted in a different order, each record can be identified by its primary key.

Although the primary key is rarely displayed, it identifies the record and all the data stored in it. If you know the primary key, you can update a record, delete it, or use it to display data. Don't worry about how you find the primary key; it's easy using Structured Query Language (SQL), the standard means of communicating with all major databases. The important thing is to assign a primary key to every record.

- A primary key doesn't need to be a number, but *it must be unique*.
- Social Security, staff ID, or product numbers make good primary keys. They may consist of a mixture of numbers, letters, and other characters but are always different.
- MySQL will generate a primary key for you automatically.
- Once a primary key has been assigned, it should never—repeat, never—be changed.

Because a primary key must be unique, MySQL doesn't normally reuse the number when a record is deleted, leaving holes in the sequence. *Don't even think about renumbering.* By changing the numbers to close the gaps, you put the integrity of your database at serious risk. Some people want to remove gaps to keep track of the number of records, but you can easily get the same information with SQL.

Although Figures 14-3 and 14-4 show the similarity between a database table and a spreadsheet, there's an important difference. With a spreadsheet, you can enter data without the need to specify beforehand what type of data it is or how it's to be structured. You can't do that with a database.

Designing a database table

Before entering data, you need to define the table structure. This involves the following decisions:

- The name of the table
- How many columns it will have
- The name of each column
- What type of data will be stored in each column
- Whether the column must always have data in each field
- Which column contains the table's primary key

14

Don't be tempted to choose the first thing that comes into your head. Experienced database developers often say at least half the total development time is spent deciding the structure of a database. Although the structure of a database can be altered, some decisions tie your hands so badly you need to redesign everything from scratch. That's not much fun when the database contains several thousand records. The time spent on these early decisions can save a lot of agony and frustration later on.

Because each database is different, it's impossible to prescribe one simple formula, but the next few pages should help guide you in the right direction. Don't attempt to commit everything to memory at the first read-through. Come back later when you need to refresh your memory or check a particular point.

Choosing the table name

The basic MySQL naming rules for databases, tables, and columns are as follows:

- Names can be up to 64 characters long.
- Legal characters are numbers, letters, the underscore, and $.
- Names can begin with a number but cannot consist exclusively of numbers.

Some hosting companies seem blissfully ignorant of these rules and assign clients databases that contain one or more hyphens (an illegal character) in their name. If a name contains spaces or illegal characters, you must surround it by backticks (`) in SQL queries. Note that this is not a single quote (') but a separate character. Dreamweaver and phpMyAdmin normally do this for you automatically.

Choose names that are meaningful. Tables hold groups of records, so it's a good strategy to use plural nouns. For example, use products rather than product. Don't try to save on typing by using abbreviations, particularly when naming columns. Explicit names make it much easier to build SQL queries to extract the information you want from a database. SQL is designed to be as human-readable as possible, so don't make life difficult for yourself by using cryptic naming conventions.

When choosing column names, there is a danger that you might accidentally choose one of MySQL's many reserved words (http://dev.mysql.com/doc/refman/5.0/en/reserved-words.html), such as date or time. A good technique is to use compound words, such as arrival_date, arrival_time, and so on. These names also tell you much more about the data held in the column.

Case sensitivity of names Windows and Mac OS X treat MySQL names as case insensitive. However, Linux and Unix servers respect case sensitivity. To avoid problems when transferring databases and PHP code from your local computer to a remote server, I recommend that you use only lowercase in database, table, and column names. Using camel case (e.g., arrivalDate) is likely to cause your code to fail when transferring a database from your local computer to a Linux server.

Deciding how many columns to create

How should you store each person's name? One column? Or one each for the family and personal names? A commercial contacts management program like Microsoft Outlook goes even further, splitting the name into five parts. In addition to first and last name, it stores title (Mr., Mrs., etc.), a middle name, and suffix (I, II, III, Jr., and Sr.). Addresses are best broken down into street, town, county, state, ZIP code, etc. Think of all the possible alternatives, and add a column for each one. Things like company name, apartment number, and extra lines in an address can be made optional, but you need to make provision for them. This is an important principle of a relational database: *break down complex information into its component parts, and store each part separately.*

This makes searching, sorting, and filtering much easier. Breaking information into small chunks may seem a nuisance, but you can always join them together again. It's much easier than trying to separate complex information stored in a single field.

Choosing the right column type in MySQL

MySQL 5.0 has 28 different column types. Rather than confuse you by listing all of them, I'll explain just the most commonly used. You can find full details of all column types in the MySQL documentation at http://dev.mysql.com/doc/refman/5.0/en/data-types.html.

Storing text The difference between the main text column types boils down to the maximum number of characters that can be stored in an individual field, and whether you can set a default value.

- CHAR: A fixed-length width text column up to a maximum of 255 characters. You must specify the size when building the table, although this can be altered later. Shorter strings are OK. MySQL adds trailing space to store them, and automatically removes it on retrieval. If you attempt to store a string that exceeds the specified size, excess characters are truncated. You can define a default value.

- VARCHAR: A variable-length character string. The maximum number must be specified when designing the table, but this can be altered later. Prior to MySQL 5.0, the limit is 255; this has been increased to 65,535 in MySQL 5.0. Another change in MySQL 5.0 affects the way trailing space is treated. Prior to MySQL 5.0, trailing space is stripped at the time of storing a record. Since MySQL 5.0, trailing space is retained for both storage and retrieval. You can define a default value.

- TEXT: Stores a maximum of 65,535 characters (slightly shorter than this chapter). You cannot define a default value.

TEXT is convenient, because you don't need to specify a maximum size (in fact, you can't). Although the maximum length of VARCHAR is the same as TEXT in MySQL 5.0, other factors such as the number of columns in a table reduce this.

Prior to MySQL 5.0, you cannot use CHAR in a table that also contains VARCHAR, TEXT, or BLOB. When creating the table, MySQL silently converts any CHAR columns to VARCHAR.

> *Keep it simple: use* VARCHAR *for short text items and* TEXT *for longer ones.*

14

Storing numbers The most frequently used numeric column types are as follows:

- TINYINT: Any whole number (integer) between –128 and 127. If the column is declared as UNSIGNED, the range is from 0 to 255. This is particularly suitable for storing people's ages, number of children, and so on.

- INT: Any integer between –2,147,483,648 and 2,147,483,647. If the column is declared as UNSIGNED, the range is from 0 to 4,294,967,295.

- FLOAT: A floating-point number.
- DECIMAL: A floating-point number *stored as a string. This column type is best avoided.*

DECIMAL is intended for currencies, but you can't perform calculations with strings inside a database, so it's more practical to use INT. For dollars or euros, store currencies as cents; for pounds, use pence. Then use PHP to divide the result by 100, and format the currency as desired.

> *Don't use commas or spaces as the thousands-separator. Apart from numerals, the only characters permitted in numbers are the negative operator (-) and the decimal point (.). Although some countries use a comma as the decimal point, MySQL accepts only a period.*

Storing dates and times MySQL stores dates in the format YYYY-MM-DD. This may come as a shock, but it's the ISO (International Organization for Standardization) standard, and avoids the ambiguity inherent in national conventions. The most important column types for dates and times are as follows:

- DATE: A date stored as YYYY-MM-DD. The supported range is 1000-01-01 to 9999-12-31.
- DATETIME: A combined date and time displayed in the format YYYY-MM-DD HH:MM:SS.
- TIMESTAMP: A timestamp (normally generated automatically by the computer). Legal values range from the beginning of 1970 to partway through 2037.

> *MySQL timestamps are based on a human-readable date and, since MySQL 4.1, use the same format as DATETIME. As a result, they are incompatible with Unix and PHP timestamps, which are based on the number of seconds elapsed since January 1, 1970. Don't mix them.*

Storing predefined lists MySQL lets you store two types of predefined list that could be regarded as the database equivalents of radio button and checkbox states:

- ENUM: This column type stores a single choice from a predefined list, such as "yes, no, don't know" or "male, female." The maximum number of items that can be stored in the predefined list is a mind-boggling 65,535—some radio-button group!
- SET: This stores zero or more choices from a predefined list, up to a maximum of 64. Although this violates the principle of storing only one piece of information in a field, it's useful when the items form a coherent unit (e.g., optional extras on a car).

The values stored in the ENUM and SET columns are stored as a comma-separated string. Individual values can include spaces and other characters but not commas.

Storing binary data Binary data, such as images, bloat your tables and cannot be displayed directly from a database. However, the following column types are designed for binary data:

- TINYBLOB: Up to 255 bytes
- BLOB: Up to 64KB
- MEDIUMBLOB: Up to 16MB
- LONGBLOB: Up to 4GB

With such whimsical names, it's a bit of a letdown to discover that BLOB stands for **binary large object**.

Deciding whether a field can be empty

When defining a database table, specifying a column as NOT NULL is the equivalent of designating a required field. Since the phpMyAdmin default is NOT NULL, you need to manually override this to make a field optional. You can change a column definition from NOT NULL to NULL and vice versa at any time.

> If you set a default value for a NOT NULL column, MySQL automatically uses that value if nothing is entered in the field. Unfortunately, Dreamweaver doesn't support this useful feature.

Storing input from the feedback form

It's time to put the knowledge from the preceding section to practical use by building a table to store the information from the feedback form from Chapters 9, 11, and 12. The form is available in the download files, so you can dive straight in. Don't be put off by the fact that it's a feedback form; working with it shows you all the basic techniques you need for inserting records into a database.

The name for the database table needs to give a clear indication of what it contains, so I'll call the table feedback. The next step is to analyze the form and decide how the feedback table should be structured.

Analyzing the form

There are seven fields in the form (see Figure 14-5), so you need at least seven columns. You need another column for the primary key. Anything else?

14

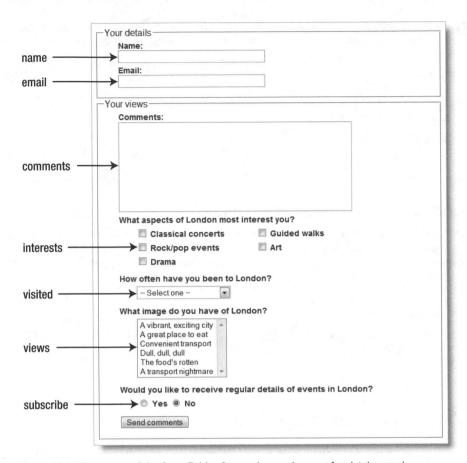

Figure 14-5. The names of the form fields often make good names for database columns.

In a real-world situation the family and given names should be stored separately, but I'm going to skip that here, because both are text fields, so they are handled in the same way.

The one extra field that I'm going to add will store the date and time that the form was submitted. So that makes a total of nine columns. As for column names, the name attributes of the form fields make a good choice, and as you'll see shortly, using them makes it a lot easier to use the Dreamweaver server behaviors. For the two extra fields, let's use message_id for the primary key, and submitted for the date.

The next step is to decide the column types (refer to "Choosing the right column type in MySQL"). By convention, the primary key column is normally the first one in a table. MySQL has a feature called auto_increment, which automatically assigns the next available number. This is ideal for a primary key, so we'll make the column an INT type. We don't want negative numbers, so we'll also make it UNSIGNED. This gives a range of nearly 4.3 billion, which is probably excessive for most tables. However, the danger of choosing a smaller number type is that you run out of numbers, particularly if records are added and deleted frequently. It's much better to err on the side of caution with the primary key column.

The first two form fields, name and email, contain short, variable amounts of text, so VARCHAR is appropriate. With VARCHAR you need to specify the maximum number of characters. For name, 50 is sufficient, but you don't want to risk truncating an email address, so 100 is a safer choice for email.

The comments field is also text. If your remote server is running MySQL 5.0 or higher, you can use VARCHAR and set a limit of 500 or 1000, but TEXT is appropriate for all versions, so we'll use that. To limit the length of comments, use the Spry Textarea Validation Widget as described in Chapter 9.

The checkbox group interests presents a dilemma. Unless you make this a required field, users can pick anything from none to five. Storing more than one piece of information in a field goes against the principles of good database design, but creating five separate columns isn't very satisfactory either. What happens if you want to add another category to the list, or remove one? Since interests are grouped together, and represent a series of closely related options, this is where SET comes in handy.

The drop-down menu visited allows only one choice. Although this sounds like a good candidate for ENUM, you may want to change the range of options later, so this is better as VARCHAR. That way, you can change the value attributes of the <option> tags without needing to change the table definition.

The views multiple-choice list is similar to the checkbox group, so that will be another SET.

The subscribe radio group is a straight yes/no choice, so it should be an ENUM column type.

Finally, submitted needs to store the date and time, so we'll make it a TIMESTAMP column. Whenever a record is inserted or updated, the current date and time are automatically inserted into the first TIMESTAMP column in a table. With a DATETIME column, you have to insert the value explicitly.

Table 14-1 summarizes this analysis. You'll use this summary to define the feedback table in phpMyAdmin, so the table headings use the same terminology as phpMyAdmin. The setting for Length/Values for the two SET columns is described in the instructions in "Defining the feedback table." Note that interests and views are specified as the only fields not required by setting them to null. I've done this because the Dreamweaver Insert Record server behavior can't handle SET columns automatically. So we'll come back to these two later.

Table 14-1. Column settings for the feedback table

Field	Type	Length/Values	Attributes	Null	Extra	Primary key
message_id	INT		UNSIGNED	not null	auto_increment	Selected
name	VARCHAR	50		not null		
email	VARCHAR	100		not null		
comments	TEXT			not null		
interests	SET	See text		null		

14

Continued

Table 14-1. Column settings for the feedback table (Continued)

Field	Type	Length/Values	Attributes	Null	Extra	Primary key
visited	VARCHAR	50		not null		
views	SET	See text		null		
subscribe	ENUM	'y','n'		not null		
submitted	TIMESTAMP			not null		

Defining a table in phpMyAdmin

Defining a database table normally requires writing a lengthy SQL query, but phpMyAdmin makes the process a lot simpler through a form-based interface. The form is quite wide and, unless you have a large monitor, you might need to scroll horizontally to see all the fields. You might find the text in some screenshots hard to read, but all important information is repeated in the instructions and Table 14-1.

Defining the feedback table

1. Launch phpMyAdmin, and select the egdwcs3 database. In the main frame, type feedback in the Name field, enter 9 as the Number of fields, and click Go.

2. This opens the form shown in Figure 14-6 with nine blank rows where you enter the column definitions. Copy the values from Table 14-1. Designate message_id as the table's primary key by selecting the radio button as indicated in Figure 14-6.

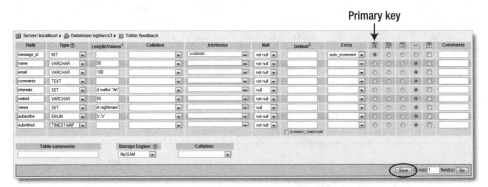

Figure 14-6. Defining the columns for the feedback table in phpMyAdmin

For the SET and ENUM columns, you need to enter in Length/Values the value attributes from the related form fields as a series of comma-separated strings. Each string needs to be enclosed in single quotes. So, for interests, it looks like this:

'Classical concerts', 'Rock/pop', 'Drama', 'Guided walks', 'Art'

For views, it looks like this:

```
'Vibrant/exciting', 'Good food', 'Good transport', 'Dull', 'Bad ➥
food', 'Transport nightmare'
```

For subscribe, it looks like this:

```
'y', 'n'
```

It's essential that the list of values matches exactly those in the form value attributes. Because the Length/Values field is so narrow, I recommend that you build the entry into this field in Notepad or TextEdit, and then copy and paste it into phpMyAdmin. Check the position of the quotes and commas carefully.

When you select the TIMESTAMP column type for submitted, phpMyAdmin adds a CURRENT_TIMESTAMP checkbox in the Default column. This applies to MySQL 5.0 and higher only. Since it's the only TIMESTAMP column in the table, all versions of MySQL assign a current timestamp, so you can leave the checkbox unchecked.

3. When you have finished, click the Save button, as highlighted at the bottom of Figure 14-6. Do *not* click the Go button alongside; this adds a new column to the table.

4. Assuming that everything went OK, phpMyAdmin creates the table and displays details of its structure, as shown in Figure 14-7. The name of the first field (column), message_id, should be underlined to indicate that it has been registered as the table's primary key. It should also have the value auto_increment in the Extra column. Check that the Default column for interests and views displays NULL.

Field	Type	Collation	Attributes	Null	Default	Extra	Action
message_id	int(10)		UNSIGNED	No		auto_increment	
name	varchar(50)	latin1_swedish_ci		No			
email	varchar(100)	latin1_swedish_ci		No			
comments	text	latin1_swedish_ci		No			
interests	set('Classical concerts', 'Rock/pop', 'Drama', 'Guided walks', 'Art')	latin1_swedish_ci		Yes	*NULL*		
visited	varchar(50)	latin1_swedish_ci		No			
views	set('Vibrant/exciting', 'Good food', 'Good transport', 'Dull', 'Bad food', 'Transport nightmare')	latin1_swedish_ci		Yes	*NULL*		
subscribe	enum('y', 'n')	latin1_swedish_ci		No			
submitted	timestamp		ON UPDATE CURRENT_TIMESTAMP	No	CURRENT_TIMESTAMP		

Figure 14-7. After you have defined the table, phpMyAdmin displays details of its structure.

If you have made a mistake, phpMyAdmin displays a lengthy error message in red. Don't panic. The major part of the message displays the SQL query that phpMyAdmin used to try to define the feedback table. Read the first part of the message, as it should contain a hint as to the problem.

The most likely things to go wrong are forgetting the length of a VARCHAR column in the Length/Values field or a missing comma or quote for the SET or ENUM columns. Since phpMyAdmin preserves your original values, you can edit them and click Save again. If you can't see the problem, click the Drop tab at the top of the page to delete the table, and start again, paying particular attention to the Length/Values field.

Check the structure of your table carefully against the values shown in Figure 14-7. If you need to amend the definition of a column, click the pencil-like icon in the Action section on the right. This redisplays a form similar to that in Figure 14-6 but with details of just the selected column, ready for editing. If you need to edit more than one column, select the appropriate checkboxes alongside the column names, and click the pencil-like icon at the bottom of the structure grid.

You're no doubt curious to know why Collation has been set to latin1_swedish_ci. The next section explains briefly what collation is all about.

Understanding collation

Collation was added in MySQL 4.1, so it doesn't affect you if your remote server is running MySQL 3.23 or MySQL 4.0. You can also ignore it if you work exclusively in English, Swedish, or Finnish (or any combination of them). However, if you work in other languages, you need to know about collation.

Collation determines the sort order of records. Different languages have their own sorting rules, so MySQL 4.1 and above lets you set the default sort order at different levels: for the entire database, for individual tables, and for individual columns. MySQL is based in Sweden, which explains why the default sort order is latin1_swedish_ci. English and Finnish share the same sort order.

If you work in a different language and your remote server is MySQL 4.1 or above, click Character Sets and Collations on the phpMyAdmin welcome screen to see the full range of supported sort orders. When defining a new database or table, select the appropriate sort order from the Collation drop-down menu. You can change the collation by selecting the database or table in phpMyAdmin, and then selecting the Operations tab. Since collation can be set at different levels, this sets the default only for new tables or columns. Existing tables and columns preserve their original collation unless you edit them individually.

> If you are working in a language, such as Spanish or French, that uses accented characters, MySQL 3.23 and 4.0 do not support UTF-8 (Unicode). This affects the way accented characters are stored. If accented characters are garbled when retrieving records from MySQL, change the default encoding of your web pages from UTF-8 to the encoding appropriate for your language. Alternatively, store accented characters as HTML entities (for example, é for é).

Inserting data from the feedback form

Most of the time, you'll want to insert the form data into a database without sending it by mail as well. So, although the ultimate goal is to combine the two operations, this section concentrates on inserting the data into the feedback table using the Dreamweaver Insert Record server behavior. For this purpose, you need to remove the mail processing script from the feedback form in Chapter 12. To make this easier for you, the download files contain feedback_start.php in examples/ch14.

However, if you want to use your own file from Chapter 12, make a copy of feedback.php, and save it in workfiles/ch14. Remove all the PHP code above the DOCTYPE declaration

(DTD). Also remove the PHP code and warning messages between the <h1> heading and the paragraph beginning "We welcome feedback . . ." Finally, remove the PHP code block in the action attribute of the <form> tag. The top of the page in Code view should look like this:

The PHP code inside the form does *not* need to be removed. It controls the validation error messages, and will be needed when the mail processing script is reintegrated later.

Before you can communicate with your database inside Dreamweaver, you need to create a MySQL connection. If you defined your site correctly in Chapter 4, it should take no more than a minute or two.

Creating a MySQL connection

A MySQL connection is simply a convenient way of storing the details needed to connect to MySQL: the server address, username, password, and database name. Dreamweaver stores them in an include file, which it automatically attaches to a web page whenever you select the connection in a server behavior.

1. Copy feedback_start.php from examples/ch14 to workfiles/ch14, and save it as feedback.php, or edit your file from Chapter 12 as described in the preceding section.

2. With feedback.php open in the Document window, open the Databases panel in the Application panel group. Alternatively, use Window ➤ Databases, or the keyboard shortcut Ctrl+Shift+F10/Shift+Cmd+F10. (Unless a PHP file is open in the Document window, the Databases panel remains grayed out.)

3. Click the plus (+) button, and select MySQL Connection as shown here.

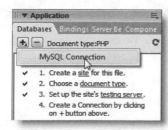

14

447

4. The dialog box that opens asks you for the following details:

- Connection name: You can choose any name you like, but it must not contain any spaces or special characters. This connection will be used by the administrator user account, so I have entered connAdmin.

- MySQL server: This is the address of the database server. If MySQL is on the same computer as Dreamweaver, you should enter localhost.

  If you are running MySQL on a port other than the default 3306 (this happens with some of the all-in-one PHP packages, such as MAMP), add the port number after a colon (e.g., localhost:8889).

  If you are using your remote server as a testing server, use the address your hosting company gave you. In most cases, this is also localhost. Dreamweaver uploads hidden files to your remote server and creates a local connection there.

  Some hosting companies locate the MySQL server on a different computer from your web files. If you are doing remote testing and have been given a server name other than localhost, enter that name now. If you are testing locally but know that your host doesn't use localhost, you will have to change this field when you finally upload your site to the remote server.

- User name: Enter the name of the MySQL user account that you want to use. This connection will be used for public pages, so I have entered egadmin.

- Password: Enter the password for the user account. I used humpty.

- Database: Enter the name of the database that you want to use. You can also use the Select button to get Dreamweaver to show you a list of databases that the named user has access to.

Fill in the necessary details. The completed dialog box should look something like the following screenshot. When you have finished, click the Test button. If all goes well, Dreamweaver will tell you that the connection was made successfully.

5. If you got the thumbs up from Dreamweaver, click OK to close both dialog boxes. If you failed to make the connection, cancel the connection setup, and check the points listed above before trying again. If that fails, see "Troubleshooting the connection."

6. In the Databases panel, you should see a database icon that has been created for connAdmin. Expand the tree menu by clicking the tiny plus button (it's a triangle on the Mac) to the left of connAdmin. It displays the database features available to the connection, including a brief description of every column in the feedback table. The columns are listed in alphabetical order, not the order they appear in the database. The little key icon alongside message_id indicates that it's the table's primary key. Both Stored procedures and Views are empty. Although MySQL 5.0 supports these features, support for them has not been implemented in Dreamweaver CS3.

If you ever need to change the connection details, double-click the database icon in the Databases panel to reopen the MySQL Connection dialog box, make your changes, and click OK. Alternatively, right-click on the connection name, and choose Edit Connection from the context menu.

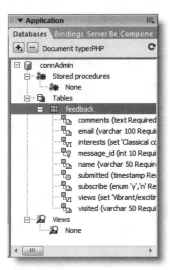

> Dreamweaver stores the MySQL connection details in a file with the same name as the connection. So connAdmin becomes connAdmin.php, which is stored in a folder called Connections that Dreamweaver creates in the site root. Don't forget to upload the contents of this folder to your remote server when deploying a PHP site on the Internet.

Troubleshooting the connection

Hopefully, everything went OK, but this section should help identify what might have gone wrong if you get an error message. Normally, you get a message about there being no testing server or saying that the testing server doesn't map to a particular URL.

All communication between Dreamweaver and MySQL is conducted through two files, MMHTTPDB.php and mysql.php, located in a hidden folder called _mmServerScripts. Dreamweaver automatically creates the hidden folder and files in the site root of your testing server. If you have defined the URL prefix incorrectly in your site definition, the folder will be in the wrong place. The solution is to use an Explorer window or Finder to see where the folder has been created. Then adjust the testing server site definition (see Chapter 4) so that both the testing server folder and URL prefix point to the site root.

If you're using your remote server as the testing server, Dreamweaver uploads the hidden folder and files to your remote server. Even if you have defined the URL prefix correctly, Dreamweaver might not be able to create the _mmServerScripts folder because of permission problems. Create the folder yourself, and make sure that it has read and write permissions.

You may see a rather unhelpful message about an unidentified error. Things to check when this happens are that MySQL and your web server are running. Also check your username and password—both are case sensitive and will fail if you use the wrong case (make sure Caps Lock isn't on by accident). A software firewall may also be blocking communication between Dreamweaver and MySQL. Try turning it off temporarily. If that solves the problem, adjust the firewall settings.

14

Applying the Insert Record server behavior

These instructions show you how to apply an Insert Record server behavior to feedback.php, but they work with any form. Because Dreamweaver doesn't handle SET columns automatically, we'll leave them blank for the time being and come back to them later in the chapter.

1. With feedback.php open in the Document window, open the Server Behaviors panel in the Application panel group (Window ➤ Server Behaviors, or Ctrl+F9/ Cmd+F9).

2. Click the plus button, and select Insert Record from the menu that appears. This opens the Insert Record dialog box. The first drop-down menu (labeled Submit values from) detects any forms on the page. In this case, there is only one, but if you have a page with more than one form, you need to select the name of the form that contains the data you want to insert into the database.

   The Connection drop-down menu detects all MySQL connections in the site but doesn't select one by default, so you need to select connAdmin manually.

   As soon as you select a connection, Dreamweaver detects all the tables in the database and automatically selects the first in alphabetical order. Since there's only one table in the egdwcs3 database, it selects feedback. However, if you're using an existing database, select the table that you want to insert the records into.

   Once the table has been selected, Dreamweaver automatically populates the Columns area. The Insert Record dialog box should now look like this:

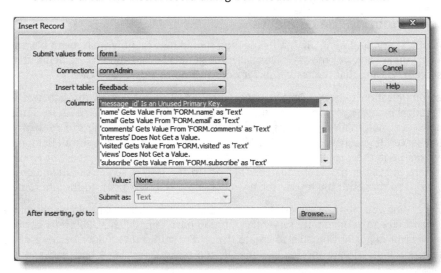

3. Since the name attributes of the form fields are the same as the column names in the feedback table, Dreamweaver automatically matches them and sets the type of data they expect. You may be surprised to see that the first entry in the Columns field says 'message_id' Is an Unused Primary Key. This is correct; MySQL automatically assigns the next available number, so you don't want to submit a value from the form.

As you go down the list in the Columns field, you'll see that three columns are marked Does Not Get a Value: interests, views, and submitted. In the case of submitted, this is fine, because it's a TIMESTAMP column that is automatically populated with the current date and time. We'll deal with interests and views later. All other columns should be listed as getting a value as text from the form field of the same name.

If any other columns are marked as not getting a value, that means you have probably given the form field and column name different spellings. Set the correct value by selecting the column in the Columns field. Then activate the Value drop-down menu, and select the form field that contains the data you want to insert into that column.

The Submit as drop-down menu should be set to the same datatype as the column. The options are Text, Integer (whole number), Double (number with decimal fraction), Date, and three varieties of Checkbox. In this form, everything should be set to Text.

4. The final field in the Insert Record dialog box lets you specify a page to go to after the record has been inserted in the database. Since this is a contact form that you want to remain onscreen, leave this field blank, and click OK.

5. Save feedback.php, and load it into a browser. If your Dreamweaver preferences use a temporary file for Preview in Browser, type the URL for the page into the browser address bar. Using a temporary file generates a series of PHP error messages.

6. Click the Send comments button without entering anything into the form. You should see a text message telling you that column name cannot be null. This is MySQL rejecting the record because a required field hasn't been filled in.

7. Click the browser back button to return to the form, and enter values for each field, except the interests checkbox group and the views multiple-choice list. Test the form by clicking Send comments. The page should reload with the form fields cleared.

8. In phpMyAdmin, select the feedback table, and click the Browse tab. If you get a red X when you click Browse, select any other tab first to refresh phpMyAdmin. You should see your form input has been stored in the database like this:

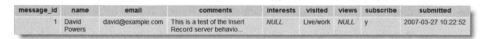

message_id	name	email	comments	interests	visited	views	subscribe	submitted
1	David Powers	david@example.com	This is a test of the Insert Record server behavio...	NULL	Live/work	NULL	y	2007-03-27 10:22:52

Check your code, if necessary, against feedback_01.php in examples/ch14.

Troubleshooting

If you get a message that a column cannot be null, even though you have entered something into the relevant form field, check that the name attributes in your form match the names of the columns in the database. Also make sure that interests and views are defined as NULL in phpMyAdmin (see Figure 14-8). If there's a mistake in your column names, you'll need to edit the Insert Record server behavior.

14

Server behaviors applied to a page are listed in the Server Behaviors panel like this:

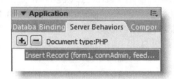

Double-click the name of the server behavior to reopen the dialog box for editing, and go back carefully over the settings for each column.

If you get a string of errors about mysql_real_escape_string() and the ODBC connection, it means you have used Preview in Browser with a temporary file. Load the actual page into a browser and try again.

If you get a fatal error about a call to undefined function virtual(), it means that your site defaults to links relative to the site root, and you're not using Apache as the web server. See the next section.

Using server behaviors with site-root-relative links

If you open feedback.php in Code view to see the PHP code that Dreamweaver has added to the page, and you use document-relative links, the top section will look like this:

```
1  <?php require_once('../../Connections/connAdmin.php'); ?>
2  <?php
3  if (!function_exists("GetSQLValueString")) {
```

The code on line 1 in the screenshot uses require_once() to include the MySQL connection details. However, if your site definition uses links relative to the site root, this will be replaced by the following:

```
<?php virtual('/Connections/connAdmin.php'); ?>
```

The virtual() function *works only on Apache*. If your code uses virtual(), make sure it is supported on both your testing and remote servers before going any further (see "Using site-root-relative links with includes" in Chapter 12 for details of how to do this).

All Dreamweaver server behaviors need to include the MySQL connection. If your server doesn't support virtual(), you have two options, namely:

- Change your site definition to use document-relative links, and manually override the default when creating links that you want to be relative to the site root. You do this in the Select File dialog box by changing the Relative to drop-down menu to Site Root, as described in "Including a text file" in Chapter 12.
- Manually replace virtual() with require_once() and a document-relative link in pages that use server behaviors. The require_once() command works on all servers.

Neither solution is ideal. I believe that Dreamweaver needs a platform-neutral way of connecting to MySQL when site-root-relative links are used, or it should use require_once() regardless of the default link type.

Inspecting the server behavior code

As you have just seen, inserting form input into a database is a breeze with the Insert Record server behavior. Many web developers are more than happy to let Dreamweaver take the strain and never venture under the hood into Code view. You don't need to understand every line of code, but it is important to know what it looks like and what the main parts of it are for. Without that knowledge, it becomes impossible to troubleshoot problems or customize the code to your own requirements. In any case, you'll need to dive into Code view to insert the values in the two SET columns, interests and views. Don't worry, the code doesn't bite, and the changes that you need to make are very simple.

As you've just seen, the first line of code creates the connection to MySQL. Without this, nothing works.

The next section of code looks like this:

```
3    if (!function_exists("GetSQLValueString")) {
4    function GetSQLValueString($theValue, $theType, $theDefinedValue = "", $theNotDefinedValue = "")
5    {
6      $theValue = get_magic_quotes_gpc() ? stripslashes($theValue) : $theValue;
7
8      $theValue = function_exists("mysql_real_escape_string") ? mysql_real_escape_string($theValue) :
     mysql_escape_string($theValue);
9
10     switch ($theType) {
11       case "text":
12         $theValue = ($theValue != "") ? "'" . $theValue . "'" : "NULL";
13         break;
14       case "long":
15       case "int":
16         $theValue = ($theValue != "") ? intval($theValue) : "NULL";
17         break;
18       case "double":
19         $theValue = ($theValue != "") ? "'" . doubleval($theValue) . "'" : "NULL";
20         break;
21       case "date":
22         $theValue = ($theValue != "") ? "'" . $theValue . "'" : "NULL";
23         break;
24       case "defined":
25         $theValue = ($theValue != "") ? $theDefinedValue : $theNotDefinedValue;
26         break;
27     }
28     return $theValue;
29   }
30 }
```

It defines a Dreamweaver function called GetSQLValueString(), which handles magic quotes and prepares user input for insertion into the database.

Next follows a short section beginning $editFormAction. This sets the action attribute of the <form> tag.

14

Finally comes the code that inserts the form data into the database by building a SQL query.

```
37  if ((isset($_POST["MM_insert"])) && ($_POST["MM_insert"] == "form1")) {
38    $insertSQL = sprintf("INSERT INTO feedback (name, email, comments, visited, subscribe) VALUES
      (%s, %s, %s, %s, %s)",
39                     GetSQLValueString($_POST['name'], "text"),
40                     GetSQLValueString($_POST['email'], "text"),
41                     GetSQLValueString($_POST['comments'], "text"),
42                     GetSQLValueString($_POST['visited'], "text"),
43                     GetSQLValueString($_POST['subscribe'], "text"));
44
45    mysql_select_db($database_connAdmin, $connAdmin);
46    $Result1 = mysql_query($insertSQL, $connAdmin) or die(mysql_error());
47  }
```

Each element of the $_POST array is passed to GetSQLValueString() together with a second argument indicating the datatype. This is designed to prevent malicious attacks on your database.

By recognizing the various sections of code, it becomes easier to see how to merge Dreamweaver's code with your own, as you'll do when integrating the mail processing script.

Now, let's sort out the two SET columns.

Inserting data into SET columns

A SET column stores values from a predetermined list. For a value to be legal, it must be specified in the table definition. The definition for interests looks like this:

'Classical concerts', 'Rock/pop', 'Drama', 'Guided walks', 'Art'

This means that you can store any combination of these (or none) in the interests column for each record in the database. However, if you change the form to add Sport to the interests checkbox group, you cannot store Sport in the interests column without first updating the table definition. Illegal values—and that includes misspellings—are ignored.

The values from a checkbox group or multiple-choice list need to be inserted into a SET column as a comma-separated string. So you pass the array that contains the form values to implode() in the same way as in the mail processing form, and then insert the values into the database as text.

Storing multiple values in SET columns

These instructions are based on feedback.php, but the technique applies to any SET column.

1. With feedback.php open in the Document window, open the Server Behaviors panel, and double-click the Insert Record server behavior listed there to edit it.

2. When you open the Insert Record dialog box to edit an existing server behavior, the first drop-down menu labeled Submit values from is grayed out, but you can change all other values. Select 'interests' Does Not Get a Value in the Columns field, and activate the Value drop-down menu. As the next screenshot shows, Dreamweaver

has listed the five checkboxes as FORM.interests[]. The square brackets prevent Dreamweaver from matching the checkbox group to the interests column.

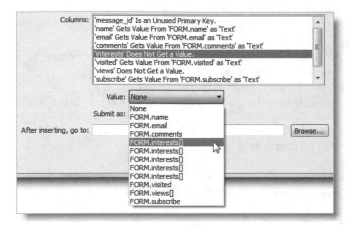

3. Select one of the instances of FORM.interests[]. Dreamweaver automatically selects Checkbox 1,0 in the Submit as drop-down menu, but you need to change this to Text.

4. Select 'views' Does Not Get a Value in the Columns field, and then activate the Value drop-down menu. There's only one instance of FORM.views[], so select that, and set Submit as to Text. Then click OK to close the Insert Record dialog box.

If you open the dialog box again for any reason, Dreamweaver sets interests *and* views *back to* Does Not Get a Value. *However, you're about to edit the server behavior in Code view, after which it ceases to be editable through the dialog box. This isn't the disaster you might think. Once you feel at home with server behaviors, you'll discover that Dreamweaver does all the tedious coding, leaving you to tidy up details, such as adjusting the code for* SET *columns.*

---

5. In Code view, the section that builds the SQL query now looks like this:

```
38    $insertSQL = sprintf("INSERT INTO feedback (name, email, comments, interests, visited, views, subscribe)
      VALUES (%s, %s, %s, %s, %s, %s, %s)",
39                         GetSQLValueString($_POST['name'], "text"),
40                         GetSQLValueString($_POST['email'], "text"),
41                         GetSQLValueString($_POST['comments'], "text"),
42                         GetSQLValueString($_POST['interests[]'], "text"),
43                         GetSQLValueString($_POST['visited'], "text"),
44                         GetSQLValueString($_POST['views[]'], "text"),
45                         GetSQLValueString($_POST['subscribe'], "text"));
```

6. Remove the square brackets after interests in $_POST['interests[]'] (line 42 in the preceding screenshot), so that it looks like this:

```
GetSQLValueString($_POST['interests'], "text"),
```

7. Remove the square brackets after views on line 44, so that it looks like this:

```
GetSQLValueString($_POST['views'], "text"),
```

14

8. You now need to convert the arrays in $_POST['interests'] and $_POST['views'] into a comma-separated string. Add the following code block highlighted in bold to the top of feedback.php:

```php
<?php require_once('../../Connections/connAdmin.php'); ?>
<?php
// if form has been submitted, convert $_POST subarrays to strings
if (array_key_exists('send', $_POST)) {
  if (isset($_POST['interests'])) {
    $_POST['interests'] = implode(',', $_POST['interests']);
    }
  else {
    $_POST['interests'] = '';
    }
  if (isset($_POST['views'])) {
    $_POST['views'] = implode(',', $_POST['views']);
    }
  else {
    $_POST['views'] = '';
    }
  }
?>
<?php
if (!function_exists("GetSQLValueString")) {
```

The block is enclosed in a conditional statement that executes the code only if the form has been submitted. It uses array_key_exists() as in the mail processing script.

Because checkboxes and multiple-choice lists don't appear in the $_POST array if nothing has been selected, the remaining code first checks whether any values have been selected for interests and views. If they have, they are converted to a comma-separated string with implode(). Otherwise, an empty string is assigned as the value. This is needed to prevent the SQL query from throwing an error.

The first argument to the implode() function is the string that you want to act as separator between array elements. It's vital to use a comma with no space on either side. If you add a space after the comma, only the first value is inserted in the SET column. This is because the space is treated as part of the string.

```php
$_POST['interests'] = implode(',', $_POST['interests']);  // this works
$_POST['interests'] = implode(', ', $_POST['interests']); // this fails
```

9. Save feedback.php, and load it in a browser. Test the form by filling in all fields, and check the results by clicking the Browse tab in phpMyAdmin. This time, you should see the selected values inserted in the interests and views columns, as shown here:

| 2 | David Powers | david@example.com | This is a test of the SET columns. | Rock/pop,Drama,Art | Live/work | Vibrant/exciting,Good food,Transport nightmare | y | 2007-03-27 17:53:47 |

Check your code, if necessary, against feedback_02.php in examples/ch14.

Putting information in a database is all very fine, but it's not much use if you can't see what it is. Of course, you can use phpMyAdmin, but it's more useful to incorporate the data in a web page.

Displaying database content

Displaying content from a database in a web page with Dreamweaver involves a three-stage process:

1. Create a connection to the database.

2. Query the database, and store the result in a recordset.

3. Insert Dreamweaver data objects (PHP code, sometimes mixed with XHTML) into your web page to display your database content.

You already have a MySQL connection for the administrator, but if you are allowed to create more than one user account on your remote database, it's a good idea to create a separate, restricted connection for visitors. By using an account limited to SELECT queries for public pages, there is no way that a malicious user can manipulate your script to alter or delete your precious data. So, if you created the eguser account earlier in the chapter, open the Databases panel to make another MySQL connection called connQuery. Enter the username and password for the restricted user (eguser and dumpty).

Creating a recordset

A recordset is the name that Dreamweaver gives to the set of results that comes from submitting a SELECT query to a database. As with the Insert Record server behavior, the code is generated automatically for you, although constructing SELECT queries for detailed searches of your data involves more work. But we'll cross that bridge later . . . Let's start with a simple query.

> **Creating a list of all records**

This exercise shows you how to query the feedback database to build a recordset containing the primary key, name, date, and time of each record. The recordset will later be used to display those details in a web page.

1. Create a new PHP page, and save it as feedback_list.php in workfiles/ch14.

2. Open the Server Behaviors panel; click the plus button, and select Recordset from the menu that appears. This opens the Recordset dialog box, which has two interfaces: Simple and Advanced. The Simple interface is smaller and has fewer options. The Advanced one is bigger and has more options. Switch between the two by clicking the Advanced or Simple button, and Dreamweaver remembers your most recent choice.

Make sure you're in the Simple interface. By default, Dreamweaver enters a generic value such as Recordset1, Recordset2, and so on, in the Name field. However, the name is used to create several PHP variables, so it's better to choose something

14

that tells you what the recordset is for. Use only letters, numbers, and the underscore. Don't use any spaces. Some people follow the convention of beginning recordset names with rs, but it's not necessary. The name I have chosen is getFeedback.

In the Connection field, select the restricted connection connQuery. The Define button lets you define a new connection if you forgot to create one for the current site.

Next, select the table that you want to retrieve the records from. There's only one at the moment, feedback.

The Columns field lists all columns in the table. By default, the All radio button is selected, and the columns are grayed out. Use this setting to retrieve the details from every column. On this occasion, though, let's select just a few. Click the Selected radio button, and hold down Ctrl/Cmd to select message_id, name, and submitted.

> *A lot of beginners select* All *every time, even if they need only one or two columns. It's easy, because it's the default, and it makes the SQL query easier to read (we'll study SQL syntax in Chapter 16). However, it's a very bad habit, as it slows down the query. You might not notice the difference in the early stages, but it can have a major impact once your database begins to grow. Always select only those columns you actually need.*

I'll explain the use of Filter later. You don't need it for this recordset.

To sort the records in reverse date order (most recent first), set Sort to submitted and the drop-down menu alongside to Descending.

When you have finished, the Recordset dialog box settings should look like this:

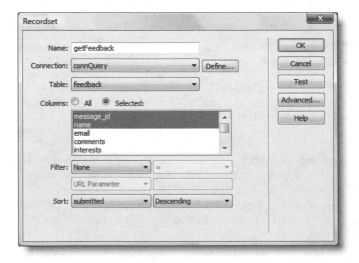

3. Click the Test button to preview the recordset. You should see a display similar to this:

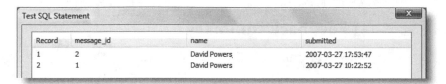

4. Click OK to close the Test SQL Statement dialog box, and OK again to close the Recordset dialog box.

5. Switch to Code view, and take a quick look at the code inserted by Dreamweaver. The first two items are the MySQL connection and GetSQLValueString() function that you saw earlier. The code that creates the recordset is only five lines long. As you can see from Figure 14-8, the name of the recordset has been incorporated into four PHP variables. These variables will be reused in the body of the page when you display the results of the recordset, so choosing a meaningful name helps identify the right code, particularly when using more than one recordset on a page.

```
32    mysql_select_db($database_connQuery, $connQuery);
33    $query_getFeedback = "SELECT message_id, name, submitted FROM feedback ORDER BY submitted DESC";
34    $getFeedback = mysql_query($query_getFeedback, $connQuery) or die(mysql_error());
35    $row_getFeedback = mysql_fetch_assoc($getFeedback);
36    $totalRows_getFeedback = mysql_num_rows($getFeedback);
```

Figure 14-8. The code for the Recordset server behavior is quite short.

6. Save feedback_list.php. In Design view it's still a blank page, but we'll fix that next.

Displaying the results of a recordset in a repeat region

Now that you have a recordset, you can display its contents in feedback_list.php. The recordset is actually an array, in which each element contains the value of a single record. To display them, you need to build a table with just two rows. The first row contains column headings, and the second row contains the data objects that display the contents of a single record. By applying a repeat region to the second row, you can loop through the recordset to display all the records.

1. Continue working with feedback_list.php from the preceding section.

2. Give the page a heading, and insert a table (use the Table button on the Common tab of the Insert bar or Insert ➤ Table). In the Table dialog box, set Rows and Columns to 2, and Table width to 400 pixels. Delete Border thickness, and set Header to Top. Give the first row the headings Date and time, and Name, as shown here.

14

3. Open the Bindings panel in the Application panel group (Window ➤ Bindings or Ctrl+F10/Cmd+F10), and expand the Recordset (getFeedback) tree menu as shown in the next screenshot. As you can see, it contains each of the columns selected in the Recordset dialog box in the previous section.

This gives you direct access to the data contained in the recordset.

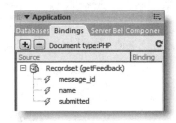

4. In Design view, click inside the first cell of the second table row. Then select submitted in the Bindings panel, and click the Insert button at the bottom right of the panel. This places a dynamic text object in the table, as shown here:

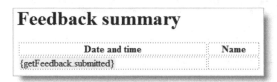

Again, the value of choosing a meaningful name for the recordset becomes clear. The dynamic text object uses the recordset and column names to identify the data that will be inserted into the web page.

5. You can also drag and drop dynamic text objects from the Bindings panel. Highlight name, and drag it into the second cell of the second table row.

6. Test the page by clicking the Live Data view button in the Document toolbar. The first result from the recordset should be displayed as shown here:

Click the Live Data view button again to toggle off the dynamic display.

7. To display multiple results from the recordset, you need to apply a Repeat Region server behavior. Click inside the second table row, and then select the whole row by clicking the <tr> tag in the Tag selector at the bottom of the Document window.

Open the Server Behaviors panel; click the plus button, and select Repeat Region from the menu that appears. Alternatively, click the Repeat Region button on the Data tab of the Insert bar, or choose Insert ➤ Data Objects ➤ Repeat Region.

This opens the Repeat Region dialog box shown here:

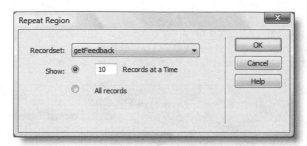

Since there's only one recordset on the current page, getFeedback is selected automatically in the Recordset drop-down menu, but if you have several record-sets, make sure the correct one is chosen. The Show radio button lets you choose whether to show a limited number of records (the default is 10, but you can enter a different number in the field), or all of them. I'll show you in Chapter 16 how to create a navigation system to page through a long recordset. For the moment, just use the default settings as shown in the preceding screenshot, and click OK.

8. The second table row should now be surrounded by a thin gray border with a gray tab at the top left, as shown in the following screenshot, indicating that it's a repeat region.

Use Live Data view again to see the effect. This time you should see up to ten rows displayed, with the latest at the top of the list. Preview the page in a browser, too. Check your code, if necessary, against feedback_list_01.php in examples/ch14.

If your page looks like a dog's dinner, you have probably made the most common mistake with a repeat region: failing to select the region accurately before applying the server behavior. When using a table row as the repeat region, you must select the surrounding <tr> tags. A lot of people drag their mouse across a table row and end up selecting only the table cells. The most accurate way of selecting the table row is to use the Tag selector, as suggested in step 7.

If you have made a mistake, highlight Repeat Region (getFeedback) in the Server Behaviors panel, and click the minus button to remove the code cleanly. Then repeat steps 7 and 8.

14

If you make a mistake with a server behavior or decide that you no longer want it on the page, always select it in the Server Behaviors *panel, and use the minus button to remove it. Just deleting dynamic elements in Design view leaves a tangled mess of unworkable code. I can't emphasize enough the importance of understanding the underlying XHTML, knowing where your insertion point is, or what's currently selected. Dreamweaver is a tool that, used correctly, speeds up dynamic website development. Used incorrectly, it's a rapid road to hell.*

Although I've used a repeat region on a table row, you can use it with any element that you want repeated. It works just as well with <li> items in a list or with <div> tags. You can also apply it to <td> tags to repeat table cells across a single row.

*Unfortunately, the built-in repeat region is unidirectional. It can repeat elements down a page or across, but not across and then down. To do that, you need either the Adobe Dreamweaver Developer Toolbox (*www.adobe.com/products/dreamweaver/ addt/*) or an extension from Tom Muck, this book's technical reviewer. Tom has created a free extension and a reasonably priced commercial one (*www.tom-muck.com/ extensions/*).*

At this point, you're probably thinking that displaying a list of names and dates is a nice party trick but doesn't really serve much purpose. You're right. Let's take a step further and link the names to a page that displays the contents of the record.

Displaying individual records

When a new record is inserted into the database table, MySQL automatically assigns the next available number to the message_id primary key. The getFeedback recordset that you created in the last section contains the message_id for each record, so you can pass the primary key to another page in a query string at the end of the URL like this:

```
http://egdwcs3/workfiles/ch14/feedback_display.php?message_id=2
```

The target page then uses the primary key to display the appropriate content. Passing variables in a query string is commonly used in search results. Dreamweaver makes it easy to build the query string.

Adding a record's primary key to a query string

These instructions continue from the previous section and assume you created feedback_list.php. They show you how to append a query string to a URL with dynamic text generated from a recordset.

1. Create a new PHP page, and save it as feedback_display.php in workfiles/ch14.

2. In feedback_list.php, select the {getFeedback.name} dynamic text object in the second cell of the second table row. You're going to create a hyperlink to feedback_display.php, but you need to do this through the Select File dialog box. So click the Browse for File icon (the one that looks like a folder) to the right of the Link field in the Property inspector.

3. In the Select File dialog box, choose feedback_display.php, and then click the Parameters button to the right of the URL field.

4. In the Parameters dialog box that opens, type message_id into the Name field. To open the field for editing, you can either click the plus button at the top of the dialog box or just click inside the field. Then click alongside, under the Value heading. Instead of typing anything in this field, click the lightning bolt icon, as shown in Figure 14-10.

5. This opens the Dynamic Data dialog box. Expand the Recordset (getFeedback) tree menu if necessary, and select message_id, as shown in Figure 14-9. Click OK in the Dynamic Data, Parameters, and Select File dialog boxes to close each one in turn.

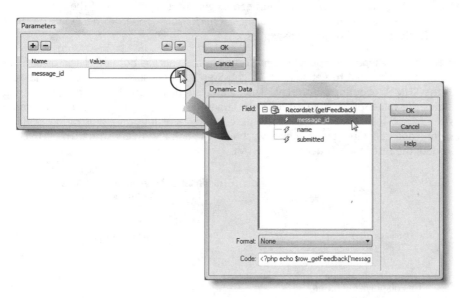

Figure 14-9. The Parameters and Dynamic Data dialog boxes build the dynamic query string.

6. Save feedback_list.php, and load it into a browser. Hover your mouse pointer over the links in the Name column, and look at the URL displayed in the browser status bar. It should point to feedback_display.php and have a query string containing message_id and the message's primary key, as shown in Figure 14-10.

14

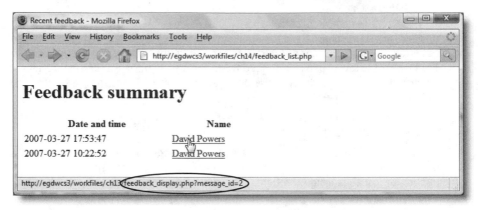

Figure 14-10. The query string has been added to the URL.

If you can't see the URL in the status bar, click the link to make sure that the query string is attached correctly to the end of the URL. Nothing will display yet in feedback_display.php, but you need to get the construction of the query string correct before moving any further. Check your code, if necessary, against feedback_list_02.php in examples/ch14.

This is a point where many people seem to go wrong. There is nothing magic or difficult about it. You just need to get steps 3–5 right. Step 3 simply surrounds the dynamic text with the XHMTL code for a hyperlink. The Parameters dialog box builds the query string and gets the value for message_id from the Dynamic Data dialog box. The most common mistake is not selecting the dynamic value correctly. The following illustration explains how the code generated by Dreamweaver builds the link and query string. The PHP code is shaded; the rest of the code is plain XHTML.

```
<a href="feedback_display.php?message_id=<?php echo $row_getFeedback['message_id']; ?>">
<?php echo $row_getFeedback['name']; ?></a>
```

This inserts the value of the primary key into the query string.

This displays the name.

Displaying the contents of the record in the details page

After you have passed the primary key to the details page, it's simply a question of creating a recordset that retrieves a single record, and then using dynamic data objects to display the contents of each field. These instructions continue from the previous section.

1. With `feedback_display.php` open in the Document window, open the Server Behaviors panel; click the plus button, and select Recordset.

2. This time, you want to retrieve all columns, but you need to filter the results of the SQL query using the primary key passed in the query string. The Filter drop-down menu contains the names of all columns in the table. Select message_id. Dreamweaver normally fills in the remaining Filter fields with the correct details. You want the value of the `message_id` column to be equal to the value of `message_id` passed through the URL query string. So reading Filter across and down, it looks like this: message_id = URL Parameter message_id (if the variable in the query string is different from the column name, you can edit the final Filter field manually).

Since there will be only one result, you don't need to set Sort.

The settings in the Recordset dialog box should look like this:

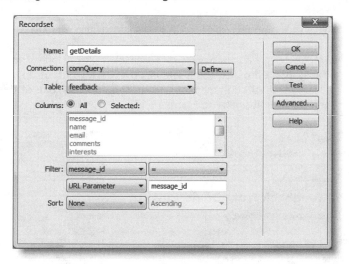

3. Click the Test button. You will be prompted to provide a test value for message_id. Enter the number of a primary key that you know exists in your feedback table, and click OK. You should see the results displayed in the Test SQL Statement panel. Click OK to close it, and then click OK in the Recordset dialog box to create the recordset.

4. All that remains now is to use the Bindings panel in the same way as before to display the contents of the recordset in `feedback_display.php`. How you lay it out is entirely up to you. Dreamweaver stores the data in the recordset, and you can be as imaginative or pedestrian as you like in how you integrate the dynamic text with your XHTML. Figure 14-11 shows a simple layout that I created. As you can see, the dynamic text objects don't need to be in the same order as they are in the record-set, and you can use them more than once (I have reused {getDetails.name}).

14

Figure 14-11. The dynamic text objects act as placeholders within your XHTML.

5. When you have designed your page, save feedback_display.php. If you attempt to load it directly into a browser, you'll see only the XHTML output. To view the page properly, load feedback_list.php into a browser, and click one of the links. You should then see output similar to Figure 14-12.

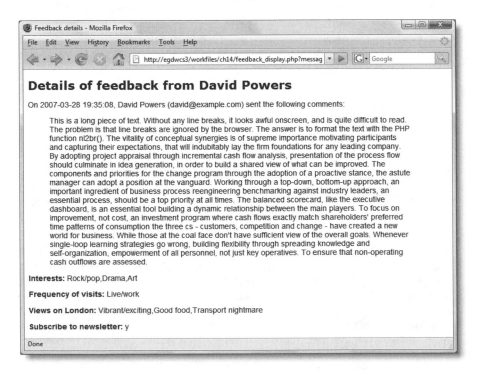

Figure 14-12. When viewed in a browser, the dynamic text objects are populated from the database.

If you're worried about the readability of that great block of text, the solution is in the next section.

Check your code, if necessary, with feedback_display_01.php in examples/ch14.

New

Displaying line breaks in text

That huge chunk of text in Figure 14-12 not only looks awful, it's difficult to read without any line breaks. The breaks are there, but new lines entered in a form text area are stored in the database as new line characters. Browsers ignore whitespace in XHTML, so everything looks bunched up. However, PHP has a nifty function called nl2br() that converts new line characters to <br /> tags. In previous versions of Dreamweaver, you needed to add nl2br() manually to dynamic text objects. Not any more . . .

Formatting dynamic text with line breaks

The Format option in the Dynamic Text dialog box makes it easy to apply a number of common string functions to data drawn from a recordset. These instructions show you how to apply nl2br() without the need to dive into Code view. The screenshot in step 3 shows the full range of available formats.

1. With feedback_display.php open in the Document window, open the Server Behaviors panel. It lists not only the recordset but also all the dynamic text objects inserted in the page, as shown here:

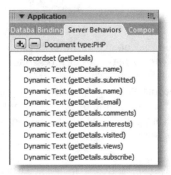

2. Double-click Dynamic Text (getDetails.comments) to open the Dynamic Text dialog box for the column that you want to format.

14

3. In the Dynamic Text dialog box, select Convert – New Lines to BRs from the Format menu, as shown here.

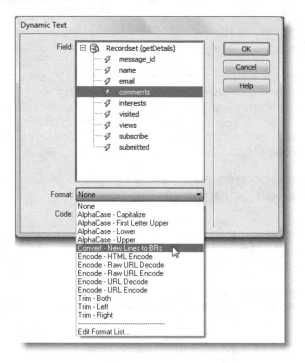

This wraps the dynamic text object in the PHP function nl2br(), which converts new line characters to <br /> tags. This ensures that any line breaks inserted into a section of text are preserved when displayed in the browser. It doesn't create genuine paragraphs, but it makes the output easier to read. As you can see from the preceding screenshot, this is just one of about a dozen formats that you can apply to dynamic text. Most are self-explanatory; the Trim formats remove whitespace from the left, right, or both ends of the dynamic text. Unfortunately, Edit Format List doesn't work.

4. Save feedback_display.php, and test it again with a long piece of text in the comments column. As Figure 14-13 shows, the line breaks in the long text are now displayed.

Check your code, if necessary with feedback_display_02.php in examples/ch14.

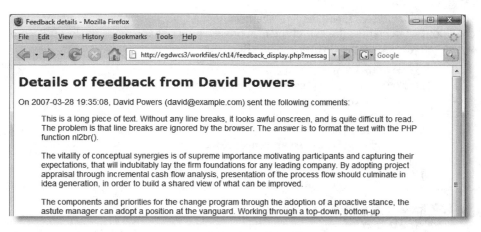

Figure 14-13. The text is now easier to read after formatting with nl2br().

Merging form input with mail processing

The final section of this chapter shows you how to combine the Insert Record server behavior with the mail processing script from Chapter 12. It's a bonus exercise that I have added in response to frequent requests in online forums. If it's not of direct relevance to your current requirements, feel free to skip it.

> *This requires the* feedback *table to be created on your remote server. The email is sent to your inbox, and the data is stored as a record in the database on your remote server. The script will not insert the data in the database in your local testing environment.*

The mail processing script in Chapter 12 and the Insert Record server behavior are both contained in conditional statements that ensure they are executed only if the form has been submitted. In theory, therefore, you could just copy the mail processing script and paste it above the Insert Record server behavior, and they would both run when a user submits the form. The drawback is that they would both run independently. Even if required fields are missing, the Insert Record server behavior would still be executed, leaving an unfriendly single-line error message onscreen. However, the mail processing script is designed to validate the input and redisplay the form with user-friendly error messages. So it makes more sense to run the Insert Record server behavior only if the mail is successfully sent.

14

Since the variable $mailSent detects whether the mail has been sent, you simply add a conditional statement at the end of the mail processing script and move the Insert Record server behavior inside the curly braces. In effect, the code outline looks like this:

```
// if the form has been submitted, process its contents
if (array_key_exists('sent', $_POST) {
  // process the mail
  // if the mail is sent successfully
  if ($mailSent) {
    // Insert Record server behavior goes here
  }
}
```

Merging the two scripts

These instructions assume that you have created the mail processing script in Chapter 12, as well as feedback.php in this chapter. The finished code is in feedback_merged.php in examples/ch14.

1. Save a copy of feedback.php in workfiles/ch14 as feedback_merged.php. If you want to move it to the site root or a different folder ready for uploading to your remote server, do so, and update the links if prompted by Dreamweaver.

2. Locate the following section of code, and cut it to your clipboard:

```
49  $editFormAction = $_SERVER['PHP_SELF'];
50  if (isset($_SERVER['QUERY_STRING'])) {
51    $editFormAction .= "?" . htmlentities($_SERVER['QUERY_STRING']);
52  }
```

This is what the Insert Record server behavior uses to set the action attribute of the <form> tag, so it needs to be moved to the top of the page to prevent it from being trapped inside the conditional statement.

3. Place your cursor immediately to the right of the opening PHP tag at the top of the page, and press Enter/Return to insert a couple of blank lines. Paste the code you cut in step 2 into the empty space. The top of the page should now look like this:

```
<?php
$editFormAction = $_SERVER['PHP_SELF'];
if (isset($_SERVER['QUERY_STRING'])) {
  $editFormAction .= "?" . htmlentities($_SERVER['QUERY_STRING']);
}

require_once('../../Connections/connAdmin.php'); ?>
```

4. Open the version of feedback.php from Chapter 12 (or use feedback_process.php in examples/ch12). Select all the mail processing code apart from the closing curly brace, as highlighted in the following screenshot, and copy it to your clipboard:

```
1   <?php
2   if (array_key_exists('send', $_POST)) {
3       //mail processing script
4       $to = 'me@example.com'; // use your own email address
5       $subject = 'Feedback from Essential Guide';
6
7       // list expected fields
8       $expected = array('name', 'email', 'comments', 'interests', 'visited', 'views', 'subscribe');
9       // set required fields
10      $required = array('name', 'comments', 'visited');
11      $headers = 'From: Essential Guide<feedback@example.com>';
12      $process = '../includes/process_mail.inc.php';
13      if (file_exists($process) && is_readable($process)) {
14          include($process);
15          }
16      else {
17          $mailSent = false;
18          mail($to, 'Server problem', "$process cannot be read", $headers);
19          }
20      }
21  ?>
22  <!DOCTYPE html PUBLIC "-//W3C//DTD XHTML 1.0 Transitional//EN"
```

5. Paste the code you have just copied onto the blank line *above* the require_once() command in step 3. Immediately after the code you have just pasted, insert the conditional statement to control the Insert Record server behavior like this:

```
mail($to, 'Server problem', "$process cannot be read", $headers);
}
if ($mailSent) {
require_once('../../Connections/connAdmin.php');?>
```

6. Scroll to the end of the Insert Record server behavior code, and insert two closing curly braces. The first one matches the opening curly brace at the beginning of the conditional statement in step 5. The second one replaces the curly brace that you didn't copy from the mail processing script.

7. Add the warning messages from the mail processing script between the <h1> heading and opening paragraph. When uploading the completed page to your remote server, don't forget to upload the Connections folder and process_mail.inc.php.

You can check your code against feedback_merged.php in examples/ch14. The code is fully commented to help you understand how the two scripts have been merged.

A great deal achieved

This chapter has concentrated heavily on the nuts and bolts of designing a database table, inserting data, and some basic retrieval and display techniques. There's a long way still to go: the date and time need formatting, and you need to know how to update and delete records. Nevertheless, I hope it's given you an insight into the power of integrating a database into a website.

In the next chapter, we continue our journey into PHP and databases by building a login system

14

```
35    $MM_dupKeyRedirect="registe
36    $loginUsername = $_POST['us
37    $LoginRS__query = sprintf("
$loginUsername, "text"));
38    mysql_select_db($database_c
39    $LoginRS=mysql_query($Login
40    $loginFoundUser = mysql_num
41
42    //if there is a row in the
43    if($loginFoundUser){
44       $MM_qsChar = "?";
45       //append the username to
46       if (substr_count($MM_dupK
47       $MM_dupKeyRedirect = $MM_
48       header ("Location: $MM_du
```

form1

connAdmin

users

'user_id' Selects Record Using 'FORM.user_id' as '
'username' Gets Value From 'FORM.username' as '
'pwd' Gets Value From 'FORM.pwd' as 'Text'
'first_name' Gets Value From 'FORM.first_name' as
'family_name' Gets Value From 'FORM.family_nam
'email' Gets Value From 'FORM.email' as 'Text'
'admin_priv' Gets Value From 'FORM.admin_priv' a

Value: FORM.user_id

Submit as: Integer   ☑ Pri

from form: form1

name field: username

sword field: pwd

connection: connAdmin

Table: users

me column: username

ord column: pwd

eds, go to: success.php

☐ Go to previous URL (if it exists)

In the last chapter, you learned how to insert information into a database and retrieve it. Once you have created a database record, you need a way to update it or delete it when it's no longer required. The principles behind updating and deleting are very similar to retrieving and displaying records. To update a record, you need to display its existing details in a form ready for editing, and to delete a record, you display sufficient information to confirm that you want to consign it to cyber oblivion.

Updating and deleting database records is something that should be entrusted only to authorized people, so I'm going to kill two birds with one stone in this chapter by showing you how to create a user registration system. This will demonstrate the basic insert, update, and deletion techniques. Once you have registered at least one user in the registration system, you can then create a login system to control access to different parts of your site.

This chapter shows you how to

- Insert, update, and delete records
- Prevent the creation of duplicate usernames
- Build your own custom server behaviors
- Preserve information related to an individual visitor with sessions
- Restrict access to your pages

Dreamweaver's Insert Record, Update Record, and Delete Record server behaviors are easy to use; and they protect you against a type of malicious attack known as **SQL injection**. An injection attack can be used to reveal sensitive information or even delete all your data by passing spurious values through form fields or URL query strings. The Dreamweaver code protects you by verifying the datatype and escaping characters in all variables passed to a SQL query.

The fundamental weakness of the server behaviors is that they do nothing to ensure that user input meets your criteria for suitable data. So you could end up with someone just pressing the space bar a couple of times, rather than typing a username or a password. This chapter shows you how to integrate your own checks into the Dreamweaver code.

Creating a user registration system

To register users for your site, you need the following elements:

- A database table to store user details, such as username and password
- A registration form
- A page to display a list of registered users
- A form to update user details
- A form to delete users

Defining the database table

Let's start with creating the necessary table to store user details in the database. I plan to use the same table for both site administrators and ordinary visitors. So it will also have columns to store an email address and the level of user privileges.

Creating the users table

These instructions show you how to define the users table in phpMyAdmin. If you're new to working with MySQL, I suggest that you work through this section step by step to familiarize yourself with table definition. More experienced users might prefer to use the phpMyAdmin Import tab to build the table structure with ch15_users.sql in the tools folder of the download files (ch15_users40.sql and ch15_users323.sql are for MySQL 4.0 and MySQL 3.23 respectively).

1. Launch phpMyAdmin, and select the egdwcs3 database. Create a new table called users. It requires seven columns, so enter 7 in Number of fields, and click Go.

2. Define the seven columns using the settings shown in the screenshot.

Primary key

The table's primary key is user_id, so Type should be set to INT, Attributes to UNSIGNED, and Extra to auto_increment.

The next five columns—username, pwd, first_name, family_name, and email—all have Type set to VARCHAR. I have set the length of username to 15, and pwd to 40. The password column must be 40 characters, because the function used to encrypt the passwords always produces a hexadecimal string exactly 40 characters long.

I've used 30 characters for both first_name and family_name, and a generous 100 characters for the email address. It's better to be over-generous than to end up with truncated data.

The final column, admin_priv, uses the ENUM column type. As I explained in the last chapter, this is typically used for "choose one of the following" situations. In this case, it's whether a user has administrative privileges. Type the permitted values in the Length/Values field as comma-separated strings like this:

'n', 'y'

In the Default column for admin_priv, enter n without any quotes.

Note that all columns have been set to not null. This is because I want all of them to be required fields. Click Save.

15

3. Check that the table structure displayed in phpMyAdmin looks like this:

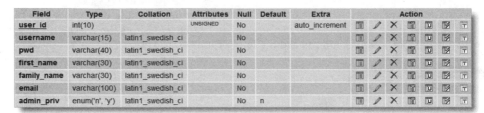

Field	Type	Collation	Attributes	Null	Default	Extra	Action
user_id	int(10)		UNSIGNED	No		auto_increment	
username	varchar(15)	latin1_swedish_ci		No			
pwd	varchar(40)	latin1_swedish_ci		No			
first_name	varchar(30)	latin1_swedish_ci		No			
family_name	varchar(30)	latin1_swedish_ci		No			
email	varchar(100)	latin1_swedish_ci		No			
admin_priv	enum('n', 'y')	latin1_swedish_ci		No	n		

Building the registration form

In the last chapter, we used a custom-built form to insert the records in the database, but Dreamweaver also has a Record Insertion Form Wizard that helps design the form for you. Personally, I don't like the insert and update wizards, because they create ugly forms with a lot of presentational code. Nevertheless, they can be useful if you want a quick way to build a form to interact with a database.

Using a wizard to build the registration form

1. Create a new PHP page called register_user.php in workfiles/ch15.

2. Give the page a title, such as Register user. Select Heading 1 from the Format menu in the Property inspector, and type the same heading at the top of the page. Then select the <h1> tag in the Tag inspector at the bottom of the Document window, and press your right keyboard arrow to move the insertion point out of the heading. If you forget to do this, Dreamweaver embeds the entire form inside the <h1> tags.

3. Open the Data tab of the Insert bar, and select Record Insertion Form Wizard. As the following screenshot shows, this is on a submenu, which automatically opens the first time you access it. On subsequent occasions, it remembers the option you used most recently, so you can just click the button. To reopen the submenu, click the small down arrow alongside the icon. If you prefer working with the main menu system, use Insert ➤ Data Objects ➤ Insert Record ➤ Record Insertion Form Wizard.

4. This opens the Record Insertion Form dialog box (see Figure 15-1). When it first loads, you need to select one of your MySQL connections. If you created two user accounts for MySQL, use the administrator connection (connAdmin). This populates the Table drop-down menu with a list of tables in the database. They are listed in alphabetical order, so you need to select users. The dialog box then presents you with its suggested values for the record insertion form, as shown in Figure 15-1.

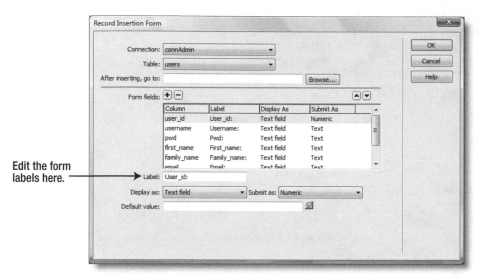

Edit the form labels here. ⟶

Figure 15-1. The Record Insertion Form Wizard helps build the insertion form automatically.

5. Dreamweaver uses the table column names to suggest labels and appropriate types of input fields for the form. The columns are listed in the same order as they appear in the database, but you can use the up and down arrow buttons at the top right of the Form fields area to rearrange the order they will be displayed in the record insertion form. If you don't want to display a particular field, remove it by clicking the minus button. To restore a deleted item, click the plus button, and select it from the list.

You can also specify where you want to go to after the record has been inserted. If you leave the option blank, the same page will be redisplayed ready for another record. That's fine for this form, but you need to edit the form fields.

6. The primary key is generated automatically, so you don't want a field for it in the form. Select user_id in the Form fields area, and click the minus button to delete it.

7. The suggested labels for the pwd, first_name, family_name, and admin_priv columns all need amending. Select each one in turn, and edit the value in the Label field (see Figure 15-1). Expand Pwd: to Password:, and change the value of Display as to Password field; remove the underscore from First_name: and Family_name:, and change admin_priv to Administrator:.

8. The admin_priv column uses the ENUM column type, so you want to use a radio button group. With admin_priv selected in Form fields, change Display as to Radio group, and then click the Radio Group Properties button that appears. This opens the Radio Group Properties dialog box as shown in the screenshot at the top of the next page. Use the plus button to create two Radio items: Yes with a value of y, and No with a value of n. These match the values defined in the ENUM column in the database table. To make No the default value, enter n in the field labeled Select value equal to, and click OK.

15

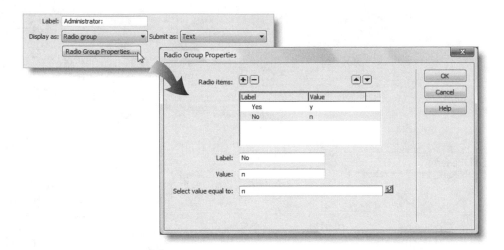

9. Before finishing the form definition, reorder the items with the up and down arrows at the top right of the Form fields area so that they look like this (the last item is the admin_priv radio button group, which is partially obscured in the screenshot):

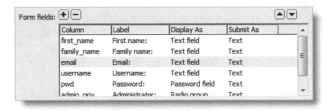

10. Click OK to create the form. In Design view, the page should now look like Figure 15-2. The form's light blue coloring indicates that it contains dynamic code.

Once you click OK in the Record Insertion Form dialog box, you cannot reopen it to make any changes. All further changes need to be made in the Document window and by double-clicking the Insert Record listing in the Server Behaviors panel. If you want to start afresh, use the minus button in the Server Behaviors panel to remove the Insert Record code before deleting the form. Otherwise, you'll end up with a tangle of impossible code.

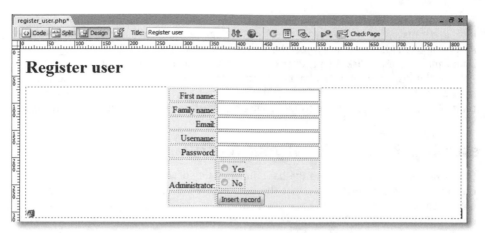

Figure 15-2. The Record Insertion Form Wizard creates the form and the necessary PHP code in a single operation.

11. Open Code view, and you'll see that the Insert Record server behavior has been added above the DOCTYPE declaration (DTD).

You'll also see that the table used to lay out the form makes extensive use of deprecated attributes, such as align. This means you need to strip them out manually if you want to redesign the form with CSS. That's why I prefer using my own forms and the Insert Record server behavior, as I showed you in the last chapter.

More importantly, scroll down to the bottom of the table, and check the code for the radio buttons. The next screenshot shows the Yes radio button:

```
84          <td><input type="radio" name="admin_priv" value="y" <?php if (!(strcmp("n","y"))) {echo
"CHECKED";} ?> />
85              Yes</td>
```

If you are using XHTML and the PHP section of code contains echo "CHECKED";, as shown in the screenshot, you need to change it to this:

echo **'checked="checked"'**;

Using CHECKED on its own is invalid in XHTML. Adobe is aware of this mistake, so it may have been corrected by an updater by the time you read this. Adobe coding style normally uses double quotes, so it may be changed to echo "checked=\"checked\"";. Either style is acceptable. You need to make the same change in the No button. The rest of the PHP code block is OK; it's just the echo part that needs changing.

12. Save register_user.php, and load it into a browser (don't use Preview in Browser with a temporary file). Enter some details in each field, and click Insert Record.

13. Launch phpMyAdmin, select the egdwcs3 database, and then select the users table. When you click the Browse tab, you should see the details listed like this:

user_id	username	pwd	first_name	family_name	email	admin_priv
1	dpowers	codeslave	David	Powers	david@example.com	y

15

The Record Insertion Form Wizard certainly makes it easy to build a form to insert records into a database, but before you start celebrating too soon, click Insert Record again. Assuming all fields were empty, you should see a message saying that the first_name column cannot be null. Click the browser's back button, and enter a single space in each field. Refresh the display in phpMyAdmin by pressing the Browse tab again. You'll see that the record has been accepted. This form is functional, but a lot of work still needs to be done on it. You can check your code so far against register_user_01.php in examples/ch15.

Preserving the integrity of your records

Dreamweaver provides you with the basic functionality of inserting records in a database, but it's up to you to make sure that the data entered by a user meets the criteria you envisaged when designing the database structure. When designing database forms, you must remember the GIGO principle—garbage in, garbage out. Unless you control carefully what you allow to go into a database, a lot of your results will be useless garbage. If your form is going to be in a controlled environment, such as an intranet, you can use the Spry validation widgets (see Chapter 9) to filter user input before it's submitted to the database. However, there's one thing that Spry cannot do, and that's check whether a username has already been registered by someone else. And on a public site, it can't stop the user from disabling JavaScript. The bottom line is that the only way to make sure data meets your criteria is to validate it with PHP before allowing it to be inserted into the database.

The first step is to make sure that the same username cannot be registered twice. Dreamweaver has a server behavior to do that. It's not very well designed but is easily adapted and saves you a lot of effort.

Preventing a username from being used twice

The Check New User server behavior queries your database to find out whether a username is already in use. Unfortunately, its default behavior results in the loss of user input if the username is already taken. These instructions show you how to adapt the code to generate an error message that can be displayed in the same page. Once you make these changes to the code generated by the server behavior, it can no longer be edited in the server behavior dialog box, but as you work through the following pages, you'll learn how to build a much more user-friendly registration system.

1. Continue working with the same file as in the preceding section. In the Server Behaviors panel, click the plus button, and select User Authentication ➤ Check New Username.

2. The Check New Username dialog box consists of two fields. The first one, Username field, is a drop-down menu listing all text columns in the table. Select username.

   The second field asks where to redirect the page if the username already exists. Nothing could be more guaranteed to annoy a user than to be taken to a different page if registration fails, but this server behavior won't let you leave the field blank. So enter register_user.php in the field labeled If already exists, go to, and click OK.

3. Open Code view, and locate the server behavior code (lines 32–51 in Figure 15-3).

```
32   // *** Redirect if username exists
33   $MM_flag="MM_insert";
34   if (isset($_POST[$MM_flag])) {
35     $MM_dupKeyRedirect="register_user.php";
36     $loginUsername = $_POST['username'];
37     $LoginRS__query = sprintf("SELECT username FROM users WHERE username=%s", GetSQLValueString(
     $loginUsername, "text"));
38     mysql_select_db($database_connAdmin, $connAdmin);
39     $LoginRS=mysql_query($LoginRS__query, $connAdmin) or die(mysql_error());
40     $loginFoundUser = mysql_num_rows($LoginRS);
41
42     //if there is a row in the database, the username was found - can not add the requested username
43     if($loginFoundUser){
44       $MM_qsChar = "?";
45       //append the username to the redirect page
46       if (substr_count($MM_dupKeyRedirect,"?") >=1) $MM_qsChar = "&";
47       $MM_dupKeyRedirect = $MM_dupKeyRedirect . $MM_qsChar ."requsername=".$loginUsername;
48       header ("Location: $MM_dupKeyRedirect");
49       exit;
50     }
51   }
```

Figure 15-3. The code for the Check New User server behavior

As you can see, it consists of two blocks. The first checks whether the username is in use, while the second handles the redirect. The second block (lines 42–50) begins with a conditional statement that executes the code inside the curly braces only if a duplicate is found. You can use this to make the page much more user-friendly.

4. Delete the code shown on lines 44–49 of the screenshot, and replace it with the code shown here in bold type:

```
if($loginFoundUser) {
  $error['username'] = "$loginUsername is already in use. Please➥
choose a different username.";
  }
}
```

This stores an error message in $error['username'], which you can display in the form to alert the user to the problem. It uses $loginUsername, a variable created by the server behavior in line 36, to store the username submitted from the registration form. I have used double quotes so that the value of $loginUsername will be displayed.

You can check your code against register_user_02.php in examples/ch15.

That's a good start, but you need to carry out a lot more checks. All fields are required, so you need to make sure that they're filled in.

Validating other fields

It's a good idea to set a minimum length for the password; and since the password won't appear onscreen, you should get the user to type it in twice to confirm the spelling. To keep the password secure, it should be encrypted before it's stored in the database. Finally, you need to check the email address for illegal characters. Quite a few checks, but not difficult to code. Continue working with the same file as in the preceding section.

15

1. You need to add a new field for the user to confirm the password. This means adding a new row to the table that contains the registration form. There are several ways to do this. Start by switching back to Design view, and clicking inside the table cell that contains the Administrator label. If you have a good memory for keyboard shortcuts, the quickest and easiest way to add a new table row is to press Ctrl+M/Cmd+M. This always inserts a new row *above* the current one.

   Alternative ways of adding a new row are to use the menu system. Modify ➤ Table ➤ Insert Row does the same as the keyboard shortcut: the new row goes above the current one. Modify ➤ Table ➤ Insert Rows or Columns opens a dialog box that lets you specify the number of rows or columns to be inserted and which side of the current selection to put them. Finally, the Layout tab of the Insert bar offers a visual way of doing it, as you can see in the following screenshot:

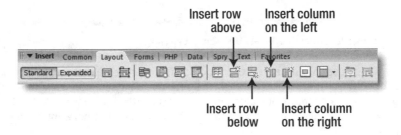

   Use whichever method you prefer to create a new row between Password and Administrator. Then type Confirm password as the label in the left cell, and insert a text field in the right cell. Name the text field conf_pwd, and set Type to Password in the Property inspector (form creation was covered in Chapter 9).

2. Switch to Code view, and amend the code shown on lines 33–36 of Figure 15-3 like this (new code is shown in bold):

```
$error = array();
// Validate form input
$MM_flag="MM_insert";
if (isset($_POST[$MM_flag])) {
  // Check name
  if (empty($_POST['first_name']) || empty($_POST['family_name'])) {
    $error['name'] = 'Please enter both first name and family name';
    }
  // remaining checks go here
  // check username
  $_POST['username'] = trim($_POST['username']);
  $loginUsername = $_POST['username'];
```

   This initializes $error as an empty array. PHP treats an array with zero elements as false (see "The truth according to PHP" in Chapter 10), so this can be used later to test whether any errors have been found.

   Line 35 in Figure 15-3 has been removed, because you no longer need to redirect the script to another page. It has been replaced by the first of a series of checks. It makes sure that neither the first name nor the family name has been left empty.

There follows a comment to indicate where all the remaining checks will go.

Finally, I have applied trim() to $_POST['username'] to remove any whitespace at either end of the string, and reassigned the value back to $_POST['username']. I've done this because the Insert Record server behavior, which remains intact further down the page, requires the original $_POST variables, so you can't reassign them to shorter variables, as with the mail-processing script in Chapter 11.

> You might think I'm contradicting myself, because the next line assigns $_POST['username'] to $loginUsername. Actually, it's part of the original Check New Username server behavior. I've left it in to avoid the need for other changes to the existing code.

3. The next check makes sure that the password contains at least six characters, and that both versions are the same. If everything is OK, the password is encrypted ready for insertion in the database. Insert the following code at the point indicated by the "remaining checks go here" comment in the code from the previous step:

```
// set a flag that assumes the password is OK
$pwdOK = true;
// trim leading and trailing white space
$_POST['pwd'] = trim($_POST['pwd']);
// if less than 6 characters, create alert and set flag to false
if (strlen($_POST['pwd']) < 6) {
  $error['pwd_length'] = 'Your password must be at least 6 characters';
  $pwdOK = false;
  }
// if no match, create alert and set flag to false
if ($_POST['pwd'] != trim($_POST['conf_pwd'])) {
  $error['pwd'] = 'Your passwords don\'t match';
  $pwdOK = false;
  }
// if password OK, encrypt it
if ($pwdOK) {
  $_POST['pwd'] = sha1($_POST['pwd']);
  }
```

The code starts by setting a variable that assumes the password is OK. After trimming any whitespace, the password is then subjected to two tests. The first test uses the PHP function strlen(), which determines the number of characters in any string passed to it, and checks that the trimmed password contains at least six characters. The second test checks whether the passwords match.

If either test fails (or both of them do), a suitable message is added to the $error array, and $pwdOK is set to false. However, if $pwdOK is still true, the password is passed to the sha1() function, which converts any string passed to it into a 40-character hexadecimal number—in effect, encrypting the string.

15

4. Create a new line immediately below the code you inserted in the previous step, open the Snippets panel, and double-click the Check email PCRE snippet in the PHP-DWCS3 folder that you installed in Chapter 11. The snippet inserts the regular expression that checks for illegal characters in an email address. Then use the regular expression to check the email, and add a message to the $error array if there's a problem like this:

```
if ($pwdOK) {
  $_POST['pwd'] = sha1($_POST['pwd']);
  }
// regex to identify illegal characters in email address
$checkEmail = '/^[^@]+@[^\s\r\n\'";,@%]+$/';
if (!preg_match($checkEmail, trim($_POST['email']))) {
  $error['email'] = 'Please enter a valid email address';
  }
```

5. The final check uses strlen() again to make sure that the username consists of a minimum number of characters. I have chosen 6, but you can use whatever number you like. This code should go after the final line of code in step 2. I have included the existing lines above and below the new code so you can see exactly where it goes.

```
$loginUsername = $_POST['username'];
if (strlen($loginUsername) < 6) {
  $error['length'] = 'Please select a username that contains at least➥
6 characters';
  }
$LoginRS__query = "SELECT username FROM users WHERE username=%s", ➥
GetSQLValueString($loginUsername, "text"));
```

6. Now that the checks are complete, you need to build the logic that determines whether the Insert Record server behavior is executed. All it requires is to wrap the server behavior in a conditional statement. Scroll down until you find the following block of code—it should be immediately above the DOCTYPE declaration:

```
85  if ((isset($_POST["MM_insert"])) && ($_POST["MM_insert"] == "form1")) {
86    $insertSQL = sprintf("INSERT INTO users (first_name, family_name, email, username, pwd, admin_priv)
    VALUES (%s, %s, %s, %s, %s, %s)",
87                       GetSQLValueString($_POST['first_name'], "text"),
88                       GetSQLValueString($_POST['family_name'], "text"),
89                       GetSQLValueString($_POST['email'], "text"),
90                       GetSQLValueString($_POST['username'], "text"),
91                       GetSQLValueString($_POST['pwd'], "text"),
92                       GetSQLValueString($_POST['admin_priv'], "text"));
93
94    mysql_select_db($database_connAdmin, $connAdmin);
95    $Result1 = mysql_query($insertSQL, $connAdmin) or die(mysql_error());
96  }
```

7. Wrap the entire block of code in the following if statement:

```
if (!$error) {
  // existing code on lines 85 through 96 in screenshot
  }
```

If no errors have been found, the $error array will contain zero elements, which, as you know, PHP treats as false. By placing the negation operator (an exclamation mark) in front of it, you get the reverse meaning. So, if $error contains no elements, this test equates to true, and the Insert Record server behavior will be executed. If errors are found, the test will equate to false, and the server behavior will be ignored.

8. The final change is within the main body of the document. Scroll down to the page heading (around line 107) just below the <body> tag, and insert the following code block between the heading and the opening <form> tag:

```
<h1>Register user </h1>
<?php
if ($error) {
  echo '<ul>';
  foreach ($error as $alert) {
    echo "<li class='warning'>$alert</li>\n";
    }
  echo '</ul>';
  }
?>
<form action="<?php echo $editFormAction; ?>" method="post" ➥
name="form1" id="newUser">
```

This uses the opposite test to the one in step 7. If the $error array contains any elements, a foreach loop iterates through the array and assigns each element to the temporary variable $alert, which is used to display the error messages as a bulleted list. (See Chapter 10 if you need to refresh your memory about foreach loops.)

Because $error is an empty array when the page first loads, the PHP script ignores this block of code unless the form has been submitted and contains errors.

9. Save register_user.php, and load it into a browser. Click the Insert record button without filling in any fields. The page should reload and display the following warnings:

Register user

- Please enter both first name and family name
- Your password must be at least 6 characters
- Please enter a valid email address
- Please select a username that contains at least 6 characters

If you have any problems, check your code against register_user_03.php in examples/ch15. The page contains no style rules, but if you add a warning class, you could make the error messages stand out in bold, red text.

10. Now, fill in several fields, but leave one blank and submit the form again. You should see the appropriate error message, but all the fields are empty.

15

Imagine the frustration of being forced to fill in all the details again because of a mistake in just one field. What you really need is a server behavior to provide the same solution you used in the contact form in Chapter 11. There isn't one, but you can make it yourself.

Building custom server behaviors

One reason for the great success of Dreamweaver is that, in addition to its massive range of features, it's also extensible. You can build your own server behaviors to take the tedium out of repetitive tasks.

To redisplay the contents of a text field after a form has been submitted, all you need to do is insert a PHP conditional statement between the quotes of the <input> element's value attribute like this:

```
value="<?php if (isset($_POST['field'])) {echo htmlentities( ➡
$_POST['field']);} ?>"
```

This checks whether the $_POST array element exists. If it does, it's passed to htmlentities() to avoid any problems with quotes, and the resulting output is inserted into the value attribute using echo. Apart from *field*, the code never changes. This consistency makes it ideal for creating a new server behavior, which involves the following steps:

1. Create a unique name for each block of code that the server behavior will insert into your page. The Server Behavior Builder generates this automatically for you.

2. Type the code into the Server Behavior Builder, replacing any changeable values with Dreamweaver parameters. The parameters act as placeholders until you insert the actual value through a dialog box when the server behavior is applied.

3. Tell Dreamweaver where to insert the code.

4. Design the server behavior dialog box.

Creating a Sticky Text Field server behavior

These instructions show you how to create your own server behavior to insert a conditional statement in the value attribute of a text field to preserve user input in any page. You must have a PHP page open in the Document window before you start.

1. In the Server Behaviors panel, click the plus button, and select New Server Behavior. In the dialog box that opens, make sure that Document type is set to PHP MySQL. Type Sticky Text Field in the Name field, and click OK.

2. This opens the Server Behavior Builder dialog box. Click the plus button next to Code blocks to insert. Dreamweaver suggests a name for the new code block based on the name of the new server behavior. Click OK to accept it. Dreamweaver fills in the remaining fields of the Server Behavior Builder like this:

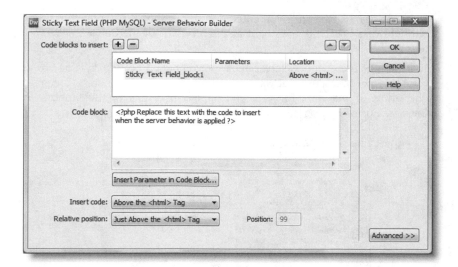

3. The Code block area in the center is where you insert the PHP code that you want to appear on the page. The value of *field* will change every time, so you need to replace it with a parameter. Parameter names must not contain any spaces, but they are used to label the server behavior dialog box, so it's a good idea to choose a descriptive name, such as FieldName. To insert a parameter, click the Insert Parameter in Code Block button at the appropriate point in the code, type the name in the dialog box, and click OK. Dreamweaver places it in the code with two @ characters on either side. You can also type the parameters in the code block directly yourself. Whichever method you use, replace the dummy text in the Code block area with this:

```
<?php if (isset($_POST['@@FieldName@@'])) {
echo htmlentities($_POST['@@FieldName@@']);} ?>
```

4. As soon as you add any parameters in the Code block area, the label on the OK button changes to Next, but first you need to tell Dreamweaver where you want the code to appear in the page. It needs to be applied to the value attribute of <input> tags, so select Relative to a Specific Tag from the Insert code drop-down menu.

5. This reveals two more drop-down menus. Select input/text for Tag, and As the Value of an Attribute for Relative position.

6. This triggers the appearance of another drop-down menu labeled Attribute. Select value. The bottom section of the Server Behavior Builder should now look like this:

15

This specifies that the code you entered in step 3 should be applied as the value attribute of a text field. Click Next at the top right of the Server Behavior Builder dialog.

7. To be able to use your new server behavior, you need to create a dialog box where you can enter the values that will be substituted for the parameters. Dreamweaver does most of the work for you, and on this occasion, the suggestions in the Generate Behavior Dialog Box dialog box are fine, so just click OK.

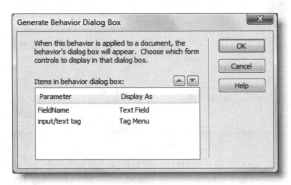

Creating a server behavior for Sticky Text Areas

The server behavior that you have just built works only with text fields, so it's worth building another to handle text areas. Unlike text fields, text areas don't have a value attribute.

1. Repeat steps 1 and 2 of the previous section, only this time, call the new server behavior Sticky Text Area.

2. In step 3 of the previous section, enter the following code in the Code block area:

```
<?php if (isset($_POST['@@TextArea@@'])) {echo ➥
$_POST['@@TextArea@@'];} ?>
```

I have split the code over two lines because of printing constraints, but you should enter the code all on a single line to avoid adding any whitespace between the <textarea> tags when this code is executed. You don't need htmlentities(), because the value is inserted directly between the tags as plain text.

3. Fill in the bottom section of the Server Behavior Builder as shown in the following screenshot. This places the content of the $_POST variable between the opening and closing <textarea> tags.

4. Click Next, and accept the defaults suggested for the server behavior dialog box.

Both server behaviors will be available in all PHP sites from the menu in the Server Behaviors panel.

Completing the user registration form

Now that you have built your own server behaviors, you can complete register_user.php.

Applying the Sticky Text Field server behavior

Applying the Sticky Text Field server behavior to each text field ensures that data already inserted won't be lost through the failure of any validation test. Continue working with register_user.php from earlier in the chapter.

1. In Design view, select the first_name text field. Click the plus button in the Server Behaviors panel. The new server behaviors are now listed. Select Sticky Text Field.

2. The Sticky Text Field dialog box appears. If you have selected the first_name text field correctly, the input/text tag field should automatically select first_name. If it's not selected, activate the drop-down menu to select it. Type the field's name in FieldName, as shown here, and click OK:

3. Dreamweaver inserts a dynamic content placeholder inside the text field in Design view. Open Split view, and as the next screenshot shows, the conditional statement you created in the Code block area of the Server Behavior Builder has been inserted, but @@FieldName@@ has been replaced by the actual name of the field:

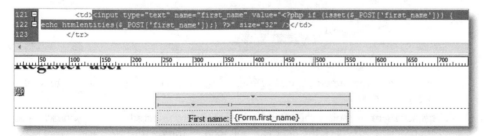

4. Apply the Sticky Text Field server behavior to the family_name, email, and username fields. Dreamweaver doesn't include password fields in the drop-down menu, so you can't apply the server behavior to them.

15

5. All instances of Sticky Text Field are now listed in the Server Behaviors panel. If you ever need to edit one, highlight it and double-click, or use the minus (–) button to remove it cleanly from your code.

6. Save `register_user.php`, and load it into a browser. Test it by entering an incomplete set of details. This time, the content of text fields is preserved. Check your code, if necessary, against `register_user_04.php` in examples/ch15.

Applying a dynamic value to a radio group

The Administrator radio buttons still don't respond to the changes. We'll fix that next. Continue working with `register_user.php` from the previous section.

1. When any errors are detected, you need checked="checked" to be inserted in the tag of the radio button that the user selected. Since the radio group is called admin_priv, the value you want is contained in $_POST['admin_priv']. Although you can type this directly into the Dynamic Radio Group dialog box, Dreamweaver lets you define $_POST, $_GET, and other super-global variables in the Bindings panel.

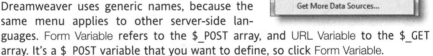

In the Bindings panel, click the plus button to display the menu shown alongside.

Dreamweaver uses generic names, because the same menu applies to other server-side languages. Form Variable refers to the $_POST array, and URL Variable to the $_GET array. It's a $_POST variable that you want to define, so click Form Variable.

2. Type admin_priv in the Name field of the Form Variable dialog box, and click OK. The new dynamic variable is now listed in the Bindings panel like this:

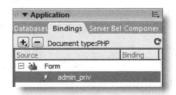

3. Select one of the radio buttons in Design view, and click the Dynamic button in the Property inspector.

4. The admin_priv radio group will be automatically selected in the Dynamic Radio Group dialog box. Click the lightning bolt icon to the right of the Select value equal to field. Then choose admin_priv from the Dynamic Data panel, as shown at the top of the next page.

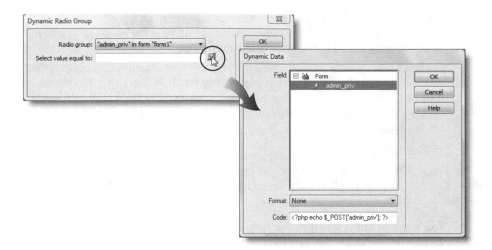

5. Save register_user.php, and load the page into a browser. If you set PHP error reporting to the level I recommended in Chapter 3, you'll see this unsightly mess:

> **Notice:** Undefined index: admin_priv in **C:\vhosts\egdwcs3\workfiles\ch15\register_user.php** on line 151
> type="radio" name="admin_priv" value="y" /> Yes
>
> **Notice:** Undefined index: admin_priv in **C:\vhosts\egdwcs3\workfiles\ch15\register_user.php** on line 155
> Administrator: type="radio" name="admin_priv" value="n" checked="checked" /> No

This is because the new code should be executed only *after* the form has been submitted. $_POST['admin_priv'] hasn't been defined when the page first loads, hence the reference to an "undefined index." Not only does this look bad, it prevents the browser from displaying the radio buttons and turns them into text fields instead.

> *Many hosting companies turn off the display of error notices, so the radio buttons would display correctly on many sites. However, it's important to eliminate all errors, because you never know when they may trip you up or leave you open to security exploits.*

6. In Design view, highlight one of the radio buttons so that you can easily locate the relevant code, and switch to Code view. The radio button code looks like this:

Delete both highlighted blocks of PHP code.

15

When you applied the dynamic value to the radio group in steps 3 and 4, Dreamweaver failed to replace the existing code, so to avoid conflicts, you need to delete it, as indicated in the preceding screenshot.

Dreamweaver uses a rather unusual PHP function called strcmp() to check whether $_POST['admin_priv'] is y or n. The function takes two arguments and returns 0 if they're exactly the same. Since 0 equates to false, the negation operator (!) converts it to true. If you find the logic difficult to follow, just take my word for it—it works.

> Note that the PHP code inserted by the Dynamic Radio Group *dialog box generates valid XHTML (*checked="checked"*), unlike the Record Insertion Form Wizard.*

7. You need to check whether the form has been submitted. Although the $_POST array is always set, it will be empty if the form hasn't been submitted. And as you should know by now, an empty array equates to false. Amend the beginning of both sections of radio button code (shown on lines 151 and 155 in the preceding screenshot) like this:

```
<input <?php if ($_POST && !(strcmp($_POST['admin_priv'],
```

8. Save the page, and load it into your browser. The radio buttons should now be back to normal. The only problem is that you don't have a default checked value when the page first loads. In one respect, it shouldn't be a problem, because you set a default value when defining the users table earlier. Unfortunately, Dreamweaver server behaviors treat unset values as NULL, causing your form to fail because admin_priv was defined as "not null." You can't even get round this by changing the column definition, because you would then end up with NULL as the default.

9. Change the code for the No radio button shown on line 155 in the preceding screenshot like this (the change made in step 7 is also shown in bold type):

```
<input <?php if (($_POST && !(strcmp($_POST['admin_priv'],"n"))) ➥
|| !$_POST) {echo "checked=\"checked\"";} ?> name="admin_priv" ➥
type="radio" value="n" />
```

I have enclosed the original test (as adapted in step 7) in an extra pair of parentheses to ensure that it's treated as a single unit. Then I added a second test:

```
|| !$_POST
```

This tests whether the $_POST array is empty. The result is this (in pseudocode):

if ((the form has been sent AND admin_priv is "n")
OR the form has not been sent) {mark the button "checked"}

10. Save register_user.php. You now have a user registration form that performs all the necessary checks before entering a new record into your database. Try it out. If all goes well, you should get no errors, but all the input fields will still be populated with the data you just input. Fortunately, that's easy to correct.

11. Scroll up to the last section of PHP code just above the DTD, which looks like this:

```
96    $Result1 = mysql_query($insertSQL, $connAdmin) or die(mysql_error());
97    }
98    }
99    ?><!DOCTYPE html PUBLIC "-//W3C//DTD XHTML 1.0 Transitional//EN"
```

Lines 96–97 in the screenshot are the last two lines of the Insert Record server behavior, followed (on line 98) by the closing brace that you inserted in step 7 of the section titled "Validating other fields."

12. Insert a new line between the braces shown on lines 97 and 98, and add this code:

```
// if the record has been inserted, clear the $_POST array
$_POST = array();
```

After the record has been inserted, you no longer need the contents of the $_POST array, so this simply turns it into an empty array.

13. If your PHP configuration has magic quotes turned on (and many hosting companies seem to use this setting), your sticky text fields will end up with backslashes escaping apostrophes in users' names. So, scroll down to the section of code that displays the error messages, and insert a new line just before the closing curly brace. Open the Snippets panel, and insert the POST stripslashes snippet that you installed in the PHP-DWCS3 folder in Chapter 11.

14. Save register_user.php, and check your code against register_user_05.php in site_check/ch10. Register a new user, and check the users table in phpMyAdmin. This time, the pwd column should contain a 40-character encrypted password.

Building an apparently simple user registration form has taken a lot of effort. You could have used it almost right away, after applying the Check New User server behavior, but before long, you would have ended up with a lot of unusable data in your database, not to mention the frustration of users when an input error results in all their data being wiped from the screen. The more time you spend refining the forms that interact with your database, the more time you will save in the long run.

Updating and deleting user records

The way you update or delete a database record is very similar to the process you used in the last chapter to display the contents of a record. First, you select the record from a list of all records and create a recordset that retrieves only the details of the selected record. In an update page, the recordset is used to populate a form identical to the one used to insert the record. After the user has made the desired changes, the form is submitted using an Update Record server behavior. In a delete page, it's not necessary to display all the details, but you should display sufficient information to identify the record and ask for confirmation. The page is then submitted to a Delete Record server behavior.

Keeping track of the selected record throughout the whole process is its primary key. It's first passed through a query string and stored in a hidden field in the update or delete page, so that when the form is submitted, MySQL knows which record to update or delete. Figure 15-4 summarizes the process.

15

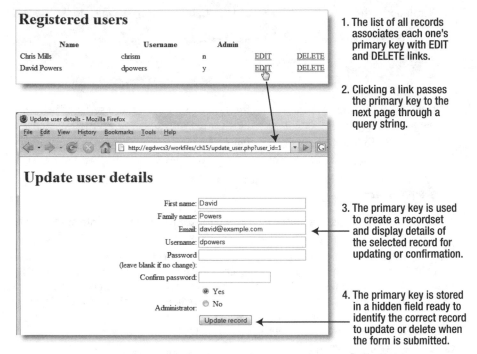

1. The list of all records associates each one's primary key with EDIT and DELETE links.

2. Clicking a link passes the primary key to the next page through a query string.

3. The primary key is used to create a recordset and display details of the selected record for updating or confirmation.

4. The primary key is stored in a hidden field ready to identify the correct record to update or delete when the form is submitted.

Figure 15-4. The primary key keeps track of the selected record in the update and delete process.

Let's start by creating the page to list all users currently registered in the database.

Listing registered users

Since the main techniques were covered in the last chapter, I have kept these instructions relatively brief.

1. Create three PHP pages, list_users.php, update_user.php, and delete_user.php, and save them in workfiles/ch15.

2. Give list_users.php a title and heading. Insert a table with two rows and five columns below the heading. Type Name, Username, and Admin in the first three cells of the first row, and EDIT and DELETE in the last two cells of the second row like this:

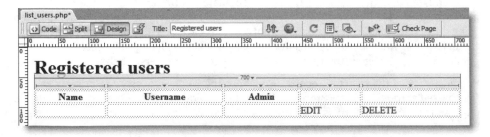

3. Open the Recordset dialog box by clicking the plus button in the Server Behaviors panel and selecting Recordset. You can also use the Recordset button on the Data tab of the Insert bar or Insert ➤ Data Objects ➤ Recordset.

4. Name the recordset listUsers, and select the connAdmin connection. This recordset only performs a SELECT operation, but you'll be editing the records later, so it's more consistent to use the same connection for all the pages.

With the Recordset dialog box in Simple mode, select the users table. Although you don't need all the columns, you do need most of them, so leave Columns set to All. Set Sort to family_name and Ascending. Click OK to create the recordset.

> *In Simple mode, you can sort by only one column. In Chapter 16, I'll show you how to use Advanced mode to sort by multiple columns.*

5. Drag first_name from the Bindings panel into the first cell of the second row of the table, and insert a space. Then drag family_name, and place it alongside. Drag username into the second cell of the second row, and admin_priv into the third cell. The table should now look like this:

Name	Username	Admin		
{listUsers.first_name} {listUsers.family_name}	{listUsers.username}	{listUsers.admin_priv}	EDIT	DELETE

6. Select the text in the fourth cell (EDIT), and turn it into a link to the update page in the same way as in "Adding a record's primary key to a query string" in Chapter 14. The necessary steps follow, but refer to the previous chapter for more details.

7. Click the Browse for File button to the right of the Link field in the Property inspector. In the Select File dialog box that opens, select update_user.php. Then click the Parameters button alongside the URL field.

8. In the Parameters dialog box, type user_id in the Name field. Then click the lightning bolt icon on the right of the Value field.

9. In the Dynamic Data dialog box, highlight user_id, and click OK. Click OK to close the Parameters dialog box. Then click OK (Choose on the Mac) to close the Select File dialog box.

10. Repeat steps 6–9 with the text in the fifth cell (DELETE). In step 7, select delete_user.php.

11. Now apply a repeat region to the second table row in the same way as in "Displaying the results of a recordset in a repeat region" in the last chapter. With your cursor inside the second row, select the entire row by clicking the <tr> tag in the Tag selector at the bottom of the Document window. Apply a Repeat Region server behavior.

12. Save list_users.php, and preview it in a browser. Mouse over the EDIT and DELETE links. The status bar of your browser should display something like this:

http://egdwcs3/workfiles/ch15/update_user.php?user_id=2

If necessary, check your code against list_users.php in examples/ch15.

15

Dreamweaver has a Record Update Form Wizard that creates the update form for you in the same way as the Record Insertion Form Wizard. The problem is that it doesn't validate the input. There's no point taking the trouble to validate data when it's first input into a database but neglecting to do so when updating it. Consequently, it makes more sense to adapt register_user.php.

The value attributes of each text field currently have the Sticky Text Field server behavior applied to them. This makes it impossible to bind the values from the record that you want to update unless you remove the Sticky Text Field server behavior. You could trust that no errors will occur when the update form is submitted. But that's trusting a great deal to fate. A better idea is to create a new server behavior that can then be reused on any update page.

Adapting the Sticky Text Field server behavior

As you have already seen, it's only when the form has been submitted—and errors detected—that the Sticky Text Field code executes. So if the $_POST variables haven't been set, you know the form hasn't been submitted, and that you need to display the values stored in the database instead.

Dreamweaver always uses the following naming convention to refer to the results of a recordset: $row_*RecordsetName*['*FieldName*']. So, all that's needed is to add an else clause to the existing code:

```php
<?php if (isset($_POST['field'])) {
  echo htmlentities($_POST['field']);
  } else {
  echo htmlentities($row_RecordsetName['FieldName']); } ?>
```

Creating the Sticky Edit Field server behavior

Most of the settings are identical to the Sticky Text Field server behavior that you built earlier, so you can use the existing server behavior to create the new one.

1. Make sure that you have a PHP page open, and click the plus button in the Server Behaviors panel. Select New Server Behavior.

2. Name the new server behavior Sticky Edit Field, and place a check mark in the box labeled Copy existing server behavior. This will populate a drop-down menu with the names of server behaviors you have already built (unfortunately, you can't base a new server behavior on one of Dreamweaver's). Select Sticky Text Field, and click OK.

3. Edit the contents of the Code block area like this:

```php
<?php if (isset($_POST['@@FieldName@@'])) {
  echo htmlentities($_POST['@@FieldName@@']);
  } else {
  echo htmlentities($row_@@RecordsetName@@['@@FieldName@@']);} ?>
```

Dreamweaver will use the new parameter—@@RecordsetName@@—in combination with @@FieldName@@ to build a variable like $row_getUser['family_name'].

> *Sometimes Dreamweaver prevents you from using the same parameter name in more than one server behavior. If that happens, change both instances of @@FieldName@@ to @@Field@@.*

4. Click Next. Dreamweaver warns you that the server behavior's HTML file already exists and asks if you want to overwrite it. The HTML file controls the server behavior's dialog box, which needs to be redesigned, so the answer is Yes.

5. In the Generate Behavior Dialog Box dialog box, reset Display as for RecordsetName by clicking to the right of the existing value and selecting Recordset Menu. Set FieldName to Recordset Field Menu, and reorder the items as shown here. Click OK.

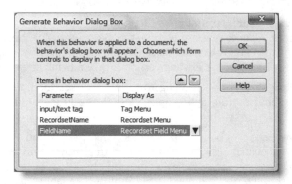

To create a similar server behavior for text areas, name it Sticky Edit Area, and select Sticky Text Area in step 2. The code block in step 3 should look like this:

```php
<?php if (isset($_POST['@@FieldName@@'])) {
  echo $_POST['@@FieldName@@'];
  } else {
  echo $row_@@RecordsetName@@['@@FieldName@@'];} ?>
```

Building the update and delete pages

Creating an update page involves the following steps:

1. Create a form to display each field of the record.

2. Create a recordset to retrieve the record's existing values. This uses the primary key passed through the URL query string as a filter to retrieve only the selected record.

3. Add a hidden field to the form to store the primary key.

4. Bind the values to each form field so that they're displayed ready for editing.

5. Apply an Update Record server behavior to implement the changes when the form is submitted.

Since you already have the form in register_user.php, step 1 simply involves making a copy of the existing page and cleaning it up in preparation for the remaining steps. There are two other issues that you need to take into consideration, as follows:

15

- The pwd and conf_pwd fields use the password type, so you can't display the value retrieved from the database. Even if you could, the password is now encrypted and cannot be decrypted. (I'll discuss encryption later in the chapter.)

- The current validation code will prevent you from updating a user's details because the same username already exists in the database—and belongs to none other than the user you're trying to update!

Applying the Update Record server behavior

Although these instructions are based on using register_user.php, only steps 1–3 are specific to this page. The remaining steps apply to all pages.

1. Open register_user.php, and press Ctrl+Shift+S/Shift+Cmd+S (File ➤ Save As) to save the page as update_user.php. In the Save As dialog box, select update_user.php in workfiles/ch15, and click Save. Dreamweaver will warn you that the page already exists, but the existing version is only a blank page, so click Yes.

2. Adjust the page's title and heading to reflect that it's for updating user details. Select the submit button, and change Value in the Property inspector to Update record.

3. In the Server Behaviors panel, highlight the Insert Record and the four Sticky Text Field server behaviors. Click the minus button to remove them from the page. The Check New Username server behavior shouldn't be listed, because you edited it in register_user.php. You still need it, but it must be adapted, as you'll see shortly.

   The page still contains all the validation code that you added earlier but is now ready for conversion. If you want to make sure that you have cleaned up the page correctly, check your file against update_user_01.php in examples/ch15.

4. Create a recordset called getUser to get the details of the record to be updated in the users table. The record's primary key, user_id, will be passed through a query string from list_users.php, so use that to filter the results, as shown here:

5. Add a hidden field to the form to store the primary key (see "Passing information through a hidden field" in Chapter 9 if you're not sure what a hidden field is). In the Property inspector, give the hidden field the same name as the primary key by entering user_id in the field on the left. It needs to get its value from the recordset, so click the lightning bolt icon alongside the Value field, as shown here:

6. In the Dynamic Data dialog box, expand Recordset (getUser), and select user_id. Click OK. This binds the value of user_id from the recordset to the hidden field, which is also called user_id. This ensures that the primary key is passed to the Update Record server behavior and updates the correct record.

7. In the Server Behaviors panel, click the plus button, and select Update Record. Alternatively, use the Update Record button on the Data tab of the Insert bar, or Insert ➤ Data Objects ➤ Update Record ➤ Update Record. If you use either of these methods, make sure you don't select Record Update Form Wizard by mistake.

8. Filling in the Update Record dialog box is simple. To update a record, you need a MySQL user account with administrative privileges, so select connAdmin as Connection. Then select the name of the table you want to update from the Update table drop-down menu. Dreamweaver should populate the Columns area with all the correct details. In the same way as with an Insert Record server behavior, it lists each column and specifies where it gets its value from and what type of data it contains. The most important one is the first, which identifies the record's primary key, as shown in the following screenshot. It gets this value from the hidden field you created in steps 5 and 6.

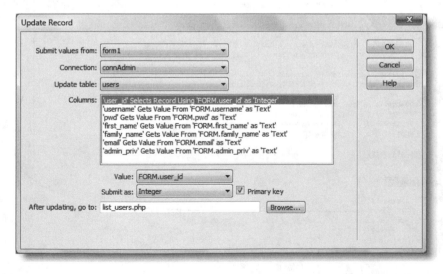

The final field, labeled After updating, go to, lets you specify where to redirect the user after the record has been updated. It's a good idea to go back to the list of records, so enter list_users.php. Check that all the details are right, and click OK.

You can check your code against update_user_02.php in examples/ch15.

That's basically all there is to applying an Update Record server behavior, apart from binding the results of the recordset to each form field. However, update_user.php has all the validation code inherited from register_user.php, so you need to merge the new code with the existing code.

Merging the Update Record server behavior with the validation code

Dreamweaver doesn't give you any choice where to locate server behavior code that goes above the DOCTYPE declaration. It follows an internal set of rules designed to ensure that each block of code exists in harmony with its neighbors. However, as long as you keep a server behavior intact, you can move it to fit in with your own conditional logic. So you need to move the Update Record server behavior code, and tweak the password and duplicate username checks.

1. Open Code view. Just above the DOCTYPE declaration, you will find an empty conditional statement, which was left behind when you removed the Insert Record server behavior in step 3 of the preceding section. You now need to move the Update Record server behavior code (shown on lines 37–56 of the following screenshot) to inside the braces shown on lines 116 and 120. I have used Dreamweaver's Code Collapse feature to hide the recordset code and all the validation checks, so take careful note of the actual code (as always, the line numbers are only a guide).

```
37   if ((isset($_POST["MM_update"])) && ($_POST["MM_update"] == "form1")) {
38     $updateSQL = sprintf("UPDATE users SET username=%s, pwd=%s, first_name=%s, family_name=%s,
       email=%s, admin_priv=%s WHERE user_id=%s",
39                          GetSQLValueString($_POST['username'], "text"),
40                          GetSQLValueString($_POST['pwd'], "text"),
41                          GetSQLValueString($_POST['first_name'], "text"),
42                          GetSQLValueString($_POST['family_name'], "text"),
43                          GetSQLValueString($_POST['email'], "text"),
44                          GetSQLValueString($_POST['admin_priv'], "text"),
45                          GetSQLValueString($_POST['user_id'], "int"));
46
47     mysql_select_db($database_connAdmin, $connAdmin);
48     $Result1 = mysql_query($updateSQL, $connAdmin) or die(mysql_error());
49
50     $updateGoTo = "list_users.php";
51     if (isset($_SERVER['QUERY_STRING'])) {
52       $updateGoTo .= (strpos($updateGoTo, '?')) ? "&" : "?";
53       $updateGoTo .= $_SERVER['QUERY_STRING'];
54     }
55     header(sprintf("Location: %s", $updateGoTo));
56   }
57
58 ⊞ $colnam...
115
116   if (!$error) {
117
118   // if the record has been inserted, clear the $_POST array
119   $_POST = array();
120   }
121   ?><!DOCTYPE html PUBLIC "-//W3C//DTD XHTML 1.0 Transitional//EN"
```

2. Although it won't do any harm, the line of code that clears the POST array (on line 119 of the preceding screenshot) is no longer necessary. You can remove it and its accompanying comment, but *don't* remove the closing brace shown on line 120.

3. If you used Code Collapse while moving the Update Record server behavior in the previous step, expand the collapsed section and scroll up to the following line of code (it should now be around line 51):

```
$MM_flag = "MM_insert";
```

Change it to

```
$MM_flag = "MM_update";
```

This is the name of a hidden field that Dreamweaver uses to check whether to execute the Update Record server behavior code. It will now ensure that the form validation checks are run before updating the database.

4. About half a dozen lines further down is the code that checks the password. When a user's record is being updated, you either want to preserve the same password or to set a new one. There are several ways to handle this, but the simplest is to decide that if pwd is left blank, the existing password will be maintained. Otherwise, the password needs to be checked and encrypted as before.

Amend the password validation code as follows (new code shown in bold type):

```
$_POST['pwd'] = trim($_POST['pwd']);
// if password field is empty, use existing password
if (empty($_POST['pwd'])) {
  $_POST['pwd'] = $row_getUser['pwd'];
  }
// otherwise, conduct normal checks
else {
  // if less than 6 characters, create alert and set flag to false
  if (strlen($_POST['pwd']) < 6) {
    $error['pwd_length'] = 'Your password must be at least 6➡
  characters';
    $pwdOK = false;
    }
  // if no match, create alert and set flag to false
  if ($_POST['pwd'] != trim($_POST['conf_pwd'])) {
    $error['pwd'] = 'Your passwords don\'t match';
    $pwdOK = false;
    }
  // if new password OK, encrypt it
  if ($pwdOK) {
    $_POST['pwd'] = sha1($_POST['pwd']);
    }
  }
```

This checks whether $_POST['pwd'] is empty. If it is, the value of the existing password as retrieved by the getUser recordset is assigned to $_POST['pwd']. Because the existing password is already encrypted, there is no need to pass it to sha1(). If $_POST['pwd'] isn't empty, the else clause executes the checks inherited from register_user.php.

15

> *If you discover that your password fields are blank after updating, make sure that the getUser recordset code is above the validation check. You can recognize it easily. It is ten lines long, and nearly every line includes getUser. If in doubt, check the download files.*

5. The final validation check that needs to be amended is the one that tests whether the username is already in use in the database. Because you're updating an existing user, it should be obvious that—unless you change the username—this test will always return true: the username already belongs to the record that you're updating.

   What's needed this time is to check that nobody other than the current user has the same username. This allows the current username to be retained or a new one to be created. The Check New Username server behavior is no longer editable through the Server Behaviors panel. What's more, it doesn't have the option that you need. So there's nothing else for it but to edit the SQL query manually. Scroll down until you find the following line of code:

```
93    $LoginRS__query = sprintf("SELECT username FROM users WHERE username=%s", GetSQLValueString(
      $loginUsername, "text"));
```

6. Insert your cursor between %s and the double quote, add a space, and type AND user_id !=. Move your cursor to the right of the double quote, so that it's just before the comma, and type a period followed by $_POST['user_id']. When you have finished, the code should look like this (new code is in bold):

```
$LoginRS__query = sprintf("SELECT username FROM users WHERE ➡
username=%s AND user_id !=" . $_POST['user_id'], GetSQLValueString( ➡
$loginUsername, "text"));
```

   This amends the SQL query so that it excludes the current record (identified by the user_id primary key) from its results. The user_id is stored in the form's hidden field, so it can be retrieved from the $_POST array. In SQL != means "is not"—the same as in PHP—so this simply looks for records where the user_id is not the same as the current one. Save the page, and check your code against update_user_03. php in examples/ch15.

> *Although SQL is an internationally recognized standard for communicating with databases, like English, it has a lot of dialects. The official standard uses <> as the "not equal" operator. However, most leading database systems, including MySQL, PostgreSQL, Oracle, and Microsoft SQL Server, also support !=, which is my preferred style. MySQL supports both <> and !=, so feel free to use whichever suits you better. We'll look at how SQL is written in the next chapter, because a basic knowledge of SQL is essential to working with server behaviors.*

Binding the field values to the update form

The final stage of building the update form involves binding the results of the getUser recordset to the form fields so that the existing values are ready for editing. The text fields are quite easy, but the radio button group needs special handling.

1. Switch to Design view, and select the first_name field in the form. In the Server Behaviors panel, click the plus button, and select Sticky Edit Field.

   Since getUser is the only recordset on this page, it's selected automatically in the Sticky Edit Field dialog box, but make sure you choose the right one if you use this server behavior on a page that has two or more recordsets. Select the field's name from the FieldName drop-down menu, as shown here:

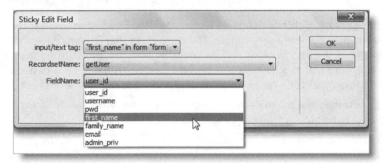

2. Apply the Sticky Edit Field server behavior in the same way to the family_name, email, and username fields. In Design view, the form should end up looking like the screenshot alongside, with dynamic text placeholders in the first four fields.

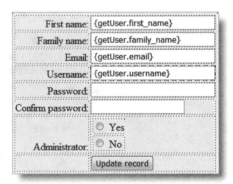

   If you're not using a validation script and don't need the edit fields to be sticky, select each form field in turn and insert its value from the recordset in the Bindings *panel. To apply the PHP* htmlentities() *function after the dynamic text has been inserted, double-click the dynamic text listing in the* Server Behaviors *panel, and select* Encode – HTML Encode *from the* Format *menu in the* Dynamic Text *dialog box.*

3. The radio buttons present an interesting challenge. When the page first loads, you want the value stored in the database for admin_priv to be selected; but if the form is submitted with errors, and you have changed the value of admin_priv, you want the new value to be shown.

15

Select one of the radio buttons in Design view, and click the Dynamic button in the Property inspector. In the Dynamic Radio Group dialog box, click the lightning bolt icon, and select admin_priv from the getUser recordset. Click OK in both dialog boxes. (This is the same as step 4 in "Applying a dynamic value to a radio group.")

4. Switch to Code view. The code for the radio group should now look like this:

```
194        <td><input <?php if (!(strcmp($row_getUser['admin_priv'],"y"))) {echo "checked=\"checked\"";}
?> <?php if ($_POST && !(strcmp($_POST['admin_priv'],"y"))) {echo "checked=\"checked\"";} ?> type="radio"
name="admin_priv" value="y" />
195            Yes</td>
196        </tr>
197        <tr>
198        <td><input <?php if (!(strcmp($row_getUser['admin_priv'],"n"))) {echo "checked=\"checked\"";}
?> <?php if (($_POST && !(strcmp($_POST['admin_priv'],"n"))) || !$_POST) {echo "checked=\"checked\"";} ?>
type="radio" name="admin_priv" value="n" />
199            No</td>
```

If the sight of all this code strikes terror into your heart, don't worry; the changes you need to make are very simple. The extra code that Dreamweaver has inserted consists of the first block of PHP on lines 194 and 198. Basically, all that you need do is ensure that this new section of code runs when the page is first loaded, and that the original code runs only after the form has been submitted.

Let's first map out the logic in terms of pseudocode. What needs to happen inside the Yes radio button's <input> tag is this:

*if (the form has NOT been submitted AND the value of admin_priv
  in the database is "y") {mark the button "checked"}
elseif (the form has been submitted AND the form value of admin_priv
  is "y") {mark the button "checked"}*

You know that when the page first loads, the form hasn't been submitted, so the $_POST array will have zero elements (and therefore equate to false). This means that the necessary check can be performed by inserting !$_POST into the conditional statements of the new code. The original code from the insert form now deals with the alternative scenario, so you need to change the if in the original code to elseif. To make the changes easier to follow, you may find it helpful to indent the code as I have done here. The changes are shown in bold type.

```php
<td><input
<?php
if (!$_POST && !(strcmp($row_getUser['admin_priv'],"y"))) {
  echo "checked=\"checked\"";
  }
elseif ($_POST && !(strcmp($_POST['admin_priv'],"y"))) {
  echo "checked=\"checked\"";
  }
?>
type="radio" name="admin_priv" value="y" />
Yes</td>
</tr>
```

```
<tr>
  <td><input
  <?php
  if (!$_POST && !(strcmp($row_getUser['admin_priv'],"n"))) {
    echo "checked=\"checked\"";
    }
  elseif ($_POST && !(strcmp($_POST['admin_priv'],"n"))) {
    echo "checked=\"checked\"";
    }
  ?>
type="radio" name="admin_priv" value="n" />
  No</td>
```

There are two other important points to note about the preceding code. First, I have removed the closing and opening PHP tags (?> <?php) immediately preceding elseif. Dreamweaver's automatic code generation normally surrounds each new block of PHP code with opening and closing tags, even when there is no XHTML code in between. In the vast majority of cases, this makes no difference. However, in this particular case, leaving the redundant tags in the code causes a syntax error. The second point to note is that some code has been removed from the final elseif clause, as shown here:

```
elseif ((($_POST && !(strcmp($_POST['admin_priv'],"n"))) || !$_POST)
```

The code is no longer appropriate, because the !$_POST situation is now covered by the if part of the conditional statement.

5. Switch back to Design view, and add some text to the Password label, indicating that the field should be left blank if the same password is being kept. Compare your code with update_user_04.php in examples/ch15 if you have any problems.

Creating the delete user page

You'll be pleased to know that deleting a record is simpler. It's similar to an update page. However, it's an irreversible action, so it's essential to get confirmation not only that the deletion should go ahead but also that the correct record is being deleted. Since you need the same recordset as in the update page, you can save time by copying it.

1. Open delete_user.php in the Document window.

2. Open update_user.php, or switch to it if it's still open.

3. In the Server Behaviors panel, highlight Recordset (getUser), right-click, and select Copy from the context menu.

4. Switch back to delete_user.php, right-click inside the Server Behaviors panel, and select Paste. Bingo, one quick, easy recordset—something I thought you'd appreciate after all that digging around inside Code view.

15

505

5. Give the page a heading and title, and insert a form. Use the Bindings panel to insert some details that will identify the user (this is the same as displaying details of the feedback record in the last chapter), and add a submit button named delete with a suitable label. The screenshot shows a suggested layout:

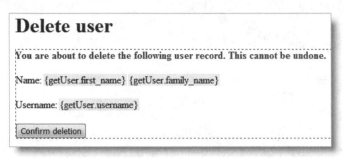

6. Insert a hidden field into the form. Name it user_id, and click the lightning bolt icon in the Property inspector to set the field's Value to user_id from the getUser record-set. The Delete Record server behavior needs this to know which record to delete.

7. Apply a Delete Record server behavior (use the plus button in the Server Behaviors panel, the Data tab of the Insert bar, or Insert ➤ Data Objects ➤ Delete Record). Fill in the Delete Record dialog box as shown in the next screenshot. Make sure that you choose the connection that has administrative privileges.

When you select the table from which the record is to be deleted, Dreamweaver should automatically select the correct value for the Primary key column. However, the server behavior uses the hidden field to identify the correct record to delete, so make sure you select Form Variable as the Primary key value, and that the primary key's name (user_id) is entered in the text field alongside. After the record has been deleted, it's a good idea to load the complete list, so enter list_users.php in the final field labeled After deleting, go to. Click OK to insert the server behavior.

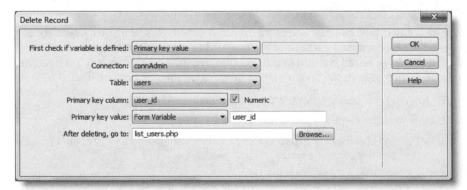

8. That's all there is to it. You can check your code against delete_user.php in examples/ch15.

Now that you have completed the user registration system, test it thoroughly, and use the DELETE links to get rid of any records that contain unencrypted passwords. When you have finished, make sure that you have at least two records in the users table: one with administrator privileges and one without.

Before showing you how to create a login system and control access to your pages, let's take a short break to look at PHP sessions, which are not only the technology behind user authentication, but also a powerful way of keeping track of information and passing it from page to page.

What sessions are and how they work

The Web is a brilliant illusion. When you visit a well-designed website, you get a great feeling of continuity, as though flipping through the pages of a book or a magazine. Everything fits together as a coherent entity. The reality is quite different. Each part of an individual page is stored and handled separately by the web server. Apart from needing to know where to send the relevant files, the server has no interest in who you are, nor is it interested in the PHP script it has just executed. PHP **garbage collection** (yes, that's what it's actually called) destroys variables and other resources used by a script as soon as they're no longer required. But it's not like garbage collection at your home, where it's taken away, say, once a week. With PHP, it's instant: the server memory is freed up for the next task. Even variables in the $_POST and $_GET arrays persist only while being passed from one page to the next. Unless the information is stored in some other way, such as a hidden form field, it's lost.

To get around these problems, PHP (in common with other server-side languages) uses **sessions**. A session ensures continuity by storing a random identifier on the web server and on the visitor's computer (as a cookie). Because the identifier is unique to each visitor, all the information stored in session variables is directly related to that visitor and cannot be seen by anyone else.

> *The security offered by sessions is adequate for most user authentication, but it is not 100 percent foolproof. For credit card and other financial transactions, you should use an SSL connection verified by a digital certificate. To learn more about this and other aspects of building security into your PHP sites,* Pro PHP Security *by Chris Snyder and Michael Southwell (Apress, ISBN-13: 978-1-59059-508-4) is essential reading. Although aimed at readers with an intermediate to advanced knowledge of PHP, it contains a lot of practical advice of value to all skill levels.*

Creating PHP sessions

Creating a session is easy. Just put this command in every PHP page that you want to use in a session:

```
session_start();
```

15

507

This command should be called only once in each page, and it must be called before the PHP script generates any output, so the ideal position is immediately after the opening PHP tag. If any output is generated before the call to session_start(), the command fails, and the session won't be activated for that page. This is exactly the same issue that affects the header() function, if any output is generated before you call the function. The solution is the same and was described in "Avoiding the 'Headers already sent' error" in Chapter 12.

Creating and destroying session variables

You create a session variable by adding it to the $_SESSION superglobal array in the same way you would assign an ordinary variable. Say you want to store a visitor's name and display a greeting. If the name is submitted in a login form as $_POST['name'], you assign it like this:

```
$_SESSION['name'] = $_POST['name'];
```

$_SESSION['name'] can now be used in any page that begins with session_start(). Because session variables are stored on the server, you should get rid of them as soon as they are no longer required by your script or application. Unset a session variable like this:

```
unset($_SESSION['name']);
```

To unset *all* session variables—for instance, when you're logging someone out—set the $_SESSION superglobal array to an empty array, like this:

```
$_SESSION = array();
```

Do not be tempted to try unset($_SESSION). *It not only clears the current session but also prevents any further sessions from being stored.*

Destroying a session

By itself, unsetting all the session variables effectively prevents any of the information from being reused, but you should also destroy the session with the following command:

```
session_destroy();
```

By destroying a session like this, there is no risk of an unauthorized person gaining access either to a restricted part of the site or to any information exchanged during the session. However, a visitor may forget to log out, so it's not always possible to guarantee that the session_destroy() command will be triggered, which is why it's so important not to store sensitive information in a session variable.

> *You may find the deprecated functions* session_register() *and* session_unregister() *in old scripts. Use* $_SESSION['*variable_name*'] *and* unset($_SESSION['*variable_name*']) *instead.*

Checking that sessions are enabled

Sessions should be enabled by default in PHP. A quick way to check is to load session1. php in examples/ch15 into a browser. Type your name in the text field, and click the Submit button. When session2.php loads, you should see your name and a link to the next page. Click the link. If session3.php displays your name and a confirmation that sessions are working, your setup is fine. Click the link to page 2 to destroy the session.

If you don't see the confirmation on the third page, go back to Chapter 3 to check your PHP configuration. Make sure that session.save_path points to a valid folder that the web server can write to. Also make sure that a software firewall or other security system is not blocking access to the folder specified in session.save_path.

Registering and authenticating users

As you have just seen, session variables enable you to keep track of a visitor. If you can identify visitors, you can also determine whether they have the right to view certain pages. There are four User Authentication server behaviors, as follows:

- **Log In User:** This queries a database to check whether a user is registered and has provided the correct password. You can also check whether a user belongs to a particular group to distinguish between, say, administrators and ordinary users.

- **Restrict Access to Page:** This prevents visitors from viewing a page unless they have logged in and (optionally) have the correct group privileges. Anyone not logged in is sent to the login page but can be automatically redirected to the originally selected page after login.

- **Log Out User:** This brings the current session to an end and prevents the user from returning to any restricted page without first logging back in again.

- **Check New Username:** This checks whether a particular username is already in use. You adapted it earlier in the chapter, when creating the user registration form

These server behaviors are identical to those in Dreamweaver 8.0.2.

Creating a login system

Now that you have a way of registering users, you need to create a way for them to log in to restricted areas of your site. Building the login system is a lot simpler than building the registration system.

15

Creating the login page

1. Create a PHP page called `login.php` in `workfiles/ch15`. Lay out the page with a form, two text fields, and a submit button, as shown here. Since you'll be applying a server behavior, there is no need to set the `action` or `method` attributes of the form.

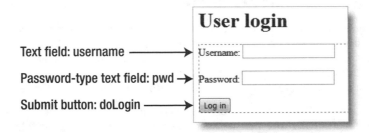

2. The Log In User server behavior expects you to designate two pages: one that the user will be taken to if the login is successful and another if it fails. Create one page called `success.php`, and enter some content to indicate that the login was successful. Call the other page `loginfail.php`, and insert a message telling the user that the login failed, together with a link back to `login.php`.

3. Make sure `login.php` is the active page in the Dreamweaver workspace. Click the plus button in the Server Behaviors panel, and select User Authentication ➤ Log In User. (You can also apply the server behavior from the Data tab of the Insert bar or from the Data Objects submenu of the Insert menu.)

4. The Log In User dialog box has a lot of options, but their meaning should be obvious, at least for the first two sections. Select the connAdmin connection, the users table, and the username and password columns, using the settings shown alongside.

The third section asks you to specify which pages to send the user to, depending on whether the login succeeds or fails. Between the text fields for the filenames is a check box labeled Go to previous URL (if it exists). This works in conjunction with the Restrict Access to Page server behavior that you will use shortly. If someone tries to access a restricted page without first logging in, the user is redirected to the login page. If you select this option, after a successful login, the user will be taken directly to the page that originally refused access. Unless you always want users to view a specific page when first logging in, this is quite a user-friendly option.

The final section of the dialog box allows you to specify whether access should be restricted on the basis of username and password (the default), or whether you also want to specify an access level. The access level must be stored in one of your database columns. For this login page, set Get level from to admin_priv. Click OK to apply the server behavior.

5. A drawback with the Dreamweaver Log In User server behavior is that it has no option for handling encrypted passwords, so you need to make a minor adjustment by hand. Open Code view, and place your cursor immediately to the right of the opening PHP tag on line 2. Press Enter/Return to insert a new line, and type the following code:

```
if (isset($_POST['pwd'])) { $_POST['pwd'] = sha1($_POST['pwd']); }
```

This checks whether the form has been submitted, and it uses sha1() to encrypt the password. I have reassigned the value back to $_POST['pwd'] so that Dreamweaver continues to recognize the server behavior; this way, you can still edit it through the Server Behaviors panel. Although Dreamweaver doesn't object to you placing the line of code here, it will automatically remove it if you ever decide to remove the server behavior.

> It's important to realize that you're not decrypting the version of the password stored in the database. You can't—the sha1() function performs one-way encryption. You verify the user's password by encrypting it again and comparing the two encrypted versions.

6. Save login.php. You can check your code against login.php in examples/ch15.

Restricting access to individual pages

Now that you have a means of logging in registered users, you can protect sensitive pages in your site. When working with PHP sessions, there is no way of protecting an entire folder. Sessions work on a page-by-page basis, so you need to protect each page individually. The Adobe Dreamweaver Developer Toolbox (formerly Kollection, developed by InterAKT, which was acquired by Adobe in 2006) does let you restrict access to a folder, but it achieves this by applying the same code to every page in the folder.

Applying the Restrict Access to Page server behavior

These instructions show you how to restrict access to one page. You need to do the same on every page that you want to protect with a password.

1. Open success.php. Click the plus button in the Server Behaviors panel, and select User Authentication ➤ Restrict Access to Page.

2. In the Restrict Access to Page dialog box, select the radio button to restrict access based on Username, password, and access level. Then click the Define button.

15

3. The Define Access Levels dialog box lets you specify acceptable values. What may come as a bit of a surprise is that it's not the column name that Dreamweaver is interested in but the value retrieved from the column. Consequently, it's not admin_priv that you enter here but y or n.

As you might have noticed, although Dreamweaver gives you the option to specify different access levels, the Log In User server behavior sends all successful logins to the same page. If you have different login pages for each type of user, this is fine; you select the appropriate value. So, for an administrator's login page, just enter y in the Name field, and click the plus button to register it in the Access levels area.

However, if you want to use the same login form for everyone, you need to register all access levels for the first page, and then use PHP conditional logic to distinguish between different types of users. So, for success.php, also enter n in the Name field, and click the plus button to register it. Then click OK.

4. After defining the access levels, hold down the Shift key, and select them all in the Select level(s) field. Then, either browse to login.php, or type the filename directly in the field labeled If access denied, go to. The dialog box should look like this:

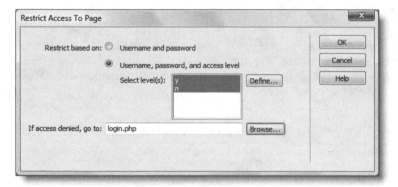

5. Click OK to apply the server behavior, and save success.php.

6. Try to view the page in a browser. Instead of success.php, you should see login.php. You have been denied access and taken to the login page instead.

7. Enter a username and password that you registered earlier, and click Log in. You should be taken to success.php. You can check your code against success_01.php in examples/ch15.

When developing pages that will be part of a restricted area, I find it best to leave the application of this server behavior to the very last. Testing pages becomes an exercise in frustration if you need to be constantly logging in and out.

I'll come back to the question of how to deal with different access levels, but first, let's look at logging out.

Logging out users

The Dreamweaver Log Out User server behavior is quick and easy to apply.

Applying the Log Out User server behavior

The Log Out User server behavior will automatically insert a logout link in your page, so you need to position your cursor at the point you want the link to be created.

1. Press Enter/Return to create a new paragraph in success.php.

2. Click the plus button in the Server Behaviors panel, and select User Authentication ➤ Log Out User.

3. The Log Out User dialog box gives you the option to log out when a link is clicked or when the page loads. In this case, you want the default option, which is to log out when a link is clicked, and to create a new logout link. Browse to login.php, or type the filename directly into the field labeled When done, go to. Click OK.

4. Save success.php, and load the page into a browser. Click the Log out link, and you will be taken back to the login page. Type the URL of success.php in the browser address bar, and you will be taken back to the login page until you log in again. You can check your code against success_02.php in examples/ch15.

Understanding how Dreamweaver tracks users

As I mentioned earlier, PHP sessions are the technology that lies behind the User Authentication server behaviors. The Log In User server behavior creates the following two session variables that control access to restricted pages:

- $_SESSION['MM_Username']: This stores the user's username.
- $_SESSION['MM_UserGroup']: This stores the user's access level.

You can use these in a variety of ways. The simplest, and perhaps most important, use is to present different content on the first page after logging in. The following exercises are based on success.php but can be used with any page that begins with session_start() after a user has logged in.

Displaying different content depending on access levels

The following instructions assume that you have created at least one administrator and an ordinary user in the users table.

1. In success.php, insert two paragraphs: one indicating that it's for administrators, the other indicating that it's for nonadministrators. The actual content is unimportant.

2. Switch to Code view, and add the PHP code highlighted in bold around the two paragraphs like this:

```php
<?php if ($_SESSION['MM_UserGroup'] == 'y') { ?>
<p>Content and links for administators</p>
<?php } else { ?>
<p>Content and links for non-administrators</p>
<?php } ?>
```

15

This is simple PHP conditional logic. If the value of $_SESSION['MM_UserGroup'] is y, display the XHTML inside the first set of curly braces. If it's not, show the other material. There's only one paragraph in each conditional block, but you can put as much as you want.

3. Save the page, and log in as an administrator. You'll see only the first paragraph. Log out and log back in as an ordinary user. This time you'll see the second paragraph. You can compare your code with success_03.php in examples/ch15.

Any content that you want to be seen by both groups should go outside this PHP conditional statement. (In success_03.php, you'll see that the page heading and the log out link are common to both groups.) By using this sort of branching logic in the first page, you can restrict access to subsequent pages according to the specific access level. So, the links in the first section would point to pages that only administrators are permitted to see.

Greeting users by name

Since the user's username is stored in $_SESSION['MM_Username'], you could use that to display a greeting, but it's much friendlier to use the person's real name. All that's needed is a simple recordset.

1. In success.php, create a recordset using the following settings in Simple mode:

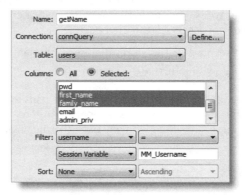

By setting Filter to username = Session Variable MM_Username, the recordset retrieves the values of the first_name and family_name columns for the currently logged in user.

2. Open the Bindings panel, and drag the first_name and family_name dynamic text placeholders into the page like this:

When the page loads, the dynamic text placeholders will be replaced by the values drawn from the recordset. You can check your code against success_04.php.

Of course, if you want other details about the user, such as user_id, amend the settings in the Recordset dialog box to retrieve all the columns you need.

Creating your own $_SESSION variables from user details

To avoid the need to create a recordset on every page where you want to use these details, store them as $_SESSION variables. The code needs to be inserted *after* the recordset code, which Dreamweaver places immediately above the DTD. The pattern Dreamweaver uses for recordset results looks like this:

```
$row_recordsetName['fieldName']
```

So, to create $_SESSION variables from first_name and family_name in session.php, you would add the following code immediately before the closing PHP tag above the DTD:

```
$_SESSION['first_name'] = $row_getName['first_name'];
$_SESSION['family_name'] = $row_getName['family_name'];
```

You're not restricted to using the same element names for the variables. You could do this instead:

```
$_SESSION['full_name'] = $row_getName['first_name'].' '. ➡
$row_getName['family_name'];
```

You can see this code in action in success_05.php in examples/ch15.

Redirecting to a personal page after login

You might want to provide users with their own personal page or folder after logging in. This is very easy to do, particularly if you base the name of the personal page or folder on the username.

If the name of the personal page is in the form *username*.php, enter the following in the Log In User dialog box in the field labeled If login succeeds, go to (see step 4 of "Creating the login page"):

```
$_SESSION[MM_Username].php
```

If the personal page is in a folder named after the username, use the following:

```
$_SESSION[MM_Username]/index.php
```

This assumes that the folder is a subfolder of the folder where the login page is located. If the username is dpowers, these values would redirect the user to dpowers.php and dpowers/index.php respectively.

> *Because of the way that PHP handles array elements in double-quoted strings,* MM_Username *must* not *be enclosed in quotes when you use it in the* If login succeeds, go to *field.*

15

Encrypting and decrypting passwords

Common questions are: What happens when a user forgets his or her password? How can I send a reminder? If you encrypt passwords using sha1(), as described in this chapter, you can't. The sha1() algorithm is one-way; you can't decrypt it. Although this sounds like a disadvantage, it actually ensures a considerable level of security. Since the password cannot be decrypted, even a corrupt system administrator has no way of discovering another person's password. The downside is that you can't send out password reminders.

If a password is forgotten, you need to verify the user's identity and issue a new password. You can also create a form for users to change their own passwords after logging in. It's simply a question of using $_SESSION['MM_Username'] as the filter for the Update Record server behavior. Don't worry if you feel that's currently beyond your capability. In the next chapter, you'll learn about the four basic SQL commands that are the key to database management.

However, it is possible to store passwords using two-way encryption. The simplest way is to use a MySQL function. If your remote server uses MySQL 3.23, you need to use the ENCODE() function. For MySQL 4.0 or higher, use AES_ENCRYPT(). Both functions work in the same way. What makes them secure is that they use a secret key to encrypt any values passed to them. The secret key is nothing more mysterious than a random string of your own choosing. When used in combination with the DECODE() and AES_DECRYPT() functions, this unlocks the encryption.

The reason I haven't covered two-way encryption in this chapter is because it involves using MySQL functions, which we haven't covered yet. You also need to edit the code in the Insert Record, Update Record, and Log In User server behaviors in such a way that they cease to be editable through the Dreamweaver dialog boxes. For more information about ENCODE() and AES_ENCRYPT(), see my book *PHP Solutions: Dynamic Web Design Made Easy* (friends of ED, ISBN-13: 978-1-59059-731-6) and the MySQL documentation at http://dev.mysql.com/doc/refman/5.0/en/encryption-functions.html.

Feeling more secure?

Hopefully, the answer is yes. But if you're beginning to wobble because of the constant need to dive into Code view, take heart. This has been another tough chapter. The danger with Dreamweaver server behaviors is they make it very easy to create record insertion and update forms, giving you a false sense of achievement. If you're just creating a dynamic website as a hobby, you might be happy with minimum checks on what's inserted into your database. But even if it's a hobby, do you really want to waste your time on a database that gets filled with unusable data? And if you're doing it professionally, you simply can't afford to.

PHP is like the electricity or kitchen knives in your home: handled properly, it's very safe; handled irresponsibly, it can do a lot of damage. Get to know what the code you're putting into your pages is doing. The more hands on experience you get, the easier it becomes. A lot of PHP coding is simple logic: if this, do one thing, else do something different.

Take a well earned rest. In the next chapter, we'll delve into the mysteries of SQL, the language used to communicate with most databases, and joining records from two or more tables.

16 WORKING WITH MULTIPLE TABLES

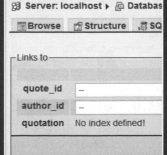

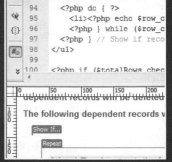

In Chapter 14, I explained that an important principle of working with a relational database was the need to break larger units, such as addresses or names, into their component elements and store them in separate columns. Another equally important principle is to get rid of columns that contain repetitive data and move them to a separate table. As long as each record has a primary key to identify it, records in separate tables can be linked by storing the primary key from one table as a reference in the other. This is known as creating a **foreign key**.

The advantage of doing this is that it eliminates inconsistency. Let's say you're creating a product catalog, you might spell a company name in different ways. For instance, friends of ED might sometimes be entered as foED, freinds of ED, or—heaven forbid—fiends of ED. Run a search for friends of ED, and anything spelled a different way will not turn up in the results. Consequently, vital data could be lost forever.

Even if you never make a spelling mistake, it's inefficient. If you store frequently repeated information in a separate table, you change it only once instead of updating every instance in the database. What's more, primary and foreign keys are normally numbers, which are much faster to search than text.

The disadvantage of using multiple tables is that it's conceptually more difficult than a single table. Also, you need to make sure that deleting a record doesn't leave references to its primary key in dependent tables. This chapter shows you how to overcome these difficulties. You'll learn how to

- Apply the rules of normalization to decide what to store in a table
- Link related information in different tables with a foreign key
- Build SQL queries with SELECT, INSERT, UPDATE, and DELETE
- Use MySQL functions and aliases
- Create a navigation bar to page through database results
- Preserve foreign key relationships

Storing related information in separate tables

The example used in this chapter uses two tables to store a selection of famous—and not so famous—quotations. The same principles apply to most multiple-table databases, so once you have mastered this chapter, you'll be equipped to create a wide variety of practical applications, such as a product catalog, contacts list, or content management system.

Deciding on the best structure

Each database is different, so there is no single "right" way to design one. However, a process known as **normalization** lays down the principles of good design. The main rules can be summarized as follows:

- Give each data record a primary key as a unique means of identification (we covered this in Chapter 14).

- Put each group of associated data in a table of its own.

- Cross-reference related information by using the primary key from one table as a foreign key in other tables.

- Store only one item of information in each field.

These principles are sometimes summed up as "Stay DRY"—don't repeat yourself.

You can find more detailed advice in *Beginning MySQL Database Design and Optimization: From Novice to Professional* by Jon Stephens and Chad Russell (Apress, ISBN-13: 978-1-59059-332-5).

Using foreign keys to link records

Figure 16-1 shows how most beginners would construct a database table to store their favorite quotations. Everything is held in one table, resulting in the need to enter the author's first name and family name for each individual record. It's not only tedious to retype the names every time; it has resulted in inconsistency. The five quotations from Shakespeare list him in three different ways. In records 25 and 34, he's William Shakespeare; in record 33, he's W Shakespeare; and in records 31 and 32, he's just plain Shakespeare.

quote_id	quotation	first_name	family_name
25	Sweet lovers love the spring.	William	Shakespeare
26	O, Wind, If Winter comes, can Spring be far behin...	Percy Bysshe	Shelley
27	In the spring a young man's fancy lightly turns to...	Alfred, Lord	Tennyson
28	It is not spring until you can plant your foot on ...		Proverb
29	The way to ensure summer in England is to have it ...	Horace	Walpole
30	’Tis the last rose of summer Left blooming ...	Thomas	Moore
31	Shall I compare thee to a summer's day? Thou art ...		Shakespeare
32	Now is the winter of our discontent Made glorious...		Shakespeare
33	Blow, blow, thou winter wind, Thou art not so unk...	W	Shakespeare
34	My age is as a lusty winter, frosty, but kindly.	William	Shakespeare

Figure 16-1. Storing repetitive information in a single table leads to redundancy and inconsistency.

It's more logical to create a separate table for names—I've called it authors—and store each name just once. So, instead of storing the name with each quotation, you can store the appropriate primary key from the authors table (on the right of Figure 16-2) as a foreign key in the quotations table (on the left).

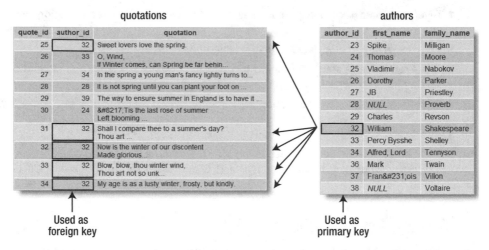

Figure 16-2. Shakespeare's primary key in the authors table (right) identifies him in the quotations table (left).

- The primary key of the authors table is author_id. Because primary keys must be unique, each number is used only once.
- The author_id for William Shakespeare is 32.
- All quotations attributed to William Shakespeare are identified in the quotations table by the same author_id (32). Because author_id is being used as a foreign key in this table, there can be multiple references to the same number.

> As long as author_id *remains unique in the* authors *table—where it's the primary key—you know that it always refers to the same person.*

I've drawn arrows in Figure 16-2 linking only Shakespeare with his quotations, but you can see that quote_id 26 comes from the poet Shelley (author_id 33) and that quote_id 27 comes from Tennyson (author_id 34). Before any sense of panic sets in about how you are going to remember all these numbers, relax. When you communicate with the database, you tell it to find the appropriate number for you. In other words, if you want to conduct a search for all quotations by Shakespeare, you issue a command that tells the database to do something like this (in pseudo-code):

```
SELECT all records in the quotation column FROM quotations
WHERE the author_id in quotations is the same as
the author_id in authors for "William Shakespeare"
```

This type of structure creates what's known as a **one-to-many relationship**: one record in one table refers to one or more records in another. In this example, it allows you to associate one author with many quotations. However, it's not suitable for a database of books, where an author is likely to be associated with multiple books and each book might have several authors. This is known as a **many-to-many relationship** and needs to be resolved through the creation of a **lookup table** (sometimes called a **linking table**). In the case of a

16

book database, each record in the lookup table stores a single pair of foreign keys linking an individual author with a particular book. To learn more about lookup tables, see my book *PHP Solutions: Dynamic Web Design Made Easy* (friends of ED, ISBN-13: 978-1-59059-731-6).

Avoiding orphaned records

The relationship between the two tables in Figure 16-2 isn't an equal one. If William Shakespeare is deleted from the authors table, author_id 32 will no longer have a value attached to it, orphaning the five Shakespeare quotations in the quotations table. However, even if you delete all five quotations from the quotations table, the authors table is unaffected. Sure, there won't be any quotations by Shakespeare (at least not in the section shown in Figure 16-2), but nothing in the authors table actually depends on the quotations table. The primary key author_id 32 continues to identify Shakespeare and can be reused if you decide to add new quotations attributed to him.

Because the foreign keys in the quotations table depend on the authors table, authors is considered to be the **parent table**, and quotations is the **child table**. Although deleting records from a child table doesn't affect the parent, the opposite is not true. Before deleting records from a parent table, you need to check whether there are any dependent records in the child table. If there are, you need to do one of the following:

- Prevent the deletion of the record(s) in the parent table.
- Delete all dependent records in the child table as well.
- Set the foreign key value of dependent records in the child table to NULL.

Making sure that the foreign key relationship between parent and child tables remains intact is known as maintaining **referential integrity**. In simple terms, it maintains the integrity of records that reference each other and means that you don't end up with incomplete records.

There are two ways to maintain referential integrity. The best way is to use **foreign key constraints**. These establish a foreign key relationship in the table definition and specify what should happen when a record in a parent table is deleted. If your hosting company supports InnoDB tables, you can use foreign key constraints to automate referential integrity.

Unfortunately, most hosting companies offer only the default MyISAM tables, which don't support foreign key constraints (they're scheduled for MySQL 5.2). However, you can reproduce the same effect with PHP. All that's required is a little conditional logic like this (in pseudo-code):

```
if (no dependent records) {
 delete;
 }
else {
 don't delete;
 }
```

I'll show you both approaches in this chapter. First of all, let's define the authors and quotations tables.

Defining the database tables

The basic table definition is the same for MyISAM and InnoDB tables. Since I have given step-by-step instructions for defining tables in phpMyAdmin in the previous two chapters, I won't go through the details again. Create two new tables in the egdwcs3 database, call them authors and quotations, and give them each three columns (fields), using the settings in Table 16-1.

 There's a setting that you haven't encountered before: Index. It's needed only on the author_id column in the quotations table. Just like the index in the back of this book, an **index** on a database column helps identify the location of its contents and speed up searches. It's also necessary when defining a foreign key relationship in an InnoDB table. To add an index to a column, select the radio button under the lightning bolt icon (see alongside) in the Action section for the column.

> *If your remote server supports InnoDB tables (see "Deciding whether to enable InnoDB support" in Chapter 13 for details of how to check), set* Storage Engine *to* InnoDB *when defining the tables in phpMyAdmin. On older versions of phpMyAdmin,* Storage Engine *is called* Table type. *Although the instructions for checking InnoDB support are in the Windows setup section of Chapter 13, they apply equally if you're developing locally on a Mac. The Mac version of MySQL supports InnoDB by default, but it's an option in the Windows Essentials version.*

Table 16-1. Settings for the authors and quotations tables

Table	Field	Type	Length/Values	Attributes	Null	Extra	Primary Key	Index
authors								
	author_id	INT		UNSIGNED	not null	auto_ increment	Selected	
	first_name	VARCHAR	30		null			
	family_name	VARCHAR	30		not null			
quotations								
	quote_id	INT		UNSIGNED	not null	auto_ increment	Selected	
	author_id	INT		UNSIGNED	null			Selected
	quotation	VARCHAR	255		not null			

As you can see in Figure 16-2, some records in the authors table don't have a value for first_name, so I have specified null in the table definition. I have done this because Dreamweaver treats not null as meaning "required," so the Insert Record and Update Record server behaviors reject a blank field.

The other thing to note is that author_id in the quotations table is set to null and does not use auto_increment, nor is the primary key radio button selected. Although author_id is the primary key in the authors table, a foreign key must not be automatically incremented. There are occasions when you might use a foreign key as a primary key (for example, in a lookup table where two foreign keys form a joint primary key), but on this occasion it's not appropriate. The reason for setting the field to null is that you might not always be able to assign author_id as a foreign key—for instance, when inserting a new quotation for someone not registered in the authors table.

After defining the quotations table, check the Indexes section at the bottom of the screen that displays the table structure. It should look like this:

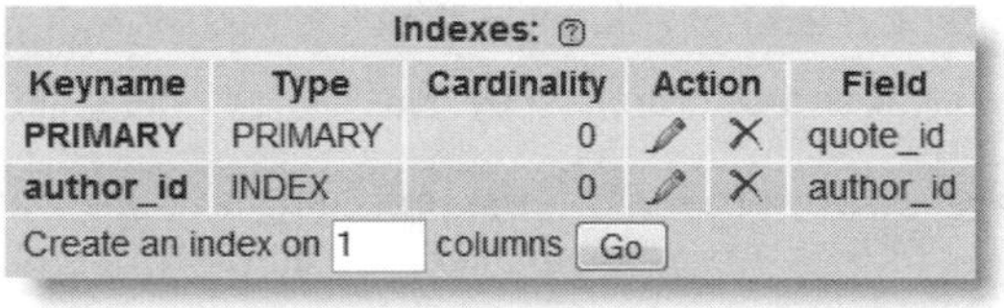

This confirms that quote_id remains the table's primary key, but that author_id is also indexed. If author_id isn't listed in the Indexes section, you can alter the table structure, as described in the next section.

Adding an index to a column

It's easy to change a table definition to add an index to a column. Select the table in the phpMyAdmin navigation frame on the left to display its structure grid, and click the lightning bolt icon in the row that describes the column you want to index. Figure 16-3 shows how to add an index to author_id in the quotations table if you forgot to do so in the original table definition.

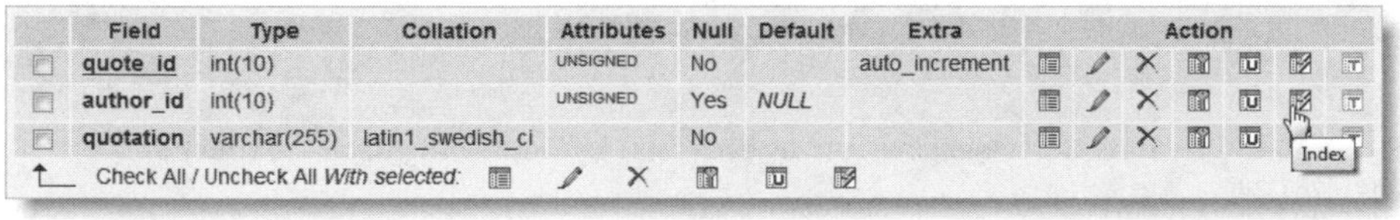

Figure 16-3. You can add an index to a column by clicking the Index icon in the table's structure grid in phpMyAdmin.

Although adding an index to a column can speed up searches, don't apply them indiscriminately. Indexing has drawbacks, the main one being that it increases the size of a table. The most important index is always the primary key. At this stage, index only foreign key columns.

Defining the foreign key relationship in InnoDB

The default MyISAM tables in MySQL don't support foreign key constraints. If your remote server doesn't support InnoDB, skip ahead to "Populating the tables."

> *This section applies only if you are using InnoDB tables. If you have converted your tables to InnoDB by mistake, refer to "Converting a table's storage engine."*

The normal way to define a foreign key relationship in MySQL is in the initial table definition. However, you can alter the structure of a table at any time, and this is the approach that phpMyAdmin takes. Defining a foreign key relationship in phpMyAdmin involves the following steps:

1. Define both parent and child tables, and set Storage Engine (Table type in older versions of phpMyAdmin) to InnoDB.
2. Confirm that the foreign key column in the child table is indexed.
3. Use Relation view to add the foreign key constraint to the child table.

Steps 1 and 2 have already been covered in the preceding sections, but you might want to convert MyISAM tables to InnoDB at a later stage, so I'll briefly describe the process.

Checking the storage engine of a table To find out whether a table uses the MyISAM or InnoDB storage engine, click the database name at the top of the main frame in phpMyAdmin or in the navigation frame on the left to display the database structure. The value for Type shows the current storage engine for each table. Figure 16-4 shows that the authors and quotations tables use InnoDB, while feedback and users use MyISAM.

	Table	Action						Records	Type	Collation	Size	Overhead
☐	**authors**	▦	☞	▨	▥	▥	✕	39	InnoDB	latin1_swedish_ci	16.0 KiB	–
☐	**feedback**	▦	☞	▨	▥	▥	✕	3	MyISAM	latin1_swedish_ci	3.9 KiB	–
☐	**quotations**	▦	☞	▨	▥	▥	✕	50	InnoDB	latin1_swedish_ci	16.0 KiB	–
☐	**users**	▦	☞	▨	▥	▥	✕	2	MyISAM	latin1_swedish_ci	2.2 KiB	20 B
	4 table(s)			Sum				94	**MyISAM**	**latin1_swedish_ci**	38.1 KiB	20 B

Figure 16-4. Check the storage engine used by each table by viewing the database structure in phpMyAdmin.

It's perfectly acceptable to mix different types of storage engines in MySQL. In fact, it's recommended that you use the most appropriate type for each table. MyISAM has the advantage of speed, but it currently lacks support for foreign key constraints and **transactions**.

> *In database terminology, a transaction is a linked series of SQL queries, in which every query must succeed. If any part of the series fails, the whole series is abandoned, and the database remains unchanged. Transactions are an advanced subject beyond the scope of this book. For details, see http://dev.mysql.com/doc/refman/5.0/en/transactional-commands.html.*

Converting a table's storage engine You can change a table's storage engine at any time, even if it already contains data. The following instructions explain how:

1. Select the table name in the list of links in the phpMyAdmin navigation frame (or click the Structure icon alongside the table name under Action in the main frame).

2. With the table structure displayed in the main frame, click the Operations tab.

3. Select InnoDB or MyISAM from the Storage Engine drop-down menu in the Table options section, as shown in the following screenshot, and click Go.

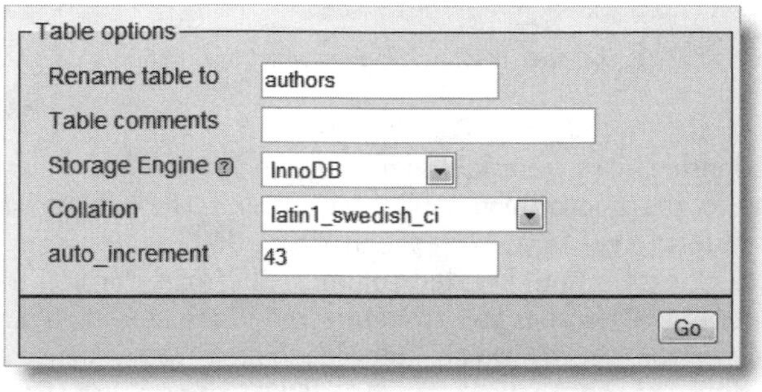

Converting a table from MyISAM to InnoDB shouldn't cause any problems. However, if foreign key constraints have been defined in an InnoDB table relationship, you must first remove them before converting from InnoDB to MyISAM. Removing a foreign key relationship simply involves reversing the process described in the next section.

Setting foreign key constraints in phpMyAdmin When a table uses the InnoDB storage engine, phpMyAdmin adds a new option called Relation view beneath the table structure (see Figure 16-5). This is where you define foreign key constraints.

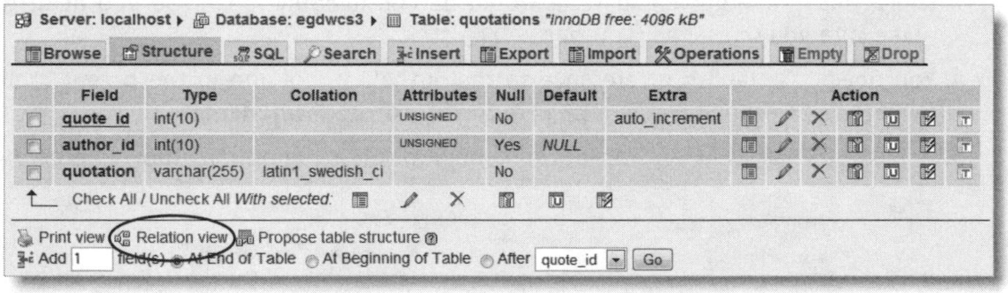

Figure 16-5. The Relation view option lets you define foreign key constraints with InnoDB tables.

The foreign key constraint must always be defined in the child table. In the case of authors and quotations, this is quotations, because it uses the authors primary key (author_id) as a foreign key. The following instructions show you how to establish the relationship:

1. Select the child table (quotations) in phpMyAdmin, and click the Structure tab to display the table grid, as shown in Figure 16-5.

2. Click the Relation view link beneath the structure grid (it's circled in Figure 16-5). This displays the screen shown in Figure 16-6.

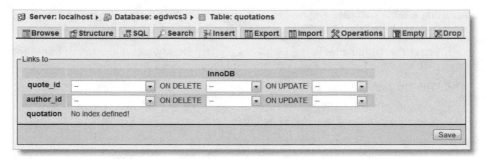

Figure 16-6. Relation view lets you specify what happens when a record in a parent table is deleted or updated.

Foreign key relationships can be established only on indexed columns. There are two indexed columns in the quotations table: quote_id is the table's primary key, and author_id is the foreign key. As you can see in Figure 16-6, phpMyAdmin displays three drop-down menus alongside both indexed columns. These are for you to set the foreign key constraint options, so the ones you are interested in are alongside author_id. The first drop-down is where you specify which indexed column you want to **reference**. (The underlying SQL command uses the keyword REFERENCES to establish the foreign key relationship.)

3. Click the down arrow on the right of the first drop-down menu. This lists all indexed columns in InnoDB tables in the database. As you can see from the screenshot alongside, they are listed in the format tableName ->columnName. Since there are only two InnoDB tables in the database, the list is very 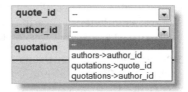 short, but in a larger database, it would be considerably longer, so you need to make sure you select the right one.

4. You need to establish a reference to the author_id column in the parent table (authors). Select authors->author_id in the first drop-down menu.

5. Activate the ON DELETE drop-down menu. It displays the options shown here:

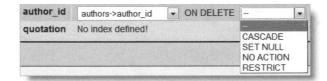

This is what each option means:

- CASCADE: If you delete a record in the parent table, MySQL cascades the delete operation to the child table. So, if you delete the record for Shakespeare in the authors table, all records in the quotations table with an author_id of 32 are automatically deleted (see Figure 16-2 at the beginning of the chapter). This is a silent operation, and there is no way of restoring the records once they have been deleted.

- SET NULL: If you delete a record in the parent table, the foreign key of related records in the child table is set to NULL. For this to work, the foreign key column in the child table must accept NULL values. Taking the Shakespeare example again from Figure 16-2, if Shakespeare is deleted from the authors table, the value of author_id is set to NULL in all records that currently have a value of 32. This leaves the quotations intact, but they are no longer related to Shakespeare. If you subscribe to literary conspiracy theories, you could now reassign those quotations to Christopher Marlowe.

- NO ACTION: This doesn't mean what you might expect. Some database systems allow you to delay foreign constraint checks. NO ACTION means a delayed check, but this is not supported in MySQL. If you select this option, MySQL treats it the same as RESTRICT.

- RESTRICT: This rejects any attempt to delete records in the parent table if related records still exist in the child table. So, attempting to delete Shakespeare from the authors table would fail unless all records with an author_id of 32 in the quotations table have already been deleted.

The fifth option is to select nothing. This applies the default action, which is the same as RESTRICT. The same options are available for ON UPDATE, although they are less useful, especially if the foreign key is the primary key in the parent table. In normal circumstances, you should never change the primary key of a record. However, in the rare cases where this might be appropriate, the most useful options are RESTRICT and CASCADE. The former prevents changes if there are dependent records in the child table; the latter propagates the changes automatically to all dependent records.

6. For the purposes of this chapter, set both ON DELETE and ON UPDATE to RESTRICT, and click Save.

7. When it confirms the creation of the foreign key constraint, phpMyAdmin displays the SQL query that it used to change the table definition. It looks like this:

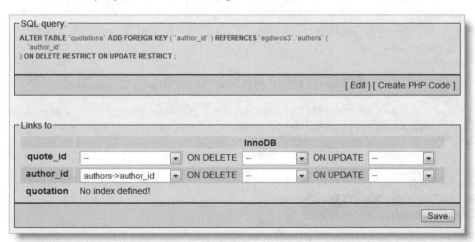

Although SQL query shows that phpMyAdmin used ON DELETE RESTRICT ON UPDATE RESTRICT, the Links to section gives the impression that your instructions were ignored.

This isn't the case, because RESTRICT is the same as the default action. In other words, the only time that you need to set values for ON DELETE or ON UPDATE is if you want to set them to either CASCADE or SET NULL.

If you need to remove a foreign key constraint (for example, when converting an InnoDB table to MyISAM), set all drop-down menus to the default value, and click Save.

Populating the tables

Later in the chapter, I'll show you how to build a content management system to insert, update, and delete records from the authors and quotations tables. First, though, I'd like to show you how to display the contents of tables linked through a foreign key. So, to save you the trouble of typing out lots of quotations and authors' names, I have created SQL scripts to populate the tables automatically.

There are six different scripts in the tools folder of the download files. They all contain the same data but are designed to work with different versions of MySQL and storage engines. If your server is running MySQL 4.1 or 5.0, use ch16_MyISAM.sql or ch16_InnoDB.sql, depending on the storage engine that is supported. The versions of files that end in 323.sql and 40.sql are for MySQL 3.23 and MySQL 4.0, respectively.

To populate the authors and quotations tables, use the appropriate file for your version of MySQL and storage engine, and follow the instructions in "Loading data from a backup file" at the end of Chapter 13.

Restoring the content of the tables

When learning, it's a good strategy to experiment. From time to time, you may need to restore the authors and quotations tables to their original state. To do so, select each table in turn in phpMyAdmin, and click the Empty tab. Click OK when phpMyAdmin asks you to confirm that you want to TRUNCATE the table. This removes all existing records in the table. After removing all records from the authors and quotations tables, you can use the SQL script to populate them again with the original records.

Selecting records from more than one table

To select records from multiple tables, you need to join them—not in the literal sense, but by using SQL commands that tell the database you want to retrieve results from more than one table. We'll look in more detail at the basic SQL commands shortly, but first let's try it out for real by displaying quotations and their associated authors from the authors and quotations tables.

Displaying a random quotation

The "Stroll Along the Thames" page that you've used in several chapters has a pull quote with a quotation from Samuel Johnson. In this exercise, you'll replace that static quotation with one drawn at random from the authors and quotations tables. This demonstrates three useful techniques: how to join multiple tables, randomize the order of recordset results, and limit the number of results. You can use an existing version of the page, as long as it has a `.php` extension. However, you will probably find it easier to use the version in examples/ch16, as it contains no other PHP script so you can see the new code in isolation.

1. Copy `stroll_quote_start.php` from examples/ch16, and save it as `stroll_quote.php` in workfiles/ch16. Click Update if Dreamweaver prompts you to update links in the page.

2. Click the plus button in the Server Behaviors panel, and select Recordset from the menu. Because you'll be selecting columns from more than one table, you need to use the Recordset dialog box in Advanced mode (see Figure 16-7). If necessary, click the Advanced button on the right of the dialog box to switch from Simple mode.

3. Your recordset should have a meaningful name, so type getQuote in the Name field.

4. The recordset will be used in a public page, so choose the non-administrative user account for Connection. If you're using the same connections as me, select connQuery. The Recordset dialog box should now look like Figure 16-7.

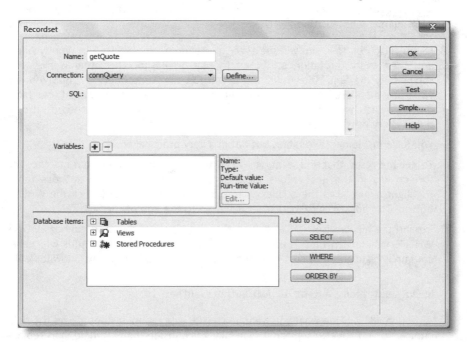

Figure 16-7. The Advanced mode of the Recordset dialog box lets you create more complex SQL queries.

The SQL field in the top half of the dialog box is where you build the query that will be sent to the database. If you're familiar with SQL, you can type your query in here manually, but the Database items field takes a lot of the hard work out of typing.

5. In the Database items field, expand Tables. You should now see both the authors and quotations tables listed. Expand quotations, highlight quotation, and click the SELECT button, as shown here:

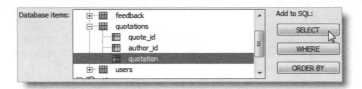

This starts building the SQL query. You should now see this code in the SQL field:

```
SELECT quotations.quotation
FROM quotations
```

6. Expand authors in the Database items area, and highlight first_name. Click SELECT.

7. Highlight family_name, and click SELECT. The SQL query should now look like this:

```
SELECT quotations.quotation, authors.first_name, authors.family_name
FROM quotations, authors
```

8. If you click Test now, you will see every quotation attributed first to Woody Allen, and then every quotation attributed to Matsuo Basho. The Dreamweaver test shows only the first 100 results, but if you run the same query in phpMyAdmin, you'll see there are 2,000 results altogether—every record in the quotations table has been matched with every record in the authors table. In other words, it produces every possible combination.

You have just joined two tables but not in a very practical way.

9. To get the result that you want, you need to add a WHERE clause that matches the foreign key in the quotations table to the primary key in the authors table. Highlight author_id in the quotations tree in Database items, and click the WHERE button. This adds WHERE quotations.author_id to the end of the SQL.

10. Expand the authors tree in Database items, and highlight the other author_id. Click WHERE again. Each time you click WHERE, Dreamweaver always adds whichever column is highlighted using AND, so the final line of the SQL query will now look like this:

```
WHERE quotations.author_id AND authors.author_id
```

Although AND is often what you want in a WHERE expression, it's not always the right choice, so you have to replace it manually. Click inside the SQL field, and replace AND with =. The SQL should now look like this:

11. Click the Test button now, and you'll see that each quotation has now been correctly matched with the right name. Adding the WHERE clause uses the foreign key to select only those records where author_id matches in both tables. Click OK to close the Test SQL Statement panel.

12. If you click Test again, the recordset appears in exactly the same order, which is the order the quotations were entered into the table. To change the order, select family_name in the authors tree in Database items, and click the ORDER BY button.

The SQL query should now look like this:

```
SELECT quotations.quotation, authors.first_name, authors.family_name
FROM quotations, authors
WHERE quotations.author_id = authors.author_id
ORDER BY authors.family_name
```

13. Click the Test button again. The quotations should be ordered according to family name.

14. Close the test panel, and add DESC at the end of the final line of the SQL query like this:

```
ORDER BY authors.family_name DESC
```

When you test the query this time, a quotation from Wordsworth will be at the top of the list, with the authors listed in reverse alphabetical order (DESC stands for "descending").

15. You want to display a random quotation in the page, so edit the last line of the SQL query like this:

```
ORDER BY RAND()
```

This uses the MySQL function RAND() to generate a random order. *Make sure there is no space between* RAND *and the parentheses.*

16. Since you need only one quotation to display in the page, it's inefficient to create a full recordset, so let's limit the result to just one record. How do you do that? Easy—change the final line of the SQL query like this:

```
ORDER BY RAND() LIMIT 1
```

17. Use the test panel several times to make sure that you're getting just one random quotation and the associated names. Once you're happy that everything is as expected, click OK to close the Recordset dialog box.

18. In Design view, highlight the quotation from Samuel Johnson, open the Bindings panel, select quotation from Recordset (getQuote), and click Insert. Then replace Samuel Johnson's name and the date with dynamic text for first_name, family_name, and a space in between.

19. Save stroll_quote.php, and load it into a browser. Each time you click the Reload button, you should see a quotation picked at random from the 50 in the quotations table (see Figure 16-8). Occasionally, you'll see the same quotation twice in succession, but that's no different from rolling two sixes twice in succession from a pair of dice.

You can check your code against stroll_quote.php in examples/ch16.

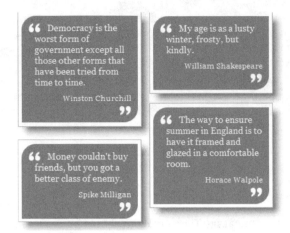

Figure 16-8. The quotations and authors' names are drawn seamlessly from separate tables.

The four essential SQL commands

As you have just seen, the advanced Recordset dialog box helps build SQL queries that work with multiple tables. Using the SELECT, WHERE, and ORDER BY buttons in conjunction with the table trees in the Database items field helps avoid spelling mistakes and always creates unambiguous references to columns. However, it cannot do everything. Not only do you need to hand-code some parts of SQL queries, you also need to have a reasonable understanding of the basic syntax. Fortunately, you don't need to be a SQL genius. You can achieve a great number of useful things with just four essential commands: SELECT, INSERT, UPDATE, and DELETE.

The following sections provide a brief overview of how each command is structured. Read through them to get a basic understanding of how SQL works, and use them later as a reference. This is not an exhaustive listing of every available option, but it concentrates on the most important ones. I have used the same typographic conventions as the MySQL online manual at http://dev.mysql.com/doc/refman/5.0/en (which you may also want to consult):

- Anything in uppercase is a SQL command.
- Expressions in square brackets are optional.
- Lowercase italics represent variable input.
- A vertical pipe (|) separates alternatives.

When working with SQL, you should follow these simple rules:

- SQL commands are case insensitive. Although the convention is to use uppercase, SELECT, select, and SeLeCt are all acceptable.
- Whitespace is ignored. This means you can split queries over several lines for increased readability.

16

- The one exception where whitespace is not ignored concerns MySQL functions, such as RAND(). There must be *no* whitespace between the function name and the opening parenthesis.

- Each section of a query *must* be in the same order as presented here. For instance, in a SELECT query, LIMIT cannot come before ORDER BY.

- Pay particular attention to punctuation. A missing or superfluous comma will cause a query to fail, so will missing quotes around a string used in a WHERE expression. However, you should read carefully "Using variables in a SQL query" later in this chapter. Since version 8.0.2, Dreamweaver automatically adds quotes where necessary around runtime variables. This subject is also discussed in depth in Chapter 17.

SELECT

SELECT is used for retrieving records from one or more tables. Its basic syntax is as follows:

```
SELECT [DISTINCT] select_list
FROM table_list
[WHERE where_expression]
[ORDER BY col_name | formula] [ASC | DESC]
[LIMIT [skip_count,] show_count]
```

The DISTINCT option tells the database you want to eliminate duplicate rows from the results.

The *select_list* is a comma-separated list of columns that you want included in the result. To retrieve all columns, use an asterisk (*).

If the same column name is used in more than one table, you must use unambiguous references by using the syntax *table_name.column_name*. In Advanced mode, the Dreamweaver Recordset dialog box always uses this syntax.

The *table_list* is a comma-separated list of tables from which the results are to be drawn. All tables that you want to be included in the results *must* be listed.

The WHERE clause specifies search criteria, for example:

```
WHERE quotations.family_name = authors.family_name
WHERE quotations.author_id = 32
```

WHERE expressions can use comparison, arithmetic, logical, and pattern-matching operators. The most important ones are listed in Table 16-2.

Table 16-2. The main operators used in MySQL WHERE expressions

Comparison		Arithmetic	
<	Less than	+	Addition
<=	Less than or equal to	-	Subtraction
=	Equal to	*	Multiplication

Continued

Table 16-2. The main operators used in MySQL WHERE expressions *(continued)*

Comparison		Arithmetic	
<>	Not equal to	/	Division
!=	Not equal to	DIV	Integer division
>	Greater than	%	Modulo
>=	Greater than or equal to		
IN()	Included in list		
BETWEEN *min* AND *max*	Between (and including) two values		

Logical		Pattern Matching	
AND	Logical and	LIKE	Case-insensitive match
&&	Logical and	NOT LIKE	Case-insensitive nonmatch
OR	Logical or	LIKE BINARY	Case-sensitive match
||	Logical or (best avoided)	NOT LIKE BINARY	Case-sensitive nonmatch

Table 16-2 contains two nonstandard operators: != (not equal to) and || (logical or). The first of these is widely used in other major database systems, but I suggest you avoid using || instead of OR because it has a completely different meaning in standard SQL.

DIV is the counterpart of the modulo operator. It produces the result of division as an integer with no fractional part, whereas modulo produces only the remainder.

```
5 / 2     /* result 2.5 */
5 DIV 2   /* result 2   */
5 % 2     /* result 1   */
```

IN() evaluates a comma-separated list of values inside the parentheses and returns true if one or more of the values is found. Although BETWEEN is normally used with numbers, it also applies to strings. For instance, BETWEEN 'a' AND 'd' returns true for *a*, *b*, *c*, and *d* (but not their uppercase equivalents). Both IN() and BETWEEN can be preceded by NOT to perform the opposite comparison.

LIKE, NOT LIKE, and the related BINARY operators are used for text searches in combination with the following two wildcard characters:

- %: matches any sequence of characters or none
- _ (an underscore): matches exactly one character

So, the following WHERE clause matches Dennis, Denise, and so on, but not Aiden:

```
WHERE first_name LIKE 'den%'
```

To match Aiden, put % at the front of the search pattern. Because % matches any sequence of characters or none, '%den%' still matches Dennis and Denise. To search for a literal percentage sign or underscore, precede it with a backslash (\% or _). The next chapter covers the use of wildcard characters in more detail.

Conditions are evaluated from left to right but can be grouped in parentheses if you want a particular set of conditions to be considered together.

ORDER BY specifies the sort order of the results. This can be specified as a single column, a comma-separated list of columns, or an expression such as RAND(), which randomizes the order. The default sort order is ascending (a–z, 0–9), but you can specify DESC (descending) to reverse the order.

LIMIT followed by one number stipulates the maximum number of records to return. If two numbers are given separated by a comma, the first tells the database how many rows to skip. For instance, LIMIT 10, 10 produces results 11–20. If fewer results exist than the limit specified, you get however many fall within the specified range. You don't get a series of empty or undefined results to make up the number.

For more details on SELECT, see http://dev.mysql.com/doc/refman/5.0/en/select.html.

INSERT

The INSERT command is used to add new records to a database. The general syntax is as follows:

```
INSERT [INTO] table_name (column_names)
VALUES (values)
```

In MySQL, the word INTO is optional; it simply makes the command read a little more like human language. The column names and values are comma-delimited lists, and both must be in the same order. So, to insert the forecast for New York (blizzard), Detroit (smog), and Honolulu (sunny) into a weather database, this is how you would do it:

```
INSERT INTO forecast (new_york, detroit, honolulu)
VALUES ('blizzard', 'smog', 'sunny')
```

The reason for this rather strange syntax is to allow you to insert more than one record at a time. Each subsequent record is in a separate set of parentheses, with each set separated by a comma:

```
INSERT INTO numbers (x,y)
VALUES (10,20),(20,30),(30,40),(40,50)
```

You'll use this multiple insert syntax in the next chapter. Any columns omitted from an INSERT query are set to their default value. *Never set an explicit value for the primary key where the column is set to* auto_increment; leave the column name out of the INSERT statement. For more details, see http://dev.mysql.com/doc/refman/5.0/en/insert.html.

UPDATE

This command is used to change existing records. The basic syntax looks like this:

```
UPDATE table_name
SET col_name = value [, col_name = value]
[WHERE where_expression]
```

The WHERE expression tells MySQL which record or records you want to update (or perhaps in the case of the following example, dream about):

```
UPDATE sales SET q3_2007 = 25000
WHERE title = 'Essential Guide to Dreamweaver CS3'
```

For more details on UPDATE, see http://dev.mysql.com/doc/refman/5.0/en/update.html.

DELETE

DELETE can be used to delete single records, multiple records, or the entire contents of a table. The general syntax for deleting from a single table is as follows:

```
DELETE FROM table_name [WHERE where_expression]
```

Although phpMyAdmin prompts you for confirmation before deleting a record, MySQL itself takes you at your word and performs the deletion immediately. DELETE is totally unforgiving—once the data is deleted, it is gone *forever*. The following query will delete all records from a table called subscribers where the date in expiry_date has already passed (as you can probably guess, NOW() is a MySQL function that returns the current date and time):

```
DELETE FROM subscribers WHERE expiry_date < NOW()
```

For more details, see http://dev.mysql.com/doc/refman/5.0/en/delete.html.

> *Although the* WHERE *clause is optional in both* UPDATE *and* DELETE, *you should be aware that if you leave* WHERE *out, the entire table is affected. This means that a careless slip with either of these commands could result in every single record being identical—or wiped out.*

Managing content with multiple tables

Now that you've seen how to use a foreign key to join tables and retrieve related records, the great mystery in life remains, "How do I insert the right foreign key in the first place?" The answer is disarmingly simple: you look it up in the database. Before I describe how to do it, let me anticipate another question: "What happens if the record I want to use as a foreign key doesn't yet exist?"

Rather than talk in abstract terms, let's use the authors and quotations tables as concrete examples. The authors table is the parent, and quotations is the child.

You can add a new record to authors at any time, because it isn't dependent on any other table. Building the insert and update forms for authors is exactly the same as for the feedback and users tables in Chapters 14 and 15. The delete form, however, needs to be different, because you shouldn't delete a record from authors if it has any dependent records in the child table (quotations). If you're using InnoDB tables, you can't anyway, but we'll come back to that issue later.

Adding a new record to the quotations table presents us with a chicken-and-egg situation. If the author has already been registered in the authors table, it's easy to look up the author's primary key and insert it in the foreign key column. What happens, though, when you want to insert a new quotation and a new author at the same time? The SQL INSERT command works with only one table, so the record in the parent table *must* exist before you can use its primary key as a foreign key in a child table. However, there's a simple way around this. The author_id column in the quotations table (where author_id is the foreign key) accepts NULL values. This means that you can insert a new quotation without assigning the foreign key. After registering the new author, you simply update the record in the quotations table to add the foreign key.

With PHP conditional logic, it is possible to build an insert form with the option to add a new author at the same time as a quotation. I have chosen this simpler approach so that you can concentrate on the basic technique of inserting the foreign key in a child table. You need four management pages for each table—insert, list, update, and delete—so you have plenty on your hands without adding further complications.

Inserting new quotations

So what's the magic secret of looking up the primary key from the authors table so you can use it as a foreign key? In the insert form for a new quotation, you have a drop-down menu that's dynamically populated by a recordset containing the names of all the authors. The drop-down menu displays the name of each author, and the value attribute contains the author's primary key. Simple, really. If you're still confused, I promise that all will come clear once you see the insert form in action.

> *From now on, I will assume that you are familiar with all the basics of building web pages and forms in Dreamweaver and will concentrate my instructions mainly on the server behaviors that interact with the database. I'll also assume that you know how to access the* Recordset *dialog box from the* Server Behaviors *panel, Data tab of the Insert bar, or* Data Objects *submenu of the* Insert *menu. I'll just tell you to open it in* Advanced *or* Simple *mode.*

Creating the quotation insert form

First, you need to design the insert form for a new quotation. It contains a text area for the quotation, a select menu for the authors' names, and a submit button.

1. Create a new PHP page, and save it in workfiles/ch16 as quote_insert.php.
2. Attach the form.css style sheet from examples/styles to give the page some minimal styling. Give the page a suitable title and heading, insert a form, and lay it out using the following illustration as a guide:

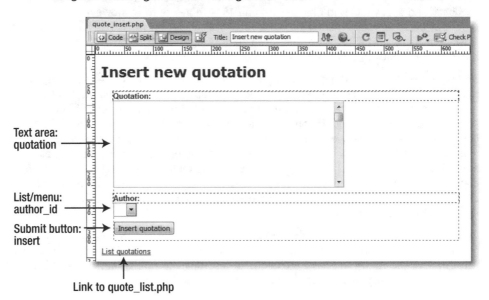

Link to quote_list.php

When inserting the form, set Method to POST, and leave Action empty.

Note that the names I've chosen for the text area and the list/menu are the same as the column names in the database.

The link to quote_list.php will display a list of all quotations (you'll create this page later). You can check your code against quote_insert_01.php in examples/ch16.

Before you can add the Insert Record server behavior, you need to populate the author_id select menu with each author's name and primary key.

Populating a drop-down menu from a database

When building drop-down menus in a static web page, you have to go through the tedious process of typing in all the values and labels manually. With a dynamic site, all this is done automatically. First, you create a recordset containing the details you want displayed in the menu. Dreamweaver then does the rest by creating a PHP loop that runs through the recordset filling in the details for you.

1. Continue working in the same page. Open the Recordset dialog box in Advanced mode. In the Name field, type listAuthors, and select connAdmin from the Connection drop-down menu. The recordset doesn't require administrative privileges, but the rest of the form does, so it makes more sense to use the same MySQL connection throughout.

2. Build the SQL query by expanding Tables and then authors in the Database items area at the bottom of the dialog box. Highlight authors in the Tables tree, and click the SELECT button. This will enter SELECT * FROM AUTHORS in the SQL field.

3. Highlight family_name, and click ORDER BY. Do the same with first_name. The top half of the Recordset dialog box should now look like this:

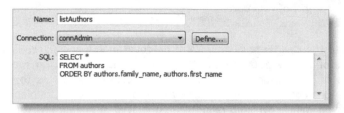

This selects all columns from the authors table and orders them first by family_name and then by first_name. Click Test to make sure you get the right results. Close the test panel, and click OK to save the recordset.

4. To populate the author_id drop-down menu with the recordset results, you need to open the Dynamic List/Menu dialog box. There are at least four ways to do this: Insert ➤ Data Objects ➤ Dynamic Data ➤ Dynamic Select List, from the Dynamic Data submenu on the Data tab of the Insert bar, from the Server Behaviors panel (choose Dynamic Form Elements ➤ Dynamic List/Menu), and the quickest way of all—through the Property inspector. Highlight the author_id menu in Design view, and click the Dynamic button, as shown here:

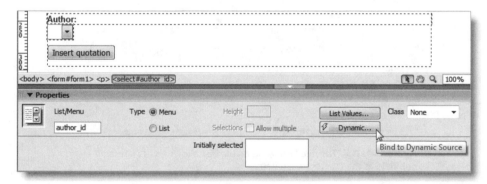

Whichever method you use, the Dynamic List/Menu dialog box automatically selects the author_id menu because it's the only one on the page.

5. In addition to the results from the database, you need a default option for the drop-down menu. Click the plus button alongside Static options. Make sure the Value field is blank, and insert Not registered in the Label field. This ensures that the foreign key will be set to NULL if Not registered is selected when inserting a new record.

Give yourself a bonus point if you spotted an apparent inconsistency with what I said in Chapter 9. The value *attribute of the* <option> *tag is optional in a drop-down menu. If it's omitted, the label is submitted instead. So how does "Not registered" become* NULL*? The Insert Record server behavior knows that the* author_id *column uses the* INT *datatype, and it converts any value that's not a whole number to* NULL *to protect the integrity of your data.*

6. Activate the Options from recordset drop-down menu, and select listAuthors. This will automatically populate the Values and Labels drop-down menus with the names of the available columns in your recordset. Set Values to author_id and Labels to family_name. Leave the final field (Select value equal to) blank. This is used when you want a dynamic value to be displayed automatically. You'll use it later when building the update form. The settings in the Dynamic List/Menu dialog box should be the same as in Figure 16-9. Click OK.

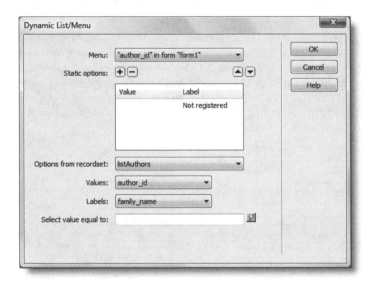

Figure 16-9. The Dynamic List/Menu dialog box allows you to use only one field as the label for each item.

7. Save quote_insert.php, and test it in a browser. Activate the drop-down menu, and you will see that it has been populated with all family names from the authors table. If you view the underlying code in your browser, you will also see that the author_id has been used as the value of each <option> tag. If necessary, check your code against quote_insert_02.php.

This is impressive, but it's far from ideal. The Dynamic List/Menu dialog box won't let you choose more than a single field to populate the labels of the drop-down menu. A simple way to get around this is to dive into Code view, find the dynamic text object for family_name, and use the Bindings panel to insert first_name and a space alongside it. However, there's a much cooler way to do it—and that's to get MySQL to manipulate the data for you. All it requires is a function and an alias.

Using a MySQL function and alias to manipulate data

Many beginners use SQL to extract raw data, and then rely on PHP or another server-side language to reformat it, whereas SQL is actually capable of doing most of the transformation itself. MySQL has an extensive range of functions (http://dev.mysql.com/doc/refman/5.0/en/functions.html) that allow you to manipulate the data in your tables in many ways. The data stored in the table remains unchanged, but you can use functions to perform calculations, format text and dates, and much, much more.

MySQL has two functions that concatenate (join together) strings, namely:

- CONCAT(): The arguments passed to CONCAT() can be literal strings (in quotes) or column names (without quotes). When a column name is used, the value of the current record is inserted into the string. CONCAT() returns NULL if any argument is NULL.

- CONCAT_WS(): This stands for "concatenate with separator." The first argument is a separator that you want inserted between the remaining arguments, which can be literal strings or column names. If the separator argument is NULL, CONCAT_WS() returns NULL, but it skips any NULL values in the remaining arguments.

Since some of the first_name fields contain NULL, you can't use CONCAT() to join the first_name and family_name columns, but CONCAT_WS() is ideal. To add a space between the two columns, you pass a pair of quotes with a space between them as the first argument like this:

```
CONCAT_WS(' ', first_name, family_name)
```

> Don't attempt to use + to concatenate strings. In MySQL, + is exclusively an arithmetic operator.

When manipulating data as part of a SQL query, you need a convenient way of referring to the result of the calculation or function. You do this by creating an **alias**. An alias is simply a temporary name that becomes part of the recordset. You assign an alias using the AS keyword. The basic syntax looks like this:

```
FUNCTION_NAME(column_name, other_arguments) AS alias_name
```

Combining the contents of two columns as a single field

In this section, you'll use CONCAT_WS() to join the first_name and family_name columns, and assign the result to an alias called author.

1. Highlight Recordset (listAuthors) in the Server Behaviors panel, and double-click to edit the recordset. Expand Tables and authors in the Database items area at the bottom of the Recordset dialog box. Highlight author_id, and click SELECT. Do the same for first_name and family_name. This changes the existing query:

```
SELECT *
FROM authors
ORDER BY authors.family_name, authors.first_name
```

to this:

```
SELECT authors.author_id, authors.first_name, authors.family_name
FROM authors
ORDER BY authors.family_name, authors.first_name
```

Both do exactly the same thing, but there is a method in my madness . . .

2. Click inside the SQL field, and amend the SQL query like this (new code in bold):

```
SELECT authors.author_id,
CONCAT_WS(' ', authors.first_name, authors.family_name) AS author
FROM authors
ORDER BY authors.family_name, authors.first_name
```

Make sure there is no space before the opening parenthesis of CONCAT_WS()—leaving a space before the opening parenthesis of a MySQL function generates a SQL error.

3. Click the Test button. You should now see the authors' names correctly formatted as a single field called author, as shown in Figure 16-10. You can now use this to populate the Labels field in the Dynamic List/Menu dialog box.

Record	author_id	author
1	1	Woody Allen
2	2	Matsuo Basho
3	3	Jeremy Bentham

Figure 16-10. The results are displayed using the alias instead of the original column names.

4. Close the test panel, and click OK to save the revised recordset. If you look at the Server Behaviors panel, you'll notice there's a red exclamation mark next to Dynamic List/Menu (author_id). This is because the recordset no longer produces a result called family_name.

5. Highlight Dynamic List/Menu (author_id) in the Server Behaviors panel, and double-click to edit it. You will be presented with a warning that the column "family_name" was not found. Click OK, and select author as the value for the Labels field. Click OK to close the Dynamic List/Menu dialog box.

6. Save the page, and preview it in a browser again. This time, the authors' names should be correctly displayed. You can check your code against quote_insert_03.php.

All that remains to complete the quotation insert form is to apply the Insert Record server behavior. This is exactly the same as you have done before, so I won't give step-by-step instructions. Use the settings shown in Figure 16-11, and compare your final code against quote_insert_04.php in examples/ch16.

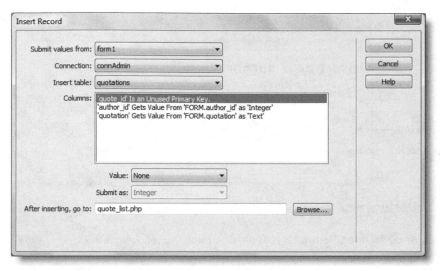

Figure 16-11. Use these settings for the Insert Record server behavior in quote_insert.php.

One of the main reasons for needing to update a quotation will be if you insert a quotation by an author who isn't already registered. So before looking at how to create the update form, it's necessary to get some new authors into the database.

Inserting new authors

Since the authors' names are in a separate table, it's vital to ensure you don't insert the same name twice. There's nothing to stop you from inserting duplicate quotations, but it won't really matter unless you decide to use quote_id as a foreign key in another table. You can delete duplicate entries in a child table without destroying the referential integrity of your database. The same cannot be said for the parent table.

When building the users table in the previous chapter, you adapted the Check New Username server behavior to prevent the same username from being used twice. That won't work this time, because you need to check the values of two fields, so I'll show you how to build the PHP logic yourself. In the process, you'll learn how to pass PHP variables to a SQL query, which forms the basis of all search operations.

Building the basic insert form

First of all, you need to create the form to insert new authors. It requires two text fields and a submit button.

1. Create a new PHP page, save it in workfiles/ch16 as author_insert.php, attach the form.css style sheet, and lay out the form as shown in the following screenshot:

Text field: first_name →

Text field: family_name →

Submit button: insert →

Link to author_list.php

2. Apply an Insert Record server behavior, using the following values:

- Submit values from: form1
- Connection: connAdmin
- Insert table: authors
- After inserting, go to: author_list.php

Compare your code, if necessary, with author_insert_01.php in examples/ch16.

As it stands, author_insert.php is now ready to insert new records into the authors table. However, it doesn't validate the input in any way. You can use the Spry validation widgets described in Chapter 9 to make sure that required fields are filled in, but this won't prevent the insertion of duplicate records. For that, you need to roll up your sleeves and dive into Code view.

Changed

Using variables in a SQL query

To find out whether an author has already been registered, you need to check the authors table to see if any record matches the values submitted in the first_name and family_name fields. In other words, you need to search the database (or in this case, a single table). If there's a match, you need to stop the Insert Record server from executing. Otherwise, the insert operation can go ahead. Since you don't know what will be entered in the form fields, you need to pass their values as variables to the query that creates the recordset.

Passing form values to a SQL query

The way you do this changed in a subtle but important way with the release of the Dreamweaver 8.0.2 updater. If you are upgrading from an earlier version of Dreamweaver, pay careful attention to the instructions in this section. Continue working with author_insert.php.

1. Open the Recordset dialog box in Advanced mode. Name the recordset checkAuthor, and select connAdmin in the Connection field.

2. Expand Tables in the Database items area, highlight the authors table, and click SELECT. Expand authors, highlight first_name, and click WHERE. Then do the same with family_name. You should now have a SQL query that looks like this:

```
SELECT *
FROM authors
WHERE authors.first_name AND authors.family_name
```

The WHERE expression needs to search for the names entered in the first_name and family_name fields. Although you don't know what the names will be, they will be stored in the $_POST array when the Insert author button is clicked. Instead of entering the PHP variables directly in the SQL query, you need to use runtime variables and define them in the Variables area in the center of the Recordset dialog box.

The runtime variables are not PHP variables, so they shouldn't begin with a dollar sign. You can use any alphanumeric characters to create the variables, as long as they don't clash with the names of columns or any other part of the SQL query. I normally call the runtime variables var1, var2, and so on, but another common convention is to use col1, col2, and so on.

Dreamweaver uses runtime variables to prevent a type of malicious attack known as **SQL injection**, which exploits poorly written scripts to inject spurious code into SQL queries. SQL injection can be used to gain unauthorized access to a database and even wipe out all the stored data. Dreamweaver changed its approach to SQL injection with the 8.0.2 updater for Dreamweaver 8, so if you're upgrading from an earlier version of Dreamweaver, the way you insert these runtime variables has changed slightly. You will probably also find that recordsets built with versions of Dreamweaver prior to 8.0.2 need to be rebuilt.

Dreamweaver replaces the runtime variables with PHP format specifiers (normally %s or %d), and uses the GetSQLValueString() function (see "Inspecting the server behavior code" in Chapter 14) to handle quotes and other characters that might cause problems with the SQL query. It also automatically adds quotes around text values. *This is an important change.* Prior to Dreamweaver 8.0.2, you needed to add the quotes around the runtime variables yourself. Now you insert the runtime variables *without quotes.*

3. I'm going to use var1 and var2 as my runtime variables, so change the last line of the SQL query like this:

```
WHERE authors.first_name = var1 AND authors.family_name = var2
```

4. You now need to define the runtime variables. Click the plus button alongside the Variables label in the Recordset dialog box. This opens the Add Variable dialog box, which has the following four fields:

- Name: This is the name of the runtime variable that you want to define.

- Type: This is a drop-down menu with four options: Numeric, Text, Date, and Double. Numeric accepts whole numbers (integers) only. Text is self-explanatory. The Date option doesn't have any practical use in PHP, so you can ignore it. Double is for floating-point numbers with a decimal fraction.

- Default value: As you'll see in the next chapter, Dreamweaver handles this value in an unexpected way. The only time it's used is when you click the Test button inside the Recordset dialog box or when the page first loads. You must enter a value in this field, because Dreamweaver uses it to prevent a MySQL error if the variable defined as Runtime value doesn't exist. Unless you want to display a default recordset result when a page first loads, set this to -1 or anything that produces no results.

- Runtime value: This is the value you want to use instead of the runtime variable.

5. When the form is submitted, you want var1 to use the value in the first_name field, so set Runtime value to $_POST['first_name']. Unless you want to check the SQL with the Test button, enter anything in the Default value field. Here are the settings that I used:

PHP is case sensitive, so make sure that $_POST is all uppercase. Click OK.

6. Define var2 in the same way, using $_POST['family_name'] as Runtime value. The central section of the Recordset dialog box should look like this:

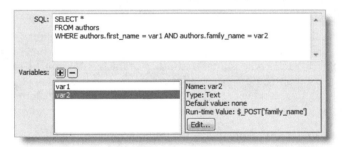

7. Click OK to close the Recordset dialog box, and save author_insert.php. You can check your code against author_insert_02.php.

Preventing duplicate entries

The recordset that you created in the preceding section checks whether there's already an author of the same name registered in the table. Unfortunately, Dreamweaver puts the code for a recordset immediately above the DOCTYPE declaration, so it's *after* the Insert Record server behavior. I know what you're thinking, but it doesn't matter which order you enter them. Dreamweaver always puts recordsets beneath Insert Record and Update Record server behaviors, so you need to move it manually.

1. Open Code view. Locate the section of code in the following screenshot:

```
53   $var1_checkAuthor = "none";
54   if (isset($_POST['first_name'])) {
55     $var1_checkAuthor = $_POST['first_name'];
56   }
57   $var2_checkAuthor = "none";
58   if (isset($_POST['family_name'])) {
59     $var2_checkAuthor = $_POST['family_name'];
60   }
61   mysql_select_db($database_connAdmin, $connAdmin);
62   $query_checkAuthor = sprintf("SELECT * FROM authors WHERE authors.first_name = %s AND
     authors.family_name = %s", GetSQLValueString($var1_checkAuthor, "text"),GetSQLValueString(
     $var2_checkAuthor, "text"));
63   $checkAuthor = mysql_query($query_checkAuthor, $connAdmin) or die(mysql_error());
64   $row_checkAuthor = mysql_fetch_assoc($checkAuthor);
65   $totalRows_checkAuthor = mysql_num_rows($checkAuthor);
```

This is the code for the checkAuthor recordset. You can easily identify it, because the first line begins with $var1_checkAuthor, which is the way Dreamweaver defines var1, which you created in step 5. The part of the code that interacts with the database begins with mysql_select_db on line 61 and continues to the end of the line that reads as follows:

```
$totalRows_checkAuthor = mysql_num_rows($checkAuthor);
```

As you can probably guess, $totalRows_checkAuthor contains the total number of records in the checkAuthor recordset. You can use this information to determine whether a record already exists for the same author. If the number of rows is zero, there are no matching records, so you can safely insert the new author. But if any matching records are found, you know it's a duplicate, so you need to skip the insert operation and display a warning.

2. Highlight the code shown on lines 53–65 in the screenshot, and cut them to the clipboard.

3. Scroll up about 17 lines, and paste the recordset in the position indicated here:

```
32   $editFormAction = $_SERVER['PHP_SELF'];
33   if (isset($_SERVER['QUERY_STRING'])) {
34     $editFormAction .= "?" . htmlentities($_SERVER['QUERY_STRING']);
35   }
36
37   if ((isset($_POST["MM_insert"])) && ($_POST["MM_insert"] == "form1")) {
38     $insertSQL = sprintf("INSERT INTO authors (first_name, family_name) VALUES (%s, %s)",
```

Paste code here →

4. Make sure your cursor is at the end of the code you have just pasted, and press Enter/Return to make room to insert the following code highlighted in bold:

```
$totalRows_checkAuthor = mysql_num_rows($checkAuthor);
// assume that no match has been found
$alreadyRegistered = false;

// check whether recordset found any matches
if ($totalRows_checkAuthor > 0) {
```

```
      // if found, reset $alreadyRegistered
      $alreadyRegistered = true;
      }
    else {
      // go ahead with server behavior
    if ((isset($_POST["MM_insert"])) && ($_POST["MM_insert"] == "form1")) {
```

> Note that false and true in this code block are keywords. They must not be enclosed in quotes.

5. Position your cursor right at the end of the code shown on line 37 in the previous screenshot (it should now be around line 60). This is the beginning of the Insert Record server behavior. Click the Balance Braces button on the Coding toolbar (or press Ctrl+'/Cmd+') to find the end of the server behavior, and insert a closing brace (}) to match the opening one at the end of the code in step 10.

   This wraps the Insert Record server behavior in an else clause to prevent it from running if a matching record is found in the authors table.

6. All that remains now is to display a warning message if the insert is abandoned. Scroll down until you find the following code (around line 86):

   ```
   <h1>Insert new author</h1>
   ```

7. Add the following code immediately after it:

   ```php
   <?php
   if ($_POST && $alreadyRegistered) {
     echo '<p class="warning">'.$_POST['first_name'].' '. ➡
   $_POST['family_name'].' is already registered</p>';
     }
   ?>
   ```

   This section of code will run only if the $_POST array has been set (in other words, the insert form has been submitted) and if $alreadyRegistered has been set to true.

8. Save the page, and preview it in a browser. Try inserting a name that you know already exists in the table, such as William Shakespeare. You should see a warning that William Shakespeare is already registered.

   Then try a name you know hasn't been registered. You'll see a warning that author_list.php wasn't found (you haven't created it yet), but when you reload quote_insert.php, the new name should be listed in the drop-down menu of authors' names. Check your code against author_insert_03.php if you have any problems.

> Although this is an adequate safeguard for a basic content management system, it won't prevent you from entering similar names or misspelled ones.

Updating authors

As you saw in the previous chapter, the way to update and delete records is to create a list of all records with EDIT and DELETE links that pass the record's primary key to the update or delete form through a query string appended to the URL. The authors table has a lot of records in it, so we'll improve the basic technique from the last chapter by adding a Recordset Navigation Bar, which lets you page through a long set of search results a specified number of records at a time.

Paging through the list of registered authors

To save space and time, I have created the basic code for the page to display a list of authors. Refer to "Creating a recordset" in Chapter 14 if you need to refresh your memory on how to build this sort of page.

1. Copy author_list_01.php from examples/ch16, and save it as author_list.php in workfiles/ch16. The page has a recordset called listAuthors, which retrieves everything from the authors table, and the EDIT and DELETE links point to author_update.php and author_delete.php with the author_id primary key appended as a query string.

2. The page doesn't yet have a repeat region, so insert your cursor anywhere in the second row of the table, and click the <tr> tag in the Tag selector at the bottom of the Document window to select the entire row. Choose Repeat Region from the Server Behaviors panel. Alternatively, use the Data tab of the Insert bar or the Data Objects submenu of the Insert menu. Set the repeat region to show 15 records at a time.

3. Before inserting the Recordset Navigation Bar, you need to make sure that your insertion point is in the right place. Select <table> in the Tag selector and press your right arrow key once to move the insertion point outside the table. Then select Recordset Navigation Bar from the Data tab of the Insert bar, as shown in the following screenshot (or go to Insert ➤ Data Objects ➤ Recordset Paging ➤ Recordset Navigation Bar):

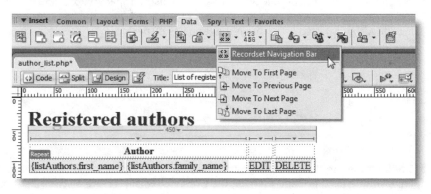

4. The Recordset Navigation Bar dialog box has two settings. The first lets you choose which recordset you want to use. There's only one on the current page, so listAuthors is selected automatically. The other setting lets you choose whether to use text or images. Select Images, and click OK.

Changed

5. The Recordset Navigation Bar is inserted beneath the table that displays the recordset. As you can see from the following screenshot, it's a rather enigmatic jumble of images with gray tabs on top.

In previous versions of Dreamweaver, the Recordset Navigation Bar was formatted with presentational markup that you needed to remove before you could style it with CSS. As part of Project Hoover (see Chapter 1), the markup has gone, and you're left with a simple table to style however you want.

6. Click anywhere in the Recordset Navigation Bar, and click the <table> tag in the Tag selector to select the whole table. Give the navigation bar an ID by typing recNav in the Table Id field in the Property inspector. Now, click the New CSS Rule icon at the bottom right of the CSS Styles panel, and create a rule for #recNav (the New CSS Rule dialog box automatically suggests the selector name if the navigation bar table is still selected).

For the purposes of this exercise, select This document only to embed the rule in the <head> of the page. In the Box category, set Width to 400 pixels, and click OK. This is 50 pixels narrower than the table that contains the recordset results, but it seems to fit better.

7. A simple way of formatting the Recordset Navigation Bar is to click inside the first cell to the right of the double arrow image and insert a space. Next, hold down the mouse button and drag-select the first two table cells. Merge the two cells by clicking the Merge selected cells icon in the Property inspector:

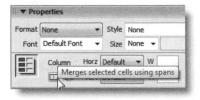

8. Do the same with the third and fourth cells by inserting a space to the right of the arrow in the third cell and merging the two cells. Finally, create a style rule (I used a class called textRight with the rule text-align: right) to move the right arrows to the right edge of the table.

9. Save author_list.php, and test it in a browser. You should see two arrows at the bottom right of the list of authors, as shown in the following screenshot:

Click the single arrow, and you'll see the continuation of the list of authors, together with arrows at the bottom left of the table for you to navigate back. The double arrows take you to the beginning and end of the list—pagination for a long list of records made easy!

You can check your code against author_list_02.php in examples/ch16.

Now that you have a list of all authors registered in the database, you can adapt the insert form to handle updates. Instead of building the whole page from scratch, it's quicker to base it on author_insert.php.

Adapting the author insert form for updates

Adapting the insert form involves removing the Insert Record server behavior—a simple, clean operation that involves just two clicks. You then create a recordset to retrieve the details of the record you want to update and bind the results to the fields in the form. This displays the existing contents of the record ready for editing. Finally, you apply the Update Record server behavior and move the code into the space originally occupied by the Insert Record server behavior.

1. Open author_insert.php, and save it (File ➤ Save As or Ctrl+Shift+S/Shift+Cmd+S) as author_update.php.

2. You now have an exact copy of author_insert.php. Change the title and heading to Update author. Use the Property inspector to change the Button name and Value of the submit button to update and Update author, respectively.

3. In the Server Behaviors panel, highlight Insert Record, and click the minus button to delete it, as shown alongside. Make sure you delete only the Insert Record server behavior, as you still need the checkAuthor recordset.

If you alter a Dreamweaver server behavior, normally, it disappears from the Server Behaviors *panel, or a red exclamation mark indicates the code is no longer editable through the server behavior's dialog box. However, when building the insert form, you simply moved the recordset code and wrapped the Insert Record server behavior in an* else *clause, without altering the actual code. Consequently, they still remain fully accessible through the* Server Behaviors *panel. When you remove the Insert Record server behavior in this way, the conditional statement you added to the insert form remains intact, ready for reuse in this page.*

4. As with the update form in the previous chapter, you need to create a recordset for the Update Record server behavior to work with. Open the Recordset dialog box in Simple mode, and use the settings shown in the following screenshot. Click OK to create the getAuthor recordset. This selects just one author identified by author_id passed in the URL query string.

5. Open the Bindings panel. You should now have two recordsets listed there: checkAuthor and getAuthor. The second one will be used to set the initial values for the text fields in the updateAuthor form. Expand the getAuthor recordset in the Bindings panel, and highlight the first_name text field in the form, followed by first_name in the recordset, as shown alongside. The label on the Insert button at the bottom of the Bindings panel changes to Bind, and the drop-down menu alongside should display input. value. Click Bind, and a dynamic placeholder will appear inside the first_name text field. The Bind button changes to Unbind. Click this if you ever want to remove dynamic text bound in this way.

6. Repeat step 5 with the family_name text field and family_name in the recordset.

7. The Update Record server behavior also needs to know the author_id. Click any blank space inside the form, and insert a hidden field (see Chapter 9). In the Property inspector, change the name of the hidden field to author_id, and click the lightning bolt icon alongside the Value field.

8. In the Dynamic Data dialog box that opens, select author_id from Recordset (getAuthor), and click OK. Make sure you use the correct recordset.

9. Apply the Update Record server behavior by clicking the plus button in the Server Behaviors panel, and select Update Record. If you have followed all the steps correctly, the Update Record dialog box will automatically apply the correct values as soon as you select connAdmin in the Connection field. Set the final field to go to author_list.php after updating. Check your settings against those shown here, and click OK.

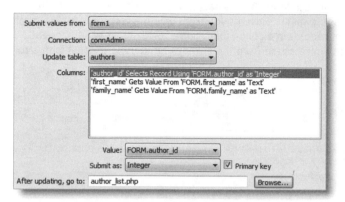

10. Switch to Code view, and locate the following section of code:

```
37  if ((isset($_POST["MM_update"])) && ($_POST["MM_update"] == "form1")) {
38    $updateSQL = sprintf("UPDATE authors SET first_name=%s, family_name=%s WHERE author_id=%s",
39                          GetSQLValueString($_POST['first_name'], "text"),
40                          GetSQLValueString($_POST['family_name'], "text"),
41                          GetSQLValueString($_POST['author_id'], "int"));
42
43    mysql_select_db($database_connAdmin, $connAdmin);
44    $Result1 = mysql_query($updateSQL, $connAdmin) or die(mysql_error());
45
46    $updateGoTo = "author_list.php";
47    if (isset($_SERVER['QUERY_STRING'])) {
48      $updateGoTo .= (strpos($updateGoTo, '?')) ? "&" : "?";
49      $updateGoTo .= $_SERVER['QUERY_STRING'];
50    }
51    header(sprintf("Location: %s", $updateGoTo));
52  }
```

This is the Update Record server behavior code. Highlight it, making sure you don't miss the closing curly brace shown on line 52 in the screenshot, and cut it to your clipboard.

11. Scroll down until you find the empty else clause just above the DOCTYPE declaration, and paste the Update Record server behavior between the braces.

Paste code here ⟶

```
71  else {
72      // go ahead with the server behavior
73
74  }
75
76  ?><!DOCTYPE html PUBLIC "-//W3C//DTD XHTML 1.0 Transitional//EN"
```

You can check your code against author_update.php in examples/ch16 if necessary.

Deleting authors

In "Avoiding orphaned records" at the beginning of the chapter, I told you that using foreign key constraints in InnoDB tables automates the preservation of referential integrity. It does—in the sense that it prevents you from deleting records in a parent table if there are still dependent records in a child table. Figure 16-12 shows what happened when I tried to delete William Shakespeare from the authors table using InnoDB with a foreign key constraint defined.

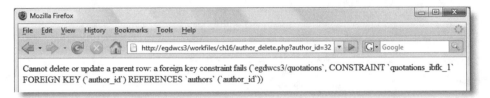

Figure 16-12. A foreign key constraint prevents the deletion of a record while it still has dependent records in a child table.

When I did the same thing with MyISAM tables, William Shakespeare vanished into cyber oblivion without so much as a by-your-leave to his children. So foreign key constraints are a good security measure, but you don't want an ugly MySQL error message like that in Figure 16-12 on your website. Consequently, even if you're using InnoDB tables, you need to incorporate the same sort of checks into a delete page as with MyISAM tables. In other words, when deleting a record from a parent table, you need to do the following:

1. Search the child table to see if the record's primary key has any matches in the foreign key column. In the example in Figure 16-2 at the beginning of the chapter, Shakespeare's primary key is 32. So, before you can delete his record, you need to check whether any records in the quotations table have the same value as the foreign key (author_id).

2. If there are any matches, display a message saying that the deletion cannot go ahead, and hide the delete button.

   If there are no matching records, display the delete button, asking for confirmation.

Adapting the author update page to handle deletes

The conditional logic that you used in the insert and update forms checked whether an author was already registered in the authors table. For the delete form, you need to perform a similar check, only this time in the quotations table. Although you're checking a different table, the script flow is exactly the same. If there are any matching records, you stop the server behavior from being executed. Otherwise, you let it go ahead. Consequently, you can adapt the existing script quite easily.

1. Open author_update.php, and save it as author_delete.php.

2. Change the title and heading to Delete author. Use the Property inspector to change the Button name and Value of the submit button to delete and Delete author, respectively.

3. In the Server Behaviors panel, highlight Recordset (checkAuthor), and delete it by clicking the minus button.

4. Do the same with Update Record.

5. Click the plus button in the Server Behaviors panel, and select Delete Record. As in the previous chapter, you get the value of the record to be deleted from a hidden field, so make sure you choose Form Variable for Primary key value. Check that your settings are the same as shown in the screenshot, and click OK.

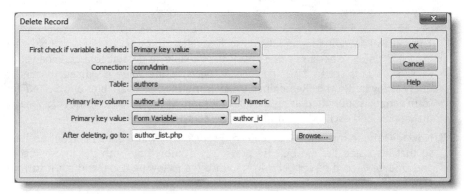

6. Before deleting a record from the authors table, you must check whether its primary key is still in use in the quotations table. Create a new recordset called checkForeign. Use the Recordset dialog box in Advanced mode with the settings shown in the following screenshot:

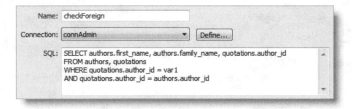

The WHERE clause selects records where quotations.author_id is equal to a variable (we'll define that in a moment) and where quotations.author_id is the same as authors.author_id. As explained in the "The four essential SQL commands" earlier in the chapter, the dot notation *tableName.columnName* eliminates ambiguity in a SQL query when columns in different tables have the same name. What this SQL query is looking for is any record where author_id matches the runtime variable var1.

7. The value of author_id is passed through the query string from author_list.php, so var1 needs to be defined in the Variables field. Click the plus button alongside Variables, and use the following settings:

The value of author_id is an integer, so Type needs to be set to Numeric. I have set Default Value to -1 because I don't want the variable to default to a genuine value. Runtime value is set to $_GET['author_id'] because the value is passed through a query string in the URL. Remember, $_GET is used for URL variables and $_POST for form variables submitted using the POST method. Click OK to close the Add Variable dialog box, and click OK again to save the recordset.

8. Now it's time to move the Delete Record server behavior from its current position so that it's inside the else clause previously occupied by both the Insert Record and Update Record server behaviors. Locate the following code, and cut it to your clipboard:

```php
32  if ((isset($_POST['author_id'])) && ($_POST['author_id'] != "")) {
33    $deleteSQL = sprintf("DELETE FROM authors WHERE author_id=%s",
34                    GetSQLValueString($_POST['author_id'], "int"));
35
36    mysql_select_db($database_connAdmin, $connAdmin);
37    $Result1 = mysql_query($deleteSQL, $connAdmin) or die(mysql_error());
38
39    $deleteGoTo = "author_insert.php";
40    if (isset($_SERVER['QUERY_STRING'])) {
41      $deleteGoTo .= (strpos($deleteGoTo, '?')) ? "&" : "?";
42      $deleteGoTo .= $_SERVER['QUERY_STRING'];
43    }
44    header(sprintf("Location: %s", $deleteGoTo));
45  }
```

9. Paste the code from your clipboard to the position indicated here:

```php
53  // assume no match has been found
54  $alreadyRegistered = false;
55
56  // check whether recordset found any matches
57  if ($totalRows_checkAuthor > 0) {
58    // if found, reset $alreadyRegistered
59    $alreadyRegistered = true;
60  }
61  else {
62    // go ahead with the server behavior
63
64  }
65
66  ?><!DOCTYPE html PUBLIC "-//W3C//DTD XHTML 1.0 Transitional//EN"
```

Paste code here ──────────▶

10. Next, amend the code shown on lines 54–59 of the preceding screenshot to match the name of the checkForeign recordset like this:

```
// assume that no match has been found
$recordsExist = false;

//check whether recordset found any matches
if ($totalRows_checkForeign > 0) {
  // if found, reset $recordsExist
  $recordsExist = true;
  }
else {
```

11. Scroll down until you find this line (it should be around line 90):

```
if ($_POST && $alreadyRegistered) {
```

The check for $_POST is not needed this time, because the checkForeign recordset will be created as soon as the page loads. You also need to change the variable to $recordsExist. Change the line to look like this:

```
if ($recordsExist) {
```

12. In the next line, $_POST['first_name'] and $_POST['family_name'] need to be replaced with dynamic data from the checkForeign recordset. Highlight $_POST['first_name'], and open the Bindings panel. Expand Recordset (checkForeign), select family_name, and click the Insert button. This will replace $_POST['first_name'] with $row_checkForeign['first_name']. Do the same with $_POST['family_name'], selecting family_name from the Bindings panel.

13. Change the remaining text in the warning paragraph, and add the opening part of an else clause so that the entire PHP code block now looks like this:

```
<?php
if ($recordsExist) {
  echo '<p class="warning">'.$row_checkForeign['first_name'].' '.➥
$row_checkForeign['family_name'].' has dependent records. Can\'t be ➥
deleted.</p>';
  }
else {
?>
```

14. Scroll all the way down to the closing </form> tag (around line 110), and insert a closing curly brace inside a pair of PHP tags like this:

```
<?php } ?>
```

What you have done is enclose the entire form in an else clause, so it will be displayed only if there are no dependent records in the quotations table.

15. Switch back to Design view, click immediately to the right of the first PHP shield, and press Enter/Return to create a new paragraph. Type a warning that the delete operation cannot be undone, and apply the warning class to the paragraph.

16. Save author_delete.php, and load author_insert.php into your browser. Select an author that you know has dependent records in the quotations table, and click DELETE. You should see a message like this:

Delete author

William Shakespeare has dependent records. Can't be deleted.

List authors

17. Now insert a new author. When the name appears in the list, click DELETE. This time you should see a screen like the following one. Click Delete author. You will be taken back to the list of authors, and the new entry will have disappeared without a trace. You can check your code against author_delete.php in examples/ch16.

Delete author

Please confirm that you want to delete the following record. This operation cannot be undone.

First name:

Invisible

Family name:

Man

[Delete author]

List authors

Improving the delete form

As the screenshot in step 16 shows, the warning message simply tells you that the author has dependent records. A simple improvement would be to display a list of the dependent records, so that you can delete them, if required. All that's needed is to add quotation to the checkForeign recordset. You can then use a repeat region to display the dependent records if any are found. Sample code showing how this is done can be found in author_delete_display.php in examples/ch16. The code is fully commented, explaining how to incorporate the display of dependent records.

Another improvement would be to remove the text fields that display the name of the author to be deleted and just display the first_name and family_name values in the same way as with delete_user.php in the previous chapter. However, it doesn't matter that the names are displayed in editable text fields. Even if you edit the names, it has no effect on the database, because the delete operation is controlled entirely by the author_id primary key.

Performing a cascading delete with InnoDB tables

Although you still need to use PHP logic in the delete form for a parent table, one advantage that InnoDB tables have over MyISAM is the ability to perform a cascading delete. This means that when you delete a record in the parent table, all dependent records are automatically deleted from the child table. To enable this behavior, you need to change the foreign key constraint to ON DELETE CASCADE.

Deleting dependent records simultaneously

The following instructions show you how to adapt author_delete.php to perform a cascading delete with InnoDB tables. You can use author_delete.php in examples/ch16 as the starting point. The completed code is in author_delete_cascade.php.

> *These instructions apply only to InnoDB tables. They do not work with the default MyISAM tables.*

1. In phpMyAdmin, select the quotations table in the egdwcs3 database. Click the Structure tab to display the table structure, and select Relation view.

2. In the Links to area, change the value of ON DELETE for author_id to CASCADE, as shown in the following screenshot, and click Save.

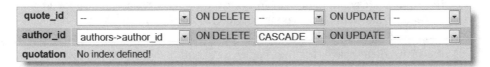

3. Open author_delete.php, and double-click Recordset (checkForeign) in the Server Behaviors panel to edit it.

4. Expand the Tables tree in the Database items area at the bottom of the Recordset dialog box, highlight quotation in the quotations table, and click the SELECT button to add it to the SQL query. This will enable you to display the dependent records about to be deleted.

5. Save the edited recordset, and locate the following section in Code view:

```
88  <h1>Delete author</h1>
89    <?php
90  if ($recordsExist) {
91    echo '<p class="warning">'.$row_checkForeign['first_name'].' '.$row_checkForeign['family_name'].' has
    dependent records. Can\'t be deleted.</p>';
92    }
93  else {
94  ?>
95  <p class="warning">Please confirm that you want to delete the following record. This operation cannot be
    undone.</p>
```

6. Delete the PHP code block shown on lines 89–94 of the preceding screenshot.

7. Delete the PHP code block immediately after the closing </form> tag. It contains only a closing curly brace to match the opening one on line 93 of the preceding screenshot.

8. Inside the form, delete the `first_name` and `family_name` text fields, leaving only the submit button and hidden field. The `<body>` section of the page should now look like this:

```
87  <body>
88  <h1>Delete author</h1>
89  <p class="warning">Please confirm that you want to delete the following record. This operation cannot be
    undone.</p>
90  <form id="form1" name="form1" method="POST">
91    <p>
92      <input type="submit" name="delete" id="delete" value="Delete author" />
93      <input name="author_id" type="hidden" id="author_id" value="<?php echo $row_getAuthor['author_id']; ?>"
    />
94    </p>
95  </form>
96  <p><a href="author_list.php">List authors</a></p>
97  </body>
```

9. Select the words the following record (shown on line 89 of the preceding screenshot), and replace them with dynamic text from the getAuthor recordset to display the author's first name and family name. Add another sentence warning that all dependent records will also be deleted at the same time.

10. You could use the page like this, but it's much better to display the dependent records that are about to be deleted. Switch to Design view, position your cursor at the end of the warning paragraph, and press Enter/Return to insert a new paragraph. Type The following records will also be deleted:.

11. Press Enter/Return, and click the Unordered List button in the Property inspector (or use Text ➤ List ➤ Unordered List).

12. Open the Bindings panel, select quotation in Recordset (checkForeign), and click Insert. Then click <li> in the Tag inspector at the bottom of the Document window to select the whole <li> element, and apply a repeat region to show all records. This will display all dependent records from the quotations table.

13. Not every record in the parent table will have dependent records, so you need to say if no records were found. Click <ul> in the Tag Inspector to select the whole unordered list, and press the right arrow key once to move the insertion point after the closing </ul> tag. Press Enter/Return to insert a new paragraph, and type No dependent records.

14. You now have contradictory displays in the page. You want to show the unordered list only if there are dependent records, and the paragraph you have just typed if there are none. Dreamweaver has another set of server behaviors for just this type of situation.

Click the <p> tag in the Tag Inspector to select the paragraph you have just typed. Then, click the plus button in the Server Behaviors panel, and select Show Region ➤ Show If Recordset Is Empty (the same option is available on the Data Objects submenu of the Insert menu). The dialog box that opens has one option: to choose the recordset. Select checkForeign, and click OK.

15. Position your cursor anywhere inside the unordered list, and click the <ul> tag in the Tag Inspector to select the whole list. Select the Show Region submenu again, and choose Show If Recordset Is Not Empty. Again, select checkForeign for Recordset.

In my testing, Dreamweaver had a problem on one occasion applying the server behavior correctly to the unordered list. In Design view, you might see a yellow highlighted </MM_HIDDENREGION> tag at the end of the list (see Figure 16-13). Yellow tags indicate incorrectly nested elements.

```php
92    <?php if ($totalRows_checkForeign > 0) { // Show if recordset not empty ?>
93    <ul>
94      <?php do { ?>
95        <li><?php echo $row_checkForeign['quotation']; ?></li>
96        <?php } while ($row_checkForeign = mysql_fetch_assoc($checkForeign)); ?>
97      <?php } // Show if recordset not empty ?>
98    </ul>
99
100   <?php if ($totalRows_checkForeign == 0) { // Show if recordset empty ?>
```

dependent records will be deleted at the same time. This operation cannot be undone.

The following dependent records will also be deleted:

Show If...

Repeat

• {checkForeign.quotation}

    </MM_HIDDENREGION>

Figure 16-13. Dreamweaver sometimes fails to position correctly the closing brace of the Show Region server behavior.

If this happens to you, reverse the order of lines 97 and 98 in Figure 16-13, to move the closing </ul> tag inside the closing curly brace of the PHP conditional statement.

You now have a user-friendly cascading delete form for use with InnoDB tables. Check your code, if necessary, against author_delete_cascade.php in examples/ch16.

Updating quotations

Now that you've dealt with all the issues involved with the parent table, authors, you can return to the child table and finish the content management system for quotations. You'll be relieved to know that building the update and delete forms doesn't involve a great deal of work. However, the presence of the foreign key in a child table does add a slight complication to creating the page that displays a list of all records. Let's start by building quote_list.php to display a list of all quotations with links to the update and delete forms.

Displaying a list of quotations

The layout of the page follows the same pattern as all other lists of records. The main difference lies in the SQL query that you build in the Recordset dialog box, because you need to draw records from the child and parent tables, using the foreign key to match records in both tables.

1. Create a PHP page called quote_list.php in workfiles/ch16, and lay it out like this:

2. Open the Recordset dialog box in Advanced mode, and build the following query:

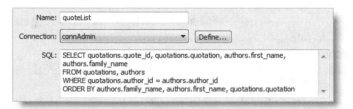

This selects the quotation and its primary key, as well as the author's first name and family name by matching the author_id in both tables. The results are ordered by family name, first name, and quotation in that order.

3. Use the Bindings panel to add the dynamic text objects to the page, building the EDIT and DELETE links in the same way as before (linking to quote_update.php and quote_delete.php and passing quote_id as a parameter through the query string.

4. Apply a repeat region and a Recordset Navigation Bar. I won't give step-by-step instructions, because you've done this before. Check your code, if necessary, against quote_list_01.php in examples/ch16.

That was easy, wasn't it? Unfortunately, it was too easy, because there's a hidden flaw in the SQL.

Load quote_insert.php into a browser, and insert a new quotation. It doesn't matter what it is, as long as you don't select an author. Leave the author drop-down menu on Not registered. Now load quote_list.php into a browser, and look for the quotation that you have just inserted. It's not listed. Double-check in phpMyAdmin, the new quotation should be at the end of the quotations table. What's going on?

Solving the mystery of missing records

The reason for the failure of quote_list.php to display quotations without an associated author lies in the WHERE expression:

```
WHERE quotations.author_id = authors.author_id
```

This works fine when there are matching records in both tables, but if the author_id foreign key hasn't been set in the quotations table, there's nothing to match it in the authors table. You need a way to find all records, even if there isn't a corresponding match for the foreign key. This is achieved in SQL by what is known as a **left join**.

The SQL queries generated by Dreamweaver are known as **inner joins**—there must be a complete match in both tables of all conditions in a WHERE expression. The difference with a left join is that when there's no match for a record in the table(s) to the "left" of the join, the result is still included in the recordset, but all the columns in the table to the "right" of the join are set to NULL. "Left" and "right" are used in the sense of which side of the keywords LEFT JOIN they appear in the SQL query. The syntax looks like this:

```
SELECT column_name(s) FROM first_table
LEFT JOIN second_table ON condition
```

If the condition is matching two columns of the same name (such as author_id), an alternative syntax can be used:

```
SELECT column_name(s) FROM first_table
LEFT JOIN second_table USING (column_name)
```

Using a left join to find incomplete records

You can now amend the SQL query in quote_list.php to use a left join. Dreamweaver doesn't have an automatic way of generating a left join, so you need to adjust the query manually. Continue working with quote_list.php from the preceding section.

1. Highlight Recordset (quoteList) in the Server Behaviors panel, and double-click it to open the Recordset dialog box.

2. Edit the SQL query by hand like this:

   ```
   SELECT quotations.quote_id, quotations.quotation, authors.first_name,
   authors.family_name
   FROM quotations LEFT JOIN authors USING (author_id)
   ORDER BY authors.family_name, authors.first_name, quotations.quotation
   ```

3. Click the Test button to make sure you haven't made any mistakes in the query. I find that I frequently forget to remove the comma after the first table name when replacing an inner join with a left join.

4. Click OK to save the recordset. Save the page, and refresh your browser. Any quotations without an author_id will now appear at the top of the list with the name column blank, as shown here:

Quotations listed by author

Name	Quotation		
	It is only with the heart that one can see rightly; what is essential is invisible to the eye.	EDIT	DELETE
Woody Allen	I don't want to achieve immortality through my work... I want to achieve it by not dying.	EDIT	DELETE

Compare your code, if necessary, with quote_list_02.php in examples/ch16.

Adapting the insert page for updates

Rather than build the update form from scratch, you can easily adapt the insert page again. Because there is no need to check for duplicate entries, this is simpler than the update page for authors. After removing the Insert Record server behavior, you create a recordset for the record being updated, bind the existing values to the quotation text area and author drop-down menu, and apply an Update Record server behavior.

1. Save quote_insert.php as quote_update.php. Change the title and heading to Update quotation. Also change the Button name and Value of the submit button to update and Update quotation, respectively.

2. Select the Insert Record server behavior in the Server Behaviors panel, and click the minus button to remove it.

3. When the EDIT link in quote_list.php is clicked, you need to display the details of the record. Open the Recordset dialog box in Simple mode, and create a recordset called getQuote, using the following settings:

4. Expand Recordset (getQuote) in the Bindings panel. Select the quotation text area in the form, and then select quotation in the recordset. Click Bind.

5. You also need the author_id drop-down menu to display the correct value. Select the menu object in the form, and click the Dynamic button in the Property inspector. All the existing values are fine, but to display the selected value dynamically, click the lightning bolt icon to the right of the Select value equal to field at the bottom of the dialog box.

In the Dynamic Data dialog box, select author_id from Recordset (getQuote), as shown in the screenshot at the top of the next page. Make sure you choose the correct recordset—both of them include author_id. The other recordset contains *all* author_id numbers; you want only the specific one associated with the quotation identified by the URL query string.

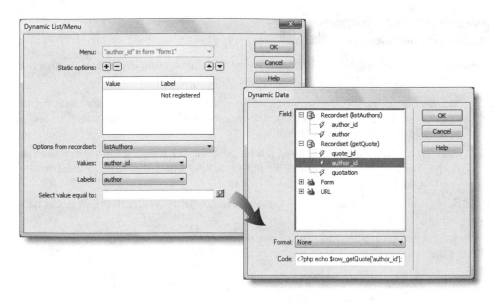

Click OK twice to close both dialog boxes. What you have just done creates the code to dynamically insert selected="selected" in the appropriate <option> tag to display the correct name from the authors table.

6. Before adding the Update Record server behavior, you need to create a hidden form field to store the correct quote_id. Click in a blank area of the form, and insert a hidden field. In the Property inspector, name the hidden field quote_id, and click the lightning bolt icon to insert dynamic data in the Value field. Choose quote_id from Recordset (getQuote), and click OK.

7. Click the plus button on the Server Behaviors panel, and choose Update Record. Use the following settings:

   - Submit values from: updateQuote
   - Connection: connAdmin
   - Update table: quotations
   - After updating, go to: quote_list.php

8. Save the page, and test it. Compare your code, if necessary, with quote_update.php in examples/ch16.

Deleting quotations

Nearly there! Just one more page to go—the page for deleting quotations is relatively simple to make, because there's no need to check for dependent records. It's only when a foreign key refers to a deleted record that you have a problem. Delete Shakespeare's records in the quotations table, and the integrity of your database remains intact. The only loss is some of the greatest sayings in the English language.

Adapting the update page for deletes

This is much simpler than the delete form for authors, because no dependent records are involved. It's a quick and easy adaptation of the update page.

1. Save quote_update.php as quote_delete.php. Change the title and heading to Delete quotation. Change the Button name and Value of the submit button to delete and Confirm deletion, respectively.

2. Insert a new paragraph between the heading and form asking for confirmation of the deletion and warning that it's not undoable. Apply the warning class to the paragraph.

3. Highlight Update Record in the Server Behaviors panel, and click the minus button to delete it.

4. Click the plus button in the Server Behaviors panel, and select Delete Record. Use the settings shown in the screenshot, and click OK.

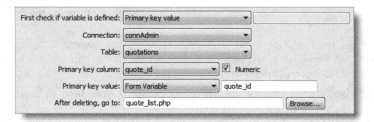

5. Save the page, and compare your code, if necessary, against quote_delete.php in examples/ch16.

You now have a complete management system for a parent and child set of tables.

What you have achieved

Creating the content management system for two tables in a parent-child relationship requires a much more complex back-end than for a single table. You may be wondering whether it's really worth the effort. The answer is *yes*. Creating a database and its related content management system is a time-consuming process, but the time spent on building a solid foundation for your database will be well rewarded.

Although this chapter has involved a lot of steps, and you've needed to dive into Code view from time to time, it's important to realize that the Dreamweaver server behaviors have taken an enormous coding burden off your shoulders. Remembering how to fill in the different dialog boxes takes time and practice, but this chapter has taken you much further by showing you how to join tables and maintain referential integrity when deleting records. This has been a relatively simple example, using just two tables. Databases frequently contain many tables with complex relationships, but the underlying principles remain the same.

In the next chapter, we'll take a more in-depth look at searching for records, as well as formatting dates.

17 SEARCHING RECORDS AND HANDLING DATES

We don't store information in a database simply for the fun of it. The idea of a database is to make it easy to find the precise information you want, when you want, and without the need to reorganize it constantly. To do this successfully, you need a good knowledge of SQL. It's a vast subject, so I'll only be able to scratch the surface by showing you some basic search techniques.

I'll also show you how to handle dates in PHP and MySQL. As you saw in Chapter 14, MySQL stores dates in the ISO format of YYYY-MM-DD. PHP takes a completely different approach, calculating dates by counting the number of seconds elapsed since January 1, 1970. It's not as complicated as it sounds, but you need to ensure that dates submitted to MySQL are in the correct format and—equally important—that you can display dates in a human-friendly way.

Specifically, this chapter shows you how to

- Display the number of results from a search
- Create striped table rows
- Troubleshoot MySQL errors
- Search for records based on full and partial matches
- Use FULLTEXT indexing
- Reuse a recordset after a repeat region
- Format dates with MySQL and PHP

To work with most of the examples in this chapter, you need to have created the authors and quotations tables and populated them with data, as described in Chapter 16. The examples with dates are based on the feedback table from Chapter 14.

Querying a database and displaying the results

By now, you should be very familiar with creating recordsets. In Chapter 14, you started off by using the Recordset dialog box in Simple mode to select all records in the feedback table and to filter a recordset by using a primary key passed through a query string. In the previous chapter, you took things a lot further by using the Advanced mode, selecting records from two tables, and even using a left join to find records that don't have a matching foreign key. As you have probably realized by now, a recordset is the result of a database search. Controlling the search is a SQL query using the SELECT command.

Dreamweaver builds the PHP code that passes the SQL query to the database and processes the result. It can also build the SQL query for very simple searches. For anything more sophisticated, it's up to you to build the query yourself. Over the next few pages, I'll show you how to tackle some common search problems. However, writing SELECT queries is a massive subject, about which whole books have been written (one of my favorite writers on MySQL is Paul DuBois). So treat this chapter as an introduction to a fascinating and rewarding subject, rather than a definitive guide to search queries.

Enhancing the look of search results

Before getting into the nitty-gritty of searching, let's take a quick look at a couple of ways to improve the presentation of a list of search results: showing the number of records retrieved and giving table rows an alternating background color. Both are quick and easy to implement.

Displaying the number of search results

The big search engines, such as Google or Yahoo!, always tell you how many records matched your criteria. In Dreamweaver, the Recordset Navigation Status data object makes this child's play.

Using the Recordset Navigation Status data object

You can do this with any page that contains a recordset, but I'll use quote_list.php from the previous chapter because it contains 50 results displayed over several pages. You can use your own file from workfiles/ch16 or copy quote_list_start.php from examples/ch17.

1. Open the page in the Document window, position the insertion point at the end of the page heading, and press Enter/Return to insert a new paragraph above the table that displays the recordset.

2. Select Recordset Navigation Status on the Data tab of the Insert bar, as shown in the following screenshot. Alternatively, use Insert ➤ Data Objects ➤ Display Record Count ➤ Recordset Navigation Status.

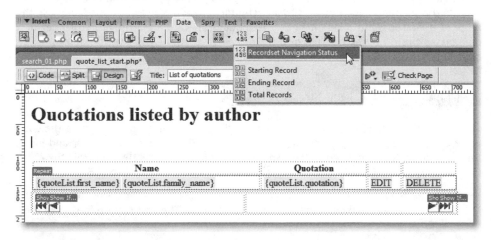

3. The dialog box has only one option: to choose the recordset that you want to use. There's only one on this page, so just click OK. Dreamweaver inserts a mixture of static and dynamic text to display the numbers of the first and last records currently being displayed, plus the total number of records in the recordset.

4. Save the page, and test it in a browser. As you move back and forth through the recordset, the numbers of the currently displayed records change dynamically, as shown in the following screenshot:

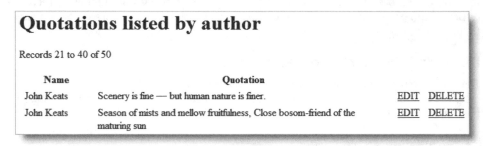

Check your code, if necessary, against quote_list_stats.php in examples/ch17.

You can edit the static text surrounding the dynamic text object to customize the display. As you can see from the screenshot in step 2, the starting record, ending record, and total records numbers can be inserted independently. These independent options can also be accessed from the Display Record Count submenu of the Server Behaviors panel.

Creating striped table rows

Viewing a long list of similar items on a computer screen can be tiring on the eyes, so it's often useful to give alternate rows a background color. This is very easy with a little bit of simple math and PHP. If you divide any number by 2, the remainder is always 1 or 0. Since PHP treats 1 as true, and 0 as false (see "The truth according to PHP" in Chapter 10), all you need is a counter; increment it by 1 each time a new table row is added, and use the modulo operator (%) to divide it by 2. The modulo operator returns the remainder of a division, so this produces 1 (true) or 0 (false) every alternate row, which you can use to control the CSS class for a different background color.

Using modulo to create stripes in alternate rows

This exercise uses the same page as in the preceding section. It involves locating the code for the repeat region and adding two short blocks of PHP to add the counter and insert the class in every alternate row. You also need to define the class that controls the background color.

1. In the Server Behaviors panel, select Repeat Region (quoteList). This highlights the repeat region, making it easy to find in Code view. The first section looks like this:

```
101      </tr>
102 ☐    <?php do { ?>
103        <tr>
104          <td><?php echo $row_quoteList['first_name']; ?>
```

The code shown on line 102 is the start of a do . . . while loop that iterates through the quoteList recordset to display the list of quotations (see Chapter 10 for details of loops).

2. Amend the code like this (new code is shown in bold type):

```
</tr>
<?php $counter = 0; // initialize counter outside loop ?>
<?php do { ?>
  <tr <?php if ($counter++ % 2) {echo 'class="hilite"';} ?>>
    <td><?php echo $row_quoteList['first_name']; ?>
```

The first new block of code initializes the counter outside the loop, while the second increments the counter by 1 inside the loop, and uses modulo to create a Boolean (true/false) test to insert the hilite class in alternate rows. I have used separate blocks to avoid breaking Dreamweaver's Repeat Region server behavior code.

The increment operator (++) performs the current calculation and then adds 1 to the variable. So, the first time through the loop $counter is 0. This leaves a remainder of 0 (false), so the hilite class isn't inserted into the <tr> tag. Next time, the calculation produces a remainder of 1 (true), and so on until the loop comes to an end.

3. Define the hilite class with the background color of your choice. Save the page, and view it in a browser. Voilà, stripes. You can check your code against quote_list_stripes.php in examples/ch17.

Name	Quotation		
Alfred, Lord Tennyson	In the spring a young man's fancy lightly turns to thoughts of love	EDIT	DELETE
Mark Twain	Familiarity breeds contempt — and children.	EDIT	DELETE
Mark Twain	Good breeding consists in concealing how much we think of ourselves and how little we think of the other person.	EDIT	DELETE
Mark Twain	Man is the only animal that blushes. Or needs to.	EDIT	DELETE
François Villon	Mais où sont les neiges d'antan? (But where are the snows of yesteryear?)	EDIT	DELETE

Some developers use slightly more complex code to insert a different class in odd-numbered rows, too. This isn't necessary. By utilizing the cascade in your CSS, you can set a default background color for the table, and override it with the hilite class like this:

```
#striped tr {background-color: #EEE;}
#striped tr.hilite {background-color: #E8F2F8;}
```

These rules will produce alternate pale gray and pale blue stripes in a table with an ID called striped. If you want to use the same effect in more than one table, change striped from an ID to a class.

To get rid of the vertical gaps between cells, set cellpadding to 0, or use text-collapse: collapse in a style rule that applies to the table.

Understanding how Dreamweaver builds a SQL query

Relying entirely on Dreamweaver to construct your queries puts you at a disadvantage when seeking help in an online forum or reading a book or tutorial not specifically aimed at Dreamweaver users. So it's important to understand the code that's generated. You don't need to learn how to write the code yourself. The purpose is to recognize various parts of the script and know what they do. With that knowledge, you can easily adapt SQL queries from other sources.

The file find_author_01.php in examples/ch17 contains a form with a single text field called first_name and a submit button. Beneath the form is a table with a single row in a repeat region, which displays the results of the search. Load the page into a browser, type William in the text field, and click Search. You should see a list of authors whose first name is William, as shown here:

Try some other names, such as John, Dorothy, and Mae, and a list of matching records is displayed. By default, text searches in MySQL are case insensitive, so it doesn't matter what combination of uppercase and lowercase you use. We'll get on to case-sensitive and partial-word searches later, but let's look at the code that Dreamweaver uses to submit the query to the database.

I created the getAuthors recordset in find_author_01.php using the following settings in the Recordset dialog box in Simple mode:

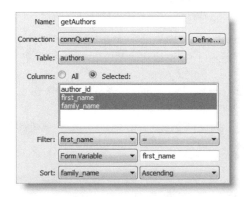

The same query looks like this in Advanced mode:

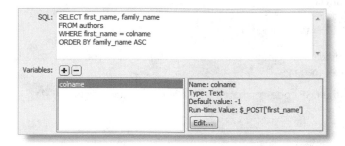

The first thing to note is that Dreamweaver doesn't add the table name in front of each column name when you use the Recordset dialog box in Simple mode. As explained in the previous chapter, adding the table name is necessary only when the same column name is used in more than one table (like author_id in the authors and quotations tables). Simple mode is capable of handling only single tables, so there's never any danger of ambiguity. However, Dreamweaver automatically adds the table names to all columns when you build a query in Advanced mode. It does so as a precautionary measure, even if there's no likelihood of ambiguity.

The other thing to note is that the Filter settings from Simple mode have been converted to this:

```
WHERE first_name = colname
```

Dreamweaver uses colname to represent the unknown value that will be passed to the SQL query through the text field in find_author_01.php. The properties of colname are defined in the Variables area below, with Type set to Text, Default value to -1, and Run-time Value to $_POST['first_name'].

> *Even though* first_name *uses a text datatype, it's perfectly acceptable to use -1 as the default value. Numbers can be stored as text. In fact, it's sometimes essential to do so. Telephone numbers usually contain nonnumeric characters, and a staff number might begin with a leading zero, which would be stripped off by a numeric datatype.*

It's important to realize that colname is not part of SQL. Dreamweaver uses the concept of replacement when dealing with unknown values in SQL queries. When you close the Recordset dialog box, Dreamweaver replaces colname with PHP code that inserts the runtime value into the query. So, in this example, it inserts "William" or whatever name is input into the search form. The choice of colname is purely arbitrary. It can be anything that doesn't clash with the rest of the query. In the previous chapter, you used var1 and var2 as the names for runtime variables.

The other important thing to know about Dreamweaver's use of runtime variables is that the PHP code automatically encloses the value in quotes unless you specify Type as Numeric. Because strings must be enclosed in quotes, the correct way to write this query in SQL is as follows (assuming that you're searching for "William"):

```
SELECT first_name, family_name
FROM authors
WHERE first_name = 'William'
ORDER BY family_name ASC
```

Because Dreamweaver handles the quotes automatically, you need to adapt SQL from other sources accordingly.

Now, look at the PHP code generated by these settings (see Figure 17-1).

```
32  $colname_getAuthors = "-1";
33  if (isset($_POST['first_name'])) {
34    $colname_getAuthors = $_POST['first_name'];
35  }
36  mysql_select_db($database_connQuery, $connQuery);
37  $query_getAuthors = sprintf("SELECT first_name, family_name FROM authors WHERE first_name = %s
    ORDER BY family_name ASC", GetSQLValueString($colname_getAuthors, "text"));
38  $getAuthors = mysql_query($query_getAuthors, $connQuery) or die(mysql_error());
39  $row_getAuthors = mysql_fetch_assoc($getAuthors);
40  $totalRows_getAuthors = mysql_num_rows($getAuthors);
```

Figure 17-1. The code Dreamweaver generates to create a recordset using a form variable

The first section of code (lines 32–35 in Figure 17-1) uses the runtime variable to create a PHP variable, which derives its name from a combination of the runtime variable (colname) and the recordset name (getAuthors) to become $colname_getAuthors.

Line 32 sets $colname_getAuthors to the default value. The conditional statement on lines 33–35 checks to see whether the form variable ($_POST['first_name']) exists. If it does, $colname_getAuthors is reset to whatever value is submitted from the form.

If further runtime variables are used in the Recordset dialog box, each one is converted to a PHP variable in a similar manner.

The code shown on line 36 of Figure 17-1 selects the appropriate database using variables that are stored in the MySQL connection you created for the site (see Chapter 14).

The SQL query that performs the search is the long section of code shown on line 37. Dreamweaver uses a PHP function called sprintf() to build the query and assigns the result to a variable called $query_*recordsetName* (in this case, $query_getAuthors).

The sprintf() function can be difficult to get your head around, but it takes a minimum of two arguments. The first of these is a string that contains one or more predefined placeholders; the number of remaining arguments matches the number of placeholders in the first argument. When the script runs, sprintf() replaces each placeholder with its corresponding argument.

Why use such a convoluted way of inserting something into the SQL query? It's a short-hand way of passing the runtime variables to another function without the need to assign the result to a variable. Dreamweaver passes all runtime variables to a custom-built function called GetSQLValueString(), which is a security measure against SQL injection. GetSQLValueString() checks a variable from an external source, such as a form, makes sure it's of the expected datatype, and prepares it for insertion into the SQL query. This involves removing magic quotes, escaping characters that cause problems with database queries, and surrounding the variable with quotes, if necessary. If Dreamweaver didn't use sprintf(), it would need to store the result of passing each runtime variable to GetSQLValueString() before building the query. It also avoids complex problems with escaping quotes with a lot of variables.

The most commonly used predefined placeholder used with sprintf() is %s, which stands for "string." So, the colname that you saw in the Recordset dialog box becomes %s, and when the script runs, it is replaced by the result of GetSQLValueString($colname_getAuthors, "text").

When there's more than one runtime variable in a SQL query, Dreamweaver replaces each one with %s, and passes it to GetSQLValueString() when listing the variable as an argument to sprintf().

> GetSQLValueString() *automatically handles quotes around text values, so you shouldn't add quotes around the* %s *placeholder in* sprintf().

The final three lines of code in Figure 17-1 pass the SQL query to MySQL, extract the first record from the recordset, and find out how many records were found. $row_*recordsetName* stores the first record, and $totalRows_*recordsetName* stores the number of records retrieved.

Troubleshooting SQL queries

At the end of line 38 in Figure 17-1 is this rather doom-laden command:

```
or die(mysql_error());
```

This tells the script to stop running if there's a problem with the SQL query, and to display the error message returned by MySQL. Figure 17-2 shows what happens if you add single quotes around the %s placeholder in the SQL query in find_author_01.php.

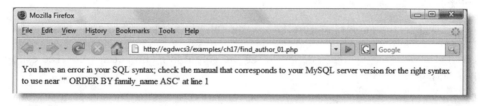

Figure 17-2. MySQL error messages look cryptic but are very useful.

The error is reported as being on line 1, because the message comes from MySQL, not PHP. MySQL sees only the query, so the error is always on line 1. The important information is the reference to the error being "near" a particular part of the query. The error is always immediately preceding the segment quoted in the message, but the only way to diagnose the problem is to study the contents of the query.

Don't waste time trying to analyze the code. As explained earlier, the SQL query is stored in a variable called $query_*recordsetName*. Dive into Code view, use echo to display the query onscreen, and comment out the section of code that submits it to MySQL, as shown in the following illustration:

1. Use echo to display the contents of the SQL query.

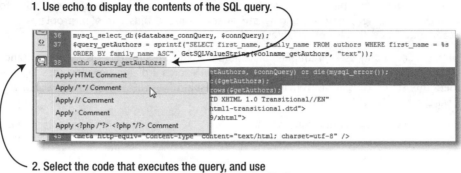

2. Select the code that executes the query, and use
   Apply /**/ Comment on the Coding toolbar to disable it.

You can then load the page into a browser and see exactly what is being sent to the database. In the case of find_author_01.php, the query is displayed as soon as you load the page (see Figure 17-3). In some cases, you need to pass the necessary values to the query through the form or as part of a query string in the browser address bar. You might see a lot of error messages onscreen, but that's not important. As long as you can see what the SQL query contains, you can get to the root of the problem.

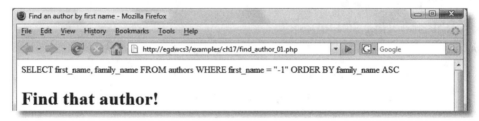

Figure 17-3. Displaying the contents of a SQL query onscreen is the best way to analyze MySQL errors.

At first glance, the output in Figure 17-3 seems OK, but on closer inspection, what looks like a pair of double quotes around -1 is, in fact, four single quotes (if you try this yourself, use the browser's View Source option to see the output in monospaced type). The extra pair of quotes is causing the error.

Even if you can't spot the problem yourself, you can copy the output and paste it into a question in an online forum. You're much more likely to get a helpful response by showing what's being passed to the database and giving details of the MySQL error message.

You can use this technique with all SQL queries, not just SELECT ones.

Setting search criteria

All the SELECT queries used so far in this book have either retrieved all records or used a single search criterion, but you often want to search on the basis of multiple conditions. As Table 16-2 in the previous chapter shows, SQL accepts multiple conditions in a WHERE clause, using AND or OR. Let's use the authors and quotations tables from the previous chapter to perform a variety of searches. We'll start with the authors table and then get more adventurous by adding the quotations table into the mix.

Using numerical comparisons

17

As you've already seen, a single equal sign in a SQL query looks for an exact match. You can also use comparison operators, such as > (greater than) and < (less than). This would be of more practical value in a price list, where you're looking for something cheaper or more expensive than a particular amount, but you can demonstrate it using the primary key column of the authors table, which uses numbers.

In find_author_02.php, I changed the Filter setting in the Recordset dialog box in Simple mode to author_id < Form Variable author_id. This changes the WHERE clause to this:

```
WHERE author_id < colname
```

The Type of colname is changed to Numeric, and its Runtime Value to $_POST['author_id']. Because the default is left at -1, nothing is displayed when the page first loads, but if you enter a number and click the Search button, you see a list of all authors with a primary key lower than the figure entered.

> *For a greater-than comparison, the default needs to be higher than any existing value in the column. If you leave it at -1, all records are displayed when the page first loads.*

This is a rather trivial example, but if you go through the various Filter options in Simple mode, and examine the SQL in Advanced mode, you'll quickly learn how the operators are used in a SQL query. Dreamweaver uses <> as the "not equal to" operator instead of !=. Either is perfectly acceptable.

At the bottom of the Filter drop-down menu are three options: begins with, ends with, and contains. These perform wildcard searches, where the user enters only part of the search term. Unfortunately, the code generated by Dreamweaver fails when you use any of these options with a numeric column. I'll come back to wildcard searches later in the chapter and explain how to perform them successfully with either text or numbers.

Although the Filter options in Simple mode have their uses, they're not very practical in a real-world situation. Normally, you want a search form to offer the user a variety of options. That's where an understanding of the code generated by Dreamweaver becomes invaluable.

Roll up your sleeves to create something a little more practical.

Performing user-controlled comparisons

This exercise enhances find_author_02.php by adding a drop-down menu that gives the user the option to choose how the comparison should be performed—greater than, less than, equal to, or not equal to. The selection is passed to the SQL query as a form variable. Since Dreamweaver has options only for numbers and text, you need to do some elementary hand-coding.

1. Copy find_author_02.php from examples/ch17, and save it as find_author_03.php in workfiles/ch17.

2. Click inside the Author_id label to the left of the text field, select the <label> tag in the Tag selector at the bottom of the Document window, and press the right arrow key once to position the insertion point correctly between the label and text field.

3. Select List/Menu from the Forms tab of the Insert bar (or use the Form submenu of the Insert menu). In the Input Tag Accessibility Attributes dialog box, enter operator in the ID field, leave Label blank, select No label tag, and click OK.

4. Click the List Values button in the Property inspector, and enter the following operators in both the Item Label and Value fields: =, !=, <, <=, >, and >=. Although you don't normally need to set the Value field if it's the same as Item Label, you need to do it on this occasion, because Dreamweaver replaces the less-than and greater-than operators with HTML entities.

5. Select the equal sign as Initially Selected.

6. Open Split view, and edit the value properties of the <option> tags to change the HTML entities to the less-than and greater-than operators. Leave the HTML entities intact between the opening and closing <option> tags. The page should look like this:

7. Switch to Code view, and scroll up to locate the recordset code, which looks like this:

```
31
32   $colname_getAuthors = "-1";
33   if (isset($_POST['author_id'])) {
34     $colname_getAuthors = $_POST['author_id'];
35   }
36   mysql_select_db($database_connQuery, $connQuery);
37   $query_getAuthors = sprintf("SELECT first_name, family_name FROM authors WHERE author_id < %s
     ORDER BY family_name ASC", GetSQLValueString($colname_getAuthors, "int"));
```

8. You need to replace the < in the WHERE clause (shown on line 37 of the preceding screenshot) with a variable and define it in the same way as Dreamweaver has done with colname. Begin by positioning your cursor on the blank line shown on line 31 and inserting the following code:

```
// define the operator variable and give it a default value
$operator = '=';
// define an array of acceptable operators
$permittedOperators = array('=', '!=', '<', '<=', '>', '>=');
// get operator value from form, if submitted
if (isset($_POST['operator']) && in_array($_POST['operator'], ➥
$permittedOperators)) {
  $operator = $_POST['operator'];
  }
```

This sets $operator to a default value of an equal sign, defines an array of acceptable operators, and reassigns the value submitted from the form, if it exists and is one of the permitted operators. Using the $permittedOperators array and in_array() like this performs a similar security check to the $expected array that you used with the feedback form in Chapter 11. Any variable that's passed to a SQL query should be scrutinized to prevent SQL injection.

9. Now edit the SQL query (shown on line 37 of the preceding screenshot) like this (new code is highlighted in bold):

```
$query_getAuthors = sprintf("SELECT first_name, family_name ➥
FROM authors WHERE author_id %s %s ORDER BY family_name ASC", ➥
$operator, GetSQLValueString($colname_getAuthors, "int"));
```

As explained earlier in "Understanding how Dreamweaver builds a SQL query," sprintf() uses %s as a placeholder and replaces each one in order by the subsequent arguments passed to the function. So, the form values are both passed to the SQL query in a secure manner; the first %s is replaced by the operator, and the second one is replaced the value entered in the text field.

10. Save the page, and test it in a browser. Enter 32 in the text field, and click Search. William Shakespeare should be displayed. Change the operator to !=, and perform the same search. All authors except Shakespeare are displayed, and so on.

You can check your code against find_author_03.php in examples/ch17.

Searching within a numerical range

There are two ways to specify a range in SQL. One is to use >= (greater than or equal to) for the bottom end of the range and <= (less than or equal to) for the top end. The alternative is BETWEEN . . . AND. Both require two input fields. This means setting two variables, so you're obliged to use the Recordset dialog box in Advanced mode. The files find_author_04.php and find_author_05.php in examples/ch17 have been modified by adding a second text input field and naming the two fields min and max. The recordset settings in find_author_04.php look like this:

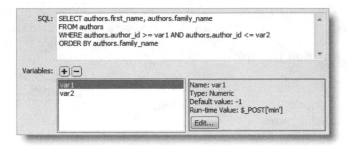

I have used var1 and var2 as the runtime variables and given them both the same settings, as shown in the preceding screenshot (Run-time Value for var2 is $_POST['max']).

The only difference in find_author_05.php is the WHERE clause in the SQL query, which looks like this:

```
WHERE authors.author_id BETWEEN var1 AND var2
```

If you test both pages in a browser, they produce identical results. As long as you enter a number in both fields, you should see a list of authors' names (unless, of course, the minimum is greater than the highest number in the table).

Now try entering a value in just the minimum field. As you might expect, there are no results. This is hardly surprising, because the default value of var2 (which controls the maximum) is set to -1. So try just the maximum field. Again, no results. This is more puzzling, because the default for the minimum field is also -1, so you would expect to get a list of authors whose primary keys belong in the range from 1 (since primary keys can't be negative) to whatever you entered in the maximum field.

You need to look at the code to understand what's happening.

Experimenting with the default value

This exercise helps explain how the default value of a runtime variable is used in a SQL query. It also shows how to tweak the Dreamweaver code to influence the way default values are used. You can use either find_author_04.php or find_author_05.php, as the PHP code is identical.

1. In the Server Behaviors panel, double-click Recordset (getAuthors) to open the Recordset dialog box. Select var2 in the Variables field, click the Edit button, and change Default value to 10. Since var2 is the runtime variable for max, this resets the default maximum.

2. Save the changes, and load the page into a browser. The names of the first ten authors are displayed after the form.

3. Enter a number between 1 and 9 in the Minimum field, but leave the Maximum field empty. Click Search. It doesn't matter what number you choose, nothing is displayed. So what's happened to the default you set in step 1?

4. To find out, open Code view, and locate the code that sets the default values. It looks like this:

```
32   $var1_getAuthors = "-1";
33   if (isset($_POST['min'])) {
34     $var1_getAuthors = $_POST['min'];
35   }
36   $var2_getAuthors = "10";
37   if (isset($_POST['max'])) {
38     $var2_getAuthors = $_POST['max'];
39   }
```

The code shown on line 36 sets the default value of $var2_getAuthors to 10. However, the conditional statement on lines 37–39 resets it if the value of $_POST['max'] has been defined. I imagine that many of you will be scratching your head at this point. Surely, if the field is left blank, the value isn't defined? Wrong. It is defined—as an empty string. As a result the WHERE clause in find_author_04.php is converted to this:

WHERE authors.author_id >= -1 AND authors.author_id <=

Similarly, the WHERE clause in find_author_05.php has no maximum. Without it, the SQL query returns no results. It doesn't trigger any error messages, either, because a valid value is passed to the query. The problem is that it's a number you want, not an empty string.

5. To preserve the default number when a blank field is submitted, change the code shown on line 37 like this:

if (isset($_POST['max']) **&& !empty($_POST['max'])**) {

6. Test the page again. This time, if you leave the Maximum field blank, the script uses 10 as its default value. Of course, you can override this by entering a different number in the field. But if you leave the Minimum field blank, you still get no results. It needs to be changed in the same way if you always want a default value to be used when the form is submitted.

Is this a bug in Dreamweaver? It depends on your point of view. When creating runtime variables in Simple mode, Dreamweaver always uses -1 as its default value. This ensures that a search form displays no results when the page first loads. This is usually what you want, but you should ask, "Why bother to run the SQL query when the page first loads?" It's inefficient to submit a query to the database when no search criteria have been defined.

The more efficient way to prevent the display of recordset results when a search form first loads is to wrap the recordset code in a conditional statement and execute the SQL query only when the search form has been submitted. If you name the submit button search, you can use the following code:

```
if (array_key_exists('search', $_POST)) {
  // recordset code goes here
  }
```

17

This is the same technique as used in Chapter 11 to make sure that the client-side valida-tion of the feedback form is run only after the form has been submitted. Since the record-set isn't created when the page first loads, you need to wrap the table that displays the recordset results in a similar conditional statement. You also need to amend this block of code below the closing </html> tag:

```php
<?php
mysql_free_result($recordsetName);
?>
```

Change it like this:

```php
<?php
if (isset($recordsetName)) mysql_free_result($recordsetName);
?>
```

A fully commented version of this code is in find_author_06.php in examples/ch17. Only the form is displayed when the page first loads. If nothing is entered in either or both of the text fields when the form is submitted, the default values are used. Otherwise, the search is based on the values entered into each field. This results in a much more efficient way of searching through a numerical range.

Searching for text

Searching for text follows the same basic principles, but there are more options, as you frequently need to base text searches on partial information. For example, you might want to find all authors whose family name begins with "S," or you might want to search for quotations that contain the word "winter." In some cases, you might also want the search to be case sensitive.

Making a search case sensitive

As explained earlier, text searches in MySQL are, by default, case insensitive. To enforce case sensitivity, you simply add the keyword BINARY in front of the runtime variable.

In find_author_01.php (see "Understanding how Dreamweaver builds a SQL query" earlier in the chapter), the SQL query looks like this:

```sql
SELECT first_name, family_name
FROM authors
WHERE first_name = colname
ORDER BY family_name ASC
```

When the form is submitted, colname is replaced by the value in the first_name field. To make the search case sensitive, change the WHERE clause like this:

```sql
WHERE first_name = BINARY colname
```

The SQL query in find_author_07.php performs a case-sensitive search. Enter John in the search field, and you get three results. Enter john, JOHN, or any other combination of uppercase and lowercase letters, and you'll see no results.

Displaying a message when no results are found

It's not very user friendly to leave users wondering whether a search is still being performed or whether it simply produced no results. The Show Region server behavior makes it easy to display a special message if nothing is found.

Using the Show Region server behavior

This brief exercise shows you how to add a message to find_author_07.php to tell a user that no results were found. The default code generated by Dreamweaver needs to be edited slightly if you don't want the message to appear when the page first loads.

1. Copy find_author_07.php from examples/ch17, and save it in workfiles/ch17 as find_author_08.php.

2. Click inside the search form, select <form#form1> in the Tag selector at the bottom of the Document window, and press your right arrow key once to place the insertion point outside the closing </form> tag.

3. Press Enter/Return to insert a new paragraph, click the Bold button in the Property inspector, and type No results found.

4. Click the <p> tag in the Tag selector to highlight the paragraph that you have just inserted, and select Show Region ➤ Show If Recordset Is Empty from the Server Behaviors panel menu (the same options are also available on the Data tab of the Insert bar and the Data Objects submenu of the Insert menu).

5. The dialog box that opens has only one option: for you to select the recordset. Since there's only one on this page, it automatically selects the correct one, so just click OK. This surrounds the selected paragraph with a gray border and a Show If tab at the top-left corner, indicating that it's controlled by a conditional statement.

6. Save the page, and load it into a browser. As the following screenshot shows, the No results found message is automatically displayed:

This is because of the way that Dreamweaver handles runtime variables (see "Searching within a numerical range" earlier in the chapter). Unless you wrap the recordset code in a conditional statement, as described earlier, the SQL query is submitted to the database when the page first loads. The default value of -1 deliberately prevents any results from being found, so the message is displayed.

There are two ways to get around this. One is to wrap the code in conditional statements as described earlier (the Show Region server behavior code needs to go inside the conditional statement that controls the display of results). The other, simpler solution is to edit the Show Region server behavior code. This time, we'll take the second option.

7. Select Show If Recordset is Empty (getAuthors) in the Server Behaviors panel to select the server behavior code, and switch to Code view. The code should be highlighted like this:

```
58  </form>
59
60  <?php if ($totalRows_getAuthors == 0) { // Show if recordset empty ?>
61      <p><strong>No results found</strong></p>
62      <?php } // Show if recordset empty ?>
63  <table width="400">
```

8. You want the code in this conditional statement to be executed only if the form has been submitted, so amend the code shown on line 60 like this:

```
<?php if (array_key_exists('search', $_POST) && $totalRows_getAuthors➥
== 0) { // Show if form submitted and recordset empty ?>
```

Changing the code like this prevents you from editing the Show Record server behavior in the Server Behaviors panel, but it tidies up the display of your search form. When you reload the page into a browser, the message is hidden until you conduct a search that genuinely produces no results.

Check your code, if necessary, against find_author_08.php in examples/ch17.

The Show Record server behavior has a companion option: Show If Recordset Is Not Empty. It's applied in exactly the same way. Its main purpose is to keep static text hidden if no results are found. For example, you might want to display a Recordset Navigation Status data object only when there's at least one result. You can also use it to keep text or column headings hidden unless there's a search result.

Searching multiple columns

Frequently, text searches are based on matching multiple criteria or alternatives. SQL uses AND and OR to build such queries. The meaning is self-explanatory. To search for an author by both first name and family name, create a second runtime variable, such as colname2, and change the WHERE clause to this:

```
WHERE first_name = colname AND family_name = colname2
```

To search on the basis of either first name or family name, change the WHERE clause to this:

```
WHERE first_name = colname OR family_name = colname2
```

Examples of this are in find_author_09.php and find_author_10.php, respectively, in examples/ch17. The file find_author_11.php shows an example of passing AND or OR as a runtime variable to the SQL query using the same technique as described earlier in "Performing user-controlled comparisons."

Searching with a partial match

In SQL, the equal sign looks only for an exact match. All the examples so far have used the authors table, where each column normally contains only a single word. A search for "William" produces two results: William Shakespeare and William Wordsworth. However, a search for "Will" produces no results. You might also want to search for all family names beginning with "S" or search the quotations table for all entries that include "winter."

When searching through columns that contain short text entries or numbers, you can use wildcard characters in your search. For longer sections of text, you should consider creating a FULLTEXT index. We'll look briefly at both approaches.

Using wildcard characters in a search

MySQL has two wildcard characters: the underscore (_) matches a single character, and the percentage sign (%) matches any number of characters. A particularly useful feature about % is that it also matches nothing. This means that a search for "Will%" matches both William and Will on its own. Consequently, most wildcard searches use %.

To use a wildcard character in a SQL query in Dreamweaver, add it to the beginning, end, or both ends of the runtime variable. Also, replace the equal sign with the keyword LIKE. So, to search for authors based on the first part of their name, change the WHERE clause in find_author_09.php like this:

```
WHERE first_name LIKE colname% AND family_name LIKE colname2%
```

You can test this in find_author_12.php. Start by entering the first part of a name in both fields. For example, if you type W in the First name field and S in the Family name field, the result is William Shakespeare. Try it again, just typing W in the First name field. You should see four results.

Pause a moment to think about this. The SQL query uses AND, so shouldn't there be something in both fields? To understand what's happened, repeat the test with find_author_13.php. The SQL query is identical, but the page displays the query along with the results (see Figure 17-4 on the next page).

Although nothing is entered in the second field, the wildcard character % is added to the end of the runtime variable. This results in the second condition matching the family_name column with %—in other words, anything.

Now try it with find_author_14.php, where the only difference is that AND has been changed to OR.

If you enter values in both fields, you'll get the results that you expect. However, if you leave one of the fields blank, you'll always get a full list of all records. This is because the query tells the database to match anything in one of the fields.

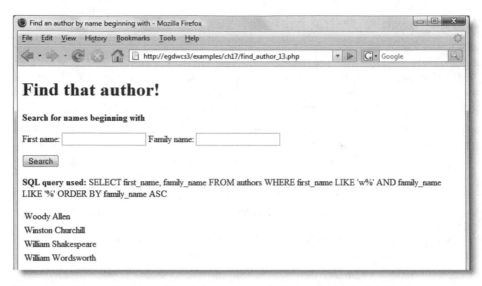

Figure 17-4. Using AND with a wildcard character search allows a field to be left blank.

> *This illustrates an important difference between SQL and PHP. When it encounters* OR, *the PHP engine doesn't bother to evaluate the second half of the condition if the first half is* true. *In a SQL query, however, both sides are evaluated. So, in the first case, the SQL query finds authors whose first name begins with "W" AND whose family name is anything. In the second case, it finds authors whose first name begins with "W" OR whose family name is anything. Creating searches with wildcards can be confusing, so it's a good idea to display the SQL query onscreen while testing to understand why you get the results you do.*

Adding % at the front of a runtime variable lets you search for words that end with a particular letter or series of characters. Putting % at both ends of a runtime variable finds the search expression in the middle of a string; and since % can also match nothing, it means the search term can be anywhere—at the beginning, in the middle, at the end, or it can even be the full string itself.

So, let's bring the quotations table into our search.

Searching for quotations that contain a word or phrase

This exercise adapts the SQL query used in quote_list.php in the last chapter. Instead of displaying a list of all quotations and their authors, it uses a runtime variable with % at both ends to search for quotations that contain a specific word or phrase. To save you time, I have created find_quote_01.php in examples/ch17 for you to use as a starting point. The finished code is in find_quote_02.php.

1. Copy find_quote_01.php to workfiles/ch17, and open it in the Document window. The page contains a form with a single text input field called searchTerm, a submit button, and code to display the results of the search.

2. Double-click Recordset (getQuote) in the Server Behaviors panel to open the Recordset dialog box. The SQL query looks like this:

```
SELECT authors.first_name, authors.family_name, quotations.quotation
FROM authors, quotations
WHERE quotations.author_id = authors.author_id
ORDER BY authors.family_name
```

It's the same as in quote_list.php. Click the Test button, and you'll see every quotation listed with its author's name.

3. To search for quotations containing a particular word or phrase, you need to add the quotation column to the WHERE clause. In the Database items section at the bottom of the Recordset dialog box, expand Tables, and highlight quotation in the quotations tree menu. Click the WHERE button to add it to the SQL query. The WHERE clause should now look like this:

```
WHERE quotations.author_id = authors.author_id AND quotation.quotation
```

4. Add LIKE %var1% to the end of the WHERE clause, click the plus button alongside Variables, and define the runtime variable var1 using the following settings:

   - Name: var1
   - Type: Text
   - Default value: -1
   - Runtime value: $_POST['searchTerm']

   The settings in the SQL and Variables fields should now look like this:

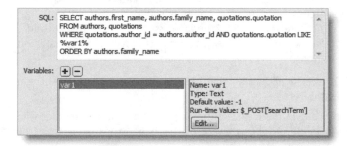

5. Click OK to close the Recordset dialog box, save the page, and load it into a browser. The quotations contain a lot of seasonal references, so enter summer or winter in the Search for field. You should see a list of quotations that contain the search term.

6. Searches with the % wildcard aren't limited to single words. Try entering just x in the Search for field. You should see a quotation from Winston Churchill that contains the word "except."

7. You can also search for a phrase. Enter red, red rose, and click the Search button. You should see the following result:

Find that quotation

Search for: [   ]

[Submit]

Robert Burns   Oh, my Luve's like a red, red rose
                            That's newly sprung in June

Note that the phrase must be exact and must not be enclosed in quotes.

Check your code, if necessary, against find_quote_02.php in examples/ch17.

In this exercise, I used only one search term, but there's no limit to the number of runtime variables that you can use. However, the more complex a search becomes, the longer it takes to process, so it's wise to limit the number of options.

This type of wildcard search works fine for even quite large databases. I use it on a database that contains more than 14,000 records, and the search results are normally displayed in one or two seconds. If you need to do a lot of text searches, you might consider FULLTEXT indexing, which offers a more sophisticated range of text search options.

Before moving on to FULLTEXT indexing, we need to take a look at using wildcard characters with numbers, because this causes a lot of confusion.

Changed

Using wildcard characters with numbers

When the Dreamweaver 8.0.2 updater was released in mid-2006, many people complained that wildcard searches for numerical columns suddenly stopped working. Dreamweaver CS3 uses the same code as the 8.0.2 updater, so to be able to use wildcard characters when searching for numbers, you need to understand why things now work differently. There are two reasons:

- The SQL specification says that LIKE is for use with strings. Dreamweaver now enforces this rule.
- There is a bug in the way that the Recordset dialog box handles wildcard searches in Simple mode. Adobe is aware of this bug, so it's likely to be corrected in an updater to Dreamweaver CS3.

The easiest way to explain how to get around both issues is with a practical exercise.

Setting the correct datatype for wildcard searches with numbers

This exercise shows you how to use wildcards with numerical columns. All that's necessary is to check that Dreamweaver treats the runtime variable as text.

1. Open `find_author_15.php` in examples/ch17. It contains all the necessary code to search for authors by primary key, using a wildcard search for `author_id`.

2. Double-click Recordset (getAuthors) in the Server Behaviors panel to open the Recordset dialog box. Switch to Simple mode, if necessary. The settings should look like this:

3. Click the Test button, and enter a test value when prompted. If you enter 3, you should see a set of results like this:

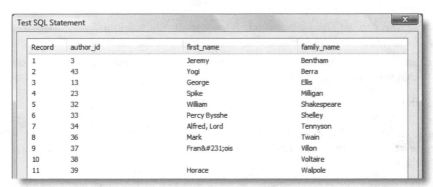

4. Close the test panel and the Recordset dialog box, and load the page into a browser. Try the same test by entering a number in the text field and clicking the Search button. This time, you'll get no results. As the following screenshot shows, the page displays the contents of the SQL query to help you understand what's happened.

Search for names where the primary key contains the following number

Author_id:

[Search]

No results found

SQL query used: SELECT * FROM authors WHERE author_id LIKE 0 ORDER BY family_name ASC

It doesn't matter what number you enter in the search field, the SQL query always uses the following WHERE clause:

WHERE author_id LIKE 0

In both SQL and PHP, numbers are not enclosed in quotes, so the absence of quotes around 0 indicates that Dreamweaver is treating the runtime variable as a number. Although that sounds logical, the SQL specification says LIKE is for *strings*. Dreamweaver now enforces that rule, but the bug in the Recordset dialog box forgets about it.

5. Open the Recordset dialog box again, and switch to Advanced mode. The settings should look like this:

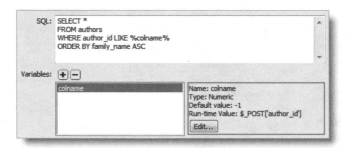

As you can see from the preceding screenshot, the value of Type for the runtime variable colname is set to Numeric. Click the Edit button, and change Type to Text.

6. Save the page, and test it again in a browser. This time, you should see a result like that shown in Figure 17-5.

Although the preceding exercise is based on the bug in the Recordset dialog box in Simple mode, the key to successful wildcard searches with numbers lies in step 5: set Type for the runtime variable to Text in Advanced mode. Although this seems counterintuitive when you're searching a numerical column, MySQL silently converts the string back to a number and performs the search correctly.

The WHERE clause uses 0 if you set Type to Numeric, because Dreamweaver adds the wildcard character to the runtime variable before passing it to GetSQLValueString(). This is the Dreamweaver function that sanitizes user input before inserting it into a SQL query. The function sees that the wildcard character isn't a number, so replaces it with 0 to protect your database from malicious attack.

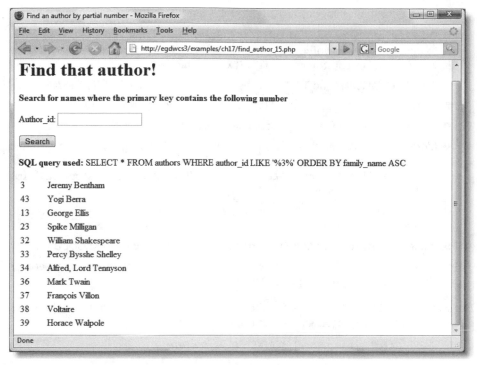

Figure 17-5. Always set the datatype to text in wildcard searches that use LIKE.

Using a FULLTEXT index

A problem with wildcard characters is that you need to design SQL queries to take into account the various combinations of search terms that users might want to use. MySQL offers a useful alternative approach: creating a FULLTEXT index on the column(s) you want to search. You can use FULLTEXT searches in a number of ways, but the following are the most useful:

- **Natural language searching**: This finds all words passed to the query as a runtime variable. So a search for "winter discontent" (without the quotes) in the quotations table returns all records that contain either "winter" or "discontent."

- **Searching in Boolean mode**: This lets the user refine the search by preceding required words with a plus sign (+) and words to be excluded by a minus sign (–). So, a search for "+winter +discontent" (without the quotes) in the quotations table would find the Shakespeare quotation about "the winter of our discontent" but exclude all other records. Boolean mode also permits the use of double quotes to specify exact phrases and the asterisk (*) as a wildcard character.

These are significant advantages to FULLTEXT, but it does have the following limitations:

- Only MyISAM tables support FULLTEXT indexes. You cannot add a FULLTEXT index to InnoDB tables. So you need to choose between maintaining referential integrity with foreign key constraints and FULLTEXT searching.

- Only CHAR, VARCHAR, and TEXT columns can be included in a FULLTEXT index.

- Words that occur in more than 50 percent of the records are ignored.

- Words that contain fewer than four characters are ignored.

- More than 500 common words, such as "the," "also," and "always," are designated as **stopwords** that are always ignored, even if preceded with a plus sign in Boolean mode. See http://dev.mysql.com/doc/refman/5.0/en/fulltext-stopwords.html for the full list of stopwords.

- Only full words are matched unless the wildcard asterisk is used in a Boolean search.

- Boolean mode requires MySQL 4.0 or higher. It does not work in MySQL 3.23.

- A FULLTEXT index can be created to search multiple columns simultaneously. However, all columns *must* be in the same table.

The syntax for a FULLTEXT search is different from a wildcard search with LIKE. The WHERE clause for a natural language search looks like this:

```
WHERE MATCH (columnName) AGAINST ('searchTerm')
```

For a Boolean search, it looks like this:

```
WHERE MATCH (columnName) AGAINST ('searchTerm' IN BOOLEAN MODE)
```

You can test FULLTEXT searching with find_quote_03.php and find_quote_04.php in examples/ch17. The SQL query in find_quote_03.php performs a natural language search and looks like this:

```
SELECT authors.first_name, authors.family_name, quotations.quotation
FROM authors, quotations
WHERE quotations.author_id = authors.author_id
AND MATCH (quotations.quotation) AGAINST (var1)
ORDER BY authors.family_name
```

The query in find_quote_04.php searches in Boolean mode and looks like this:

```
SELECT authors.first_name, authors.family_name, quotations.quotation
FROM authors, quotations
WHERE quotations.author_id = authors.author_id
AND MATCH (quotations.quotation) AGAINST (var1 IN BOOLEAN MODE)
ORDER BY authors.family_name
```

Since these are text searches, it goes without saying that the Type of the runtime variable must always be set to Text.

Before you can use the example files, you need to add a FULLTEXT index to the quotations table. If you used the InnoDB version of the quotations table, you also need to convert it to MyISAM first.

Converting the quotations table from InnoDB to MyISAM

Follow these instructions only if you installed the InnoDB version of the quotations table. If you installed the MyISAM version, skip ahead to "Adding a FULLTEXT index."*

1. Launch phpMyAdmin, select the egdwcs3 database, and click quotations in the left navigation frame to display the quotations table structure in the main frame.

2. Click Relation view under the table structure grid (see Figure 16-5 in the previous chapter). Reset the drop-down menu alongside author_id to remove the link to author_id in the authors table, as shown in the following screenshot, and click Save:

3. Click the Operations tab at the top of the screen. In the Table options section of the screen that opens, change Storage Engine to MyISAM, as shown in the next screenshot, and click Go:

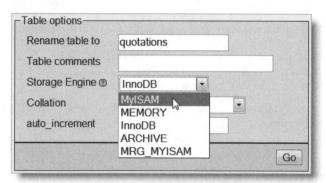

4. Click the Structure tab at the top of the screen to return to the table structure grid. There is no need to convert the authors table to MyISAM unless you want to add a FULLTEXT index to it also.

Adding a FULLTEXT index

Adding a FULLTEXT index to a MyISAM table in phpMyAdmin is as simple as clicking a button.

1. If it's not already open, launch phpMyAdmin, and display the quotations table structure in the main frame.

2. Click the Fulltext icon in the quotation row, as shown in the following screenshot:

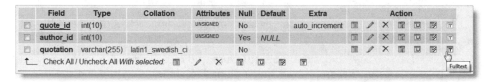

As you can see from the screenshot, the Fulltext icon is grayed out for quote_id and author_id, because they're not capable of taking a FULLTEXT index. If the icon is also grayed out for quotation, it probably means that the table is still using the InnoDB storage engine. You must convert the table to MyISAM first.

That's all there is to adding a FULLTEXT index.

A FULLTEXT index is best suited to very large text databases. When building the database, it's recommended to add the index *after* the data has been imported.

Working with multiple-column indexes A multiple-column FULLTEXT index allows you to search several columns simultaneously. To create a multiple-column index in phpMyAdmin, select the checkbox alongside each column name in the table structure grid, and click the Fulltext icon at the bottom of the grid.

To create a SQL query for a multiple-column FULLTEXT index, list the column names separated by commas in the parentheses after MATCH like this:

```
WHERE MATCH (column1, column2, column3) AGAINST ('searchTerm')
```

The index must include all columns listed. You cannot create a FULLTEXT index for each column and list them in a MATCH definition. You need to create a separate index for each combination of columns that you want to use in searches.

See http://dev.mysql.com/doc/refman/5.0/en/fulltext-search.html to learn more about FULLTEXT searches.

Solving common problems

This section deals with frequently asked questions about SQL queries. Although the solutions are relatively simple, you need to use the Recordset dialog box in Advanced mode for all of them.

Counting records

In Chapter 14, I warned you to resist the temptation to renumber primary keys to keep track of how many records you have in a table. To count the number of records, just use this simple query:

```
SELECT COUNT(*) FROM tableName
```

There must be no gap between COUNT and the opening parenthesis.

You can also combine this with a WHERE clause like this:

```
SELECT COUNT(*) FROM tableName WHERE price > 10
SELECT COUNT(*) FROM tableName WHERE first_name = 'John'
```

With SELECT COUNT(*), it's a good idea to use an alias (see Chapter 16) like this:

```
SELECT COUNT(*) AS num_authors FROM authors
```

You can then access the result as num_authors from the Bindings panel. If you don't use an alias, Dreamweaver displays COUNT(*) in the Bindings panel, but when you insert the value in Design view, you see a gold PHP shield instead of a dynamic text object. It works, but the ability to see dynamic text objects makes it easier to understand what's in your page.

The code for this example is in Recordset (countAuthors) in count.php in examples/ch17. There are gaps in the author_id sequence, so the result is 40.

Eliminating duplicates from a recordset

SQL uses the keyword DISTINCT to eliminate duplicates from a SELECT query. You simply insert DISTINCT immediately after SELECT. The authors table has three Johns and two Williams. The following query results in John and William being listed only once:

```
SELECT DISTINCT first_name FROM authors
```

You can combine this with the COUNT() function to find out the number of distinct records. The query looks like this:

```
SELECT COUNT(DISTINCT first_name) AS num_names FROM authors
```

The code for this example is in Recordset (countUnique) in count.php in examples/ch17. The result for Recordset (countAuthors) is 40 and for Recordset (countUnique) is 34.

Hang on a moment . . . If you eliminate the two duplicate Johns and one duplicate William, the result should be 37. The discrepancy comes from the fact that the first_name column permits NULL values. Three records are NULL. COUNT(DISTINCT) ignores NULL values, making 34 the correct result.

Reusing a recordset

It's sometimes useful to use the same recordset more than once on a page, but you might get a bit of a shock if you try to do so. A practical example will help explain the problem—and the solution.

Rewinding a recordset for reuse

The following exercise shows what happens when you attempt to reuse a recordset after displaying its contents in a repeat region. To gain access to the data, you need to reset the MySQL result resource. If you just want to look at the finished code, it's in `rewind_04.php` in `examples/ch17`.

1. Copy `rewind_01.php` from `examples/ch17` to `workfiles/ch17`, and open it in the Document window. The page has been laid out like this:

The `getAuthors` recordset retrieves the first five authors alphabetically by family name and displays them in a repeat region as an unordered list.

2. Test the page by clicking the Live Data view button in the Document toolbar or by loading the page into a browser. You should see the first five names displayed in the unordered list. Nothing will be displayed after the paragraph that reads "Let's display the first one again:" because there's no dynamic text object there yet.

3. Open the Bindings panel, and insert dynamic text objects for first_name and family_name at the bottom of the page, as shown here:

4. Test the page again. There should be no difference from what you saw in step 2. Check your code against `rewind_02.php` in `examples/ch17`, if you need to make sure.

So, why do the dynamic text objects no longer work? The answer, as always, lies in the code. A repeat region is simply a PHP do . . . while loop. In Code view, the repeat region that creates the unordered list to display the recordset looks like this:

```php
47   <ul>
48     <?php do { ?>
49       <li><?php echo $row_getAuthors['first_name']; ?> <?php echo $row_getAuthors['family_name']; ?></li>
50   <?php } while ($row_getAuthors = mysql_fetch_assoc($getAuthors)); ?></ul>
```

In pseudo-code, the PHP code is doing this:

```
do {
  display the first_name and family_name fields in an <li> element
} while (records are still left in the recordset)
```

As the loop progresses, the recordset (or to be more precise, the MySQL result resource) keeps track of its current position by moving an internal pointer. With each iteration, the pointer moves to the next record, and when it gets to the last record, the do . . . while loop comes to a halt. That's why you can't display anything else from the recordset. You have reached the end of the line. But a recordset is just like a fishing line. You can rewind it and use it again.

To rewind a MySQL result resource, you use the mysql_data_seek() function like this:

```
mysql_data_seek(resultResource, 0);
```

This resets the pointer and moves it back to the first record.

In Dreamweaver, the MySQL result resource is stored in a variable that has the same name as your recordset. To reuse a recordset, you also need to prime the variable that holds the current record. The name of this variable is made up of $row_ followed by the recordset name (see why I told you to choose memorable names for your recordsets). You prime the variable with the first record like this:

```
$row_recordsetName = mysql_fetch_assoc($recordsetName);
```

Unfortunately, Dreamweaver doesn't let you apply a repeat region to the same record more than once, so you need to code it manually. Let's fix the code in our example page.

5. Place your cursor at the end of the do . . . while loop, and insert the code high-lighted in the following screenshot:

```
47  <ul>
48    <?php do { ?>
49      <li><?php echo $row_getAuthors['first_name']; ?> <?php echo $row_getAuthors['family_name']; ?></li>
50    <?php } while ($row_getAuthors = mysql_fetch_assoc($getAuthors)); ?></ul>
51  <?php mysql_data_seek($getAuthors, 0);
52  $row_getAuthors = mysql_fetch_assoc($getAuthors); ?>
53  <p>Let's see the first one again: <?php echo $row_getAuthors['first_name']; ?> <?php echo
    $row_getAuthors['family_name']; ?></p>
```

The name of the recordset is getAuthors, so the variables for the recordset and the current record become $getAuthors and $row_getAuthors, respectively.

6. Test the page again. This time, the name of the first author should be displayed again at the bottom of the page (you can check your code against rewind_03.php).

If you simply want to display the unordered list of authors' names again, you can copy the code shown on lines 47–50 of the preceding screenshot and paste them anywhere on the page after the highlighted section that rewinds the recordset. However, you rarely want to use a recordset in exactly the same way, so let's use a table this time and see how to insert the repeat region code manually.

7. In Design view, position your cursor at the end of the paragraph that displays the name of the first author again. Insert a table with two columns and two rows, put some column headings in the first row and dynamic text objects for first_name and family_name in the second row, so the page now looks like this:

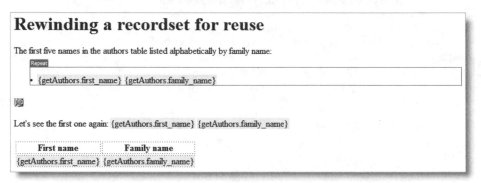

8. Click inside the second table row, and select the entire row by clicking the <tr> tag in the Tag selector at the bottom of the Document window. Although you can't use the Repeat Region server behavior again, this highlights the section of code that you want to repeat. This makes it easier to see where to insert the repeat region code.

9. Switch to Code view, copy the highlighted sections of code from the original repeat region, and paste them into the positions indicated in Figure 17-6.

```
48    <?php do { ?>
49        <li><?php echo $row_getAuthors['first_name']; ?> <?php echo $row_getAuthors['family_name']; ?></li>
50    <?php } while ($row_getAuthors = mysql_fetch_assoc($getAuthors)); ?></ul>
51    <?php mysql_data_seek($getAuthors, 0);
52    $row_getAuthors = mysql_fetch_assoc($getAuthors); ?>
53    <p>Let's see the first one again: <?php echo $row_getAuthors['first_name']; ?> <?php echo
      $row_getAuthors['family_name']; ?></p>
54    <table width="300">
55      <tr>
56        <th scope="col">First name</th>
57        <th scope="col">Family name</th>
58      </tr>
59      <tr>
60        <td><?php echo $row_getAuthors['first_name']; ?></td>
61        <td><?php echo $row_getAuthors['family_name']; ?></td>
62      </tr>
63    </table>
```

Figure 17-6. Creating a repeat region manually involves copying two short PHP code blocks.

10. Save the page, and test it again. The table should now display the names of the first five authors. Check your code, if necessary, against rewind_04.php in examples/ch17.

Understanding how a repeat region works

Note that the first name (Woody Allen) is displayed three times: in the original repeat region, in the paragraph after the rewind code, and in the manually coded repeat region. This is because the do . . . while loop doesn't move to the next row of the recordset until the end of the loop.

The code that controls the repeat region is highlighted on lines 48 and 50 of Figure 17-6. In effect, what it does is this:

```
<?php do { // start the repeat region ?>
  Display the contents of the current record
<?php } while (retrieve and store the next record); ?>
```

The code inside the parentheses following while looks like this:

```
$row_getAuthors = mysql_fetch_assoc($getAuthors)
```

It's exactly the same as the code on line 52 of Figure 17-6, which is used to prime the variable that holds the current record. The mysql_fetch_assoc() function retrieves the next available record from a MySQL query result as an associative array (see Chapter 10 for an explanation of associative arrays), and moves the internal pointer to the next record. The array is stored in $row_getAuthors. The name of each column is used as the array key, so $row_getAuthors['first_name'] contains the first_name field of the current record, and $row_getAuthors['family_name'] contains the family_name field. You can use these values as often as you like until the next iteration of the loop, when the next record replaces all the values in the array.

Many books and online tutorials use a for or a while loop and place this code at the beginning of the loop. Dreamweaver takes a slightly different approach by retrieving the first record outside the loop and getting each subsequent record at the end of the loop. Either approach is perfectly acceptable. The only reason you need to be aware of this is in case you want to incorporate code from another source. Mixing two styles of coding without understanding how they work might result in records being skipped as the conflicting styles iterate through a set of database results.

Formatting dates and time in MySQL

Let's turn now to the thorny subject of dates. The calendars of most countries now agree on the current year, month, and date (at least for international purposes—some countries have different calendars for domestic use). What they don't agree on is the order of the component parts. In the United States, it's month, date, year. In Europe, it's date, month, year. And in China and Japan, it's year, month, date.

To avoid this mess, MySQL stores dates and time in the ISO-approved order of largest unit (year) first, followed by the next largest (month), and so on down to the smallest (second). In all versions of MySQL, dates are stored in the format YYYY-MM-DD, and times as HH:MM:SS. In Chapter 14, we used a TIMESTAMP datatype for the submitted column of the feedback table. In MySQL 4.1 and above, this is stored in the following format: YYYY-MM-DD HH:MM:SS. Earlier versions of MySQL omit the punctuation, which makes a TIMESTAMP column less readable, but the underlying format is the same. The following examples show how MySQL stores a TIMESTAMP created at 1:21 PM on May 7, 2007:

```
2007-05-07 13:21:00   /* MySQL 4.1 and above */
20070507132100        /* MySQL 4.0 and earlier */
```

17

This inevitably leads to the question, "But how can I store dates in the American (or European) style?" The simple answer is, "You can't. Or as Star Trek fans might put it: resistance is futile."

The situation isn't as bad as you might think. By storing dates and time in a standard format, you're never in any doubt as to the meaning. If the date in the preceding example were stored as 5/7/2007, it would mean May 7 to an American, but 5 July to a European. Love it or hate it, 2007-05-07 is unambiguous. Moreover, MySQL makes it very easy to display the date (or part of it) in just about every imaginable format.

I'll come back at the end of the chapter, in the section "Storing dates in MySQL," to discuss the best way of handling dates in user input, but, for the moment, let's concentrate on how to display a date that has already been stored in this format.

Using DATE_FORMAT() to output user-friendly dates

MySQL has a wide range of date and time functions. The one that concerns us here is DATE_FORMAT(), which does exactly what its name suggests. The syntax for DATE_FORMAT() is as follows:

DATE_FORMAT(*date, format*)

Normally, *date* is the name of the table column that you want to format, and *format* is a string that tells MySQL which format to use. You build the format string from specifiers. Table 17-1 lists those most commonly used.

Table 17-1. Frequently used MySQL date format specifiers

Period	Specifier	Description	Example
Year	%Y	Four-digit format	2007
	%y	Two-digit format	07
Month	%M	Full name	January, September
	%b	Abbreviated name, three letters	Jan, Sep
	%m	Number, with leading zero	01, 09
	%c	Number, no leading zero	1, 9
Day of month	%d	With leading zero	01, 25
	%e	No leading zero	1, 25
	%D	With English text suffix	1st, 25th

Period	Specifier	Description	Example
Weekday name	%W	Full text	Monday, Thursday
	%a	Abbreviated name, three letters	Mon, Thu
Hour	%H	24-hour clock, with leading zero	01, 23
	%k	24-hour clock, no leading zero	1, 23
	%h	12-hour clock, with leading zero	01, 11
	%l (lowercase "L")	12-hour clock, no leading zero	1, 11
Minute	%i	With leading zero	05, 25
Second	%S	With leading zero	08, 45
AM/PM	%p		

The specifiers can be combined with ordinary text or punctuation in the format string. As always, when using a function in a SQL query, there must be no space between the function name and the opening parenthesis. It's also a good idea to assign the result to an alias using the AS keyword (see Chapter 16). Referring to Table 17-1, you can now format the date in the submitted column of the feedback table in a variety of ways. To present the date in a common U.S. style and retain the name of the original column, use the following:

```
DATE_FORMAT(submitted, '%c/%e/%Y') AS submitted
```

To format the same date in European style, reverse the first two specifiers like this:

```
DATE_FORMAT(submitted, '%e/%c/%Y') AS submitted
```

You can now format the TIMESTAMP value in the feedback table in a way that's easier to read.

Formatting the date and time in the feedback table

The following exercise shows you how to use DATE_FORMAT() to transform the TIMESTAMP value stored in the feedback table. The same technique applies to any date or time column. By using different aliases, you can extract different parts of the date or time to use in a variety of ways in your web pages. The exercise uses the feedback table created in Chapter 14. Use ch17_feedback.sql, ch17_feedback40.sql, or ch17_feedback323.sql in the tools folder to import the table and sample data, if necessary.

1. If you created feedback_list.php in Chapter 14, open the page in the Document window. Otherwise, copy feedback_list_01.php from examples/ch17, and save it in workfiles/ch17. Test the page in a browser to make sure that it displays a list of dates and names, as shown in the following screenshot:

Feedback summary

Date and time	Name
2007-03-28 19:35:08	David Powers
2007-03-27 17:53:47	David Powers
2007-03-27 10:22:52	David Powers

2. In the Server Behaviors panel, double-click Recordset (getFeedback) to edit the SQL query. Switch to Advanced mode if necessary.

   The first line of the SQL query looks like this:

   ```
   SELECT message_id, name, submitted
   ```

3. For a U.S.-style date, amend it like this:

   ```
   SELECT message_id, name, DATE_FORMAT(submitted, '%b %e, %Y') AS ➥
   submitted
   ```

   Reverse the order of the first two specifiers for a European-style date.

4. Click the Test button to make sure that everything is working correctly. You should still have a column called submitted, but the dates will now be formatted as shown here:

Record	message_id	name	submitted
1	3	David Powers	Mar 28, 2007
2	1	David Powers	Mar 27, 2007
3	2	David Powers	Mar 27, 2007

If Dreamweaver displays a MySQL error message instead, check that you have not left any space between DATE_FORMAT and the opening parenthesis of the function. Although some computer languages allow you to leave a space, MySQL doesn't. Also, make sure that the format string is enclosed in matching quotes. Although I have used single quotes, double quotes are equally acceptable.

5. Close the test panel. You now have a nicely formatted date, but the time is missing. Let's experiment a little. The format string can contain any text in addition to the format specifiers, so change the format string to this:

   ```
   '%b %e, %Y at %l:%i %p'
   ```

6. Click the Test button again. The date and time should now be formatted like this:

7. You could leave it like that, but it's sometimes convenient to have the date and time available as separate variables, so let's create a new alias for the time. Close the test panel, and edit the first line of the SQL query like this:

```
SELECT message_id, name, DATE_FORMAT(submitted, '%b %e, %Y') ➥
AS the_date, DATE_FORMAT(submitted, '%l:%i %p') AS the_time
```

This extracts two formatted values from the same column: one as the_date and the other as the_time.

8. Close the Recordset dialog box. The page now has a dynamic text object for submitted, which is no longer part of the recordset. Select Dynamic Text (getFeedback. submitted) in the Server Behaviors panel, and click the minus button to delete it.

9. Use the Bindings panel to insert dynamic text objects for the_date and the_time. The actual layout is not important, but I inserted "at" as plain text between them like this:

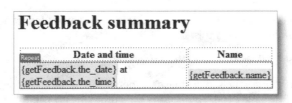

10. Save feedback_list.php, and view it in a browser. The dates should now be formatted in a more user-friendly way. You can check your code against feedback_list__02.php in examples/ch17.

This gives you just a brief glimpse of working with dates in MySQL. Other functions allow you to perform useful calculations, such as working out people's ages from their birthdates, calculating the difference between two dates, and adding to or subtracting from dates. You can find details of all MySQL date and time functions, together with examples at http://dev.mysql.com/doc/refman/5.0/en/date-and-time-functions.html.

Working with dates in PHP

PHP handles dates in a very different way from MySQL that's not as easy to visualize in everyday terms. Whereas MySQL timestamps are based on the human calendar, it's impossible for anyone—except, perhaps, a mathematical genius—to read the date from a PHP time-stamp, as this example shows:

```
1178544060   // Unix timestamp for 13:21:00 UTC on May 7, 2007
```

This seemingly arbitrary figure is the number of seconds since midnight UTC (Coordinated Universal Time) on January 1, 1970—a point in time commonly referred to as the **Unix epoch** and used as the basis for date and time calculations in many computing languages. Except when referring to the current time, all dates in PHP need to be converted to a Unix timestamp. After performing any calculations, you format the result in a more human-readable way by using the date() or strftime() function, which I'll describe shortly. But first, let's take a look at time zones and Unix timestamps.

Setting the correct time zone

The internal workings of the PHP date and time functions were revised in PHP 5.1 and require a time zone to be defined. Normally, this should be done by setting the value of date.timezone in php.ini; but if your hosting company forgets to do so, or you want to use a different time zone, you need to set it yourself. You can do this in three different ways.

The simplest way is to add the following at the beginning of any script that uses date or time functions:

```
ini_set('date.timezone', 'timezone');
```

You can find a full list of valid time zones at www.php.net/manual/en/timezones.php. The correct setting for where I live is this:

```
ini_set('date.timezone', 'Europe/London');
```

ini_set() fails silently if your server doesn't support the date.timezone setting. As long as you use a valid PHP time zone, your scripts will automatically use this setting whenever your server is upgraded.

A slightly longer way is to add this (with the appropriate time zone) before using date and time functions:

```
if (function_exists('date_default_timezone_set')) {
  date_default_timezone_set('Europe/London');
}
```

If your remote server runs Apache, you may be able to set a default time zone for your entire site by putting the following in an .htaccess file in the site root (use the correct time zone for your location):

```
php_value date.timezone 'Europe/London'
```

This works only if Apache has been set up to allow .htaccess to override default settings.

Creating a Unix timestamp

PHP offers two main ways of creating a Unix timestamp. The first uses mktime() and is based on the actual date and time; the other attempts to parse any English date or time expression with strtotime().

The mktime() function takes six arguments as follows:

> mktime(*hour, minutes, seconds, month, date, year*)

All arguments are optional. If a value is omitted, it is set to the current date and time. However, you can't skip arguments; as soon as you leave one out, all remaining ones must also be omitted. Consequently, if you are interested only in the date, you need to set the first three arguments to 0 (midnight) like this:

> $Xmas2007 = mktime(0, 0, 0, 12, 25, 2007);

The strtotime() function attempts to parse dates from American English but holds some unpleasant surprises. The following expressions produce the correct timestamp for Christmas day 2007:

> $Xmas2007 = strtotime('12/25/2007');
> $Xmas2007 = strtotime('2007-12-25');

However, replacing the slashes with hyphens in the first example, as follows, produces a false result:

> $notXmas = strtotime('12-25-2007'); // produces Jan 1, 1970 timestamp

To avoid such problems, it's best to use the name of the month, either spelled out in full or just the first three letters, and to place the year at the end of the string.

The real value of strtotime(), however, lies in its ability to add or subtract from dates by parsing simple time-related expressions. For instance, strtotime() understands all these expressions:

> strtotime('tomorrow');
> strtotime('yesterday');
> strtotime('last Monday');
> strtotime('next Thursday');
> strtotime('-3 weeks');
> strtotime('+1 week 2 days');

> *Be careful when using* next *in a* strtotime() *expression. In versions prior to PHP 4.4, it is incorrectly interpreted as +2, instead of +1.*

The previous examples calculate the timestamp based on the current date and time. However, you can supply a specific timestamp as a second, optional argument to strtotime(). This means you can add or subtract from a particular date. The following example calculates the timestamp for January 6, 2008:

> $Xmas2007 = mktime(0, 0, 0, 12, 25, 2007);
> $twelfthNight = strtotime('+12 days', $Xmas2007);

If you ever need to generate a Unix timestamp from a date-type column in MySQL, you can use the UNIX_TIMESTAMP() function in a SELECT statement like this:

```
SELECT UNIX_TIMESTAMP(submitted) AS PHPtimestamp FROM feedback
```

Formatting dates in PHP

PHP offers two functions that format dates: date(), which displays the names of weekdays and months in English only, and strftime(), which uses the server's locale. So, if the server's locale is set to Spanish, date() displays Saturday, but strftime() displays sábado. Both functions take as their first, required argument a string that indicates the format in which you want to display the date. A second, optional argument specifies the timestamp, but if it's omitted, the current date and time are assumed.

There are a lot of format characters. Some are easy to remember, but many seem to have no obvious reasoning behind them. You can find a full list at www.php.net/manual/en/function.date.php and www.php.net/manual/en/function.strftime.php. Table 17-2 lists the most useful.

Table 17-2. The main format characters used in the date() and strftime() functions

Unit	date()	strftime()	Description	Example
Day	d	%d	Day of the month with leading zero	01 through 31
	j	%e*	Day of the month without leading zero	1 through 31
	S		English ordinal suffix for day of the month	st, nd, rd, or th
	D	%a	First three letters of day name	Sun, Tue
	l (lowercase "L")	%A	Full name of day	Sunday, Tuesday
Month	m	%m	Number of month with leading zero	01 through 12
	n		Number of month without leading zero	1 through 12
	M	%b	First three letters of month name	Jan, Jul
	F	%B	Full name of month	January, July
Year	Y	%Y	Year displayed as four digits	2007
	y	%y	Year displayed as two digits	07

Unit	date()	strftime()	Description	Example
Hour	g		Hour in 12-hour format without leading zero	1 through 12
	h	%I	Hour in 12-hour format with leading zero	01 through 12
	G		Hour in 24-hour format without leading zero	0 through 23
	H	%H	Hour in 24-hour format with leading zero	01 through 23
Minutes	i	%M	Minutes with leading zero if necessary	00 through 59
Seconds	s	%S	Seconds with leading zero if necessary	00 through 59
AM/PM	a	%p	Lowercase	am
AM/PM	A		Uppercase	PM

* Note: %e is not supported on Windows.

You can combine these format characters with punctuation to display the current date in your web pages according to your own preferences. For instance, the following code (in dates.php in examples/ch17) produces output similar to that shown in the following screenshot:

```
<p>American style: <?php echo date('l, F jS, Y'); ?></p>
<p>European style: <?php echo date('l, jS F Y'); ?></p>
```

Storing dates in MySQL

There's one outstanding issue—the problem of converting user-supplied dates to the format expected by MySQL. Using a TIMESTAMP column in the feedback table to get MySQL to format the date and time automatically was very convenient, but it's not an approach that is appropriate to all situations. So this final part of the chapter is devoted to dealing with human-generated dates.

A very simple way to handle dates in user input is to use the Spry Validation Text Field widget (see Chapter 9) to enforce a particular format. One of the available formats is YYYY-MM-DD. So, if you're in an enclosed environment, such as an intranet, where you can guarantee compliance—and that JavaScript won't be disabled—this might be your solution.

However, getting Internet users to adhere to rules is rather like herding cats. It's far safer to ensure accurate date input by providing separate fields for month, day of the month, and year, and then to use PHP to verify and format the input.

Validating and formatting dates for database input

In the examples/ch17 folder of the download files, you will find a page called date_converter.php. When you load it into a browser, it displays a drop-down menu preset to the current month, together with two text fields for the date and year, as shown in the screenshot. The Max Chars settings for the text fields have been set to 2 and 4, respectively, to limit the range of mistakes that can be made.

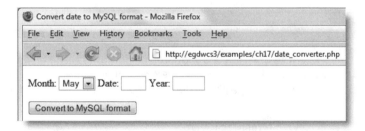

Experiment with the page, inserting a variety of valid and invalid input. When you click the Convert to MySQL format button, either the correctly formatted date or an error message is displayed at the foot of the page. You can incorporate the construction and validation techniques used in this example page in any of your PHP forms.

The drop-down menu for the month is created in two parts. The first section of code goes in a PHP block above the DOCTYPE declaration and consists of an array of the names of the months, plus the PHP getdate() function. This is how it looks:

```
$months = array('Jan','Feb','Mar','Apr','May','Jun','Jul','Aug',➥
'Sep','Oct','Nov','Dec');
$now = getdate();
```

The getdate() function produces an associative array that contains a number of useful date parts, such as the year, weekday name, and so on. When used without an argument like this, getdate() returns information about the current date, so we can find the number of the current month in $now['mon'] and use it to preset the drop-down menu. There's a full list of the array elements returned by getdate() at www.php.net/manual/en/function.getdate.php.

The code for the form looks like this (the section that builds the drop-down menu is highlighted in bold):

```
<form id="convert" name="convert" method="post" action="<?php➡
$_SERVER['PHP_SELF']; ?>">
  <p>
    <label for="select">Month:</label>
    <select name="month" id="month">
      <?php for ($i=1;$i<=12;$i++) { ?>
      <option value="<?php echo $i < 10 ? '0'.$i : $i; ?>"
      <?php if ($i == $now['mon']) {
        echo ' selected="selected"'; } ?>><?php echo $months[$i-1]; ?>
      </option>
      <?php } ?>
    </select>
    <label for="day">Date:</label>
    <input name="day" type="text" id="day" size="2" maxlength="2" />
    <label for="year">Year:</label>
    <input name="year" type="text" id="year" size="4" maxlength="4" />
  </p>
  <p>
    <input type="submit" name="Submit" value="Convert to MySQL format"
/>
  </p>
</form>
```

The PHP code uses a for loop to populate the menu's <option> tags. Although counters normally begin at 0, I have set the initial value of $i to 1, because I want to use it for the value of the month.

The second line highlighted in bold uses the conditional operator (see Chapter 10) to test whether $i is less than 10. If it is, a leading zero is added to the number; otherwise it is left alone. Another way of writing it would be to use this:

```
if ($i < 10) {
  echo '0'.$i;
  }
else {
  echo $i;
  }
```

The third line of PHP checks whether the value of $i is the same as $now['mon']. If it is, the following line inserts selected="selected" into the opening <option> tag. The final part of the script displays the name of the month by drawing it from the $months array. Because indexed arrays begin at 0, you need to subtract 1 from the value of $i to get the right month.

I have not created similar drop-down menus for the day and year because PHP is a server-side language. Although you could create a script to display the correct number of days for the month, you would have to reload the page every time the month was changed. You could create an intelligent date input system with JavaScript, but that makes the dangerous assumption that all users will have JavaScript enabled.

The code that validates the input and formats the date for MySQL also goes above the DOCTYPE declaration. It's a straightforward chain of if . . . else statements, which looks like this:

```
if ($_POST) {
  $m = $_POST['month'];
  $d = trim($_POST['day']);
  $y = trim($_POST['year']);
  if (empty($d) || empty($y)) {
    $error = 'Please fill in all fields';
    }
  elseif (!is_numeric($d) || !is_numeric($y)) {
    $error = 'Please use numbers only';
    }
  elseif (($d <1 || $d > 31) || ($y < 1000 || $y > 9999)) {
    $error = 'Please use numbers within the correct range';
    }
  elseif (!checkdate($m,$d,$y)) {
    $error = 'You have used an invalid date';
    }
  else {
    $d = $d < 10 ? '0'.$d : $d;
    $mysqlFormat = "$y-$m-$d";
    }
}
```

You don't need to perform any checks on the value of the month, because the drop-down menu has generated it. So, after trimming any whitespace from around the day and year, they are subjected to the first three checks: to see if they are empty, not numeric, or out of range. You have met the empty() function before. The second check uses is_numeric(), which is basically self-explanatory. It takes advantage of PHP's loose typing. In strict terms of datatypes, the content of a text field is always a string, but is_numeric() also returns true if a string contains a number, such as '5'. (No, it's not clever enough to recognize 'five' as a number.) The third test looks for numbers within acceptable ranges. It looks like this:

```
elseif (($d <1 || $d > 31) || ($y < 1000 || $y > 9999)) {
```

The values set for the day (1–31) are immediately understandable, even though they don't apply to every month. The range for years (1000–9999) is dictated by the legal range for MySQL. I suggest that you use a narrower range, more in line with the requirements of the application you're building. In the unlikely event that you need a year out of that range, you must choose a different column type to store the data. MySQL was not designed to handle stardates from *Star Trek: The Next Generation*!

By using a series of `elseif` clauses, this code stops testing as soon as it meets the first mistake. If the input has survived the first three tests, it's then subjected to the PHP function `checkdate()`, which really puts a date through the mill. It's smart enough to know the difference between February 29 in a leap year and an ordinary year.

Finally, if the input has passed all these tests, it's rebuilt in the correct format for insertion into MySQL. The first line of the final `else` clause uses the ternary operator, as described earlier, to add a leading zero to the day of the month if necessary.

The way to integrate this routine into your own pages is by testing whether the `POST` array has any values, and whether the `$error` or `$mysqlFormat` variables have been set. The following code shows the way that it's done in date_converter.php:

```
if ($_POST) {
  echo '<p>';
  if (isset($error)) {
    echo $error;
    }
  elseif (isset($mysqlFormat)) {
    echo $mysqlFormat;
    }
  echo '</p>';
  }
```

In the case of the example file, the tests are used to display the result. When adapting it for an insert form, for example, you would use the tests like this:

```
if (isset($error)) {
  // abandon insertion of data and display error messages
  }
elseif (isset($mysqlFormat)) {
  // go ahead with insertion of data
  }
```

Continuing the search for perfection

As I said at the outset of this chapter, building SQL queries is a vast subject. The more you learn, the more you realize just how much more there is to know. Even when working with a single table, you can fine-tune your searches by using MySQL functions and aliases. So it's important to break out of the confines of the Recordset dialog box in Simple mode and learn how to build queries that extract the information that you want—and in the format you want. When you have a moment to spare, visit `http://dev.mysql.com/doc/refman/5.0/en/functions.html`, and take a look at the impressive range of functions that you can use in MySQL queries. The most useful categories are the string and date and time functions. The online documentation has lots of examples showing how to use the functions. Experiment with them and take your SQL skills to a new level.

18 USING XSLT TO DISPLAY LIVE NEWS FEEDS AND XML

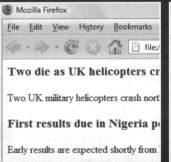

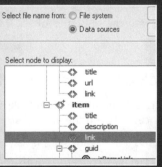

Extensible Markup Language (XML) is probably one of the most hyped and least understood aspects of web development. XML has the simple objective of storing data in a format that both humans and computers can easily understand. It's not a database, nor is it a programming language. It's a highly structured way of presenting data. Because it uses tags like HTML and XHTML, XML looks very familiar to web developers. However, there is no master list of tags or attributes, and although XML frequently contains data intended for display on the Web, it provides no way of displaying it.

That's where programs like Dreamweaver come in. Dreamweaver CS3 offers two important ways of processing raw XML and incorporating it in a web page, which we'll look at in the remaining chapters of this book. In this chapter, we'll explore Extensible Stylesheet Language Transformations (XSLT), a language for transforming XML into XHTML. Then, in Chapters 19 and 20, we'll look at using Spry, the Adobe implementation of Ajax, to manipulate XML data sets. The final chapter will also show you how to generate your own XML documents from data stored in MySQL.

In this chapter you'll

- Learn what XML and XSLT do
- Determine whether your host supports XSLT within PHP
- Draw data from a live news feed into your site
- Experiment with the XPath Expression Builder

A quick guide to XML and XSLT

XML became a W3C standard in February 1998, and XSLT followed almost two years later, in November 1999. Because of the "stylesheet" in its name, the role of XSLT is often described as being to format XML documents in a similar way to CSS. However, there is no real similarity. The real strength of XSLT lies in its ability to manipulate data, sorting and filtering it in much the same way as SQL does with a database. Unfortunately, it's not an easy language to learn, but the XSL Transformation server behavior in Dreamweaver eases the process considerably.

Before delving into the mysteries of XSLT, let's take a look at the structure of an XML document.

What an XML document looks like

XML is closely related to XHTML, so it looks reassuringly familiar, but there are two fundamental differences between them:

- XHTML has a fixed range of tags and attributes. In XML, you create your own.
- XHTML tags are concerned with the structure of a page (<head>, <body>, <p>, <table>, and so on), whereas XML tags normally describe the data they contain (for instance, the following example uses <Book> to store details of individual books).

The following is a simple example of an XML document:

```
<?xml version="1.0" ?>
<BookList>
  <Book ISBN13="9781590598597">
    <Title>The Essential Guide to Dreamweaver CS3 with CSS, Ajax, ➥
and PHP</Title>
    <Authors>
      <Author>David Powers</Author>
    </Authors>
    <Publisher>friends of ED</Publisher>
    <ListPrice>49.99</ListPrice>
  </Book>
  <Book ISBN13="9781590598610">
    <Title>Foundation Flash CS3 for Designers</Title>
    <Authors>
      <Author>Tom Green</Author>
      <Author>David Stiller</Author>
    </Authors>
    <Publisher>friends of ED</Publisher>
    <ListPrice>39.99</ListPrice>
  </Book>
</BookList>
```

The first line is the **XML declaration**, often also referred to as the **XML prolog**, which tells browsers and processors that it's an XML document. The XML declaration is recommended but not required. However, if you do include it, the XML declaration *must* be the first thing in the document. The W3C recommends using XML 1.0 unless you need the highly specialized features of XML 1.1 (www.w3.org/TR/2004/REC-xml11-20040204/#sec-xml11). The XML declaration can also contain an encoding attribute. If this attribute is omitted, as in the previous example, XML parsers automatically use Unicode (UTF-8 or UTF-16).

As you can see from the example document, the tags give no indication as to how the document is intended to look. In fact, it's normally recommended that they shouldn't, because XML is intended primarily to store data in a hierarchical structure according to meaning and without any reference to presentation. Unless you are working in a large collaborative project, which needs to use a standardized vocabulary, you can make up your own tags, as I have done here. They can be made up not only of alphanumeric characters but also accented characters, Greek, Cyrillic, Chinese, and Japanese—in fact, any valid Unicode character. However, they cannot include any whitespace or punctuation other than the hyphen (-), underscore (_), and period (.), nor can they begin with xml in any combination of uppercase or lowercase letters.

The goals of XML include being human-legible, and terseness is considered of minimal importance. So, instead of using <pub>, which could mean publisher, publication date, or somewhere to get a drink, I have been specific and used <Publisher>. The most important thing about an XML document is that it must be **well formed**. The main rules of what constitutes a well-formed document are as follows:

- There can be only one root element.

- Every start tag must have a matching closing tag.

- Empty elements can omit the closing tag, but, if they do so, must have a forward slash before the closing angle bracket (/>).
- Elements must be properly nested.
- Attribute values must be in quotes.
- In the content of an element or attribute value, < and & must be replaced by < and &, respectively.

An empty element is one that doesn't have any content, although it can have attributes that point to content stored elsewhere. To borrow a couple of examples from XHTML, which is HTML 4.01 reformulated to adhere to XML rules, <img> and <br> are empty elements. The src attribute of the <img> tag points to the location of the image, but the tag itself is empty. The <br> tag simply creates a line break, so never has any content. To comply with XML rules, they can be written as <img></img> and
</br> or use the shorthand <img/> and <br/>. To avoid problems with older browsers, a space is normally inserted before the closing forward slash in XHTML, but this is *not* a requirement of XML.

If you look at the previous example, you will see that it has only one root element: <BookList>. All other elements are nested inside the root element, and the nesting follows an orderly pattern. Even when a book has only one author, the <Author> tag is still nested inside <Authors>, and the value of the ISBN13 attribute is always in quotes. While these strict rules make XML more time-consuming to write, the predictability of a well-formed document makes it a lot easier to process. As you will see shortly, when you define an XML source, Dreamweaver instantly builds a diagrammatic representation of the document structure that enables you to manipulate its content with XSLT.

Using HTML entities in XML

Among the conditions of being well-formed is the need to replace < and & with the HTML entities < and & in the content of an element or attribute value. This often leads to the misconception that XML supports the full range of HTML entities, such as é (for é). It doesn't. XML understands only the following five entities: < (<), & (&), > (>), " ("), and ' (').

When creating an XML document in an accented language, such as Spanish, French, or German, you should use accented characters in the same way as in ordinary text. A key principle of XML is that it should be human-readable. You can use other HTML entities in XML, but they will not be automatically rendered as their text equivalent. The XSL Transformation server behavior defines the most frequently used HTML entities so they render correctly. If your XML source contains other HTML entities, you can add your own definitions to the XSL page, as described in "Understanding how XSLT is structured" later in the chapter.

> A good starting place to learn more about XML is the XML FAQ, edited by Peter Flynn, at http://xml.silmaril.ie.

Using XSLT to display XML

There are two ways of using XSLT: client-side and server-side. With client-side XSLT, you create an XSL page and link it to the XML document just like linking a CSS style sheet to an ordinary web page. The job of interpreting the XSLT instructions is then left up to the visitor's browser. Most modern browsers are now capable of handling client-side XSLT, but support is by no means universal. This lack of universal support means that you can use it only in controlled environments, such as an intranet, where you know that everyone is using a compatible browser.

Another drawback of client-side XSLT is that the XSL and XML documents must both reside in the same folder on the web server. So, if you want to display the contents of a news feed from another site, you must first download the XML feed and store it locally.

To get round these problems, you can use PHP to process the XSLT on the server. This converts the XML into XHTML before it's sent from the server, providing your visitors with exactly the same page regardless of which browser they're using. Moreover, with server-side transformation, you can pull the XML feed from any publicly available source on the Internet.

As I mentioned earlier, XSLT is a difficult language, but Dreamweaver automatically builds the XSL page for you. All you need to do is embed the XSL fragment in a PHP page. We'll take a look at XSLT code in "Understanding how XSLT is structured" later in the chapter, but first let's see it in action.

Checking your server's support for XSLT

PHP 4 and PHP 5 handle XSLT completely differently, but Dreamweaver's XSL Transformation server behavior has been designed to work seamlessly with both by automatically detecting the version of PHP running on your server. However, XSLT isn't enabled by default, so you need to check that it is supported.

Use test.php from examples/ch03 to display the PHP configuration page that you used in Chapter 3. Scroll almost to the bottom of the page, and look for a section similar to that shown in the following screenshot.

xsl	
XSL	enabled
libxslt Version	1.1.17
libxslt compiled against libxml Version	2.6.26
EXSLT	enabled
libexslt Version	0.8.13

The screenshot shows what you are likely to see on a server running PHP 5 if it has been configured to handle XSLT. The configuration details will look slightly different on a PHP 4 installation. Instead of xsl, it should say xslt, but it should be in the same position just above the Additional Modules section, close to the bottom of the page. The difference in name reflects the functions they use.

If you can't find either xsl or xslt, contact your host, and ask for the server to be upgraded. If hosts realize there is a genuine demand for new features, they are likely to respond, or risk losing business. If your host doesn't support XSLT, you can build the pages in the rest of this chapter and test them on your local computer, but you won't be able to upload them to your website. If you set up PHP as described in Chapter 3, the XSL extension should be enabled in your local testing environment.

> The XSL Transformation server behavior relies on allow_url_fopen *being on. As explained in Table 3-1 in Chapter 3, this is the default setting, but many hosting companies turn it off as a security measure. Unfortunately, there is no simple way around this problem, although Adobe hints that this might be addressed in an updated version. A comment in version 0.6.3 of the file that processes the remote feed,* MM_XSLTransform.class.php, *lists adding support for socket connection. If your hosting company's security policy prevents the XSL Transformation server behavior from working, submit an enhancement request to Adobe at* www.adobe.com/cfusion/mmform/index.cfm?name=wishform, *urging support for socket connection. The same URL is the best way to submit bug reports and other requests for improvements in Dreamweaver and other Adobe products.*

Pulling in an RSS news feed

You can use the XSL Transformation server behavior with any XML file, but one of its most useful applications is working with a live news feed. For this book, I have chosen one of the feeds from BBC Online primarily because it offers very good news coverage. The feed is also very easy to work with, and the BBC welcomes its use on websites, subject to certain simple terms and conditions. You can find the full details at http://news.bbc.co.uk/2/hi/help/rss/4498287.stm, but the main conditions are as follows:

- You cannot use the BBC logo on your site.
- You must provide a link back to the original story on the BBC website.
- You must attribute the source, using a specified formula, such as "From BBC News."
- You are not allowed to edit or alter the content in any way.
- You cannot use the content on sites that promote pornography, hatred, terrorism, or any illegal activity.

Of course, another reason for choosing the BBC is sentimental. I worked in BBC News for nearly 30 years, both as a correspondent and as an editor. I remember sitting in a basement in Marylebone High Street more than a decade ago talking to Mike Smartt about the Internet's potential for news. In spite of skepticism all around, he was convinced it was the way of the future. I knew he was right, but without Mike's vision and drive as the first editor of BBC Online, it wouldn't have become the force that it is today.

To see all RSS feeds available from BBC News, go to http://news.bbc.co.uk/2/hi/help/3223484.stm. There are nearly 20 specialist news feeds, ranging from world news, health, science, and business to British news and entertainment. If you prefer news with an

American flavor, try the New York Times (www.nytimes.com/services/xml/rss/index.html) or CNN (www.cnn.com/services/rss). In fact, you can get RSS feeds wherever you see the orange RSS or XML logos shown alongside. Much RSS content is copyright protected, so always make sure that you study the terms of use carefully.

RSS is one of those sets of initials that no one can agree on what they really stand for. Some say it means Really Simple Syndication. Others say it's Rich Site Summary. Yet others insist that it stands for RDF Site Summary, and that RDF is the Resource Description Framework. They're all equally valid; the important thing is that RSS feeds all conform to the rules of XML, so they're ideal for handling with the Dreamweaver XSL Transformation server behavior.

Figure 18-1 shows what the news feed looks like when it's incorporated into the sidebar of the "Stroll Along the Thames" page that has been used in several chapters throughout this book.

Figure 18-1. Live news headlines from an external news feed can add constantly changing interest to a site.

How Dreamweaver handles server-side XSLT

When a visitor requests the page shown in Figure 18-1, it looks and works in exactly the same way as any other web page. However, what goes on in the background is considerably more complex.

The XSL Transformation server behavior relies on two external files, as follows:

- **MM_XSLTransform.class.php**: Dreamweaver creates this file automatically and stores it in the MM_XSLTransform subfolder of the includes folder. If you don't already have an includes folder, Dreamweaver creates it. This file is similar to the Spry JavaScript libraries in that it contains all the PHP code needed to process XSLT and XML. It's also responsible for importing the XML source. All you need to do is remember to upload this file to your remote server when deploying your site.

- An XSL file that contains details of the XML source and how you want to display the data it contains. Dreamweaver calls this an **XSLT Fragment**.

You create the XSLT Fragment using the same drag and drop interface as for all dynamic data. Instead of PHP code, everything in the XSLT Fragment uses XSLT syntax. The great thing from the developer's point of view is that you don't need to know any XSLT syntax for it to work. Of course, if you *do* know XSLT syntax, you can get the XSL Transformation server behavior to do a great deal more.

Figure 18-2 shows a simplified outline of what happens when a visitor to a site requests a page that includes code generated by the XSL Transformation server behavior.

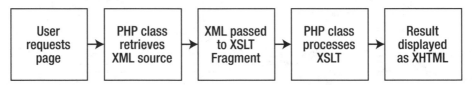

Figure 18-2. How the XSL Transformation server behavior communicates with an XML data source

Using XSLT to access the XML source data

Using the XSL Transformation server behavior is a two-stage process, as follows:

1. Create an XSLT Fragment to access the XML source, and extract the data that you want.
2. Embed the XSLT Fragment in a PHP page.

The following instructions use the BBC Online world news feed. The principles behind displaying any XML source are the same, but I suggest you use the same feed until you are comfortable with the process, because some of the concepts might be unfamiliar.

Creating the XSLT Fragment

Because you are working with a live feed, you need to be connected to the Internet for several steps during the following section.

1. From the Dreamweaver File menu, choose New. In the New Document dialog box, select Blank Page, and XSLT (Fragment) as Page Type. Click Create.

> *Make sure you choose* XSLT (Fragment). *The* New Document *dialog box has another option for* XSLT (Entire page), *which is used only for client-side XSLT. For a tutorial on client-side XSLT, visit* www.adobe.com/devnet/dreamweaver/ articles/display_xml_data.html.

2. Dreamweaver immediately presents you with the Locate XML Source dialog box shown here. It offers two options: to work with a local XML file or a remote one on the Internet. Select the radio button labeled Attach a remote file on the Internet, and insert the following URL: http://newsrss.bbc.co.uk/rss/newsonline_world_edition/ front_page/rss.xml. Click OK.

3. If you don't know the URL of the XML file, clicking Cancel doesn't stop Dreamweaver from creating a page for the XSLT Fragment. You can reopen the Locate XML Source dialog box by clicking either Source or XML in the Bindings panel, as shown here.

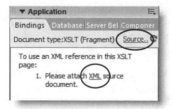

4. As long as you are connected to the Internet, Dreamweaver will contact the BBC Online site and populate the Bindings panel with a document tree like that shown in Figure 18-3. This shows you the structure (Dreamweaver uses the technical term, **schema**) of the XML document sent by the RSS feed.

5. Before working with the XML data, save the page as bbc_feed.xsl. On Windows, Dreamweaver will automatically add the .xsl on the end of the file name, even if you delete it in the Save As dialog box.

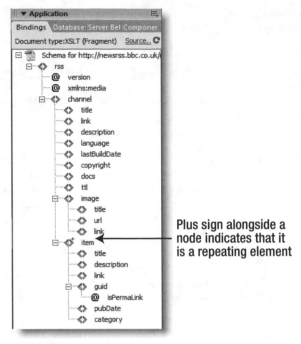

Plus sign alongside a
node indicates that it
is a repeating element

Figure 18-3. Dreamweaver builds a tree (or schema) of the
XML source in the Bindings panel.

Take a good look at Figure 18-3 or the actual schema in your own Bindings panel. You'll see
that it's like a family tree. The angle brackets (<>) represent the different elements or
nodes of the source document, with the name shown alongside. The top level or **root
element** of the XML document is rss. As you go up and down the structure, nodes share a
parent-child relationship. Go up a level to reach the parent; go down a level to reach the
child or children. This genealogical terminology also extends to nodes on the same level,
which are called **siblings**. So item is a child of channel and a sibling to image. Dreamweaver
builds this diagrammatic hierarchy to make it easier for you to identify the elements you
want to manipulate, and XSLT uses it as a sort of road map to perform the transformation.

Attributes that appear within XML tags are designated by @. So at the top of Figure 18-3,
you can see that rss has an attribute called version. The channel and image nodes contain
child nodes that describe the feed. The news comes much further down: in the seventh
node from the bottom labeled item.

The important thing to note about item is that it has a tiny plus sign to the upper-right of
the angle brackets. This indicates that it's a repeating element.

Branching off item are six child nodes: title, description, link, guid (with an attribute
isPermaLink), pubDate, and category. The ones we are interested in are title, which contains
the headline; description, which contains a summary of the news story; and link, the URL to
the full story.

6. Make sure you're in Design view, select title from the item node in the Bindings panel, and drag it into the page.

> It's very easy to go wrong when selecting nodes, because several share the same name. There are three nodes each called title and link, and two called description. All the nodes that you need to select are children of the item repeating node.

7. You should now see a dynamic placeholder inside the page. The placeholder indicates the path to title within the hierarchy of the XML document. Select the placeholder and select Heading 3 from the Format dropdown menu in the Property inspector. The page should now look like the screenshot alongside.

8. Click to the right of the dynamic placeholder, and press Enter/Return to insert a new paragraph. Highlight description in the item node, and drag it into the paragraph that you have just created. You should now have a similar dynamic placeholder for {rss/channel/item/description}.

9. The news feed contains a large number of news items, so you need to apply a repeat region to it. The simplest way to do this would have been to put the news feed into a table or surround each item with a <div>, but either solution results in unnecessary code. Open Split view, and click inside Code view to highlight all the code from the opening <h3> tag to the closing </p> tag, as shown in the following screenshot:

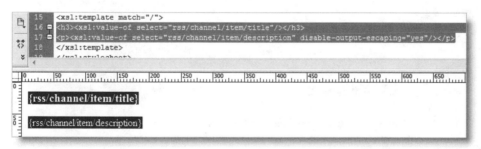

Don't worry about the meaning of the code. It's simply the XSLT way of inserting dynamic data in the same way as PHP does with echo and a variable. Just make sure that the opening and closing XHTML tags are properly selected.

10. Look at the Insert bar. You'll see a new XSLT tab has appeared. It's displayed only when the current document is an XSL file. Select the XSLT tab, and click the Repeat Region button as shown here. Alternatively, use the menu option: Insert ➤ XSLT Objects ➤ Repeat Region.

11. This brings up a completely different dialog box from the one you used with the PHP server behavior. It's the XPath Expression Builder.

XPath is the W3C standard that describes how to identify parts of an XML document. In many ways, it's very similar to ordinary file paths and URLs, but it has many more options (www.w3.org/TR/xpath), including functions. The XPath Expression Builder incorporates a lot of these functions and builds an XPath with the correct syntax for you.

All you need to do is highlight the parent node of the elements that you want to repeat—in other words, item. In the XPath Expression Builder (Repeat Region) dialog box, scroll down to the bottom of the section labeled Select node to repeat over, and select item. Dreamweaver inserts rss/channel/item into the Expression field at the bottom. Click OK.

12. When the XPath Expression Builder closes, the dynamic placeholders will have changed to just the node names. This is because the XPath expression created in the previous step tells the underlying XSLT code where to find them. There will also be a gray border around the placeholders with a tab labeled xsl:for-each at the top-left corner, as shown alongside, indicating that this is now a repeat region.

13. Save bbc_feed.xsl, and press F12/Opt+F12 to view the page in a browser. If you are connected to the Internet, you should see something like Figure 18-4, except with the very latest headlines, not something from all those months ago when I was writing this book.

Look in the browser address bar, and you'll see that Dreamweaver is using a temporary file, even if you have set your preferences not to use temporary files. You can't use an XSLT Fragment in a browser on its own, nor can you use Live Data view, but Dreamweaver processes it internally so you can check that everything is working as expected before embedding it into a PHP file.

You can check your code against bbc_feed_01.xsl in examples/ch18.

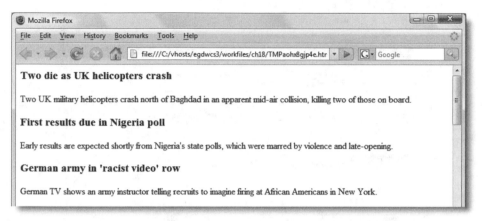

Figure 18-4. Dreamweaver uses a temporary file to confirm that the XSLT Fragment is working as expected.

As part of the BBC conditions of use, you must either provide a link back to the complete story or insert a link to the part of the BBC site from which the feed was drawn. Since the XML source contains a link node (see the schema in Figure 18-3), it's easy to provide a link to each story by converting its headline into a link.

Converting the headlines into links

Continue working with the XSLT Fragment from the previous exercise. Alternatively, use bbc_feed_01.xsl in examples/ch18.

1. In Design view, select the title dynamic placeholder, and click the Browse for File icon to the right of the Link field in the Property inspector.

2. When the Select File dialog box opens, choose Data sources as the option for Select file from. (It's a radio button at the top of the dialog box in Windows, but an ordinary button at the bottom of the dialog box in the Mac version.) Scroll down inside the area labeled Select node to display, and select link, as shown in the screenshot at the top of the next page. Leave the other options at their default settings, and click OK.

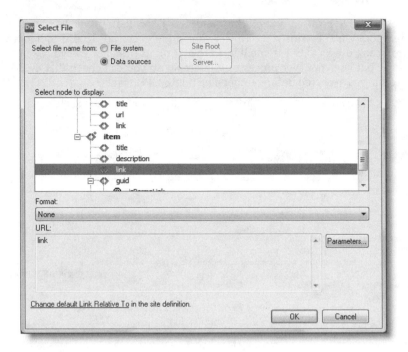

3. Look in the Link field in the Property inspector. It should contain {link}, indicating that it will draw its value from the link node in the XML source.

4. Save bbc_feed.xsl, and press F12/Opt+F12 to test it again. This time, the headlines should have been converted to links. Click one of them to check that it takes you to the relevant story on the BBC website.

   You can check your code against bbc_feed_02.xsl in examples/ch18.

The BBC news feed normally contains 20 or more items. Unlike the Repeat Region server behavior, the XPath Expression Builder (Repeat Region) dialog box has no option to limit the number of items displayed. Instead, you need to use an XSLT conditional region, as shown in the following exercise.

Restricting the number of items in an XSLT repeat region

Continue working with the XSLT Fragment from the previous exercise. Alternatively, use bbc_feed_03.xsl in examples/ch18. The following instructions show you how to limit the page to displaying the first five items.

1. Open Split view, and click in Code view to select all the code from the opening `<h3>` tag to the closing `</p>` tag in the same way as in step 10 in "Creating an XSLT Fragment." Then click the Conditional Region button in the XSLT tab of the Insert bar, as shown in the following screenshot:

2. The Conditional Region dialog box contains just one field, Test. Enter the following code and click OK:

```
position() <= 5
```

XSLT uses the position() function to determine a node's position in the XML hierarchy. Unlike PHP or JavaScript, it begins counting at 1, so you need to use <= 5 to display the first five items.

3. Save bbc_feed.xsl, and press F12/Opt+F12 to test it again. This time, just the first five items should be displayed. You can check your code against bbc_feed_03.xsl.

Dreamweaver places another gray border around the dynamic placeholders in Design view, with an xsl:if tab at the top-left corner. Confusingly, Dreamweaver positions the xsl:if tab above the repeat region's xsl:for-each tab, giving the incorrect impression that the repeat region is nested inside the conditional one. In Figure 18-5, the conditional region has been selected by clicking the xsl:if gray tab. As you can see, lines 17–20 are highlighted in the underlying code. The code that controls the repeat region is on line 16 and the closing tag of the repeat region is on line 21. If in doubt about the order of code, check the Tag selector at the bottom of the Document window, as it always displays the correct hierarchy of parent and child tags.

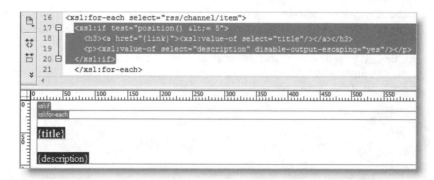

Figure 18-5. XSLT uses <xsl:if> tags to create a simple conditional region.

As you can see on line 17 of Figure 18-5, Dreamweaver has converted the less-than operator from < to <. XSLT follows the rules of XML and cannot use < within the test attribute value. Although it looks strange, it's the way that XSLT expects it. More important, it works!

Displaying the news feed in a web page

Now that you have got the XSLT Fragment to display the items that you want, it's time to embed the XSLT into a PHP page. To save time, I have created a copy of the "Stroll Along the Thames" page with a <div> called news in the sidebar. The style sheet contains a small number of extra rules to adjust the font size, margins, padding, and colors of the news <div>. The rules use basic CSS, so I'll leave you to study the style sheet yourself and just concentrate on the mechanics of embedding the XSLT Fragment into the page.

Embedding the XSLT Fragment in a dynamic page

You can't use the XSLT Fragment on its own; you need to serve it through a dynamic page so that the PHP server behavior can perform the necessary server-side transformation.

1. Copy stroll_xsl_start.php from examples/ch18 to workfiles/ch18, and save it as stroll_xsl.php. It uses stroll_xsl.css, which is in examples/styles, so update the links when Dreamweaver prompts you.

2. Open Split view, and highlight the placeholder text in the news <div>. Make sure that only the placeholder text is selected, and press Delete. The insertion point should be between the opening and closing <div> tags.

3. Click the XSL Transformation button in the Data tab of the Insert bar, as shown in the next screenshot. Alternatively, select Insert ➤ Data Objects ➤ XSL Transformation.

4. In the XSL Transformation dialog box that opens, click the top Browse button, and navigate to bbc_feed.xsl. When you click OK in the Select XSLT File dialog box, Dreamweaver will automatically populate the XML URI field. This is the address of the BBC RSS feed, which Dreamweaver gets from the XSLT Fragment. You don't need to bother with XSLT parameters, so just click OK. The use of XSLT parameters is explained later in the chapter.

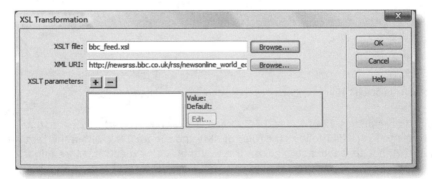

5. Your page should now look like Figure 18-6. Although it looks as though the XSLT Fragment has just been included in the page in the same way as a PHP include file, the underlying code is completely different. Notice that the embedded version displays the repeat region and conditional region tabs in the correct order.

Figure 18-6. The XSLT Fragment embedded in a PHP page

6. You can test the page by clicking the Live Data view icon in the Document toolbar. (Although it won't work with an XSLT Fragment on its own, you can use it after embedding the fragment in a dynamic page.)

7. Save the page, and test it in a browser. It should now look like Figure 18-1. Compare your code, if necessary, with stroll_xsl.php in examples/ch18.

When deploying on the Internet a page that contains an embedded XSLT Fragment, don't forget to upload the XSL page and the PHP class that does all the hard work: MM_XSLTransform.class.php, which is located in includes/MM_XSLTransform.

If instead of the latest news headlines, you see an MM_XSL Transform error message, it means that your remote server doesn't have the necessary support for XSLT. Pressure your hosting company to provide support, or move to one that does. As noted earlier, another problem might be that your hosting company has turned off allow_url_fopen. In that case, use the URL at the end of "Checking your server's support for XSLT" to urge Adobe to upgrade the XSL Transformation server behavior.

Being a bit more adventurous with XSLT

Up to now, I have deliberately avoided discussing most of the code that's being generated. There's actually very little of it in the XSLT Fragment and PHP page, because all the processing is done by an external PHP class. What's more, the code in the XSLT Fragment is very different from what you've been working with in previous chapters. In the remaining pages of this chapter, I'd like to show you just a few of the things you can do if you decide to experiment with XSLT and XPath. Instead of using a live news feed as the XML source, I've prepared an XML document that contains details of the friends of ED and Apress catalog. (In Chapter 20, I'll show you how to generate XML from your own data in MySQL.)

Setting up a local XML source

Getting XML data from a local source involves nothing more complicated than telling Dreamweaver where to find it. You will find a copy of booklist.xml in the examples/ch18 folder, and you can access it directly from there. Open it, and take a look at its structure. The root element is called BookList, and it contains ten elements each called Book, which look like this:

```
<Book ISBN13="9781590598597">
  <Title>The Essential Guide to Dreamweaver CS3 with CSS, Ajax, ➡
and PHP</Title>
  <Authors>
    <Author>David Powers</Author>
  </Authors>
  <Publisher>friends of ED</Publisher>
  <ListPrice>49.99</ListPrice>
</Book>
```

Each Book element or node has an attribute called ISBN13 and four child elements: Title, Authors, Publisher, and ListPrice. In turn, Authors can have one or more child elements called Author.

The following series of exercises shows you how to access the XML structure for use in a web page.

> *Each exercise builds upon the previous one. The finished code for each exercise is in* examples/ch18.

Displaying the node tree (schema) of booklist.xml

Before you can do anything with the XML data, you need to create an XSLT Fragment and display the node tree or schema.

1. Choose File ➤ New ➤ Blank Page ➤ XSLT (Fragment).

2. In the Locate XML Source dialog box, choose the default option (Attach a local file on my computer or local area network), and click the Browse button to navigate to booklist.xml in examples/ch18.

   Notice that the dialog box you use to locate the XML file is called Locate Source XML for XSL Template. Although XSL templates are very different from Dreamweaver templates, the idea is the same: an XSL template defines the basic pattern that will be applied to all the data passed to it.

   After locating booklist.xml, click OK (or Choose on a Mac). Click OK to close the Locate XML Source dialog box.

3. This attaches booklist.xml to the XSLT Fragment and displays the structure of the document in the Bindings panel, as shown in Figure 18-7. Although the document tree is much shorter than the BBC RSS feed, it contains two repeating nodes: Book

and Author. Moreover, Author is a grandchild of Book. In other words, you have a repeating region within a repeating region. Each book can have more than one author, so this makes handling this XML document more complex than the BBC feed.

Figure 18-7.
The node tree (schema) of booklist.xml

4. Save the XSLT Fragment page as books1.xsl in workfiles/ch18.

Displaying the book list in a table

Since the purpose is to show you a few of the things you can do with XSLT in Dreamweaver, I don't plan on styling the content. The data in the book list is best displayed in a table, so that's what I'll use.

1. Insert a table in books1.xsl. The table should have two rows and five columns. I also set Table width to 80 percent, and Cell padding to 4, leaving both Border thickness and Cell spacing blank.

2. Give the first row the following headings: Title, Author(s), Publisher, ISBN13, and Price.

3. Drag the Title node from the Bindings panel, and drop it in the second row, so that the dynamic placeholder sits beneath the Title heading in the first row. Do the same for Publisher, ISBN13, and ListPrice, dropping them in the appropriate cells in the second row. What should you do about the Author(s) cell? You want to show the names of all the authors, so you probably think you should use the Author node. Illogical though it may seem, drag the parent node, Authors, *not* the child node.

4. Click anywhere in the second row, and then select <tr> in the Tag selector to highlight the entire table row.

5. In the XSLT tab of the Insert bar, click the Repeat Region button, and select the Book node in the XPath Expression Builder (Repeat Region) dialog box. Click OK. Your page should now look like this:

6. Save books1.xsl, and press F12/Opt+F12 to view the XSLT Fragment in a browser. Surprise, surprise . . . all the authors' names are listed. To understand why, you need to dive into the mysteries of XSLT syntax.

Understanding how XSLT is structured

Now's the time to look at an XSLT Fragment in detail in Code view. The first line of books1.xsl looks like this:

```
<?xml version="1.0" encoding="utf-8"?> ➡
<!-- DWXMLSource="../../examples/ch18/booklist.xml" -->
```

The first part is the XML declaration, which must go at the beginning of every XML document. By default, Dreamweaver inserts the encoding attribute using the same value as in your Dreamweaver preferences. If your XML source uses a different encoding, you should change the setting for your XSLT Fragment and any dynamic page that you intend to embed it in. Do this by choosing Page Properties from the Modify menu. In the Page Properties dialog box, select the Title/Encoding category, and set Encoding to the appropriate value.

The second part of the first line is an XML comment (the same format as HTML is used), where Dreamweaver stores the location of the XML source.

The next ten lines define common HTML entities. As mentioned earlier, only five entities are predefined in XML, so Dreamweaver anticipates the need for others that are likely to occur in XML feeds. You can also define others, if necessary.

Defining new entities If you discover that your XSLT Fragments are having problems with unrecognized entities, add a new definition on a new line within this section, using the same format. For example, if you want to add the entity for lowercase e acute (é), add this line:

```
<!ENTITY eacute   "&#233;">
```

In other words, remove the leading & and trailing semicolon from the HTML entity, and put the character entity equivalent in quotes. You can find a full list of HTML entities and their character entity equivalents at www.w3.org/TR/html4/sgml/entities.html.

Embedding XHTML in XSLT The rest of the code in the page is a mixture of XSLT and XHTML. The two fit together in a very similar way to PHP and XHTML. The XSLT processor handles anything in an XSLT tag (they all begin with <xsl:), and it treats anything outside as literal text. I have reproduced here the main XSLT code from books1.xsl, and highlighted some key points in bold:

```
<xsl:stylesheet version="1.0" xmlns:xsl="http://www.w3.org/1999/ ➡
XSL/Transform">
<xsl:output method="html" encoding="utf-8"/>
<xsl:template match="/">
<table width="80%" cellpadding="4">
  <tr>
    <th scope="col">Title</th>
    <th scope="col">Author(s)</th>
```

```
        <th scope="col">Publisher</th>
        <th scope="col">ISBN13</th>
        <th scope="col">Price</th>
      </tr>
      <xsl:for-each select="BookList/Book">
        <tr>
          <td><xsl:value-of select="Title"/></td>
          <td><xsl:value-of select="Authors"/></td>
          <td><xsl:value-of select="Publisher"/></td>
          <td><xsl:value-of select="@ISBN13"/></td>
          <td><xsl:value-of select="ListPrice"/></td>
        </tr>
      </xsl:for-each>
    </table>
  </xsl:template>
</xsl:stylesheet>
```

The first line that I have highlighted creates an XSLT template. XSLT templates match a certain part of the XML source (hence the attribute match). The closing </xsl:template> tag is on the second line from the bottom, so all the code in between is part of the template. The value of match is /, which is the XPath way of indicating the document root. In other words, this set of XSLT instructions will be applied to the whole of the XML source, rather than just a specific part of it.

The next highlighted line uses <xsl:for-each>. As you can probably guess, this is the way that XSLT creates a loop or repeat region. The value of select is BookList/Book, so the loop applies to every Book node or element in the XML document. As the loop goes through each Book node, the <xsl:value-of> instruction gets the selected value. When it gets to the Author node, it also loops through the child nodes. That's why you see all the author's names displayed in the table, even though you haven't selected the Author node in your XSLT Fragment.

Accessing nested repeating elements

In some respects, the way that XSLT loops through the child nodes is quite useful, but there are no commas between the authors' names. You need a way of getting to the Author nodes and manipulating them. This is where things get interesting or fiendishly complicated, depending on your point of view. I'll try to keep things as simple as possible. Once you understand what's happening, it's a lot simpler than it may seem at your first attempt.

Accessing the Author elements directly

This uses the same XSLT Fragment as in the previous exercise. Save books1.xsl as books2.xsl before continuing, and then work with the new version.

1. Select the {Authors} placeholder in the second row of the table, and press Delete. The second cell of the second row should now be empty.

637

2. Select the Author repeating node in the Bindings panel, and drag and drop it into the empty cell. Instead of inserting an Author dynamic placeholder, as you might expect, Dreamweaver inserts an XSLT repeat region with a text placeholder, as shown here:

3. Highlight the words Content goes here, and press Delete. Make sure you remove only the text and not the gray tab labeled xsl:for-each. Don't click anywhere in the document, because the cursor *must* remain inside the repeat region.

4. In the XSLT tab of the Insert bar, click the Dynamic Text button (or choose Insert ➤ XSLT Objects ➤ Dynamic Text). This opens the XPath Expression Builder. Select Author. It may appear as though Dreamweaver hasn't created anything in the Expression field, but look a bit closer. There's a single period (.) there, which is the XPath way of saying "current node." Click OK.

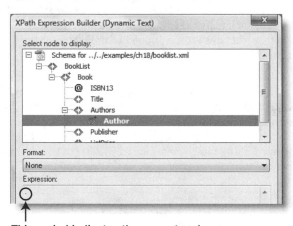

This period indicates the current node.

5. You should now have a current-node dynamic placeholder inside the repeat region.

6. Save books2.xsl, and press F12/Opt+F12 to view the output in a browser. The authors' names are there, but things have gotten worse—there's no space between them any more. Switch back to Dreamweaver, where you'll put it right.

7. Select the current-node dynamic placeholder that you created in step 5. Open Split view. You will see the following line highlighted in the underlying code:

```
<xsl:value-of select="."/>
```

8. Click inside Code view, and add the following code on a new line underneath. I've shown the preceding and following lines to help you get the right location.

```
<xsl:value-of select="."/>
<xsl:text>, </xsl:text>
</xsl:for-each></td>
```

When you start typing, Dreamweaver code hints will display the available XSLT tags. To save typing, you can scroll down to xsl:text and press Enter/Return. Automatic code completion will also insert the correct closing tag after you type </.

This inserts a comma followed by a space after the name of each author. You could just type the comma, but to get the space you need to wrap it in the <xsl:text> tags.

9. Save books2.xsl, and view it in a browser. This is progress, but you don't want a comma after the last name. To deal with that, you need to use a conditional region.

Creating conditional regions

When working with an XSLT Fragment, there are two options on the XSLT tab of the Insert bar (and XSLT Objects submenu of the Insert menu) for creating a conditional region— Conditional Region and Multiple Conditional Region. We'll take a closer look at both of them. First, a simple conditional expression.

Testing a single condition

You used a simple conditional expression in "Restricting the number of items in an XSLT repeat region" earlier in the chapter. As Figure 18-5 shows, the code inserted by Dreamweaver is very similar in structure to a PHP if statement. In the same way as a pair of curly braces, the <xsl:if> tags surround the code you want to display only if the condition is met. The condition is specified as the test attribute in the opening <xsl:if> tag.

Removing the final comma from authors' names

This builds on the XSLT Fragment from the previous exercise and shows you how to get rid of the comma following the name of the last author. Save books2.xsl as books3.xsl, and work on the new document.

1. Open Split view, and highlight the line that you inserted in step 8 of the previous exercise. Alternatively, click the xsl:text tab in Design view. Click the Conditional Region button in the XSLT tab of the Insert bar.

2. Earlier in the chapter, you used the position() function to select the first five elements in the item node. Another very intuitively named function, last(), determines whether an element is the last one in the current node. You don't want the comma to be displayed if the author's name is the last one, so type position() != last() in the Test field of the Conditional Region dialog box. != has the same meaning as in PHP.

3. Save books3.xsl, and view it in a browser. The final comma is no longer displayed, so single author's names appear on their own, but the names of multiple authors are nicely formatted as a comma-separated list.

If you look in Code view, you'll see that the `<xsl:text>` tags that insert the comma and space have been surrounded by `<xsl:if>` tags like this:

```
<xsl:if test="position() != last()">
  <xsl:text>, </xsl:text>
</xsl:if>
```

Testing alternative conditions

Although there's a comma between each of the author's names when there are more than one, it would be more natural to replace the comma with "and" or "&" before the last name. The logic behind how you do this is simple. Instead of placing the comma *after* each author's name, create a conditional statement that decides whether to put a comma or "and" *before* the name. In pseudo-code this becomes:

```
if (position is greater than 1 AND position is not last) {
  insert a comma before the name
  }
else if (position is greater than 1 AND position is last) {
  insert "and" before the name
  }
```

The if . . . else structure is exactly what you would use in PHP, but the XSLT syntax is a little more complex. XSLT wraps the whole conditional block in `<xsl:choose>` tags; `<xsl:when>` equates to if; and `<xsl:otherwise>` equates to else. Dreamweaver takes care of inserting the correct tags when you select Multiple Conditional Region from the XSLT tab of the Insert bar or from the XSLT Objects submenu of the Insert menu.

Inserting "and" before the final author's name

Save books3.xsl as books4.xsl, and continue working with the new file. In this exercise, you'll use a multiple conditional region to replace the final comma in a list of authors' names with "and."

1. Things are beginning to look rather crowded in the table cell that contains the dynamic placeholders for the authors' names. You need to click the xsl:if tab indicated by the arrow in the screenshot alongside.

   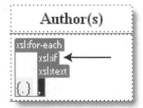

   You will know that you have selected it correctly if the Property inspector displays the test expression for the conditional region as shown here (this is also how you would edit it).

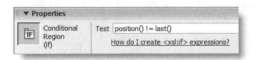

If you have difficulty selecting the tab, use the Zoom tool (it looks like a magnifying glass) at the bottom right of the Document window. When you select the Zoom tool, click on the area that you want to magnify until it's big enough to work with. Then choose the Select tool (an arrow). To zoom out, select the Zoom tool again and hold down Alt/Opt while clicking.

2. Open Split view. The conditional region that you inserted in the preceding exercise should be highlighted. Since the syntax for a multiple conditional region is completely different, press Delete to remove the highlighted code.

3. In Code view, your cursor will be just below `<xsl:value-of select="."/>`. This is what XSLT uses to display the name of each author. This time, the comma needs to go in front of the author's name, so insert it as `<xsl:text>` on a new line above, like this:

```
<td><xsl:for-each select="Authors/Author">
  <xsl:text>, </xsl:text>
  <xsl:value-of select="."/>
```

4. Highlight the line that you have just inserted, and click the Multiple Conditional Region button on the XSLT tab of the Insert bar, as shown in the following screenshot:

5. Type the following in the Test field of the Multiple Conditional Region dialog box:

```
position() > 1 and position() != last()
```

This will show the comma and space if the element is neither first nor last. Click OK.

6. If you thought the table cell was crowded before, just look at it now! Dreamweaver inserts Content goes here as a placeholder inside `<xsl:otherwise>`. This is where you are expected to create a default value if all tests fail. However, you don't want a default for this conditional region, so highlight Content goes here and delete it. Keep Split view open to make sure you don't delete any XSLT tags.

7. To create the second condition, you need to position your cursor inside Code view immediately before the opening `<xsl:otherwise>` tag. Then click the Conditional Region button on the XSLT tab of the Insert bar. Make sure you click the one for a single condition (marked with IF), and *not* the icon for a multiple condition.

8. Type the following in the Test field of the Conditional Region dialog box, and then click OK:

```
position() > 1 and position() = last()
```

You'll use this test to insert "and" surrounded by a space on either side before the last author's name. It's necessary to check that the position is greater than 1, because you don't want "and" to appear before the names of single authors. Also notice that XSLT uses a single equal sign to test for equality.

9. There's now a severe overcrowding problem in the table cell, as Dreamweaver inserts another Content goes here to indicate where to insert what will be displayed when the test evaluates to true. It's easier to work in Code view at this stage, so click inside Code view, and replace Content goes here with the following:

```
<xsl:text> and </xsl:text>
```

> As you're typing, you'll notice that the greater-than sign you added in step 8 has been replaced by >. This is because > indicates the end of a tag, so XSLT conditional expressions use the HTML entity instead. XSLT also requires quotes in expressions. Dreamweaver handles all the necessary conversions automatically if you use the appropriate dialog boxes.

10. Save books4.xsl, and view it in a browser. You should see commas between names, with "and" separating the final two.

11. Change `<xsl:text> and </xsl:text>` to `<xsl:text> & </xsl:text>`, and view the page again. It won't work. You get the following error:

SAXParseException: Expected entity name for reference (books4.xsl, line 33, column 25)

This is because & is used by XML-related languages, such as XSLT, to designate an entity. Replace & with &, and all will be well.

Sorting elements

XSLT has many powerful features, including the ability to sort nodes, so they appear in a different order from the original XML source. Dreamweaver doesn't generate the code for you automatically, but it's very easy to do by hand.

Sorting the book list by title and publisher

Save books4.xsl as books5.xsl, and continue working with the new document. This exercise shows you how to sort the books first by title, and then by publisher and title.

1. In Code view, locate the following line (it should be around line 24):

```
<xsl:for-each select="BookList/Book">
```

2. Insert a new line immediately below, and add the code shown in bold:

```
<xsl:for-each select="BookList/Book">
<xsl:sort select="Title"/>
```

3. Save the page, and view it in a browser. The value of select determines which node is used to sort the document. The list is now sorted by the books' titles.

By chance, most of the books that I chose from the Apress catalog have titles that start with *B*, so they appear first in the list, but *Pro CSS Techniques* is lurking among the friends of ED titles. You can use multiple sort conditions by adding similar tags in the order of priority that you want to give each element.

4. To sort by publisher and then by title, use the following:

```
<xsl:for-each select="BookList/Book">
<xsl:sort select="Publisher"/>
<xsl:sort select="Title"/>
```

5. Test the page again and *Pro CSS Techniques* will have joined its Apress buddies.

6. But, hey, this is a friends of ED book. Surely the order should be reversed. No problem. Just add an order attribute to the <xsl:sort> tag like this:

```
<xsl:sort select="Publisher" order="descending"/>
```

Note that, as you type the code, Dreamweaver displays code hints for XSLT, showing you the available options.

7. The friends of ED books now appear first, with their titles sorted in correct alphabetical order, followed by all Apress books similarly sorted. Like PHP, *XSLT is case sensitive*, so make sure you use the correct case for the node names.

Formatting elements

You may have noticed that there's a drop-down menu labeled Format in the middle of the XPath Expression Builder. This allows you to apply 22 preset formats to the content of a node. Most of them deal with formatting numbers or currency.

Formatting the book prices

Save books5.xsl as books6.xsl, and continue working with the new file. This exercise shows you how to format the book prices using the dollar and other currency symbols.

1. In Design view, select the ListPrice dynamic placeholder in the second row of the table, and click the Dynamic Text button in the XSLT tab of the Insert bar. This opens the XPath Expression Builder.

2. Activate the Format drop-down menu, and select Currency – Leading 0, 2 Decimal Places. The Expression field displays the XPath function that will be inserted in the underlying code: format-number(ListPrice, '$#0.00'). Click OK.

3. Save `books6.xsl`, and view it in a browser. Nothing is different—the prices don't have any currency symbol. This is because the parser used by Dreamweaver can't process all XSLT functions.

4. Create a PHP page called `books.php`. The only reason you need this page is to embed the XSLT Fragment, but it's best to insert some ordinary text. Otherwise, you won't be able to click inside the Document window after the fragment has been embedded. Type a heading, such as Good Books. Move the cursor out of the heading, and select the XSL Transformation button on the Data tab of the Insert bar.

5. In the XSL Transformation dialog box, click the top Browse button, and select `books6.xsl` as the XSLT file. Click OK (or Choose on a Mac) to close both dialog boxes.

6. Save `books.php`, and view it in a browser. The currency symbols now appear correctly.

At the bottom of the Format drop-down menu in the XPath Expression Builder is an option to edit the format list. Ideally, this should be the place to create a custom currency format for sterling or euros. Unfortunately, Dreamweaver converts both the £ and € symbols to their HTML equivalents, which not only prevents them being displayed in the final page but also prevents you from using the XPath Expression Builder to edit any element to which you apply the format. The solution, fortunately, is very simple: apply one of the standard currency formats and edit it manually in Code view.

Change this:

```
format-number(ListPrice, '$#0.00')
```

to this (for pounds sterling):

```
format-number(ListPrice, '£#0.00')
```

or this (for euros):

```
format-number(ListPrice, '€#0.00')
```

You may wonder why the actual symbol is used instead of an entity. It's because the second argument to `format-number()` is a string literal. If you use an entity, it will be ignored.

Displaying output selectively

There are two ways of displaying output that meets certain criteria. One is to use an XPath filter. The other is to use a parameter. Let's take a quick look at both of them.

Filtering nodes with XPath

The XPath Expression Builder has an option that lets you build filters to display XML data selectively. The filters work in a very similar way to a WHERE clause in a SQL query, so you should have little difficulty understanding how they work.

Selecting books by price

Save books6.xsl as books7.xsl, and continue working with the new file. This exercise shows you how to select books cheaper than or equal to a specified price.

1. Select the repeat region for the second table row by clicking the xsl:for-each tab above the {Title} dynamic placeholder. You can tell that you have selected it correctly by checking the Property inspector, which should look like this:

2. Click the lightning bolt icon to the right of the Select field in the Property inspector to open the XPath Expression Builder (Repeat Region) dialog box.

3. Click the triangle to the side of Build Filter in the middle of the XPath Expression Builder to expand the filter builder.

4. Click the plus button at the top of the Build Filter area. Click in the Where field to activate the drop-down menu that contains a list of all nodes. Select ListPrice.

5. Click in the Operator field and choose <= (less than or equal to).

6. Click in the Value field, and type 40. Click anywhere inside the dialog box to remove the focus from the Value field. The Build Filter area should now look like this:

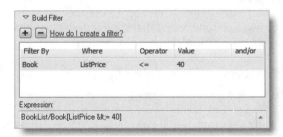

The Expression field below the Build Filter area shows you the XPath expression that Dreamweaver will insert into the XSLT code.

7. Click OK. Save books7.xsl, and view the page in a browser. Instead of the previous ten books, you should now see just seven—all priced $40 or less.

Selecting books by price and publisher

As you can see from the preceding screenshot, the Build Filter area has an and/or option. This exercise shows you how to filter XML data using more than one condition. Save books7.xsl as books8.xsl, and continue working with the new file.

1. Repeat steps 1 and 2 of the previous exercise to open the XPath Expression Builder. Expand the Build Filter area if it's not already open.

2. Click in the and/or field, and select and from the drop-down menu.

3. Click the plus button at the top left of the Build Filter area to add another filter.

4. Click the Where field and select Publisher.

5. Leave Operator at the default =.

6. Click the Value field and type 'Apress'—it *must* be in quotes (single or double: it doesn't matter). The Build Filter area should now look like this.

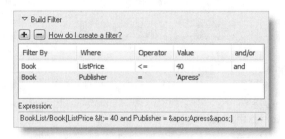

7. Click OK, save the page, and view it in a browser. You will now see just three titles listed.

Look at the Expression field and the underlying code, and you will see that Dreamweaver has converted the quotes and the less-than operator to HTML entities, saving you a lot of effort with building XPath expressions. Remember to use the normal characters in the dialog boxes so that Dreamweaver can convert them correctly. It's also vital to remember that strings entered in the Value field must always be in quotes.

Using XSLT parameters to filter data

The other way of selecting output is by passing one or more parameters from the PHP page to the XSLT Fragment. This is much more interactive, because the decision about what to display is dynamically generated, unlike filters, which are hard-coded into the XSLT instructions.

Creating a default parameter to select the publisher

Before using a parameter to change the content dynamically, you need to create a default parameter inside the XSLT Fragment. Save books8.xsl as books9.xsl, and continue working with the new page.

1. Insert an XSLT parameter after the opening <xsl:output> tag (around line 14) like this:

```
<xsl:output method="html" encoding="utf-8"/>
<xsl:param name="pub" select="'friends of ED'"/>
<xsl:template match="/">
```

The <xsl:param> tag takes two attributes: name, which is self-explanatory, and select, which sets the parameter value. Note that there are two sets of quotes around friends of ED. The double quotes surround the value of select, which is a string and must itself be enclosed in quotes. To avoid a clash, single quotes are used for the inner pair.

By declaring the parameter immediately after the <xsl:output> tag, you make it global in scope—in other words, available throughout the XSLT script.

2. Switch to Design view, select the xsl:for-each tab that controls the repeat region for the entire table row, and click the lighting bolt icon in the Property inspector to open the XPath Expression Builder. You should see the same two filters as in step 6 of the last exercise.

3. Highlight the first filter (based on ListPrice), and click the minus button to remove it.

4. Click inside the Value field of the remaining filter to reveal a drop-down menu. You should now see your XSLT parameter listed with a dollar sign in front of it. Select $pub in place of 'Apress', as shown in the following screenshot:

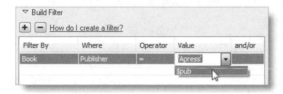

The Expression field should now read: BookList/Book[Publisher = $pub]. Click OK.

5. Save books9.xsl, and view it in a browser. Only friends of ED books should be listed.

Once you have defined a default parameter, you can use it to change the content of an XSLT fragment dynamically when it's embedded in a PHP page.

Sending a parameter from a PHP page

This simple exercise demonstrates how you can toggle between displaying books published by Apress and friends of ED, using a jump menu to send the parameter to the XSLT Fragment through a URL query string.

1. Create a new PHP page called books_param.php.

2. From the Insert menu, select Form ➤ Jump Menu.

3. In the Insert Jump Menu dialog box, insert Apress in the Text field, and ?pub=Apress in the field labeled When selected, go to URL. This will add the name and value of the parameter to a query string that will be added to the URL when the page reloads.

18

4. Click the plus button to add a second menu item. Insert friends of ED in the Text field and ?pub=friends of ED for When selected, go to URL. Leave the other options in the dialog box unchanged. When you have finished, it should look like this:

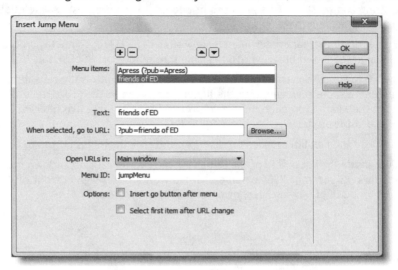

5. Click OK to insert the jump menu, and then select the menu object in Design view. In the Property inspector, change the name of the menu to pub. You also need the menu to display the currently selected value. Apart from the first time the page loads, this comes from the value of pub in the URL query string. Before clicking the Dynamic button in the Property inspector, you need to create a URL variable for Dreamweaver to use.

6. Open the Bindings panel, click the plus button, and select URL variable. Type pub in the Name field, and click OK.

7. Make sure the menu item is still selected in Design view, and click the Dynamic button in the Property inspector. When the Dynamic List/Menu dialog box opens, click the lightning bolt icon alongside the field labeled Select value equal to.

8. Expand the URL tree in the Dynamic Data dialog box, select pub, and click OK. Also click OK in the Dynamic List/Menu dialog box to close it.

9. Unfortunately, the code created by Dreamweaver needs tweaking slightly. Open Code view or Split view. The jump menu code should look like this:

```
17  <form name="form" id="form">
18    <select name="pub" id="pub" onchange="MM_jumpMenu('parent',this,0)">
19      <option value="?pub=Apress" <?php if (!(strcmp("?pub=Apress", $_GET['pub']))) {echo
    "selected=\"selected\"";} ?>>Apress</option>
20        <option value="?pub=friends of ED" <?php if (!(strcmp("?pub=friends of ED", $_GET['pub']))) {echo
    "selected=\"selected\"";} ?>>friends of ED</option>
21      </select>
22  </form>
```

Delete the two highlighted sections.

10. Delete the two sections indicated in the preceding screenshot by removing ?pub= from the PHP code. This is necessary because $_GET['pub'] contains just the value of the pub variable, not the whole query string. Be careful to remove the correct sections—you still want the full query string in the value attribute of each <option> tag.

11. $_GET['pub'] won't be set when the page first loads, so add the following code immediately above the opening <form> tag:

```php
<?php if (!isset($_GET['pub'])) {$_GET['pub'] = 'Apress';} ?>
```

This sets the default value of pub to Apress and prevents any error from being generated if the query string is missing. I've deliberately chosen the opposite default from the one in the XSLT Fragment to show how passing a parameter from outside takes precedence over the value of select in <xsl:param>.

12. Position your cursor just after the closing </form> tag, and switch back to Design view.

13. Embed the XSLT Fragment by clicking the XSL Transformation button in the Data tab of the Insert bar. In the XSL Transformation dialog box, click the top Browse button, and select books9.xsl as the XSLT file. Then click the plus button alongside XSLT parameters. Type pub in the Name field of the Add Parameter dialog box, and click the lightning bolt icon to the right of the Value field. This opens the Dynamic Data dialog box, where you should select pub from the URL tree.

14. When you click OK to close the Dynamic Data dialog box, the Default value field is no longer grayed out in the Add Parameter dialog box. This is where you can insert a default value to be passed to the XSLT Fragment. However, it's not necessary because you created a default value in the <xsl:param> tag in the previous exercise.

15. When you click OK to close the Add Parameter dialog box, you'll see the pub parameter listed, as shown in the following screenshot. An Edit button has been added in case you need to make any changes. Click OK to close the XSL Transformation dialog box.

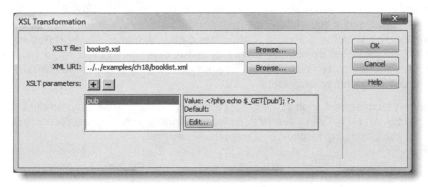

16. Save books_param.php, and press F12/Opt+F12 to view it in a browser. It should look like Figure 18-8. Even though the default parameter in the XSLT Fragment was set to friends of ED, the parameter sent from the PHP page takes precedence.

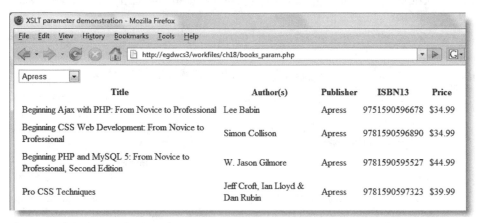

Figure 18-8. The contents of the XML document have been sorted, formatted, and displayed selectively through a combination of XSLT and PHP.

17. Select friends of ED from the jump menu, and the display will change, showing only foED books.

More XML to come . . .

This has been only a brief introduction to working with XSLT. It's a massive and complex subject, but I think Dreamweaver has done a good job of making it more accessible to nonexperts. However, in spite of its power, XSLT has failed to take the web development community by storm. Although lack of browser support for client-side XSLT has played some part in holding it back, I think the main reason probably lies in the fact that XSLT on its own doesn't style the output. It manipulates data in a similar way to PHP, and since most XML is generated dynamically from a database, developers prefer to go straight to the source and use more familiar server-side technologies. The nonintuitive syntax is also a major put off for many developers.

In the next chapter, we'll look at a different approach to XML, using Spry, Adobe's implementation of Ajax. The Dreamweaver interface for handling Spry data sets is very similar to XSLT, but the underlying technology is completely different.

19 USING SPRY TO DISPLAY XML

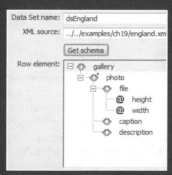

The ability to manipulate XML data without the need to refresh the web page lies at the very heart of Ajax. It's also the prime motivation behind Adobe's decision to develop the Spry framework. In theory, it's the most exciting development in Dreamweaver CS3. The reality leaves much to be desired, partly because of the accessibility problems that I outlined in Chapter 2, but also because Spry is still work in progress. The original release of Dreamweaver CS3 incorporated Spry 1.4. Only a month later Spry 1.5 was made available on Adobe Labs (http://labs.adobe.com/technologies/spry/), raising expectations of an update for Dreamweaver. It took a further month before Adobe announced that an extension to update Dreamweaver would be made available for the "production release" of Spry during summer 2007. Details were still hazy at the time this book went to press, but it's anticipated that there may be three or four releases of Spry before the next version of Dreamweaver. At the time of this writing, it had not been decided whether to release extensions on a regular basis to allow Dreamweaver to keep pace with new features in Spry.

This chapter focuses on creating and using Spry data sets through the Dreamweaver interface, so it is based on Spry 1.4, the version supported at the time of publication. Once you have learned the basics, you can study the latest version by visiting Adobe Labs at the URL in the preceding paragraph. In this chapter, you'll learn how to

- Create a Spry data set from an XML document
- Display data in a sortable table
- Use a Spry detail region to display related information
- Distinguish the different types of Spry repeat regions
- Build a Spry online photo gallery

You don't need a deep knowledge of JavaScript to use Spry data sets. In fact, you don't need any knowledge at all. Nevertheless, you'll get more out of working with Spry if you know what the code looks like and what it's for. So, throughout this chapter, you'll be diving regularly into Code view to see what's going on under the hood.

I assume that you're familiar with the basic structure of an XML document and the role of XPath, both of which are described in the previous chapter.

How Spry handles XML data

Before you can display or manipulate the content of an XML document with Spry, you need to create a Spry data set. Dreamweaver analyzes the structure of the XML and displays dynamic data objects in the Bindings panel for you to incorporate into a web page in much the same way as with a database recordset or an XSL fragment. If you have worked through the previous chapter, you will see a lot of similarities between the way you create an XSL fragment and a Spry data set. However, there are some important differences, namely:

- Browser security restrictions mean that the XML source must originate from the same domain as the web page. This means you can't normally use a remote XML or RSS feed unless you fetch the remote file with a proxy script and serve it as though it comes from the same domain. I'll show you how to do this in the next chapter. It's very easy to do with PHP.

- Spry 1.4 ignores XML nodes that have child nodes of their own. This means that the version of Spry that shipped with Dreamweaver CS3 is unsuitable for handling complex XML with deeply nested information.

This second limitation has been overcome in Spry 1.5, but if you want to use the Dreamweaver interface to work with Spry data sets, you will probably find it easier to structure your XML documents to eliminate nesting.

Making sure Spry can find data

To give a practical example of the problem caused by child nodes, let's look at the data in booklist.xml from the previous chapter. The basic XML structure looks like this:

```
<BookList>
  <Book ISBN13="number">
    <Title>Book title</Title>
    <Authors>
      <Author>Name</Author>
      <Author>Name</Author>
    </Authors>
    <Publisher>Name</Publisher>
    <ListPrice>Price</ListPrice>
  </Book>
</BookList>
```

Figure 19-1 displays this as a node tree. The <Authors> node and its <Author> child nodes are shaded in gray to illustrate how Spry treats them.

Figure 19-1. A Spry data set ignores nodes that have child nodes of their own.

When creating a Spry data set, you need to specify the XPath to the repeating element from which you want to extract the data. If you set the XPath to BookList/Book, Spry 1.4 is capable of extracting the ISBN13 attribute. It can also extract the values of <Title>, <Publisher>, and <ListPrice>, but it ignores <Authors>. If you attempt to access <Authors>, Spry 1.4 displays undefined.

You can create a Spry data set by specifying BookList/Book/Authors as the XPath, but that gives you access only to the <Author> child nodes. You cannot get to the <Author> nodes from their grandparent <Book>. In other words, with Spry 1.4 you get either the values shown with a white background or those with a gray background but not both.

The implication of this is that your XML documents should ideally have no more than three levels: the root node, a repeating element such as `<Book>`, and all details should be stored either in attributes of the repeating element or in child nodes that have no children of their own. So, for booklist.xml to work with Spry, the structure needs to be altered like this:

```
<BookList>
  <Book ISBN13="number">
    <Title>Book title</Title>
    <Authors>Names</Authors>
    <Publisher>Name</Publisher>
    <ListPrice>Price</ListPrice>
  </Book>
</BookList>
```

Some of the Adobe sample files rely heavily on attributes. The Spry gallery shown in Figure 2-11 in Chapter 2 uses `<gallery>` as the root node, `<photos>` as the repeating element, and `<photo>` for each individual image. To get around the child node issue, the `<photo>` nodes contain all the details in six different attributes like this:

```
<photo path="china_01.jpg" width="263" height="350"  ➡
thumbpath="china_01.jpg" thumbwidth="56" thumbheight="75"></photo>
```

> *Spry 1.5 addresses the problem of accessing grandchildren nodes by introducing nested data sets. See* http://labs.adobe.com/technologies/spry/samples/data_region/NestedXMLDataSample.html.

Creating a Spry data set

You can create a Spry data set from either a static XML document or XML data generated on the fly from a database. To keep things simple, let's start with a static XML document.

Later in the chapter, you'll create an online gallery using Spry. One of the XML documents used in the gallery, england.xml, contains details of photos. The basic XML structure looks like this:

```
<gallery>
  <photo>
    <file width="number" height="number">filename</file>
    <caption>text</caption>
    <description><![CDATA[XHTML formatted text]]></description>
  </photo>
</gallery>
```

The root node is `<gallery>` and each photo's details are in a repeating node called `<photo>`. Each `<photo>` node has three child nodes, as follows:

- `<file>`: This contains the photo's file name as a text node, and the file's width and height as attributes.

- `<caption>`: This contains a text node with a caption that can double as alternate text.

- `<description>`: This contains a description of the photograph formatted as XHTML. To avoid conflicts with the XML structure, the contents of this node are enclosed in a CDATA section.

In XML, < is always treated as the opening of an XML tag, and & is always treated as the beginning of an entity (such as —, which represents an em dash). If you want to use them in any other context, < and & must be replaced by < and &. The alternative is to use a **CDATA section**, which allows you to embed literal code—or raw character data—inside an XML document. In simple terms, this means that the opening < of an XHTML tag inside a CDATA section is treated as ordinary text and not as the opening of an XML tag. To create a CDATA section, just place the literal code between opening `<![CDATA[` and closing `]]>` tags like this:

```
<description><![CDATA[<p><em>This is XHTML.</em></p>]]></description>
```

In this example, `<description>` is treated as an XML element, but the `<p>` and `<em>` tags inside the CDATA section are regarded as part of the text node. They're ignored in the XML, but will be recognized as XHTML markup when the text node is extracted and displayed in a web page.

Right, let's use `england.xml` to create a Spry data set.

I have created all the example files for this chapter in PHP pages. However, PHP is not required to work with Spry data sets, except for the accessible examples in the next chapter. If you don't have a local PHP testing environment, you might find it easier to use .html pages for the exercises in this chapter.

Creating a Spry data set from a static XML document

This exercise examines the various options in the Spry XML Data Set dialog box (see Figure 19-2).

1. Create a new web page, and save it as `spry_data.php` in `workfiles/ch19`.

2. To create a Spry data set, click the Spry XML Data Set button on the Spry tab of the Insert bar, as shown in the following screenshot.

You can also use Insert ➤ Spry ➤ Spry XML Data Set, or click the plus button in the Bindings panel and select Spry XML Data Set from the menu that appears.

3. This opens the Spry XML Data Set dialog box, as shown in Figure 19-2. You need to give a data set a name in the same way as a recordset. Dreamweaver automatically assigns the name ds1 to the first data set on a page, but it's a good idea to change this to something more meaningful. So, change ds1 in the Data Set name field to dsEngland.

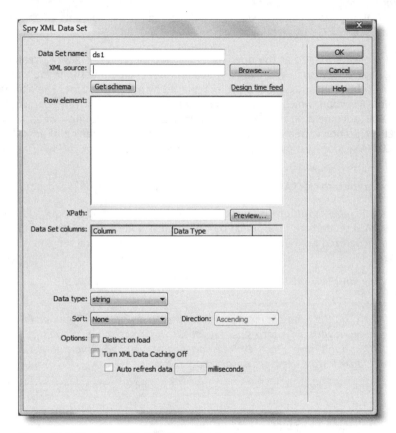

Figure 19-2. The Spry XML Data Set dialog box

4. Next, tell Dreamweaver where to find the XML source. Click the Browse button alongside the XML source field, and navigate to examples/ch19/england.xml. Click OK (Choose on a Mac) to return to the Spry XML Data Set dialog box. Then click the Get schema button to load the XML structure into the Row element area, which should now look like this:

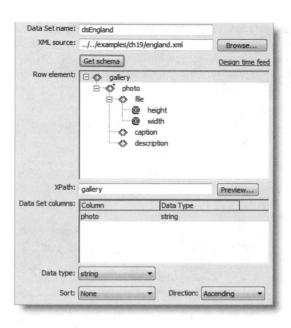

The XML node tree uses the same conventions as the XSL Transformation server behavior in the previous chapter. A pair of angle brackets (<>) indicates an XML node. A repeating node or element is indicated by a small plus sign at the top right of the node symbol. In the preceding screenshot, you can see that photo is a repeating element. Attributes are indicated by an @ mark. In england.xml, you can see that height and width are attributes of the file node.

The Design time feed link to the right of the Get schema button is rather confusing. If you click it now, a dialog box opens telling you that Dreamweaver failed to get a schema from the dynamic feed and suggesting that you provide a sample feed for design time. As I explained earlier, you can create a Spry data set from XML data generated on the fly. If the dynamic data source isn't available at design time, you need to use a static XML document with sample data. Since that's exactly what you're doing with england.xml, this message is both misleading and pointless. Just ignore the Design time feed link.

> *In Windows, the* Select XML Source *dialog box shows only files with an* .xml *extension. If your XML data is dynamically generated by PHP, you need to set the* Files of type *drop-down menu to* All Files (*.*) *before you can select the source file. As you'll see in the next chapter, Dreamweaver works with dynamically generated XML in exactly the same way as with a static XML document.*

5. To create the data set, you need to select the repeating element from which you want to extract the data. In this case, there's only one, so select photo in the Row element area. As the next screenshot shows, this changes XPath from gallery to gallery/photo and populates the Data Set columns area with the names of all the child nodes and attributes.

6. Click the Preview button to check what the data set contains. You should see something similar to Figure 19-3.

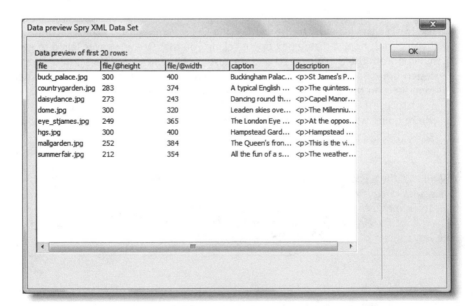

Figure 19-3. You can check that you're getting the right data by previewing the first few rows.

The Data preview panel shows a maximum of the first 20 rows of the data set. There are only eight in england.xml, so the panel shows them all. Click OK to close the panel and return to the Spry XML Data Set dialog box.

7. By default, all columns are treated as strings, which can cause problems for sorting numbers, so the Data type drop-down menu lets you specify how you want individual columns to be treated. The height and width attributes are numerical, so select file/@height in the Data Set columns area and set Data type to number. Do the same for file/@width.

8. As you can see from Figure 19-3, the file column is in alphabetical order. This reflects the order in which I created england.xml, and the same order will be used for the data set. However, you can tell Spry to order the data differently by setting the Sort and Direction options. Just for the sake of demonstration, let's sort the data according to width from largest to smallest.

   Set Sort to file/@width and Direction to Descending.

9. On this occasion, you don't need to change the last three options at the bottom of the Spry XML Data Set dialog box (see Figure 19-2), but let me explain what they're for:

   - Distinct on load: Selecting this checkbox eliminates duplicate records in the data set.

   - Turn XML Data Caching Off: By default, Spry caches the data set when it first loads. This is the most efficient way. Select this option only if you know that the XML data source is likely to be updated frequently.

   - Auto refresh data: This option is grayed out unless you select the previous option. Enter the interval at which you want the browser to check for new data. The interval must be stated in milliseconds, so 60000 represents one minute. Don't use a thousands separator. Also remember that constantly checking for new data could increase server load and bandwidth use dramatically.

10. When you have made all the changes to the Spry XML Data Set dialog box, click OK to save your settings. Then save spry_data.php. If this is the first Spry data set that you have created in the site, Dreamweaver displays an alert telling you that it is saving two dependent files, xpath.js and SpryData.js, to the Spry assets folder. These contain all the necessary JavaScript libraries to manipulate a data set.

    You can check your code against spry_data_01.php in examples/ch19.

At this stage, you have nothing to show for your efforts in Design view, but if you switch to Code view, you can see how Dreamweaver has defined the Spry data set. All the code goes into the <head> of the document, as shown in Figure 19-4.

19

```
5   <title>Spry data example</title>
6   <script src="../../SpryAssets/xpath.js" type="text/javascript"></script>
7   <script src="../../SpryAssets/SpryData.js" type="text/javascript"></script>
8   <script type="text/javascript">
9   <!--
10  var dsEngland = new Spry.Data.XMLDataSet("../../examples/ch19/england.xml", "gallery/photo",{
    sortOnLoad:"file/@width",sortOrderOnLoad:"descending"});
11  dsEngland.setColumnType("file/@height", "number");
12  dsEngland.setColumnType("file/@width", "number");
13  //-->
14  </script>
15  </head>
```

Figure 19-4. A Spry data set is initialized in the <head> of a page so that it's ready for use when the main body loads.

The code shown on lines 6–7 attaches the two external JavaScript libraries; the dsEngland data set is initialized on line 10; and lines 11–12 apply the setColumnType() method to the data set. The data set is a Spry object with methods and properties (see "Understanding Spry objects" in Chapter 8) just like the user interface widgets you used in the first half of this book. If you're feeling ambitious later, you can study details of the Spry framework by visiting www.adobe.com/go/learn_dw_spryframework, but for the time being, let's content ourselves with the Dreamweaver interface and build a Spry table to display the contents of the data set.

Displaying a data set in a Spry table

Building a Spry table is very simple. Unfortunately, Dreamweaver CS3 has forgotten an important aspect of usability—there's no way to edit a Spry table after you have created it, other than diving into Code view or scrapping it and starting all over again. So, before diving into creating a Spry table, you need to do a little planning and decide how you want the table to look. The Insert Spry Table dialog box has the following options for setting CSS classes:

- Odd row class: This sets the styles for odd-numbered rows.
- Even row class: This sets the styles for even-numbered rows.
- Hover class: This determines how you want a row to look when the mouse hovers over it.
- Select class: This styles the currently selected row.

Although you can set these classes later in Code view, it's easier to create skeleton style rules first. I have created some simple styles in spry_table.css, which you can find in examples/styles. The rules look like this:

```
body {
  color:#000;
  background-color:#FFF;
  font-family:Verdana, Arial, Helvetica, sans-serif;
  }
div {
```

```
    font-size:85%;
    width:650px;
    margin-left:30px;
    }
th, td {
    padding:3px 10px;
    }
th {
    cursor:pointer;
    }
.odd {
    background-color:#EEEEEE;
    }
.even {
    background-color:#E8F2F8;
    }
.hover {
    cursor:pointer;
    background-color: #B4C6DB;
    }
.selected {
    color:#FFFFFF;
    background-color: #999999;
}
```

When using a Spry data set in a web page, you need to create Spry regions, which must be in a <div> or <span>, so I have used the div Type selector to control the width and font size. I have also added some padding inside the table headers and table cells. The four classes are for the Spry table. The odd rows will have a light gray background and even rows a light blue one.

Spry tables are interactive but don't use <a> tags, so you need to change the cursor explicitly to look like a hand when the mouse pointer passes over a table row. Spry applies the Hover class action only over table rows, so you must create a separate rule to change the cursor for table headers. The color I have chosen for table rows when the mouse passes over them is dark blue, with white text on a dark gray background for the selected row.

Figure 19-5 shows the simple Spry table that you'll build in the next exercise. When the page first loads, the table is sorted according to the width of the images, so hgs.jpg and its associated caption (Hampstead Garden Suburb in North London) appears in the top row. Clicking the File or Caption column header reorders the rows according to which column you clicked. The description is displayed in a <div> below the table and is automatically updated depending on the currently selected row—all without the need to refresh the page.

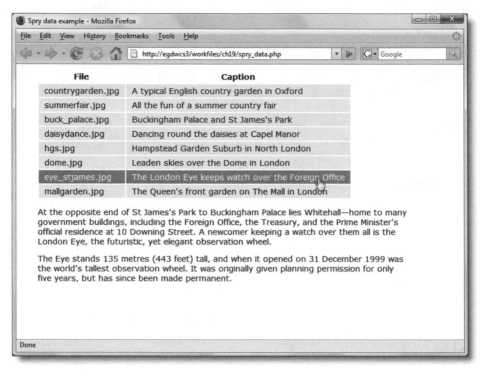

Figure 19-5. A Spry table can be sorted and display related information in a detail area without the need to refresh the page.

Displaying the photo details

This exercise shows you how to define a Spry table to display the <file> and <caption> nodes from the dsEngland data set. You'll also learn how to create a detail region that is updated when its related row is clicked in the table. The instructions assume that you created the dsEngland data set earlier in the chapter. Alternatively, use spry_data_01.php in examples/ch19. If you just want to look at the finished code, it's in spry_data_02.php.

1. Attach spry_table.css in the examples/styles folder to spry_data.php (attaching a style sheet was covered in Chapter 5).

2. Click the Spry Table button in the Spry tab of the Insert bar, as shown in the following screenshot, or choose Insert ➤ Spry ➤ Spry Table.

3. This opens the Insert Spry Table dialog box, as shown here:

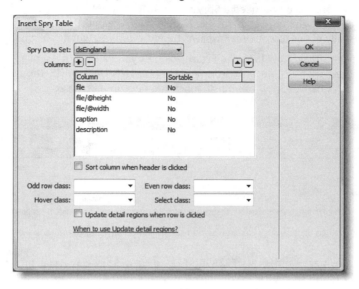

The layout and functionality of the dialog box should be immediately familiar from other parts of Dreamweaver. There's only one data set on the current page, but if there are more, select the data set you want to use from the Spry Data Set drop-down menu at the top. This populates the Columns area with the names of XML nodes and attributes in the data set.

You can remove a column by selecting it and clicking the minus button; and if you change your mind, restore it using the plus button.

By default, the columns are not sortable. To make a column sortable when its header is clicked, select the column name and select the sort option at the bottom of the Columns area.

The remaining options set the CSS classes discussed earlier and let you update one or more detail regions when a row is clicked.

The table in Figure 19-5 displays just the file and caption columns, so highlight the rest and delete them, make both columns sortable, and set the remaining options so that the dialog box looks like this:

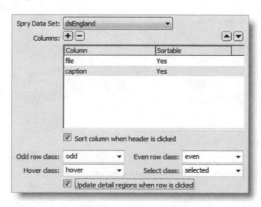

4. Click OK to create the Spry table. Dreamweaver will ask you if you want to insert a Spry region. Since you need a Spry region or detail region to display the contents of a data set, the answer is Yes (you could have created the Spry region first, but it's usually easier to get Dreamweaver to add it for you when inserting the table).

5. The page should now look like Figure 19-6. As you can see, it's similar to what you might get with a table built from a PHP recordset. Unlike PHP, though, Live Data view can't handle Spry. You must launch the page in a browser.

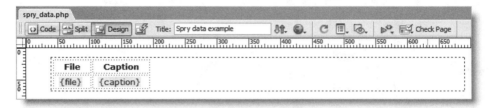

Figure 19-6. In Design view, a Spry table gives no real indication of what it will look like in a browser.

Save the page, and press F12/Opt+F12 to view spry_data.php in a browser. It should look like Figure 19-5 minus the description at the foot of the table. We'll add that in a moment, but first, test the page by running the mouse over the rows and clicking the column headers to sort the data. As long as you're using a modern browser with JavaScript enabled, it should work very smoothly without needing to refresh the page.

6. Return to Dreamweaver, and click anywhere inside the table. The <div> and <tr> tags in the Tag selector at the bottom of the Document window are highlighted in orange, indicating that they contain Spry data set code. Select the <div> tag and press the right arrow key once to move the insertion point outside the <div>.

7. To display the description, you need to create a Spry detail region. Click the Spry Region button on the Spry tab of the Insert bar, as shown alongside, or select Insert ➤ Spry ➤ Spry Region.

8. This opens the Insert Spry Region dialog box, as shown here:

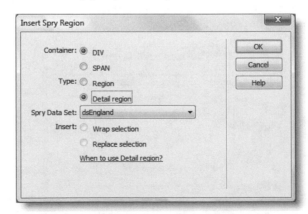

The options let you choose a <div> or <span> as the container. Most of the time, you'll want to use a <div>, unless you want the region to appear inline. You also have the choice of Region or Detail Region. The link at the bottom of the dialog box opens the Dreamweaver help files to explain the difference. Basically, a Spry region is used to display multiple elements from a data set, as in the table you built in steps 2–5. A Spry detail region gives you access to the currently selected element within the data set. In this case, you're going to display the description of whichever file name or caption the user clicks in the table.

The remaining options in the dialog box let you choose the data set if there's more than one on the page and whether to wrap the region around the current selection or to replace it. Since nothing is currently selected in spry_data.php, the Wrap selection and Replace selection options are grayed out.

Use the settings shown in the preceding screenshot, and click OK.

9. Dreamweaver inserts the Spry region with placeholder text, as shown here:

10. Open the Bindings panel. As you can see from the screenshot alongside, dynamic objects for the data set values are listed in the same way as for a recordset or in an XSLT fragment. At the bottom of the list are three Spry data objects that can be used to get access to the row ID, current row ID, and row count.

The data object that we're interested in at the moment is description. Select it, and use it to replace the placeholder text in the Spry detail region. You can either drag and drop it, or use the Insert button at the bottom of the Bindings panel.

11. The page should now look like this:

In Design view, it still looks very unimpressive, but when you save the page and test it in a browser, it should look like Figure 19-5 and be fully interactive.

You can check your code against spry_data_02.php in examples/ch19.

Understanding the Spry data code

I don't intend to go into great detail about how the code works. The whole idea of incorporating Spry into Dreamweaver CS3 is to make it easy to use Ajax without needing to become a JavaScript guru, but it does help to recognize the code and have a basic understanding of what it's for.

The table and detail region use remarkably little code, as you can see from the following listing (all the Spry code is highlighted in bold):

```
<div spry:region="dsEngland">
  <table>
    <tr>
      <th spry:sort="file">File</th>
      <th spry:sort="caption">Caption</th>
    </tr>
    <tr spry:repeat="dsEngland" spry:setrow="dsEngland" spry:odd= ➡
"odd" spry:even="even" spry:hover="hover" spry:select="selected">
      <td>{file}</td>
      <td>{caption}</td>
    </tr>
  </table>
</div>
<div spry:detailregion="dsEngland">{description}</div>
```

Even if you don't know how it works, the Spry syntax is easy to follow. Everything begins with spry: followed by the name of a property and its value. The property names are all very intuitive: region, sort, repeat, and so on.

Take the code in the second table row. It begins with spry:repeat="dsEngland". This turns the row into a repeat region that draws data from the dsEngland data set. The spry:setrow property controls the display in the detail region. When the row is clicked, Spry sets it as the current row, which sends a message—or triggers an event, to use the correct terminology—that tells any dsEngland detail region to update its contents.

The data objects that hold the contents are in curly braces. So {description} tells the browser to display the current value of the <description> node.

> *If you forget to set one of the classes in a Spry table, you can easily edit the repeat row by adding* spry:odd, spry:even, spry:hover, *or* spry:select *and the name of the class. Dreamweaver code hints speed up the process by displaying the available options after you type* spry: *in Code view.*

Validating pages that use Spry

If you submit a page that uses Spry to the W3C validator at http://validator.w3.org/, you get a series of errors saying, for example, that there is no attribute spry:region or spry:repeatchildren. This happens even though Dreamweaver amends the <html> tag at the top of the page like this:

```
<html xmlns="http://www.w3.org/1999/xhtml" ➥
xmlns:spry="http://ns.adobe.com/spry">
```

The code highlighted in bold declares spry as a **namespace**. This tells the browser not to confuse anything prefixed with spry: with standard XHTML attributes or custom attributes from other namespaces, such as other Ajax frameworks. While this prevents conflicts, it's not sufficient for W3C validation. You need to tell the validator where to find the Spry document type definition (DTD) by amending the top of each page like this:

```
<!DOCTYPE html PUBLIC "-//W3C//DTD XHTML 1.0 Transitional//EN" ➥
 "http://www.w3.org/TR/xhtml1/DTD/xhtml1-transitional.dtd"
[
  <!ENTITY % SPRY SYSTEM "http://www.adobe.com/dtd/spry.dtd">
  %SPRY;
]>
<html xmlns="http://www.w3.org/1999/xhtml" ➥
xmlns:spry="http://ns.adobe.com/spry">
```

So why doesn't Dreamweaver add the necessary code? Figure 19-7 shows why. Internet Explorer, Firefox, and Safari all fail to understand the <!ENTITY> tag and display %SPRY;]> at the top of the page if you include it (see http://labs.adobe.com/technologies/spry/articles/validation/validating_spry.html).

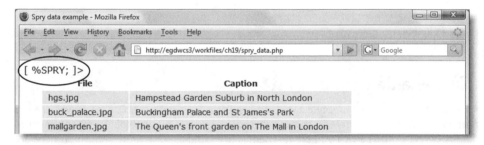

Figure 19-7. Most leading browsers can't cope with the code needed to ensure that Spry validates.

If W3C validation is a mandatory requirement for your website, you have two options: don't use Spry, or use the <!ENTITY> tag to prove compliance but remove it when the site goes live.

The fly in Spry's ointment

Dreamweaver CS3 makes it incredibly easy to create a master/detail display of data as in spry_data.php, but it's important to remember that the underlying content seen by search engines is exactly the same as the listing in "Understanding the Spry data code." Search engines don't interpret JavaScript, so putting vital content in Spry regions is a high-risk strategy.

The other thing to remember is that Spry content remains inaccessible to anyone using an old browser or one with JavaScript disabled. You can see the effect for yourself by turning off JavaScript temporarily in your browser. Here's how you do it:

- **Firefox**: Go to Tools ➤ Options, and select the Content tab. Deselect Enable JavaScript, and click OK.

- **Internet Explorer for Windows**: Go to Tools ➤ Internet Options. Select the Security tab, then the Internet icon. Click the Custom level button, and in the Security Settings – Internet Zone dialog box, locate Scripting ➤ Active Scripting, and set it to Disable. Click OK to close all the dialog boxes.

- **Safari**: Open Preferences from the Safari menu. Click the Security icon, and deselect Enable JavaScript. Close Preferences.

When you reload spry_data.php in your browser, all you'll see is what's shown in Figure 19-8. Unlike the Spry widgets covered in Chapters 7 and 8, Spry data sets do not degrade gracefully unless you combine them with static links or server-side technology. I'll show you how to do that in the next chapter.

Figure 19-8. With JavaScript disabled, the page shown in Figure 19-5 displays only meaningless code.

Displaying a data set as a list

As well as automatically creating tables to display a Spry data set, Dreamweaver creates four types of lists: unordered (<ul>), ordered (<ol>), definition (<dl>), and drop-down menus (<select>). The way you create them is the same as for a table, although there are no options for setting CSS classes. You can either create a Spry region first and insert the list, or you can leave it up to Dreamweaver to wrap the list in a Spry region when you have finished.

Unordered and ordered lists have only two options: the data set and the name of the column that you want to display. Definition lists and drop-down menus have an extra option because both have a label and value for each item in the list. I'll show you how to create a drop-down menu when building the photo gallery later, but let's look briefly at creating a Spry definition list. To keep things simple, we'll adapt spry_data.php from the previous exercise.

Creating a Spry definition list

This exercise converts the Spry table in spry_data.php into a definition list. The result won't look very elegant, but the purpose is simply to demonstrate how to create a list with Spry. Use spry_data_02.php in examples/ch19 if you don't have your own copy of the file. The finished code is in spry_data_03.php.

1. Select the <div> that encloses the Spry table, and press Delete to remove it. You should be left with the <div> that contains the detail region and the {description} data object. In Split view, your page should now look like this, with the insertion point immediately after the opening <body> tag:

2. Click the Spry Repeat List button in the Spry tab of the Insert bar, as shown in the following screenshot, or select Insert ➤ Spry ➤ Spry Repeat List.

3. This opens the Spry Repeat List dialog box, as shown here:

The Container tag drop-down menu contains the following four options:

- UL (Unordered List): This creates an unordered list using `<ul>` tags and populates the `<li>` tags with the values stored in the XML node selected as Display column. Only one node can be selected.

- OL (Ordered List): This creates an ordered (numbered) list using `<ol>` tags. In other respects, it's identical to the previous option.

- DL (Definition List): This creates a definition list using `<dl>` tags. When you select this option, the Display column option is replaced by DT Column and DD Column, which let you choose what to display in the `<dt>` and `<dd>` tags.

- SELECT (Drop-down List): This creates a drop-down menu using `<select>` tags. When you select this option, a Value column option is added at the bottom of the dialog box. Display column determines the value displayed in the drop-down, and Value column sets the value attribute of each `<option>` tag. You'll see this in operation when building the Spry gallery later in the chapter.

Whichever option you choose for Container tag, the Spry Data Set option selects the data set to be used. There's only one data set on the current page, so it's selected by default.

4. Select DL (Definition List) for Container tag, and set DT column to file and DD column to caption. This will display the same information as in the original Spry table, but as a definition list. Click OK to save the settings, and click Yes when Dreamweaver asks if you want to insert a Spry region. The page should now look like this in Split view:

As you can see from the preceding screenshot, Dreamweaver has inserted a `<div>` on lines 19–24, and set the `spry:region` property to dsEngland, the name of the data set to use.

The opening tag of the definition list on line 20 contains the `spry:repeatchildren` property, which is also set to dsEngland. This tells the browser to loop through the dsEngland data set for each child element of the `<dl>` tag—in other words, the `<dt>` and `<dd>` tags.

Lines 21–22 insert {file} and {caption} data objects in the `<dt>` and `<dd>` tags, respectively.

Dreamweaver does all this coding for you automatically, so you don't need to bother about it unless you want to start using Spry in more sophisticated ways.

5. Save spry_data.php, and press F12/Opt+F12 to view the page in a browser. It should look like Figure 19-9. However, clicking any of the list items no longer changes the description at the bottom of the page. To do that, you need to hand-code some Spry properties.

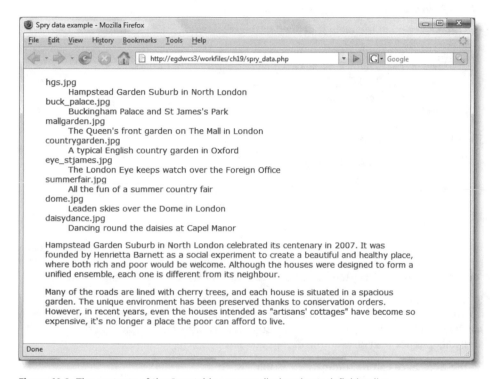

Figure 19-9. The contents of the Spry table are now displayed as a definition list.

6. Just as an example of how to add some Spry interactivity to the definition list, edit the `<dd>` tag by adding a `<span>` around the data object like this (new code is shown in bold):

```
<dd><span spry:setrow="dsEngland" spry:hover="hover" ➥
spry:select="selected">{caption}</span></dd>
```

I have used a `<span>` to limit the width of the background color to the text. When you start typing in Code view, code hints pop up. As soon as you select spry:setrow, another code hint displays the name of the available data set; and when you select spry:hover and spry:select, you are presented with a list of classes defined in the page's style sheet. Make sure you don't use spry:selected instead of spry:select, as they have different meanings.

7. Test the page again. This time, the hover and selected classes are applied to the caption, and the spry:setrow property triggers an event that updates the description at the bottom of the page. You can check your code, if necessary, with spry_data_03.php in examples/ch19.

What's the difference between repeat and repeatchildren?

If you're interested in taking Spry further, look more closely at the code in the Spry table and the Spry definition list. Both use Spry repeat regions, but there's a subtle difference between them.

The repeat region in the table is defined in the <tr> tag of the second row like this:

```
<tr spry:repeat="dsEngland" spry:setrow="dsEngland" spry:odd="odd" ➡
spry:even="even" spry:hover="hover" spry:select="selected">
  <td>{file}</td>
  <td>{caption}</td>
</tr>
```

The repeat region in the definition list is defined like this:

```
<dl spry:repeatchildren="dsEngland">
  <dt>{file}</dt>
  <dd><span spry:setrow="dsEngland" spry:hover="hover" ➡
spry:select="selected">{caption}</span></dd>
</dl>
```

In the table, the spry:repeat property repeats an element and all of its content for each row in the data set. In other words, it repeats the table row (<tr>) and its two cells (<td>) for each row in the dsEngland data set. This results in the creation of eight table rows.

In the definition list, on the other hand, spry:repeatchildren repeats all the children of a given element for each row in a data set. The property is defined in the <dl> tag, which has two children: <dt> and <dd>. As a result, Spry creates *one* definition list with a <dt> and <dd> pair for every row in the dsEngland data set.

So the difference can be summarized as follows:

- spry:repeat repeats the element in which it is declared.
- spry:repeatchildren doesn't repeat the element itself but does repeat its children.

Because Spry manipulates the content in the browser window without creating any underlying source code for you to inspect, it can sometimes be difficult to grasp the difference between what's happening. For example, if you change the code in the <dl> tag from spry:repeatchildren to spry:repeat, the output seems to be identical. However, if you create a style rule to add a visible border around a definition list, the difference becomes obvious. With spry:repeatchildren, there's a single border around the list, but with spry:repeat, you get a border around each list item (see Figure 19-10). In other words, the <dl> element is also repeated, so you end up with eight definition lists instead of one.

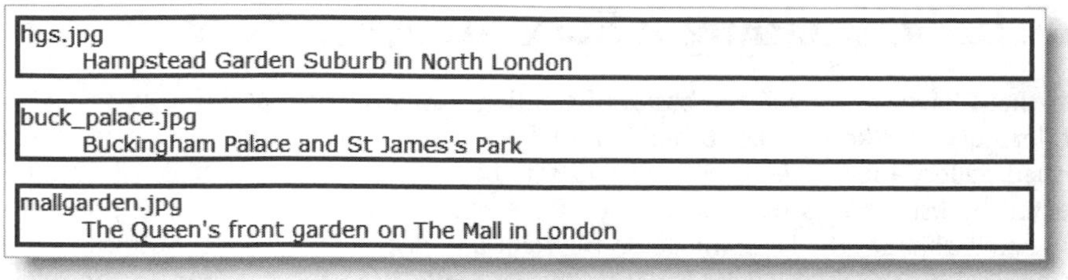

Figure 19-10. Using spry:repeat with the <dl> tag creates a separate definition list for each row of the data set.

This might tempt you to remove the Spry property from the <dl> tag, and use spry:repeat directly on the <dt> and <dd> elements like this:

```
<dl>
  <dt spry:repeat="dsEngland">{file}</dt>
  <dd spry:repeat="dsEngland">{caption}</dd>
</dl>
```

Figure 19-11 shows what happens—all the <dt> elements are repeated first, followed by all the <dd> elements.

Figure 19-11. Using the wrong type of Spry repeat region brings unwanted results.

You get equally undesirable results if you use spry:repeatchildren in the <tr> tag of the table. Instead of eight table rows with two table cells each, you get one table row with 16 table cells.

Case study: Building a Spry image gallery

Now that I have shown you the basics of creating a Spry data set and displaying text output, let's use that knowledge to build an online gallery. Figure 19-12 shows you what the finished gallery looks like. There are two sets of images and thumbnails, which can be selected by using the drop-down menu at the top left of the page. Clicking any of the thumbnails changes the large image on the right and displays the appropriate caption and description. All the interactivity is controlled by Spry within the browser, so the relevant sections of the page are updated without reloading.

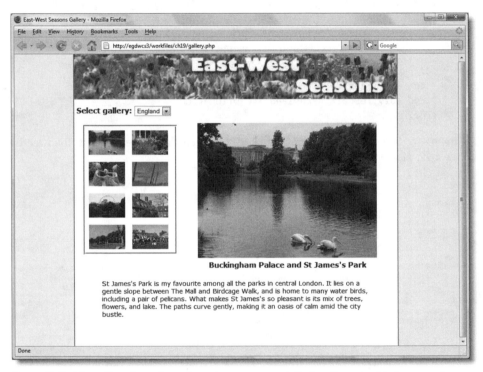

Figure 19-12. The gallery draws from three data sources and displays the output in two repeat regions and two detail regions.

Planning the gallery

The gallery uses two Spry data sets: one to select the currently displayed photo gallery and the other to load details of the selected gallery. The first data set uses a very simple XML document called galleries.xml, which looks like this:

```
<?xml version="1.0" encoding="utf-8"?>
<galleries>
  <gallery file="england.xml">
    <name>England</name>
  </gallery>
```

```
      <gallery file="japan.xml">
        <name>Japan</name>
      </gallery>
    </galleries>
```

Dynamically selecting the gallery data set

The file attribute of the repeating <gallery> element tells Spry where to find the data source for the selected gallery, and the <name> node is displayed as the label in the drop-down menu. This generates a data set, which we'll call dsGalleries, which always exists. The second data set, dsPhotos, is generated dynamically depending on which option is selected in the drop-down menu, as shown in the following illustration:

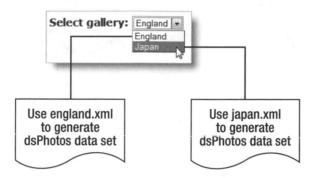

In effect, this means that the gallery has three data sets, but only two exist at the same time. The contents of dsPhotos change whenever a different option is selected in the drop-down menu.

The details of the galleries are contained in england.xml and japan.xml. The first of these is the same file that you have been using throughout the chapter. It contains a repeating element called <photo> with three child nodes: <file> (which has the file's width and height properties), <caption>, and <description>. The other file, japan.xml, is identical in structure and contains details of eight photographs of Japan.

The photos are in the gallery subfolder of the main images folder. Each photo has a corresponding thumbnail in the thumbs subfolder of gallery. To simplify the code, I have given each thumbnail the same name as the large photo. So, images/gallery/thumbs/basin.jpg is the thumbnail version of images/gallery/basin.jpg.

Controlling the structure with CSS

Figure 19-13 shows the underlying structure of the page. The whole page is enclosed in a <div> called wrapper with a fixed width of 720 pixels. The left and right margins are set to auto, which centers the content in the page and aligns it with the background image. The background image is also centered and tiled vertically and is 1,200 pixels wide. Each side has a subtle gradient that fades to the same light pink as the background color (#F9F2F8), so the two blend if the browser viewport is wider than 1,200 pixels.

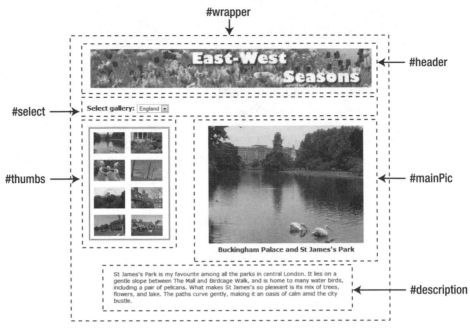

Figure 19-13. The gallery is held together by a series of <div> elements enclosed in a wrapper <div> that centers the page.

The rest of the positioning is achieved through margins and by floating to the left the thumbs and mainPic elements. A Spry table can't loop both horizontally and vertically, so the thumbs <div> is given a fixed width that accommodates only two thumbnails side by side. The thumbnails are all a standard 80 pixels × 54 pixels.

The large images vary in size up to a maximum width of 400 pixels. When a large image is displayed, it is centered within the mainPic <div> by placing it and its accompanying caption in a paragraph styled with the CSS property text-align: center.

The style rules in gallery.css are fully commented, so I'll leave you to study them at leisure.

Putting everything together

To save time, I have prepared all the basic files for you. The images are already in the correct folders. You need to copy the following files from examples/ch19 to workfiles/ch19:

- gallery_start.php
- galleries.xml
- england.xml
- japan.xml

The style sheet gallery.css is already attached to gallery_start.php. You can leave gallery.css in the examples/styles folder by clicking Update when prompted to update the links in gallery_start.php. Alternatively, if you want to experiment with the styles, copy gallery.css to workfiles/styles, and leave the relative links unchanged.

Before starting, open the XML files to examine their structure. Make sure you understand what they contain. See "Creating a Spry data set" earlier in the chapter for a description of england.xml; the structure of japan.xml is identical. The structure and purpose of galleries.xml was described at the beginning of the preceding section.

Right, let's begin. By the time you have finished, you might be surprised at how little code has been created. However, getting everything right involves a lot of steps. Give yourself plenty of time and follow the instructions carefully.

Creating the data sets and displaying the thumbnail

In this section, you'll create the initial data sets, insert the drop-down menu that selects the gallery, and build the thumbnail display on the left of the page. The drop-down menu will eventually switch dynamically between two versions of the dsPhotos data set. However, Dreamweaver cannot generate the schema from a dynamically selected data source, so you need to work initially with a static version. Don't worry if you find this confusing; it should become clear once you have built the page.

1. Rename gallery_start.php as gallery.php.

2. Open the Spry XML Data Set dialog box by clicking the Spry XML Data Set button on the Spry tab of the Insert bar or choosing Insert ➤ Spry ➤ Spry XML Data Set.

   Name the data set dsGalleries, and use galleries.xml in workfiles/ch19 as the XML source.

   In the Row element area, select the repeating element gallery, and click the Preview button. You should see the following data set displayed:

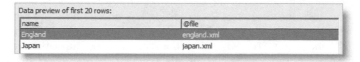

3. Close the Data preview panel, and click OK to close the Spry XML Data Set dialog box.

4. Create another Spry data set. Call this one dsPhotos, and use england.xml in workfiles/ch19 as the XML source. In the Row element area, select the repeating element photo, and in Data Set columns, set file/@height and file/@width to number.

Your settings should look like this:

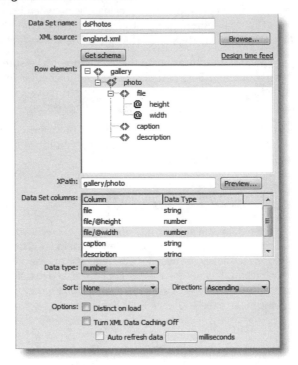

This is almost identical to the dsEngland data set in the earlier exercises. The only difference is that I have left the data set in its original order, rather than sorting it by the width of each photo.

Click OK to close the Spry XML Data Set dialog box.

5. Next, you need to start inserting the Spry regions. Although Spry regions normally use <div> tags, the Insert Spry Region dialog box doesn't have the same option as the Insert Div Tag dialog box, which lets you specify where to put it in the page. If you use the Insert Div Tag dialog box first, select the <div>, and instruct Dreamweaver to replace the current selection with a Spry region, the id attribute is deleted. This leaves you with a messy Catch 22 situation, so the best approach is to know exactly where your insertion point is before inserting a Spry region, table, or list.

You want the select <div> that contains the drop-down menu to go after the header <div>, but inside the wrapper <div>. So, click the image of tulips at the top of the page, and select <div#header> in the Tag selector at the bottom of the Document window. Press the right arrow key once to move the insertion point into the correct position. Check in Split view, if you're not sure.

6. Click the Spry Repeat List button on the Spry tab of the Insert bar (or use the Insert menu), and use the following settings in the Insert Spry Repeat List dialog box:

This uses the dsGalleries data set to create a drop-down menu, displaying the name node (England or Japan), and setting the value attribute of the <option> tag to the value of the file attribute (england.xml or japan.xml).

Click OK to insert the drop-down menu, and click Yes when asked if you want to insert a Spry region. The top of the page should now look like this:

7. Select the menu element to bring up its details in the Property inspector, and change its name from the default select to chooseGallery. Press Enter/Return to effect the change. Now move the insertion point into the correct position to add a label by selecting <select#chooseGallery> in the Tag selector and pressing the left arrow key once.

8. Click the Label button on the Forms tab of the Insert bar (or use Insert ➤ Form ➤ Label). This opens Split view with the insertion point between two <label> tags. Type Select gallery followed by a colon and a space. Then edit the opening <label> tag to add the for attribute and set its value to chooseGallery. Click back in Design view to view the change. The page should now look like this:

9. Right-click the orange-colored <div> in the Tag selector (click inside the <div> that contains the drop-down menu if you can't see it), and choose Set ID from the context menu. Because all the ID selectors have been declared in the style sheet, they are listed on a flyout. Choose select from the list of IDs.

   This applies the styles to the <div> and changes the listing in the Tag selector to <div#select>. Press the right arrow key once to move the insertion point into the correct position for inserting the thumbs <div>. In Design view, it looks as though the cursor is still inside the select <div>, but you can verify that it's in the right position by checking in Split view.

10. Insert a Spry region for the thumbnails by clicking the Spry Region button on the Spry tab of the Insert bar (or use the Insert menu). Use the following settings, and click OK:

    - Container: DIV
    - Type: Region
    - Spry Data Set: dsPhotos

11. This inserts a <div> as a Spry region with some placeholder text. You now want to nest a repeat region within this <div> to display the thumbnails.

    With the placeholder text still highlighted, click the Spry Repeat button on the Spry tab of the Insert bar (or use the menu equivalent). This time, use the following settings:

    - Container: SPAN
    - Type: Repeat
    - Spry Data Set: dsPhotos
    - Insert: Replace selection

    When you click OK, the placeholder text is still there. What's happened is that the old placeholder text has been replaced by the repeat region, but new placeholder text has been inserted inside the repeat region to aid with inserting the real content.

12. Your instinct is probably to press Delete to get rid of the placeholder text. If you do so, the repeat region is also deleted. So, insert a thumbnail by selecting Insert ➤ Image, navigating to images/gallery/thumbs, and selecting one of the images. It doesn't matter which one, because you're going to replace it in a moment with a dynamic object. However, inserting a real image has the advantage of setting the correct path to the thumbs folder, as well as setting the correct values for height and width. When prompted for alternate text, type something generic like "thumbnail."

13. Inserting the thumbnail doesn't get rid of the placeholder text, so delete it. Go into Code view, and replace the file name of the image with {file}. This is a Spry dynamic object that contains the value of the file node from england.xml in the dsPhotos data set. As soon as you type the opening curly brace, code hints display the dynamic objects you can use in this repeat region, as shown in the following screenshot:

```
<span spry:repeat="dsPhotos"><img src="../../images/gallery/thumbs/{" alt="thumbnail" w
                                                    file
                                                    file/@height
                                                    file/@width
                                                    caption
                                                    description
                                                    ds_RowID
                                                    ds_CurrentRowID
                                                    ds_RowCount
```

Use your mouse to double-click file or select it with your down arrow key, and press Enter/Return to insert it. Dreamweaver automatically adds the closing curly brace.

14. When you click back in Design view, the thumbnail is replaced by a broken image icon. This is perfectly normal. Before checking your code so far, let's first harness the thumbnails.

In the Tag selector, right-click the <div> that contains them, and select thumbs from Set ID on the context menu. The thumbs <div> is styled, but still contains only one broken image icon. You need a good imagination or to have carefully planned your page layout when using Spry data sets.

15. Save gallery.php, and test the page in a browser. Eight thumbnails should be displayed in a neat box at the side of the page, as shown in Figure 19-14.

Figure 19-14. The Spry gallery begins to take shape—the thumbnails are all there.

If things don't look like Figure 19-14, check your code against gallery_01.php in examples/ch19. There's remarkably little code when working with Spry data sets, but it's easy to nest elements incorrectly. Also make sure that you have the correct path and file names. Spry and XML are case sensitive.

The next stage is to create the sections that display the large version of the selected image, its caption, and its description. Although the caption and photo can go together in a single <div>, the description looks better in a separate <div>. This presents no problem, because you can have as many Spry detail regions as you like. All of them automatically register **event listeners** with the data set they are associated with. As the name suggests, an event listener sits in wait listening for a specific event and reacts accordingly when it receives notification. So, when the currently selected row in the data set changes as the result of clicking a thumbnail, the detail regions respond by displaying the data corresponding to that row.

Adding the detail regions

In this section, you'll add two detail regions that listen for changes to the dsPhotos data set.

1. Select <div#thumbs> in the Tag selector, and press the right arrow key once to move the insertion point to the correct place for inserting the mainPic <div>.

2. Click the Spry Region button on the Spry tab of the Insert bar (or use the menu equivalent), use the following settings, and click OK:

   ▪ Container: DIV

   ▪ Type: Detail region

   ▪ Spry Data Set: dsPhotos

3. You want the image and caption to be in a paragraph so that they can be centered, so format the placeholder text as a paragraph. Make sure that only the text inside the paragraph is selected, and press Delete. This leaves behind a pair of <p> tags with a nonbreaking space in between. This is where you'll insert the main image.

4. Because the large photos vary in size, we'll use a different way to insert the image this time. Select Insert ➤ Image, and navigate to the images/gallery folder.

   As well as selecting an image from the file system, Dreamweaver lets you specify a data source. However, when you do so, Dreamweaver assumes that the data source will supply the full path, so it deletes the path from the dialog box. However, this is easily overcome. The Windows and Mac interfaces are subtly different, so I'll give separate instructions. First, Windows . . .

   Highlight the path to the images/gallery folder in the URL field at the bottom of the Select Image Source dialog box (see Figure 19-15), and copy it (Ctrl+C) to your clipboard. Then select the Data sources radio button at the top of the dialog box.

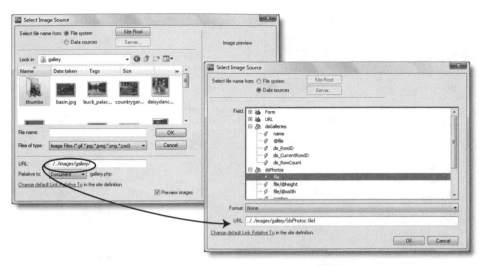

Figure 19-15. Selecting the data source for the main image in Windows

The Select Image Source dialog box changes as shown on the right of Figure 19-15. Expand the dsPhotos tree menu if necessary, and select file. This inserts {dsPhotos::file} into the URL field. Click inside this field, and move your cursor so that it's immediately in front of the opening curly brace. Paste (Ctrl+V) the path to images/gallery. Skip to step 5 *before* clicking OK.

If you're using the Mac version of Dreamweaver, select the path to the images/gallery folder in the URL field at the bottom of the Select Image Source dialog box (see Figure 19-16 on the next page), and copy (Cmd+C) it to your clipboard. Then click the Data Sources button at the bottom of the dialog box.

This opens the Dynamic Data dialog box, as shown on the right of Figure 19-16. Expand the dsPhotos tree menu if necessary, and select file. This inserts {dsPhotos::file} into the Code field. Click inside this field, and move your cursor so that it's immediately in front of the opening curly brace. Paste (Cmd+V) the path to images/gallery. The path you have just pasted doesn't end with a forward slash, so insert a forward slash between gallery and the opening curly brace of {dsPhotos::file}. Check the contents of the Code field as described in the next step.

19

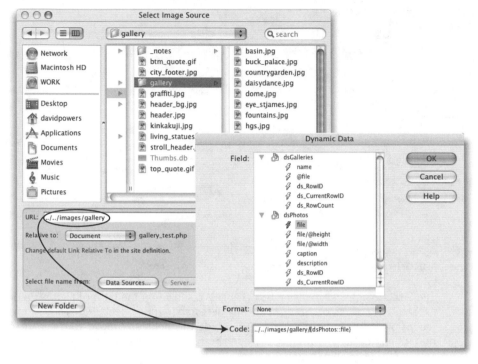

Figure 19-16. Selecting the data source for the main image in the Mac version

5. If you're using document-relative links, the URL (Windows) or Code (Mac) field should look like this:

```
../../images/gallery/{dsPhotos::file}
```

If you're using site-root-relative links, it will look like this:

```
/images/gallery/{dsPhotos::file}
```

Click OK to insert the image. When prompted for alternate text, just click OK, because you'll make that dynamic, too. You'll have another broken image icon in your page (you need to get used to them with Spry). Leave the image selected, and open the Bindings panel.

You can use the caption as alternate text. So, expand the dsPhotos tree menu, if necessary, and select caption. Then select img.alt from the Bind to drop-down menu at the bottom of the Bindings panel, as shown alongside, and click the Bind button.

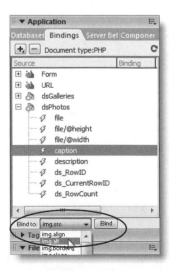

6. Do the same with file/@height and file/@width, binding them to img.height and img.width, respectively. This adds the XHTML attributes inside the <img> tag, and assigns dynamic objects as the value to each one. The code in the <img> tag should now look like this:

```
<img src="../../images/gallery/{file}" alt="{caption}" ➜
width="{file/@width}" height="{file/@height}" />
```

7. In Design view, click alongside the image you have just been working on, and press Shift+Enter/Shift+Return to insert a single line break (
 tag). Select caption in the Bindings panel, and click the Insert button (this is the same as the Bind button that you used in steps 5–6, but Dreamweaver's context sensitivity changes its name and function because nothing is currently selected).

8. In the Tag selector, right-click the <div> that contains the image and caption, and select mainPic from the Set ID submenu.

9. Press the right arrow key to make sure the insertion point is outside the mainPic <div>, and insert another detail region, using the same settings as in step 2.

10. With the placeholder text still highlighted, select description in the Bindings panel, and click Insert. This replaces the placeholder text with {description}.

11. Select the new <div>, and set its ID to description in the same way as with all the other Spry regions. In Design view, your page should now look like Figure 19-17. To say the least, it looks rather nondescript.

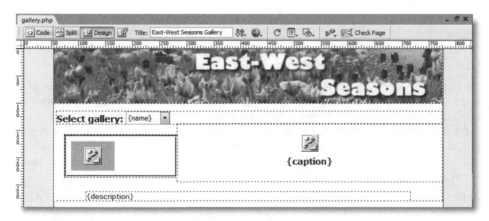

Figure 19-17. You need a lot of imagination to visualize what a Spry page will look like in a browser.

12. Save gallery.php, and test it in a browser. It should look like Figure 19-12 earlier in the chapter. However, nothing happens if you try clicking the thumbnails or changing the drop-down menu. You still need to wire up the event handling manually.

Check your code, if necessary, against gallery_02.php in examples/ch19.

Activating the event handling

As explained in "Understanding the Spry data code" earlier in the chapter, the spry:setrow property controls what is displayed in the detail region. You set its value to the name of the data set that you want to control. Internally, a Spry data set is like a database recordset, and each row has an ID, rather like a database primary key. This ID is called ds_RowID (you can see it listed in the Bindings panel in step 5 of the preceding section). When an element that contains the spry:setrow property is clicked, Spry checks the ds_RowID, and broadcasts it to all registered event listeners. "Hey, guys, ds_RowID 5 is now the current row. Time to get in line."

Counting from 0 in dsPhotos, ds_RowID 5 represents hgs.jpg. So by adding the spry:setrow property to the <img> tag in thumbs <div> and setting its value to dsPhotos, whenever the hgs.jpg thumbnail is clicked the detail regions automatically update to display the large image, caption, and description.

Edit the <img> tag in thumbs <div> like this:

```
<div id="thumbs" spry:region="dsPhotos"><span spry:repeat="dsPhotos">➡
<img src="../../images/gallery/thumbs/{file}" alt="thumbnail"➡
width="80" height="54" spry:setrow="dsPhotos" /></span></div>
```

Save the page, and test it in a browser. The addition of that tiny snippet of code has activated the thumbnails. The code is in gallery_03.php, if you need to check your own version.

The next step is to activate the drop-down menu. This works on the same principle but requires different code.

Distinguishing between data sets

All the dynamic objects placed in the code up to now have consisted of the XML node name enclosed in curly braces. So the <description> node is represented as {description}. An XML attribute consists of the node name followed by a forward slash, the @ sign, and the attribute name. So, the height attribute of the <file> node is represented as {file/@height}. If the attribute belongs to the repeating element, as is the case with the file attribute of the <gallery> node in the dsGalleries data set, the node name is omitted: {@file}.

Although there are two data sets on the same page, there's no danger of confusion, because Spry dynamic objects must always be inside a Spry region. The spry:region or spry:detailregion property specifies the data set that the region utilizes.

However, there are times when you want to refer to another data set. To do so, you add the name of the data set followed by two colons and the node or attribute name. So, a fully qualified reference to the <file> node in dsPhotos becomes {dsPhotos::file}, and to the file attribute in dsGalleries becomes {dsGalleries::@file}.

Creating a data set dynamically

The code that initializes the two data sets in the <head> of gallery.php looks like this:

```
var dsGalleries = new Spry.Data.XMLDataSet("galleries.xml", ➥
"galleries/gallery");
var dsPhotos = new Spry.Data.XMLDataSet("england.xml", ➥
"gallery/photo");
```

Two arguments are passed to the Spry.Data.XMLDataSet() method: the location of the XML source and the XPath to the repeating element.

The XML source for dsPhotos is contained in the file attribute of the <gallery> node of galleries.xml. Since the same information is held in {dsGalleries::@file}, change the initialization code for dsPhotos to this:

```
var dsPhotos = new Spry.Data.XMLDataSet("{dsGalleries::@file}", ➥
"gallery/photo");
```

As soon as you type the double colon after dsGalleries, Dreamweaver shows you the available properties, so you can use code hints to auto-complete the dynamic object. The other thing to notice is that all the dynamic objects disappear from the Bindings panel, as shown in Figure 19-18. This is why I told you to use england.xml as the XML source while building the page. Once the name of the source is generated dynamically, Dreamweaver has no way of accessing the XML structure. But this no longer matters, since you have already laid out the page.

The dynamic objects have disappeared ⟶

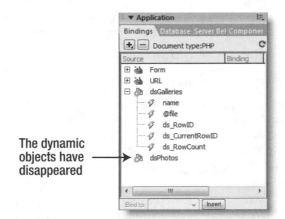

Figure 19-18. You no longer have access to dynamic objects when the XML source is specified dynamically.

For Spry to generate the dsPhotos data set, it now needs to know the current selection in the drop-down menu. So, instead of sending the file name, the drop-down menu needs to send the ds_RowID of the currently selected item, as shown in the following illustration:

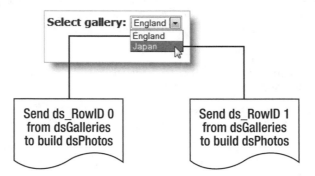

When you inserted the drop-down menu, the Insert Spry Repeat List dialog box didn't offer the opportunity to use ds_RowID, so you need to edit the value attribute of the <option> tag manually like this:

```
<option value="{ds_RowID}">{name}</option>
```

You also need to add an onchange event handler to the <select> tag to change the current row number of the dsGalleries data set whenever a new value is selected in the drop-down menu. The Spry method that does this is called, appropriately enough, setCurrentRow(). By passing this.value as the argument, it obtains ds_RowID from the <option> tag. Insert the following code in the <select> tag:

```
onchange="dsGalleries.setCurrentRow(this.value)"
```

After editing, the select <div> should look like this:

```
<div id="select" spry:region="dsGalleries">
  <label for="chooseGallery">Select gallery: </label><select ➥
name="chooseGallery" spry:repeatchildren="dsGalleries" ➥
id="chooseGallery" onchange="dsGalleries.setCurrentRow(this.value)">
    <option value="{ds_RowID}">{name}</option>
  </select>
</div>
```

Save gallery.php, and load it into a browser. Select Japan from the drop-down menu, and you should see a different set of thumbnails, as shown in Figure 19-19. Click the thumbnails: the gallery works exactly the same as before, except the dsPhotos data set is drawing details of the photos from japan.xml. Select England again, and the original gallery is displayed again—but the page never reloads; only the content changes.

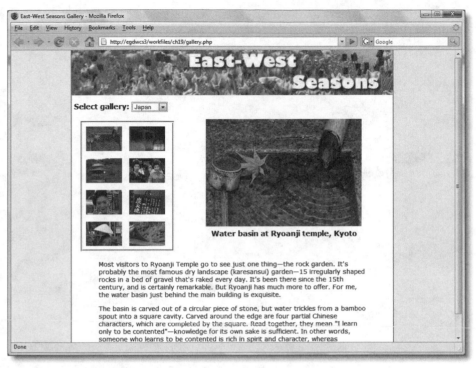

Figure 19-19. Changing the selected value in the drop-down menu displays a completely new gallery without reloading the page.

You can check your code against gallery_04.php.

To add a little more Spry interactivity to the gallery, you can also apply the Spry Highlight effect to add a border to each thumbnail as it's moused over. You can find the code for that in gallery_05.php.

Nearly there . . .

Throughout this chapter, you have worked with static XML documents. No doubt, many of you are probably wondering, "What's the point of storing information in a database if you need to type everything out again as XML? It's just as time consuming as creating a static web page, and nowhere near as intuitive." So, in the next chapter, I'll show you how to generate XML on the fly from a MySQL database. I'll also show you how to adapt the Spry gallery from this chapter so that it remains accessible when JavaScript is disabled. Equally important, it's search engine friendly, too.

20 GETTING THE BEST OF BOTH WORLDS WITH PHP AND SPRY

The Spry gallery that you built in the previous chapter has two important shortcomings. First, the page's content is generated entirely inside the browser using JavaScript, leaving nothing for a search engine to index and failing miserably in an older browser or if JavaScript is disabled. Second, although the content is generated dynamically, the XML sources are static. In the case of a photo gallery, this might not be a major drawback, but one of the main reasons for creating dynamic web pages is to exploit the ability to update content on the fly without the need to build everything from scratch again. Rather than creating a new XML document every time a new photo is added or deleted, it's more convenient to add or delete the details from a database and generate the XML dynamically. This has the added advantage that you can use the database content for other purposes, greatly increasing your efficiency.

In this, the final chapter, we'll address both of these shortcomings. You can incorporate Spry into a static or PHP-driven page, giving you and your site visitors the best of both worlds. The content remains accessible to both search engines and browsers that don't understand the Spry code, but anyone using a modern browser gets updated content without the page needing to reload for every change. The Spry functionality needs to be added manually in Code view, but it's quite easy with the help of Dreamweaver code hints. We'll also look at several ways of generating XML with PHP, as well as using PHP as a proxy to access XML hosted on a different domain.

What this chapter covers

- Using the XML Export extension
- Adapting a recordset to generate XML
- Using PHP as a proxy for a remote XML source
- Building Spry pages that still work with JavaScript turned off
- Adapting the Spry gallery from Chapter 19

Since the new version of the Spry gallery draws the image details from a MySQL database, let's start by looking at ways to generate XML on the fly.

Generating XML dynamically

Some people think that XML is a new way of writing web pages or an alternative to using a database. Although you *can* use XML as a database substitute, it's not a very efficient way of storing large amounts of data. An XML document is simply a platform-neutral way of presenting information in a structured manner. Because each repeating element contains the same nodes, it's very easy to automate the creation of an XML document by querying a database and using a loop to insert the data in each node. To use the Dreamweaver terminology, it's the same as creating a recordset and using a repeat region to display all results.

Before I can show you how to do this, you need to insert the data in your MySQL database.

Preparing the database table

To save time, I'm not going to show you how to build the content management system for the ch20_gallery table. You should be able to create the pages to insert, update, delete, and list records yourself, using the knowledge from earlier chapters. Instead, let's get straight to the heart of the matter by loading the necessary data into your database. There are three versions of the SQL file in the tools folder of the download files: ch20_gallery.sql, ch20_gallery323.sql, and ch20_gallery40.sql. If you're running MySQL 4.1 or higher, use ch20_gallery.sql. For MySQL 3.23 or 4.0, use the file with appropriate number at the end of the file name.

> *I have chosen the name* ch20_gallery *to avoid clashing with an existing table if you're restricted to only one database. In the highly unlikely event that you have a table with the same name, do* not *run this SQL file unless you are prepared to lose all existing data in that table. The SQL commands in the file drop any table called* ch20_gallery *and build a completely new one. To use a different name, open the SQL file in Dreamweaver, and use* Edit ➤ Find and Replace *to replace all instances of* ch20_gallery.

The following instructions show you how to create the ch20_gallery table and populate it with data:

1. Open phpMyAdmin, navigate to the egdwcs3 database, and select the Import tab (on older versions of phpMyAdmin, use the SQL tab).

2. Use the Browse button alongside the field labeled Location of the text file to navigate to the appropriate SQL file in the tools folder, and click Go.

3. When the SQL file has finished executing its commands, click the Browse tab at the top of the screen to see the table you have just created. Figure 20-1 shows the first five records.

photo_id	filename	category	width	height	caption	description
1	basin.jpg	JPN	350	237	Water basin at Ryoanji temple, Kyoto	\<p\>Most visitors to Ryoanji Temple go to see just ...
2	buck_palace.jpg	GB	400	300	Buckingham Palace and St James's Park	\<p\>St James's Park is my favourite among all the p...
3	countrygarden.jpg	GB	374	283	A typical English country garden in Oxford	\<p\>The quintessential English country garden is a ...
4	daisydance.jpg	GB	243	273	Dancing round the daisies at Capel Manor	\<p\>Capel Manor, just to the North of London, has 1...
5	dome.jpg	GB	320	300	Leaden skies over the Dome in London	\<p\>The Millennium Dome in Greenwich never lived up...

Figure 20-1. The details of the photos are now stored in a database table.

The table consists of seven columns. The width and height attributes are in columns of their own, and there's a category column that identifies which set of photos a particular image belongs to (JPN for Japan, and GB for England).

4. Click the Structure tab to examine the structure of the ch20_gallery table (see Figure 20-2).

Field	Type	Collation	Attributes	Null	Default	Extra
photo_id	int(10)		UNSIGNED	No		auto_increment
filename	varchar(30)	latin1_swedish_ci		No		
category	enum('GB', 'JPN')	latin1_swedish_ci		No		
width	int(10)		UNSIGNED	No		
height	int(10)		UNSIGNED	No		
caption	varchar(255)	latin1_swedish_ci		No		
description	text	latin1_swedish_ci		No		

Figure 20-2. The structure of the ch20_gallery table

There's nothing new or unusual here. The category column uses the ENUM datatype with two options: GB and JPN. The caption column uses the VARCHAR datatype with a perhaps overly generous maximum of 255 characters, and the description column uses the TEXT datatype to allow for a lengthy description. You don't need any special settings to store XHTML in a TEXT or other datatype designed for storing strings.

Now that the data has been loaded into the database, you can use PHP to build the XML sources for the gallery. Since you have phpMyAdmin open, let's see what it's capable of doing.

Using phpMyAdmin to generate XML

The XML capabilities of phpMyAdmin are very basic, but they're worth knowing about if you need a quick and easy way to generate a static XML document. You can export data from a single table or from several tables. The structure always looks like this:

```
<DatabaseName>
  <TableName>
    <ColumnName>Data</ColumnName>
    <ColumnName>Data</ColumnName>
  </TableName>
</DatabaseName>
```

The name of the table becomes the repeating element that contains each record, and the column names make it easy to identify the data you want to use. The XML that phpMyAdmin creates from the ch20_gallery table looks like this (for space reasons, I have included only the first two records and shortened the descriptions):

```
<egdwcs3>
  <!-- Table ch20_gallery -->
  <ch20_gallery>
    <photo_id>1</photo_id>
    <filename>basin.jpg</filename>
    <category>JPN</category>
```

```
    <width>350</width>
    <height>237</height>
    <caption>Water basin at Ryoanji temple, Kyoto</caption>
    <description>&lt;p&gt;Most visitors to Ryoanji Temple go to see ➥
just one thing&amp;#8212;the rock garden . . . &lt;/p&gt;</description>
  </ch20_gallery>
  <ch20_gallery>
    <photo_id>2</photo_id>
    <filename>buck_palace.jpg</filename>
    <category>GB</category>
    <width>400</width>
    <height>300</height>
    <caption>Buckingham Palace and St James's Park</caption>
    <description>&lt;p&gt;St James's . . . &lt;/p&gt;</description>
  </ch20_gallery>
</egdwcs3>
```

As you can see, the XHTML <p> tags in the <description> nodes have been converted to <p>. The ampersand at the beginning of the em dash entity (—) has also been converted into an HTML entity, so it becomes &#8212;. This isn't a mistake, but you do need to know how to handle it with Spry. I'll explain the situation in "Using XHTML with Spry" later in the chapter.

Use the following steps to create an XML document with phpMyAdmin:

1. In the phpMyAdmin navigation frame, select the database from which you want to create the XML document. If you want to use just one table, navigate to that table.

2. Click the Export tab at the top of the main frame.

3. If you are creating an XML document from more than one table, select the tables that you want to use in the Export list at the top left of the page. This list is not displayed if you selected an individual table in step 1.

4. Select the XML radio button at the bottom of the Export section.

5. Select the Save as file checkbox at the bottom of the page.

6. If you are exporting data from several tables, the field labeled File name template should contain __DB__. This creates a file using the database name, for example, egdwcs3.xml. For a single table, it will be __TABLE__, which creates a file using the table name, for example, ch20_gallery.xml. You can add other text at the beginning or end of the file name template.

   Make any changes you want to the file name, and click Go. Depending on your browser setup, you might be prompted to specify a location to save the file in. Otherwise, it will be saved to your normal download destination.

Using the XML Export extension

When planning the features in Dreamweaver CS3, Adobe made the strange decision not to include the ability to export XML from a database, even though XML plays such a crucial role in Spry data sets. Instead, it was decided to offer the XML Export extension as one of the bonuses that you can claim after registering your version of Dreamweaver CS3 or one of the Creative Suite packages.

The XML Export extension was originally created by InterAKT, the Romanian company that was responsible for Kollection, a suite of popular Dreamweaver extensions. Adobe acquired InterAKT in September 2006 and released a modified version of Kollection as the Adobe Dreamweaver Developer Toolbox (ADDT). The XML Export extension is part of ADDT, so if you have ADDT or selected the extension as your registration bonus, this section is for you. If you don't have ADDT and chose a different bonus, skip to "Building XML manually from a recordset."

The XML Export extension is very easy to use, and it has the advantage that you have much more control over the structure of the XML. This is because the XML is generated from a recordset, so you could create an XML source from the authors and quotations tables used in Chapter 16, associating the correct author with each quotation by using a left join. This would be impossible with the phpMyAdmin XML export feature described in the preceding section.

> The minimum requirement for the XML Export extension is PHP 4.4.0. The PHP `mbstring` extension must also be enabled. If you used the instructions in Chapter 3 to set up a local testing environment, `mbstring` should already be enabled. See "Checking installed extensions" in Chapter 3 for details of how to check your remote server.

Since the purpose of this chapter is to show you how to generate an XML source for the Spry gallery from Chapter 19, the following instructions show you how to use the XML Export extension to generate XML with details of the Japanese images in the ch20_gallery table. They assume that you have installed the XML Export extension or ADDT.

1. Create a new PHP page called japan_xe.php in workfiles/ch20. The page should contain nothing apart from the default code inserted by Dreamweaver.

2. Open the Recordset dialog box in Simple mode, and create a recordset called getPhotos. This doesn't need administrative privileges, so use connQuery for Connection, and select ch20_gallery in the Table field.

   You don't need the photo_id and category columns for the XML output, so select all other columns except those two.

   However, you do want to retrieve only those records where category is set to JPN. Set Filter to category, and leave the second drop-down set to =. Since JPN is a fixed value, select Entered Value from the third drop-down, and type JPN in the field alongside.

   When you have finished, the settings should look like this:

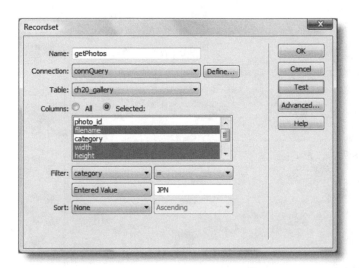

3. Use the Test button to make sure the recordset works, and then click OK to save it.

4. How you access the Export Recordset As XML server behavior depends on whether you installed the extension on its own or have the full version of ADDT. If you installed the extension on its own, it sits in splendid isolation on the Developer Toolbox tab of the Insert bar, as shown in the following screenshot:

Alternatively, click the plus button in the Server Behaviors panel, and select Developer Toolbox ➤ Export Recordset As XML.

If you have the full version of ADDT, it's not on the Insert bar. Your only options are to access it through the Server Behaviors panel or add it to the Developer Toolbox Favorites button.

5. This opens the Export Recordset As XML dialog box, as shown in the screenshot at the top of the next page.

The dialog box has two tabs: Basic and Advanced. The Basic tab lets you choose the recordset to use, but in most cases, you're unlikely to have more than one on the page.

The Columns area lets you exclude columns from the XML output by highlighting them and clicking the minus button. However, this shouldn't be necessary if you selected the columns you want in the recordset. You can also use the up and down arrows to change the order the nodes or attributes appear in the XML.

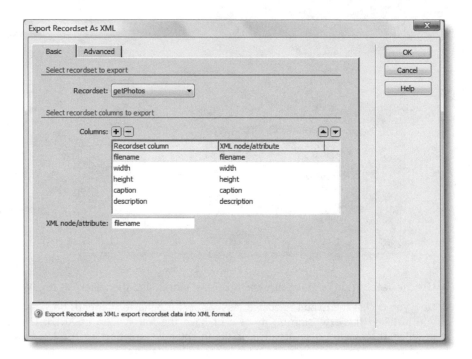

You can change the name of individual nodes or attributes by selecting them in the Columns area, and entering a new value in the XML node/attribute field at the bottom of the Basic tab.

As the labels suggest, the extension lets you choose whether to export data as XML nodes or attributes. You make that choice in the Advanced tab.

6. Select the Advanced tab, which presents you with the options shown in the next screenshot.

The help hints at the bottom of the tab explain briefly what each option is for. The first option lets you choose whether to export columns as XML nodes or as attributes of the repeating element (referred to in the fifth option as the "Row node"). This is an all or nothing option: all columns are treated the same way. You cannot choose, for example, to make the height and width columns attributes of the <filename> node.

The Export all records checkbox is selected by default. If you deselect it, enter how many records you want to include in the XML in the Number of records field. This field is grayed out and ignored when Export all records is selected.

The next two options, Root node and Row node, let you specify the names of the root and repeating nodes. The defaults are deliberately neutral: export signifying that the XML has been exported from a recordset, and row representing each record or row in the recordset.

When working with dynamic data, I find it's always a good idea to use meaningful names so that you know instantly what you're working with. Change Root node to gallery and Row node to photo.

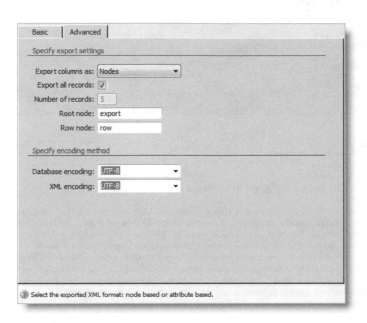

The final two options let you specify the encoding of the database and XML output. The choices are unrealistically limited: UTF-8 (the default) or ISO-8859-1 (Western European). The encoding values are not vital in the case of unaccented English, because it uses a subset of ISO-8859-1, which uses identical coding to UTF-8. However, you need to select the appropriate encoding if you are using other languages.

7. Click OK when you're happy with the settings.

8. The page remains blank in Design view. This is perfectly normal. Save japan_xe.php, and press F12/Opt+F12 to view the page in a browser. You should see raw XML output, as shown in Figure 20-3 at the top of the next page.

9. View the page source in the browser. The <p> tags in the <description> node have been converted to <p> in the same way as when you export XML with phpMyAdmin. Again, I'll explain the implications in "Using XHTML with Spry" later in the chapter.

The XML Export extension doesn't create a static XML document—that's not the idea. It's intended to provide a live XML feed from a database. When creating a Spry data set or XSLT fragment, you use the PHP page as the XML source, and—as long as you have a testing server defined for your site—Dreamweaver treats it as XML. On Windows, you need to select All Files (*.*) in the Files of type field of the Select XML Source dialog box to be able to find the PHP file.

When you save the PHP page, Dreamweaver creates a new subfolder called XMLExport in your site's includes folder. It also creates the includes folder, if it doesn't already exist. The XML Export folder contains two files, XMLExport.class.php and XMLExport.php.

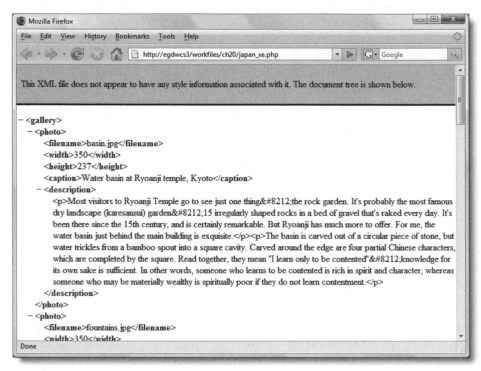

Figure 20-3. The XML Export extension generates XML on the fly from a MySQL database.

You must upload the XML Export *folder and its contents to your remote site when deploying on the Internet a page made with the XML Export extension. You also need to upload the* Connections *folder to connect to the database. If you forget either folder, the page will generate a fatal error.*

As long as you don't attempt to put anything else in the PHP page, japan_xe.php or any other page created using this extension should generate XML successfully. However, the PHP code uses the header() function to ensure that the output is treated as XML. If you make any changes to the code generated by Dreamweaver, you might see a warning that the headers have already been sent and XML cannot be exported. See Chapter 12 for details about the "headers already sent" error.

Updating the includes folder

If you access the XML Export extension through the Server Behaviors panel, there's another option called Control Panel on the Developer Toolbox submenu. This opens the ADDT Control Panel. A full installation of ADDT contains a large number of options, but a stand-alone version of the XML Export extension has just a single option labeled Update includes folder. Click the icon on the left, as shown in the following illustration, to open the Update Includes Folder dialog box:

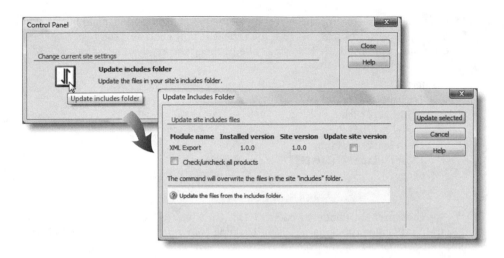

This checks the version of the XML Export files installed in Dreamweaver and compares it with the version currently uploaded to your remote server. If the remote version is older than the one in Dreamweaver, select the Update site version checkbox, and click Update selected to upload the newer version.

Building XML manually from a recordset

The XML Export extension is a very quick way to create the code to generate XML on the fly, but it gives you very little control over the format of the XML. If you don't have the extension or want to fine-tune the structure of your XML, it takes only a little effort to roll your own. Before getting down to the detail, here's a brief outline of the steps involved:

1. Create a recordset.
2. Build a skeleton of XML tags for the repeating element and its child nodes.
3. Populate the child nodes with dynamic text objects from the recordset.
4. Apply a Repeat Region server behavior to the repeating element.
5. Remove the XHTML code from the page.
6. Add the XML declaration and root node tags.
7. Add headers to tell Dreamweaver and browsers to treat the output as XML.

You build everything in a similar way to an ordinary web page and remove the DOCTYPE declaration and XHTML tags, leaving behind just the code to create the XML feed. However, it's important to leave all the XHTML code in the page until you have applied the server behavior. Otherwise, Dreamweaver gets rather upset.

The following instructions show you how to create an XML feed of details of the Japanese images in the ch20_gallery table:

1. Create a new PHP page called japan_manual.php in workfiles/ch20.
2. Create a recordset using the same settings as in step 2 of the preceding section.

3. Now build a skeleton for the repeating element, <photo>, and its child nodes. You need just one set of tags, because the repeat region generates the rest. Switch to Code view, and insert the following code between the <body> tags:

```
<body>
  <photo>
    <filename></filename>
    <width></width>
    <height></height>
    <caption></caption>
    <description><![CDATA[]]></description>
  </photo>
</body>
```

The <description> node contains XHTML, so I have added opening and closing CDATA tags inside the node tags (see "Creating a Spry data set" in Chapter 19 if you need a reminder of the role of CDATA sections). When building your own XML, create a similar skeleton using the node names of your choice.

As you're typing, you'll notice that Dreamweaver code hints recognize your custom XML tags, making it easier to complete the closing tags.

> *You need to insert the XML skeleton between the <body> tags in order to use the Repeat Region server behavior.*

4. Now populate the child nodes with dynamic text objects from the recordset. Position the insertion point between the opening and closing <filename> tags.

5. Open the Bindings panel, expand the recordset, select filename, and click the Insert button. This inserts a dynamic text object inside the <filename> child node.

6. Repeat steps 4 and 5 with the other child node tags, positioning the insertion point between the CDATA tags for the <description> node. The XML skeleton should now look like this:

```
<photo>
  <filename><?php echo $row_getPhotos['filename']; ?></filename>
  <width><?php echo $row_getPhotos['width']; ?></width>
  <height><?php echo $row_getPhotos['height']; ?></height>
  <caption><?php echo $row_getPhotos['caption']; ?></caption>
  <description><![CDATA[<?php echo $row_getPhotos['description']; ?> ➥
]]></description>
</photo>
```

7. Select the XML skeleton, and apply a Repeat Region server behavior (use the Server Behaviors panel, the Data tab of the Insert bar, or the Insert ➤ Data Objects submenu). In the Repeat Region dialog box, select Show All Records.

8. Once the Repeat Region server behavior has been applied, you can get rid of the unwanted XHTML. Select everything from the opening tag of the DOCTYPE declaration to the opening PHP tag at the start of the repeat region that you have just created, as shown in the following screenshot:

```
36   $totalRows_getPhotos = mysql_num_rows($getPhotos);
37 ▣ ?><!DOCTYPE html PUBLIC "-//W3C//DTD XHTML 1.0 Transitional//EN"
     "http://www.w3.org/TR/xhtml1/DTD/xhtml1-transitional.dtd">
38   <html xmlns="http://www.w3.org/1999/xhtml">
39   <head>
40   <meta http-equiv="Content-Type" content="text/html; charset=utf-8" />
41   <title>Untitled Document</title>
42   </head>
43
44   <body>
45 ▣     <?php do { ?>
46        <photo>
47          <filename><?php echo $row_getPhotos['filename']; ?></filename>
```

9. Delete the selected code, and replace it with the XML declaration and the opening tag of the XML root node like this:

```
$totalRows_getPhotos = mysql_num_rows($getPhotos);
?>
<?xml version="1.0" encoding="utf-8"?>
<gallery>
<?php do { ?>
```

10. Scroll down and replace the closing </body> and </html> tags with the closing tag of the XML root node (</gallery>).

11. The last change that you need to make is to insert headers to tell Dreamweaver and browsers to treat the output as XML. Without them, they treat it as plain text. The headers go just before the closing PHP tag shown on line 37 of the preceding screenshot, like this:

```
$totalRows_getPhotos = mysql_num_rows($getPhotos);
// Send the headers
header('Content-type: text/xml');
header('Pragma: public');
header('Cache-control: private');
header('Expires: -1');
?>
<?xml version="1.0" encoding="utf-8"?>
```

Forgetting the headers is a common cause of problems when generating XML on the fly. The XML declaration added in step 9 isn't sufficient on its own (in fact, an XML document is perfectly legal without it). Since you're using a file with a .php extension, the web server doesn't know that it's meant to treat the output as XML without sending the Content-type *header. The remaining three headers are optional but are designed to prevent the XML output from being cached.*

20

12. Save japan_manual.php, and test the page in a browser. It should look the same as Figure 20-3. The only difference is that the <p> tags are in a CDATA section and use <p> in the underlying source code, rather than <p>. It makes no difference to the XML, although using a CDATA section does have an important advantage when used with Spry 1.4, the version distributed with the original release of Dreamweaver CS3. This is discussed in "Using XHTML with Spry" later in the chapter.

You can compare your code with japan_manual.php in examples/ch20.

Using a proxy script to fetch a remote feed

Security restrictions in browsers prevent Spry and other Ajax frameworks from accessing an XML source that's hosted on a different domain from the web page. To get around this restriction, you need to use a proxy script. If your server supports allow_url_fopen (see Table 3-1 in Chapter 3), a few of lines of code will do the trick. The following example, which can be found in proxy.php in examples/ch20, acts as a proxy for the friends of ED RSS feed:

```php
<?php
$url = 'http://friendsofed.com/news.php';
// Make sure the remote feed is accessible, then fetch it
if (file_exists($url) && is_readable($url)) {
  $remote = file_get_contents($url);
  // Send an XML header and display the feed
  header('Content-Type: text/xml');
  echo $remote;
  }
else {
  echo "Cannot open remote file at $url";
  }?>
```

This script checks that the remote feed is available and stores it in a variable called $remote. The two lines highlighted in bold create an XML header and output the content of $remote. If the feed can't be found, an error message is displayed instead.

If your hosting company doesn't allow you to open remote files directly, it might have provided an alternative through the cURL (Client URL Library) extension. You can tell whether cURL is available by displaying the output of phpinfo() using test.php in examples/ch03. If you can see a listing similar to Figure 20-4, cURL is enabled.

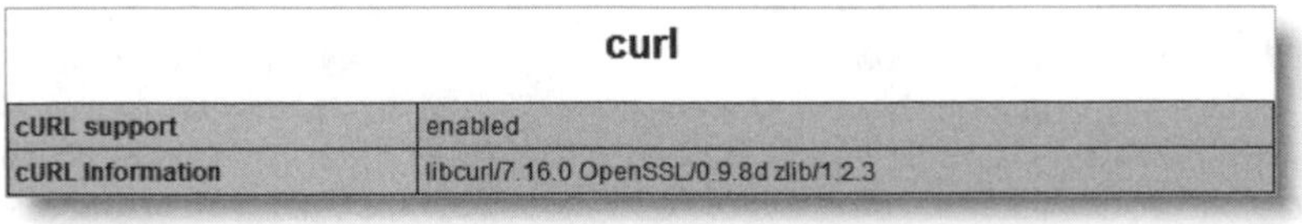

curl	
cURL support	enabled
cURL Information	libcurl/7.16.0 OpenSSL/0.9.8d zlib/1.2.3

Figure 20-4. Confirmation that the PHP cURL extension is enabled

The cURL extension lets you communicate with many different types of servers with a large number of protocols. The following script, which is in curl.php in examples/ch20, does the same as proxy.php, using a cURL session to retrieve the friends of ED RSS feed:

```php
<?php
$url = 'http://friendsofed.com/news.php';
// Open the cURL session
if ($session = curl_init($url)) {
  // Block HTTP headers, and get XML only
  curl_setopt($session, CURLOPT_HEADER, false);
  curl_setopt($session, CURLOPT_RETURNTRANSFER, true);
  // Get the remote feed
  $remote = curl_exec($session);
  // Close the cURL session
  curl_close($session);
  // Check that the feed was retrieved successfully
  if ($remote) {
    // Send an XML header and display the feed
    header('Content-Type: text/xml');
    echo $remote;
    }
  else {
    echo "No content found at $url";
    }
  }
else {
  echo "Cannot initialize session";
  }
?>
```

Again, the content of the feed is stored in a variable called $remote. If the cURL session succeeds, the lines highlighted in bold output an XML header and the content of $remote. For more details about cURL, visit www.php.net/manual/en/ref.curl.php.

In both files, all you need to do to fetch a different feed is replace the value of $url with a different address.

> *When using a remote XML or RSS feed, remember to check ownership of copyright and any restrictions on reuse of material contained in the feed. Using copyrighted material without permission could land you with a hefty legal bill.*

Creating an XML document from a dynamic source

A potential problem with XML generated on the fly from a database or through a proxy script is that slow network connections will slow down the response. Even worse, the dynamic source may be unavailable. So you might want to consider generating a static

XML document and using that instead. This is particularly appropriate if the XML content is unlikely to change very often. Instead of putting repeated strain on the database server, for example, the static document acts as a cache, which is faster and more efficient.

The principle behind creating a static document from a dynamic source is very simple: capture the XML output in a PHP variable and use PHP file system functions to write the document to your site or local hard disk. Before you can do this, you need to make sure that the web server has permission to write to the target folder.

Setting permission for PHP to write files

Most hosting companies use Linux servers, which impose strict rules about the ownership of files and directories. Writing a file creates a new version of the file on the server, so the user needs all three privileges—read, write, and execute. However, in most cases, PHP doesn't run in *your* name, but as the web server—usually nobody or apache. Unless your hosting company has configured PHP to run in your own name, you need to give global access (chmod 777) to every directory to which you want to be able to write files. Since 777 is the least secure setting, you need to adopt a cautious approach. Begin by testing the scripts in this section with a setting of 700. If that doesn't work, try 770, and use 777 only as a last resort.

Windows servers use a different system of setting permissions. Consult your hosting company if you have problems writing files.

When testing locally, there are usually no permissions issues on Windows.

However, on Mac OS X, you need to change the permissions of any folder that you want PHP to be able to write to like this:

1. Select the folder in Finder, and press Cmd+I or choose File ➤ Get Info.
2. In the Ownership & Permissions section at the bottom of the Info window, click the triangle alongside Details to reveal the permissions for all users, as shown in Figure 20-5.
3. Change the setting for Others from Read only to Read & Write, and close the Info window. The folder is now writable.

Using PHP to write to a file

Writing to a file with PHP isn't difficult, but it involves three steps, as follows:

1. Create a resource handler to open the file.
2. Write the contents to the file.
3. Close the file.

Each step uses an intuitively named function: fopen(), fwrite(), and fclose(). Unfortunately, fopen() has a bewildering range of options that prepare the file for reading and writing in different ways. If you're interested in the details, study the PHP online manual at www.php.net/manual/en/function.fopen.php or read Chapter 7 of my book *PHP Solutions: Dynamic Web Design Made Easy* (friends of ED, ISBN-13: 978-1-59059-731-6).

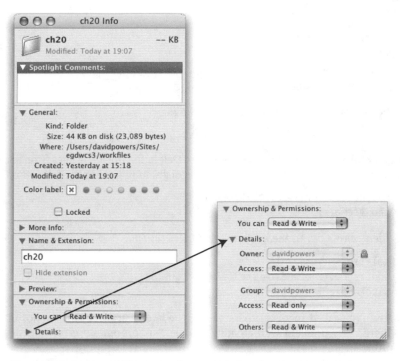

Figure 20-5. On Mac OS X, you need to set global read and write permissions on the folder you want to write to.

The option that I'm going to use overwrites any existing content in the file. This is ideal for creating a static XML document from a dynamic source. All you need to do is run the script, and the XML document is automatically updated. I have wrapped the script in a custom function and put it in an include file, so you can use it in conjunction with any script that you want to write the contents of a variable to an external file.

The function, complete with inline comments, follows (it's in write_file.inc.php in examples/includes):

```php
<?php
// function to overwrite content in a file
function writeToFile($content, $targetFile) {
  // open the file ready for writing
  if (!$file = fopen($targetFile, 'w')) {
    echo "Cannot create $targetFile";
    exit;
    }
  // write the content to the file
  if (fwrite($file,$content) === false) {
    echo "Cannot write to $targetFile";
    exit;
    }
  echo "Success: content updated in $targetFile";
```

```
// close the file
fclose($file);
}
?>
```

The writeToFile() function takes two arguments, as follows:

- The content that you want to write to the file
- The name of the target file

Creating an XML document from a remote source Delete the following lines from proxy.php or curl.php in the previous section (they are highlighted in bold in the full listings):

```
header('Content-Type: text/xml');
echo $remote;
```

Replace them with a call to the writeToFile() function like this:

```
$xmlfile = 'foed.xml';
require('../includes/write_file.inc.php');
writeToFile($remote, $xmlfile);
```

This creates a file called foed.xml that contains the latest version of the friends of ED RSS feed. If there's any problem with creating the file, an appropriate error message is displayed instead.

Creating an XML document from a local dynamic source You can use the writeToFile() function to create a static XML document from an XML source generated dynamically using either the XML Export extension or the technique described in "Building XML manually from a recordset." It involves using an adaptation of proxy.php.

The script in proxy.php uses the file_get_contents() function to retrieve the XML from a remote source. If you try to use this on a local file, such as japan_manual.php, instead of the XML, you get the PHP script that generates the XML. So, instead of using the file name, you need to use the full URL, so that the file is processed by the web server in your local testing environment.

However, proxy.php uses a conditional statement that checks whether the remote feed exists and is readable. This causes the script to fail when accessing a local dynamic source. The simple answer is to leave it out. This leaves the following script (it's in local_proxy_write.php in examples/ch20):

```
<?php
// URL to file that generates local dynamic XML source
$url = 'http://egdwcs3/workfiles/ch20/japan_manual.php';
// Get the XML and store it in a variable
$xml = file_get_contents($url);
// Set the name of the file to write the XML to
$xmlfile = 'japan_proxy_manual.xml';
// Include the writeToFile() function and call it
require('../includes/write_file.inc.php');
writeToFile($xml, $xmlfile);
?>
```

This gets the XML generated by japan_manual.php (the file that created XML from a recordset earlier in the chapter) and writes it to a file called japan_proxy_manual.xml. It also works with japan_xe.php, the file created using the XML Export extension. Just change the value of $url at the beginning of the script.

The following three values (highlighted in bold in the preceding listing) are the only things you need to change:

- $url: To find the correct value, open in the Document window the page that generates the XML source, and press F12/Opt+F12 to view the XML output in the browser. Select the URL in the browser address bar, and paste it into local_proxy_write.php. This won't work if you have set your Dreamweaver preferences to use a temporary file for Preview in Browser (see Chapter 4 for details of how to change the setting).

- $xmlfile: This is the name of the file you want to write to. The preceding example writes the file to the same folder as local_proxy_write.php. If you want to write to a different folder, use a relative address or a full pathname.

- require(): This needs to point to the location of write_file.inc.php. As explained in Chapter 12, this should be a relative address or a full pathname.

> *Although I designed the* writeToFile() *function to write an XML source to file, it is completely generic. It writes any string stored in the first argument to the file named in the second argument.*

Using Spry in pages that work without JavaScript

There are no two ways about it: Spry doesn't work without JavaScript. However, it is possible to use Spry to refresh content seamlessly in pages that not only provide content for search engines to index but also continue to work normally in browsers that have JavaScript turned off or don't understand the latest scripting standards. The technique involves building a standard web page first and adding some simple code that refreshes the page's content if JavaScript is enabled.

How to incorporate a Spry data set in an ordinary web page

In Chapter 19, you created a Spry table that displayed the captions of a set of photos, and when you clicked a caption, the related description was displayed in a <div> at the foot of the table. To create a similar effect with PHP, you need two recordsets: one that contains details of each caption and the record's primary key, and the other that retrieves a single description based on the primary key passed through the URL.

Let's build the PHP version.

Building the PHP table

This creates a PHP version of the Spry table in spry_data_02.php in Chapter 19. Since all of the techniques have been covered in previous chapters, I'll keep the details to a minimum. I won't bother with any styling either, because the purpose is to concentrate on the code.

1. Create a new PHP page called accessible.php in workfiles/ch20.

2. Open the Recordset dialog box in Simple mode, and use the following settings:

   - Name: getCaptions
   - Connection: connQuery
   - Table: ch20_gallery
   - Columns (Selected): photo_id, filename, caption
   - Filter: category = Entered Value GB

3. Insert a table with two rows and two columns. Enter column headings in the first row and dynamic text objects for filename and caption in the second row. Apply a repeat region to the second row. The page should now look like this in Design view:

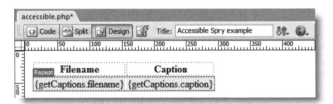

4. Select the dynamic text object for caption, and create a link using the Browse for File icon in the Property inspector. Select accessible.php, and click the Parameters button. In the Parameters dialog box, set Name to photo_id, and click the lightning bolt icon in the Value field. Select photo_id from the getCaptions recordset.

5. Open the Recordset dialog box in Simple mode, and use the following settings:

   - Name: getDescription
   - Connection: connQuery
   - Table: ch20_gallery
   - Columns (Selected): description
   - Filter: photo_id = URL Parameter photo_id

6. Before closing the Recordset dialog box, switch to Advanced mode, and edit the colname variable to set Default value to 2. This is the photo_id of the first record in the getCaptions recordset. As explained in Chapter 18, Dreamweaver always sets Default value to –1 to prevent anything from displaying when the page first loads. On this occasion, you need the description of the first record to display by default.

7. Insert a <div> after the table, and replace the placeholder text with a dynamic text object for description.

8. Save accessible.php, and load it into a browser. It should look like Figure 20-6. Test the links, and the content of the description `<div>` should change. You can check your code against accessible_01.php in examples/ch20.

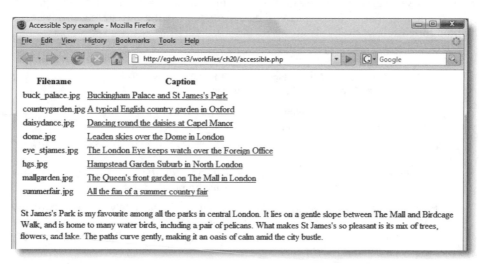

Figure 20-6. Although not styled as elegantly, this has roughly the same functionality as the Spry table in Chapter 19.

What drives the page is passing the primary key of the selected caption through a query string appended to the URL. Each time you click a link, the URL changes, the page reloads, and the changed content is displayed.

Use the browser's View Source feature to check the underlying code. Each time the page reloads, the content of the description `<div>` also changes in the source. Although the content is generated dynamically, what's being sent by the web server each time is, in effect, a static page.

By contrast, what Spry does is to load the data set into the browser's memory and manipulate the Document Object Model (DOM) to refresh the content without reloading the page.

To create an accessible version of the Spry table, you need to add a Spry data set and tell the page to use Spry instead. This involves just two steps, as follows:

1. Add an onclick event handler to each link. The event handler takes this form:

```
onclick="datasetName.setCurrentRowNumber(number); return false"
```

This sets the current row number for the Spry data set to update the detail region. Adding return false prevents the browser from following the link. However, if the browser doesn't understand JavaScript, it follows the link in the normal way.

2. Add the spry:detailregion and spry:content properties to the element that you want to act as the Spry detail region. The spry:detailregion property takes the Spry data set name as its value, and the spry:content property requires the name of the data set node in curly braces.

So, let's add the necessary code to accessible.php.

Adding Spry functionality to the PHP table

In this exercise, you'll add the Spry data set and the code that controls the detail region. A self-incrementing PHP counter inserts the row number in the setCurrentRowNumber() method for each link.

1. Continue working with accessible.php from the previous exercise.

2. Create a Spry data set called dsPhotos, using england.xml in examples/ch19 as the XML source, and selecting photo as Row element.

3. Switch to Code view, and insert the following PHP code block anywhere before the code that applies the repeat region to the second table row:

   ```php
   <?php $i = 0; ?>
   ```

   This initializes a variable called $i that will act as a counter to insert the correct row number in the event handler for each link in the repeat region.

4. To insert the event handler, position your cursor immediately to the left of the closing angle bracket of the <a> tag in the table cell. There are a lot of angle brackets in there, so make sure you get the right place. Use the following screenshot to guide you:

   Insert onclick event handler here

   ```
   71    <td><a href="accessible.php?photo_id=<?php echo $row_getCaptions['photo_id']; ?>"><?php echo
         $row_getCaptions['caption']; ?></a></td>
   ```

   Insert a space and enter the following code:

   ```
   onclick="dsPhotos.setCurrentRowNumber(<?php echo $i++; ?>)"
   ```

   As you type, Dreamweaver code hints will appear, first showing you the available attributes and event handlers for the <a> tag, and when you type the period after dsPhotos, the available methods and properties for a Spry data set. The setCurrentRowNumber() method is self-explanatory: it sets the current row number of the dsPhotos data set. It takes one argument: the number of the current row. Because this code is in a repeat region, you need the counter ($i) to increment by 1 for every row in the recordset. By placing the ++ operator after $i, PHP performs the increment after inserting the number. As a result, the first row is 0; the next one is 1, and so on. Since Spry data sets use JavaScript and count from zero, this is exactly what you want. However, you don't want the browser to follow the link if it understands Spry.

5. To prevent the browser from following the link, you need to add a semicolon followed by return false to the event handler. The entire line of code shown in the preceding screenshot should now look like this (new code is in bold):

   ```
   <td><a href="accessible.php?photo_id=<?php echo ➥
   $row_getCaptions['photo_id']; ?>" ➥
   onclick="dsPhotos.setCurrentRowNumber(<?php echo $i++; ?>); ➥
   return false"><?php echo $row_getCaptions['caption']; ?></a></td>
   ```

6. You now need to tell Spry that you want to use description <div> as a detail region for the dsPhotos data set, and that it should draw its content from the <description> node. Add the spry:detailregion and spry:content properties to the <div> tag like this:

<div id="description" **spry:detailregion="dsPhotos"** ➥
spry:content="{description}">

Dreamweaver code hints suggest available options as you type, helping you get the correct combination of uppercase and lowercase. Note that you enclose description in curly braces when specifying the value of spry:content.

7. Save accessible.php, and test it in a browser. If you use the browser reload button, remove the query string from the end of the URL. As long as JavaScript is enabled in your browser, the description should change at the bottom of the page each time you click a link.

8. Click any of the links apart from the first one, and view the source code in the browser. Figure 20-7 shows what happened when I clicked the final link. The description of the summer country fair is displayed, but the underlying source code still shows the description of Buckingham Palace and St James's Park—proof that Spry is in action.

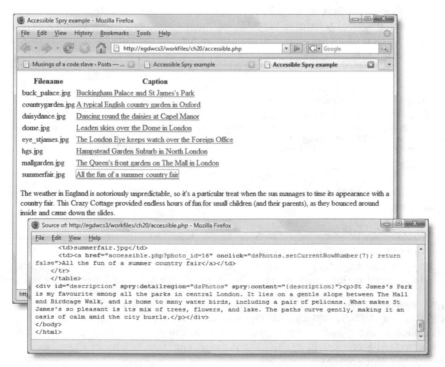

Figure 20-7. Although Spry changes the content in the browser, the underlying code remains unchanged.

You can check your code against accessible_02 in examples/ch20.

If you temporarily turn off JavaScript in your browser, the page will act the same way as before you added the event handler and Spry code. This not only makes the page accessible to the admittedly small number of people who surf the Web with JavaScript disabled, but it also leaves content in your page for a search engine to index. Search engines are capable of following dynamic links that use query strings, so all your links can be followed.

The disadvantages of this approach are that specific content can't be bookmarked, and the browser back button takes you to the last URL, not to the most recently displayed content. However, these failings are common to all Ajax pages at the moment. The other disadvantage is that it involves more effort, but the payoff of greater accessibility is probably worth it.

Using XHTML with Spry

The exercise in the previous section uses england.xml as the XML source for the Spry data set. The XHTML tags in that XML document are stored in CDATA sections, so the <p> tags use angle brackets. However, the XML generated by phpMyAdmin and the XML Export extension converts the angle brackets into entities like this: <p>. This is a perfectly acceptable way of treating XHTML tags in XML.

However, due to an oversight in Spry 1.4, the version that shipped with the original release of Dreamweaver CS3, Spry is incapable of handling these tags correctly. Figure 20-8 shows what happened when I generated the XML for the previous exercise with the XML Export extension. Instead of interpreting the <p> tags as XHTML markup, the browser displayed them as though they were part of the text.

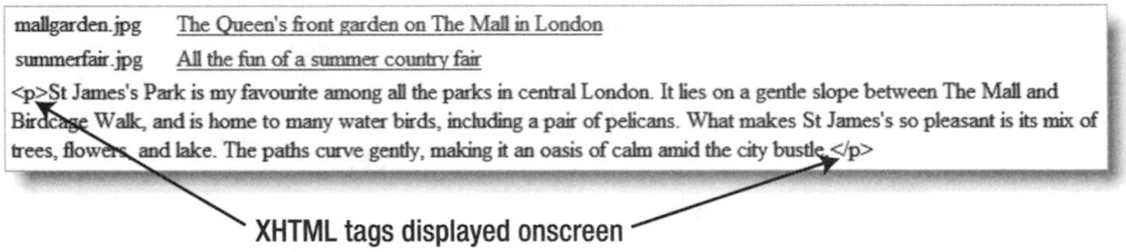

Figure 20-8. Version 1.4 of Spry fails to handle XHTML tags correctly if the XML source uses entities instead of angle brackets.

This problem has been corrected in Spry 1.5. As noted in the previous chapter, Adobe has promised to release an extension to update the Spry functionality in Dreamweaver. However, the precise details were still not available at the time this book went to press, so the following instructions are based on updating the Spry data JavaScript library manually.

If you replace SpryData.js in the Spry assets folder with version 1.5 or later, you can fix the display of XHTML tags by applying the setColumnType() method to the data set initialization in the <head> of your page. In the case of accessible.php, this is how you need to edit the code (I have used a file called england_xe.php in examples/ch20 to generate the XML source):

```
<script src="../../SpryAssets/SpryData.js" type="text/javascript"> ➥
</script>
<script type="text/javascript">
<!--
var dsPhotos = new Spry.Data.XMLDataSet("england_xe.php", ➥
"gallery/photo");
dsPhotos.setColumnType("description", "html");
//-->
</script>
```

For more details, see http://labs.adobe.com/technologies/spry/samples/data_region/
HTMLFragsInXMLSample.html. Hopefully, the Dreamweaver updater will add this option to
the Spry XML Data Set dialog box. Changes that affect this book will be listed on my website at http://foundationphp.com/egdwcs3/updates.php.

Case study: Making the Spry gallery accessible

In the previous chapter, you used Spry to create an online gallery to display photos of
England and Japan, together with captions and brief descriptions. Although it looks and
works well in a JavaScript-enabled browser, it's not search engine friendly, and it fails miserably in a browser that doesn't support Spry. To round off this book, I'd like to show you
how to get the best of both worlds by combining Spry with PHP. The XML sources will also
be generated dynamically by PHP, so the gallery contents can be updated automatically by
changing only the records in the database.

The techniques involved have all been covered in earlier parts of the book, so I won't go
into minute detail of each step. You can study the completed files in examples/ch20. In
addition to the ch20_gallery table in the database, the accessible version of the gallery
requires just three files, as follows:

- hijax_gallery.php: This displays a PHP-driven version of the gallery but uses Spry
  if the browser is capable of understanding it.

- england.php: This draws information from the database to generate the XML
  source for the England photos.

- japan.php: This generates the XML source for the Japan photos. It's identical to
  england.php, except for the SQL query.

Let's start by building the PHP version of the gallery. By the way, if you don't want to use
Spry, this page on its own creates an online gallery that works in any visual browser.

Creating the gallery with PHP

Instead of using a Spry data set to populate the page, the PHP version of the gallery uses
two recordsets like this:

- One recordset gets details of all the images in either the GB or JPN category. This is used to display the thumbnails of the selected category, as well as to display the large image, caption, and description of the first photo when the page loads initially.

- Each thumbnail is enclosed in a link that appends its primary key as a query string to the URL, which reloads the page and passes the primary key to the second recordset. This retrieves the details of the selected image to display the large version, its caption, and its description.

The <select> drop-down menu also reloads the page and appends the selected category to the URL as a query string. This changes the category in the first recordset, determining which set of thumbnails is displayed.

Because the page is rebuilt every time, the recordsets are also refreshed, so the dynamically generated links always have the right details. Basically, what is happening is the same as with a search page: runtime variables are being passed through the URL, and the results are displayed on the same page. However, instead of displaying only text, you also use the result details to build the <img> tags for the thumbnails and main image.

Although the gallery uses the same basic page and layout as gallery.php in Chapter 19, it's quicker to start from scratch. We'll use the same start page and style sheet, and build everything afresh. This has the advantage of showing you how to build a PHP gallery on its own if you decide that Spry isn't for you.

Creating the Select gallery menu

Dreamweaver has a jump menu that could be used to switch between galleries, but the whole idea of this case study is to create a page that doesn't rely on JavaScript. Since the jump menu uses JavaScript, that rules it out. Instead, we'll insert the <form>, <select>, and submit button elements separately. But, first, you need to lay out the structure of the page.

1. Copy gallery_start.php from examples/ch20 to workfiles/ch20, and rename it hijax_gallery.php. The page should look like this in Design view:

If it's unstyled, check the link to styles/gallery.css and that the display of styles isn't turned off in the Style Rendering toolbar or View ➤ Style Rendering.

2. The rules for the `select`, `thumbs`, `mainPic`, and `description` ID selectors are already defined in the style sheet, making it easy to insert the `<div>` elements that form the structure of the page (refer to Figure 19-13 in the previous chapter).

Select Insert Div Tag from the Common category of the Insert bar (or Insert ➤ Layout Objects ➤ Div Tag). In the dialog box that opens, set Insert to After tag, and select `<div id="header">` from the drop-down menu alongside. You can then set the ID for the first `<div>` by choosing select from the ID drop-down menu, as shown here:

> The ID menu displays only ID selectors that are already defined in the style sheet and haven't yet been used in the page. As you add the remaining three `<div>` elements, you'll see this list getting shorter. This is designed to prevent you from using the same ID in more than one element on a page. If you're building a new page and haven't yet defined the styles, you can type the name of the new ID into the ID field and define its style rules by clicking the New CSS Style button (it's hidden behind the ID drop-down menu in the preceding screenshot).

3. Click OK to insert the select `<div>`. Then repeat step 2 three times to insert the remaining `<div>` elements in this order: thumbs, mainPic, and description, each time setting Insert to After tag and selecting the name of the `<div>` you have just inserted from the drop-down menu alongside. By the time you have finished, the page should look like this:

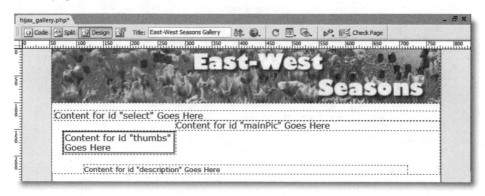

4. You need to replace the placeholder text in each <div> with the code that generates the actual content, so it's a good idea to open Split view to make sure that you delete only the placeholder text and don't affect the surrounding tags.

   Highlight the placeholder text in the select <div>, and press Delete to remove it.

5. With the insertion point between the empty <div> tags, insert a form, using the Forms tab of the Insert bar or Insert ➤ Form ➤ Form.

   In the Property inspector, set Method to GET. Leave Action blank. You want the form to reload the same page.

6. Insert a <select> element by choosing List/Menu from the Forms tab or Insert ➤ Form ➤ List/Menu. In the Input Tag Accessibility Attributes dialog box, use the following settings:

   - ID: category
   - Label: Select gallery:
   - Style: Attach label tag using 'for' attribute
   - Position: Before form item

7. Select the menu element in Design view to bring up its details in the Property inspector, and click the List Values button.

   Create two menu items by entering England in the Item Label field and GB in the Value field for the first item, and Japan and JPN for the second one.

8. The purpose of this gallery is to work even without JavaScript, so click to the side of the menu element in Design view, and insert a submit button. In the Input Tag Accessibility Attributes dialog box, give the button an ID called go, but no label. In the Property inspector, change Value from Submit to Go.

   The top of the page should now look like this:

Save the page, and compare your code, if necessary, with hijax_gallery_01.php.

Creating the thumbnail gallery and links

The thumbnails are displayed using a repeat region. It's common practice to put thumbnails in a table, but the Dreamweaver Repeat Region server behavior is unidirectional—it can't go across and down in the same operation—so we'll do the same as with the Spry data set, which is to let the width of the thumbs <div> control the number of thumbnails displayed in a row. Each thumbnail needs to be wrapped in a link that loads the same page and passes the photo_id of the selected image in a query string. This will be used later to display the main image and its details.

1. Create a Recordset called getThumbs in Advanced mode. It needs to retrieve only the photo_id and filename columns, where category is specified by a runtime variable. Set the default value of the runtime variable to GB, and the runtime value to $_GET['category']. Your settings should look like this:

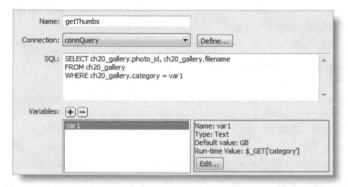

2. Select the placeholder text in the thumbs <div>, and press Delete to remove it.

3. With the insertion point still inside the thumbs <div>, insert the image basin.jpg from images/gallery/thumbs. When prompted, set alternate text to thumbnail. As with the Spry data set, by inserting an actual thumbnail image, Dreamweaver sets the width and height attributes automatically. You now need to replace the image with a dynamic object.

4. Go into Code view, and delete the file name basin.jpg from the src attribute of the <img> tag. Then open the Bindings panel, and select filename from the getThumbs recordset. *Do not click the* Bind *button*. If you do so, Dreamweaver deletes the rest of the path inside the src attribute and removes the width and height attributes.

   Drag and drop filename from the Bindings panel so that the dynamic text object forms the last part of the src attribute. If you find it difficult to drop it in the right place the first time, choose Edit ➤ Undo, or just cut and paste the PHP code into the right place. The <img> tag should now look like this:

```
<img src="../../images/gallery/thumbs/<?php echo ➥
$row_getThumbs['filename']; ?>" alt="thumbnail" width="80" ➥
height="54" />
```

20

5. Click the Live Data view button to check that the first thumbnail is displayed correctly. Toggle Live Data view off before continuing. Notice that Dreamweaver has placed a dynamic image placeholder in the thumbs <div>, as shown in the next screenshot, not a broken image icon, as happens with Spry.

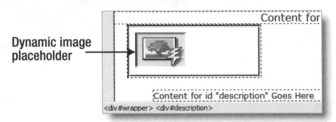

6. You now need to wrap the thumbnail in a link. Make sure the dynamic image placeholder is selected, and click the Browse for File icon to the right of the Link field in the Property inspector.

Select hijax_gallery.php in the Select File dialog box, and click the Parameters button.

In the Parameters dialog box, set Name to photo_id, and click the lightning bolt icon in the Value field to select photo_id from the getThumbs recordset.

7. The repeat region needs to be applied to both the link and the image. The <a> tag might not be displayed in the Tag selector, so click anywhere in Design view. Then select the dynamic image placeholder again. You should now be able to select the <a> tag in the Tag selector.

8. Apply the Repeat Region server behavior, and select the option to show all records.

9. Save the page, and test it in a browser. You should see all eight thumbnails from the England gallery displayed in four rows of two. Mouse over each thumbnail to check that it displays a link with a query string on the end like this:

```
http://egdwcs3/workfiles/ch20/hijax_gallery.php?photo_id=12
```

You can check your code with hijax_gallery_02.php in examples/ch20.

Displaying the main image

A second recordset that selects the details of just one image controls the display in the rest of the page. There's just one problem: no photo_id is passed through a query string when the page first loads or when you change the selected gallery. The solution is to use the photo_id from the first record of the getThumbs recordset as the default value. That way, the main image and description match the first thumbnail when a new gallery first loads, but as soon as a thumbnail is clicked, the second recordset gets its runtime value from the query string.

1. Create a recordset called getDetails. You want all columns from the ch20_gallery table, filtered by the URL parameter photo_id, so you can use the Recordset dialog box in Simple mode with the following settings:

20

Although the default value set by Dreamweaver produces no result when the page first loads, let's first insert the dynamic objects for the main image, caption, and description. We can deal with the default later.

2. Click inside the mainPic <div> placeholder text and format it as a paragraph. Then select the text and delete it. Insert the main image using the same technique as shown in Figures 19-15 and 19-16 in the previous chapter. Select Insert ➤ Image, navigate to the images/gallery folder, and copy the path from the URL field. Then select Data sources, and choose filename from Recordset (getDetails). Make sure you choose the correct recordset, as both have a filename field. Finally, paste the path in front of the PHP code in the URL field, as shown in the following screenshot (in the Mac version, it's the Code field, and you need to add the trailing slash after gallery):

Paste the path in front of the PHP code ——

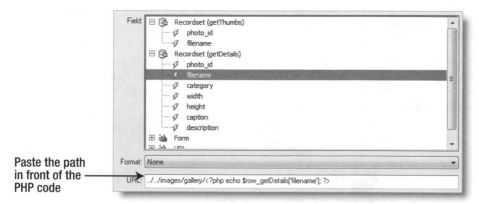

The alternate text is set dynamically using the caption, so just click OK when prompted for alternate text.

3. You now need to bind the alt, width, and height attributes to the image. This is all done through the Bindings panel in the same way as you did in the previous chapter with a Spry data set.

   With the dynamic image placeholder for the main image still selected, open the Bindings panel, and highlight caption in Recordset (getDetails). Choose img.alt from the Bind to drop-down menu at the bottom of the panel, and click the Bind button, as shown in the screenshot alongside.

   Do the same with width and height, binding them to img.width and img.height, respectively.

4. Click alongside the dynamic image placeholder for the main image, and press Shift+Enter/Shift+Return to insert a single line space (<br />).

5. Select caption in the Bindings panel, and click Insert (this was previously labeled Bind—nothing is selected in Design view, so there's nothing to bind the data to).

6. Delete the placeholder text in the description <div>, and replace it with a dynamic text object for description.

7. Save the page, and test it in a browser. The main image and description won't display when the page first loads, but they should when you click any thumbnail. The Japanese gallery also loads if you select Japan and click Go, but as soon as you click a thumbnail, everything reverts to the England gallery.

   We'll fix those issues next, but first you might want to check your code against hijax_gallery_03.php in examples/ch20.

Fixing the code

There are just two things that need to be fixed in the code to make the gallery work properly. First, the default value of the getDetails recordset needs to be made the same as the photo_id of the first record in getThumbs. Second, you need to tell the page which gallery has been selected. It's time to dive into Code view . . .

1. The code that sets the default value of the getDetails recordset is shown on lines 42–45 of the following screenshot:

```
39  $row_getThumbs = mysql_fetch_assoc($getThumbs);
40  $totalRows_getThumbs = mysql_num_rows($getThumbs);
41
42  $colname_getDetails = "-1";
43  if (isset($_GET['photo_id'])) {
44    $colname_getDetails = $_GET['photo_id'];
45  }
```

Three lines higher (on line 39) is the code that retrieves the first record of the getThumbs recordset (see "Reusing a recordset" in Chapter 17 for an explanation of this code). This is important, because we want to use a value from the getThumbs recordset, so it must come before we use it.

Dreamweaver stacks recordset definitions above the DOCTYPE declaration in the same order that you create them. Since getThumbs was created first, I knew they would be in the order I wanted. If they're in the wrong order, you can reorder recordsets, as long as you keep the code for each one together.

Instead of –1, you want the default value of getDetails to be the photo_id of the first record in getThumbs, so change the code shown on line 42 of the preceding screenshot to this:

```
$colname_getDetails = $row_getThumbs['photo_id'];
```

Dreamweaver gets upset that you have changed part of the recordset code and puts a red exclamation mark in the Server Behaviors panel, but it's nothing to worry about. All it means is that you won't be able to edit this recordset in the Recordset dialog box (if you try, it deletes the runtime variable).

2. Next, you need to insert code in the drop-down menu so that it displays the name of the currently selected gallery. This value is stored in $var1_getThumbs, so edit the <select> menu like this:

```
<select name="category" id="category">
  <option value="GB" <?php if ($var1_getThumbs == 'GB') {echo ➡
'selected="selected"';}?>>England</option>
  <option value="JPN" <?php if ($var1_getThumbs == 'JPN') {echo ➡
'selected="selected"';}?>>Japan</option>
</select>
```

This inserts selected="selected" in the <option> tag of the selected gallery.

3. Finally, you need to add the value of the selected gallery to the query string when the user clicks a thumbnail. Edit the opening <a> tag for the thumbnails like this:

```
<a href="hijax_gallery.php?photo_id=<?php echo ➡
$row_getThumbs['photo_id']; ?>&amp;category=<?php echo ➡
$var1_getThumbs; ?>">
```

This adds &category=GB or &category=JPN at the end of the query string.

4. Save the page, and test it again. It should now work exactly the same way whether JavaScript is enabled or not. You can check your code against hijax_gallery_04. php in examples/ch20.

Generating the XML sources with PHP

Earlier in the chapter, I showed you how to generate an XML source manually from a recordset. To adapt the PHP version of the gallery to use Spry, yet remain accessible if

20

JavaScript is disabled, you need to generate two XML sources: one for the photos of England, the other for the photos of Japan. The XML structure for each one looks like this:

```
<gallery>
  <photo>
    <file width="number" height="number">filename</file>
    <thumb>path/to/thumbs/filename</thumb>
    <url><![CDATA[<img> tag for main image]]></url>
    <caption>caption</caption>
    <description><![CDATA[description]]></description>
  </photo>
</gallery>
```

Figure 20-9 shows a sample of the output this produces.

```
- <gallery>
  - <photo>
      <file width="400" height="300">buck_palace.jpg</file>
      <thumb>../../images/gallery/thumbs/buck_palace.jpg</thumb>
    - <url>
        <img src="../../images/gallery/buck_palace.jpg" alt="Buckingham Palace and St James's Park" width="400"
        height="300" />
      </url>
      <caption>Buckingham Palace and St James's Park</caption>
    - <description>
        <p>St James's Park is my favourite among all the parks in central London. It lies on a gentle slope between The Mall
        and Birdcage Walk, and is home to many water birds, including a pair of pelicans. What makes St James's so pleasant
        is its mix of trees, flowers, and lake. The paths curve gently, making it an oasis of calm amid the city bustle.</p>
      </description>
    </photo>
  - <photo>
      <file width="374" height="283">countrygarden.jpg</file>
      <thumb>../../images/gallery/thumbs/countrygarden.jpg</thumb>
```

Figure 20-9. Part of the XML source generated for the Spry-enhanced gallery

The SQL query for the XML source for the gallery of photos of England is this:

```
SELECT * FROM ch20_gallery WHERE category = 'GB'
```

For the Japanese photos, it's

```
SELECT * FROM ch20_gallery WHERE category = 'JPN'
```

To build the PHP pages to generate the XML sources, it's just a question of building the XML skeleton as earlier in the chapter and binding the dynamic text objects to them. You can find the full scripts in england.php and japan.php in examples/ch20.

> *Since the only difference between* england.php *and* japan.php *is the value passed to the* WHERE *clause in the SQL query, you could use just one page and pass the value as a runtime variable. I used two separate pages to keep the code simple and concentrate on the integration with Spry.*

Enhancing the accessible gallery with Spry

Converting the gallery to utilize Spry to refresh the main image, caption, and description involves the same process as earlier in the chapter, namely:

- Create a Spry data set to load the XML data. You can use PHP logic to choose the correct data set, so Spry will use only one, and reload the data set when the gallery changes. As before, we'll call the data set dsPhotos.

- The thumbnails act as the trigger to refresh the other areas, so you add an onclick event handler to the opening <a> tag and set it to return false so that the link isn't followed if JavaScript is supported. A PHP counter sets the correct row number in the underlying code.

- The areas to be refreshed—the main image, caption, and description—will be designated as Spry detail regions, using the spry:content property to load the appropriate content from the current row of the data set.

So, without further ado, let's get coding.

20

Creating the enhanced gallery

Apart from creating the data set, everything involves hand-coding, but it's basically the same as the simple example with the table earlier in the chapter.

1. Create a Spry data set called dsPhotos, using england.php in examples/ch20 as the XML source (if you're on Windows, select All Files (*.*) for Files of type in the Select XML Source dialog box).

Select photo as Row element.

Change Data type for url to image link. You don't need to change Data type for file/@height or file/@width because the numbers are not required for sorting.

2. In Code view, initialize the PHP counter variable between the opening tag of thumbs <div> and the repeat region code like this:

```
<div id="thumbs">
  <?php $i = 0; // initialize counter for row number ?>
  <?php do { ?>
```

3. Add the onclick event handler in the opening <a> tag of the thumbnail like this:

```
<a href="hijax_gallery.php?photo_id=<?php echo ➥
$row_getThumbs['photo_id']; ?>&amp;category=<?php echo ➥
$var1_getThumbs; ?>" onclick="dsPhotos.setCurrentRowNumber(<?php ➥
echo $i++; ?>); return false">
```

This was explained in "How to incorporate a Spry data set in an ordinary web page" earlier in the chapter, so I won't go into details again.

4. Both the main image and the caption are embedded in a paragraph, so wrap them in <span> elements, and add the spry:detailregion and spry:content properties like this:

```
<div id="mainPic">
  <p><span spry:detailregion="dsPhotos" spry:content="{url}"><img ➡
src="../../images/gallery/<?php echo $row_getDetails['filename']; ➡
?>" alt="<?php echo $row_getDetails['caption']; ?>" width="<?php ➡
echo $row_getDetails['width']; ?>" height="<?php echo ➡
$row_getDetails['height']; ?>" /></span><br />
    <span spry:detailregion="dsPhotos" spry:content="{caption}"> ➡
<?php echo $row_getDetails['caption']; ?></span></p>
</div>
```

5. The description is in a <div> of its own, so the spry:detailregion and spry:content properties can be added to its opening tag like this:

```
<div id="description" spry:detailregion="dsPhotos" spry:content= ➡
"{description}"><?php echo $row_getDetails['description']; ?></div>
```

6. All that remains is to use some PHP logic to choose the correct XML source. Locate the section of code that sets the default value of the getThumbs recordset (around line 32), and edit it like this:

```
$var1_getThumbs = "GB";
// use england.php as the default XML source
$set = 'england.php';
if (isset($_GET['category'])) {
  $var1_getThumbs = $_GET['category'];
  // if the Japan gallery has been selected, change XML source
  if ($_GET['category'] == 'JPN') {$set = 'japan.php';}
}
```

Although Spry changes the content of the Spry detail regions, it's not affected by clicking the Go button. This submits the form and passes the selected category through the URL. So, if category is set to JPN in the $_GET array, the value of $set changes to japan.php. Otherwise, it remains the default, england.php.

7. Edit the data set initialization to use the selected data source like this:

```
var dsPhotos = new Spry.Data.XMLDataSet("../../examples/ch20/<?php ➡
echo $set; ?>", "gallery/photo");
```

This builds the path to the XML source file, so make sure there is no gap between the forward slash and the opening PHP tag.

8. Save the page, and test it in a browser. With JavaScript enabled, the gallery refreshes the main image, caption, and description without reloading the page. The only time the page is reloaded is when you switch galleries. This isn't quite as slick as the pure Spry version, but it's much more accessible and search engine friendly. With JavaScript disabled, it continues to work as an ordinary dynamic web page, whereas the pure Spry version fails.

You can check your code against hijax_gallery_05.php in examples/ch20.

The end of a long journey . . .

Congratulations if you have stayed with me all the way from page 1. We've covered a lot of ground and crunched a lot of code. I hope you've found it an interesting and not too difficult journey. Most of all, I hope it has stimulated your interest in exploring further. Over the past 700 pages or so, we have worked with a wide range of web technologies: XHTML, CSS, JavaScript, Spry, PHP, MySQL, XSLT, and XML. One of the great attractions of web design and development is the low threshold of knowledge required to get started. But if your knowledge remains in the foothills, you'll be greatly limited in what you can do. You need to start climbing the slopes of the various technologies; at times, the learning curve can be steep, but the rewards are often well worth the effort.

One of the difficulties of writing this sort of book is that it can give you only a brief insight into the possibilities. Don't treat the exercises and case study as definitive "answers" but rather as starting points for your own ideas and experimentation. The great thing about dynamic web development is that it lets you present information in an infinite variety of ways. Some ideas work better than others, but it's only by trying out different techniques that you get a feel for what's right for a particular situation.

This book has dealt with PHP and MySQL primarily in a Dreamweaver context. If you have found the techniques taught here useful, I urge you to expand your knowledge by visiting the online documentation at www.php.net/manual/en/ and http://dev.mysql.com/doc/refman/5.0/en/index.html. Although they're not suitable for reading from end to end, they are well written and crammed with useful examples. The PHP manual has a section for frequently asked questions at www.php.net/manual/en/faq.php; and if you run into difficulties with MySQL, a good place to start is http://dev.mysql.com/doc/refman/5.0/en/problems.html.

Thanks for reading.

20

INDEX

Numbers and symbols